Walking in Britain

David Else

Sandra Bardwell, Belinda Dixon, Peter Dragicevich, Des Hannigan,
Becky Ohlsen, Simon Richmond

Destination Britain

Walking in Britain means travelling through a stunningly varied landscape – from the high peaks of Scotland and the wild moors of Yorkshire, to the pristine coast of West Wales and the tranquil farmland of the Cotswolds. Walking is also one of the best ways to meet people and, whether you're a local or a visitor, the slow pace means it's easy to learn about the country you're passing through, not just skim the surface.

Britain's other major draw card is its size and compact nature. You spend less time going between places and more time in them. You get the chance to slow down and get off the beaten track, the opportunity to combine your walking with a relaxed lunch in a friendly café, or maybe watching a cricket match, or simply sitting on a high summit drinking in the vista before your eyes.

More than anything else, walking in Britain means freedom. You can enjoy the extensive public-footpath network and the traditional 'right to roam' in many areas, letting you walk unencumbered over hills and mountains, beside rivers and lakes, through valleys and across moors.

Some walkers rave about hardy, week-long expeditions through the untamed wilderness of the Cairngorms, while others love the human scale of a stroll along the River Thames. The choice is yours. There really is something for everyone.

To top it all, access is easy for walkers in Britain, regulations are few and permits virtually unheard of. All you need to do is look at the map, put on your boots and go!

ANDREW MARSHALL & LEANNE WALKER

Southern England

Chalk and cheese: Beachy Head lighthouse (p133) rises from the sea beneath chalk cliffs on the final section of the long-distance South Downs Way

In elemental Dartmoor (p97), your walking companions will be herds of wild ponies

View chocolate-box scenery in the rolling hills of the quintessentially English Cotswolds (p107)

Northern England

The final four days of the Cleveland Way (p252) amble along the Yorkshire coast

GRANT DIXON

ANDREW MARSHALL & LEANNE WALKER

World Heritage–listed Hadrian's Wall (p213) doubles as an 84-mile national trail

Bamburgh Castle (p231) is a regal staring point for the Northumberland Coast Walk

DAVID ELS

DAVID TOMLINSON

Autumn brushes the lakes, fells and farms of Elterwater (p205) in the Lake District

JON DAVISON

Take it as a sign: a typical walking welcome in Grassington (p179)

Dip a toe in the North Sea at Robin Hood's Bay (p239) for a symbolic end to the Coast to Coast Walk

GRANT DIXON

Wales

Mt Snowdon is Wales' highest peak and the centrepiece of the Snowdon Traverse (p311)

GARETH McCORMACK

The empty, arched windows of Tintern Abbey (p336) mark a graceful beginning to the Offa's Dyke Path

GREG GAWLOWSKI

The Pembrokeshire Coast Path (p291) clings to cliffs above the impressive sweep of Marloes Sands

MARK DAFFEY

Scotland

GRAEME CORNWALLIS

Enjoy high times in the Cairngorms (p374), one of Britain's wildest highland areas

The Skye's the limit with views across the Black Cuillin from Bruach na Frithe (p404)

GARETH M^cCORMACK

Beinn Alligin (p390), the 'Mountain of Beauty', reflected in the waters of Loch Torridon

GARETH M^cCORMACK

Scotland

GARETH M°CORMACK

Slioch (p393) towers above the remote Great
Wilderness in the Western Highlands

GRANT DIXON

The mountains of Glen Coe (p369)
shadow an isolated farmhouse

Britain's highest mountain, Ben Nevis (p360) is also one of the country's major walking drawcards

MARTIN MOOS

Foreword Christine Elliott

Writers the world over have extolled the virtues of Britain's landscape, which offers thrilling choices to suit your walking preferences: gentle countryside, dramatic hills and mountains, awe-inspiring antiquities and breathtaking modern sculpture await the walker's discovery. During each season there is a vista rich with flora and fauna. To punctuate your walking, Britain welcomes its on-foot explorers through a community of character-filled towns and villages, brimming with delightful refreshment and accommodation options. Whether you know it or not, we walkers also benefit from decades of campaigns to save and reinstate footpaths and to protect the countryside. Most recently, the British government introduced a statutory right to walk in huge areas of land that were previously out of bounds. So, traditions and history underpin the recreation and activities you are about to enjoy.

With the right to access millions of acres of uncultivated countryside and inspiring landscapes, come responsibilities as members of a worldwide fellowship of walkers. Intuitively, we all know that the world's resources are under threat from our overly disposable culture and lifestyle. Henri-Frederic Amiel wrote that, 'Any landscape is a condition of the spirit'. That being so, walking in an environment where you can 'get away from it all' brings a welcome break from career or lifestyle pressures. However, the walking environment is about much more than the ground on which we place our steps. Our endangered environment has become the urgent global issue, joined up in what is arguably the greatest-known threat to humanity and earth – climate change.

The fact that global warming dominates the political radar confirms there is no room for complacency. Yet what the Ramblers' Association's president describes as a huge 'elephant trap' is at our feet: energy choices in how we live our lives, especially transport. Which of us hasn't travelled by car to reach an otherwise inaccessible walk? Or enjoyed a marvellous holiday that involved air travel? We may only have 10 years in which to halt and reverse otherwise inexorable climate change. However, the environmental cost of air travel is huge and there is great pressure to restrict carbon-selfish practices.

It is as unrealistic and impractical to expect humankind to relinquish cars and planes as it is to pretend we can tackle global warming without making real sacrifices. The Ramblers' Association is keen to use shared travel to connect our communities with the pleasures of the outdoors. To help conserve the environment we love, each of us can make personal lifestyle choices, so that our children and theirs do not pay for the luxury of the last-minute culture.

Meanwhile, have a wonderful experience as you enjoy the best of outdoor Britain. Nathaniel Howe was right to say that, 'Leisure is the time for doing something useful'. You will not only be walking, you will be walking for our world.

Christine Elliott is chief executive of the Ramblers' Association, Britain's largest and most active national walking organisation.

Contents

Regional Map Contents

Scotland p344

Northern England p150

Wales p280

Southern England p52

The Walks	Duration	Difficulty	Best time	Transport
Southern England				
London & the Southeast				
The Jubilee Walkway	3-4hr	easy	all year	bus, train, tube
The Centenary Walk	6-7hr	easy	all year	train, tube
The Thames Path (East)	6 days	easy	all year	train
Wessex				
The Clarendon Way	9-11hr	easy	Apr-Oct	bus
The Kennet & Avon Canal Path	4-5hr	easy	Apr-Oct	train
The Ridgeway (West)	3 days	easy	Apr-Oct	bus
The Thames Path (West)	6 days	easy	all year	train, bus
Dartmoor				
A South Dartmoor Traverse	7-8hr	moderate	all year	train, bus
A North Dartmoor Circuit	5-6hr	moderate	all year	bus
The Cotswolds				
The Cotswold Way	7 days	easy-moderate	all year	train, bus
Bourton & the Slaughters	6hr	easy	all year	bus
Southern England Long-Distance Paths				
The South Downs Way	8 days	moderate	all year	train, bus
The South West Coast Path (Padstow to Falmouth)	14 days	moderate-demanding	Apr-Sep	bus, train
Northern England				
The Peak District				
The Edale Skyline	5¼-7½hr	moderate	Mar-Oct	bus, train
The Limestone Way	2 days	easy-moderate	Mar-Oct	bus, train
The Yorkshire Dales				
Wharfedale & Littondale	5-6hr	easy-moderate	Mar-Oct	bus
The Three Peaks	9-12hr	demanding	Mar-Oct	bus, train
The Dales Way	6 days	moderate	Mar-Oct	bus, train
The Lake District				
The Fairfield Horseshoe	5-7hr	moderate	Apr-Sep	bus
Helvellyn & Striding Edge	5-6hr	moderate-demanding	Apr-Sep	bus
Dovedale & Fairfield	5-7hr	moderate-demanding	Apr-Sep	bus

The Walks	Duration	Difficulty	Best time	Transport
A High Street Circuit	6-8hr	moderate	Apr-Sep	bus
A Scafell Pike Circuit	5-6½hr	moderate-demanding	Apr-Sep	bus
The Cumbria Way	5 days	moderate	Apr-Sep	bus, train
Northumberland				
Hadrian's Wall Path	7 days	moderate	Apr-Sep	bus, train
A Northumberland Coast Walk	5-6½hr	easy	Apr-Sep	bus
Northern England Long-Distance Paths				
The Coast to Coast Walk	12 days	moderate-demanding	Apr-Oct	train, bus
The Cleveland Way	9 days	moderate	all year	bus, train
The Pennine Way	16 days	moderate-demanding	Apr-Oct	train, bus

Wales

The Walks	Duration	Difficulty	Best time	Transport
The Brecon Beacons				
Brecon Beacons Ridge Walk	7½-9½hr	moderate	Apr-Sep	bus
Pembrokeshire				
Pembrokeshire Coast Path	15 days	moderate-demanding	Apr-Sep	bus
Preseli Hills & History	6-8hr	moderate	Apr-Sep	bus
Snowdonia				
A Snowdon Traverse	5-7hr	moderate-demanding	May-Sep	bus
Tryfan & the Glyders	5-7hr	demanding	May-Sep	bus
A Carneddau Circuit	4-6hr	moderate	May-Sep	bus
Wales Long-Distance Paths				
The Glyndŵr's Way	9 days	moderate	Apr-Sep	bus, train
The Offa's Dyke Path	12 days	demanding	Apr-Sep	bus, train

Scotland

The Walks	Duration	Difficulty	Best time	Transport
Central Highlands & Islands				
The Ptarmigan Route	4½-5hr	moderate	Apr-Oct	ferry
The Cobbler	5-5¾hr	demanding	Apr-Oct	bus, train
A Goatfell Circuit	6-7½hr	moderate-demanding	Apr-Oct	bus, ferry

The Walks	Duration	Difficulty	Best time	Transport
Ben Nevis & Glen Coe				
Ben Nevis	6-8hr	moderate-demanding	May-Sep	bus
The Road to the Isles	6½hr	moderate	Apr-Oct	train, bus
Buachaille Etive Mór	5½hr	moderate-demanding	Apr-Oct	bus
The Cairngorms				
Cairn Gorm High Circuit	4hr	moderate-demanding	May-Sep	bus
Chalamain Gap & the Lairig Ghru	6hr	moderate-demanding	Apr-Oct	bus
The Western Highlands				
The Five Sisters of Kintail	6¾-8hr	demanding	May-Oct	private
Beinn Alligin	6-8hr	moderate-demanding	May-Oct	private
Slioch	7½hr	moderate-demanding	May-Oct	bus
Isle of Skye				
Coast & Cuillin	8hr	moderate	Apr-Oct	bus
Bruach na Frithe	6-7hr	moderate-demanding	May-Oct	bus
Scotland Long-Distance Paths				
The Southern Upland Way	9 days	moderate-demanding	Apr-Sep	bus, train
The West Highland Way	7 days	moderate	Apr-Oct	bus, train

The Authors

DAVID ELSE

A full-time professional writer, David has authored more than 20 walking and travel guidebooks, including Lonely Planet's *England* and *Trekking in East Africa*. His knowledge of Britain comes from a lifetime of travel around the country – often on foot – a passion dating from university years, when heading for the hills was always more attractive than visiting the library. Originally from London, David slowly trekked northwards via Wiltshire, Bristol and Derbyshire (with periods of exile in Wales and Africa) to his present base in Yorkshire, close to the Peak District National Park – and once again he's often tempted from his desk by the view of the nearby hills.

My Favourite Walks

While researching this book, I revisited many of my favourite places in Britain. I remember the misty day I walked up the valley from Seathwaite in the Lake District, suddenly popping out above the cloud near Styhead Pass (p199), looking across to Scafell and other high peaks glowing in the light of the low autumn sun. Then there was that beautiful summer stroll along the Pembrokeshire Coast Path (p291) near St David's Head, where gorse-topped cliffs plunged down to shining sand and crystal-clear water. In sharp contrast, I enjoyed a wintry outing on Beinn Alligin (p390), cracking on to keep warm in the chill wind, but loving the endless views and solitude, and really earning that pie and pint back down in the pub.

Beinn Alligin,
Torridon,
Western Highlands

Eskdale & Scafell,
Lake District

St David's Head,
Pembrokeshire
Coast Path

SANDRA BARDWELL

When Sandra discovered a Scottish great-grandmother, she knew it must be in the genes. The first time she set eyes on the Highlands' hills, she felt she'd come home. When she settled beside Loch Ness, she flung herself into the hills, walked the glens, loch shores and coast with huge enthusiasm. This happened well into a lifetime of walking in wild, remote and not-so-remote places, mainly in Australia, and writing the odd bushwalking article and book there. With Lonely Planet she's explored some other wonderful European countries, but Scotland – and especially the Highlands, in their infinite variety and ever-changing beauty – are closest to her heart.

BELINDA DIXON

Living near Dartmoor and having developed a late – and to her friends baffling – interest in archaeology, Belinda can often be seen setting out, map in hand, to investigate stone rows and hut circles. That love of hiking and old bones also came in handy for Cotswold hillforts and Neolithic mortuary practices. Almost 20 years of living in southwestern England have given her an understanding and love of its ridges and moors, while years of guidebook writing have left her, despite all the efforts, thanking her lucky stars that you can actually get paid to do this.

PETER DRAGICEVICH

Peter's first taste of long-distance walking was a four-day *hikoi* (a Maori protest/pilgrimage) in his native New Zealand/Aotearoa. Since then the walking's been mainly for pleasure, and the protests much shorter. During his dozen years in publishing he's written numerous travel features for newspapers and magazines, on subjects as varied as Welsh castles and gay life in Brighton. This is the fourth book he's co-authored for Lonely Planet.

DES HANNIGAN

Des has been exploring the Cornish coast, both onshore and offshore, by footpath and rock climb, for over 30 years. He lives in the tiny parish of Morvah (Cornish for 'by the sea') on the beautiful north coast of the Land's End Peninsula, where the South West Coast Path passes through one of its most scenic sections. Des has written several walking guides to various parts of Britain, as well as numerous general travel guides to such diverse places as the down-to-earth Netherlands and the high-in-the-sky mountains of North Pakistan. He has worked on Lonely Planet's *Greece*, *Ireland*, *Spain* and *Denmark* guides.

BECKY OHLSEN

Becky has been walking since she was a small child, but had no idea until a few years ago that it could be used as a means of getting from one pub to another. Most of her hiking time has been spent in the largely pub-free forests of Colorado and Oregon. She has also completed some hilly treks in Switzerland and northern Sweden. After covering three of Britain's long-distance national trails, she is permanently hooked on the white acorn.

SIMON RICHMOND

Travel writer, photographer and hiking enthusiast Simon Richmond has slung on his backpack and laced up his boots for walks on five continents. Among many projects for Lonely Planet he's covered walks in Australia's Blue Mountains, traipsed up an active volcano in Kamchatka, sweated it out in Malaysia's jungles and puffed his way across Table Mountain in Cape Town. Despite the inevitable rain, covering both the Coast to Coast and Pennine Way routes was an ideal way to spend an August.

Walk Descriptions

This book contains 52 route descriptions, ranging from six-hour strolls through to multiday megawalks, as well as suggestions for other walks, side trips and alternative routes. Each route description has a brief introduction outlining the natural and cultural features you may encounter, plus extra information to help you plan your walk, such as transport options, the level of difficulty and time-frame involved, and any permits that are required.

All the routes we describe pass through national parks and scenic areas. The multiday walks tend to be linear, while many of the day walks are circular. For all routes we include information on camp sites, mountain huts, hostels and other accommodation, and point out places where you can obtain water and supplies.

TIMES & DISTANCES

These are provided only as a guide. Times are based on actual walking time and do not include stops for snacks, taking photographs, rests or side trips. Be sure to factor these in when planning your walk.

Distances are provided but should be read in conjunction with the altitudes you expect to reach, as significant elevation changes can make a greater difference to your walking time than lateral distance. In this book we have reflected the rather wacky British system of mixing imperial and metric measurements. In route descriptions, daily distances along footpaths are given in miles, with some kilometre equivalents, while distances of less than half a mile are given in metres and heights of mountains are given in metres. When converting from one to the other, we have usually rounded up or down to the nearest half-mile or 0.5km. This may give rise to small inconsistencies between measurements, but nothing significant.

In most cases the daily stages are flexible and can be varied. It is important to recognise that short stages are sometimes recommended because of difficult terrain in mountain areas, or perhaps because there are interesting features to explore en route.

The times given in this book reckon on most walkers going at about 2.5mph (4km/h), with an extra hour for every 300m to 500m of ascent. This gives walking times that allow for a few short stops (eg for map reading), but not for long stops (eg a good pub lunch). It also assumes good weather. If you prefer to linger longer, or there's a chance of bad weather (always a possibility in mountains), then you should add extra time – about 10% for straightforward walks and up to 50% for serious mountain routes. If you are carrying a heavy load, then your speed will drop even more.

LEVEL OF DIFFICULTY

Grading systems are always arbitrary. However, having an indication of the grade may help you choose between walks. Our authors use the following grading guidelines:

Easy – A walk on flat terrain or with minor elevation changes, usually over short distances on well-travelled routes with no navigational difficulties.

Moderate – A walk with challenging terrain, often involving longer distances and steep climbs.

Demanding – A walk with long daily distances and difficult terrain with significant elevation changes; may involve challenging route-finding and periods of scrambling.

DIRECTIONS

Throughout the walk descriptions we have used general compass bearings (eg 'head northwest', or 'aim east away from the river'). Precise compass bearings have been used rarely, and only where necessary.

The terms 'true left' and 'true right', used to describe the bank of a stream or river, sometimes throw readers. The 'true left bank' simply means the left bank as you look downstream.

THE LONG & THE SHORT

There are two main types of walk in this book. Day walks have been chosen as the best examples in each region. They are usually circular, and we give details of where to stay before and afterwards. The route is broken into natural stages, such as from a village to a mountain pass, from the pass to the mountain summit, then from the summit back to the village.

Long-distance path (LDP) descriptions in this book are divided into daily stages, each ending at a place with accommodation, usually a hotel, B&B or hostel (often a choice of all three – plus camping), as is usual in Britain. Obligatory wilderness camping – because there's simply no B&B or hostel – on LDPs in Britain is very rare. In LDP descriptions in this book, suggestions are given for different stages so you can adjust the daily mileage to suit your own ability.

Planning

This edition of *Walking in Britain* is for visitors from overseas looking for a single book that covers the whole country. It's also for people living in British eager to explore their own backyard. We describe a wide selection of walking routes, ranging from gentle half-day rambles on river-side paths to multiday treks across wild mountains, plus anything in between, with something suitable for everyone. You can base yourself in an interesting spot for a week and go out on day walks to explore the surrounding countryside, or you can travel from place to place on foot in true backpacking style. The options for walking in Britain are almost limitless, so providing a complete list is impossible, but what we have included is enough to keep you busy for a long time.

Walking is one of the most popular pastimes in Britain, so an infrastructure for walkers already exists and makes everything easy for visitors or first-timers. Most towns and villages in walking areas have shops selling maps and local guidebooks, while Britain's excellent chain of tourist offices can provide walking leaflets and other information. National parks offer guided walks. All this means you can arrive in a place for the first time, pick up a leaflet or guidebook, put on your boots and within an hour you'll be walking through some of Britain's finest landscapes. No fees. No permits. No worries. It really is almost effortless.

Where you go first may depend on your own experience. Generally speaking, the lower and more cultivated the landscape, the easier the walking, with clear paths and signposts – ideal for beginners. On popular routes in mountain and moorland areas, there will be a path (although sometimes it's faint) but not many signposts. If the route is rarely trodden, there may be no visible path at all and absolutely no signposts, so you'll need a detailed map and compass for navigation.

As well as the wonderful scenery, two aspects make walking in Britain unlike hiking, tramping or trekking in many other parts of the world. The first is the principle of 'right of way', allowing walkers to cross private land on paths or tracks open to the public. At the last count, the right-of-way network totalled about 140,000 miles (225,000km) – more than enough to keep any walker busy – and many of the paths have existed for hundreds or thousands of years. Even though nearly all land in Britain is privately owned, from tiny cultivated areas to vast tracts of wilderness, the right of way cannot be overruled by the actual owner. If there is a right of way, you can walk through fields, woods and even farmhouse yards as long as you keep to the correct route and do no damage.

The second aspect is the principle of 'freedom to roam'. Landmark laws introduced in 2003 and 2004 allow walkers to move *beyond* the right of way in mountain and moorland areas, and effectively go anywhere – opening up vast tracts of wild and remote landscape that were previously off limits. Of course, with freedom comes responsibility (for more details see the boxed texts on p32 and p448) but for many walkers in Britain these new opportunities are like opening the doors of a sweet shop.

In this book, we've described our favourite walking areas, and picked a selection of day walks as the best samples of each area. Most day walks are circular, so you start and finish in the same place. Some of the day walks can be extended into two days – ideal for a weekend, or if the weather's fine and you simply want to keep going. We also outline shorter alternatives; good if you only want to walk for a morning or afternoon.

The Ramblers' Association's annual publication *Walk Britain* is an invaluable planning tool, outlining many routes and walking areas, with handy lists of walker-friendly B&Bs all over Britain.

We've also selected our favourite long-distance paths (LDPs), ranging from about four days to 20 days. Freedom is key here too: the LDPs don't have to be followed in their entirety – you can do just a couple of days if you prefer. In this book, we've selected some day walks and LDPs that deliberately overlap, giving you even more scope for several walks in the same area.

When it comes to a place to stay, all walking areas and LDPs are well served by a mix of hotels, B&Bs and hostels, plus camp sites and bunkhouses. On the long routes you may want to camp but you certainly don't *have* to. You don't even have to carry all your gear, thanks to a marvellous system of baggage-carrying services.

In this book, we have concentrated on the national parks and other rural or remote areas, simply because these are where the walking is best. Some of the routes are long-time classics; others are personal favourites based on our own local knowledge. We have also described a few out-of-the-way routes and provided brief outlines of many more places that you can enjoy exploring on your own. Have fun!

> As Australians in Britain we like our routes to go through villages, and we stop overnight in old inns when possible. We are keen bushwalkers at home, but in Britain do not wish to duplicate our Australian walks. A pint in a pub at the end of a day's walking through English fields and meadows is most enjoyable.
>
> *Phillip Crampton*

WHEN TO WALK

The best seasons for walking in Britain are spring, summer and autumn (March to October) – the conditions are likely to be better and there's more daylight. July and August are school holidays and the busiest months, especially around the coast and in national parks. In winter (November to February) some accommodation closes, restaurants have shorter hours and public transport options are reduced.

In summer in northern England it's light from around 5am to 9pm, while in winter it's light between 8am and 5pm. In southern England the differences are less pronounced, but in Scotland during summer it gets dark for only a few hours around midnight and your days are luxuriously long. Conversely, during winter in southern Scotland or northern England you only have about seven or eight hours of daylight to play with – down to just five or six in northern Scotland.

Generally speaking, the farther north you go, the longer the winter and the shorter the walking season. This especially applies to Scotland; while lower and coastal areas may enjoy seasons similar to those in England and Wales, in the high mountains of Scotland the best time for walking is from May to September. (During the Scottish winter, most walking routes

DID YOU KNOW?

On many long-distance paths in Britain, baggage services will arrange to transport your kit between overnight stops, while you travel light all day. See p437.

See Climate (p439) for more information on Britain's climate.

DON'T LEAVE HOME WITHOUT...

▪ Your passport and visa, if you're from overseas (p452)

▪ Good boots and gaiters, if you're heading for the moors and mountains (p467)

▪ At least some basic map-reading skills (p468)

▪ Midge repellent, if you're heading for Scotland in summer (p462)

▪ A taste for real ale (p443)

require an ice axe, crampons and specialist knowledge; technical winter walks of this nature are beyond the scope of this book.)

Away from the high mountains, you can walk the rest of Britain at any time of the year. Even in winter the weather is never bad enough to make conditions technical. In fact, a beautiful, crisp midwinter day is always preferable to one of the damp and misty days that can easily occur in high summer.

See p439 for more details on regional climates.

COSTS & MONEY

More than anything, your choice of accommodation will determine how much you'll spend while walking in Britain. Camp sites cost around £3 to £8 per person, or £5 to £15 per 'pitch' (usually two people and a tent), but may be more if the site has many facilities. Bunkhouses are around £7 to £10 per person per night, and hostels around £10 to £20. At a simple B&B you'll pay £20 per person, and up to £30 in smarter places. A night in a midrange hotel can be anything from £20 to £50 per person, although £35 to £50 is more likely. These prices assume you're sharing a double or twin room. Single rooms are usually around 75% of the double-room rate. Wherever you stay, prices are usually higher at busy times – in Britain this means from around Easter to early September. The rates we quote throughout this book are high-season prices, but you may discover an extra peak at the busiest time – late July and August. For more details about accommodation, see p432.

For food, in towns and cities you can get by on £5 per day by purchasing basic supplies from supermarkets. When walking, camping or hostelling you may be self-catering anyway, so £10 per day will see you through. If you have meals at hostels, cafés or cheap restaurants, £15 to £20 per day will be your baseline. A bar meal in a pub will be about £7, while a restaurant main course will set you back around £8 to £10. Beer may not be classed as an essential by some but – just for the record – a pint will cost £2.50 to £3 in London and the Southeast, and £1.50 to £2.50 around the country.

Transport will be your other big expense, but its cost is harder to quantify as it depends not on how long you stay, but on how far you go and how many different areas you visit. More details are given in the Transport chapter (p453).

For more money details, see p447.

BACKGROUND READING

To get you in the mood for walking in Britain here's a selection of our favourite travelogues. Details on specific area guidebooks are given in the individual route descriptions.

- *As I Walked Out One Midsummer Morning* by Laurie Lee. A young man leaves the time-warped 1930s Cotswolds, then carves out a life in London before heading off to Spain.
- *Journey Through Britain* by John Hillaby. An intrepid adventurer explores his own backyard on foot in the mid 1960s and captures the spirit of that age.
- *On Borrow's Trail* by Hugh Oliff. Retracing the journeys through Wales made by 19th-century writer George Borrow, combining a rich synopsis of the original observations with modern photos and colour illustrations.
- *Two Degrees West* by Nicholas Crane. Walking a perfectly straight line across Britain, the author wades across rivers, cuts through towns, sleeps in fields and meets an astounding selection of people.

HOW MUCH?

Camp site (for 2 people)
£10

YHA hostel (dorm bed)
£10-20

B&B (double or twin)
£40-60

Map £5-8

Mars Bar 60p

GUIDED WALKS & ORGANISED WALKING TOURS

In national parks and other countryside areas (and in some cities), guided walks ranging from an hour to all day – many with a theme such as wildlife or history – are organised by rangers or local experts. More details are given in the chapters throughout this book, and you can find out more from national park websites or tourist offices.

For something longer, a great option is an organised walking tour with a commercial operator. These are ideal if you're new to walking or simply enjoy the company of others. Some operators offering walking tours in Britain are listed below. Even if you don't book a tour, the itineraries outlined in their websites and their brochures can be handy for planning and a great source of information.

- **Adventure Plus** (☎ 01678-521109; www.advplus.co.uk) Friendly team offering guided or self-guided walking in North Wales.
- **Bath & West Country Walks** (☎ 01761-233807; www.bathwestwalks.com) Guided and self-guided trips in the Southwest.
- **Brigantes Walking Holidays** (☎ 01729-830463; www.brigantesenglishwalks.com) Self-guided tours in northern England (Coast to Coast, Cleveland Way, Cumbria Way, Dales Way etc).
- **Contours Walking Holidays** (☎ 01768-480451; www.contours.co.uk) Long-standing outfit with a very wide range of self-guided tours throughout Britain.
- **Cotswold Walking Holidays** (☎ 01242-254353; www.cotswoldwalks.com) Does exactly what it says on the tin, and comes in thee varieties: guided, self-guided and luxury.
- **Country Adventures** (☎ 01254-690691; www.country-adventures.co.uk) Offers walking and activity holidays around Britain, especially the Lake District, North York Moors and Wales.
- **Countrywide Holidays** (☎ 01707-386800; www.countrywidewalking.com) Part of well-respected and long-standing **Ramblers Holidays** (www.ramblersholidays.co.uk), with a very wide selection of tours throughout Britain.
- **Footpath Holidays** (☎ 01985-840049; www.footpath-holidays.com) Guided and self-guided hotel-based walking trips throughout Britain.
- **Greenways Holidays** (☎ 01834-862109; www.greenwaysholidays.com) Self-guided walking holidays in Pembrokeshire, Wales.
- **Make Tracks** (☎ 0131-229 6844; www.maketracks.net) Self-guided walks along many of Scotland's long-distance routes.
- **River Deep Mountain High** (☎ 01539-531116; www.rdmh.co.uk) Outdoor activities, including walking, in the Lake District.
- **Sherpa Expeditions** (☎ 020-8577 2717; www.sherpa-walking-holidays.co.uk/britain) International trekking company that offers a very good range of self-guided walking tours in Britain.
- **SYHA Holidays** (☎ 0870 155 3255; www.hostelholidays.org.uk) Walking tours in Scotland based in youth hostels.
- **Walking Women** (☎ 01926-313321; www.walkingwomen.com) Female-only walking tours in the Lake District, around Britain and beyond.
- **Wandering Aengus** (☎ 01697-478443; www.wanderingaengustreks.com) Specialising in guided tours for small groups, including a 'Three Peaks' trip to Snowdon, Scafell and Ben Nevis.

Many more companies can be found under 'tours' links in several of the walking websites listed under Internet Resources (opposite). One of the most comprehensive lists is at www.ramblers.org.uk/info/Contacts/hols.html. For more ideas, type words such as 'walking tours', 'walking holidays' and 'hiking vacations' into internet search engines.

WALKING FESTIVALS

During summer, many towns and country areas organise walking festivals featuring a few days of guided walks, often coinciding with an annual carnival or other event. The aim is to encourage more people to get into walking, or for established walkers to meet like-minded people. For more details contact local tourist offices, do an internet search for 'walking festivals' or see www.ramblers.co.uk.

- *Slow Coast Home* by Josie Dew. A cross between journal of miscellany and chatty letter to a friend. Yes, it's about a cycling tour of England and Wales, but walkers will identify with the pace and offbeat observations.
- *The First Fifty* by Muriel Gray. The perfect antidote to male-dominated tales of peak bagging and other hardy walking ploys.
- *Hamish's Mountain Walk* by Hamish Brown. The extraordinarily long (and first) continuous round of the Munros, by an extremely well-known Scottish mountain writer.
- *Plowright Follows Wainright* by Alan Plowright. Follows the footsteps of legendary 'AW' (see the boxed text, p188) along the Pennine Way and Coast to Coast, with evocative landscapes and eccentric fellow walkers encountered along the way.

INTERNET RESOURCES

The internet is a wonderful planning tool for walkers and travellers, and there are millions of sites about Britain. Before plunging into the cyber-maze, try these for starters:

Backpax (www.backpaxmag.com) Cheerful info on cheap travel in Britain, plus details about visas, activities and work.

BBC (www.bbc.co.uk) For an overview of British news and culture, see this immense and invaluable site from the world's best broadcaster.

i-UK (www.i-uk.com) The official government site for all British business, study and travel information.

Lonely Planet (www.lonelyplanet.com) Loads of travel news, a bit of merchandise and the legendary Thorn Tree bulletin board, complete with a Walking, Trekking & Mountaineering forum.

Long Distance Walkers Association (www.ldwa.org.uk) The name says it all, and the site includes details of long day or multiday walks in rural or mountainous areas. The club also promotes challenge walking (covering set distances within a set time).

Mountaineering Council of Scotland (www.mountaineering-scotland.org.uk) The MCofS represents climbers and hillwalkers in Scotland, and provides mountains of information, particularly on issues of access and freedom to roam.

Ramblers' Association (www.ramblers.org.uk) Britain's largest and most active national walking organisation; the website has details of routes, events, places to stay, campaigns, walking festivals and guided walks, plus general advice for walkers and a list of publications for sale online.

Sherpa Van (www.sherpavan.com) One of Britain's leading tour operators and baggage-carrying services, the website is also packed with useful route information, walker-friendly accommodation listings and a lively walkers' forum – especially good for first-timers.

Visit Britain (www.visitbritain.com) The country's official tourism website: accommodation, attractions, events and much more.

Walking Britain (www.walkingbritain.co.uk) A comprehensive list of walking routes, recommended books and maps, organised walking tours and a lively walkers' forum.

Walking Pages (www.walkingpages.co.uk) A great source of information on all aspects of walking Britain – destinations, festivals, rights, equipment and more – also with an online shop for buying local guidebooks.

Walkingworld (www.walkingworld.com) The largest of many commercial walking information sites, with more than 3000 route descriptions in all parts of Britain – and growing daily.

TOP THREES

Major positives of walking in Britain include variety of the landscape, the compact nature of the country, and the sheer range of options from short strolls to multiday epics. These 'top threes' will help you find what you're looking for.

Coast Walks

■ **The South West Coast Path** (p133) The cliff-top paths of the Southwest Peninsula are hard to beat; the ups and downs can sometimes be hard work, but this is the place for jolly seaside resorts, great views, sand and surf.

■ **The Pembrokeshire Coast Path** (p291) Another top choice for roller-coaster seaside walking, with birds, seals, wildflowers and a great mix of busy beaches and secluded traditional fishing villages.

■ **Scotland's west coast and islands** (p398) For coastal walks with wilder edge, there's simply nothing better.

High Walks

■ **Ben Nevis and Glen Coe** (p359) When it comes to high walks, in Scotland you're spoilt for choice, but the peaks in this iconic area are a great starting point.

■ **Snowdonia** (p308) The highest mountains in Wales, with wonderful high-level walking and a great mix of terrain.

■ **The Lake District** (p185) The heart and soul of walking in England; inspiration for poets, and summits and ridges for walkers.

River Walks

■ **The Thames Path** (p64 and p88) A long-distance river-side classic, meandering through countryside to the capital.

■ **The Dales Way** (p174) A gem of northern England, following the beautiful River Wharfe through Yorkshire.

■ **The Speyside Way** (p427) A lowland Scottish path beside the famous 'silvery Spey' from the sea to the Cairngorm foothills.

History Walks

■ **Dartmoor** (p97) An ancient landscape dotted with standing stones, burial mounds and Bronze Age settlements.

■ **The Ridgeway** (p83) Walk from Avebury's time-worn stone circle past Neolithic grave mounds and mysterious figures carved in chalk hillsides.

■ **Hadrian's Wall Path** (p213) A route that has it all: Roman remains, medieval castles, battle-fields, even rich industrial heritage.

Wilderness Walks

■ **Northwest Scotland** (p384) Most serious and most rewarding and, without doubt, Britain's finest wilderness area, with its rugged and far-flung mountains.

■ **Cheviot Hills** (p277) One of the wildest parts of England, crossed by the Pennine Way.

■ **The Glyndŵr's Way** (p324) A long-distance route through the remote heart of Mid Wales.

Environment

The island of Britain consists of three nations: England in the south and centre, Scotland to the north and Wales to the west. Further west lies the island of Ireland. Looking southeast, France is just 20 miles away.

THE LAND

Geologically at least, Britain is part of Europe. It's on the edge of the Eurasian landmass, separated from the mother continent by the narrow English Channel (the French are not so proprietorial, and call this strip of water La Manche – the Sleeve). About 10,000 years ago Britain was *physically* part of Europe, but then sea levels rose and created the island we know today. Only in more recent times has there been a reconnection, in the form of the Channel Tunnel.

When it comes to topology, Britain is not a place of extremes. There are no Himalayas or Lake Baikals here. But the geography of Britain is undeniably varied, with plenty to keep you enthralled, and even a short journey can take you through a surprising mix of landscapes. Here we outline the main features by focusing on each country.

RESPONSIBLE WALKING

Walkers as a group tend to care about the environment, and some of the following points you'll have heard before, so hopefully they will just be handy reminders.

When walking in rural areas:

- Guard against all risk of fire – is the great outdoors the place for a cigarette anyway?
- Fasten all gates, or leave them as you found them if they're obviously supposed to be open (to let stock reach water, for example).
- Avoid damaging buildings, fences, hedges, walls, wild plants and trees – or anything else for that matter.
- Leave no litter – take it home. All of it. Don't bury it. For extra points, pick up some of the stuff others have dropped.
- Keep dogs under control – that usually means on a lead or near to you, as a dog chasing a bird or sheep rarely comes when called (whatever their owner thinks)
- Safeguard water supplies – don't pollute streams, rivers or lakes.
- Respect the privacy of people who live and work in the countryside.

Some of the general advice above also applies when you're camping 'wild'. Remember that all land in Britain is privately owned, and wild camping is generally not permitted. Where it is tolerated (in some areas of open mountain and moorland), please ensure that you heed the following:

- Don't wild camp somewhere for more than one night.
- Camp out of sight of roads, houses or popular recreational areas.
- Don't camp in fields enclosed by walls without permission.
- Avoid lighting fires – and handle stoves carefully.
- Keep groups small and avoid pitching where other tents have recently been.
- Leave wild camp sites exactly as you found them – or better.

England

Covering just over 50,000 sq miles, England can be divided into five main geographical areas: northern, central, southwestern, eastern and southeastern.

Northern England is dominated by the Pennines, a chain of mountains, hills and valleys – often dubbed the 'backbone of England' – stretching for 250 miles in a central ridge from Derbyshire to the border with Scotland. The Pennine Way (p261) winds through this range. To the west are the Lake District's scenic Cumbrian Mountains, especially popular with walkers, containing England's highest point, Scafell Pike (978m). Not surprisingly, the bulk of England's best walking areas are in the north of the country.

The central part of England is known as the Midlands, which is mainly flat, heavily populated and an industrial heartland since the 19th century. In the southern part of this region lie the Cotswold Hills, an area of farmland, quaint villages and small market towns, also blending into the northern part of southwest England.

Southwestern England's most notable geographic feature is the Southwest Peninsula, also known as the West Country, with a rugged coastline, good beaches and a mild climate, making it a favourite holiday destination. The South West Coast Path (p133), Britain's longest national trail, and the wild, grass-covered moors of Dartmoor and Exmoor are popular areas with walkers.

Eastern England, or East Anglia is it's usually called, is the flattest part of the country, and a major agricultural area.

The rest of the country is usually lumped together as the Southeast, a region of rolling farmland and several densely populated towns and cities, including London, the capital of both England and Britain. In the southern part of this region are hills of chalk known as 'downs', including the North Downs and South Downs, both crossed by national trails and stretching to the coast where the chalk is exposed as England's iconic white cliffs.

Fascinating interviews with farmers, anglers, walkers, surfers, park rangers and everyday people from around Britain, compiled onto CD as 'audio books', are available from www.rovingear.co.uk. It's like meeting an interesting local in the pub…

WALKING IN WHERE?

It won't have escaped your notice that this title of this book is *Walking in Britain*. The state of Great Britain (shortened to 'Britain') is made up of three countries – England, Wales and Scotland – and those are the areas we describe in this book.

The United Kingdom (UK) consists of Great Britain and Northern Ireland. The island of Ireland consists of Northern Ireland and the Republic of Ireland. The latter, also called Eire, is a completely separate country. We don't cover Irish walks in this book – although there are plenty of options there, as detailed in Lonely Planet's *Walking in Ireland*.

The British Isles is a geographical term for the whole group of islands that make up the UK and the Republic of Ireland, and also includes autonomous or semiautonomous islands such as the Isle of Man and the Channel Isles.

It is quite usual to hear 'England' and 'Britain' used interchangeably but you should, if possible, avoid this – especially in Wales or Scotland. Calling a Scot 'English' is like calling a Canadian 'American' or a New Zealander 'Australian'. Visitors can plead ignorance and get away with an occasional mix-up, but some of the worst offenders are the English themselves, many of whom seem to think that Wales and Scotland *are* parts of England. This naturally angers the Scots and Welsh, fuelling nationalist sentiments, and is completely misunderstood by the English, who simply think their neighbours carry ancient and unreasonable grudges.

NEVER MIND THE BEALACHS

In different parts of Britain geographical features have various names, according to local dialect. For example, a stream is a 'beck' in the Lake District and a 'burn' in Scotland; a valley can be a 'cwm' in Wales, a 'glen' or 'strath' in Scotland and a 'coombe' in southern England. A low point between hills is a 'bwlch' in Wales, a 'haus' in the Lake District and a 'bealach' in Scotland. For more local words, see the Glossary (p472).

Wales

Covering just over 8000 sq miles, Wales is surrounded by sea on three sides. Its border to the east with England still runs roughly along Offa's Dyke, a giant earthwork constructed in the 8th century, today followed by a national trail (see p333). Wales has two major mountain national parks: Snowdonia (with Mt Snowdon, at 1085m, the highest peak in Wales) in the north and the Brecon Beacons in the south. In between is the wild and empty landscape of the Cambrian Mountains. The population is concentrated in Wales' southeast, along the coast between the cities of Cardiff (the capital) and Swansea, and in the Valleys (a former mining centre) that run north from here.

Scotland

Scotland covers about 30,000 sq miles, two-thirds of which is mountain and moorland and therefore very popular with walkers. The Central Lowlands run from Edinburgh (the capital and financial centre) in the east to Glasgow (the industrial centre) in the west, and include the industrial belt and the majority of the population. A coastal plain runs most of the way up the east coast. Between the Central Lowlands and the border with England are the Southern Uplands, an area of rolling hills and deep valleys. To the north of the Central Lowlands are the Highlands, a vast, sparsely populated area where most of the major mountain ranges are found. Ben Nevis, at 1344m the highest mountain in Scotland and Britain, is near the town of Fort William. The most spectacular (and most remote) mountains are those in the northwest.

Scotland has 790 islands, 130 of them inhabited. The Western Isles comprise the Inner Hebrides and the Outer Hebrides. Two other island groups are Orkney and Shetland, the northernmost part of the British Isles.

WILDLIFE

Britain may be a small country but it boasts a surprisingly diverse range of natural habitats, thanks partly to the country's wide range of climatic influences – from cold Arctic winds howling down the glens of northern Scotland, to the warm waters of the Gulf Stream lapping the beaches in southern Cornwall.

Some native plant and animal species are hidden away but it's easy to spot undoubted gems, from woods carpeted in shimmering bluebells to a stately herd of red deer in the mountains. This wildlife is part of the fabric of Britain, and having a closer look as you walk will enhance your trip enormously.

Animals

When you're walking through farmland and woodland areas, you'll easily spot small birds such as the robin, with its red breast and cheerful whistle, and the yellowhammer, with its 'little-bit-of-bread-and-no-cheese' song. You might also hear the warbling cry of a skylark as it

For in-depth information on the nation's flora and fauna, www.wild aboutbritain.co.uk is a comprehensive, accessible, interactive, award-winning site.

LINE OF DUTY

A particularly important aspect of responsible walking in Britain concerns rights of way, meaning you can cross private land, as long as you keep to the path (for more details see p448). It's the duty of walkers not to deviate from the right of way and to do no damage. If a right of way is obstructed, you can remove enough of the impediment to pass. Sometimes, though, a right of way may go straight across a field sown with crops. In such cases you can go legally (but carefully) through the crops, but discretion is advised and it is usually more responsible to walk round the edge of the field.

Considering the size of Britain, in practice there are surprisingly few rules and regulations. Mostly it comes down to common sense. If there's no stile and you have to climb over a wall to cross a field, chances are you shouldn't be there.

Away from cultivated areas, up on mountains and moorlands, paths can get very boggy and walkers often seek the drier ground on the edge of the path, gradually making it wider and exposing soil or peat and damaging sensitive vegetation. The advice here is to stick to the path rather than widen it, even if it means getting your boots dirty. In some other areas, however, walkers are encouraged *not* to keep to a single line, to spread the load and avoid creating lines of bare earth through the grass. In the area around Hadrian's Wall, for example, notice boards specifically ask people to walk side by side since keeping a solid cover of vegetation means archaeological remains are better protected.

---

flutters high over the fields – a classic, but now threatened, sound of the British countryside.

Between the fields, hedges provide cover for flocks of finches, but these seed-eaters must watch out for the sparrowhawk – a bird of prey that comes from nowhere at tremendous speed. Other aerial predators include the barn owl, a wonderful sight as it flies silently along hedgerows listening for the faint rustle of a mouse, or other mouse-like creatures such as a vole or shrew. In rural Wales or Scotland you may see a buzzard, Britain's most common large raptor.

Also in fields, look out for the increasingly rare brown hare; it's related to the rabbit but is much larger, with longer legs and ears. Males who battle for territory in early spring are, of course, as 'mad as a March hare'.

A classic British mammal is the red fox. As you walk though the countryside – especially towards dusk – you may see one, but these wily beasts adapt well to any situation, so you're just as likely to see them scavenging in towns and even in city suburbs. A controversial law banning the hunting of foxes with dogs was introduced in 2005, but it's too early to see what impact this has had on population numbers.

Another well-known British mammal is the black-and-white-striped badger. This animal is nocturnal so you'll probably only see its large burrows when you're walking in lowland areas, but if you're driving at night you might catch sight of 'old Brock' in your headlights. Some farmers believe badgers spread tuberculosis to cattle, although the evidence is inconclusive, and the debate rumbles on between the agricultural and environmental lobbies.

In woodland areas, mammals include the small, white-spotted fallow deer and the even smaller roe deer. They're timid, so you're only like to see them if you're walking along very quietly. Also in woodland, if you hear rustling among the fallen leaves it might be a hedgehog – a cute, spiny-backed insect-eater – though it's an increasingly rare sound these days. Conservationists predict that hedgehogs will be extinct in Britain by 2025,

(Continued on page 45)

Ridges, Rivers & Romans

A meandering descent on Ben Hope (p430), Scotland's northernmost Munro

MARK DAFFEY

The fertile Long Man of Wilmington (p132), seen along the South Downs Way

DAVID TOMLINS

On a map of the world Britain appears small, but this island boasts a spectacular and varied landscape. From the rolling whaleback hills of Dartmoor to the airy mountain peaks of Snowdonia, this is a country tailor-made for walkers. In the space of a few days, or even a few hours, you can walk along cliff tops overlooking the sea, trot across moors with only the sound of the breeze for company, and scramble up to rocky summits with views in all directions.

Britain boasts many thousands of miles of footpaths, a network that can take you rambling through picturesque Cumbrian villages or striding along remote Scottish glens. In addition, there are vast areas of mountain and moorland where you can leave the paths and explore the wilderness as much and as far as you like.

The only possible downside to this wonderful variety is deciding where to go. We hope this chapter will help. Instead of dividing walking routes into geographical areas, we've divided them into themes: Walking through History, Flora & Fauna, City Escapes, Mountain Challenges and Rugged but Reachable. Of course, there are some overlaps – the Thames Path, for example, is rich in history *and* a great place to spot watery wildlife – but we hope this gives you a few pointers when you're planning your trip.

As well as the walks and areas covered in detail by this book, we also suggest a few places off the beaten track that you can go and discover for yourself. With a map, a backpack and a sense of adventure (and sense of direction!), the rest is up to you.

Stonehenge

DAVID RYAN

Housesteads Fort (p225), Hadrian's Wall

VERONICA GARBUTT

WALKING THROUGH HISTORY

Britain may be a small island on the edge of Europe, but it was never on the sidelines of history. For thousands of years, invaders and incomers have arrived, settled and made their mark. The result is Britain's fascinating mix of landscapes, cultures and historic sites – and walking through Britain is one of the best ways of seeing them.

Perhaps Britain's best-known historic sites are Stonehenge, a circle of menhirs on windswept Salisbury Plain, and the nearby, larger, stone circle at Avebury. In the surrounding area are many more relics from past eras: 5000-year-old Bronze Age burial mounds, Iron Age forts and mysterious figures carved in the chalk – even a place where horses will be magically re-shod overnight. And you can see them all on the Ridgeway (p83), where hikers follow the footsteps of the ancient people who walked this route many millennia ago.

Jump forward a few centuries and you reach another famous historic site: Hadrian's Wall, a battlement stretching 75 miles across the country, built by the Romans in the 2nd century AD to mark the edge of their great empire – and to keep out rowdy Scots. Despite the passing of almost 2000 years, much of Hadrian's Wall has survived the ages remarkably well and, with various forts, turrets and castles, it's protected as a World Heritage Site. It's also followed by the Hadrian's Wall Path (p213), a week-long national trail that's fast becoming one of the most popular in Britain.

For another border walk, you could follow Offa's Dyke Path (p333), a national trail based on a defensive ditch or 'earthwork' constructed in the 8th century by King Offa, ruler of

Barn owl (p32)   Puffin (p46)

DAVID TIPLING   DAVID TIPLI

Mercia, to mark the boundary between his kingdom and Celtic stronghold of Wales, and – you guessed it – to keep out the rowdy Welsh. Even today, though only 80 miles of the dyke remains, the modern Wales–England border roughly follows its line. The Offa's Dyke Path crosses and recrosses that border around 30 times, passing castles and battlefields, and heading through Welsh and English villages that are notably different in character, even though they may be just a few miles apart.

Other walks with a historic theme include the Thames Path (p64 and p88), the definitive walk through the annals of England, from Roman remains near the source in the Cotswolds, to Windsor Castle and the giant wheel of the London Eye, a monument to the second millennium. Then there's the Pembrokeshire Coast Path (p291), especially around St David's; the Clarendon Way (p74) between the cathedrals of Winchester and Salisbury; the valley of Glen Coe (p369); the Pilgrim's Way to Canterbury (see North Downs Way on p70); and just about anywhere on the southern edge of Dartmoor (p97), where you can hardly walk without tripping over a medieval marker stone, a Bronze Age village or granite blocks originally destined for London Bridge.

FLORA & FAUNA

Britain's varied landscape means a surprisingly diverse range of plants and animals, although you won't find vast deserts or wild beasts such as bears here, as you might when hiking elsewhere in the world – but, then, that's a major plus for walkers…

Some of Britain's most spectacular walks follow the coastline – a dramatic melee of high cliffs, sandy beaches, wave-cut rocky platforms, tidal flats, marshes and estuaries – and this is also one of the finest places to spot wildlife, especially during spring and early summer (March to June) when they are home to thousands of breeding sea birds. Guillemots, razorbills and kittiwakes fight for space on impossibly crowded rock ledges, while comical puffins with their distinctive rainbow beaks burrow into sandy banks to make their nests. Up above, gannets are one of Britain's largest sea birds, making dramatic dives for fish. These avian delights can all be seen on Britain's two finest long-distance seaside routes, the Pembrokeshire Coast Path (p291) and the South West Coast Path (p133), and on many of the coastal walks in Scotland's Western Highlands (p384) and around islands such as Skye (p398), Arran (p353) and the salt-splashed northern outliers of Orkney and Shetland (p430). In the water itself you'll see seals bobbing around, and with a keen eye you'll spot dolphins and even sharks.

Inland, many of Britain's best walking routes take you though meadows and farmland, where fields that escape artificial fertilizers and pesticides come alive with wildflowers – especially in spring and summer. In places such as the Cotswolds (p107), look out for the fairy-tale-named cowslips, primroses and buttercups. These flowers also grow in areas such as the Yorkshire Dales (p165) and the limestone valleys of the Peak District (p151), alongside several species of orchid.

Britain may not have rainforest or jungle, but it does have some beautiful swathes of woodland. The Centenary Walk (p59) winds through Epping Forest, a surprisingly sylvan outing so close to London's outskirts, while there are lovely patches of tree-shaded walking along the Cleveland Way (p252), Wye Valley Walk (p341) and North Downs Way (p70).

Heather (p253) in bloom GREG GAWLOWSKI

Bluebells in beech woodland DAVID TIPLING

Tryfan's north ridge (p315)

DAVID ELSE

TOP FIVES

Still can't decide where to go? Here's a no-prisoners list of our favourite walking destinations in Britain. You may disagree, and that's fine – as long as you've been to all the other places first.

Mountains

- Beinn Alligin (p390)
- Buachaille Etive Mór (p370)
- Pen-y-Ghent (p172)
- Scafell Pike (p197)
- Tryfan (p315)

Flora & Fauna

- The Cotswolds (p107)
- Isle of Skye (p398)
- Norfolk (p71)
- The Pembrokeshire Coast Path (p291)
- The Yorkshire Dales (p165)

City Escapes

- Cardiff to the Brecon Beacons (p281)
- Glasgow to Ben Lomond (p347)
- Liverpool to Snowdonia (p308)
- London to Corrour and the Road to the Isles (p365)
- Manchester to the Pennines (p261)

Other areas great for wildlife walking include Norfolk (p71), where the coast has some of Britain's best bird reserves, while the meadows around the inland waterways of the Broads are rich in flowers and butterflies.

CITY ESCAPES

When you're walking through the wilds of Scotland, or the mountains of Mid Wales, you wouldn't think for a moment that Britain is a heavily urbanised nation. Even following the Pennine Way, as it snakes along the high moors separating Manchester and Leeds, you can be less than an hour from city streets while enjoying clean air, wide views and good paths though fabulous open countryside.

So turn this to your advantage. Whether you're a visitor from overseas or just looking for a weekend break from work, there are many great walking options within easy striking distance of the major cities.

Let's start with London. The Thames Path (p64 and p88) is on the doorstep, of course, so why not catch a train upstream then spend a day or two (or longer) walking back home? Or sample the great chalky hills of the South Downs, offering one-day strolls or longer walks along the South Downs Way (p123), a roller-coaster hike from Winchester to the sea. The nearby Clarendon Way (p74) is also perfect for a weekend getaway. In the other direction sit Norfolk and Suffolk (p71), with plenty of relaxing rambles.

Good train services mean you can strike out further. A long weekend in the Brecon Beacons (p281) is eminently possible for Londoners, although these great rolling hills and deep corries are more easily reached from Cardiff, the Welsh capital. For a real sense of changing places, from London you can get an overnight train to Scotland, wake up to the sight of scenic glens, and get off at remote Corrour, heading into the wilds on the Road to the Isles (p365) straight from the station platform.

From the northwestern cities of Liverpool or Manchester you can easily reach the Pennines, the 'backbone of England'. Or get a bit organised, make an early start, and by mid-morning you can be striding up Snowdon (p311) or another fine peak in North Wales.

From the West Country gateways of Bath and Bristol you can easily reach the Cotswolds (p107), or simply follow the Kennet & Avon Canal Path (p80). Further north, the cities of Carlisle and Newcastle-upon-Tyne are good jumping-off points for walks along Hadrian's Wall (p213), through the stark and beautiful hills of the North Pennines (p261) or across the empty, big-sky landscape of the Cheviot Hills (p234).

Then, of course, there are the northern centres of Edinburgh and Glasgow, from where the walkers' paradise of Scotland lies within reach. It's a mere hop to the glens and peaks around famous Loch Lomond (p346), or to Arran (p353), the island billed as 'Scotland in miniature', with several great and varied choices for walkers. With a skip and a jump you could be in the Southern Uplands (p408), or stepping off the train in Fort William and heading up Ben Nevis (p360), or alighting in the fine port town of Oban and catching the ferry across to Mull (p431).

Standing stones below Goatfell (p354) on the Isle of Arran

GRAEME CORNWALLIS

YOU WOULDN'T THINK FOR A MOMENT THAT BRITAIN IS A HEAVILY URBANISED NATION

Dawn mist wrapped around Glen Coe's mighty Buachaille Etive Mór (p370).

GARETH McCORMACK

MOUNTAIN CHALLENGES

Britain has plenty of options for strollers, and those who like to tie in walks with a relaxed pub lunch, but if you like to get high on the big hills and work up a sweat with a serious outing, there's a massive choice as well.

Post box and mountains, Great Langdale (p205), Lake District

DAVID TOMLINSON

A great place to start is the Lake District, the heart and soul of walking in England. To reach the summit of Scafell, England's highest peak, we describe a classic route (p197), plus a longer alternative taking in neighbouring peaks; it's a walk that'll take your breath away – in more ways that one. On Helvellyn (p192), another major Lakeland mountain, the walk up and down is stiff enough, especially if you enjoy the scramble along the narrow ridge of Striding Edge, but for a really good long day out you can extend the loop, taking the alternative route over the summits of neighbouring Dollywaggon Pike and Fairfield. Or head north, over Helvellyn and along a broad ridge to Great Dodd and Stybarrow Dodd (p210) – a stunning route known as the 'Backbone of the Eastern Fells'. And if all that still sounds like a stroll in the park, you can start bagging the 214 separate summits known as 'Wainwrights' (see the boxed text, p188); some people take years to do it, others do the lot in a week. For an even more serious challenge, the Bob Graham Round (see www.bobgrahamround.co.uk) takes in 42 Lake District peaks, covering around 75 miles with a total ascent of more than 8700m, all within 24 hours. Some superhuman fell-runners do it in just over half that time.

For mere mortals, other mountain challenges include the famous Three Peaks of Yorkshire (p170), a 25-mile circular hike over the summits of Whernside, Ingleborough and Pen-y-ghent, that keen walkers try to do within 12 hours. In Wales, the Brecon Beacon Ridge Walk (p283) is a long enough walk, over the famous summits of Pen y Fan and Fan y Big ('fan' simply means 'peak' in Welsh), but can always be turned into a longer route by tying in peaks to the west, including Fan Frynich – a route known as the Fan Dance by soldiers who train in this area.

An airy view to Llyn Llydaw on the Snowdon Traverse (p311)

GRANT DIXON

Also in Wales, the Snowdonia mountains offer more challenges. Many walkers aim for a traverse of Snowdon (p311), the country's highest peak, but a tougher challenge is the classic Snowdon Horseshoe, taking in the knife-edge ridge of Crib Goch, where a wrong step can send you plummeting down sheer cliffs. The neighbouring mountains of Tryfan ('three peaks'), Glyder Fawr and Glyder Fach are another great mountain challenge when done in one hit (see p315). For more fun and games, tie Snowdon, Tryfan and the Glyders together, or go for the best-known mountain challenge in the region, the Welsh Three-Thousanders (p321), summiting 15 peaks over 3000ft (914m) in less than 24 hours.

And then there's Scotland, where the mountain vistas go on for ever and the challenges are virtually endless as well. Classic summits include Ben Nevis (p360), the highest peak in the whole of Britain, and nearby sit the iconic mountains of Buachaille Etive Mór (p370) and Buachaille Etive Baeg – the 'great shepherd' and 'small shepherd' of Etive – overlooking Glen Coe. For yet more walks from base-town Fort William, head for the wilder ranges: the Mamores (p372) and Grey Corries (p373).

Further north, even greater challenges lie in the Cairngorms (p376), one of the country's most serious mountain ranges, equally renowned for its stunning beauty, remote atmosphere and fearsome weather. Come here for a taste of the tundra, especially in winter – although snow in high summer isn't unknown.

Skye's Black Cuillin (p400) is a favourite with walkers and nimble scramblers

GARETH McCORMAC

To the west is Skye (p398), dominated by the long, serrated ridge of the Black Cuillin. A classic route to the crest follows Bruach na Fríthe (p404), but for one of Britain's best-known mountain challenges you can go *along* the ridge, a very serious undertaking for only the most experienced high-level walkers with legs of steel and a head for heights, not to mention a rope and some rock-climbing knowledge.

> Perhaps it's time to get serious and start ticking off Munros... there are 284 in total

In the Western Highlands the landscape is covered by peaks, many providing mountain challenges to satisfy even the most demanding walker. For starters, sample the Five Sisters of Kintail (p386), a classic line of summits overlooking Glen Shiel. In the Torridon area, Beinn Alligin (p390) is another classic, as are neighbouring Beinn Eighe (p393), Beinn Dearg and Liathach, a famously massive wall of a mountain festooned with pinnacles and buttresses.

Still hungry for more? Try an ascent of double-tiered Slioch (p393), rising majestically from the shores of Loch Maree; attack An Teallach (p397), another Scottish classic; or explore wild and rarely visited Glen Affric (p396). And still you're just skimming the surface. Perhaps it's time to get serious and start ticking off Munros (p349) – all the mountains in Scotland over 3000ft. There are 284 in total and, as with the Wainwrights and other groups of peaks with collective names, some people take a lifetime bagging them all, while others seem to saunter over them in a season. The record for a single 'round' of the Munros is less than seven weeks, but then we're back in the realm of superhumans again.

THE LONG WALKS

Where Nepal has the Annapurna Circuit and America has the Appalachian Trial, Britain has the Pennine Way and the Coast to Coast Walk – plus many other long-distance routes. They may not match their overseas cousins in length or altitude but the long walks of Britain certainly lack nothing in terms of scenery, variety, quality and – the big plus – feasibility. Most of the best-known routes are easily reached and can be done virtually on a whim, often in just two or three weeks, although others such as the South West Coast Path and Monarch's Way (both around 600 miles) may take up to eight.

The long routes are not necessarily hard – you can potter along at 10 miles per day, if you're not strapped for time. And most are not wilderness walks – they pass through villages with walker-friendly B&Bs and welcoming pubs. But as you settle into a long walk there's a very special enjoyment of travelling from place to place through the landscape.

Below is a short list of our favourite classic long walks. For an idea of other options, see the website of the **Long Distance Walkers Association** (www.ldwa.org.uk).

Walk	Distance	Duration	Page
The Coast to Coast Walk	191 miles (307.5km)	12 days	237
The Cotswold Way	102 miles (164km)	7 days	109
The Dales Way	84 miles (135km)	6 days	174
The Offa's Dyke Path	177.5 miles (285km)	12 days	333
The Pennine Way	255 miles (411km)	16 days	261
The South Downs Way	107 miles (172km)	8 days	123
The South West Coast Path	630 miles (1014km)	50-60 days	134
The Thames Path	173 miles (278km)	12 days	64 & 88
The West Highland Way	95 miles (153km)	7 days	418

South West Coast Path (p133), Dorset
DAVID TOMLINSON

Peak District (p151) stile
DAVID ELSE

Peak conditions: a misty view across the Peak District National Park from Froggatt Edge (p164)

RUGGED BUT REACHABLE

So if you're *not* looking for a mountain challenge but still want a flavour of Britain's more rugged landscapes, as well as cosy strolls through bucolic countryside, where can you go? Dartmoor (p97) is a great place to start; this vast expanse of wild grassland is ringed by towns and villages, offering relatively straightforward access to the high hills, Bronze Age remains and characteristic spiky rock tors.

In the Peak District, the Edale Skyline (p154) is no idle jaunt, but it gives a great taste of the wild Pennine moors, and you can still have a pint in the pub at lunchtime. For a mix of wild beaches and good pit stops, the Northumberland coast (p229) is ideal.

In Wales, head for the Preseli Hills (p304), an area rich in history and mystery, where paths are clear and the views across farmland, heath and seascape, simply divine. Or follow the Glyndŵr's Way (p324), a national trail through the heart of seldom-visited Mid Wales, walking over rolling, grassy mountains by day, and staying in friendly village inns by night.

Though Scotland is best known for its challenging walks, even non-hardcore walkers can experience its rugged landscape. A good starter is the ascent of Ben Lomond (p347), or coast walks on the easily reached islands of Arran (p353), Jura (p358) and Skye (p398). Further north, there's the steep-sided but surprisingly accessible Stac Pollaidh (p430). And, finally, out across the sea, you can delight in relatively easy options on the islands of Rum, Harris, Barra (p430), Orkney and Shetland (p430), forever tempting the walker as they bask in the glow of a rich Scottish sunset.

(Continued from page 32)

possibly thanks to increased building in rural areas, the use of insecticides in farming and the changing nature of both the countryside and the city parks and gardens that once made up the hedgehog's traditional habitat.

In the trees, you're much more likely to see a grey squirrel. This species was introduced from North America and has proved so adaptable that the native British red squirrel is severely endangered (see the boxed text, below). Much larger than squirrels is the pine marten, which is seen in some forested regions, especially in Scotland. With a beautiful brown coat, it was once hunted for its fur but is now fully protected.

Out of the trees and up in the moors, birds you might see include the red grouse, a popular 'game bird', and the curlew, with its elegant curved bill. Also in the moorland, as well as some lower farmed areas, the golden plover is beautifully camouflaged so you have to look hard. But you can't miss its cousin, the lapwing, often showing off with its spectacular aerial displays, although unfortunately it's one of Britain's fastest-declining species – conservationists are making efforts to maintain the well-watered upland farm habitat it needs to survive.

The most visible moorland mammal is the red deer. Herds survive on Exmoor and Dartmoor, in the Lake District and in larger numbers in Scotland. The males are most spectacular after June, when their antlers have grown ready for the rutting season. The stags keep their antlers through the winter and then shed them again in February. (For information on hunting deer with guns, as opposed to with dogs, in Scotland, and how this impacts walkers, see the boxed text, p388.)

Birds you may see when walking in mountain areas include the red kite (in Wales there has been a successful project to reintroduce this spectacular fork-tailed raptor), while on the high peaks of Scotland you may see the grouse's northern cousin, the ptarmigan, dappled brown in the summer but white in the winter. Also in the Scottish mountains, keep an eye peeled for the golden eagle, Britain's largest bird of prey.

If you're walking near rivers, look along the banks for signs of the water vole, an endearing rodent also called a 'water rat' (and the inspiration for Ratty in *Wind in the Willows*). It was once common but has been all but wiped out by wild mink (introduced from America to stock fur farms).

Handy wildlife guides (*Trees, Birds, Wild Flowers, Insects* etc) are produced by the Wildlife Trusts (www.wildlifetrusts.org). The website is a great source of information, and proceeds from book sales support environmental campaigns.

SEEING RED

The red squirrel was once a common species in many parts of woodland Britain, but it's now one of the country's most endangered mammals. Where they once numbered in the millions, populations have declined significantly over the last 60 years to about 150,000 – confined mainly to Scotland, with isolated groups in the Lake District, Norfolk and the Isle of Wight – and the simple reason for this is the arrival of larger grey squirrels from North America.

The problem isn't grey squirrels attacking their red cousins; the problem is food. Greys can eat hazelnuts and acorns when they're still tough, whereas reds can only eat these nuts when they're soft and ripe. So the greys get in first, and there's little left over for the reds. So thorough are the greys that once they arrive in an area the reds are usually gone within about 15 years.

One place where reds can do well is pine plantations, as they're more adept than greys at getting the seeds out of pine cones, but even this advantage is threatened as, in recent years, the indomitable and adaptable greys have started learning the technique.

The red squirrel fills an important ecological niche in Britain and is a legally protected species, with various national and local schemes in place to hopefully ensure its survival. Websites with more information include www.squirrelweb.co.uk and www.red-squirrels.org.uk.

In contrast to water voles, the formerly rare otter is beginning to make a comeback after suffering from polluted water, habitat destruction and persecution by anglers. In southern Britain it inhabits the banks of rivers and lakes, and in Scotland it frequently lives on the coast. Although its numbers are growing, it's mainly nocturnal and hard to see, but keep alert and you might be lucky. Also near water, you have a chance of spotting an osprey, a magnificent fish-eating bird of prey; the Cairngorms are among best places in Britain for a sighting.

On the coasts of Britain, particularly in Cornwall, Pembrokeshire and northwest Scotland, the dramatic cliffs are a marvellous sight in early summer (around May), when they are home to hundreds of thousands of breeding sea birds. Guillemots, razorbills and kittiwakes, among others, fight for space on impossibly crowded rock ledges. The sheer numbers of birds makes this one of Britain's finest wildlife spectacles, as the cliffs become white with droppings and the air is filled with their shrill calls.

Another bird to look out for in coastal areas is the comical puffin (especially common in Orkney and Shetland), with its distinctive rainbow beak and underground nests burrowed in sandy soil. In total contrast, the perfectly designed gannet is one of Britain's largest sea birds, most spectacular when it makes dramatic dives for fish, often from a great height.

And, finally, the sea mammals. Two species of seal frequent British coasts, with the larger grey seal more often seen than the (misnamed) common seal. Walking along the cliff-top paths in Cornwall, Pembrokeshire and particularly Scotland, you may see dolphins and porpoises, and even minke whales. With luck you may also spot basking sharks, especially from May to September when viewing conditions are best. For more reliable sightings it might be best to combine your walking with a wildlife-watching boat trip – we mention where this is possible in the walk descriptions throughout this book.

Plants

In any part of Britain, the best places to see wildflowers are in areas that have evaded large-scale farming. For example, in April and May some grazing fields erupt with great profusions of cowslips and primroses in the chalky hill country of the South Downs and Wiltshire Downs in southern England – crossed by the South Downs Way (p123) and the Ridgeway (p83) – and in limestone areas such as the Peak District (p151) and Yorkshire Dales (p165) in northern England.

Some flowers prefer woodland, and the best time to visit these areas is also April and May. This is because the leaf canopy of the woods hasn't at that time fully developed, allowing sunlight to break through to encourage plants such as bluebell – a beautiful and internationally rare species.

Another classic British plant is gorse – you can't miss the swathes of this spiky bush in sandy heathland areas, most notably in the New Forest in southern England. Legend says that it's the season for kissing when gorse blooms; luckily, its vivid yellow flowers show year-round.

In contrast, the blooming season is quite short – though spectacular – for heather, a low, woody bush found mainly on moors. On the Scottish mountains, the Pennines of northern England and Dartmoor in the south, the hill tops are covered in a riot of purple in August and September.

Britain's natural deciduous trees include oak, ash, hazel and rowan, with seeds and leaves supporting a vast range of insects and birds. The New Forest in southern England and the Forest of Dean on the Wales–England border are good examples of this type of habitat. In some parts of Scotland, stands of indigenous Caledonian pine can still be seen. As you

Complete British Birds by Paul Sterry is full of excellent photographs and handy notes, ideal for identifying anything feathered you may see on your walk.

Complete Guide to British Wildlife by Norman Arlott, Richard Fitter and Alastair Fitter is a highly recommended single volume ideal for walkers, covering mammals, birds, fish, plants, snakes, insects and even fungi.

travel through Britain you're also likely to see non-native pines, standing in dark plantations devoid of wildlife. Thankfully for Britain's wildlife (and for walkers who like to see birds, plants and animals), large-scale conifer planting is on the decline, and an increasing number of deciduous trees are being planted instead.

NATIONAL PARKS

Way back in 1810, famous poet and walker William Wordsworth suggested that the Lake District should be 'a sort of national property, in which every man has a right and interest who has an eye to perceive and a heart to enjoy'. But it took more than a century for the Lake District to become a national park and it was very different from the 'sort of national property' Wordsworth envisaged.

Other national parks in Britain are the Brecon Beacons, Cairngorms, Dartmoor, Exmoor, Loch Lomond and the Trossachs, New Forest, Norfolk and Suffolk Broads, Northumberland, North York Moors, Peak District, Pembrokeshire Coast, Snowdonia and Yorkshire Dales. A new park, the South Downs in southern England, was in the process of being created at the time of research. In this book we describe a range of walks – long and short – in most of these areas.

Combined, Britain's national parks now cover more than 10% of the country. It's an impressive total, but the term 'national park' can cause confusion. First, these areas are not state-owned: nearly all land is private, belonging to farmers, companies, estates and conservation organisations. (Just to increase the confusion, large sections of several national parks are owned by the National Trust but, despite the similar name, this private charity has no direct link with the national park administrative authorities.) Second, Britain's national parks are not total wilderness areas, as in many other countries. In Britain's national parks you'll see roads, railways, villages and even towns. Development is strictly controlled, but about 250,000 people live and work inside national park boundaries. Some of them work in industries such as quarrying, which ironically does great damage to these supposedly protected landscapes. On the flip side, these industries provide vital jobs (although sometimes for people outside the park), and several wildlife reserves have been established on former quarry sites.

But don't despair! Despite these apparent anomalies, national parks still contain vast tracts of wild mountains and moorland, rolling downs and river valleys and other areas of quiet countryside, all ideal for long walks, easy rambles, or just lounging around. They are still among the most scenic areas of Britain, but being aware of their actual status will lessen the surprise for some visitors, especially if you're used to places like Yellowstone or Kakadu. To help you get the best from Britain's national parks, there are information centres, and all provide various recreational facilities (trails, car parks, camp sites etc) for visitors.

The current number of visits to British national parks is more than 100 million every year. That's a lot of footsteps – though many visitors don't get far beyond the car park. Some conservationists believe national parks are counterproductive, claiming that giving an area a precise name and boundaries creates an increase in visitors, putting unsustainable pressure on the land and local resources. It seems there's never an easy solution.

It's also worth noting that there are many beautiful parts of Britain that are *not* national parks (such as the Cambrian Mountains of Mid Wales, the North Pennines in England and many parts of Scotland). These can be just as good for exploring on foot, and – as the anti-park conservationists point out – are often less crowded than the national parks.

The Woodland Trust (www.woodland-trust.org.uk) buys and conserves woods and forests all over Britain – and allows walkers free access to many of them.

The Royal Society for the Protection of Birds (www.rspb.org.uk) runs more than 100 bird reserves across the UK.

Other Protected Areas

Wildlife Walks, edited by Malcolm Tait (with a foreword by the nation's favourite ecologist, David Bellamy), suggests days out in more than 500 wildlife reserves across the country.

As you enjoy your walking in Britain, you'll undoubtedly pass through protected areas other than national parks – most are identified by a bewildering array of acronyms. First up are Areas of Outstanding Natural Beauty (AONBs), the second tier of protection for landscapes in England and Wales, all of which have excellent walking opportunities. There are about 40 such areas – including famous regions such as the Cotswold Hills (crossed by the Cotswold Way, p109) and less-known parts of the country such as the Solway Firth, a tranquil part of north Cumbria crossed by Hadrian's Wall Path (p213).

In Scotland, National Nature Reserves (NNRs) are usually sizeable areas, more or less wild, or at least uninhabited. These reserves are owned or leased by Scottish Natural Heritage, or by conservation organisations such as the Royal Society for the Protection of Birds and National Trust for Scotland. For walkers, some of the finest NNRs are Beinn Eighe (p393) and Creag Meagaidh (p396). Others include Hermaness (Shetland), Ben Lawers (Central Highlands), Glen Affric in the Highlands and Loch Lomond. There's also a vast NNR within Cairngorms National Park. Most NNRs are readily accessible, and the most popular reserves offer ranger-led guided walks.

Another protected area popular with walkers is a Heritage Coast. Once again, the clue's in the name – these are particularly scenic or environmentally important areas of coastline. You'll also encounter Sites of Special Scientific Interest (SSSIs), protecting the most important areas of wildlife habitat and geological formation in Britain; Environmentally Sensitive Areas (ESAs); and Countryside Stewardship Schemes (CSSs), which are intended to help farmers protect or manage their land in a more environmentally positive manner.

Conspiracy theorists claim that the sheer number of protected areas and governmental organisations charged with environmental protection is a deliberate move to prevent any one body becoming too powerful. Whether this is true or not, there are two important points to remember:

BRITAIN'S WORLD HERITAGE

Some areas in Britain have been declared World Heritage Sites – places of great environmental or cultural significance. There are around 700 sites globally, of which about 20 are in Britain. Those on or near walking routes described in this book include:

- The Georgian city of **Bath** – at the start of the Cotswold Way (p109)

- The mills of the **Derwent Valley** – near the start of the Limestone Way (p158)

- **Hadrian's Wall** – followed in its entirety by Hadrian's Wall Path (p213)

  The stone circles of **Stonehenge** and **Avebury** – the latter near the start of the Ridgeway (p83)

- The castles of **Caernarfon, Conwy, Beaumaris** and **Harlech** – near the mountains of Snowdonia (p308)

- **Cornwall's** coastal mining heritage and the **Dorset and East Devon coast** – both followed by the South West Coast Path (p133)

  The maritime sites of **Greenwich**, the **Royal Botanic Gardens** in Kew, the **Tower of London**, and **Westminster Palace** and **Westminster Abbey** – all passed on the Thames Path (p64)

For more details see www.culture.gov.uk, following the Tourism and Leisure link to 'historic environment'.

THE ANSWER IS BLOWING IN THE WIND

As we go through the early years of the 21st century, renewable energy – most notably in the form of wind turbines – is a major environmental issue in Britain. Of course, these giant towers (and accompanying lines of transmission pylons) ideally need to be sited in high areas away from habitation – just the kind of areas that walkers and conservationists would like to see untouched. Plans to establish vast banks (or 'farms') of wind turbines in areas of outstanding scenery, such as Mid Wales and much of Scotland, have generally been opposed, but the debate is far from over, and demand for energy shows no sign of ebbing. Meantime, walkers still blithely jump into cars and drive considerable distances in pursuit of their hobby. Since public transport services have improved in recent times, perhaps we should all slow down, use less energy at an individual level and think about the future.

like national parks, most protected areas consist of privately owned land; and these special designations do not normally affect rights of way – where they exist, you can use them without worry.

ENVIRONMENTAL ISSUES

With Britain's long history of human occupation, it's not surprising that the landscape's appearance is almost totally the result of people's interactions with the environment. Ever since Neolithic farmers learnt how to make axes, trees have been cleared so that crops could be planted – a trend that has continued into our own time. In Scotland particularly, the Clearances of the 18th century meant that poor tenant farmers were moved off the land by powerful estate owners to make room for sheep, and these animals nibbled to death any saplings brave enough to try growing on the mountainsides. Today, the Highlands is undoubtedly a wilderness, devoid of human habitation in many areas, and a place of rugged beauty, but don't be under any impression that it's 'natural' or 'unspoilt'.

The most dramatic environmental changes hit rural areas of Britain after WWII, especially in England, when a drive to be self-reliant in food meant new farming methods. This changed the landscape from a patchwork of small fields to a scene of vast prairies as walls were demolished, trees felled, ponds filled, wetlands drained and, most notably, hedgerows ripped out.

For many centuries, these hedgerows had formed a network of dense bushes, shrubs and trees that stretched across the countryside protecting fields from erosion, supporting a varied range of flowers and providing shelter for numerous insects, birds and small mammals. But in the postwar rush to improve farm yields, thousands of miles of hedgerow were destroyed. The destruction continued into our own time; from 1984 to 2002 another 25% disappeared. Some remain though, and as you walk through areas such as the Cotswolds or the dales of Derbyshire you'll still see examples of great British hedgerows. A 2006 report from the Countryside Agency indicates that hedgerow destruction has virtually ended, partly because farmers are now encouraged to set aside hedges and other uncultivated areas as havens for wildlife.

Of course, environmental issues are not exclusive to rural areas. In Britain's towns and cities, topics such as air pollution, light pollution, levels of car use, road building, airport construction, public transport provision and household-waste recycling are never far from the political agenda, although some might say they're not near enough to the top of the list. Ironically, Britain's new 'hedgerows' are motorway verges.

The National Trust (www.nationaltrust.org.uk) is one of Britain's major conservation charities and a major landowner, with estates, wilderness areas, parks and woods all over England and Wales, plus about 600 miles of coastline.

Totalling almost 30,000 hectares, these long strips of grass and bushes support many rare plant species, insects and small mammals – that's why kestrels are often seen hovering nearby.

Meanwhile, back in rural Britain, hot environmental issues include farming methods such as irrigation, monocropping and pesticide use. Environmentalists say the results of these unsustainable methods are rivers running dry, fish poisoned by run off, and fields with one type of grass and not another plant to be seen. These 'green deserts' support no insects, which in turn means populations of some wild bird species dropped by an incredible 70% from 1970 to 1990. This is not a case of old, wizened peasants recalling the idyllic days of their forebears; you only have to be over 30 in Britain to remember a countryside where birds such as skylarks or lapwings were visibly much more numerous.

But all is not lost. In the face of apparently overwhelming odds, Britain still boasts great biodiversity, and some of the best wildlife habitats are protected to a greater or lesser extent, thanks to the creation of national parks and similar conservation zones – often within areas privately owned by conservation campaign groups such as the Woodland Trust, National Trust, Wildlife Trusts and the Royal Society for the Protection of Birds. Many of these areas are open to the public, and are ideal spots for walking, bird-watching or simply enjoying the peace and beauty of the countryside.

Also on the plus side, and especially important for an island such as Britain, sea protection is better than it's ever been – a definite plus for walkers as so many excellent routes, such as the Pembrokeshire Coast Path and the South West Coast Path, follow the shoreline, sometimes along beaches, and at other times striding across dramatic cliffs. Major efforts have been made to stem the flow of sewage into the sea, and while oil spills still occur, the clean-up process is quick and efficient. While some coastal areas may still be dirty and polluted, there are many other areas (around southwestern England and much of Wales and Scotland, for example) where the water is clear and many popular holiday beaches are proud holders of 'blue flag' awards. These awards show they meet international standards of cleanliness – on the sand and in the waves. The wild birds, dolphins and whales like clean water, the tourists are happy, the locals make some money and the scenery is stunning for walkers and everyone else to enjoy. It's a win-win-win situation!

The National Trust for Scotland (www.nts.org.uk) has similar objectives to its namesake south of the border, concentrating on buildings and large estates such as Glencoe and Torridon.

The John Muir Trust (www.jmt.org) owns several large estates, including Ben Nevis and three on Skye, and is committed to protecting and conserving wild places in Scotland.

DO WALKERS SHIT IN THE WOODS?

Yes – quite often. So it is something that has to be discussed and not coyly skirted around.

Ideally, when out walking you should use public toilets where provided, but sometimes that's just not possible, so if you have to 'go' in the great outdoors, please do it responsibly. Defecate at least 100m away from water, paths and camp sites; dig a hole and bury your excrement if possible – it will break down in the soil. The hole should be deep enough (around 15cm) to prevent animals from being attracted by the smell and digging it up – which can spread disease. Do *not* simply cover excrement with a stone. If you really can't bury it, it is better out in the sun, where it breaks down more quickly.

Bury toilet paper (biodegradable paper is good for this) or, ideally, carry it out in a bag and dispose of it properly. Tampons and sanitary pads should always be carried out. A sealable plastic bag (nappy sacks are ideal) inside a supermarket carrier bag keeps things safe and out of sight.

After all this malarkey, don't forget to wash your hands! But, please, *not* in a river or stream. Collect some water in a cup and wash you hands away from the waterway. Packs of moist tissues are useful – but carry these out too.

Southern England

GLENN BEANLAND

Southern England

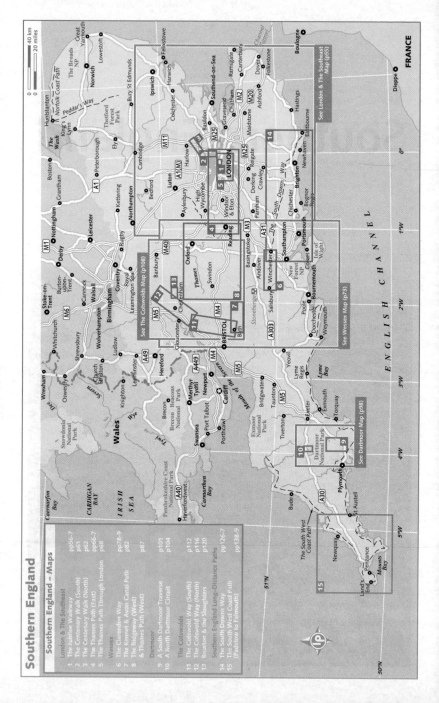

Southern England – Maps

London & The Southeast

0   20 miles
0   40 km

FRANCE

ENGLISH CHANNEL

See London & The Southeast Map (p55)

See Wessex Map (p73)

See Dartmoor Map (p98)

See The Cotswolds Map (p108)

London & the Southeast

Welcome to London – capital of Britain, cosmopolitan melting pot, the world in one city. Visitors come to see the famous sights – Buckingham Palace, Tower Bridge and all – but if you're a local, or you've come to Britain specifically for walking, you'll probably be tempted to skip the big smoke and head straight for the hills. But hold on there! Perhaps surprisingly, London has one of the largest footpath networks of any city in the world, and walking (along with cycling and increased public transport use) is positively encouraged by the city authorities.

We're not talking trackless wilderness, of course, but exploring London on foot can be one of the best ways to see Britain's largest city. Pounding the pavement – not to mention miles of parkland, woodland and river-side path – provides a great opportunity to get under London's skin a little, to see the famous monuments from an unusual angle and to simply explore parts of the city that many visitors never reach.

Beyond London, there are many more opportunities for walking in the surrounding counties of southeastern England – Essex, Hertfordshire, Berkshire, Surrey and Kent – and this chapter outlines one of the finest routes in the region, the Thames Path, leading walkers beside Britain's best-known river from its semi-rural hinterland to the landmark barrier holding back the ever-rising waters of the North Sea. We also describe the 100%-urban Jubilee Walkway through the heart of the capital, and the Centenary Way – an unexpected Cinderella route through green parks and patches of ancient forest little more than a stone's throw from the high-rise buildings of the city centre.

HIGHLIGHTS

- Strolling along **London's South Bank** (p58) from Westminster to Tower Bridge
- Discovering tranquil glades in **Epping Forest** (p61), surprisingly near central London
- Watching the rowers in a quintessential English scene at **Henley-on-Thames** (p65)
- Admiring **Hampton Court Palace** (p68), Henry VIII's splendid Thames-side home
- Drinking in history at one of the many old pubs along the **River Thames** (p64)

INFORMATION
Maps
For route planning and orientation, the Ordnance Survey (OS) 1:250,000 *Southeast England* map covers this large region (with London at the centre) on one sheet. Maps covering individual walks in this chapter are listed in the Planning section of each route description. Homing in on the capital, Lonely Planet's *London City Map* includes several maps of different scales, from the whole of Greater London down to detail of the inner centre. For ultra-detail, a street directory such as the iconic *London A-Z* is always useful.

Books
Walking guidebooks covering London and the Southeast include *London: The definitive walking guide* by Colin Saunders and *Walks in the Country Near London* by Christopher Somerville. Also good for ideas is *100 Walks in South East England* (published by AA).

For before and after your walk, you'll need a general guidebook to help you get around, to recommend places to stay and eat, and to provide more information on places of interest. Lonely Planet's *London* and *Best of London* guides also include descriptions of short walking tours. There's also *The Rough Guide to Walks in London and South East England* by Judith Bamber and Helena Smith. For a different angle, *Eccentric London* by Benedict le Vay guides you well beyond the usual sights.

Guided Walks
The weekly listings magazine *Time Out* includes details of guided walks in and around London in its Around Town section. These range from literary walks through the city streets to pub walks in the parks and leafy suburbs.

Information Sources
For general tourist information, there are tourist offices throughout London and the Southeast – those useful for specific walks described in this chapter are listed in the individual route descriptions. You're probably better off using one of the countless websites covering the capital and its environs; good places to start include www.visit london.com and www.londontown.com.

The **Ramblers' Association** (☎ 020-7339 8500; www.ramblers.org.uk), Britain's largest and most active national walking organisation, is another very useful contact for information on walking in London (as well as the rest of Britain). From its website you can order the excellent *Walking in London* booklet. Other good walking sites include www.london-footprints.co.uk.

GATEWAYS
As well as being the start and end point for a couple of the walks in this chapter, London is the gateway to the Southeast region and a major gateway to Britain for many visitors. The city has a wide range of places to stay, from basic hostels to the finest hotels, and if you're peckish there are about 10,000 restaurants to chose from.

From London you can reach the rest of the country by train or long-distance bus – for details see p458 and p456.

THE JUBILEE WALKWAY

Duration	3–4 hours
Distance	8 miles (13km)
Difficulty	easy
Start/Finish	Leicester Square, central London
Transport	bus, train, tube

Summary A fascinating walk through the streets of ancient and modern London, taking in many popular sights along both sides of the River Thames.

The Jubilee Walkway strides through the heart of London and is a great introduction to walking in the capital. The route was created in 1977 (as the Silver Jubilee Walkway) to celebrate the 25th anniversary of Queen Elizabeth II's accession to the throne, and remains a legacy enjoyed by Londoners and visitors alike. The Walkway passes some of the best-known sights in the city, including Buckingham Palace, Big Ben, St Paul's Cathedral, Tower Bridge, Trafalgar Square and the Tower of London. The route also goes along the south bank of the River Thames, providing excellent views of the great buildings on the northern side, while crossing and recrossing the famous Thames bridges gives some of the finest views of the city.

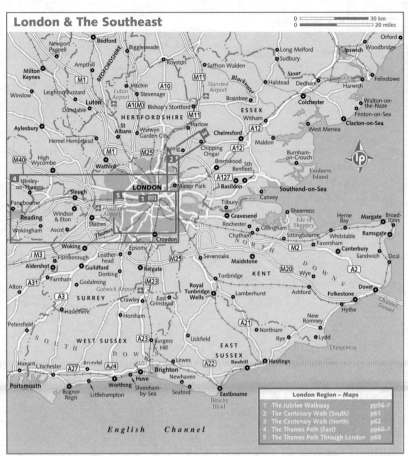

London & The Southeast

London Region – Maps	
1 The Jubilee Walkway	pp56-7
2 The Centenary Walk (South)	p61
3 The Centenary Walk (North)	p62
4 The Thames Path (East)	pp66-7
5 The Thames Path Through London	p68

PLANNING

The main route is circular, with three additional (or optional) loops, running mainly through city streets north of the River Thames and along the traffic-free embankment path along the south side. The official start and finish is Leicester Square. We describe the main route clockwise, but you can start anywhere and go in either direction. The route is signed with silver metal discs marked with a crown and set into the footpaths and pavements; many are scuffed by the passing of countless feet but most have survived the years since 1977 pretty well.

The Jubilee Walkway's total distance is 14 miles (including the three additional loops). The route we describe is 8 miles.

You'll need to at least double the suggested walking time if you stop to look at the sights – and probably double again if you go into just some of the famous buildings along the way. It's best to allow all day, or even two days. Another option is to do the walk as a whole, then come back and separately visit the sights that take your fancy. If you can't do the whole route, we recommend the Leicester Square to Tower Bridge sections.

Maps & Books

A booklet called the *Jubilee Walkway Route Map & Guide* is available from local tourist offices, libraries and museums, although this is one route where you could use the map in our book alone.

The Jubilee Walkway

Information Sources

Your first stop for information should be www.jubileewalkway.com. Numerous information boards along the route explain the history of landmark buildings or interpret the scenes from bridges and other view points. As you walk along the South Bank, you can also pick up a very nice series of *Walk this Way* leaflets from local tourist offices, shops, museums and cafés, describing in detail the various points passed on this section. See also www.southbank london.com.

If you want to know more about all the famous buildings and fascinating sights along the Jubilee Walkway, you'll need a good local guidebook to give more details. See p54 for some suggestions.

THE WALK
Leicester Square to Lambeth Bridge
1 hour, 2 miles

Setting off for your walk from Leicester Square, it's hard to believe this busy London landmark was once a quiet public garden. Today it's most famous for its cinemas – and for its movie premieres when the stars pose for pictures and make handprints in brass plaques in the pavement.

From here, the route heads south to **Trafalgar Square**, dominated by Nelson's Column, then along the Mall for a short distance (with Buckingham Palace, the London home of the Queen, at its western end) before turning left into Horse Guards Rd, with the parade ground on your left and St James's Park on your right. (One of the optional loops takes you down the Mall, past **Buckingham Palace** then along the south side of St James's Park.)

From Trafalgar Square, you may prefer to leave the route briefly, and go along Whitehall instead, past the entrance to **Downing St**, where the prime minister lives at No 10, rejoining the Walkway at the **Houses of Parliament**, dominated at the north end by St Stephen's Tower, commonly called **Big Ben** (actually the name of the bell inside).

The route goes south past **Westminster Abbey** (the coronation place of monarchs since at least the 11th century, and final resting place of Geoffrey Chaucer, Charles Darwin and many other famous names) and just south of Parliament cuts into Victoria Tower Gardens, from where you get your first sight of the Thames, crossed nearby by **Lambeth Bridge**. Some benches, thoughtfully raised so you can see over the embankment wall, provide a good rest spot.

Lambeth Bridge to Tower Bridge
1–1½ hours, 3 miles

Cross the River Thames on Lambeth Bridge, from the north to the south bank. For the next few miles the route stays off the roads and follows walkways beside the river. After passing **Lambeth Palace** (London residence of the Archbishop of Canterbury), there are excellent views of the Houses of Parliament and the nearby Westminster Bridge. Go past the **London Eye**, a giant wheel giving spectacular views over the city, and under Waterloo Bridge. From here the south bank becomes the **South Bank**, an area of theatres, studios, museums, galleries and concert halls, with a lively atmosphere despite the ugly concrete 1960s architecture.

Next, you pass the **Tate Modern**, a former power station now a world-class art gallery, and the silver thread of the **Millennium Bridge** spanning the river. There's a fine view of St Paul's Cathedral, dominating the near skyline on the north side of the river. Walk past **Shakespeare's Globe**, a re-creation of the Bard's original theatre, and go under Southwark Bridge and then a rail bridge rattling with trains (and home to flocks of pigeons – so walk fast and don't look up).

Now you're in **Southwark** (pronounced 'suth-ark'), once a separate town outside London, famous for its taverns, brothels and theatres that flourished beyond the control of the city's lawmakers. From here, the route moves inland slightly away from the river and down Clink St (site of a former prison so notorious that 'clink' became a byword for prison everywhere), then past ancient **Southwark Cathedral** (dating back to Saxon times).

The next feature is **London Bridge**, but the route goes underneath almost without noticing (if you want to stand on the bridge, for great views up and down the river, go up the steps on the left) and past a large office block called St Olaf's House, before cutting down an alley (virtually under the office block) called St Olaf's Stairs to reach the river-side path again. Be sure to visit **Hay's Galleria**, a converted warehouse and dock (one of many that used to line the south bank), now with shops and cafés centred round a large and fantastical metal sculpture.

As you pass the spherical, glass-clad headquarters of the mayor of London and the London Assembly (back by popular demand after being abolished in the 1980s), your view over the river is dominated by **Tower Bridge** – one of London's most famous landmarks. Before crossing to the north bank, with luck you may see the roadway swing open to let a ship through.

Tower Bridge to Leicester Square
1–1½ hours, 3 miles

On the north bank of the River Thames, the official route loops through **St Katharine's Dock**, now a fancy marina with waterside pubs, shops and cafés, but it's more interesting to walk west along the embankment between the river and the **Tower of London**. Built originally by William the Conqueror shortly after the Battle of Hastings in 1066, the tower has been added to by many subsequent monarchs; it is now home to the Crown Jewels and ceremonial guards called Beefeaters. (More prosaically, there are some cafés, snack bars and public loos nearby, so this might be a good spot for a lunch break.)

For the remainder of the route, the path leaves the river and hits the streets. You're now in the **City of London** – usually just called the City or the Square Mile, a separate entity within the metropolis governed by a corporation more than 900 years old that today is London's banking and financial centre. If you thought the City was ancient, next stop is **All Hallows-by-the-Tower**, a church dating from AD 675.

Turn back to more recent times as you pass near the **Monument**, commemorating the 1666 Great Fire of London, and wander up King William St to the **Mansion House**, the residence of the Lord Mayor of London since around 1750. (Just to keep you on your toes, this is a different figure to the Mayor of London based at the London Assembly back by Tower Bridge.) Nearby is a potent symbol of Britain's financial prowess: the **Bank of England**.

From Mammon to God, and the next highlight is **St Paul's Cathedral**, designed by Sir Christopher Wren, one of London's greatest architects, and built between 1675 and 1710. (From the Mansion House, the official route runs the length of Queen Victoria St, but at the junction with Queen St it's more pleasant to take Watling St and reach St Paul's at its eastern end.)

The route then takes you up a street called Ludgate Hill and over a road junction called Ludgate Circus (once an execution site), down Fleet St (once London's newspaper centre), past the Royal Courts of Justice (where TV crews wait for the latest celebrity trial to end) and through Lincoln's Inn Fields (London's legal centre), crossing **Drury Lane** (past a cluster of famous theatres) and continuing down Bow St (where the 'Bow Street Runners' in the 1750s became the forerunner of London's police force).

Round the corner and back to the present: **Covent Garden**, the epitome of trendy modern London, with shops, cafés and a lively street atmosphere. (Even this place has its roots in history though; it was a fruit and flower market for centuries, and the name comes from a convent that stood here for centuries before that.) Time to sit down, have a coffee, watch a busker, or buy an 'I love London' hat. It's a short stroll back to Leicester Square and the end of the walk.

THE CENTENARY WALK

Duration	6–7 hours
Distance	15 miles (24km)
Difficulty	easy
Start	Manor Park
Finish	Epping (p60)
Transport	train, tube

Summary An eclectic mix of ancient forest and urban parkland, with historical highlights and some fine pubs for sustenance.

The Centenary Walk offers good walking surprisingly close to the centre of London – the starting point is a mere 5 miles from St Paul's Cathedral – through Epping Forest on the northern edge of the city. A look at the map shows that the 'forest' tag may be a little misleading – perhaps woodland would be more accurate, and there are large areas of open parkland too – but the swathes of trees are indeed remnants of the great royal forest that covered much of the county of Essex in the 12th century. For the people of London today, it's still a much-loved oasis and respite from suburbia.

HISTORY

Epping Forest has a continuous biological history dating from the last Ice Age, but for more than 1000 years it has been greatly influenced by human activity, managed for firewood, timber and grazing, and as a hunting ground for the monarch. Common forest trees include beech, oak and hornbeam, many of which have been pollarded – 'beheaded' around 3m above ground level to produce a cluster of branches that are later cut for firewood. Pollarding mostly ceased in the 19th century but left a remarkable legacy of weirdly contorted trees still easily seen all along the route.

Over the centuries, as kings lost interest in hunting, the forest diminished. By the 1850s the possible loss of a much-used recreation area (allied to early stirrings of the environmental movement) caused the City of London to act. In 1878 legislation was introduced that made the City of London 'conservator' of the forest with a charter to keep it public and preserve its natural aspect. Since then the forest has remained popular, particularly among walkers who make good use of the network of paths and bridleways. It was to celebrate the 100th anniversary of the Epping Forest Act that the Centenary Walk was devised in 1978.

PLANNING

This linear walk can be done in either direction, but south to north is more pleasing as you head out of town into the countryside. From Manor Park to Epping is 15 miles, requiring about six to seven hours of walking. With stops for lunch and places of interest, you should allow seven to eight hours. The walking is mostly on flat or undulating tracks. All are straightforward, although they can be muddy after rain.

On the southern part of the route Epping Forest is embedded in urban development, but its setting becomes much more rural to the north. Some parts of the route are heavily used on summer Sundays, so if you prefer a solitary walk choose another day.

There are very few waymarks for this route, so you need a good map. In some parklands and forest areas there's a maze of paths, but don't worry too much. Keep heading in roughly the right direction and you'll soon find a landmark that will help you get back on track.

You can reduce the length of the walk (and cut the more urban sections) by starting at Leytonstone or Chingford, reducing the distance to Epping to 12 miles or 7 miles, respectively.

For sustenance along the way, there's one café and a selection of good pubs serving meals and bar snacks. More details are given in the route description. Epping (below) also has a choice of restaurants.

Maps

The Centenary Walk is on OS Explorer 1:25,000 map No 174 *Epping Forest & Lee Valley*. An inexpensive *Epping Forest* pictorial map, marking the Centenary Walk, is available from the Epping Forest Information Centre (below).

Books

The most useful book is *The Centenary Walk* booklet, published by Epping Forest Conservators. For more options, get *Short Walks in Epping Forest* by Fred Matthews. For history and background, try *Epping Forest Through the Ages* by Georgina Green or the *Official Guide to Epping Forest*. All are available at the Epping Forest Information Centre (below) and can be posted on request.

Information Sources & Guided Walks

The **Epping Forest Information Centre** (☎ 020-8508 0028; www.cityoflondon.gov.uk/epping) at High Beach, south of Epping (and on the Centenary Walk), has a bookshop, plenty of free leaflets, displays about the forest's history and ecology, and an extensive program of guided walks on forest topics.

NEAREST TOWNS

London is of course the 'nearest town' to the start of this route, and if you're staying in the city centre it's very easy to reach Manor Park (and return from Epping) by public transport (see p61).

Epping

At the end of the route, the old market town of Epping has a small selection of places to stay, including the **Duke of Wellington Inn** (☎ 01992-572388; 30 High St; r £45), although no breakfast is available here, and **Thatched House Hotel** (☎ 01992-578353; 236 High St; s/d £55/65). About 3 miles south of Epping, bang on the route at High Beach, the charming **Epping Forest YHA Hostel** (☎ 0870 770 5822; epping@yha.org.uk; dm £12) maintains the forest theme. The **Epping Forest Information Centre** (☎ 020-8508 0028; www.cityoflondon.gov.uk/epping) at High Beach can provide an accommodation list with more options

GETTING TO/FROM THE WALK

From central London, the start of the walk at Manor Park is easily reached by suburban train from Liverpool Street train station. At the end of the walk, you can easily return to central London on the tube (London's underground railway) – Epping is the northern terminus of the Central Line. Train and tube services start early in the morning and end late in the evening, with several trains an hour in each direction daily, with a reduced service on Sunday.

THE WALK
Manor Park to Chingford
3–3½ hours, 8 miles (13km)

From Manor Park train station, begin by turning left along a street called Forest Dr, which soon brings you out to a large, grassy open space called Wanstead Flats. Head diagonally across the grass in a northwesterly direction.

After 1 mile, you cross a road and continue towards the left edge of some houses on the far side of another road, which you also cross. Go along a track with grassland on your left and houses on your right, fork right then left, and follow the path through woodland to reach a busy main road and the **Green Man Roundabout** – named after a former pub, in turn named after the ancient spirit of the woods, a reminder that the forest has existed here for millennia.

Use the pedestrian tunnel to go under the roads feeding the roundabout, then over a bridge crossing the railway to reach Leyton Flats, another largely grassland area. Head across this, through a belt of trees, past Hollow Pond and straight ahead through woodland to meet a road that you cross. Go past a pond and some attractive houses on your right to enter a road called College Pl. At its end, veer left through the forest, crossing a road to reach the **Rising Sun Pub**. It's probably too early for a drink, so re-enter the woodland with Bullrush Pond on your right, then turn right and go along a

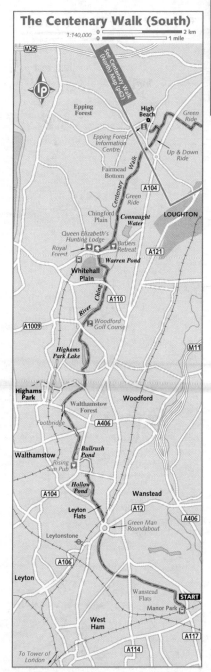

The Centenary Walk (South)

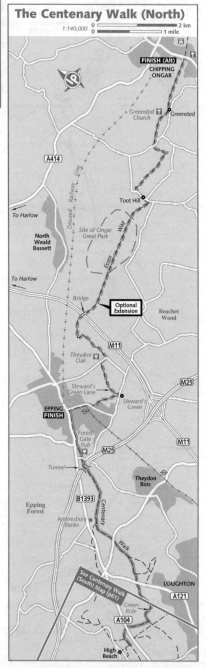

The Centenary Walk (North)

1:140,000

FINISH (Alt)
CHIPPING
ONGAR

Greensted
Church   Greensted

A414

Disused Railway Line

Toot Hill

To Harlow

North
Weald
Bassett

Site of Ongar
Great Park

Essex Way

To Harlow

Bridge

Beachet
Wood

Optional
Extension

M11

Theydon
Oak

Steward's
Green Lane

Steward's
Green

M25

EPPING
FINISH

Forest
Gate
Pub

M25   M11

Tunnel

Theydon
Bois

B1393

Epping
Forest

Ambresbury
Banks

Centenary Walk

See Centenary Walk
(South Map) (p61)

LOUGHTON
A121

Green
Ride

A104

High
Beach

white-posted track (for horses) until a narrow path on your left leads up a grassy bank to cross a footbridge over a road. From here there are panoramic views over the city and suburbs of London.

To continue, fork left, following the path over another footbridge, this time above the busy North Circular Rd, then down into the woods of **Walthamstow Forest** and past an area where, in 1992, the Epping Forest Conservators repollarded trees as an experiment. For perhaps 1000 years much of the forest would have looked like this.

Cross a road and continue with a high-rise building on the left. Keep left as you go downhill and then over a road and along the right (east) side of Highams Park Lake. At its end go uphill through trees to pick up a grassy track leading onto and over a road to Woodford Golf Course. Continue on the track, later with a fairway on the right, then go uphill and through trees along a wide grassy strip.

The route skirts round the eastern edge of the suburb of Chingford, crossing a road to reach Whitehall Plain. It then continues alongside the little River Ching, turning left over a bridge. Go uphill to the left of Warren Pond to meet and cross a road opposite distinctive **Queen Elizabeth Hunting Lodge** (see opposite). Just to the left is the **Royal Forest**, a good pub serving no-nonsense food like liver and bacon or steak pie for around £6. To the right, **Butlers Retreat** also provides refreshments.

Chingford to Epping
3–3½ hours, 7 miles (11km)

From Queen Elizabeth Hunting Lodge go towards the fountain behind Butlers Retreat and turn right (with a pond on the right) and down a wide grassy track to the right of Chingford Plain. This is **Green Ride**, cut through the forest in the 1880s so Queen Victoria could go on a commemorative carriage tour, and it soon becomes a gravel-surfaced track continuing through woodland. Go over a junction of tracks and continue uphill, round an overgrown pond on the right, and on for 1.5 miles, to eventually reach a large grassy area called Fairmead Bottom. Go left and uphill as the track winds through beech woods, crosses a small road and becomes **Up and Down Ride**.

Take a left fork after about 800m and then left again down a hard track to reach Epping Forest Information Centre at High Beach (not a misspelt tree name – so called because the soil is quite sandy), where Queen Victoria dedicated the forest to the people in 1882. Years later the dedication is not forgotten and this area is busy at weekends. Nearby, the **King's Oak** pub serves lunches, while the green **tea hut** serves drinks and cakes.

From High Beach retrace your steps to the main route and go left at the fork. Cross the main road to a car park and continue ahead on a surfaced track, which after 500m joins another main track, where you turn left. You're on Green Ride again; follow it for 2.5 miles through woodland and across two roads.

After the second road and 200m beyond another track on the left, it is worth a short detour slanting left into the woodland to the impressive **Ambresbury Banks** earthworks – an Iron Age defensive structure dating from around 500 BC. According to local legend, a British uprising led by Queen Boudicca was put down here by the Romans in AD 60.

Eventually the track arrives at a grassy area with a cricket pitch to the left. In the 1970s this part of the forest was threatened with the construction of the M25 motorway and major environmental battles were fought to prevent it being severed. These were successful and today the motorway goes through a tunnel a couple of metres below your feet.

Go past the cricket pavilion to a gravel track and turn right onto a footpath with

---

ONWARDS OVER ESSEX

Epping is the end of the Centenary Walk, but it's also the start of a long-distance path called the Essex Way, extending for 81 miles through farmed countryside and sizable woodlands to the North Sea port of Harwich. If you enjoyed the Centenary Walk, you could keep going along the Essex Way for a day or two. The historic market town of Chipping Ongar is just 8 miles (13km) from Epping, three to four hours of walking along the Essex Way. Highlights of this section include **Ongar Great Park**, the first recorded deer park in England, mentioned in early-11th-century documents, and **Greensted Church**, possibly the oldest wooden church in the world, a remarkable survivor from the 10th century or earlier. Another option is to start the Centenary Walk at Chingford and go all the way to Chipping Ongar – a comfortable day's walk of six to 7½ hours (15 miles), avoiding the more urban part of the route. For details see www.ramblers.org.uk/info/paths/essex.html.

---

a pond on the left. Follow this over a road (the nearby **Forest Gate** pub does excellent lunches) and continue over Bell Common – a narrow strip of scrub, grass and trees between a main road to the left and houses to the right.

At the end of the common follow Hemnall St (past a little house where Lucien, son of Camille Pissarro the French impressionist painter, lived for many years) to Station Rd, then turn right to reach Epping train station – the end of the Centenary Walk.

TEMPER & TEMPERANCE

The Queen Elizabeth Hunting Lodge is centuries old but, despite its name, dates from a period *before* the well-known eponymous queen. It was built for King Henry VIII in the mid-16th century, and from here the monarch would ride out to hunt deer or simply escape the pressures of court in the city. Henry is of course famous (or infamous) for his impatient desire to ensure a male heir for the throne – a quest that led to the break up of the Church and his marrying six wives. Tradition says that he waited here to hear the cannon signalling that Anne Boleyn (wife No 2) had been beheaded at the Tower of London, meaning he was clear to marry Jane Seymour (wife No 3). To celebrate, so the legend goes, he went hunting!

In contrast, nearby Butlers Retreat is a symbol of restraint. It was one of many 'retreats' established in the late 19th and early 20th centuries to provide an alcohol-free alternative to the pubs that were a major cause of drunkenness for the working people who escaped to Epping Forest on Sunday from the factories and docks of London's East End.

THE THAMES PATH (EAST)

Duration	6 days
Distance	90 miles (145km)
Difficulty	easy
Start	Pangbourne (p91)
Finish	Thames Barrier
Transport	train

Summary Take the main artery to the country's heart, ticking off Britain's best-known sights along the way.

The Thames Path National Trail follows Britain's best-known river from its source in the countryside of Gloucestershire all the way to the sea barrier on the edge of the capital. Picking up from Pangbourne, the eastern section is like taking a walk through time, from semi-wild and rural beginnings to increasing industrialisation and urbanisation, finishing in London's gritty suburbs.

Along the way you'll pass a veritable Greatest Hits of British tourist attractions, making it the perfect path for first-time visitors wanting an alternative to tour-bus hell. For locals it gives a fascinating insight into the importance of the Thames in shaping their history. There isn't a long-distance path more accessible from London or gentler in its gradient – making it perfect for both day-trippers and those wanting the taste of a longer challenge.

The genteel western half of the route is described on p88.

PLANNING

Most of the general information covering the whole route is in the Thames Path (West) section (p88). For this eastern section, we break the walk into the following stages. Every suggested overnight stop has shops and ATMs.

Alternatives

On Day 1, although Pangbourne is a pleasant town, you can avoid the tedious suburban section to Reading by starting *at* Reading and heading to Henley from there.

Many walkers end the route at Kew or Richmond on the outer limits of London. This misses a large section of the walk through the capital, which, although built up and urban, provides views and experiences not found on the standard walking trails.

To stretch this walk into a sightseeing extravaganza, stop at Windsor on Day 3, carrying on to Staines on Day 4, Hampton Court Palace on Day 5 and then allow a few days for London's numerous river-side attractions.

When to Walk

Especially on this eastern section, the Thames Path can be easily walked at any time of the year and the path conditions are suitable for children. If the weather turns bad you're never too far from the next town or village.

Maps

The eastern section of this route is covered by the OS Landranger 1:50,000 maps No 175 *Reading & Windsor,* 176 *West London* and 177 *East London.* For a single map of the whole route, Geoprojects' *Thames – the river & the path* is excellent.

For the first five days along this eastern section, as you pass each lock you can collect free *River Thames Out & About Guides,* featuring maps of the upcoming section of the river.

NEAREST TOWNS

The eastern section of the Thames Path begins in Pangbourne (p88) – also the end the western section of the Thames Path. The

Day	From	To	Miles/km
1	Pangbourne	Henley-on-Thames	15/24
2	Henley-on-Thames	Maidenhead	15/24
3	Maidenhead	Staines	14/22.5
4	Staines	Kingston upon Thames	15/24
5	Kingston upon Thames	Battersea	15/24
6	Battersea	Thames Barrier	16/25.5

> **WARNING**
>
> Upstream from London you'll see many people swimming in the river on hot days. If you choose to join them, be extremely careful. Stay close to the banks, as currents can be strong and the water unexpectedly deep. Don't attempt to swim across the river or near weirs and locks, and don't swim alone. Certainly don't dive off bridges.

'nearest town' to the end of the walk is the giant city of London.

GETTING TO/FROM THE WALK

There are numerous daily trains from London to Reading (30 minutes) and also from Reading to Pangbourne (10 minutes). Reading is equally well served by National Express coaches from London (1½ hours) and other centres.

The walk ends at the Thames Barrier in Eastmoor St, off the A206, about 1 mile west of Woolwich. At the end of the route, walk 10 minutes south to catch the No 472 bus from Woolwich Rd to North Greenwich tube station (Jubilee line). A wonderfully triumphant coda is to catch the River Thames Boat Service from Thames Barrier Pier to Westminster (1½ hours, five daily).

THE WALK
Day 1: Pangbourne to Henley-on-Thames
6 hours, 15 miles (24km)
The peaceful river-side stroll takes a turn for the worse leading into Reading, but quickly recovers with the most unspoilt section of the route.

It's unfortunate that the first sign on this otherwise well-marked route points the wrong way out of Pangbourne, but you should have no trouble picking up the path following the south side of the river, heading east from the bridge.

The trail gets off to a good start, following the river as it winds through pretty fields to Mapledurham Lock. Suddenly it detours through farmland and then climbs through drab suburbia to follow a busy road before dropping back down to the water just past **Beethoven's Hotel** to follow the railway line into Reading. This is the worst section of the whole itinerary. You could hardly be blamed for skipping it.

Aside from hosting a legendary annual rock festival, Reading (pronounced 'redding') is a dull, sprawling town, but a good lunch stop nonetheless.

After leaving its industrial fringes, the route swiftly becomes incredibly beautiful, especially after crossing the bridge at Sonning. There are plenty of secluded spots to be found if you're tempted to cool off in the clear water (see the boxed text, left). From here, continue on an idyllic 6-mile shady stretch leading to charming Henley-on-Thames.

HENLEY-ON-THAMES

This picturesque old town hugging the river banks makes a great first pit stop. Henley-on-Thames has a **tourist office** (☎ 01491-578034; www.visithenley-on-thames.co.uk; King's Arms Barn, Kings Rd), loads of shops and excellent restaurants. It's all rather posh, but surprisingly stylish. Be sure to book ahead during the internationally renowned **rowing regatta** (late June/early July).

On the northern outskirts of town **Swiss Farm** (☎ 01491-573419; www.swissfarmcamping.co.uk; Marlow Rd; camp site for 2 £10-14; ⚹) is about as upmarket a camp site as you'll find. **Alushta** (☎ 01491-636041; www.alushta.co.uk; 23 Queen St; s/tw/tr £45/50/95, d £75-85, d without bathroom £60) and **Lenwade** (☎ 01491-573468; www.w3b-ink.com/lenwade; 3 Western Rd; s £45-50, d £65; 💻) both exude old-world charm, while modern, minimalist **Milsoms** (☎ 01491-845789; www.milsomshotel.co.uk; 20 Market Pl; r £95) is a beautifully designed boutique hotel.

The river-side setting makes up for the average grub and paper plates at **Angel on the Bridge** (☎ 01491-410678; Thames Side; mains £6-9; ⌚ lunch & dinner). The seafood, wine list and service are exceptional at **Loch Fyne** (☎ 01491-845780; 20 Market Pl; mains £9-18; ⌚ breakfast, lunch & dinner), while the **Three Tuns Food House** (☎ 01491-573260; 5 Market Pl; mains £10-18; ⌚ lunch & dinner) is a gastro pub with lots of ambience.

Day 2: Henley-on-Thames to Maidenhead
6 hours, 15 miles (24km)
This is more like it – a consistently beautiful walk through the English countryside, book-ended by pretty towns.

Crossing the bridge, a pleasantly rural start takes you alongside meadows for about 3 miles before leaving the river to head through tiny Aston, then through a

The Thames Path (East)

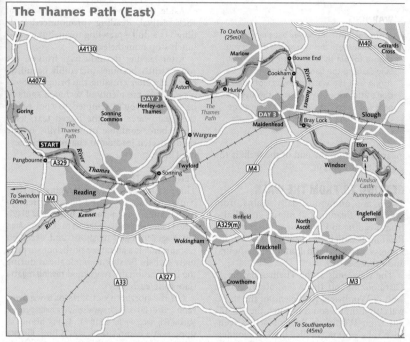

farming estate with a manor house. Back to the river there are more meadows until **Hurley Lock** (☎ 01628-824334; Mill Lane; camp sites for 2 £7), where camping is permitted on the idyllic lock island (book well in advance).

The path crosses the river three times in quick succession, ending up on the north side heading towards Marlow, a busy riverside town with a **tourist office** (☎ 01628-483597; 31 High St) and several places for lunch. After a further 3 miles you'll cross again, where the path wanders through the grounds of Cookham's Holy Trinity Church. From here you follow what is now the western bank of the river to Maidenhead.

MAIDENHEAD

The town of Maidenhead has an air of faded glory. Some large hotels by the river are testimony to its pre-WWI peak, when it was a playground for toffs. Comfortable, walker-friendly B&B is offered at **Ray Corner Guest House** (☎ 01628-632784; www.raycornerguesthouse.co.uk; 141 Bridge Rd; s £40-45, d/tw £55/60) and the nearby **Bridge Cottage** (☎ 01628-626805; www.bridgecottagebb.co.uk; Bath Rd, Taplow; s with/without

bathroom £47/37, d/tw with bathroom £55/60). For more options, enquire at the **tourist office** (☎ 01628-796502; Library, St Ives Rd).

Thai Orchid (☎ 01628-777555; 2 Ray Mead Rd; mains £5-15; ☹ lunch Sun-Fri, dinner daily) serves delicious meals, as does the upmarket **Blue River Café** (☎ 01628-674057; The Bridge; mains £8-18; ☹ breakfast, lunch & dinner), with a wonderful river-side setting.

Cross the bridge and continue along the path for 1 mile to reach the excellent **Amerden Caravan & Camping Park** (☎ 01628-627461; Old Marsh Lane, Dorney Reach; sites for 2 £8), just past Bray Lock. Neighbouring **Amerden Lodge** (☎ 01628-673458; Old Marsh Lane, Dorney Reach; r £55) is a 16th-century cottage and serves great breakfasts.

Day 3: Maidenhead to Staines
5½ hours, 14 miles (22.5km)
A country vibe feel still dominates in this moneyed stretch, although opportunities for posh-house spotting increase as it starts to get more developed.

Maidenhead to Windsor is another gorgeous leafy stretch, with intriguing views

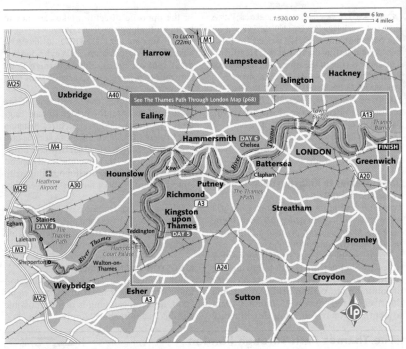

of manor houses on the other side of the river. Eventually the woods open up to a stunning view of **Windsor Castle** (☎ 01753-831118; www.royalcollection.org.uk; adult/child £14/free), one of Britain's greatest surviving medieval strongholds and the residence of royalty since 850. Surrounding the castle, Windsor has fine old cobbled streets, historic buildings and the prestigious **Eton College**.

If you decide to stay overnight to explore properly, there are dozens of B&Bs. Try **Dee & Steve's** (☎ 01753-584489; 169 Oxford Rd; s with/without bathroom £40/30, d with bathroom £58), **Barbara's Bed & Breakfast** (☎ 01753-840273; www.bbandbwindsor.com; 16 Maidenhead Rd; s £30, d with/without bathroom £60/55) or the central **Clarence Hotel** (☎ 01753-864436; www.clarence-hotel.co.uk; 9 Clarence Rd; s/d £65/77). Otherwise the **Royal Windsor Information Centre** (☎ 01753-743900; www.windsor.gov.uk; Old Booking Hall, Windsor Royal Station) can help you find a place (£5 fee), as well as providing a free city map.

At the very least Windsor makes for a great lunch stop before tackling the 9 miles to Staines. **Spice Route** (☎ 01753-860720; 18a Thames St, Boots Passage; mains £8-15; ☼ lunch & dinner)

serves a killer curry, with lots of vegetarian choices.

Beyond Windsor, the towpath was closed by Queen Victoria so walkers have to divert along a busy main road for a stretch. Any republican feelings this engenders can be given full vent at the meadow of **Runnymede** – where the powers of absolute monarchy were limited in 1215 when barons forced King John to sign the Magna Carta. Today it's a popular swimming spot.

From here it's a few more miles to Staines, the end of the day.

STAINES

Once an important river crossing, Staines is now a lacklustre commuter town that serves primarily as a convenient stopping point rather than a place to explore.

It's a further 3 miles to **Laleham Camping Club** (☎ 01932-564149; Laleham Park; sites for 2 £10). Otherwise **Penton Guest House** (☎ 01784-458787; 39 Penton Rd; s with/without bathroom £40/30, d £60/50) and **Rose Villa** (☎ 01784-440022; www.rosevillaguesthouse.co.uk; 75 Gresham Rd; s £35, d £50-70) are good B&B options. **Thames Lodge Hotel**

(☎ 0870 400 8121; www.thameslodge-hotel.co.uk; Thames St; s/d Fri-Sun £75/110, r Mon-Thu £120-180) is right on the path, but midweek it's priced for businesspeople jetting in to nearby Heathrow. The same is true of the upmarket **Runnymede Hotel & Spa** (☎ 01784-436171; www.runnymedehotel .com; Windsor Rd, Egham; s Fri-Sun £88-98, Mon-Thu £211-234, d Fri-Sun £140-175, Mon-Thu £253-287; ❌ ▣ ⤢), on the river side as you're nearing the town. **Baroosh** (☎ 01784-452509; High St; mains £7-9; ☽ breakfast, lunch & dinner) is a friendly, modern bar serving seafood, pasta and grills, with plenty for vegetarians to choose from.

Day 4: Staines to Kingston upon Thames
6 hours, 15 miles (24km)
Less posh and more built-up, there are still some traces of countryside, but river-living becomes more evident, with lots of permanently moored houseboats.

From Staines, it's a straightforward 8 miles to Shepperton Lock, following the northeastern bank. Here you have a choice of continuing to Walton Bridge or crossing the river by ferry (every 15 minutes 10am to 6pm). If you're following this itinerary

in the opposite direction, take care not to branch off along the path.

The **Minnow** (☎ 01932-831672; 104 Thames St; mains £7-18; ☽ lunch & dinner) at Weybridge is a great spot for lunch, although there is no shortage of picturesque river-side pubs over the next few miles.

The path follows the south side of the river until crossing the bridge to pass England's grandest Tudor structure, **Hampton Court Palace** (☎ 0870 751 5175; www.hampton-court -palace.org.uk; adult/concession/child £13/10/free), home to King Henry VIII. You could easily spend a day exploring this beautiful building, with superb grounds and a famous 300-year-old maze.

The path continues past Christopher Wren's baroque wing for a pleasant 3.5-mile stretch alongside meadows, while suburbia begins in earnest on the opposite bank.

KINGSTON UPON THAMES
On the fringe of Greater London, Kingston upon Thames is a town in its own right. From here on, camping is nigh impossible and B&Bs are in short supply.

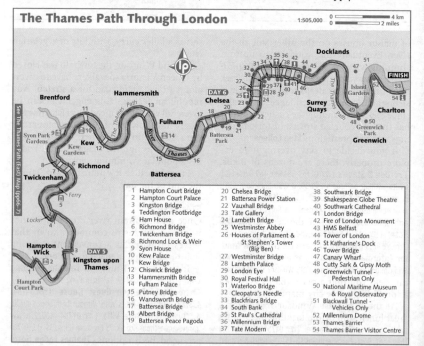

The Thames Path Through London   1:505,000

1	Hampton Court Bridge	20 Chelsea Bridge	38 Southwark Bridge
2	Hampton Court Palace	21 Battersea Power Station	39 Shakespeare Globe Theatre
3	Kingston Bridge	22 Vauxhall Bridge	40 Southwark Cathedral
4	Teddington Footbridge	23 Tate Gallery	41 London Bridge
5	Ham House	24 Lambeth Bridge	42 Fire of London Monument
6	Richmond Bridge	25 Westminster Abbey	43 HMS Belfast
7	Twickenham Bridge	26 Houses of Parliament &	44 Tower of London
8	Richmond Lock & Weir	St Stephen's Tower	45 St Katharine's Dock
9	Syon House	(Big Ben)	46 Tower Bridge
10	Kew Palace	27 Westminster Bridge	47 Canary Wharf
11	Kew Bridge	28 Lambeth Palace	48 Cutty Sark & Gipsy Moth
12	Chiswick Bridge	29 London Eye	49 Greenwich Tunnel -
13	Hammersmith Bridge	30 Royal Festival Hall	Pedestrian Only
14	Fulham Palace	31 Waterloo Bridge	50 National Maritime Museum
15	Putney Bridge	32 Cleopatra's Needle	& Royal Observatory
16	Wandsworth Bridge	33 Blackfriars Bridge	51 Blackwall Tunnel -
17	Battersea Bridge	34 South Bank	Vehicles Only
18	Albert Bridge	35 St Paul's Cathedral	52 Millennium Dome
19	Battersea Peace Pagoda	36 Millennium Bridge	53 Thames Barrier
		37 Tate Modern	54 Thames Barrier Visitor Centre

One B&B option is **Annand** (☎ 020-8547 0074; 16 Chivenor Grove; r £50), close to the river just past the town. **Bushy Park Lodge** (☎ 020-8943 1917; www .ashortlet.com; 6 Sandy Lane; s £65-75, d £75-80), 800m west of Kingston Bridge, offers self-contained apartments. Both **Chase Lodge** (☎ 020-8943 1862; www.chaselodgehotel.com; 10 Park Rd; s £65, d £85-98) and the **White Hart** (☎ 020-8977 1786; www.fullershotels.com/main/1014; 1 High St; r/ste Fri & Sat £95/125, Sun-Thu £125/155) are hotels in neighbouring Hampton Wick. There are dozens of eateries to choose from on Kingston's high street.

Day 5: Kingston upon Thames to Battersea

6 hours, 15 miles (24km)

Despite journeying from London's transport zone 6 to zone 2, there's still plenty of green space on this penultimate leg.

From Kingston Bridge the Thames Path runs simultaneously along both banks of the river – although as far as Kew the east bank is definitely preferable. As you head through Richmond you'll pass an extraordinary cluster of stately homes – including **Ham House** (1610), reputedly the most haunted house in England – before reaching fascinating **Kew Gardens** (☎ 020-8332 5655; www.kew.org.uk; Kew Green, Richmond; adult/child £12/free) and **Fulham Palace**, home to the bishops of London from the 8th century through to 1973.

From Putney the buildings finally drag themselves up to dominate both sides of the river, and from now on you're well and truly in the city. Finish the day under the shadow of the magnificent **Battersea Power Station**, immortalised on the cover of Pink Floyd's 1977 album *Animals*. Now you're in London proper, make use of public transport and check into a hotel for two nights, returning at the end of the next day.

Day 6: Battersea to the Thames Barrier

6½ hours, 16 miles (25.5km)

The sights just don't stop coming.

Again you can choose either side, although we'd recommend the south bank to **Tower Bridge**, as this passes several interesting sites and has superb views across the river. For more details of the section between Lambeth Bridge and Tower Bridge, see p58.

Beyond Tower Bridge, the final sections of the Thames Path weave through the detritus of the old London docks and industry. Some follow pleasant river-side embankments past yacht marinas and renovated warehouses; others take dirty streets or dodge through forlorn parks, tower blocks and waste-ground.

At Greenwich the two routes rejoin and there's plenty to see: the **Cutty Sark** (☎ 020-8858 2698; www.cuttysark.org.uk; King William Walk; adult/child £5/free) sailing ship, the **National Maritime Museum** (☎ 020-8312 6565; www.nmm.ac.uk; Romney Rd; admission free) and, of course, the prime meridian marked out at the **Royal Observatory** (☎ 020-8312 6565; Greenwich Park; admission free), giving its name to Greenwich Mean Time. The **Trafalgar Tavern** (☎ 020-8858 2437; Park Row; bar snacks £6-11; ☽ lunch & dinner) is an atmospheric spot to stop for lunch, with outdoor benches by the river.

Beyond Greenwich, the route takes a post-apocalyptic turn, as you wander past abandoned buildings and factories. It's a fascinating contrast to the pyramid-peaked **Canary Wharf** business hub across the river, a testimony to the brash aspirations of the plutocratic 1980s.

Next iconic structure: the **Millennium Dome**, the world's largest dome (365m in diameter) lying abandoned at the time of research – having opened on 1 January 2000 at a cost of £789 million, but closing on 31 December, only hours before the 3rd millennium began. Negotiations are taking place to convert the site into Britain's first super-casino, and it's expected to house the gymnastics and trampolining at the 2012 Olympic Games.

As you round the peninsula, the giant silver shells of the **Thames Barrier** come into view, marking the end of the route. The Barrier was built in 1984 with hydraulic gates to protect the capital from flooding. As you pass under the control tower, you can retrace your journey on the river map etched into the wall. The barrier's **visitor centre** (☎ 020-8305 4188; adult/child £1.50/1) tells the story of the Thames through history and has a **café** attached. Time for a cake and cup of tea to celebrate the end of your walk!

MORE WALKS

The Jubilee Walkway (p54) takes in many great sights of London, but this is only a taster and the city offers many more opportunities for exploring on foot. If you're looking for ideas, a good place to start is Transport for London's walking website (www .tfl.gov.uk/streets/walking) and the London and Southeast sections of the Ramblers' site (www.ramblers.org.uk).

PARK WALKS

To get off the streets, take a long walk through London's glorious parks. You could start in St James's Park and go east to west through Hyde Park and Kensington Gardens. Or try a south-to-north route, tying in all or any of Battersea Park, Ranlagh Gardens, Hyde Park, Regent's Park and Hampstead Heath, using buses or the tube to skip the street sections in between. To the southwest are the larger open areas of Richmond Park and Wimbledon Common. On a clear day, and armed with a picnic, a walk here is guaranteed to banish urban blues.

GREEN CHAIN

The Green Chain is a well-signposted 40-mile (64km) network of walks in southeast London connecting parks, commons, woods and other open spaces. The Chain stretches from the outer suburbs of Thamesmead and Erith, on the banks of the River Thames, through Plumstead, Eltham and Beckenham to Crystal Palace. A major branch goes through Charlton, linking this line to the Thames Barrier. Access is easy as the whole route is well served by public transport, and you can do short or long stretches. For more details see www.greenchain.com.

LEA VALLEY WALK

The Lea Valley Walk is a 50-mile (80km) linear route from Limehouse, in the East End, along the valley of the River Lee, past the site of the 2012 Olympic Games, then winding a green way between the suburbs and towns of Tottenham, Enfield, Waltham Abbey, Hertford and Harpenden to reach Luton, north of the capital. Of course, you don't have to do the whole route; it's very well served by public transport all along the walk. The route passes through country parks and nature reserves, beside lakes and reservoirs, over golf courses and beside canals. The southern sections are undoubtedly urban but the walk becomes surprisingly rural as you go north. For more details see www.leevalleypark.org.uk, following the links to 'Outdoor Recreation'.

The best guidebook is *Lea Valley Walk* by Leigh Hatts; as well as describing the main route it includes an Olympic Park chapter for those wanting to explore the developing site before 2012.

CAPITAL RING & LONDON LOOP

The Green Chain walk (left) is part of a complete circuit of London called the Capital Ring – a 72-mile (115km) route divided into 15 stages, mixing city streets, parks, gardens and other open suburban spaces. For a longer option try the London Loop, a 150-mile (240km) outer circuit taking full advantage of the many green spaces that line the capital's fringe – many with a surprisingly rural feel. The route also passes several villages with attractive pubs for lunch. This is an ideal way to sample the countryside and yet still be in reach of the city centre.

You don't have to do the Ring or the Loop in one go. In fact they're designed to be done in short sections, tied in with a circular route, or using bus and train to get back to your start. *The Capital Ring* by Colin Saunders and *The London Loop* by David Sharp are the best guidebooks, and you can order handy leaflets (free) from **Transport for London** (www.tfl.gov.uk/streets/walking), or pick them up from local libraries and tourist offices.

THE NORTH DOWNS WAY

The North Downs Way takes you further away from London, and is a popular national trail along with the neighbouring South Downs Way (p123).

As the name suggests, the North Downs Way National Trail follows the North Downs – an elongated area of hills and chalk ridges running through southeastern England between Farnham, south of London, and Dover, on the coast of the English Channel. Never far from towns and roads (although they're often out of sight), the walk does have a commuter-belt feel in some places, but also passes through two Areas of Outstanding Natural Beauty (AONB), with panoramic views, leafy woods, grassy downland, nature reserves, farmland, orchards and vineyards, and ends with a grand finale across the famous white cliffs of Dover.

For history fans, part of the modern walkers route parallels the Pilgrims Way, a Victorian interpretation of the ancient route taken by Christians from Canterbury to Winchester for the festival of St Swithen, and more recently from Winchester to Canterbury in celebration of St Thomas Becket. Other historical features include Neolithic long barrows (burial mounds), medieval castles, 1970s motorways and the entrance to the Channel Tunnel.

The total length of the North Downs Way is 157 miles (251km), walkable in around 12 to 14 days. For more details see www.nationaltrail.co.uk/northdowns. A recommended guidebook is *North Downs Way* by John Curtin.

NORFOLK & SUFFOLK

Although not really in the southeast of England, the two counties of Norfolk and Suffolk deserve a mention, as they're within easy reach of London – ideal for a weekend getaway. The landscape is mainly (some say unforgivingly) flat, so don't come here looking for hills and dales. The main attraction for walkers is a coastline ideal for gentle walking, with wide sandy beaches, great expanses of salt marsh, nature reserves rich in bird life, tiny villages and several busy seaside resorts. A good base with a range of accommodation, walks and activities is the visitor-friendly village of **Burnham Deepdale** (www.burnhamdeepdale.co.uk).

The region's other main attraction is the **Broads**, a vast network of navigable rivers and lakes between Norwich (the Norfolk county capital) and the coast. The Broads Special Area is effectively a national park, and there are many opportunities for walking along lake shores and river banks.

For a longer walk, two quite separate routes together form a national trail, the **Peddars Way & North Norfolk Coast Path** (www.nationaltrail.co.uk/peddarsway), usually completed by walkers in about a week. For a taste of seaside walking, the final three days are highly recommended.

Further south, another enjoyable route with salt in the air is the **Suffolk Coast & Heaths Path** (www.suffolkcoastandheaths.org), running through the AONB of the same name.

Wessex

The land of Wessex has a rich past. In prehistoric times, the chalky, grass-covered hills were inhabited by Stone Age and Bronze Age peoples and here they built their great monuments, such as Avebury and Stonehenge – magical, mystical sights that still awe visitors today.

In the 9th century, Wessex was one of several British kingdoms, and was ruled most famously by King Alfred the Great from his capital at Winchester. The name is a derivation of 'West Saxons' – the modern-day counties, elsewhere in Britain, of Essex and Sussex have similar derivations (although there's no place called Nossex) – and at its greatest extent the kingdom of Wessex included much of western and southern England.

In more recent times, the Wessex name was resurrected and immortalised by the author Thomas Hardy (1840–1928). Hardy based many of his pastoral novels in this part of Britain, including the much-read *Tess of the d'Urbervilles* and *Far from the Madding Crowd*.

Today, Wessex no longer officially exists as a county or a kingdom, but the name is used as a convenient catch-all for the area covered by the counties of Dorset, Hampshire, Somerset, Wiltshire and Berkshire, and much of the western Thames Valley.

As in Thomas Hardy's day, Wessex is still a largely rural region, and there are many opportunities for walking within easy travelling distance of the popular tourist centres of London, Salisbury, Winchester and Bath. Most routes are straightforward, often spectacular without being overbearing, and can be walked at any time of the year. If you're new to walking in Britain, or just new to walking, Wessex could be a very good place to start.

HIGHLIGHTS

- Going mystic at **Avebury Stone Circle** (p85)
- Striding through history, past burial mounds and forts, on **The Ridgeway** (p83)
- Marvelling at audacious early engineering on the **Kennet & Avon Canal Path** (p80)
- Strolling along the leafy banks of the **River Thames** (p88), Britain's best-known waterway
- Following Roman footsteps on the **Clarendon Way** (p74) between Salisbury's and Winchester's awesome cathedrals

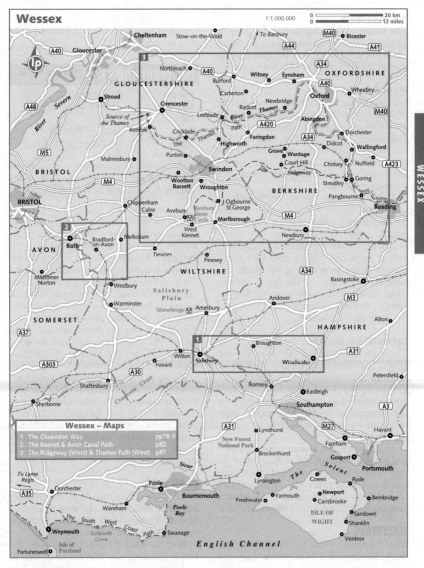

Wessex

1:1,000,000

0 ———— 20 km
0 ———— 12 miles

WESSEX

Wessex – Maps		
1	The Clarendon Way	pp78-9
2	The Kennet & Avon Canal Path	p82
3	The Ridgeway (West) & Thames Path (West)	p87

INFORMATION

This chapter covers a wide area – a good third of southern England – with four contrasting routes suggested as walking tasters: the shorter Clarendon Way and part of the Kennet & Avon Canal Path, plus sections of the timeworn Ridgeway and the bucolic Thames Path.

Together, these trails make up a fascinating set of walks through varied scenery and many centuries of history, from the Neolithic stone circles at Avebury to the grand designs of the early industrial era. They will take you along Roman roads, medieval manor houses, through battlefields and past cathedrals and castles.

When to Walk

The walks in this chapter can be done at any time of year, although there's a better chance of good weather in the spring, summer or autumn months (April–October).

Maps & Books

For route planning, Wessex is covered by three maps in the Ordnance Survey (OS) *Travel Map – Tour* 1:100,000 series: No 7 *Hampshire*, No 9 *Dorset & Somerset East* and No 22 *Wiltshire*. For more detail, maps covering individual walks in this chapter are listed in the Planning section of each route description.

There seems to be no single walking guidebook for the Wessex region covered by our chapter. Most 'Wessex' guidebooks tend to concentrate on Dorset – for example, *Walk Dorset* by Charles David, with colour maps and photos, and GPS information – and most cash in on Hardy too, such as *Pub Walks in Hardy's Wessex* by Mike Power and *In the Steps of Thomas Hardy: Walking Tours of Hardy's England* by Anne-Marie Edwards.

Information Sources

There are many tourist offices in Wessex. Useful ones near the walks we describe are listed in the individual route descriptions. Online, good tourism websites include www.visitsouthwestengland.com and www.visit-hampshire.org.uk. Also good is www.dorsetforyou.com; follow links to 'Enjoying' and 'Tourism'.

Also worth a look is www.wessex.me.uk – a slightly homespun but very comprehensive website, centred on Chard in Somerset but covering the entire Wessex region, with lots of links and information on subjects ranging from King Arthur to soccer clubs.

GATEWAYS

Major gateway cities for Wessex include Bath, Salisbury and Winchester. Although not *in* Wessex, Oxford is a handy gateway to the eastern side of the region and Cheltenham is a handy gateway for the northwest. All these places can be very easily reached from London and all parts of Britain by National Express coach and train services.

The main Transport chapter at the end of this book has more information about travel around the country, and lists several public transport inquiry lines providing details of both national and local bus and train services.

THE CLARENDON WAY	
Duration	9–11 hours
Distance	27 miles (43.5km)
Difficulty	easy
Start	Salisbury (opposite)
Finish	Winchester (p76)
Transport	bus
Summary A long but straightforward walk on good paths and tracks, through woods, farmland and villages, and over rolling hills.	

This is an ideal introduction to walking in Wessex, with a clear route and sense of direction, plus a healthy dollop of history. It starts and finishes at the ancient cathedral cities of Salisbury and Winchester, respectively, and takes its name from the medieval Clarendon Palace, now ruined, which is passed on the walk a few miles east of Salisbury. The route also passes several Bronze Age tumuli (ancient burial mounds) and a Civil War battle site, and just for good measure follows the remains of a Roman road. There's even a pyramid.

It's also a walk through today's Britain – a classic southern English landscape of water meadows, crystal-clear chalk streams, tranquil woods and farmland, plus cosy pubs, noble manor houses, neat thatched cottages, comfortable homes and narrow country lanes frequented by large, expensive cars.

PLANNING

The Clarendon Way can be walked in either direction, although going west to east, as described here, is likely to be more comfortable, with the wind (or rain) behind.

Even though the landscape is mostly flat and undulating, the Way requires nine to 11 hours' walking, so you're looking at 10 to 12 hours overall. This can be quite a push in one day, particularly if you make any sightseeing pauses, so you may prefer to do the walk over two days. Access to the start and finish is good from London, and it makes an ideal weekend break from the city, with some comfortable accommodation options.

> **WARNING: CLARENDON MARATHON**
>
> In early October each year, the Clarendon Marathon takes place. Thousands of runners cover the route we describe here – from Winchester to Salisbury – some in less than four hours. If you want inspiration, come and watch. If you want a quiet walk, come at another time!

If you're on a tight budget, though, there are no camping or hostel options along the route and you're forced to do the walk in one go. In that case it's worth staying a night in Winchester, taking the first bus to Salisbury and walking back, unencumbered by a large backpack, to spend a second night. Alternatively, you can do the first 20 miles or so, as far as Farley Mount, then get a taxi into Winchester.

Maps
Waymarking along the Clarendon Way is mostly good – the symbol is a bishop's mitre (ceremonial hat) – but a map is definitely required.

The route is covered by the Ordnance Survey (OS) Landranger 1:50,000 maps No 184 *Salisbury & the Plain* and No 185 *Winchester & Basingstoke*. For more detail, you'll need OS Explorer 1:25,000 maps No 130 *Salisbury & Stonehenge*, No 131 *Romsey, Andover & Test Valley* and No 132 *Winchester, New Alresford & East Meon*.

Books
The only book on this route is *The Test Way & the Clarendon Way* by Barry Shurlock, but it's out of print and hard to find – although some tourist offices may have copies.

Information Sources
There are large and efficient tourist offices at both ends of the walk – in **Salisbury** (☎ 01722-

334956; www.visitsalisbury.com; Fish Row), near Market Sq, and **Winchester** (☎ 01962-840500; www .winchester.gov.uk; The Guildhall, High St; ☯ closed Sun Oct-Apr). Both have comprehensive accommodation lists and will make free bookings for you on their patch (ie in the city and immediate surrounds). For accommodation outside the area there may be a charge. These two tourist offices also sell a good selection of maps and local walking guidebooks. The websites also include walking information.

Other useful websites include www.visit salisburyuk.com and www.visitwinchester .co.uk

NEAREST TOWNS
The 'nearest towns' to this route are the cities of Salisbury (at the start) and Winchester (at the end) – both of which have many sleeping and eating options. Places to stay and eat along the route are detailed in the walk description.

Salisbury
pop 43,335
For many visitors, Salisbury means one thing: **Salisbury Cathedral** (☎ 01722-555100; www.salisburycathedral.org.uk; requested donation adult/ child £4/2), a truly majestic place of worship, topped by the tallest spire in England. But there's more. **Markets** have been held twice weekly for more than 600 years and the stalls still draw large crowds. The town's architecture, including some very beautiful half-timbered buildings, is a blend of every style since the Middle Ages, while just beyond the outskirts stands the ancient site of **Old Sarum**, with remains from the Iron Age and Roman eras, and a place of council for William the Conqueror.

SLEEPING & EATING
The busy **YHA Hostel** (☎ 0870 770 6018; salisbury@ yha.org.uk; Milford Hill; dm £18) is an attractive old

> **SALISBURY CATHEDRAL**
>
> Salisbury Cathedral is, quite simply, one of the most beautiful cathedrals in Britain. The architecture is uniformly Early English, a style characterised by pointed arches, graceful flying buttresses and a rather austere feel. This uniformity is thanks to its rapid construction, between 1220 and 1266 – a remarkably short time for such a mammoth project in the days before tower-cranes and reinforced concrete. Inside the cathedral there's a model of how the medieval construction site would have looked. Note the wooden scaffolding and not a hard hat in sight.

building surrounded by gardens, just east of the city centre. Nearby, just off Millford Hill, **Byways House** (☎ 01722-328364; www.bed-breakfast-stonehenge.co.uk; 31 Fowlers Rd; s/d £45/65) is a good-value, walker-friendly place.

The main street for B&Bs is Castle Rd (between the inner ring road and Old Sarum); it's a busy road but very handy for the centre. Nearest the city is a cluster of B&Bs including **Leena's** (☎ 01722-335419; 50 Castle Rd; d £56-80), **Victoria Lodge** (☎ 01722-320586; www.viclodge.co.uk; 61 Castle Rd; s/d £50/65); **Edwardian Lodge** (☎ 01722 413329; www.edwardianlodge.co.uk; 59 Castle Rd; d from £54) and **Hayburn Wyke** (☎ 01722-412627; www.hayburnwykeguesthouse.co.uk; 72 Castle Rd; d from £46).

Salisbury has a wide range of places to eat, from greasy fast-food outlets to very fine restaurants; with a quick stroll around the market square and surrounding streets, you'll soon find something to suit your taste and budget. Of the good pubs doing food, we like the **Haunch of Venison** on Minster St and the **Wig & Quill** on New St.

GETTING THERE & AWAY
Salisbury is linked by regular National Express coaches to London and other parts of the country. For train travel, Salisbury is effectively on the outer edges of London's commuter belt, so there are frequent trains to/from the capital, as well as to/from the Midlands and the southern coast of England. For local transport between Winchester and Salisbury, see right.

Winchester
pop 41,420
The venerable city of Winchester has a long and varied history. It was an Iron Age fort, a Roman town and a Saxon settlement, and most famously the capital of King Alfred the Great – making it the most important city in England for many years until a young upstart called London took the mantle in the 12th century.

The top sight here is **Winchester Cathedral** (☎ 01962-857200; www.winchestercathedral.org.uk; adult/child £4/free) – though it's less dramatic on the outside (and arguably more impressive on the inside) than its neighbour. According to tradition, the weather on St Swithin's feast day (15 July) dictates the weather for the next 40 days. A quick prayer here for good conditions during your walk couldn't hurt.

The centre has a lively high street, a fascinating array of old buildings and a good collection of bars and restaurants.

SLEEPING & EATING
As a major stop on the tourist track, Winchester has an etremely wide choice of places to stay – although many get full in the summer months.

Budget accommodation options include **St Margaret's** (☎ 01962-861450; www.winchesterbandb.com; 3 St Michael's Rd; s/d £30/50), which has basic accommodation with shared bathrooms. More attractive is **29 Christchurch Rd** (☎ 01962-868661; www.fetherstondilke.com; s £30-50, d £60-70), an elegant Regency home with a lovely garden, en suite rooms and great vegan breakfasts on request. Out of the city centre, in the St Cross area, **Brymer House** (☎ 01962-867428; www.brymerhouse.co.uk; 29 St Faith's Rd; d £65) offers similar quality, but charges a £10 supplement for single-night stays on the weekend.

Also in St Cross, and handy for Clarendon Way walkers, **67 St Cross Rd** (☎ 01962-863002; s/d £35/55) is an unassuming-looking but welcoming place on St Cross Rd near where it's crossed by the Clarendon Way. Nearby **54 St Cross Rd** (☎ 01962-852073; martinblockley@uwclub.net; s/d £32/52) is another walker-friendly place. Also just off the route, but back up the hill near the junction of Romsey Rd and Stanmore Lane, is charming and peaceful **Dawn Cottage** (☎ 01962-869956; dawncottage@hotmail.com; 99 Romsey Rd; d £70).

For food, the **Bishop on the Bridge** (☎ 01962-855111; 1 High St; mains £8-10; ☺ lunch & dinner) offers pub grub, with a pleasant terrace next to the river. Other pubs we like include the old-style **Eclipse Inn**, near the cathedral, serving homely food in quaint surroundings, and the eclectically decorated **Wykeham Arms** (Kingsgate St) for good beer and meals.

Up a step, **Chesil Rectory** (☎ 01962-851555; www.chesilrectory.co.uk; 1 Chesil St; lunch £15, 3-course dinner £49) serves great meals and occupies the oldest house in Winchester.

For food and drink on the walk, there are many shops and supermarkets in Winchester city centre.

GETTING THERE & AWAY
Winchester is easily reached by train from London (one hour, up to 50 services daily) and many parts of the country, such

as Southampton (20 minutes, 40 daily), Brighton (1½ hours, four daily), Birmingham (2½ hours, 12 daily) and Manchester (four hours, three daily).

National Express (☎ 08705 808080; www.national express.com) coaches link Winchester with London (two hours) and various other parts of the country, with frequent services throughout the day.

To get back to the start of the walk, local bus 68 runs between Winchester and Salisbury (1⅓ hours, roughly every two hours, less frequently on Sunday); all services go via Stockbridge, some via Broughton and some via King's Somborne.

If travelling by car, Winchester is just off the M3 motorway, which links Southampton with London.

THE WALK
Salisbury to Broughton
4–5 hours, 11 miles (17.5km)

The route starts at Salisbury Cathedral and heads east out of town along Milford St (the street between the cathedral and Market Sq). Begin by following signs for the YHA hostel ('Youth Hostel') – there are no specific signs for the Clarendon Way. Go under the inner ring road, up Millford Hill, down a suburban path called Millford Hollow and along Millford Mill Rd, which crosses the River Bourne. Surprisingly quickly, you're out of the city and in the country.

Keep heading east along a lane called Queen Manor Rd, and – about 2 miles from the start of the walk – look out for the first noticeable waymarks on the right, directing you onto a path across a field and up King Manor Hill. Looking behind, the path points straight back towards the cathedral, still towering above any other building in Salisbury.

From the top of the hill, continue through woodland and pass the ruined remains of **Clarendon Palace** where, in 1164, Henry II hosted an early skirmish in the long power struggle between crown and church. Present was the infamous 'turbulent priest', Thomas à Becket, who was killed six years later in Canterbury at the king's behest.

At a fork just after the palace, keep straight on the main track for 100m, then branch left (do not follow the wider track that leads eventually to Pitton Lodge) and follow narrow footpaths and tracks through pleasant woodland all the way to the pretty little village of Pitton. From the crossroads, head southeast briefly (nearby, the **village shop** sells drinks, food and ice creams), pass the **Silver Plough** pub, and turn immediately left (north) into a lane lined with houses. The lane leads to a path that takes you over the hill to reach a road opposite the very attractive flint **church** in the tiny settlement of West Winterslow.

Cross the road and go down a track with the church on your left. Go through a gate and follow the paths across a couple of fields (potentially confusing, so keep a close eye on your map), eventually leading northeastwards to the village of Middle Winterslow.

Go through the village to its northern side, where the route turns sharp right along a road called the Causeway. This former Roman road originally ran between Old Sarum, near Salisbury, and the port of Clausentum, near Southampton. The map reading becomes easier for a while – you pretty much go straight ahead for several miles – and, now that you've crossed from Wiltshire to Hampshire, the signposting is much better, too.

Follow the route of the Roman road along a track along the northern edge of Middle Winterslow with fields on your left and the backs of houses on your right. On the eastern edge of the village (called The Common) the route comes down, meets the tar lane for a few hundred metres, then rejoins the route of the Roman road down a gravel track called Eastern Common Hill. Follow this though a nice section of fields and woodlands, over a lane, then up the farm lane to Buckholt Farm. Beyond here, the Clarendon Way leaves the Roman road, veering directly east over a hilly area before descending into the sleepy village of **Broughton**.

If it's time for a rest, Broughton's fine brace of pubs, the **Greyhound** and the **Tally Ho**, await the weary walker. There's also a **village shop**. If you plan to spread the walk over two days, this is pretty much the halfway point. Local B&Bs include the clean-lined and modern **Old Coach House** (☎ 01794-301527; www.ochouse.co.uk; d £50), and the cosy and historic **Yew Tree House** (☎ 01794-301227; pandjmutton@onetel.com; s/d £35/56).

WESSEX

The Clarendon Way

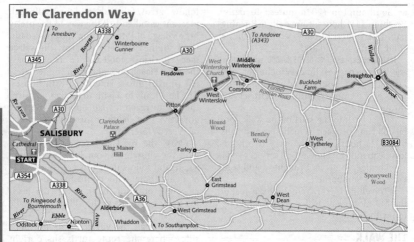

Broughton to King's Somborne
1 hour, 3 miles (5km)

Before leaving Broughton, take a few moments to admire **St Mary's Church** and the fine dovecote in its churchyard, demonstrating that intensive animal rearing is not a new invention. Battery pigeons were raised in this circular structure in medieval times, and 3½ tons of young pigeons were slaughtered each year.

The route now leads along Rectory Lane out of Broughton, over Wallop Brook and behind some large houses. It then heads across fields to Houghton, from where a narrow lane leads to two footbridges across the crystal-clear waters of the River Test. A rash of 'private' signs indicates that this is a premier trout stream. If there is one thing that the English value highly, it's their fishing rights, and rumour has it that even Prince Charles was made to join a waiting list to gain membership of the local angling club.

Just after the river, the route crosses an old railway track, which is part of the Test Way, another long walking route through Hampshire. If you want to call it a day, turn left (north) here along the Test Way to reach the small town of Stockbridge, where you can catch a bus to Winchester or Salisbury. Stockbridge also has several pubs and B&Bs.

If you're carrying on, go up the steep hill, then follow the lane down to King's Somborne – yet another pretty little village

although, straddling the busy A3057 road, it's not as peaceful as others.

If you're going for the all-in-one-day option and didn't stop in Broughton, then you might be tempted by the **Crown Inn** at King's Somborne – good beer and bar meals will slake any walking thirst or hunger. Across the green on the other side of the main road, the **village shop** (✍ closed Sun), with a bench by the stream, is an alternative spot for refreshment and rest.

King's Somborne to Winchester
4½–5½ hours, 13 miles (21km)

Leave King's Somborne on the lane that heads northeast towards Ashley, then at the edge of the village take a path on the right. This leads uphill through fields and woods to briefly join the Roman road once again, before zigzagging its way through more fields and taking you up to the summit of **Beacon Hill**. This splendid view point is topped by a curious, pyramid-like monument marking the burial place of a horse that, in 1733, tumbled into a local quarry during a hunt. Apparently, neither the horse nor its rider was injured, and the grateful owner changed his mount's name to Beware Chalkpit. The horse would go on to win several races.

If it's a weekend, you're likely to meet a few more horses and a few more people as, for the next couple of miles or so, the route crosses **Farley Mount Country Park**, with a rather confusing tangle of walking

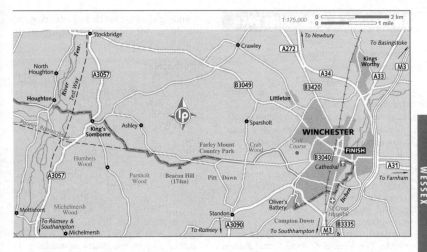

paths and bridleways. The Clarendon way-marks disappear at some junctions but, if in doubt, follow the bridleway (marked by red poles with horseshoe symbols) through the woods. The Clarendon Way once again meets the Roman road, which is now also a modern road, then branches off to loop north and then south past farms and a golf course.

The country lane becomes a suburban street as you enter the outskirts of Winchester. At a junction with the busy B3040, go straight onto Stanmore Lane, then immediately right on Oliver's Battery Rd. Go along this for 500m, under a busy road, then past **Oliver's Battery**, the site where Cromwell forced the city to surrender during the Civil War – though today it looks like a patch of grass surrounded by a housing estate.

Keep going through the fiddly minor suburban streets until you reach the open grassland of Compton Down. Turn sharp left (almost back the way you have just come) along a couple of narrow footpaths, over the main road on a footbridge and down a narrow sunken track (the remains of an old road into the city) to finally reach a railway line, which you cross on a bridge to meet a main road (the B3335).

Turn right here, then turn left just before a pub called The Bell. Nearby is St Cross' Hospital, a charitable home founded in 1137 for '13 poor impotent men so reduced in strength as rarely or never able to raise themselves without the assistance of one another'.

From here the Way leads across beautiful water meadows beside the River Itchen, before going through a series of narrow streets and arches round ancient Winchester College. At **Wolvesey Castle**, the official Clarendon Way goes to the right, through a little stretch of river-side park, to end at the City Mill. Nearby is the **Bishop on the Bridge** pub, which has a nice terrace overlooking the river – this may be just the spot for a celebratory pint and bite. You can then continue along the main street to end your walk at the grand door of **Winchester Cathedral**.

WINCHESTER CATHEDRAL

Winchester Cathedral was built between 1079 and 1093, shortly after the Norman Conquest of 1066. Compared with Salisbury, the architecture is a mix: in the 13th century the cathedral was extended in the Early English style, and from the mid-14th century the nave was rebuilt in a late Gothic style called 'perpendicular', characterised by large windows, fan vaults and an emphasis on vertical lines. The cathedral's internal detail is truly awe-inspiring and outshines the comparatively mundane exterior. This makes an interesting contrast with Salisbury Cathedral, where the outside is wonderful and the inside less dramatic.

THE KENNET & AVON CANAL PATH

Duration	4–5 hours
Distance	10 miles (16km)
Difficulty	easy
Start	Bath (p110)
Finish	Bradford-on-Avon (opposite)
Transport	train

Summary A flat and easy waterway walk through delightful countryside with a good taste of Britain's early industrial heritage.

Canals were the railroads and motorways of their day; busy routes transporting cargo across the country. Now they're loved as tranquil leisure routes for boaters, cyclists and walkers, and are a great way to stroll effortlessly through some of Britain's countryside. The Kennet & Avon Canal Path is just such a route, and the walk we describe here follows one of its most interesting sections, from the historic city of Bath to the neat market town of Bradford-on-Avon, following the canal as it traverses the landscape via a fascinating series of bridges, tunnels and aqueducts. Other attractions include decorated boats, good bird life and some very nice canal-side pubs.

PLANNING

This linear walk can be done in either direction. We describe the route from Bath to Bradford-on-Avon, assuming you'll return to Bath by train. You could, however, overnight in Bradford-on-Avon, catch the train to Bath, then walk back.

Adding time for lunch and admiring the aqueducts, you will probably need about six hours to complete the walk.

Alternatives

If you don't want to go all the way to Bradford-on-Avon, you can walk as far as Avoncliff (8.5 miles from Bath), and from there catch a train back to Bath.

If you've got more time, you can continue along the canal from Bradford-on-Avon to Devizes. This provides a change of scenery – from enclosed river valley to open farmland – and includes the 'flight' of 16 closely stepped locks at Caen Hill, one of the most spectacular features on Britain's entire inland waterway system. The distance from Bradford-on-Avon to Devizes is 11.5 miles (18.5km), requiring another five to six hours of walking. If you do the extension, it brings the total distance from Bath to Devizes up to 21.5 miles (34.5km), which most people will need nine to 11 hours to cover. However, because the route is flat and easy underfoot, strong walkers could do it in around seven or eight hours – not too demanding on a long summer's day.

Maps & Books

The OS Landranger 1:50,000 maps No 172 *Bristol & Bath* and No 173 *Swindon & Devizes* cover the route described here. For more detail on the whole canal and a bargeful of very useful information, the *Kennet & Avon Canal Map & Guide*, published by GeoProjects, is highly recommended.

BARGE BACK IN

The Kennet & Avon Canal was built between 1794 and 1810 to join London and Bristol, two of the most important ports in the country, by an inland route. The canal linked the River Avon to the River Kennet, a tributary of the Thames, so that barges called narrowboats, towed by horses, could carry goods up one river, along the canal, then down the other river. The project was completed before the days of mechanisation, so most construction was done by workmen called navigators ('navvies') using little more than picks and wheelbarrows.

In the late 19th and early 20th centuries, canals had to compete with railways for the movement of freight. Then came road transport. Trains and trucks were quicker than barges, and by the 1960s much of the Kennet & Avon Canal was abandoned and in an unusable state. However, since the early 1980s dedicated enthusiasts have rebuilt the canal, providing a modern waterway for a whole new generation of narrowboat owners – not to mention many more activities never foreseen by the navvies. Today, people in pleasure cruisers, rowing boats and canoes enjoy the canal, while anglers sit on the bank, and walkers and cyclists (and still the occasional horse) follow the towpath.

The Kennet & Avon Walk by Ray Quinlan covers the whole canal, plus river walks at either end, from the mouth of the Avon, near Bristol, to Westminster in central London.

Information Sources

Tourist offices are located at **Bath** (☎ 01225-477101; www.visitbath.co.uk) and **Bradford-on-Avon** (☎ 01225-865797; www.bradfordonavon.co.uk). A very handy information source is the site of the **Kennet & Avon Canal Trust** (www.katrust.org), responsible for much of the canal's restoration work. See also www.bathcanal.com. For more general information, see www.waterscape.com/walking.

NEAREST TOWNS

The nearest town to the start of this walk is the city of Bath (see p110) – regularly linked to all parts of the country by train and National Express coach, and with accommodation and facilities for all tastes and budgets, as befits a major tourist destination.

Bradford-on-Avon

Before you catch your train back to Bath from the end of the walk, there are several options in Bradford-on-Avon for food and drink. Our favourites include the **Dandy Lion** pub, the bar at the **Swan Hotel** (note the Moulton bicycle hanging on the wall – it was invented here) and delightful **Mr Salvat's Coffee Room**, last modernised in the 17th century.

GETTING THERE & AWAY

From Bradford-on-Avon, buses go regularly back to Bath, but it's far easier to use the train, with about 20 trains per day each way (about 15 on Sunday). For onward travel, you can also get a bus or train from Bradford-on-Avon to Salisbury or the south coast.

GETTING TO/FROM THE WALK

Getting to the start of the walk is easy. With your back to the Bath Spa train station entrance, go right and follow the footpath sign under the railway arch, then over a footbridge crossing the River Avon. Turn left, then after 50m turn left again to reach the start of the canal near the lock gates separating it from the river. That's the tricky navigational bit over! You keep to the towpath now for the rest of the walk.

For transport from the end of the walk, see left.

THE WALK

Leaving the lock-gates that mark the start of the Kennet & Avon Canal, you also leave behind the hubbub of trains and traffic. Indeed, there's probably no quieter, or more attractive, way of leaving Bath.

The towpath sits nicely beside the canal as you pass a few more lock-gates and grand **Cleveland House**, straddling the canal, where you cross to the opposite bank. Next the path runs beside **Sydney Gardens**, once a very fashionable quarter where two more bridges were built to hide the lowly narrowboats from sensitive aristocrats. It's worth leaving the canal briefly for a quick stroll around.

You soon reach Bathampton (2.5 miles from the start) where the **George Inn** serves

---

HISTORY-ON-AVON

Largely thanks to its position on the river, Bradford-on-Avon holds plenty of historic interest, so it's worth having a look around. The **Town Bridge** dates from 1610 and is noted for its 'lockup' (small prison) built into the central pier.

Near the bridge, some magnificent **mill buildings** line the river. These date from the 17th and 18th centuries when Bradford-on-Avon reached its peak as a weaving centre and West Country wool was highly prized across Britain and Europe.

Up on the hill overlooking the town is the tiny Saxon **church of St Laurence**. It was established in the 7th or 8th century, but was put to secular use and eventually forgotten when a new church was constructed. It was rediscovered around 1856 and has been returned to its original condition.

On the edge of town, near the canal, is the medieval **Packhorse Bridge**, over which produce was carried to the immense **Tithe Barn** – built in 1341 and still standing today despite 100 tons of stone tiles on the roof.

drinks and food, and the **Raft Café** (on a tied-up barge) serves coffee and sandwiches to take away. If it's too early for a stop, continue along the path, now heading south. After Bridge No 181 (they are numbered from Reading, so you can start counting down) there are woods on the right, while a beautiful stretch of countryside unfolds to your left.

About 5 miles from Bath, a footbridge takes you onto the right (west) bank, just before the main canal does a sharp left turn and leaps across the River Avon at the remarkably ornate **Dundas Aqueduct**, named after the first chairman of the canal company but designed by engineer John Rennie.

Just before the aqueduct, another small canal branches off (ie goes straight) from the Kennet & Avon. This is the Somerset Coal Canal, another long-term restoration project – worth following for 500m or so along to **Brassknocker Basin** and the very pleasant **Angelfish Café** (open daily for teas, snacks and lunches). Also here are some public loos, a bike- and boat-hire outlet and an exhibition about the canal's history.

The main route continues along the towpath and over Dundas Aqueduct, then clings to the wooded valley side, skirting above the village of Limpley Stoke. Look out for the sign in the hedge to the **tearoom** if you need hot drinks or cakes.

Another few miles brings you to **Avoncliff Aqueduct** – longer, higher and even more splendid than Dundas. This takes you back across the River Avon, and you have to loop down under a tunnel to reach the towpath on the other side of the canal.

If it's time for refreshment, the popular **Cross Guns** (☎ 01225-862335; www.crossguns.net) serves good beer and food, with tables outside if it's a sunny day and a fire inside if it's cold. There's also a nearby **tearoom**.

The last 1.5 miles of towpath takes you into Bradford-on-Avon. Look out for the famous medieval **Tithe Barn** on your left – this is well worth a visit (see boxed text, p81). Just behind the barn are several craft shops and a small friendly **café** around a courtyard-like garden.

The end of this walk is marked by a bridge over the canal. Next to the bridge is the **Lock Inn Cottage** (☎ 01225-868068; www .thelockinn.co.uk; ☻ breakfast, lunch & dinner), a busy pub-café with canal-side gardens, no-frills interior and a vast array of drinks, snacks and meals, including the famous Boatman's Breakfast. You can also rent bicycles and canoes, which may provide an alternative way of covering the route. Nearby, the **Canal Tavern** does a range of bar meals.

Before leaving the canal, cross the road to see the lock and basin – once Bradford-on-Avon's port. Nearby, the **Barge Inn** (can you see the theme here?), with its pleasant canal-side garden, is another option for drinks or meals.

From the end of the walk it's less than 800m to the centre of **Bradford-on-Avon** (p81).

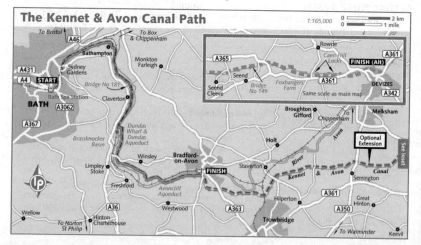

The Kennet & Avon Canal Path

1:165,000

THE RIDGEWAY (WEST)

Duration	3 days
Distance	44 miles (71km)
Difficulty	easy
Start	Avebury (p85)
Finish	Goring (p86)
Transport	bus

Summary A popular and straightforward national trail through high, rolling chalk hills and farmland, with great views and a rich historical background.

The Ridgeway is dubbed 'Britain's oldest road'. Archaeological evidence confirms that this ancient route has been used for at least 5000 years, and as you walk here today the landscape oozes a palpable sense of human history.

In reality, the original Ridgeway did not follow a single linear route, but rather a series of tracks and paths across high chalk hills, avoiding swampy plains or forested valleys and making travel easier for early Stone Age walkers. It was one of many such ancient routes that linked southwest England with the east coast. For today's walker, the western part of the Ridgeway National Trail is an ideal year-round route, especially good in summer when mild gradients, dry paths and fine views make the walking effortless and enjoyable.

Although the original Ridgeway crossed the country, the modern Ridgeway National Trail follows only part of this ancient route and is divided into two very distinct sections. The western section, described here, crosses the North Wessex Downs Area of Outstanding Natural Beauty (AONB) over open country with few roads and villages, providing excellent views when the skies are clear and a bleak grandeur when the storm clouds brew. Historical reminders abound, as the route passes Stone Age burial mounds and Iron Age forts, as well as passing near the massive stone circle at Avebury.

PLANNING

This route description covers the western section of the Ridgeway, from Avebury to Goring in the Thames Valley. Beyond Goring, the eastern section of the Ridgeway winds through the very different landscape of the Chiltern Hills – also an AONB, but more densely populated with numerous villages and small towns, along with notably more woodland. If you want to do the whole Ridgeway, see boxed text, p88, for some brief information. As with all LDPs, you can do just a small section of the Ridgeway or a circular route taking in a stretch of the main trail.

Whether you do all or just some of it, the Ridgeway is a linear route and, as a national trail, is well waymarked with acorn symbols and signs. We recommend going west to east, to keep the wind mostly behind you.

The national trail officially starts at Overton Hill, an uninspiring car park next to the busy main A4 road west of Marlborough (although the 5000-year-old burial mounds nearby, where archaeologists have found the remains of adults and children, are somehow made all the more poignant by the lorries that rumble past obliviously). A much more interesting option is to start at the fascinating Avebury Stone Circle – an appropriate introduction to this walk through ancient British history – and join the Ridgeway from here, missing the first few miles of the official route.

You will need to add a few extra miles to the stated distance to get to/from your accommodation as there's only one village actually *on* the route. All others are a mile or two away, and even then places to stay and eat are limited, so careful planning is required (as are advance reservations in summer).

Most walkers do this section in three days, and the most convenient stages are:

Day	From	To	Miles/km
1	Avebury	Ogbourne St George	9/14.5
2	Ogbourne St George	Court Hill	21/34
3	Court Hill	Goring	14/22.5

Hours given in the description are walking times only – remember to add extra for lunch, sightseeing, rests etc.

Alternatives

Day 1 is short (to allow for a visit to Avebury Stone Circle before setting out) and Day 2 is long, although not too arduous, and easily possible for fit walkers. Alternatively, on Day 1 you can continue beyond Ogbourne St George to either Bishopstone or Ashbury; both villages have B&B options. This makes Days 1 and 2 about 15 miles each.

When to Walk

You can do this route at any time of year. In winter the paths can be muddy and the bare chalk slippery, but it's not too difficult if you take care – although you'll need good waterproofs if the rain comes in when you're up on the high sections!

Maps

The western section of the Ridgeway is on OS Landranger 1:50,000 maps No 173 *Swindon & Devizes* and No 174 *Newbury & Wantage*; these maps are fine, as the going is straightforward. Very useful is Harvey Maps 1:40,000 *The Ridgeway* strip map; the strips are wide enough to show villages off the route where you might divert for accommodation and, like all Harvey maps, are waterproof and hard-wearing. It also very usefully shows water points.

Books

The official national trail guide is *The Ridgeway* by Anthony Burton, with good detailed description, background information and extracts from OS 1:25,000 maps, although these are only useful if you don't detour more than a few miles off the route. Highly recommended is *The Ridgeway* by Nick Hill, full of background and route information with easy-to-read, walker-specific line maps.

Absolutely invaluable is *The Ridgeway National Trail Companion*, published by the National Trails Office and covering accommodation, services and facilities along or near the trail. Organised in a logical fashion, it also lists recommended maps and books, provides background historical and wildlife information, and even shows where your horse can get a drink.

The National Trails Office also produces *Walks Around the Ridgeway*, which describes a good selection of circular walks including sections of the main national trail.

Information Sources

For general accommodation and transport inquiries, the main tourist website for this area is www.visitkennet.co.uk. Tourist offices near the route include **Avebury** (☎ 01672-539425; all.atic@kennet.gov.uk), **Swindon** (☎ 01793-530328; www.visitswindon.co.uk), **Marlborough** (☎ 01672-513989) and **Wantage** (☎ 01235-760176; www.visitvale.co.uk).

For walking information, your first contact should be the **National Trails Office** (☎ 01865-810224; www.nationaltrail.co.uk/ridgeway). For information on Avebury and some other historic sites, see also www.national trust.org.uk/Wessex.

Guided Walks

The National Trails Office organises a series of guided walks along the Ridgeway, ranging from a few hours to all day long.

GETTING AROUND

The Ridgeway is well served by various local buses, including the handy X47, which runs close to the central section of this route on Saturdays. For more details, the *Ridgeway Bus & Train Guide* is a very handy leaflet, available (free of charge) from local tourist offices or by mail from the national trails office. You can also download the leaflet as a PDF from the national trails website (http://nationaltrail .co.uk/ridgeway).

WARNING – WATER & RUTS

Just because you're in comfortable southern England, don't be lured into complacency on the Ridgeway. There are very few settlements along the way (meaning very few cafés or pubs for lunch-stops), so it's best to carry supplies and enough water – especially in summer – as this route through pervious chalk land is above the spring line, with only occasional opportunities for refills.

Most of the western section of the Ridgeway consists of rights of way defined as 'Byway'. This means walkers share the route with mountain bikers, horse riders and 4WDs that churn up the ground in wet weather, making walking tricky. In some areas, separate footpaths run parallel to the main track, giving walkers a chance to avoid the ruts.

NEAREST TOWNS
Avebury
The village of Avebury is surrounded by a gigantic **stone circle** (see boxed text, below), larger than Stonehenge, plus several other historic sites and an excellent **museum** to draw the crowds, so there are several accommodation options.

SLEEPING & EATING
Places to stay in Avebury include **Manor Farm** (☎ 01672-539294; High St; d from £70). Nearby is **The Lodge** (☎ 01672-539023; www.aveburylodge.co.uk; d £95-225) – luxurious, eclectic and historic.

There are other options outside Avebury. Just west of the village, in the 'suburb' of Avebury Trusloe, is small and down-to-earth **6 Beckhampton Rd** (☎ 01672-539588; d £50). A mile north, in Winterbourne Monkton, the **New Inn** (☎ 01672-539240; www.thenewinn.net; s/d £50/60) offers good pub food and accommodation. About 1.5 miles southwest of Avebury at East Kennet, the **Old Forge** (☎ 01672-861686; www.theoldforge-avebury.co.uk; d from £50) offers good quality rooms with en suite bathrooms. Two miles southeast of Avebury at West Overton, there's comfortable B&B at **Cairncot** (☎ 01672-861617; www .cairncot.co.uk; d £50).

For a drink, lunch or evening meal, the **Red Lion** (☎ 01672-539266; ⏲ breakfast, lunch & dinner) is picture-postcard twee on the outside but a regular pub on the inside. It serves pretty standard pub fare, plus breakfast is available until 10am.

When it comes to retail, aspiring druids can stock up on charms and Celtic goodies at **Henge Shop**, while walkers can load their rucksacks with chocolate bars and takeaway sandwiches from the **village store**. There's also a **tearoom** next to the museum, and the National Trust's very own **Circles Restaurant**.

GETTING THERE & AWAY
The gateway town of Swindon can be easily reached from most parts of the country by National Express coach and by train (Swindon is on the main line between London and Bristol). You can then take the 49 Trans-Wilts Express bus, running about 10 times daily (less on Sunday) between Swindon and Trowbridge via Avebury and Devizes.

Alternatively, you could get a train to Pewsey (on the main line between London and southwest England), from where Avebury is a scenic 6-mile walk.

AVEBURY STONE CIRCLE

The stone circle at Avebury dates from around 2600–2100 BC, making it roughly the same age as Stonehenge, its more famous neighbour. With a diameter of about 350m, Avebury is also one of the largest stone circles in Britain, and it's well worth spending some time here before you set off along the Ridgeway.

The site originally comprised an outer circle of 98 standing stones, many weighing up to 20 tons, although they're not worked to shape as at Stonehenge. The stones remained largely intact through the Roman period, when the site may already have been a tourist attraction, and from around AD 600 a Saxon settlement grew up inside the circle. In medieval times, when the power of the church was strong and fear of paganism stronger, many of the stones were deliberately buried. Then, in the early 18th century, stones were broken up for building material as the village began to expand.

Modern archaeological surveys commenced in the early 20th century. In 1934, under the supervision of Alexander Keiller, buried stones were located and resurrected, and markers were placed where stones had disappeared. The wealthy Keiller actually bought Avebury in order to restore 'the outstanding archaeological disgrace of Britain'.

The modern roads into Avebury neatly cut the circle into four sectors. To see everything, start from the High St and walk round the circle in an anticlockwise direction. In the southwest sector there are 12 standing stones, including the Barber Surgeon Stone where the skeleton of a man was found buried. The southeast sector starts with the huge Portal Stones – the entry into the circle from an ancient road. The northwest sector has the most complete collection of standing stones, including the massive 65-ton Swindon Stone – one of the few never to have been toppled.

WESSEX

Goring

The western section of the Ridgeway National Trail ends at the sleepy little town of Goring, a historic crossing point on the River Thames and also on the Thames Path National Trail (see p88).

SLEEPING & EATING

Budget options are limited to the basic but friendly **Streatley YHA Hostel** (☎ 01491-872278; streatley@yha.org.uk; dm £16), on the west bank across the bridge from Goring. Nearby, **The Bull** (☎ 01491-872392; www.thebullatstreatley .com; d £70), a 15th-century former coaching inn, serves meals and has six cosy rooms. Solo walkers can stay at **3 Ickneild Cottages** (☎ 01491-875650; s £25), a traditional place with one single guest room.

In Goring itself, budget options start with the **Queens Arms** (☎ 01491-872825; s/d £30/60), a straightforward pub near the station on the edge of town, with no-frills accommodation (and no breakfast available). Two other options include **Melrose Cottage** (☎ 01491-873040; melrose@fsmail.net; 36 Milldown Rd; s/d £30/50), a family-run B&B about 800m from the path, and **Northview House** (☎ 01491-872184; hi@goring-on -thames.freeserve.co.uk; Farm Rd; s/d £30/50), a conveniently located B&B surrounded by trees.

For cosy rooms and good food, the cottage-like **John Barleycorn Inn** (☎ 01491-872509; s/d £45/55, mains £8-13) is worth a stop. Just up Station Rd is the **Catharine Wheel** (☎ 01491-872379; £8-12), another recommended place to eat and drink. Top of the lot is the **Miller of Mansfield Hotel** (☎ 01491-872829; www.millerof mansfield.com; High St; s £90, d £100-130) with classy rooms, contemporary decor and fine food in the restaurant.

GETTING THERE & AWAY

Goring is on a main train line between London and Reading, Oxford and Stratford-upon-Avon, with very frequent trains in both directions.

THE WALK
Day 1: Avebury to Ogbourne St George
4–5 hours, 9 miles (14.5km)

This first day of the route leads through classic Wiltshire Downs scenery, with rolling hills of grass and wheat, and occasional clumps of trees on the horizon. The whole area is dotted with mysterious mounds and ancient standing stones.

From the Red Lion pub, cross the main road, pass the tourist office on your right, and head east along a narrow lane called Green St, which soon becomes a rough track, leading uphill through fields to meet the Ridgeway 1.5 miles from the village. Turn left here and keep going for three days!

About 5 miles from Avebury the route goes through the dramatic earthworks of **Barbury Castle**, an Iron Age hillfort. The area is now a country park with public toilets and a good **café** at the warden's bungalow. There's also a water tap.

Beyond Barbury the route approaches the northern edge of the downs and the views get better – across to the giant town of Swindon and the more scenic Vale of White Horse. Follow Smeathe's Ridge across open farmland and descend to the village of Ogbourne St George.

OGBOURNE ST GEORGE

On the edge of the village, a good budget choice is **Foxlynch Farm** (☎ 01672-841307; camp sites for 2 £10, B&B s/d £20/40). The **Parklands Hotel** (☎ 01672-841555; www.parklandshoteluk.co.uk; s/d £50/75) is also a bar and restaurant, and the friendly owners can provide packed lunches and baggage transfer by arrangement. The nearby **Inn with the Well** (☎ 01672-841445; www .theinnwiththewell.com; s/d £40/50) has more of a pub atmosphere, serving up good beer and traditional bar food, with more elaborate meals in the restaurant.

Day 2: Ogbourne St George to Court Hill
8–10 hours, 21 miles (34km)

This is a long day, but the route is straightforward and not too tiring. With an early start you should have no problems.

From Ogbourne St George you soon burn off breakfast with a stiff ascent to rejoin the Ridgeway. The trail continues up to **Liddington Hill**, the highest point on the route at a dizzying 277m. Nearby is Liddington Castle, another Iron Age fort, reached by a permissive footpath and offering a fine panorama, spoilt only by the scar of the M4 motorway.

You descend a chalky track and walk along a busy road for about 200m, before turning right onto a lane that crosses the M4 and leads to the hamlet of Fox Hill and the welcoming sight of the **Shepherds Rest**

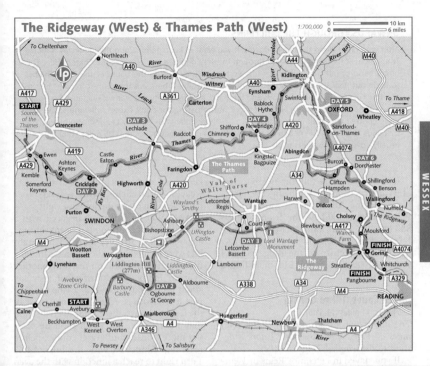

The Ridgeway (West) & Thames Path (West)

(the only pub actually *on* the western section of the trail), offering breakfasts, fresh coffee, lunches and evening meals.

About 200m beyond the pub, the Ridgeway leaves the asphalt behind and rejoins the rough track. Over the next few miles the surface switches between grass, shale, gravel and bare chalk – slippery when wet. If it's dry, this is one of the finest sections of the route, passing over high ground with more wonderful, sweeping views to the north. (If the weather is hot, remember to carry enough water for this stretch.)

The next feature on the Ridgeway is **Wayland's Smithy**, where legend tells of horses being left overnight and reshod by morning, although in reality it's an unusual 'chamber barrow' burial site. About a mile further along the trail is yet another fine Iron Age fort, **Uffington Castle**, from where you get views across the Vale of White Horse, with the chalky outline of the aforesaid animal cut in the turf just below. (For more on white horses, see the boxed text, p95.)

Another fine, rolling section of open downland follows, with the path ahead often visible for miles. As you continue, do stop occasionally and look back – the views are stunning that way, too. The route crosses a main road at Sparshot Firs, and the final few miles of today's stage lead past Letcombe Castle (you guessed it: another Iron Age fort) to reach another main road (the A338) at Court Hill.

COURT HILL & LETCOMBE REGIS

About 500m north of the trail are the **Ridgeway Information Centre**, with a good exhibition, and delightful **Ridgeway YHA Hostel** (☎ 0870-770 6064; www.yharidgeway.org.uk; dm £16), which has an appropriately historic atmosphere in a series of converted barns with an oak-beamed dining room, excellent views over the Vale and a choice of family rooms.

The nearest B&Bs are at Letcombe Regis, about 1.5 miles northwest. They include **Quince Cottage** (☎ 01235-763652; www.rboden.supanet.com; s/d £35/60), a lovely 18th-century thatched building. You can also stay and get evening bar food Tuesday to Saturday at the **Greyhound Inn** (☎ 01235-771093; d £60).

ONWARDS THROUGH THE CHILTERNS

After your jaunt along the chalky downs, if you want to keep going along the Ridgeway National Trail, the next three days take you through the very different landscape of the Chiltern Hills. This broad band of hills runs roughly southwest to northeast, from the banks of the River Thames to fizzle out near the towns of Aylesbury and Dunstable. These are the nearest 'proper' hills to London, covered in a mix of woods and farmland, and are a very popular walking area, especially at weekends. There's an excellent network of footpaths, but don't expect wilderness: the area is also dotted with well-to-do villages, especially popular with wealthy London commuters. The trail ends at Beacon Hill near Ivinghoe and the whole Ridgeway route is 85 miles (136km) long, usually covered by walkers in six days.

If these places are full, the nearby town of Wantage (famous for being the birthplace of King Alfred) has a wider choice. First choice should be the friendly **Regis B&B** (☎ 01235-762860; www.regisbandbwantage.co.uk; 12 Charlton Rd; s/d £35/65), which offers free pickup from and return to the Ridgeway and three-course dinners for £14 including a glass of wine.

Day 3: Court Hill to Goring
5–6 hours, 14 miles (22.5km)
This day is one of transition, with your final miles on high, open downland before a descent to the wooded Thames Valley.

If you stayed in Letcombe Regis or Wantage, retrace to the Ridgeway and continue along the northern edge of the downs, now also following the route of an ancient defensive dyke called **Grim's Ditch**. About 2 miles from Court Hill – as the route follows a wide, grassy track – look to the right for the **Lord Wantage Monument**. The noble lord commemorated here was a philanthropic landowner and commander of a battle in the 19th-century Crimean War; it's said he planted clumps of trees on his estate in the same formation as troops on a battlefield.

Along this stretch you'll see signs of the racehorse training activity for which the area is famous, as well as the cooling towers of Didcot power station and the former Atomic Energy Research Establishment at Harwell – but none of this affects the calmness of the surrounding downland.

About 6.5 miles from Court Hill, the Ridgeway goes under the busy A34 by way of a pedestrian tunnel (with some murals added for your enjoyment). A mile beyond here, the track is paved with concrete and there is a broad grass verge. Look for the sharp left turn off the paved section and

keep your eye open for signs as the route weaves round fields, with several other paths leading off to the left and right.

After Warren Farm you're faced with 3 miles of almost continuous descent through an area called **Streatley Warren**, where rabbits were farmed in medieval times. Initially the track is stony but, on reaching another Warren Farm (you know what they say about rabbits), it turns into a lane running past a few houses. After the remoteness of the last few hours, these signs of civilisation may be a shock, but you'll soon be passing more houses and a golf course, before reaching a junction with the busy A417. Turn right to reach a junction with the even busier A329 and then go straight into the village of Streatley, where a left turn at the traffic lights leads onto a bridge crossing a very scenic stretch of the River Thames and marking the end of this route. On the east bank is Goring, with several fine old pubs and cafés where you can celebrate finishing your walk through 5000 years of history.

THE THAMES PATH (WEST)

Duration	6 days
Distance	83 miles (133.5km)
Difficulty	easy
Start	Thames Head
Finish	Pangbourne (p91)
Nearest Town	Kemble (p90)
Transport	train, bus

Summary A classic and pleasurable river-side walk passing beautiful English countryside and fascinating historical sites.

The River Thames marks the northern limits of the legendary land of Wessex and is followed from its source to London by the Thames Path National Trail. The total length of this route is 173 miles and it usually takes around 12 to 14 days to walk, but it's divided very neatly at the town of Reading into two sections that can each be traversed in a week. Reading is also a transition point, where the Thames changes from a rural river to a major waterway with urban overtones.

Here we describe the western section of the Thames Path National Trail and also include most of the introductory information. For a description of the eastern section, see p64.

The Thames is a lowland river and its source is a mere 107m above sea level. Geological barriers are few so the river has an easy time of it, ambling towards the sea, losing height slowly with no tumbling falls or rapids to ripple its surface. The walking is correspondingly straightforward and leisurely, and the Thames Path takes the walker through a rich vein of English countryside, history and culture, past unspoilt pastures and old market towns, across broad floodplains and slicing through large settlements.

While the scenery around the river can be beautiful, the history is fascinating. Some of the most historically significant towns and villages of southern England grew up on the Thames and it's often worth a brief diversion from the side of the river to look at old town halls and coaching inns, market squares and grand houses.

The Thames is also a working river, and in its upper reaches you'll see where the immature river has been diverted to provide water for millponds. As you progress downstream you'll see locks, weirs and cuts (canals), all customising the Thames for human use. But nature can never be completely controlled, and you'll also see evidence of occasional rebellion where the river has escaped its artificial boundaries and flooded the surrounding lands. Regular commemorative stones mark high floods, particularly those of 1897 and 1947, which caused enormous devastation. In our own time, and as global warming and its effects becomes an increasingly topical issue, there were also major floods in the autumn of 2000, when the owners of many river-side houses found their ground floors swamped with water.

PLANNING

Combining the western and eastern sections of the Thames Path, as described in this book, creates a 12-day walk that takes you from the source of the river to the Thames Barrier. The route can be walked in either direction, but going downstream is more satisfying, following the rural stream as it develops into a magnificent river. The Thames Barrier (a series of massive flood-prevention gates, raised in high-water conditions to prevent London from being flooded) is a fitting end to the walk, whereas arriving at the source, an indistinct depression in a field, can be a bit of an anticlimax.

The total length of the Thames Path is between 170 and 180 miles. You will see some references to distances nearer 200 miles, but this includes the trail in London where it runs along both sides of the river simultaneously. Our western section measures 83 miles, and we suggest the following stages:

Day	From	To	Miles/km
1	Thames Head	Cricklade	10/16
2	Cricklade	Lechlade	11/17.5
3	Lechlade	Newbridge	16/25.5
4	Newbridge	Oxford	14/22.5
5	Oxford	Dorchester	16/25.5
6	Dorchester	Pangbourne	16/25.5

Hours given for each day's distance are walking times only. You will need to add extra for lunch, sightseeing etc.

The Thames Path is a trail undergoing continuous improvement; the aim is for the route to be next to the river as much as possible. Waymarking is mostly good, but be prepared for detours away from the river, or brand-new sections where maps have not kept up with recent developments and you *can* now walk beside the Thames.

Maps

Even though you're following a river, a map is essential to put the trail in a wider context and to help guide you through the diversions or away from the trail to your accommodation. The western section is covered by the OS Landranger 1:50,000 maps No 163 *Cheltenham & Cirencester,* No 164 *Oxford* and No 175 *Reading & Windsor.*

A very useful single map showing the whole route is *Thames – the River & Path,* published by GeoProjects, available in local tourist offices and online bookstores. It is not quite detailed enough to be relied upon totally for walking, but used in conjunction with the maps in *The Thames Path National Trail Guide* (see below) it will be fine. It also includes a wealth of background information and many useful phone numbers.

Books

The Thames Path National Trail Guide by David Sharp is the official guide and the most comprehensive book available, describing the route from the source to the Thames Barrier; it also features the relevant sections of OS maps. *The Thames Path* by Leigh Hatts describes the route going upstream from the Thames Barrier to the source.

Also very useful is *The Thames Path National Trail Companion,* a compendium of practical information, including details of camping, B&B and hotel accommodation along the river. It's available from local tourist offices or from the Thames Path National Trail Office (see right), which can also supply you with useful leaflets on public transport to points along the trail.

For background, get a copy of *River Thames in the Footsteps of the Famous* by Paul Goldsack, a fascinating introduction to nobles and notables with Thames connections, from Shakespeare and Dickens to Henry VIII and Toad of Toad Hall.

MESSING ABOUT IN BOATS

Two classics of English literature are *Three Men in a Boat* by Jerome K Jerome, a whimsical tale of a trip up the Thames, and *The Wind in the Willows* by Kenneth Grahame, an animal story for kids and a morality tale for all. Both are worth putting in your backpack for evening reading.

Information Sources

For general advice on accommodation and transport, tourist offices along this section of the Thames Path can be found at **Cirencester** (☎ 01285-654180; www.cotswold.gov.uk/tourism), **Oxford** (☎ 01865-726871; www.oxford.gov.uk) and **Abingdon** (☎ 01235-522711; www.visitvale.co.uk).

For route specifics, your first contact should be the **Thames Path National Trail Office** (☎ 01865-810224; www.nationaltrail.co.uk/thamespath). The excellent website is a wealth of information, and you can order maps and guides online.

The comprehensive website of the **Environment Agency** (www.visitthames.co.uk) has sections on walking, eating and drinking, as well as fishing, boating and other watery pursuits.

Although aimed mainly at boaters, www.the-river-thames.co.uk is a good source of background information on wildlife, history and traditions. For more history, see www.thames.me.uk.

Guided Walks

The National Trail Office organises a series of guided walks along the Thames Path ranging from a few hours to all day long. Various commercial organisations offer guided walks in Oxford, Windsor and London; local tourist offices have details.

A WELCOME LEGACY

The Thames, having being a major trading route, retains a legacy of inns, hotels, guesthouses and B&Bs. These are less common in the early sections (the unnavigable part of the river), but once you pass Lechlade the options increase. If you're intending to camp, get information and a copy of the *River Thames Camping* leaflet from www.visitthames.co.uk/ecamping.html.

NEAREST TOWNS
Kemble

The nearest town to the start of the walk is Kemble, a small place of fewer than 100 houses but enjoying a direct rail link to London (thanks to once having been the home of a senior railways figure). This facility is now enjoyed by the stockbrokers who combine rural living with work in the capital. Note the copies of *Horse & Hound* magazine neatly stacked on the polished table in the station waiting room.

SLEEPING & EATING

B&Bs include **The Willows** (☎ 01285-770667; 2 Glebe Lane; s/d £30/50), conveniently near the train station. Just about a mile from the source, in the village of Coates, is **Southfield**

NOT IN MY BACK YARD

The national trail downstream from Lechlade is loosely based on the towpath that used to run beside the navigable river. The towpath was developed by the Thames Commissioners in the 17th century to improve the river as a business route. However, construction was sometimes hindered by powerful river-side landowners, forcing the towpath to frequently cross from one side of the river to the other. Once, ferries operated at these points, to carry across the horses that pulled the barges, but these have now disappeared, obliging modern walkers to divert away from the river in some sections. The long-gone facilities are still remembered in some Thames-side villages by names such as Horseferry Rd and Horseferry Lane.

House (☎ 01285-770220; www.bandbinthecotswolds .com; s/d £40/70), which has lovely, country-style rooms. The **Thames Head Inn** (☎ 01285-770259; www.thamesheadinn.co.uk; camp sites for 2 £5 s/d £40/60) is 1 mile north of Kemble and (as the name suggests) very near the source; accommodation is in simple rooms with exposed beams.

In Ewen (1 mile east of Kemble and on the route), **Brooklands Farm** (☎ 01285-770487; s/d £30/40) is a real working farm, while the **Wild Duck Inn** (☎ 01285-770310; www.thewildduckinn.co.uk; s £70-100, d £95-150) has romantic, high-quality rooms and a seriously good reputation for food. There are more sleeping and eating options in the larger town of Cirencester, about 4 miles to the northeast of Kemble.

If you're arriving in Kemble in the morning, and need sustenance before walking straight to Cricklade, there's a **café** at the train station.

GETTING THERE & AWAY
By far the easiest way to reach Kemble by public transport is to use the regular train services between London and Cheltenham.

Pangbourne
The comfortable town of Pangbourne is little more than a smart commuter enclave of Reading (and London) but it makes the perfect place to end this route, before the Thames Path becomes more urban in feel.

SLEEPING & EATING
The homely **Weir View House** (☎ 0118-984 2120; www.weirview.co.uk; 9 Shooters Hill; d £75) is a good B&B with uncluttered but classically styled rooms. Up the price-band a little, the half-timbered **George Hotel** (☎ 0118-984 2237; www .georgehotelpangbourne.co.uk; s £69-85, d £75-90) – once home to *Wind in the Willows* author Kenneth Grahame, now part of Best Western –

has comfortable if predictable rooms. For food, **The Swan** (☎ 0118-984 4494; www.swanpang bourne.com; Shooters Hill; mains £6-11), a 17th-century inn opposite, is recommended.

On the opposite side of the Thames, in Whitchurch, the **Ferry Boat Inn** (☎ 0118-984 2161; d £50) is a good budget choice with no-frills rooms.

GETTING THERE & AWAY
Pangbourne is on the railway between London and Oxford, with regular trains to/from Reading and London. Reading is also linked to London and other parts of the country by National Express coach and local bus.

GETTING TO/FROM THE WALK
To reach Thames Head from Kemble, leave the village on the minor road past the station car park on your left, heading northwest towards Tarlton. On reaching a busy main road (the A433) turn right and walk along the road (take care – there's no footpath), past the Thames Head Inn, then a little further towards the railway bridge. Just before the bridge, go through a broken gateway and an abandoned goods yard, parallel to the railway line, to reach a stile, and cross the tracks (beware of trains). On the other side, you're finally free of danger from fast-moving transport. Follow paths roughly north across a couple of fields towards a copse of trees. Under one of these trees, in an inauspicious field corner, you will find the official source of the Thames marked by an engraved stone.

For a much more pleasant route to the start (if you don't mind a bit of backtracking), leave the village on the minor road towards Tarlton, as described above. You pass the station car park on your left, and about 20m later there's a footpath on your right, signposted 'Wysis Way' (a route through

Gloucestershire, linking the Wye and the Thames). Follow this path for 500m to meet the Thames Path near a bridge carrying the main road over the fledgling river. Turn left and follow the Thames Path 'upstream' for 1.5 miles to reach the source.

Whichever way you reach the source, don't expect a gushing fountain! Most of the year this 'source' is dry, although the surrounding field can be boggy from underground water. But this is the official source, so this is where our walk begins.

For transport from the end of the walk, see p91.

THE WALK
Day 1: Thames Head to Cricklade
4 hours, 10 miles (16km)

This is a day of anticipation as the minor dip in a field develops into a real river, which flows past cultivated fields, fallow meadows and picturesque villages.

From the river's source, follow the trail southwards through quiet fields, over the main roads to the east of Kemble and then through the edge of the village of Ewen (from the Saxon word *aewylme,* meaning 'river source'). By this time you should indeed be beside the infant Thames (also called the Isis as far as Abingdon), even if the first few miles were dry. Walk beside the river to Neigh Bridge (there are public toilets at the county park car park) and then enjoy more aquatic flavours as the route winds between the ponds and lakes of the Cotswold Water Park – once extensive gravel pits, some now providing leisure amenities such as sailing, others converted to wildlife reserves.

The old and pretty village of **Ashton Keynes** has a couple of pubs and makes a suitable lunch stop. The route carries on – effortless walking – through the water park, briefly touching the Thames' banks as the last couple of miles take you into Cricklade.

CRICKLADE
The sleepy old Roman town of Cricklade has churches and buildings with fine examples of architecture from Norman times to the present. Accommodation is available in two old coaching inns, both in the main street – the **White Hart Hotel** (☎ 01793-750206; whitehart-cricklade@arkells.com; s/d £45/65) and the **Old Bear Inn** (☎ 01793-750005; s/d £30/60); both also serve meals.

Another good option is in Latton, about 1 mile from the path (come off at Weaver's Bridge) before you reach Cricklade; it's the **Dolls House** (☎ 01793-750384; s/d £32/55).

Day 2: Cricklade to Lechlade
4½ hours, 11 miles (17.5km)

The river is now well established, but not yet navigable. Accordingly, there is no continuous river-side path and the trail also meanders through fields and farmland.

From Cricklade, the trail follows the river to Castle Eaton, the largest settlement you will pass today, where the **Red Lion** has a garden overlooking the river and serves filling pub food. A good lunch will set you up for the second half of today's stage, a mix of quiet lanes, paths, a rather unpleasant road and (with relief) a final stretch of river into Lechlade. About a mile before reaching the town, look out for the **Roundhouse**, marking the point where the Thames & Severn Canal once met the river, allowing barges and other watercraft to cross the Cotswolds and reach the River Severn. Downstream of here, the river is navigable, as illustrated by the boats in the marina.

LECHLADE
This is a quintessential Cotswold town that owes its wealth to trade on the Thames, although it's slightly back from the river. The church spire is visible from afar. At St Johns Lock, look out for the reclining figure of **Old Father Thames**, a concrete statue with a colourful history. Originally placed at the river source, it was relocated in 1974 because of problems with vandals.

There is a wide choice of accommodation. Campers can head for **Bridge House Campsite** (☎ 01367-252348; sites for 2 £8), just a short distance off the river. B&Bs include the **Apple Tree Guesthouse** (☎ 01367-252592; emreay@aol.com; High St; s/d £35/55), almost on the river, and **Cambrai Lodge** (☎ 01367-253173; www .cambrailodgeguesthouse.co.uk; Oak St; s £30-45, d £50-65) with bright, homely rooms. Other good options include the **Swan Inn** (☎ 01367-253571; 7 Burford St; s/d with bathroom £38/55, s/d with shared bathroom £25/45. mains £7-14), with simple rooms upstairs and good pub food downstairs; the **New Inn Hotel** (☎ 01367-252296; www.newinnhotel .com; Market Sq; s/d £45/55), with comfy, old-style rooms and good food; and the **Crown Inn** (☎ 01367-252198; www.crownlechlade.co.uk; High St;

s/d £45/55)), with cosy new-built rooms, pine furniture and patchwork quilts.

In the market square the **Red Lion** (☎ 01367-252373; High St; d £70, mains £7-9) has predictable rooms, and no meals on Sunday nights. The 13th-century **Trout Inn** (☎ 01367-252313; mains £10-14) right on the river serves a good selection of meals.

Day 3: Lechlade to Newbridge
6½ hours, 16 miles (25.5km)
The remote and rural feel of the Thames is retained, although the river is now a substantial waterway, crossed by historic bridges and locks.

From Lechlade it's 5 miles of lovely riverside to Radcot, scene of Civil War clashes and the site of the oldest existing bridge on the Thames, where **The Swan** (☎ 01367-810220; www.swanhotelradcot.co.uk; r £45-55) has cosy, traditional rooms. Along the way you'll also see reminders of a later conflict: pillboxes (small fortified emplacements) built in WWII as a defence against invasion.

Another 3 miles and you reach **Rushey Lock** (☎ 01367-870218), where camping is allowed, then Tadpole Bridge, where the 17th-century **Trout Inn** (☎ 01367-870382; www .troutinn.co.uk; s/d £55/80; mains £12-15) provides real ales, an excellent wide-ranging menu, mismatched furniture, old flagstones, log fires, cosy atmosphere and tastefully decked-out bedrooms.

Beyond here, riverside paths lead past Chimney Nature Reserve to Shifford Lock, from where you continue for 2 miles into Newbridge.

NEWBRIDGE
This old river crossing has a pub on each side: the **Maybush Inn** on the south bank and the **Rose Revived** (☎ 01865-300221; www .roserevived.com; s £43-48, d £53-58, mains £7-10) on the north bank, with accommodation that blends contemporary style and period character, and good meals. There are more options in the village of Kingston Bagpuize, about 2 miles south, or you could push on to Bablock Hythe.

Day 4: Newbridge to Oxford
5½ hours, 14 miles (22.5km)
Today's walk is another scenic section, but as you approach Oxford the river banks get perceptibly busier.

From Newbridge, it's 3.5 miles to Bablock Hythe, where the **Ferryman Inn** (☎ 01865-880028; s/d £35/60) provides functional rooms. Beyond here you leave the river for 2.5 miles. As an alternative, ask the landlord of the Ferryman Inn about his irregular ferry service – in more or less continuous operation for the last 1000 years – across the river. This will allow you to follow the path that runs along the east bank and rejoin the official trail at Pinkhill Lock.

It's another mile to Swinford Bridge, one of the last two remaining toll bridges over the river, where the **Talbot Inn** (☎ 01865-881348) on the north bank serves good pub food and makes an ideal lunch stop.

For the next few miles the trail is better defined and the distant hum of traffic comes as quite a shock after four days of quiet. More leisure craft are moving on the river and, before you realise it, the Thames has brought you into the heart of Oxford.

OXFORD
Much of Oxford's fascinating history and architecture is based around the university, but the city has also been a regional trade centre since medieval times. In later years, heavy industry (notably car manufacturing) was established here. Being a working city, rather than just a university town, means that Oxford isn't 'quaint', but 650 buildings officially designated with historical or architectural merit mean it's certainly worth discovering. If you were planning a rest day from the National Trail, this would be a good place.

Accommodation is plentiful. Budget possibilities include student-oriented **Oxford Backpackers** (☎ 01865-721761; www.hostels .co.uk; 9 Hythe Bridge St; dm £14-18; 💻), with big dorms and lots of partying at weekends. More restful are **Central Backpackers** (☎ 01865-242288; www.centralbackpackers.co.uk; 13 Park End St; dm £14-18; 💻), with small dorms and a nice roof terrace, and **Oxford YHA Hostel** (☎ 01865-727275; oxford@yha.org.uk; 2a Botley Rd; dm/d £21/55; 💻).

B&Bs include **Beaumont** (☎ 01865-241767; www.oxfordcity.co.uk/accom/beaumont; 234 Abingdon Rd; s £50-72, d £58-72) a good, bright place close to the river, and **Cornerways** (☎ 01865-240135; jeakings@btopenworld.com; 282 Abingdon Rd; s/d £45/64) with simple modern rooms. If you don't want to forget the Thames for a moment, the **Head of the River** (☎ 01865-721600;

headoftheriver@fullers.co.uk; Folly Bridge; s/d £75/95) is a popular river-side pub and hotel right in the centre of town with comfortable rooms.

As a university town and tourist honeypot, Oxford's eating options are virtually endless. Most of the pubs do evening bar meals, and there's a range of cheap takeaways, mid-priced eateries and very fine restaurants. With a short stroll around the centre you'll soon find something to suit your taste.

Day 5: Oxford to Dorchester
6½ hours, 16 miles (25.5km)
This stage could be described as the heart of the walk, with a fascinating mix of river-side views and historical buildings, especially ecclesiastical remains. The river is active and you'll likely see punts, rowing eights and hired cruisers out and about.

From Oxford the trail runs along the west bank, past Iffley Lock and Sandford Lock (4 miles from today's start), where the **Kings Arms** makes a pleasant refreshment spot. Then it's another 4 miles of tranquil river-side walking to Abingdon – an attractive and well-established market town with plenty of lunch opportunities. Look out for the fine range of former **monastic buildings** near the river, and a very handsome 17th-century **County Hall** in the marketplace. Don't linger too long, though – it's still another long 8 miles of classic Thames scenery, past locks and weirs, and over bridges, to reach Dorchester. At Clifton Hampden, about 2 miles before you reach Dorchester, the traditional thatched **Plough Inn** (☎ 01865-407811; www.ploughinns.co.uk; s/d £75/90) has good-quality, period-style rooms. Across the river the **Barley Mow Inn** (☎ 01865-407847) draws the crowds for its food and its Jerome K Jerome links: the author wrote most of his timeless classic *Three Men in a Boat* here and described the pub as '…without exception the quaintest most old-world inn up the river'.

DORCHESTER
Sometimes called Dorchester-on-Thames to distinguish it from its namesake in Dorset, this was a Roman garrison town and a Saxon bishopric. It still has a historical atmosphere, sustained in part by the large number of antique shops. B&B options include **Buena Vista** (☎ 01865-340903; www.buenavistabnb.co.uk; 34 Watling Lane; s/d £40/60)

with cosy, modern rooms, while on the high street there's the **George Hotel** (☎ 01865-340404; www.thegeorgedorchester.co.uk; s/d £70/95) and the **White Hart** (☎ 01865-340074; www.white-hart-hotel-dorchester.co.uk; s/d £95/105), both good options for food.

Day 6: Dorchester to Pangbourne
6½ hours, 16 miles (26km)
Today the Thames wanders through the serene Chiltern Hills and the trail occasionally strays onto higher ground away from the river.

From Dorchester, the trail continues to meander alongside the river, and passes through the historic town of Wallingford (with the remains of a castle, a market square and more accommodation options). The Chiltern Hills, marking the end of today's stage, are visible in the distance.

About 9 miles from today's start, at the village of Moulsford, you'll pass the **Beetle & Wedge** (www.beetleandwedge.co.uk), yet another literary location, as characterised in *The History of Mr Polly* by HG Wells. Next comes Goring (p86), another lunch or overnight possibility. The Ridgeway National Trail crosses the river and the Thames Path here.

Beyond Goring, the nature of the path changes. The valley sides are steeper, and the route passes through woods and copses. You're now skirting the southern edge of the Chiltern Hills, and it's a few easy miles to Pangbourne.

If this is the end of your walk, Pangbourne has some fine pubs and restaurants for a celebratory drink or meal. If you're continuing downstream, the rest of the Thames Path route is described in the London & the Southeast chapter (see p64).

MORE WALKS

THE WILTSHIRE DOWNS
The Wiltshire Downs is an area of chalky grassland and sparsely wooded hills, forming a broad west–east band between the towns of Devizes, Marlborough, Swindon, Wantage and Newbury. Also known as the **North Wessex Downs**, this area is combined with the Chiltern Hills, north of the Thames Valley, to form an important Area of Outstanding Natural Beauty (AONB).

The Wiltshire Downs area is traversed by the Ridgeway National Trail (see p83) but there are many more good walking opportunities in this area. From Avebury, a walk with major historic interest takes in the mysterious Neolithic earth pyramid of **Silbury Hill** and the nearby West Kennet Long Barrow – an ancient burial mound.

To the west of Avebury, **Cherhill Down** (pronounced cheh-ril) is high, easily accessible, and topped by a monument and a giant white horse carved in the chalk (see boxed text, below).

South of Avebury is the quiet, rural **Vale of Pewsey**, between the Wiltshire Downs and Salisbury Plain. The small town of Pewsey makes a good walking base; destinations include two white horse figures carved on the hillsides, several tumuli and other prehistoric remains. The **Kennet & Avon Canal Path** (p80) runs through the Vale of Pewsey and is a good focus for day walks. Pewsey train station is on a main line between London and the West Country, so access is easy.

To the west of Salisbury Plain lie the **West Wiltshire Downs**, an area of grassy hills and escarpments near the town of Westbury, southeast of Bath. Nearby is yet another famous white horse figure carved on the hillside. Together with the farmland and heath of **Cranborne Chase**, this forms another important AONB, with more good walking opportunities.

A great way to explore the West Wiltshire and North Wessex Downs is on **Wiltshire's White Horse Trail**, a 90-mile route linking eight white horses and many other historical sites, passing through tranquil farmland, meadows, hills and quiet villages. The route can be done in one week, but it's ideal for following shorter sections for just a day or two, either on a circular walk or returning to the start by public transport. Good bases are Devizes, Avebury, Marlborough, Westbury or Pewsey. Route cards are available from local tourist offices. For general tourist information, see www.visitwiltshire.co.uk.

SALISBURY PLAIN

Salisbury Plain is a wide, empty area of rolling grassland surrounded on the north by a steep escarpment and on the south by the rivers Wylie and Test. Much of the area is an army training ground, usually (and understandably) closed to the public, so most options for walkers keep pretty much to the edge of the plain rather than crossing it.

On the southern edge of the plain, the quiet villages and classic English farmland of the **Hampshire Avon Valley** are a good easy-walking area. The tourist office in Salisbury (see p75) has books and maps. If you like a challenge, ask about the **Sarcen Way**, a 26-mile route across the rarely visited heart of the plain, linking the stone circles of Stonehenge and Avebury. Unfortunately, some sections open only on certain days of the year but, if you coincide with these, it is well worth doing.

WESSEX CHALK FIGURES

Much of the rolling downland of Wessex covers a large area of chalk. The vegetation is only a thin, green cloak of grass, and gives rise to the practice of cutting pictures into hillsides. The technique is simple: mark out your picture and cut away the grass and topsoil to reveal the white chalk below. The picture needs periodic maintenance, but not much. Some of the chalk figures may date back to Bronze Age times, although the histories of the oldest figures are uncertain.

Wessex has many chalk figures and Wiltshire has more than any other county. Most are horses, and these include one at Cherhill and one at Uffington (near the Ridgeway), which lends its name to the nearby Vale of White Horse), plus several more near Pewsey and Westbury. There's another good one at Osmington near Weymouth.

The tradition has continued into the 20th century. During WWI, soldiers based at Fovant, west of Salisbury, cut a series of army badges into a nearby hillside, and a New Zealand regiment left a gigantic kiwi on a hillside at Bulford, a few miles east of Stonehenge.

Although Wiltshire goes for sheer quantity, in other parts of Wessex the locals go for sheer style. Probably the most impressive chalk figure is Dorset's 180ft-tall Cerne Giant (on a hillside near the village of Cerne Abbas), with his even more notable 30ft penis.

WESSEX

THE WESSEX RIDGEWAY

If you want a long-distance walk through the heart of the region, the Wessex Ridgeway (not to be confused with the Ridgeway National Trail) is an excellent 140-mile route. From Marlborough in Wiltshire it heads south and includes Avebury Stone Circle, the northern and western edge of Salisbury Plain, a section of the picturesque Wylie Valley, Cranborne Chase and the huge chalk giant of Cerne Abbas, then runs through the heart of Thomas Hardy country to finish on the South Devon coast at Lyme Regis – famous for its fossils. The best guidebook is *The Wessex Ridgeway* by Anthony Burton.

THE SOUTH WEST COAST PATH IN WESSEX

A highlight of the southern part of Wessex is the English Channel coast of Dorset and southeast Devon – sometimes billed as the 'English Riviera' thanks to the mild climate (although don't expect Cannes). Walkers can follow this coast from Exmouth to Poole Harbour on a section of the South West Coast Path (SWCP; see p133).

From Exmouth the SWCP rambles pleasantly along red sandstone cliffs and through the resorts of Budleigh Salterton, Sidmouth and Seaton before passing through the deeply wooded 'Undercliffs' to reach Dorset at Lyme Regis.

East again is pretty, thatched Abbotsbury with its unique swannery. The next feature is Chesil Beach, a huge curving bank of stones, which eventually leads you to Portland Bill and the large town of Weymouth.

East of Weymouth there's more stunning coastal scenery at Lulworth Cove, Kimmeridge Bay and Durlston Head until resort Swanage is reached. A short hop north from here is Studland Point – official end of the SWCP – from where a ferry ride brings you to Poole and a well-deserved journey's end.

SOLENT WAY & BOURNEMOUTH COAST PATH

East along the coast from the Dorset section of the South West Coast Path is the Solent Way (www.hants.gov.uk/walking/solentway), a 60-mile walking route from Milford-on-Sea to Emsworth, and linking these two routes is the Bournemouth Coast Path (www .bournemouthcoastpath.org.uk). This 23-mile route embracing Poole Harbour, the wooded Bournemouth chines, Christchurch Harbour and Bay, two castles and great views across the water to the Isle of Wight. The route is described in *The Bournemouth Coast Path* by Leigh Hatts.

ISLE OF WIGHT

Just a few miles off the south coast of Wessex lies the Isle of Wight, 23 miles (37km) long by 13 miles (21km) wide. Its name is thought to come from 'wiht', an ancient word meaning 'lifted' – ie from the sea. During their occupation of Britain, the Romans named the island Vectis and built several villas here; perhaps the mild climate and sea views were reminders of their Mediterranean home.

Today, the pleasant weather still attracts visitors and holiday-makers, particularly to the busier eastern side of the island. Conditions are good for walking and, particularly on the quieter western side, there's a marvellous network of footpaths through the fields and villages, over the downs (rolling hills) and along the coast, so you could easily stay a week or longer here. For all tourism details, see www .islandbreaks.co.uk.

Popular routes include the Coastal Path and the Tennyson Trail (named for the famous poet, who lived on the island). For details of these and other routes, see www .wightstay.co.uk/walking.

Tourist offices are well stocked with maps and guidebooks, and the local authorities have put a lot of work into maintaining and signposting their paths. The island also has a very good bus service for getting to the start or back from the end of walks. If you're new to walking in Britain, or you're not looking for high peaks and wilderness, the Isle of Wight is an excellent place to start. If you're just looking for a place to relax, maybe after doing some longer walks through Wessex, the island is a very good place to end your trip.

Dartmoor

Anchored in granite and topped by bracken; huge and spectacular – Dartmoor provides an elemental, ancient walking environment. Straddling the centre of Devon, its rounded hills are dotted with piles of granite rocks, or tors, looking for all the world like abstract sculptures or the remains of fantastical castles. Dartmoor's past is very present – this moody chunk of southwest England is studded with an extraordinary variety of ancient remains. You can't walk far without stumbling across stone circles, prehistoric burial mounds, stone rows and the largest concentration of Bronze Age hut circles in Britain. You'll also see 1000-year-old stone bridges and medieval crosses (from the days when monks would walk between abbeys), while abandoned mines and dismantled tramways are reminders of more recent, but now forgotten, industrial days. Herds of semi-wild ponies introduce a picturesque element to the mix.

Although once heavily populated, Dartmoor is today the emptiest and wildest area in southern England – more livestock lives here than humans. There's a great feeling of space and you can be further from a road or village than anywhere else in England and Wales. For keen walkers this is its attraction, but the notoriously fickle weather patterns (hazards range from blistering temperatures to mist, rain and even snow) make some of the walking surprisingly challenging – be prepared for highland weather conditions.

Most of Dartmoor lies within the 365-sq-mile Dartmoor National Park (DNP). The northwest slice is the highest and wildest, peaking at 621m at High Willhays – the highest point in southern England. In the southwest, the moor is mostly between 400m and 500m and is particularly rich in ancient remains.

DARTMOOR

HIGHLIGHTS

▪ Clambering to the top of **Belstone Tor** (p104) for a view of swathes of rolling moorland – and absolutely nothing else

▪ Walking the **Abbot's Way** (p102) in the footsteps of medieval monks

▪ Sitting in your very own stone circle near **Hound Tor** (p105)

▪ Dangling your feet from an ancient **clapper bridge** (p102) into a cool Dartmoor stream

DARTMOOR

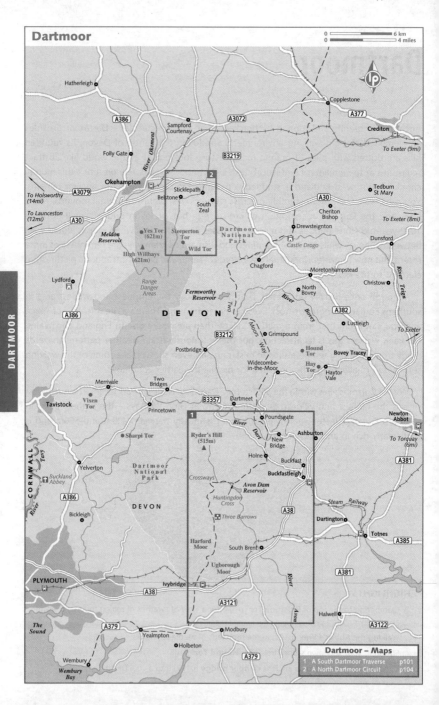

Dartmoor – Maps	
1 A South Dartmoor Traverse	p101
2 A North Dartmoor Circuit	p104

INFORMATION

Maps

The Ordnance Survey (OS) Explorer 1:25,000 map No 28 *Dartmoor* covers the whole of Dartmoor in good detail. It encompasses our two featured walks and is strong on ancient sites.

Books

Of the guidebooks covering Dartmoor, *Walking on Dartmoor* by John Earle is full of fascinating history but can be tricky to use on the ground. More useful is the *Pathfinder Dartmoor* guide, published by Jarrold, with a good selection of routes and clear mapping. *Weekend Walks – Dartmoor & Exmoor* by Anthony Burton is ideal for keen walkers.

The first walk described in this chapter includes part of the Two Moors Way, well described in *The Two Moors Way* by James Roberts.

For background information, *Dartmoor* by Richard Sale is excellent and has beautiful photos. For archaeological information, local tourist offices stock a huge range of books, covering everything from Bronze Age hut circles to the quarries that produced the London Bridge stone. Most useful as an introduction are the *Dartmoor Pocket Guides*, a series of inexpensive, weatherproof cards covering archaeology and many other subjects.

Guided Walks

The DNP organises excellent guided walks throughout the year. Details are on its website, in the *Dartmoor Visitor* and on leaflets in tourist offices. If you're visiting in spring or autumn, ask about the North Devon and Ivybridge Walking Festivals, which include many guided walks.

Information Sources

The Princetown-based **Dartmoor Tourist Association** (☎ 01822-890567; www.discoverdartmoor.com; High Moorland Visitor Centre, Tavistock Rd) produces an annual accommodation and visitors guide, but isn't generally open to people dropping in. In the same building, however, the DNP's main **visitor centre** (☎ 01822-890414; www.dartmoor-npa.gov.uk) definitely is.

Among other tourist offices and information points are those at Okehampton (p103), Ivybridge (p100) and Buckfastleigh (p100).

The free *Dartmoor Visitor* newspaper also contains lots of useful information.

South Devon (☎ 0870 608 5531; www.discoverdevon .com) is a very popular tourist destination with a wealth of tourist offices.

GATEWAYS

The main gateway cities for Dartmoor are Exeter and Plymouth, both served by train and National Express coach from London and other parts of the country. From Exeter and Plymouth you can reach any of the 'border towns' around the moor – including Okehampton, Ivybridge and Buckfastleigh – by public transport. **Traveline** (☎ 0870 608 2608; www.traveline.org.uk) has local timetables. For more on public transport services around Dartmoor, pick up a copy of the *Dartmoor Public Transport Guide* from local tourist offices.

A SOUTH DARTMOOR TRAVERSE

Duration	7–8 hours
Distance	14 miles (22.5km)
Difficulty	moderate
Start	Ivybridge (p101)
Finish	Buckfastleigh (p100)
Transport	train, bus

Summary A sweeping hike over high ground, past evocative burial mounds and Bronze Age hut circles. It finishes with a trek down a track established by medieval monks.

This route follows an inspiring section of the Two Moors Way (p105), taking you far from civilisation and deep into a Dartmoor rich in history and thick with bracken. You pass striking remnants of an industrial heritage spanning centuries – from medieval rabbit farming to early-20th-century quarrying. Later stages pick up a part of the ancient Abbot's Way and provide a great cross section of southern Dartmoor scenery.

PLANNING

You can walk in either direction, but from Ivybridge clear waymarking ensures you make a good start as the early miles follow a winding, dismantled tramway, where it's very hard to get lost. Problems can arise when you turn off east along the Abbot's Way. Here the route is less defined and landmarks are hard to spot if it's misty. On the moor itself there are very few signs – so this walk should only be done on a clear day and if you're confident with a map and compass. If the weather changes unexpectedly, turn back rather than risk getting lost on the moor.

You might prefer to start from Buckfastleigh and get the potentially difficult bit done first, knowing that the disused tramway will guide you home with few surprises. Most fit people should be able to do the walk in eight to nine hours with time for lunch, map reading and playing historical detective along the way.

What to Bring
There's nowhere to buy food or water once out of town on this walk, so stock up before you go.

Maps
This route is covered by the OS Explorer 1:25,000 map No 28 *Dartmoor*.

Information Sources
Ivybridge's tourist office is inside **Global Travel** (☎ 01752-897035; 19 Fore St; ⌚ closed Sun), while in Buckfastleigh the national park has an information point inside the **Valiant Soldier Museum** (☎ 01364-644522; 80 Fore St; ⌚ 12.30-4.30pm Mon-Sat).

NEAREST TOWNS
Buckfastleigh
The old market town of Buckfastleigh lies just off the A38 between Exeter and Plymouth. Two miles north is **Buckfast Abbey**, which was founded in 1018 and flourished until 1539. Today's abbey, which is still in use, was rebuilt in the early part of the 19th century in mock-Gothic style.

The town has no ATM but does have a post office, supermarket and several smaller shops.

SLEEPING & EATING
Campers can head for the pleasant little site at **Churchill Farm** (☎ 01364-642844; Church Hill; sites for 2 £9), between Buckfast and Buckfastleigh. The friendly owners are happy to advise on local walking routes. It's near a ruined chapel (marked on the OS 1:25,000 map) and can be reached on foot from Buckfastleigh up a steep path from the eastern end of the main street – much better than the long way around by road.

Otherwise, the **Globe Inn** (☎ 01364-642223; Plymouth Rd; s/d £38/63; ⌚ lunch & dinner) does reasonable B&B and meals. On the northeast edge of the village, near the A38 off-ramp, is **Furzeleigh Mill Hotel** (☎ 01364-643476; www.furzeleigh.co.uk; Ashburton Rd; s/d £34/62, mains £10; ⌚ lunch & dinner), a charming converted corn mill, offering meals and low-season discounts.

Other eating options include the snug **Baker's Oven** (☎ 01364-642531; 71 Fore St; mains £6; ⌚ dinner Tue-Sat) for good pizza and pasta, and the chintzy **Singing Kettle Tearoom** (☎ 01364-642383; 54 Fore St; mains £7; ⌚ 10am-5pm, dinner Fri & Sat). On the main road between Buckfast and Buckfastleigh, the **Abbey Inn** (☎ 01364-642343; Buckfast Rd; bar meals £7, mains £13; ⌚ lunch & dinner) has lovely river-side dining. Of the pubs in town, the **White Hart** (☎ 01364-642337; Plymouth Rd; ⌚ lunch & dinner) is by far the most appealing.

GETTING THERE & AWAY
There are at least eight buses every day between Exeter and Plymouth; they stop by the entrance to the steam-train station in Buckfastleigh.

DARTMOOR LETTERBOXING

If you should see the word 'Letterbox' marked on your map, don't expect to send your postcards home. Letterboxing is a peculiar (and typically British) pastime, unique to Dartmoor, in which people hide small boxes in remote areas and other people try to find them.

Each box has an owner, and inside the box are a rubber stamp with a unique pattern or picture, which finders use to mark their logbooks, and a visitor book that the finders sign or stamp with their own personal insignias. The aim is to find as many letterboxes as possible. The craze goes back more than a century, although it really became popular about 25 years ago, and there are several hundred such letterboxes all over Dartmoor. Only a few particularly old or important ones are marked on maps, and these are considered 'too easy' by aficionados. You can get a leaflet with more information from tourist offices.

There's also a bus service hourly Monday to Saturday (five on Sunday) between Newton Abbot (for train connections) and Buckfastleigh.

The nearest main-line train stations to Buckfastleigh are at Newton Abbot and Totnes, both on the line between London and Plymouth and served by regular trains. From Newton Abbot you can reach Buckfastleigh by local bus. From Totnes, buses to Buckfastleigh aren't so handy but in the summer months you can travel in old-fashioned style – steam trains run several times a day along the private South Devon Railway from Totnes all the way to Buckfastleigh.

Buckfastleigh is just off the A38 between Exeter and Plymouth.

Ivybridge

Ivybridge is larger than Buckfastleigh, with more in the way of B&Bs, restaurants, cafés and pubs plus shops, banks and other services. If you decide to stay in Ivybridge instead of Buckfastleigh, the tourist office (opposite) can help you with accommodation suggestions.

SLEEPING & EATING
Kevela (☎ 01752-893111; www.kevela.co.uk; 4 Clare St; s/d £30/45) has a compact room in a handily central, Dartmoor-granite B&B. It's strong on floral and peach furnishings.

The four-poster rooms at the **Sportsmans Inn** (☎ 01752-892280; www.thesportsmansinn.co.uk; Exeter Rd; standard s/d £48/70; superior s £60-80, superior d £80-100, roast dinner £6, fish & steak £16) are positively plush, and the others still comfortable. There's a snugly beamed bar and a large restaurant.

The **Duke of Cornwall** (☎ 01752-892867; 3 Keaton Rd; ☺ lunch & dinner Tue-Sun), in the centre of town, serves fairly standard bar food; **Meghna Tandoori House** (☎ 01752-698138; 2 Kimberly Ct, Fore St; ☺ dinner) does good takeaway; while the **Old Smithy** (☎ 01752-892490; 45 Fore St), a few steps down the road, is a good pub for a pint.

GETTING THERE & AWAY
The same eight or more daily Exeter–Plymouth buses that go every day to Buckfastleigh also stop on the main road about 1 mile outside Ivybridge (not in the town itself). If you're staying in Buckfastleigh, the handiest bus to Ivybridge and the start of the walk comes through at about 9.20am and takes 15 minutes.

Ivybridge is on the main rail line between London and Plymouth but not all express trains stop here; you may have to change in Exeter.

Ivybridge is just off the A38 between Exeter and Plymouth. From Buckfastleigh, **K Kars** (☎ 01364-643531, 0771-844 8673) will transport you to Ivybridge for £20.

THE WALK
Ivybridge to Crossways
4½ hours, 8 miles (13km)

The route starts at the car park just north of the South Dartmoor Leisure Centre. The Two Moors Way is clearly waymarked north out of town, up a footpath and then a narrow street called Costly St. On your right, handily enough, is a small supermarket at which to buy lunch.

Cross the main road in front of the supermarket and carry on walking north, up a lane (signposted to Harford) that climbs steeply for about 800m, continuing straight

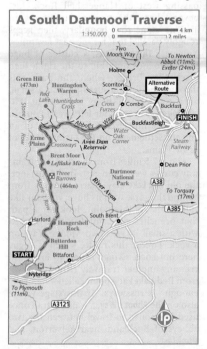

A South Dartmoor Traverse

1:350,000

0 — 4 km
0 — 2 miles

on at Cole Lane, then immediately over the railway on Stowford Bridge. Look for the signs for 'Dartmoor National Park' and 'Two Moors Way'. (If you've come by train, walk west from Ivybridge train station along the south side of the line to Stowford Bridge.)

Cross the bridge and continue for another 250m to Stowford Farm Cottage, then turn right onto a track signposted 'To the Moor'. After a few steps turn left (north) and continue along an old track, uphill between hedges. At the top, a gate leads invitingly onto the open moor. Follow a gradually climbing path through the grass and bracken towards the cairn on Butterdon Hill. Within 800m of the gate you'll meet the old, dismantled **tramway**; turn left (north).

The tramway was constructed in 1910 to carry china clay from a quarry on the moors at Red Lake to a factory near Ivybridge. It was closed in 1932, but now provides a firm footpath for 6 miles. It takes a rather circuitous route but apparent short cuts don't save much time.

Continue aiming mostly northwards, passing west of Hangershell Rock. Just beyond here, the tramway intersects an ancient 'stone row' boundary, then keeps roughly parallel to it for the next few miles. You pass **Three Barrows**, a cluster of huge burial mounds on a hill to the right, then reach Clay Bridge, where the path cuts through the eerie disused pit and a small, grass-covered spill-heap and pool at **Left-lake Mires**. Over to your left (west) you can clearly see hut circles, the remains of an ancient settlement, on the facing slopes of Erme Plains.

About 7.5 miles from the start, the tramway curves west, then east. In the distance, the old **Red Lake** clay quarry emerges from behind the gorse with its huge, volcano-like spill-heap. At this point, look for a path that branches off right (south), marked with a small 'MW' (Two Moors Way) on a rock. Follow this route, which is vague here but soon swings round to aim east, crossing another tramway (running down from Red Lake) at a point called – naturally enough – Crossways. At this stage you're also on the **Abbot's Way**, a walking trail once used by monks to travel between the two abbeys of Buckland, near Yelverton, and Buckfast.

Crossways to Buckfastleigh
3–3½ hours, 6 miles (9.5km)

From Crossways, the combined Two Moors Way and Abbot's Way trail aims northeast, but the path is difficult to see in the long grass so you will definitely need that compass. It becomes clear again as you drop into a valley to reach a wonderful and ancient **clapper bridge** (made of stone slabs), which you cross to the north bank of the River Avon.

Follow the path (boggy in places) down the north side of the river to **Huntingdon Cross**, a standing stone used as a route and boundary marker in medieval times. To the north are the slopes of Huntingdon Warren, a former rabbit farm with the remains of artificial burrows and huts for the 'warreners' who looked after them.

Just after Huntingdon Cross, you ford a small stream, where the Two Moors Way splits off to head northeast up Hickaton Hill. Stay on the Abbot's Way, following the north bank of the River Avon, then heading across the slopes above the Avon Dam Reservoir. To your left (north) you will see several more Bronze Age hut circles in good condition.

The path crosses Brockhill Stream. Here, instead of following the line of the reservoir, you should turn to head east up the steep hillside, then continue across a small, featureless plateau called Dean Moor. Head down to Water Oak Corner, where the open moor ends and you enter private farmland. There's a gate with a very clear sign: 'Abbot's Way, Exit from Moor, to Cross Furzes'.

Keep to the path, following the marker poles through the fields to a stream, which you cross on a little clapper bridge, in a dappled patch of woodland. Continue on a track to the junction just south of Cross Furzes. The easiest way home is to the right, following the quiet lane southeast and east to Buckfastleigh.

There is another, more scenic, route to the finish. From the lane junction go straight on (east) for 1.5 miles, then turn right (southeast) through Button Farm. Make sure you keep to the legal path through the fields, which leads to, and through, the lovely shade of Bilberryhill Copse. From here, an old walled track leads down into Buckfastleigh.

A NORTH DARTMOOR CIRCUIT

Duration	5–6 hours
Distance	10.5 miles (17km)
Difficulty	moderate
Start/Finish	Sticklepath (right)
Transport	bus

Summary An exhilarating walk through wooded valleys and over high ground into the very heart of the moor. Solitude, stone circles and Dartmoor streams await.

This is the northern moor at its best – remote and rugged, with satisfying panoramic views to reward your scrambling ascents of the tors. But it's not all sweeping moorland: this circular walk is also an excellent introduction to Dartmoor's remarkably diverse scenery. Quiet villages lead to captivating woods, where streams are flanked by boulders flecked with moss. The contrast between this sheltered world and the expanse of the higher ground as you stride onto the moor ensures a varied day's wandering.

PLANNING

You can do the walk in either direction, but we describe it anticlockwise so you can limber up in the valley before heading for the tors. Allowing extra time for lunch and sitting in stone circles, the walk will take about six to seven hours. Two notes of caution: first, there's no waymarking on the moor, so only attempt it in clear weather and if you're comfortable with a map and compass; and second, the route fringes a military live-firing area – see the boxed text, below.

What to Bring

Buy your lunch before you leave Sticklepath as, apart from an early stop at the pub in Belstone, there's nowhere to get food or water on the way.

Maps

This route is covered by the OS Explorer 1:25,000 map No 28 *Dartmoor*.

Information Sources

The nearest **tourist office** (☎ 01837-53020; 3 West St; ◷ closed Sun) proper is in Okehampton. Sticklepath has an information point (the village shop) – look here for the excellent leaflets describing short walks in the area.

NEAREST TOWNS
Sticklepath & Belstone

The delightful little village of Sticklepath is about 3 miles east of Okehampton. **Finch Foundry** is a cottage-sized, water-powered forge dating from the 19th century, sitting in the middle of its main street. It is run by the National Trust, is still working and has a small museum. The nearest ATM is in Okehampton.

SLEEPING & EATING

Sticklepath's camping barn, still marked on many maps, isn't there any more. The nearest budget accommodation is **Okehampton YHA Hostel & Adventure Centre** (☎ 01837-53916; www.okehampton-yha.co.uk; Station Rd, Okehampton; dm/s/d £16/19/35).

In Sticklepath's main street, the **Devonshire Inn** (☎ 01837-840626; d £40) will, intriguingly,

---

WARNING

This route skirts the edge of Okehampton Range, one of three Dartmoor ranges used by the army for training with live ammunition.

In general, you're advised to check if the area you're planning to walk over falls within a range. If it does, you need to find out if firing is taking place on the day or night you want to walk. You can call (free) the **Firing Information Service** (☎ 0800 458 4868; www.dartmoor-ranges .co.uk). On the Okehampton range there's usually no firing in April, May, July, August and early September, nor at weekends, public holidays or Mondays all·year. You can walk here then and at other times if no firing is taking place. If the range is being used, red flags fly during the day and red lights burn at night at regular points along the edge of the danger area. Even when there's no firing, you should beware of unidentifiable metal objects lying in the grass. If you do find anything suspicious, don't touch it. Make a note of the position and report it to the police or the **Commandant** (☎ 01837-650010). Some unexploded shells may lie beneath the surface, so use common sense if you need to relieve yourself in the open. While burying your excrement is recommended in most country areas, random digging around Dartmoor is not a good idea.

only put you up if you have a dog with you. It also serves good beer and meals if you're staying. The other pub in the village, the **Taw River Inn** (☎ 01837-840377; ☼ lunch & dinner), will feed and water you irrespective of canine accompaniment.

Dog-less walkers can opt to start and finish the walk at the pretty village of Belstone, west of Sticklepath. Here, the **Tors** (☎ 01837-840689; s/d £30/60; ☼ lunch & dinner) pub has very comfortable rooms.

There are also B&Bs at South Zeal, a few miles to the east, where you can easily join the walk.

GETTING THERE & AWAY

There are eight buses a day (two on Sunday) between Exeter and Okehampton via Sticklepath. An alternative way into and out of the village is the Okehampton–Sticklepath–Moretonhampstead bus, which runs three or four times daily.

The nearest and most useful rail connection is with Exeter. Technically, the nearest train station is Okehampton, but it's a very limited option: the Exeter–Okehampton service consists of three or four trains, on Sunday only, from late May to mid-September.

By car, Sticklepath is just south of the A30 (dual carriageway) between Exeter and Okehampton.

THE WALK
Sticklepath to Steeperton Tor
2½–3 hours, 5.5 miles (9km)

From Sticklepath's main street, aim east, over the main road bridge at the end of the village, and then turn immediately right (south) onto a path alongside the River Taw, signed to Skaigh Wood. Follow this path, going right at the fork to keep close to the river (on your right), with gardens and the backs of cottages on the opposite bank. You then enter the beautiful Skaigh Wood and cross a wooden footbridge, inscribed with a quote from *Tarka the Otter* by Henry Williamson, onto the north bank of the river.

Shortly afterwards, you cross another footbridge back to the south bank, turning right (west) to continue upstream along the river through a steep-sided valley called Belstone Cleave – quite possibly the inspiration for the quote on the bridge you crossed earlier. The path climbs diagonally up the

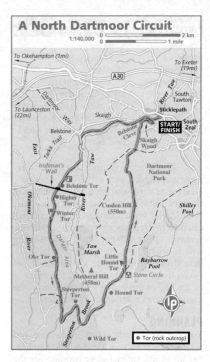

valley, then down, and crosses another footbridge before leading up to an open grassy area and a lane on the fringes of the village of Belstone. Time for a breather and to admire the view – fortunately, there's a choice of benches provided.

Continue south along the lane, taking a right fork to reach a gate, which leads to the open moor. There's a noticeboard here about firing days so have a final check before you stride out.

The track leads south, with the River Taw to your left. At a suitable point – there's no set path – branch right (broadly southwest) off the track and go steeply uphill to the summit of **Belstone Tor**. Time for another look at the view: to the south, swathes of open moorland fill the horizon; to the north, farmland leads to the distant hills of Exmoor, with (on a clear day) the sea visible behind.

Aim southwest, down from Belstone Tor, through a gap in a huge dry-stone wall (called **Irishman's Wall** – a 19th-century job-creation project) and up to **Higher Tor**. Then it's down again to meet a track coming up from the valley to your right. Near Winter Tor, you'll also notice the line of red-and-white poles marking the edge of the danger area – which you now enter.

The track follows the broad ridge southwards – a wonderful section with wide views on both sides. You pass just east of Oke Tor, getting an increasingly clear view of Steeperton Tor, marred only slightly by the radio mast on the summit.

After another 800m or so, with the tip of Steeperton Tor directly to the east, take the left fork of the track, leading southwards, into a little valley called Steeperton Gorge. Just before you cross the stream there's a patch of grass on the left that makes a lovely, sheltered lunch spot.

Once across the stream, the path continues, climbing up the other side of the valley, reaching a junction after 300m, where another path turns sharply back (northeast) to reach **Steeperton Tor**. The summit offers great views of the ridge you've just followed from Belstone, and of the next section towards Cosdon Hill.

Steeperton Tor to Sticklepath
2½–3 hours, 5 miles (8km)

From Steeperton Tor it seems Hound Tor is just a short hop across the valley, but don't be tempted – that valley floor is very boggy. Instead, follow the path southeast for about 500m to cross Steeperton Brook by the ruins of an old hut. Then turn northeast, passing more red-and-white posts (you are now leaving the danger area). The path edges west of the rounded summit of **Hound Tor**, then just to the west of a **stone circle**, which is in good condition and well worth a stop.

A path leads directly from the stone circle, north over Little Hound Tor and then gradually up to the summit of **Cosdon Hill**, marked by a trig point. Here you say goodbye to the deserted, open moor to the south and look north to where the bracken gives way to the fields of farming country.

It's all downhill now as you follow a path north from the summit. Be careful not to go too far east towards South Zeal but keep aiming north, straight at Sticklepath and down into a corner formed by the moor boundary wall. Here there are two gates. One leads towards South Zeal. Take the other one and head north down an old sunken lane into Skaigh Wood. Turn right

(northeast) through the gate to run along the top of the steep valley, then zigzag down to meet the same river-side path you walked along at the very start. Turn right to reach the village along the path or go over the small footbridge leading past a small graveyard and into the car park at the back of Finch Foundry.

MORE WALKS

TWO MOORS WAY

Our South Dartmoor Traverse (p99) follows a stage of a wonderful long-distance path: the Two Moors Way. This crosses the southwest peninsula via the rugged national parks of Dartmoor and Exmoor. If you can't resist the urge to keep heading north, most people take a week to complete this 117-mile (188km) trail. Extended in its 30th year to connect with the south coast, it passes through some of the finest (and wildest) scenery in southern England. The **Two Moors Way Association** (☎ 01392-467094; 'Coppins', The Poplars, Pinhoe, Exeter, EX4 9H) has produced an official guide, which also includes maps, and an accommodation sheet. There are rail then bus links to the start at Wembury and from the finish at Lynmouth.

THE DARTMOOR WAY

If walking over moors doesn't appeal, how about walking around one? The circular, 90-mile (145km) Dartmoor Way snakes through the unique, gentle landscape that fringes the national park. Crisscrossing moors and fields, and travelling through peaceful villages and Devon market towns, this six-day ramble also cuts across the southern moor itself to take in Princetown. It's ideal if you're not confident or prepared to tackle the wilder, higher remote moors. See our featured Dartmoor walks for some information and accommodation options. You can get more by contacting the **Dartmoor Way** (☎ 0870 241 1817; www.dartmoorway.org. uk). The vast majority of the route, except for some east/west fringes, is covered by the OS Explorer 1:25,000 map No 28 *Dartmoor*.

A GRIMSPOUND GAMBOL

This circular stroll covers thousands of years of Dartmoor history in just 4.5 miles (7.3km). Start at the car park just north of the Warren House Inn, on the Postbridge–Moretonhampstead road. Pick up the track heading east, cross a stream then navigate up towards Headland Warren Farm. Next it's round to Grimspound – the remains of a massive settlement of 24 Bronze Age hut circles, all enclosed by a stone wall. When you're done wandering amid the ruins, pick up the Two Moors Way head-

ing northwest, before joining the path alongside the road and back (southwest) to the Warren House Inn. This fine old pub makes a fitting finish; check out the black-and-white photos showing it cut off by snow for six weeks. Then warm yourself by the fire – reputed not to have gone out since 1845. Use the OS Explorer 1:25,000 map No 28 *Dartmoor*.

The Cotswolds

Intimate and benign, the Cotswold Hills beckon you, in a polite, English sort of way, to their central ribbon of rolling countryside. North of Bath, east of Gloucester and west of Oxford, this is the land of afternoon tea, warm beer and bicycling vicars – it is quintessentially English. Neat fields, lush woodland, clear rivers and narrow, hedge-lined lanes crisscross a network of pretty villages. In them the houses, churches, cottages and farms are built of the famous warm, honey-coloured Cotswold stone. Walking here is a delight.

The region is defined by that stone. It's the golden building blocks of the villages, but it's also the limestone bedrock of the hills, and peeps out beneath your feet where the topsoil has peeled away. The Cotswold Way traces the spine of these hills, often along the steep escarpment that slices down their western edge, offering exhilarating views over the River Severn and Wales beyond.

The human landscape of the Cotswolds is down to wool. Sheep here produced a large portion of medieval England's wealth, and some of that money was clearly spent locally, on still-fine buildings. In the 17th century the wool trade died but the massive physical changes of the Industrial Revolution bypassed the Cotswolds. Of course, the hills are not set in aspic and have, thankfully, engaged with the modern world, but today this is England at its most affluent. Villages exude a heady aroma of solid bank accounts and abound with expensive public schools, new cars and golf courses. But beneath the picture-postcard views, high property prices make it impossible for many locals to buy a home in their home town.

THE COTSWOLDS

HIGHLIGHTS

- The better-than-bird's-eye view over Cheltenham and the River Severn, and towards the Brecon Beacons, from **Leckhampton Hill** (p116)
- Wandering the Windrush Way to cross tiny bridge after tiny bridge in the 'Venice of the Cotswolds' – **Bourton-on-the-Water** (p120)
- With only 30 miles of the Cotswold Way to go, being smoothed, stretched and soothed at a luxury spa in **Cheltenham** (p117)
- The gorgeous golden buildings of **Chipping Campden** (p111) – a fitting finish to a fantastic trail

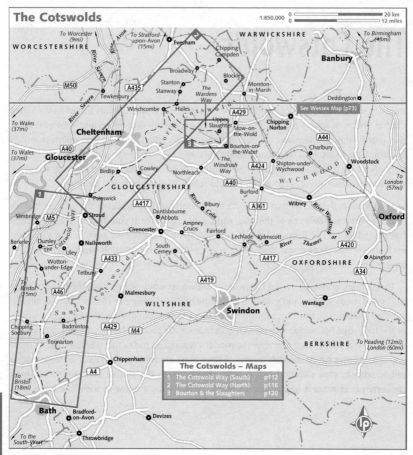

The Cotswolds

1:850,000

The Cotswolds – Maps

1	The Cotswold Way (South)	p112
2	The Cotswold Way (North)	p116
3	Bourton & the Slaughters	p120

INFORMATION

Maps

Useful maps for walking include Ordnance Survey (OS) Landranger 1:50,000 maps No 172 *Bristol & Bath*, 162 *Gloucester & Forest of Dean*, 163 *Cheltenham & Cirencester*, 150 *Worcester & the Malverns* and 151 *Stratford-upon-Avon*. The OS Explorer 1:25,000 map No 45 *The Cotswolds* covers only the northern part of this area (north of Cirencester and east of Cheltenham).

For maps covering individual walks, see the Planning sections for each walk.

Books

There are shelves-full to choose from. Try *Cotswold Teashop Walks* by Jean Patefield,

and *Pub Walks in the Cotswolds* by Nigel Vile. For a quieter atmosphere, *Discovery Walks in the Cotswolds* by Julie Meech avoids the tourist honey pots. For a range of walks, with good maps and route descriptions, *The Cotswold Pathfinder Guide* (published by Jarrold) is ideal. The AA's *50 Walks in the Cotswolds* by Christopher Knowles provides an excellent variety of clear, concise routes, while Jarrold's *The Cotswolds* offers 20 routes of up to 5.5 miles.

For books specific to the Cotswold Way, see p110.

Guided Walks

The **Cotswolds Area of Outstanding Natural Beauty** (☎ 01451-862000; www.cotswoldsaonb.org)

organises a series of guided walks. Tourist offices also have details. As well as the national companies organising trips (see p26), one local specialist is **Cotswold Walking Holidays** (☎ 01242-254353; www.cotswoldwalks.com).

Information Sources

A good starting point is the Southwest's official **tourist board** (☎ 0870 442 0880; www.visit southwest.com). The local authority site is www .cotswold.gov.uk, while www.cotswolds.info is also useful. Key tourist offices include those in Bath (p110), Cheltenham (p117), Chipping Campden (p111) and Bourton-on-the-Water (p119).

GETTING AROUND

The most useful train service for walkers is the Worcester–Oxford–London line, which runs through the northern part of the Cotswolds and includes a very handy stop at Moreton-in-Marsh. Many other places can be reached from here by local bus.

GATEWAYS

Key gateway cities and transport hubs for the Cotswolds are Bath, Gloucester, Cheltenham, Oxford and Stratford-upon-Avon. These are easily reached by National Express coach and car. Train stations in the Cotswolds include Moreton-in-Marsh, Kemble and Stratford-upon-Avon.

Traveline (☎ 0870 608 2608; www.traveline.org .uk) has local travel timetables, while the *Explore the Cotswolds by Public Transport* leaflet has general information and is available from tourist offices.

THE COTSWOLD WAY

Duration	7 days
Distance	102 miles (164km)
Difficulty	easy–moderate
Start	Bath (p110)
Finish	Chipping Campden (p111)
Transport	train, bus

Summary A delightful jaunt through picture-book English countryside. Walking a spine of steep hills, you step through rolling farmland, dappled woods and enchanting villages.

Always picturesque, at times dramatic, the Cotswold Way charts a course between two exquisite tourist towns and delivers England at its most enchanting en route. From Bath to Chipping Campden, via a steep, exhilarating escarpment, you constantly track up and down; from villages in intimate valleys to expansive ridges with bird's-eye views. The Way is also a trail through time, passing prehistoric hillforts and burial mounds, reminders of the Romans, and some fine monuments and stately homes.

It's a comfortable walk compared with wilder options in this book, but underestimate it at your peril. The days are long, the walking is often demanding and the weather can turn nasty very quickly. But the huge number of delightful pubs and B&Bs mean a pint, a warm bed and a good meal are never far away.

PLANNING

You can walk the Cotswold Way in either direction, although we describe it from south to north, giving you the sun and the wind at your back. It was upgraded and relaunched as a national trail in 2007, and with few exceptions the waymarking is very good – either small arrows with a white dot in the centre or the national trail acorn symbol. But it is still possible to miss turns simply because there are so many interconnecting paths, so it's wise to carry maps.

We outline the stages where you need to buy lunch before setting out. In terms of cash, the only ATMs directly on the route we describe are at Bath, Wotton-under-Edge, Dursley, Painswick, Cheltenham, Winchcombe, Broadway and Chipping Campden.

The following itinerary covers the walk in seven days. The most convenient places to start and finish each day are shown in the table:

Day	From	To	Miles/km
1	Bath	Tormarton	16/26
2	Tormarton	Wotton-under-Edge	13.5/22
3	Wotton-under-Edge	Uley	10.5/17
4	Uley	Painswick	13/21
5	Painswick	Cheltenham	19/31
6	Cheltenham	Winchcombe	12.5/20
7	Winchcombe	Chipping Campden	17.5/28

Alternatives

Each of Days 1, 5 and 7 can be comfortably split into two, with overnight stops at Cold Ashton or Marshfield and Broadway.

THE COTSWOLDS

The fifth night, in Cheltenham or Charlton Kings, is the only overnight stop that takes you a couple of miles off the Way.

Hours given are for walking times only, and a few days to rest and explore the many churches, manor houses, villages and monuments you encounter would give you a relaxed and entertaining 12-day jaunt.

Maps

The Harvey Long Distance Route 1:40,000 map *Cotswold Way* covers the whole trail in a strip map, although we've based our description on OS references.

The OS Explorer 1:25,000 map No 45 *The Cotswolds* covers only about a quarter of the route (in the north) so detail addicts need to supplement it with OS Explorer 1:25,000 maps No 155 *Bristol & Bath*, 167 *Thornbury, Dursley & Yate*, 168 *Stroud, Tetbury & Malmesbury* and 179 *Gloucester, Cheltenham & Stroud*.

Good waymarking, however, means the following combination is perfectly adequate: OS Landranger 1:50,000 maps No 172 *Bristol & Bath*, 162 *Gloucester & Forest of Dean* and 163 *Cheltenham & Cirencester* with OS Explorer 1:25,000 map No 45 *The Cotswolds*.

Books

The one book you shouldn't be without is *The Cotswold Way Handbook & Accommodation List*, produced by the **Ramblers' Association** (☎ 0207-339 8500; www.ramblers.org.uk) and available from the association or from tourist offices along the route.

A new National Trail Official Guide, *The Cotswold Way* by Anthony Burton, complete with OS 1:25,000 maps, accompanies the Way's relaunch. *The Cotswold Way* by local expert Mark Richards is a brief and affectionate account of the walk. Other titles include *The Cotswold Way* by Kev Reynolds, which describes the route in both directions.

Accommodation

B&Bs and hotels here often cost above the British average – allow for £30 to £50 a night and be prepared to book early. The only hostel directly on the Way is in Bath and there are relatively few places to camp. We've listed recommended places to stay; for more options consult *The Cotswold Way Handbook & Accommodation List*.

Information Sources

The best starting point is the official Cotswold Way website at www.nationaltrail.co.uk/cotswold, which also has updates on route alterations. Also useful are www.cotswold-way.co.uk and the **Cotswold Way National Trail Office** (☎ 01453-827004). Individual tourist offices are outlined in the route description.

Baggage Services

Sherpa Van (☎ 0871 520 0124; www.sherpavan.com) provides baggage transfers along the Cotswold Way. *The Cotswold Way Handbook* also has contact details for baggage services.

NEAREST TOWNS

Bath

pop 90,144

Bath is undoubtedly one of Britain's most beautiful cities. The short-sighted developmental approach that's disfigured so many places has left Bath relatively unscathed, and the splendid Georgian architecture is a delight to explore. You might be itching to hit the trail but try to build in at least a day to experience this lovely place.

There's a **tourist office** (☎ 0906 711 2000; www.visitbath.co.uk) in the Abbey Churchyard and the **Guide Friday Tourism Centre** (☎ 01225-444102) at the train station. If the 102 miles ahead isn't enough for you, clock up some more on a free **two-hour walking tour** (☒ 10.30am & 2pm Sun-Fri, 10.30am Sat); they leave from the Abbey Churchyard.

Bath's blockbuster sight is the **Roman Baths** (☎ 01225-477785; www.romanbaths.co.uk; Abbey Churchyard; adult/child £10/6; ☒ 9am-5pm Mar-Jun, Sep & Oct, 9am-9pm Jul & Aug, 9.30am-4.30pm Nov-Feb), where you get to wander the complex the invaders built.

Bath is also a city of **festivals** (☎ 01225-463362; www.bathfestivals.org.uk), the main one being the International Music Festival (late May to early June).

SLEEPING

Bath's cheaper options get snapped up fast, especially in the summer and during festivals. Many also charge more at weekends so we've indicated the range of prices below. Our recommendations are all central.

The nearest camp site to Bath, **Newton Mill Camping Park** (☎ 01225-333909; www.campinginbath.co.uk; Newton Rd; sites for 2 £16), is 3 miles west

BATH'S PAINFUL REBIRTH

What's in a name? For Bath – everything. Its waters have been the source of its moniker and its money ever since the Romans first built a system of baths and a temple to Sulis-Minerva on the site of what they called Aquae Sulis.

Those waters still mattered in the 18th century when Bath was the most fashionable and elegant haunt of English society. Aristocrats flocked here to gossip, gamble and flirt. Fortunately, they also paid the brilliant architects who designed the Palladian terraced housing, circles, crescents and squares that still define the city today. But two centuries later the thermal bubble finally burst when, in 1970, what was then the last spa closed for reasons of health. For more than a quarter of a century, bathers and visitors were denied access to the mineral-rich reason for the city's name and fortune.

Fast forward 25 years to **Thermae Bath Spa** (☎ 01225-335678; www.thermaebathspa.com; 2hr spa session £19, 50min treatments from £64), a stunningly high-tech glass-and-steel project – complete with roof-top pool, thermal waters and steam rooms. Trouble is, it went £20 million over budget and almost four years over schedule. Now open, but still an infant in terms of this city's spa past, the next twist in the saga is anybody's guess. But it has left the people of Bath hoping their thermal future is as clear as their thermal past.

of town at Newton St Loe. The funky **Bath Backpackers** (☎ 01225-446787; www.hostels.co.uk; 13 Pierrepont St; dm £13, d £35-45) is the best budget option. There's also the slightly institutional **YMCA** (☎ 01225-325900; www.bathymca.co.uk; Broad St Pl; dm £13-15, s £24-28, d £36-44), in a small square just off Walcott St.

The **Henry Guest House** (☎ 01225-424052; www.thehenry.com; 6 Henry St; s/d £35/60) is charming; all rooms have shared bathrooms. **Romany Guest House** (☎ 01225-424193; 9 Charlotte St; d £45) also has shared bathrooms and rates don't include breakfast. Across the river around Poultney Rd there's a cluster of B&Bs charging around £35 for singles and £55 for doubles; check with the tourist office.

For some pre-trail luxury, try the pleasant **George's Hotel** (☎ 01225-464923; www.georgeshotel.co.uk; 2-3 South Pde; s/d £60/75), or **Three Abbey Green** (☎ 01225-428558; www.threeabbeygreen.com; 3 Abbey Green; s £85-112, d £95-125), which is delightful.

EATING

In Bath, you're spoilt for choice. Northumberland Pl has the **Hub** and **La Croissanterie**, which both serve tasty pastries and baguettes.

Near the Abbey, the groovy **Café Retro** (☎ 01225-339347; 18 York St; lunch £5; breakfast & lunch daily, dinner Thu-Sat) offers an excellent, varied menu. The Indian restaurant **Jamuna** (☎ 01225-464631; 10 Cheap St; lunch & dinner) has a set dinner for £8. **Tilley's Bistro** (☎ 01225-484200; www.tilleysbistro.co.uk; 3 North Pde Passage;

lunch & dinner) does wonderful food in intimate surroundings – bargains include a two-course early dinner from £10. Meanwhile, dishes at **Demuth's** (☎ 01225-446059; www.demuths.co.uk; mains £12; lunch & dinner) will make vegetarians smile. The **Moon and Sixpence** (☎ 01225-460962; 6A Broad St; mains £17; lunch & dinner) provides fine bistro dining with an alfresco seating option.

The central streets are heaving with good pubs. The best is the **Old Green Tree** (Green St), a cosy little place that exudes warmth and charm. Others include the **Pig & Fiddle** (with its outside tables), on the corner of Walcott St, and the tiny **Coeur de Lion** (Northumberland Pl).

GETTING THERE & AWAY

Bath is easy to reach; it's on the main railway line between London and Bristol, and is also served by National Express coach. By car, it's south of the M4 motorway between London and Bristol.

Chipping Campden

Locals claim the stonework in the houses of Chipping Campden is the finest in the Cotswolds and it certainly is gorgeous – making this town a fitting finale to the Cotswold Way. Buildings of interest include the medieval **town hall**, **St James' Church** and the 1627 **market hall**. Further up the street, William Grevel's **late-14th-century house** can lay claim to being the oldest and finest in the village.

THE COTSWOLDS

SLEEPING & EATING

B&B options include the **Old Bakehouse** (☎ 01386-840979; Lower High St; s/d £30/60), the beautifully restored **Bantam Tea Rooms** (☎ 01386-840386; www.thebantam.co.uk; High St; s/d £49/75) and the **Red Lion** (☎ 01386-840760; www .redlionchippingcampden.co.uk; High St; s/d £65/79) – full of dark beams and creaky floors. You can also stay at the lovely **Badgers Hall** (☎ 01386-840839; www.badgershall.com; High St; d £80), but there's a minimum two-night stay. The **tourist office** (☎ 01386-841206; High St) can give further suggestions.

For food, pubs that offer meals include the **Kings Arms**, the **Red Lion** and the **Eight Bells**. Otherwise, **Joel's Restaurant** (☎ 01386-840598; mains £8-17; ☾ lunch & dinner) serves delicious food and has a wide-ranging menu. Next door is **Huxley's** (☎ 01386-840520; mains £11; ☾ lunch & dinner), while there's also (another) **Lygon Arms Hotel** (☎ 01386-640318; mains £18; ☾ lunch & dinner). All are on the high street.

GETTING THERE & AWAY

Local buses run Monday to Saturday only between Chipping Campden, Stratford, Evesham and Moreton-in-Marsh – so you can't arrive at, or leave, Chipping Campden via public transport on Sunday.

Moreton is on the Worcester–Oxford–London railway line, and you can link up with trains or National Express coaches from Stratford or Evesham to other destinations.

By car, Chipping Campden lies north of the A44 between Evesham and Oxford, about 12 miles south of Stratford-upon-Avon.

THE WALK
Day 1: Bath to Tormarton
7–8 hours, 16 miles (26km)

A moderately difficult but rewarding introduction to the Way, with a couple of steep ascents early on. There are interesting historical sites to delay you so it's wise to get an early start.

From the Abbey, walk northwest past the beautiful Georgian architecture of the **Circus** and around the **Crescent** before heading north to pick up the Cotswold Way markers, which point you across the Approach Golf Course and through a couple of suburbs. A short, sharp push up Penn Hill rewards you with fine views of Bath and the River Avon, and you're in the countryside proper at last.

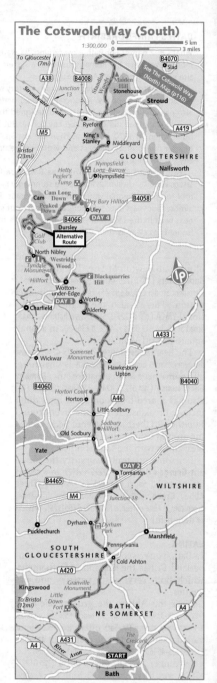

The next couple of miles offer good walking along tracks before you skirt Bath Racecourse. Immediately after, you come to a series of grassy ridges: the remains of **Little Down Fort** and the first of scores of Iron Age hillforts to dot the route. After some more fields you encounter the **Granville Monument**, which commemorates a 1643 Civil War battle. Here 'more officers and gentlemen of quality than private soldiers were slain'. Calamity indeed…

The Way wanders bridleways and fields before a long, steep hill takes you up to the village of **Cold Ashton**. You can break for the night at the **Chestnuts** (☎ 01225-892020; camp sites for 2 £6, s/d £39/58). A few places in nearby Marshfield, including **Knowle Hill Farm** (☎ 01225-891503; Beeks Lane; s/d £25/50), offer a pick-up service.

Leaving Cold Ashton you cross the A420, then pass the **White Hart** (☎ 01225-891233; ⓨ lunch & dinner) pub. Across a short field is Pennsylvania, where **Old Swan Cottage** (☎ 01225-891419; www.old-swan-cottage.co.uk; s/d £35/50) offers comfortable accommodation. More fields and woods lead to the pretty village of Dyrham, noted for **Dyrham Park**, a grand mansion and deer park run by the National Trust. A footpath leads directly from the Way into the grounds. You weave north, then east across fields and the A46 before joining a lane at Lower Lapdown Farm, which leads over the M4 motorway and into Tormarton.

TORMARTON

This tiny village is noted for its Norman **church of St Mary Magdalene**. The best place to stay is the traditional **Portcullis Inn** (☎ 01454-

218263; s/d £30/44; ⓨ lunch & dinner). Other options include **Noades House** (☎ 01454-218746; Old Hundred Lane; camp sites for 2 £5, s/d £30/50). Two miles further on, Old Sodbury (see below) has other choices.

Day 2: Tormarton to Wotton-under-Edge
6–7 hours, 13.5 miles (22km)
An easy day of undulating countryside with plenty of farmland and a brace of hillforts. You pass several small villages but no shops, so bring lunch with you.

Leaving Tormarton, ignore the old metal 'Cotswold Way' signs, continue past the Portcullis Inn and pick up the wooden waymarks across a lovely series of ancient stone stiles and into **Old Sodbury**. Here, **1 The Green** (☎ 01454-314688; s/d £30/50) is tucked just behind the petrol station. The beautifully beamed **Dog Inn** (☎ 01454-312006; s with/without bathroom £50/30; d with/without bathroom £70/50; ⓨ lunch & dinner) opposite is an excellent choice and offers tasty meals.

Out of the village the Way passes a series of medieval stepped terraces before going up a steep escarpment to the prominent ramparts of the Iron Age **Sodbury Hillfort**. Going straight ahead along the public path avoids the steep bit, but it's a shame to miss the huge fortified expanse at the top. Next, it's down into the small village of **Little Sodbury**, where William Tyndale worked on the first translation of the Bible into English (see boxed text, below).

From Little Sodbury you cross fields, pass through the pretty village of Horton and then come to **Horton Court**, the oldest house on the Way, dating from Norman times. This is beautiful, peaceful, green and

---

WILLIAM TYNDALE – MARTYR TO THE ENGLISH WORD

Born in the mid-1490s in North Nibley, William Tyndale is remembered as the man who first translated the Bible into English – and got himself executed for his trouble.

Forced by pressure from the Catholic Church to go to Germany to work on his translation, Tyndale led a precarious existence, one step ahead of vengeful authorities. His first edition of the New Testament was printed in 1526 and condemned by English church leaders, but proved immensely popular with their congregations. Fearing Tyndale's influence, Henry VIII sent men to the Continent to track him down – he was eventually tried for heresy in Belgium and burnt at the stake. In a dubiously merciful gesture, he was spared the flames by being strangled before the fire was lit. His last words reportedly were: 'Oh Lord, open the King of England's eyes'.

Ironically, the Lord apparently did. A scant two years later, Henry VIII passed a law requiring every church in England to hold an English-language copy of the Bible – it was cold comfort to Tyndale's friends and family that it was based largely on his work.

pleasant England – all birdsong and gushing streams. A long gravelled section skirts fields to the fringe of Hawkesbury Upton and the grandiose 1846 **Somerset Monument**, commemorating Battle of Waterloo hero General Lord Somerset. After a stroll through some lovely woods to Alderley, the Way continues to the edge of Wortley, where the route swings to the east of **Wotton-under-Edge** (usually called Wotton) and climbs to a viewpoint. There's a sharp left at Blackquarries Hill before going down and then up towards Coombe Hill and finally into Wotton.

WOTTON-UNDER-EDGE

Wotton is another once-prosperous wool town, but it's retained its charm and boasts a host of fine buildings plus an excellent array of pubs and eateries. The ancient **St Mary the Virgin church** dates from at least 1283, while the **Hugh Perry's Almshouses** have a daunting list of regulations inside the entrance. There's a **tourist office** (☎ 01453-521659; 15 Bradley St; ☯ 9am-12.30pm Mon-Fri) inside the civic centre; if it's closed, try the **Heritage Centre** (☎ 01453-521541).

Wotton Guest House (☎ 01453-843158; 31a High St; s/d £45/55) welcomes walkers and has charming rooms and a walled cottage garden in which to put your feet up. Another option is the **Ridings** (☎ 01453-842128; s/d £25/50); it's about 1 mile north of town, but provides lifts to walkers. For food, there's the atmospheric **Falcon Inn** (☎ 01453-521005; Church St; ☯ lunch & dinner) or, a few doors down, the **India Palace** (☎ 01453-843628; mains £9; ☯ lunch & dinner), doing excellent curries. The **White Lion**, in the high street, is a good place for a (well-deserved) pint at the end of the day.

Day 3: Wotton-under-Edge to Uley

4½–5½ hours, 10.5 miles (17km)
One of the best days on the route, with the most exhilarating views so far. Accommodation is thin at the end of the day, so ensure you have a booking.

Leaving town, go steeply up Wotton Hill to the curious **Jubilee Clump**, a circle of trees planted in 1815 to commemorate the Battle of Waterloo. A delightful section of path through the dappled Westridge Wood (rich in birdsong) leads you past Brackenbury Hillfort. Here you enter a plateau with almost aerial views – a lovely mishmash of fields and woods, toy tractors and model sheep. The 111ft **Tyndale Monument** (adult 50p), erected in 1866 to commemorate William Tyndale's work to produce a Bible in the vernacular (see the boxed text, p113), looms next. You can climb hundreds of steps to the top; if it's not open, get the key from the village shop in North Nibley.

North Nibley also has a few B&Bs, including the wonderful **Nibley House** (☎ 01453-543108; www.nibleyhouse.co.uk; camp sites for 2 £4, s/d £30/50), a mini-mansion on the western fringe of the village. Or there's the welcoming **Black Horse Inn** (☎ 01453-543777; s/d £45/65; ☯ lunch & dinner) in the centre, which also does great food. Next, the path edges downhill, over a stream beside an old mill, then climbs steeply to the golf course that sprawls across Stinchcombe Hill. The route hugs the edge for a couple of miles but, apart from the breadth of views, there's little of interest. You can miss this section by heading for the clubhouse, cutting right (east) down the public footpath just before it, and then descending a steep hill into **Dursley**.

Here, facing Dursley's 1738 Market House, is **St James' Church** – minus its spire. In January 1699, the bells were rung to celebrate the completion of major repairs but the vibrations brought stonework tumbling down, killing a number of spectators. Queen Anne, who helped pay for the rebuild, was rewarded with a singularly unattractive statue in a niche in the Market House.

You can sleep at the traditional **Old Bell Hotel** (☎ 01453-542821; 15 Long St; s/d £30/47). For food there's a host of cafés along Parsonage Lane, **Dursley Tandoori** (☎ 01453-548833; 41 Long St; mains £8; ☯ lunch & dinner) or the **Old Spot Inn** (☎ 01453-542870; May Lane; ☯ lunch daily, dinner Mon-Thu), a great old pub.

Leave Dursley down Long Street, go up a lane and through fields towards Peaked Down, where you ascend steadily, skirting its eastern edge. From here it's a stiff climb up to **Cam Long Down**, then time for another aerial-photo moment. Here the views are 360-degree and extraordinary – back to the Tyndale Monument and across the Severn to Wales. Follow this ridge for several hundred metres, perform a switchback descent, then climb again towards the wide sweep of Uley Bury hillfort. Here the Way goes through the delightful **Hodgecombe Farm** (☎ 01453-860365; www.hodgecombefarm.co.uk; camp sites for 2 £6, s/d £37/55; ⦿ Apr-Oct). If you stay the owners will even ferry you to the pub in the evening. Continuing uphill, if you're walking into **Uley** itself, leave the Way just before the B4066 and take the public bridlepath on the right (south), which winds into the village and saves risking life and limb on the road.

ULEY & NYMPSFIELD

Uley is a tiny place nestled in a valley below the hillfort. The friendly **Old Crown Inn** (☎ 01453-860502; s/d £45/80; ⦿ lunch & dinner), on the main street, is the best place to stay. You can also B&B at **Little Meadow** (☎ 01453-861608; South St; s/d £26/52), a modern bungalow a few minutes walk from the centre.

There's a fabulous pub in Nympsfield, a couple of miles through Coaley Wood – the **Rose and Crown Inn** (☎ 01453-860240; www.roseandcrown-nympsfield.com; s/d £59/70; mains £10; ⦿ lunch & dinner). All old beams and wooden floors, it also serves imaginative food.

Day 4: Uley to Painswick
5½–6½ hours, 13 miles (21km)
Woodland and a short section of town walking lead to a wonderfully scenic section and a picture-perfect village to finish. Despite the urban areas, you don't actually pass a shop, so stock up before you leave Uley.

Haul yourself out of Uley's valley, then descend into Coaley Wood to follow the contour along a pleasant track. A short detour to the impressive prehistoric burial site of **Hetty Pegler's Tump**, a long barrow, is worth the short climb. A little later you come to the **Nympsfield Longbarrow** before another long but enjoyable stretch through the steep-sided Buckholt and Stanley woods.

The Way cuts north at Pen Hill, transfers onto pavement at Middleyard, then back onto fields, before another road-side stretch round King's Stanley and across the A419. (An alternative is planned here, over Selsley Common and along the Stroudwater Canal.) Turn right (east) for 200m before cutting north between houses and across the railway line. Then it's fields beneath your feet once more as you head to Maiden Hill and the cool of Standish Woods.

Next comes more ridge walking, around the edge of the plateau on **Haresfield Hill**, its dramatic views down onto the Severn Valley providing you with a textured, living

map. A circuit around Haresfield Beacon and back leads you through more woods, which open to reveal the highly picturesque village of **Painswick** nestling in the valley below. Farmland ushers you down to pass a stone marker in a field, telling you Chipping Campden is 47 miles away; you're nearly halfway there.

PAINSWICK

The compact town of Painswick attracts plenty of visitors and it's certainly a place with a history: New St was new in 1253. The town is remarkably preserved, and pretty much all built of the now-familiar Cotswold stone. The 14th-century **St Mary's Church** features a large collection of table-top tombs and 99 neatly trimmed yew trees – legend has it no more than 99 will grow at any one time. On the same street (Stroud Rd) you'll find the **tourist office** (☎ 01452-813552; ⦿ closed Sun & Mon) in the local library.

Painswick can be pricey, but try the chintzy **Hambutt's Mynd** (☎ 01452-812352; Edge Rd; s/d £30/60) – it's to the right of the Way as it enters the village from the south. In the centre, lush hanging baskets frame the lovely **Thorne** (☎ 01452-812476; Friday St; s/d £30/60), with its old beams at crazy angles, while the old **Falcon Inn** (☎ 01452-814222; New St; s/d £45/72, mains £11; ⦿ lunch & dinner) is hugely atmospheric. Or you can experience the extraordinarily sumptuous **Cardynham House** (☎ 01452-814006; www.cardynham.co.uk; The Cross; s/d from £50/69). Here, four-poster luxury awaits, but prices rise at the weekend, and if you want a room with its own private pool (and who doesn't?) it'll cost even more – from £160.

For food, there's decent pub grub at the **Royal Oak** (☎ 01452-813129; St Mary's St; ⦿ lunch & dinner), the **March Hare Thai Restaurant** (☎ 01452-813452; The Cross; set menu £25; ⦿ dinner Tue-Sat) or the rather grand **Painswick Hotel** (☎ 01452-812160; Kemps Lane; 3-course meal £30; ⦿ lunch & dinner).

Day 5: Painswick to Cheltenham
8–9 hours, 19 miles (31km)
A long and tough day, not helped by the fact that you have to leave the Way at the end to find a bed. But the walking is lovely, dominated by woodland and peppered with hillforts and golf courses.

From Painswick the path climbs steadily beside a golf course, heading northeast

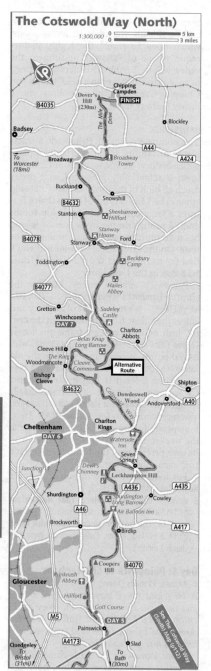

The Cotswold Way (North)

across more fairways and past the Painswick Beacon hillfort. Then it's into the woods, past Prinknash Abbey. Here the waymarking become slightly haphazard – hunt out the yellow arrows, accompanied by the Cotswold Way white dots, painted on trees. Eventually you emerge at **Coopers Hill**, where there's a painfully steep field. This is the site of the annual bank holiday cheese-rolling contest (www.cheese-rolling. co.uk) – an insanely dangerous pursuit dating from medieval times at which broken bones are still not uncommon.

A couple of miles of woods take you past the village of **Birdlip** – a short but steep climb away. You can break for the evening if you want, but the only option, the **Royal George Hotel** (☎ 01452-862506; www.theroyalgeorge-hotel .com; s/d £70/90; ☽ lunch & dinner), isn't cheap and feels more like a motel than the old coaching inn it is.

Another sharp uphill section leads eventually to a roundabout where the **Air Balloon Inn** (☎ 01452-862541; ☽ lunch & dinner) offers snacks and meals. You pass another hillfort just before the Crickley Hill Country Park and the well-preserved Neolithic Shurdington Long Barrow. A few miles more and you're at the vertiginous **Leckhampton Hill**, where the view stretches from the Brecon Beacons in Wales to Cheltenham spread out like a model town below. Next, a signed, and very short, detour leads to the rock pillar that's come to symbolise the Cotswold Way – the intriguing **Devil's Chimney** reaching for the sky.

The Way edges south, then across the A435 at Seven Springs (some say, the source of the River Thames) and under fizzing power lines. After heading northeast through Chatcombe Wood, Cheltenham swings into view again and you scramble down a perilously steep path and into the pretty Lineover Wood. This leads you to the A40 by the **Waterside Inn**; from here you can walk, take the bus coming in from Bourton-on-the-Water or catch a **taxi** (☎ 01242-514341, 07850-982899) into Charlton Kings or Cheltenham for the night.

At Charlton Kings, **Detmore House** (☎ 01242-582868; www.detmorehouse.com; London Rd; s/d £35/55) is a glorious melange of architectural styles spanning centuries. More impersonal is the upmarket **Charlton Kings Hotel** (☎ 01242-231061; www.charltonkingshotel.co.uk; London Rd; s/d £65/95).

CHELTENHAM
pop 98,875

The elegant Regency town of Cheltenham hasn't survived the 20th century quite as well as Bath, but numerous sights and a good selection of places to stay and eat may tempt you to rest for a day. The town is also a handy escape point as transport links are good.

The **tourist office** (☎ 01242-522878; www.visit cheltenham.info; 77 Promenade; ❤ closed Sun) stocks Cotswolds walking guides. If you want a break from pounding the hills, pound some pavements instead on a **walking tour** (1hr £3; ❤ 11am Mon-Fri & 11.30am Sat late Jun–mid-Sep) of Regency Cheltenham; tours leave from the tourist office. Alternatively, have your calves caressed and your hamstrings made happy at the luxurious **Chapel Spa** (☎ 01242-518075; www.chapelspa.co.uk; North Pl; 55min £45), but be sure to book well in advance.

The **YMCA** (☎ 01242-524024; www.cheltenham ymca.com; 6 Vittoria Walk; dm/s £17/21) is institutional but cheap, while over the summer holidays, **Cheltenham & Gloucester College** (☎ 01242-532774; www.glos.ac.uk; The Park; s £24) lets out student rooms.

The best place to search out B&Bs is the trendy Montpellier area, just southwest of the centre. Here, **Montpellier Hotel** (☎ 01242-526009; www.montpellier-hotel.co.uk; 33 Montpellier Tce; s/d £30/54) has pleasant rooms. Nearby, the highly engaging **Lonsdale House** (☎ 01242-232379; lonsdalehouse@hotmail.com; Montpellier Dr; s with/without bathroom £44/30, d with/without bathroom £65/55) offers a Regency feel. Moving up a price bracket, the gorgeously Georgian **Lypiatt House Hotel** (☎ 01242-224994; www.lypiatt.co.uk; Lypiatt Rd; s/d £70/80) is resolutely unstuffy, while the **Beaumont House Hotel** (☎ 01242-578450; www .bhhotel.co.uk; 56 Shurdington Rd; s/d/ste from £56/79/129) is the place to go if your tastes extend to African-themed creations with whirlpool baths.

Bath Rd, to the southeast of town, is full of cheap cafés and takeaways, while the Montpellier and neighbouring Suffolks areas are good for restaurant and bar hunting. Try the vibrant **Beehive pub** (☎ 01242-702270; 1-3 Montpellier Villas; mains £9; ❤ lunch daily, dinner Mon-Sat) or, for a taste of Spain, head to the funky **Ole Tapas Bar** (☎ 01242-573556; 50 Suffolk Rd; tapas from £4; ❤ lunch Wed-Sat, dinner Tue-Sat). There's Mediterranean–British fusion at **Laze Daze** (☎ 01242-257878; 81 Promenade;

mains £11; ❤ lunch & dinner Mon-Sat); check out its weekday early-evening two-course supper for £11.

For drinks, you'll find the slightly chic **Residence Bar** (Montpellier Walk) next to the very Irish pub **O'Neils**, while the relaxed **Montpellier Wine Bar** (Montpellier St) is on a parallel road.

Day 6: Cheltenham to Winchcombe
5–6 hours, 12.5 miles (20km)

A comfortable day's walk through quintessential English countryside. The windswept views and a remarkable ancient site add extra spice. Buy your lunch before you set out.

From the Waterside Inn the path climbs steeply up the edge of Dowdeswell Wood, then continues through farmland for a couple of miles to **Bill Smiley's Reserve**, an area alive with butterflies. There are plans to make the route round Cleeve Common less circuitous; currently you can cut off a couple of miles by taking the footpath heading northeast, but you miss some excellent views and relatively wild terrain.

The Way skirts the edge of golf links, past the rugged ramparts of a hillfort (popular with climbers) and an Iron Age earthwork dubbed the **Ring**. Here the views are expansive, and you get a real sense of walking the spine of these hills. There are lots of crisscrossing paths here, so keep your eyes peeled for the waymarks.

Farmland soon returns, bringing with it more clouds of butterflies, and you turn left (northeast) onto a track at the derelict Wontley Farm. This leads you to **Belas Knap**, a 4000-year-old Neolithic long barrow (burial mound). With dry-stone walls at the false entrances, it's in remarkably good condition. Its history is gloriously grisly: bits of bone from 38 people have been found in the chambers. There's also evidence ritual feasting went on alongside the burials – something to think about as you munch your lunch…

From here it's a steep descent through a wood, along a short stretch of road and down past the ruins of a Roman villa, hidden by a dense copse. A few more fields and you're in **Winchcombe**.

WINCHCOMBE
The small and engaging town of Winchcombe was once a medieval abbey but after Henry VIII conducted his monastic

THE COTSWOLDS

land-grab in 1539 it almost completely disappeared. One exception is **St Peter's Church** (1465) with its outstanding collection of leering gargoyles. The other principal attraction is **Sudeley Castle**. The home of Henry VIII's sixth wife, Catherine Parr, it was deliberately damaged after the Civil War and not rebuilt for nearly 200 years.

B&Bs include **Gower House** (☎ 01242-602616; 16 North St; s/d £35/55), just off the high street, and ivy-clad **Blair House** (☎ 01242-603626; 43 Gretton Rd; s/d £30/50), a 10-minute walk up North St. Highly recommended is the charming, and surprisingly Swedish, **White Hart Inn** (☎ 01242-602359; www.the-white-hart-inn.com; High St; s £30-50, d £40-70). Its cheaper 'ramblers rooms' (shared bathroom) are a bargain, and the smorgasbord buffet breakfast is a delight. Check at the **tourist office** (☎ 01242-602925; ⏰ 10am-1pm & 2-4pm Mon-Sat, 10am-4pm Sun) in the old town hall for more options.

For food, the **Plaisterer's Arms** (Abbey Tce; ⏰ lunch & dinner) does good pub grub and meals at the **White Hart Inn** (mains £9; ⏰ lunch & dinner) are excellent, while the plush **Wesley House** (☎ 01242-602366; High St; 2-course dinner £30; ⏰ lunch & dinner) also has a tapas bar next door.

Day 7: Winchcombe to Chipping Campden

7½–8½ hours, 17.5 miles (28km)

Another taxing day to finish the Cotswold Way, but the route takes in stunning views and another two hillforts before culminating with a stately finish along the Mile Dr.

Leaving Winchcombe via Puck Pit Lane, the path goes gently upwards to the ruins of **Hailes Abbey**, which once attracted streams of medieval pilgrims to see its famed sample of Christ's blood (later proven to be coloured honey).

After **Hayles Fruit Farm** (☎ 01242-602123; www.hayles-fruit-farm.co.uk; camp sites for 2 £8), which does snacks and camping, you enter Hailes Wood and go steeply up to Beckbury Camp – a large Iron Age fort and a good place for a breather. Dropping down again, the Way wanders past the extraordinary Jacobean gatehouse of **Stanway House**, then into the pretty village of Stanton, where the **Mount Inn** (☎ 01386-584316; ⏰ lunch daily, dinner Mon-Sat) has a decent lunch menu. It's another long climb out of town, this time to Shenbarrow hillfort, before you descend steadily to **Broadway**.

The village of Broadway today veers towards kitsch, but it started life as part of a nearby monastery before expanding to become an important stagecoach stop. The golden stone buildings, topped with tile and thatch, ensure many – albeit more modern – coaches still visit today. Book early if you want to spend the night.

Camping is available at **Leedon's Park** (☎ 01386-852423; Childswickham Rd; sites for 2 £10). B&Bs include the **Olive Branch Guest House** (☎ 01386-853440; www.theolivebranch-broadway.com; 78 High St; s/d £44/75), which is chintzy but cosy, and the welcoming **Crown & Trumpet** (☎ 01386-853202; Church St; s/d £50/65), although this pub has a two-night minimum stay at weekends. You could decide to splash out at the extremely grand **Lygon Arms** (☎ 01386-852255; www.paramount-hotels.co.uk/lygonarms; High St; s/d/ste £290/300/550) – all oak panelling and antiques. The **tourist office** (☎ 01386-852937; 1 Cotswold Ct; ⏰ closed Sun & Jan-Feb) has other options.

Eateries include the **Swan Inn** (☎ 01386-852278; The Green; mains £8; ⏰ lunch & dinner), which does pub/bistro meals. There's also the traditional **Horse & Hound** (High St; ⏰ lunch daily, dinner Mon-Sat), while the **Lygon Arms** (mains £18, 3 courses £40; ⏰ lunch & dinner) offers fine dining.

If you're walking to the end, it's another long ascent to **Broadway Tower**, an incongruous little folly dating from 1798. From here it's plain sailing as the path gradually descends to the Mile Dr, an extremely broad, grassed avenue that takes you quickly along to one last dogleg up **Dover's Hill** (which takes its name from Robert Dover, who instituted a local 'Olympick Games' in 1612, featuring such fine sports as shin kicking), before you enter **Chipping Campden** (p111).

BOURTON & THE SLAUGHTERS

Duration	6 hours
Distance	12 miles (19.5km)
Difficulty	easy
Start/Finish	Bourton-on-the-Water (opposite)
Transport	bus

Summary Delightful walking through farmland and valleys, over rolling hills, along river banks and past chocolate-box villages.

No, Bourton & the Slaughters is not the name of a local rock band; instead, they are some of the prettiest places in the Cotswolds. Both the villages of Upper and Lower Slaughter and the town of Bourton-on-the-Water (usually called just Bourton) attract crowds – Bourton is dubbed the 'Venice of the Cotswolds'. While this is optimistic, the River Windrush's gentle course through the village (and the numerous tiny bridges over it) does create a charming atmosphere. This walk sidesteps the coach parties and presents the villages and the surrounding country in idyllic peace and quiet.

PLANNING

Our circular walk follows sections of two longer routes, the Windrush Way and the Wardens Way (p121), both of which are well waymarked – although a map is still recommended. If you want a shorter route, you can cut south from Naunton and meet the Windrush Way just east of Aylworth.

Maps

The route is on the OS Explorer 1:25,000 map No 45 *The Cotswolds*.

NEAREST TOWN
Bourton-on-the-Water

The Bourton-on-the-Water **tourist office** (☎ 01451-820211; www.bourtoninfo.com; Victoria St; ✆ closed Sun) can provide information on accommodation, transport and local walks.

Campers should head, surprisingly, to the local football club, **Bourton Rovers** (☎ 01451-821977; Rissington Rd; sites for 2 £6); you don't actually pitch on the pitch, but at one end. **Rose Cottage** (☎ 01451-821033; Sherborne St; s/d £25/50) is lovely – packed full of character and wonky beams; there isn't a straight line in the house. **Broadlands Guest House** (☎ 01451-822002; Clapton Row; s/d £35/55) is friendly, while **Manor Close** (☎ 01451-820339; High St; s/d £50/55) is right at the start of the walk and has its own walled cottage garden.

For food, Bourton has sandwich shops and plenty of pubs and restaurants. The **Duke of Wellington** (☎ 01451-820539; www.dukeofwellingtoninn.com; Sherbourne St; mains £5-9; ✆ lunch & dinner) is a relaxed pub, while the **Rose Tree Restaurant** (☎ 01451-820635; High St; mains £8; ✆ lunch & dinner) is also recommended.

GETTING THERE & AWAY

The easiest route is by train to Moreton-in-Marsh (on the London–Worcester line),

---

Unlike most other places in the Cotswolds, and throughout Britain, Upper Slaughter has no war memorial – extraordinarily, the local men who fought in WWI and WWII all came home again. Such places are known as 'thankful villages', and a plaque in Upper Slaughter church thanks God for their protection. In contrast, of the 65 men from nearby Naunton who served in WWI, 13 were killed.

---

then by bus. Buses tie in with train times and run to Cirencester via Bourton-on-the-Water and Stow-on-the-Wold. They run about 10 times a day Monday to Saturday only. Alternatively, if coming from the West Country, it may be easier to get a train to Kemble (on a main line to/from London), then a bus to Bourton-on-the-Water from there. Again, this bus does not run on Sunday.

On summer Sundays (May to September) your only options are the one or two buses that run between Moreton-in-Marsh and Cheltenham via Stow-on-the-Wold and Bourton-on-the-Water. Check with the tourist office for the latest times.

By car, Bourton-on-the-Water is on the main A429 between Cirencester and Stow-on-the-Wold.

THE WALK
Bourton-on-the-Water to Naunton

2 hours, 4 miles (6.5km)

The first part of the route follows the Wardens Way, signposted from the church at the centre of Bourton. From here a footpath leads northeast past a school. When it meets the road, go left (northwest, signed 'Heart of England Way'), then right across the A429, then left (northwest) 50m later (signed 'Wardens Way').

From here you're out in the country; the route crosses fields and meets up with lanes to lead into the village of Lower Slaughter. (On some maps the Wardens Way is shown slightly further north than the route described but both ways lead you to Lower Slaughter.)

Lower Slaughter is a smaller version of Bourton, with a shallow river running between grassy banks through the heart of

Bourton & the Slaughters

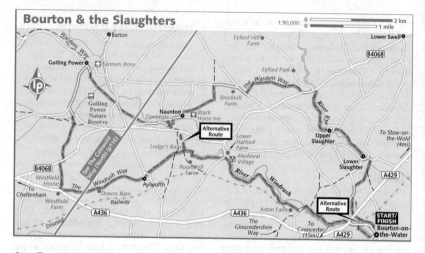

the village. Its name has nothing to do with killing but comes from Schlotre, the family name of the original Norman landowner. Head west through the centre of the village, cross the river on a small stone-slab footbridge, passing some cottages on your right, then turn left (northwest) onto a footpath again just after the Old Mill (which has a **tearoom**). From here it's a gentle riverside walk across fields before entering **Upper Slaughter**. Here, make sure you swing right (north) and then left around the church to follow a small path through a patch of woodland, then across fields and into woodland again.

About 1 mile later you come to a road and turn left (take care, as there's no path) and follow it for 300m. Here, on the right, two tracks appear very close together – take the second track. This leads you through fields, around a barn and along a track to meet another lane near Brockhill Farm, where you turn right (northwest), looking out for the path in the fields running parallel to the road.

Soon the road forks – take the route on the left, then a short while later turn left again (south) onto a track. This leads you through more fields, then steeply down into the quiet and not-too-cutesy village of **Naunton**. Turn back east a short distance along the village main street to reach the **Black Horse Inn** (☎ 01451-850565; mains £8; ☾ lunch & dinner), which serves coffee, good beer and excellent lunches.

Naunton to Bourton-on-the-Water
4 hours, 8 miles (13km)

Go westwards along Naunton's main street, then turn south (look for the 'Wardens Way' signs), down to the river and along a back lane past the 17th-century **Dovecote**, where hundreds of pigeons used to be farmed for their meat. The lane out of the village goes up a hill before waymarks lead you clearly at a northwest slant across fields all the way to **Guiting Power**, another charming village featuring sturdy Cotswold stone houses around a little square. The **Farmers Arms** (☎ 01451-850358; ☾ lunch & dinner) makes a good lunch, while **Well House** (☎ 01451-850298; s/d £25/50) offers traditional B&B. You can buy cakes and snacks from the time-warped village **shop** behind the **bakery**, where the friendly lady also makes sandwiches to order (cheese or ham – that's the choice).

Here we say farewell to the Wardens Way. Heading back the way you came, turn right (southwest) down the lane in front of the school. Follow this for 1 mile to a fork, where you go left (south). Just before a bridge, go through a gate on your right and across a field to reach a junction of footpaths, one of which is the **Windrush Way** and the route home.

Head south through a lovely patch of woodland, then fields, to meet the B4068, where you go right, then almost immediately left, into a field that runs along the back of some cottages. This path cuts just left of Westfield House then south towards the A436. Just before you get there, it swings left (east) along a wonderful old track that winds beside hedgerows and through cornfields. Pass through the settlement of Aylworth and then walk gradually downhill beside a stream (a tributary of the Windrush) to eventually meet a lane near Lower Harford Farm. Turn left (north), go down the lane for 100m, then right (east) onto the path and through a field. The bumps here are the remains of the medieval **Harford village**. Now the route traces a beautiful course beside the River Windrush before turning uphill and entering woodland. Just to the south of the path are the remains of an old railway and the large, dark bridge hidden deep in the wood comes as a sudden surprise.

You cross the River Windrush only once more, after Aston Farm, on a bridge by an old mill. The path climbs up to and follows the old railway for 100m before jumping down into fields again for a lovely finish through water meadows. The busy A429 has to be crossed and then you can walk down the street called Lansdowne, but it's best to turn right onto one last, gorgeous section of river-side path and into the centre of Bourton.

MORE WALKS

DIAMOND WAY

A 60-mile (96km) circular meander through the heart of this beguiling, essentially English region. Starting from Moreton-in-Marsh, it winds north to Chipping Campden, west to Guiting Power and south to Northleach before taking in Bourton-on-the-Water on the way home.

It's a pretty, rural route that also connects with many of the area's long-distance paths – the Cotswold, Monarch's and Macmillan Ways (see p148) – and you'll need around five days to do it justice. You'll find relevant transport and tourist information in this chapter's introduction, while Elizabeth Bell's *North Cotswold Diamond Way* guides you through the whole route. The

walk itself is covered by the OS Explorer 1:25,000 map No 45 *The Cotswolds*.

THE WARDENS & WINDRUSH WAYS

This delightful, 27-mile (43km), two-day route – pretty much a region highlight – traces an oval from Bourton-on-the-Water in the east to the incredibly picturesque Winchcombe, on the Cotswold Way, in the west. Following the entire length of the Windrush and Wardens Ways, it also includes the Bourton & the Slaughters walk (p118). Adding the hilly western section, the extra day and an overnight stop in Winchcombe makes for a much more rounded journey.

Day 6 of our Cotswold Way description (p117) covers Winchcombe, while our Bourton & the Slaughters day walk (p118) features transport information. The map to guide you round this lovely piece of English wandering is the OS Explorer 1:25,000 map No 45 *The Cotswolds*.

AN AVON AMBLE

This half-day walk shepherds you out of Bath via the famous Crescent to climb the first hills of the Cotswold Way (see the Cotswold Way Day 1 description, p112). Once at Little Down Fort head down and then through the pretty village of North Stoke. Follow the road south out, admiring views of the River Avon on the way. At the busy A431 turn right then immediately left to join the footpath that parallels the River Avon for over 800m. Your legs then lead you past a picturesque weir, locks and a row of lovely old cottages. At a gloomy railway tunnel, hop up onto the raised old railway track itself. Built in the 1860s, this line linked Bristol to London before closing a century later – it's now a popular foot and cycle path. You leave it just under 1 mile later – immediately after crossing the bridge at Kelston Park. Take the steps on the left (north) that lead down to the River Avon Trail then turn right (east) to shadow the river all the way back into Bath.

This lush 8.5-mile (14km) wander is best accompanied by the OS Explorer 1:25,000 map No 155 *Bristol & Bath*.

Southern England Long-Distance Paths

This chapter covers two of the longest and best-known long-distance paths (LDPs) in southern England – the South Downs Way and the South West Coast Path. These sharply contrasting routes have their own chapter simply because they do not fit neatly into any other chapter in this book.

For most walkers, the South Downs Way takes around a week. It starts in historic Winchester, winding gently at first through farms and woodland then gathering pace and confidence as it leaves the trees behind to stride across rolling, grassy hills, with great views and big, dramatic skies, to finally plunge to the English Channel at the seaside resort of Eastbourne.

At the other end of southern England, the South West Coast Path is the longest national trail in Britain – a whopping 630 miles – easily taking a couple of months to complete. In this book, we've described the most popular two-week section, taking in beaches, cliff tops and fishing ports along the way. One walker we heard from who'd done both routes said he 'loved the contrast between the neat hills of the posh Southeast and the wild coast of raggedy Cornwall'.

For all you mile-eaters out there, the South Downs Way and South West Coast Path are by no means the only long-distance options in southern England. Other LDPs described in this book are the Ridgeway (p83), the Cotswold Way (p109) and the Thames Path (p64 and p88), and further ideas are given in the More Long-Distance Walks section on p148.

HIGHLIGHTS

- Wandering the atmospheric main street of **Alfriston** (p131)
- Watching the waves crash around the **Beachy Head lighthouse** (p133)
- Stopping for a quick dip at any one of the north coast's fabulous golden beaches on the **South West Coast Path** (p133)
- Turning the corner at **Land's End** (p143) and then heading along exhilarating granite cliff tops

THE SOUTH DOWNS WAY

Duration	8 days
Distance	107 miles (172km)
Difficulty	moderate
Start	Winchester (p76)
Finish	Eastbourne (p124)
Transport	train, bus

Summary Follow the ancient chalk and flint highway along the ridges of rolling downs, past picture-perfect villages and prehistoric sites.

There's something quintessentially English about the South Downs Way (SDW). From high on the ridges of the downs (grassy chalk hills), Albion's pastoral idyll stretches out as far as the eye can see. It's difficult to resist the word 'quaint' when describing the villages strung along the route, nearly all with their own Norman church, 500-year-old pub and cottages of flint, wood and thatch. And as if the Shire-like surroundings weren't Tolkien-esque enough, the place names compound the impression – Long Bottom, Cheesefoot Head, Ditchling Beacon, the Rivers Arun and Adur, Big Bottom, Devil's Dyke, Cocking, Didling and Fulking.

This ancient route was first used by Neolithic people, keen to avoid the marsh and dense forest below the downs. Later settlers all left their marks, including Bronze Age burial barrows, Iron Age hillforts and a Roman road, now part of the track. As you leave Hampshire and head into Sussex the views become increasingly panoramic, over chequerboard farmland to the north and south to the sea.

Waymarking is generally good, although there are a few points where signs are missing and vigilance is required. At any branch of the trail, look around for either the wooden signs or the plastic disks marked with an acorn. There are also disks pointing to bridleways, public footpaths and other walks, so always check that you're following the right path. Where there are no SDW markers it's generally safe to assume that you can keep marching straight ahead on the most obvious trail.

Walkers share much of the route with bicycles and the occasional horse, although there are large segments where nonwalkers are diverted away from the main path (including the whole of the last leg from Alfriston).

ENVIRONMENT

The South Downs fall within two official Areas of Outstanding Natural Beauty – East Hampshire and Sussex Downs – and there have been moves for a number of years to have the area designated as a national park.

This is farming land, where crops and livestock have coexisted for centuries. Grazing plays an important part in preserving the downland environment, keeping back the scrub and allowing wild flowers such as orchids and bluebells to bloom. However, intensive farming methods, involving the use of fertilisers, herbicides and the introduction of imported ryegrass, continue to threaten the native turf. The National Trust has been trying to turn the tide by reintroducing sheep grazing on its estates along the SDW, while a **Sustainable Development Fund** (www.southdowns.gov.uk) seeks to encourage other landowners to do the same.

There are a few wild patches of woodland along the way, some dating back to the Iron Age. If you're lucky (and quiet) you might spot deer. Keep an eye out for peregrine falcons and fulmars along the cliffs on the last day.

PLANNING

Finding accommodation along the SDW can be a problem. Campers will struggle to find an official site every night and there are few hostels. B&Bs may be your only option, but it pays to book early, as even these are thin on the ground. If there happens to be a wedding or major polo game on, you might find all the available beds booked up in villages for quite a radius.

While you can follow the path in either direction, our description goes west to east, with prevailing winds propelling you from the more enclosed part of the trail to open and dramatic scenery, with a spectacular cliff-top finish.

There are no baggage services along the SDW so you'll have to be your own mule.

Cycling the route should only take three days, but be sure to bring a puncture kit, as the sharp flint can be murder on your tires.

The walking days as we've described them are as follows:

Day	From	To	Miles/km
1	Winchester	Exton	12/19.5
2	Exton	Buriton	14/22.5
3	Buriton	Cocking	12/19.5
4	Cocking	Amberley	12/19.5
5	Amberley	Steyning	13/21
6	Steyning	Kingston-near-Lewes	20/32
7	Kingston-near-Lewes	Alfriston	12/19.5
8	Alfriston	Eastbourne	12/19.5

Alternatives

Our itinerary is fairly gentle, except for Day 6. You could split this leg up by catching the bus from Pyecombe to Brighton and staying overnight there. If you're feeling strong, more challenging combinations are possible; for instance, amalgamating Days 3 and 4, or Days 4 and 5. If you're short of time, you can omit the first two days and get the best of the route by joining at Buriton.

As with all LDPs, you can do just a single-day linear section of the SDW, or a circular route taking in a stretch of the main track. See the boxed text on p132 for suggestions.

When to Walk

Since the land is generally well-drained and the climate mild, the SDW can be walked at any time of year, although spring and summer unleash a riot of wildflowers and butterflies.

Maps

Harvey Maps produces an excellent 1:40,000 *South Downs Way* strip map, which covers the whole route on one sheet. Like all strip maps it's useless once you get a few miles away from the trail but does include most of the walkable towns and villages where accommodation is available. The SDW is covered by Ordnance Survey (OS) Landranger 1:50,000 maps No 185 *Winchester & Basingstoke*, 197 *Chichester & the Southern Downs*, 198 *Brighton & Lewes* and 199 *Eastbourne & Hastings*.

Information Sources

The South Downs Way official website (www.nationaltrail.co.uk/Southdowns) is an excellent resource, with information on the route, maps, photos, accommodation listings and links to public-transport sites. Also covering accommodation and transport is www.visitsouthdowns.com, with a particular focus on sustainable tourism.

The **Winchester tourist office** (☎ 01962-840500; www.visitwinchester.co.uk; The Guildhall, High St; ☼ closed Sun Oct-Apr) sells walking maps and can assist with finding accommodation along the route for a £5 fee plus 10% of the total booking.

NEAREST TOWNS

For Winchester, see p76.

Eastbourne

pop 106,562

At the end of the route, Eastbourne's a bit like Brighton for the over-60s, who make up 30% of the population. There's not a lot to see or do here and, given its large community of retirees, it's hardly a party town. Its tidy buildings are riddled with hotels and B&Bs that hug the seafront, especially around the pier. The **tourist office** (☎ 0906 711 2212; www.visiteastbourne.co.uk; Cornfield Rd; ☼ closed Sun Nov-Apr) has a number of free pamphlets, as well as maps and guides for sale. It charges slightly less for booking accommodation than other tourist offices (£3 fee plus 5% of the total booking).

SLEEPING & EATING

Eastbourne's surfeit of accommodation makes for some good bargains.

Channel View Hotel (☎ 01323-736730; schanvw7@nildram.co.uk; 57 Royal Pde; s £21, d £24-28) is right on

---

WARNING

There's no shelter from the elements along the ridges, so the sun and wind can be brutal and electrical storms rather scary. If you hear thunder you're best to leave the ridges and seek shelter in a building. If you can't find one, go to a low-lying, open place away from trees or poles and squat low to the ground.

Make sure you pack plenty of water, as all the villages are at the foot of the downs and you won't fancy leaving the path to refuel. Taps are provided along the trail (and marked on some maps), but it's still worth carrying 1L with you.

the main seaside promenade and has some rooms with balconies.

Just back from the water, **Cromwell Private Hotel** (☎ 01323-725288; www.cromwellhotel.co.uk; 23 Cavendish Pl; s £27-32, d £54-64) has eight rooms in a Victorian townhouse not far from the pier.

You can rest your weary legs in a canopied bed at the elegant **Albert & Victoria** (☎ 01323-730948; www.albertandvictoria.com; 19 St Aubyns Rd; s £30-40, d £70-80), although it doesn't take single-night bookings on the weekend.

If you're looking for a supermarket, there's a **Sainsbury's** (☎ 01323-639344; 63 Arndale Centre) in the mall next to the train station.

Pomodoro e Mozzarella (☎ 01323-733800; 23-24 Cornfield Tce; mains £6-15; ✞ lunch & dinner) serves traditional Italian food with plenty of vegetarian options.

GETTING THERE & AWAY

Trains are the best option. **Southern** (☎ 0845 127 2920; www.southernrailway.com) operates direct lines from Brighton (40 minutes, 14 daily) and London Victoria (1½ hours, 11 daily), stopping at Gatwick airport.

National Express (☎ 08705 808080; www.national express.com) has one daily coach from London (2¾ hours) and two from Brighton (45 minutes).

By car, take the A22 from London or the A27 from Brighton.

THE WALK
Day 1: Winchester to Exton
4–6 hours, 12 miles (19.5km)
Ease into the walk with a gentle stroll through woods, farms and fields.

Start the route with a right royal send-off, at the grandiose statue of **King Alfred the Great** at the end of the high street. Cross the bridge and turn right into Chesil St. After 200m turn left up East Hill then bear right along Petersfield Rd, through leafy suburbs. At the 'Welcome to Highcliffe' sign, veer right onto Fivefields Rd and continue straight ahead along the footpath when the road ends at a cul de sac. Once you clear the houses, turn right, take the footbridge over the busy M3 motorway, veer left at the end and you're on your way. Relax – there are no navigation problems for several miles as the trail follows tracks and lanes through farmland.

A natural resting point is the **Milbury's** (☎ 01962-771248; www.themilburys.co.uk; Beauworth;

mains £6-15; ✞ lunch & dinner), a 17th-century pub serving hearty food about 8 miles along the path. From here, further easy walking takes you to wooded **Beacon Hill** (there are more such hills to come, where fires were lit four centuries ago to warn of the approaching Spanish Armada) and the route's first tricky bit of navigation. At the car park the path splits, with cycles and horses directed to the northeast and walkers to the southeast. This takes you through a wheat field where, after 50m, a pile of flint (with no sign) marks the point where you should cut diagonally across the field on a path no more than 1ft wide. At the end, a stile leads onto a road where, before long, another stile directs you across more fields. From here the route is clearly marked, taking you over several more stiles (some crossing electric fences) and through open farmland heading down towards Exton.

EXTON

Accommodation is extremely limited in this quiet village and its twin sister Meonstoke across the river.

The **Buck's Head** (☎ 01489-877313; Bucks Head Hill, Meonstoke; s/d £45/65, mains £7-14; ✞ lunch daily, dinner Mon-Sat) offers B&B in a cosy pub with good beer and reasonable food.

Although it's about 1.5 miles southwest of the village, the friendly folks at the **Copper Room** (☎ 01489-877506; Corhampton Lane Farm; camp sites for 2 £10, s/d £35/60) will collect you from Exton and return you the next day. The sheltered camp site has access to a toilet but no shower.

There are further accommodation choices in Droxford, 2 miles south along the A32.

In Exton village, the **Shoe Inn** (☎ 01489-877526; Shoe Lane; mains £9; ✞ lunch & dinner) is a flash pub serving meals and bar snacks, with more tables in a small garden across the road.

The **Meonstoke Post Office** (☎ 01489-877374; Warnford Rd, Meonstoke) doubles as the village store and sells just about everything you might possibly need.

Day 2: Exton to Buriton
4–6 hours, 14 miles (22.5km)
The path yo-yos through pastures and fields, with a couple of stretches of woodland and the (literal) high point of the route.

The irony of the Downs is that there are at least as many ups, which is something you begin to appreciate today. From Exton the trail climbs to **Old Winchester Hill**, the most impressive Iron Age fort on the route. It's an excellent viewpoint; you can look over the Meon Valley to the New Forest and the silver line of sea that splits the Isle of Wight from the coast.

After Salt Hill, hurry past HMS Mercury, a landlocked naval station with grim razor-wire fences and derelict outbuildings. Of more interest is the nearby **Sustainability Centre** (☎ 01730-823166; www.earthworks-trust.com; Droxford Rd, East Meon; admission free; ☼ 10am-4pm), where you can examine different technologies relating to environmentally friendly living. Its **Wetherdown Hostel** (☎ 01730-823549; hostel@earthworks-trust.com; camp sites for 2 £7, s/d/tr tepees £15/20/30, dm/s £20/25) uses solar energy and a wood-chip biomass boiler.

Next comes butt-crunching **Butser Hill** – at 270m the highest point on the SDW, although the path skirts about 20m below the peak. Savour a rolling descent, heading under the A3 to reach the **Queen Elizabeth Country Park Visitor Centre** (☎ 02392-595040; www .hants.gov.uk/countryside/qecp; ☼ closed 21 Dec-6 Jan),

with a café, toilets and shop. Carefully follow the SDW signs (ignore the multicoloured waymarks for circular trails in the forest) until you reach Hall's Hill car park, where a lane drops down to Buriton and bed.

BURITON

This village could hardly be cuter if it tried. There's a fine 12th-century Norman church set alongside a duck pond, an impressive manor house, flint cottages and two pubs, both offering food and accommodation.

The more atmospheric of the two is the **Five Bells** (☎ 01730-263584; www.fivebellsburiton .co.uk; High St; s £50-60, d £70, mains £8-10; ☼ lunch daily, dinner Mon-Sat), parts of which date from the 16th century, although it was heavily altered 200 years later. It serves an interesting menu, including vegetarian options and a great wine list, in its low-beamed dining room (which once was the village butcher, and occasionally doubled as the morgue) and in the garden. Accommodation is provided in self-catering cottages next door.

The **Master Robert** (☎ 01730-267275; master .robert@btconnect.com; 1 Petersfield Rd; s/d £40/50, mains

The South Downs Way

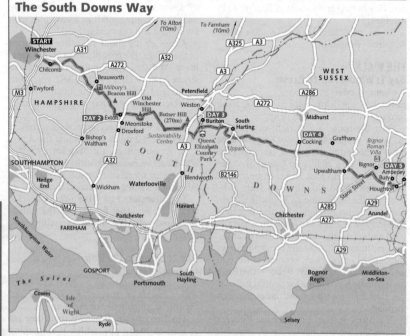

£7-8; ✆ lunch daily, dinner Mon-Sat) attracts a younger crowd, but is rather less impressive.

A better option for B&B is **Nurstead Farm** (☎ 01730-264278; s/d £22/44), just outside the village in a 17th-century farmhouse.

If you get stuck for a place to rest your weary legs, catch a taxi 3 miles north to the attractive town of Petersfield where there are several more options.

Day 3: Buriton to Cocking
4–6 hours, 12 miles (19.5km)
A couple of steep climbs don't dent a wonderful day's walk along the ridge of the Downs proper, with the best views thus far.

Upon regaining the trail from Buriton you'll find yourself on wooded paths, skirting around farms for around 4 miles before you cross the B2146, just south of South Harting. A 200m diversion south along this road will bring you to the gates of **Uppark** (☎ 01730-825415; www.nationaltrust.org.uk; admission to house adult/child £7/4, garden only £3/2; ✆ 11.30am-5pm Sun-Thu Apr-Oct), a handsome 17th-century manor house with terrific gardens and amazing views. You can easily indulge in a

quick look around and an early lunch at the restaurant before heading back to the trail.

You'll be glad of the rest once you reach the succession of steep, grass-covered domes, including Tower Hill and Harting Down. At Beacon Hill (yes, another one) and a place called Devil's Jumps, take care as the SDW switches back sharply on itself – it's easy to go striding straight on. After this you'll pass through a wonderful patch of wild woods, where you may get to see some ostentatiously antlered stags. As you leave the woods, look out for a cluster of grassy mounds that are actually Bronze Age **burial barrows**. Back into the open, it's time for the first long, straight stretch of high ridge, passing grazing sheep and breathtaking views out to sea. You'll see the neat village of Cocking to the north as you come down the hill towards the busy A286; follow the road into the village.

COCKING
Any day, another perfect village – complete with a Norman church, popular pub and flint cottages. A unique new attraction is

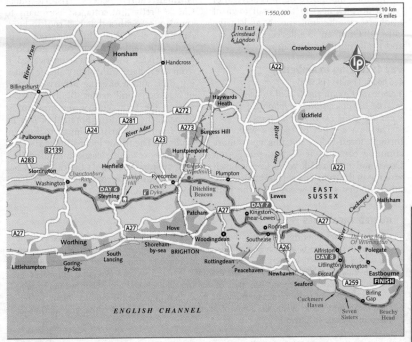

the **History Column**. Erected for the millennium, bronze images of 14 centuries of village life twist their way around and up the structure like a mini Trajan's Column.

You'll be cocking up (hey, there had to be one bad pun) if you don't try to stay at the super-friendly **Moonlight Cottage** (☎ 01730-813336; www.moonlightcottage.co.uk; Chichester Rd; s/tw/d £33/55/60), which goes so far as to offer a foot spa in some rooms. If you're not lucky enough to find a vacancy here, you can still enjoy scrummy cakes, sandwiches and meals in the tearooms.

The **Blue Bell Inn** (☎ 01730-813449; www.the bluebell.org.uk; Chichester Rd; s/d £40/60, mains £8-12; ☯ lunch Tue-Sun, dinner Tue-Sat) has a friendly pub, excellent grub (including veggie options) and comfortable B&B accommodation.

While the eccentric **Cinque Port** (☎ 01730-813594; Bell Lane; s/d £28/56) is rather cluttered, the enigmatic hostess proffers wonderful hospitality and an excellent yarn.

Next door, the walker-friendly **Downsfold** (☎ 01730-814376; www.downsfold.co.uk; Bell Lane; s/d £33/55) has attractive rooms and a lovely garden.

There are more B&B options (several of which do pick-ups) in the small town of Midhurst, another mile north, and in the village of Graffham, 3 miles east of Cocking and 1 mile north of the trail.

Day 4: Cocking to Amberley
4–5 hours, 12 miles (19.5km)
Today, all Roman roads lead to, well, Eastbourne, as you continue to follow the escarpment along the Down's flinty spine.

The first section of today's walk cuts through forest before opening up to more stunning pastoral views. Between Sutton Down and Bignor Hill you'll find yourself walking in the footsteps of legionnaires and other sundry sandal-wearers as the path

follows Stane Street, a Roman road dating from AD 70 that ran between London and Noviomagus (New Port), today called Chichester.

If you're interested in further exploring the area's imperial connections, the **Bignor Roman Villa** (see the boxed text, below) is 2 miles north of the route. Just to the south, the wondrously named **Gumber Bothy** (☎ 01243-814484; Gumber Farm, Slindon; camp sites per person £8, dm £8) has camping and bunk beds in a barn. Facilities include a shared kitchen.

Pressing on, allow yourself some contentment as you cross the busy A29, in the knowledge that you're at the halfway point of your journey. The cluster of impossibly sweet villages in the Arun Valley below provides your choice of stops tonight. Head down the hill and south at Houghton Lane for Houghton. For Amberley Station/Houghton Bridge, continue on the SDW until you reach the river and follow it south. For Amberley proper, stick on the path until you reach the B2139 and head north.

AMBERLEY
Norman church? Check. Historic pubs? Check. Pretty flint cottages? Too many to count, most with a thatched roof to boot. Anything else? Well, this one's got a ruined castle, although you can't get close, as its private owners have barricaded it from the village with high walls, foreboding signs and a *Sleeping Beauty*–like wall of blackberry and nettles. Built in 1103, it was, in the 13th century, the home of St Richard, the unwitting librettist of *Day By Day* from '70s Christian-hippy rock-opera *Godspell*. The firmly locked Richard's Gate once connected the castle to the village's 12th-century **St Michael's Church**, which has the remains of frescoes and some interesting stone columns.

BURIED TREASURES

In 1811 a local farmer got more than he bargained for when ploughing his field. Excavations revealed the remains of a lavish Roman villa with some wonderfully preserved mosaics, including a 24m intact section of corridor. With the finds properly protected and displayed, **Bignor Roman Villa** (☎ 01798-869259; Bignor; adult/child £5/2; ☯ closed Nov-Feb & Mon Mar & Apr) makes an interesting detour. You can still see parts of the original walls and underfloor heating system, plus a collection of tools, coins and domestic items. Best of all are the mosaics: Venus, winter-snug in a warm cloak, eyeing up a pair of gladiators; a Rasta-haired Medusa; and Ganymede, the androgynous shepherd boy.

Stream Cottage (☎ 01798-831266; www.stream cottage.co.uk; Church St; s/d £50/70) offers B&B in a thatch-roofed, fairy-tale setting.

Just opposite, parts of the **Black Horse Inn** (☎ 01798-831552; www.theblackhorseinnamberley.co.uk; High St; mains £10-17; ☾ lunch & dinner) date from the 17th century. The pub has a large beer garden and the restaurant has home-cooked veggie options.

The **Amberley Village Stores** (☎ 01798-831171; The Barn, High St) also doubles as the post office.

A five-minute walk to the east of the village will bring you to Cross Gates, where, behind a beautifully trim garden, **Woody-banks** (☎ 01798-831295; www.woodybanks.co.uk; Rackham Rd; s £27-32, d £50-65) has two tidy rooms with a shared bathroom, run by a friendly Christian couple.

Next door, there's another pub, the **Sportsman** (☎ 01798-831787; www.amberleysportsman.co.uk; Rackham Rd; s/d/tr £45/70/90, mains £7-10, ☾ lunch & dinner), with great views back over the Downs, basic meals and comfortable rooms.

Near the Amberley train station there's a cluster of traveller-friendly activity around the pretty Houghton Bridge.

Riverside House (☎ 01798-831558; s/d/ste £35/70/90) is a friendly place to stay in an idyllic setting. The owner also runs the **café & bistro** (mains £8-9; ☾ breakfast & lunch daily, dinner Thu-Sat) next door, with tables right by the river – a great spot to enjoy a late summer sunset over the Downs.

Across the road, the **Bridge Inn** (☎ 01798-831619; mains £9-13; ☾ lunch & dinner) is a welcoming pub, serving a mix of sandwiches, traditional pub fare and, bizarrely, Greek dishes.

An altogether fancier option is the **Boathouse Brasserie** (☎ 01798-831059; set 2-course lunch/ dinner £17/19).

In Houghton, the friendly **Houghton Farm** (☎ 01798-831327; s/d £33/60) offers B&B with shared amenities.

Nearby, the **George & Dragon** (☎ 01798-831559; mains £7-10; ☾ lunch & dinner) is a compulsory pit stop. Built in 1276, Charles II stopped here for an ale in 1651 while on the run from Cromwell. It even has a resident ghost who moves glasses around – a young boy called Charlie who got stuck and died while sweeping the chimney.

There are further B&B options in Bury and a **YHA hostel** (☎ 01903-882204; www.yha.org.uk; Warningcamp; dm/d/tr £23/50/72) 4 miles off the route in Arundel.

> **NOT SO HEAVY INDUSTRY**
>
> **Amberley Working Museum** (☎ 01798-831370; www.amberleymuseum.co.uk; adult/child £9/5; ☾ Wed-Sun mid-March–Oct) spreads over 36 acres of former chalk pits, focusing on the industrial heritage of the area. You can take a ride on vintage buses and trains, and watch craftspeople at work.

Day 5: Amberley to Steyning
4–6 hours, 13 miles (21km)

Once you've conquered the initial ascent, relax into another enjoyable, none-too-strenuous day's walk along the backbone of southern England as the views get better and better.

By now you'll be accustomed to the initial steep trek up to the top of the ridges. Once you're here it's fairly easy going as the path leads through classic, wide-open downland scenery – beautiful in clear weather but exposed in wind and rain. At a fork by a barn (the first feature for several miles), make sure you keep left, nearer the edge of the Downs, before dropping down to scuttle across the A24 just south of Washington.

From here it's a stiff push up to **Chanctonbury Ring**, a coppice of beech trees planted in 1760 by a local landowner on a site that probably dates back to the Neolithic. It gained earthen ramparts around the 6th century BC and later a Roman temple, although there's not a lot to be seen from vaulting the unpopular barbed-wire fence added by the present landowner. For more on this fascinating site, linked in folklore to witches, fairies, druids, ghosts, UFOs and, predictably, the devil, there's a fascinating article at www2.prestel.co.uk/aspen/sussex /chanctonbury.html.

It's an easy 2 miles from here to Steyning. Turn off the path when you reach the memorial to a local farmer and take the incredibly steep road 1 mile down into town, turning left into the high street. Alternatively, to shorten tomorrow's tough walk, you may consider pressing on a further 4 miles to the **Truleigh Hill YHA Hostel** (☎ 01903-813419; www.yha.org.uk; Tottington Barn; dm/d £17/34).

STEYNING
Not a village this time but a proper town, the biggest since Winchester. It's still unbearably quaint (flint cottages, pubs, churches,

ruined castle – you know the drill), but it's also got banks, shops and a supermarket.

There's basic camping available (no showers) at **White House Caravan Site** (☎ 01903-813737; Newham Lane; sites for 2 £6).

Springwells Hotel (☎ 01903-812446; www.springwells.co.uk; 9 High St; s £41-62, d £69-117; ☒) is an attractive building on the main street, offering a choice of en suite rooms or cheaper rooms with shared bathrooms.

Further along, **Chequer Inn** (☎ 01903-814437; www.chequerinnsteyning.co.uk; 41 High St; s/d/tr £45/70/80, mains £6-11; ☺ breakfast, lunch & dinner) has rooms above an atmospheric, wood-beamed, 500-year-old pub, which serves food. On the southern outskirts of town, technically in Bramber village, there are more rooms at the **Castle Inn Hotel** (☎ 01903-812102; www.castleinnhotel.co.uk; The Street, Bramber; s/d £50/70, mains £6-11; ☺ lunch daily, dinner Mon-Sat).

For a break from pub food, and a magnificent one at that, the misleadingly named **Saxons** (☎ 01903-813533; 76 High St; mains £6-15; ☺ lunch & dinner), serves the best Indian food this side of Brick Lane.

Day 6: Steyning to Kingston-near-Lewes
7–9 hours, 20 miles (32km)
By far the toughest day of the route; a number of steep climbs towards the end will test your endurance.

Rather than retracing yesterday's steep steps uphill, it's not really cheating to pick up the trail where it dips to the River Adur. Follow High St south then southeast past the roundabout. After 800m you'll cross the river, where you'll find the SDW just after the next roundabout.

After your first climb of the day, Brighton appears on the horizon and there are sea views for most of the way. The view from **Devil's Dyke** attracts tourist buses to its large **pub**. A few miles from here, the path descends rapidly to cross the extremely busy A23 linking London and Brighton. Although it's not scenic, the **Plough Inn** (☎ 01273-842796; London Rd, Pyecombe; mains £7-9; ☺ lunch & dinner) is a convenient lunch stop.

The route skirts a golf course and passes near **Clayton Windmills**, more popularly known as Jack and Jill, then climbs steeply to **Ditchling Beacon**, the site of another Iron Age fort. Like Devil's Dyke, this area is popular with day-trippers. It's busiest on weekends when there's a bus that runs from Brighton to both sites.

Quickly the path becomes more isolated. Take care not to go straight on just after a hill called Plumpton Plain, but follow tracks zigzagging endlessly through the fields and a patch of woodland to meet the A27, 3 miles west of Lewes (pronounced 'lewis'). After backtracking to an overbridge the path turns east along the motorway and then – just when you think you've finished – sharply south under the railway tracks, through some woods and then up a ridge, climbing a soul-destroying 200m before circling back, high above Kingston-near-Lewes.

BRIGHTON & HOVE

Simultaneously tacky and elegant, trashy and refined, the conjoined city of Brighton & Hove is like no other place in England. **Brighton Pier** is all funfair flashing lights and rock candy, jutting over the broad sweep of the popular pebbly beach. The **Royal Pavilion** (☎ 01273-292820; www.royalpavilion.org.uk; adult/child £8/5), right in the centre of town, is a mad Orientalist fantasy – Indian exteriors and Chinese interiors, complete with the nodding heads of Mandarin mannequins. Built by George VI when he was still Prince Regent, the future king's exploits gave the town a reputation as the home of the dirty weekend.

This libertine tradition may have created the environment that has resulted in Brighton having the highest concentration of gays and lesbians of any British city, with the community based around the beachside suburb of Kemptown (aka Camp Town, Tramp Town or Soho-On-Sea). Music has also played a part in the city's mystique. In 1964 there were riots between mods and rockers, immortalised in The Who's rock opera *Quadrophenia*. Dance-music legend Fatboy Slim is one of the city's favourite sons, entertaining a crowd of 250,000 people in a free concert on the beach in 2002.

If you want to break up Day 6 of the walk into more manageable chunks, Brighton would make an excellent overnight option – see p124 for details.

KINGSTON-NEAR-LEWES

The sight of this leafy little village at the foot of the Downs will come as a great relief after an exhausting day.

From **Settlands** (☎ 01273-472295; diana-a @solutions-ink.co.uk; Wellgreen Lane; s/d/tw £40/58/60) there are views back over the South Downs Way.

Both **Bethel Bed & Breakfast** (☎ 01273-478658; www.lewes-area-bed-and-breakfast.com/bethel; Kingston Ridge; s/d £45/65) and **Nightingales** (☎ 01273-475673; www.users.totalise.co.uk/~nightingales; The Avenue; s £45, d £65-70) offer comfortable rooms in quiet properties surrounded by gardens and trees.

The nearby village pub, the **Juggs** (☎ 01273-472523; mains £7-14; ✷ lunch & dinner), dates from the 15th century. With a great beer garden and an excellent and varied menu, once you sit down you may have trouble getting up again.

Nearby Lewes is a very interesting town, well worth a visit in its own right. If you get stuck for accommodation in the village, it has plenty more options. If you can't face the 2-mile walk, ask nicely at the pub for someone to call you a cab.

Day 7: Kingston-near-Lewes to Alfriston
5–7 hours, 12 miles (19.5km)
On this penultimate day, the route finally leaves the spine of the Downs behind. It's a simply spectacular farewell.

From Kingston-near-Lewes you stride along a gently undulating route, with a few short, sharp dips and rises, enjoying your last extensive views north over the Weald before dropping down to skirt the little village of Southease. In nearby Rodmell, the **Abergavenny Arms** (☎ 01273-472416; mains £6-12; ✷ lunch daily, dinner Mon-Sat) does good pub food. Although it's only 5 miles from Kingston, there are few other options for lunch. About 2 miles south is **Telscombe YHA Hostel** (☎ 01273-301357; www.yha.org.uk; Bank Cottages; dm £12).

From Southease the trail follows a lane over flat floodplains then across the surprisingly large River Ouse on a bridge. Southease train station also comes as a surprise, but the hourly trains are handy for accessing Lewes or Brighton.

It's a tough haul up the east side of the valley, before a final stroll along the tops and a descent into Alfriston.

THE LEWES REVOLUTIONARY

Tom Paine, a major intellectual inspiration for the American Revolution, lived at Bull House, 92 High St, and expounded his ideas to the Headstrong Club at the **White Hart Hotel** (☎ 01273-476694; www.whitehartlewes .co.uk; 55 High St; s/d £65/94), where you can still see a copy of the *Declaration of Independence*. His seminal work, *Rights Of Man*, was written in defence of the French Revolution, and he later had a hand in drafting the French constitution.

Ironically, Lewes is also well known for its events celebrating the execution of another would-be revolutionary. More than 70,000 people turn out annually to watch Lewes' bonfires on 5 November, marking the foiling of the 1605 plot by Guy Fawkes to blow up parliament.

In another American connection, John Harvard, founder of the American university of the same name, also lived here.

ALFRISTON

At risk of sounding like a broken record, Alfriston ticks all the 'quaint' boxes, just like other villages on the route, but somehow outdoes them all in sheer English, chocolate-box cuteness. The high street is a procession of characterful pubs lined up like choirboys in front of a Norman church with a grassy moat, for heaven's sake!

Even the **Alfriston YHA Hostel** (☎ 01323-870423; www.yha.org.uk; Frog Firle; dm/d/tr £17/38/46), about 1 mile from the village centre, is housed in a Tudor flint cottage.

Only three houses from the SDW, **5 The Broadway** (☎ 01323-870145; janetandbrian@dingley56 35.freeserve.co.uk; s/d £30/60) is a walker-friendly B&B.

Chestnuts (☎ 01323-870298; 8 High St; s/tw/d £35/48/55, lunch £3-7) is in a rambling 18th-century house with shared facilities, and doubles as tearooms.

Dating from 1397, the **George Inn** (☎ 01323-870319; www.thegeorge-alfriston.com; High St; s £50, d £80-120, mains £10-15; ✷ lunch & dinner) is a spectacularly character-filled place to spend your last village night. It also serves candlelit meals, ranging from pork belly to tofu with noodles. Across the road, the **Star Inn** (☎ 01323-870495; www.star-inn-alfriston.com; High St; s £69-109, d £98-158, 2-course meal £23; ✷ lunch & dinner),

THE LONG MAN OF WILMINGTON

Carved into the chalk-face around 2 miles east of Alfriston, the Long Man of Wilmington stands nearly 70m tall, looking rather like an enthusiastic English rambler holding oversized walking poles. In 1874 the outline was lined with bricks to maintain the image. These had to be painted green during WWII to prevent German planes using it for navigation, and eventually they were replaced with white-painted concrete blocks, which are repainted annually.

The jury is still out on his age, purpose and what he's holding in his hands. Were they once tools, Roman standards, spears, or is he standing in a doorway? Has he been standing there since the Iron Age (somebody get the man a chair)? Does shagging on his outline increase the chance of conception (as suggested by some neo-pagans)?

Given the ambiguity, we can adopt him as the first SDW walker with impunity. And shagging on his outline couldn't really hurt, either. The best view of our man is from the road leading into Wilmington village, a 45-minute walk from Alfriston.

with its frontage covered in wonderful painted wooden carvings of dragons, saints and serpents, is around the same age and reputedly haunted. There are a few character rooms remaining, but there is a chain hotel feel to the remainder.

By comparison, the upmarket Victorian villa **Wingrove House** (☎ 01323-870276; www .wingrovehousehotel.com; tw £95, d £120-150, mains £11-15; ☺ lunch Tue-Sun, dinner Tue-Sat) is a youngster – it has a great terrace for summer dining.

There are more ghost stories associated with Ye Old Smugglers Inne on Waterloo Sq and Deans Place, once a moated manor house and now an expensive hotel. A common ghost story throughout the Downs is of ghostly black dogs with red eyes wandering the paths at night.

Day 8: Alfriston to Eastbourne

4–6 hours, 12 miles (19.5km)
You have (if only in principle) a choice today. You could take the inland bridleway, but this is best left to mountain bikers. Or you can follow the walkers' route, which, with an exhilarating finale along the cliff tops, is undoubtedly the better option.

The trail leaves Alfriston from the old Market Sq and crosses the River Cuckmere. Where the bridleway goes straight on, you go right and south along the riverbank to Litlington, then through the woodland of Seven Sisters Country Park to rejoin the Cuckmere at Exceat – the park visitor centre, with toilets and a **café**. The trail then continues south with views over the meandering river. You pass near **Foxhole Bottom Camping Barn** (☎ 01323-870280; www.sevensisters .org.uk; sites for 2 £5, dm £8), where you can pitch a tent or sleep in the dorm. Bookings are recommended.

Route and river meet the open sea at Cuckmere Haven, where the home stretch lies before you. Turning east to follow the coast, the trail soon climbs steeply to the crest of Haven Brow, the first of the **Seven Sisters** cliffs (there are, in fact, eight but this doesn't alliterate so neatly). With stagger-

THE BEST BITS

If you want to get a feel for the South Downs but you have only a couple of days to spare, the most spectacular section is at the end. One option is to catch the train via Lewes to Southease and pick up the itinerary partway through Day 7, overnighting in Alfriston before heading on to Eastbourne.

An alternative is to follow a circular route, starting in Eastbourne and heading north through Jevington (allegedly the home of the banoffee pie), continuing over the head of the Long Man of Wilmington (see the boxed text, above) and down into Alfriston. This follows the official alternative part of the trail that bikes and horses are required to take. The next day, continue on the Day 8 itinerary back to Eastbourne.

Both these options give something of the essence of the walk: some excellent downland ridge walking, an overnight stay in a pretty village and the finale of the Seven Sisters cliffs.

ing views over the English Channel, the Sisters can't fail to thrill.

About halfway along, you'll pass the small hamlet of Birling Gap. Press on to **Beachy Head**, where the Downs finally tumble into the sea. Here the candy-striped lighthouse below makes a fine landmark for the end of the route, and the nearby **Beachy Head Pub** (☎ 01323-728060; Beachy Head Rd; mains £6-12; ✆ lunch & dinner) may tempt you for a celebratory pint or meal.

Savour all this because the official end of the trail, a couple of miles further on at the edge of Eastbourne, beside a snack bar, is a complete anticlimax. For a proper finish, continue along the promenade and proudly put down your backpack at the end of Eastbourne's fine **19th-century pier**.

THE SOUTH WEST COAST PATH (PADSTOW TO FALMOUTH)

Duration	14 days
Distance	168 miles (268km)
Difficulty	moderate–demanding
Start	Padstow (p136)
Finish	Falmouth (p136)
Transport	bus, train

Summary An inspiring, invigorating and sometimes strenuous journey that includes cliff tops, beaches and resort towns, plus some rural inland sections.

Always exhilarating and with ever-changing views, the South West Coast Path (SWCP) is a tough proposition, but the rewards are plentiful. This is Britain's longest national trail – 630 miles (1014km) – and one of the longest continuous footpaths in the country. It follows the coast of the Southwest Peninsula from Minehead in Somerset, along the north Devon coast and around Cornwall, turning the corner at Land's End on the way. After Cornwall the SWCP traces its way along the south Devon coast to Poole in Dorset.

The Cornwall section of the SWCP is the most popular, not least because of the drama and beauty of the county's coastline. From Padstow to Falmouth is a particularly beautiful part and is described here in detail. (The other sections of the SWCP are outlined briefly in the boxed text on p134.) The views along the way are often breath-

taking. The cornucopia of dramatic cliffs, sandy beaches, remote coves, ancient burial chambers, castles, disused mineral mines and engine houses, plus the chance of spotting seals, dolphins and a wide range of bird life, makes binoculars a necessity.

ENVIRONMENT

About two-thirds of this beautiful coastline is designated Heritage Coast and one-third is in the care of the National Trust. The trail passes through several Areas of Outstanding Natural Beauty and Areas of Special Scientific Interest. One section skirts the Exmoor National Park, while the mining coasts of West Cornwall are part of a World Heritage Site. Adding balance to all this wilderness splendour are the several large seaside resorts, picturesque fishing villages and working ports through which the trail passes.

Bird life along the coast is particularly impressive. There are chances of spotting peregrine falcons as well as a range of sea birds, including gannets, fulmars, kittiwakes and guillemots. On the north coast of the Land's End Peninsula, and in the Lizard area, Cornwall's 'national' symbol, the glossy-black, red-beaked, red-legged chough, has been reintroduced and is reported as having bred successfully, although sightings are still rare (but enthralling). Seals, dolphins and huge basking sharks are often seen close inshore, especially in the far west.

Cornwall's wildflower extravaganza is outstanding in spring and summer. Expect acres of pink thrift and creamy bladder campion, and a palette of purple heather, yellow gorse, orchids, squill, wild carrot and foxgloves.

PLANNING

Accommodation, food and drink are often found just off the trail, but there are sections where there are no conveniences for several miles at a time. It's essential to book accommodation in advance for Easter, July and August. We have quoted average prices in this section, but some places charge more in August and sometimes less in winter.

The route is well served by camp sites (some open only from Easter to October), YHA hostels and several independent backpackers hostels.

The trail is waymarked with national-trail acorn symbols, but these are often missing. Transiting towns and large villages can be complicated in a few instances. Junctions with other paths crossing the area can sometimes be confusing; careful checking of maps is strongly advised.

GPS-based measurement, by the authoritative and well-informed South West Coast Path Association (SWCPA), of the trail as described here gives a distance of 168 miles (268km). Accurate distance over the ground is only half the story, however; the coastline of the Southwest Peninsula is a

---

THE SOUTH WEST COAST PATH

The 600-mile (966km) South West Coast Path is one of the longest routes in Britain, usually divided into four handy sections – each of them considerable undertakings in their own right. We describe the Padstow-to-Falmouth section in this chapter. If you're thinking of doing the whole thing, these basic outlines will be useful.

Minehead to Padstow

Passing through a part of Somerset, along the coast of north Devon and into north Cornwall, this section leads from the official start of the SWCP at the seaside resort of Minehead, whose delights are soon left behind as you enter Exmoor National Park, where steep, hogback hills make for strenuous coastal walking.

The delightful Devon villages of Lynton and Lynmouth soon follow and then the steepness eases as you head for Ilfracombe, the exclamatory Westward Ho! and lovely Clovelly, perched like a postcard on steep cliffs.

Cornwall greets you with more high cliffs that relent at the popular beach resort of Bude before rising again at Tintagel, where dramatic ruins are awash with Arthurian fancy. From here a beautiful, lonely coast leads to tiny Port Isaac and then the village of Rock and a ferry across the River Camel to Padstow.

Padstow to Falmouth

This section of the SWCP is covered in the main walk description in this book, beginning on p133.

Falmouth to Exmouth

From Falmouth, you can cross by ferry to St Mawes, before heading along the delightful Roseland Peninsula to the archetypal fishing village of Mevagissey.

The popular resorts of Fowey, Polperro and Looe follow and then you reach Cornwall's border at the River Tamar and a ferry from Cremyll to bustling Plymouth. Beyond the city the trail leads to Bigbury-on-Sea and the South Devon Heritage Coast, through pretty Bantham, the busy yacht haven of Salcombe, and then on to delightful Dartmouth, where a ferry crosses the River Dart to Kingswear. The trail then takes you to Brixham and the busy resorts of Torquay, Teignmouth and Dawlish, and finally the broad estuary of the River Exe to end at Exmouth.

Exmouth to Poole

This section leads along the coast of east Devon, with the SWCP rambling pleasantly above red sandstone cliffs and through the resorts of Budleigh Salterton, Sidmouth and Seaton before passing through the deeply wooded 'Undercliffs' to reach Dorset at Lyme Regis.

East again is pretty, thatched Abbotsbury, with its unique swannery. The next feature is Chesil Beach, a huge curving bank of stones, which eventually leads you to Portland Bill and the large town of Weymouth.

East of Weymouth there's more stunning coastal scenery at Lulworth Cove, Kimmeridge Bay and Durlston Head until the resort of Swanage is reached. A short hop north from here is Studland Point – the official end of the SWCP – from where a ferry ride brings you to Poole and a well-deserved journey's end.

gloriously corrugated and undulating entity and the SWCP includes numerous steep ascents and descents where streams and rivers slice their way to the sea and where sandy bays bite into the land. Brace yourself for a glorious switchbacking trek and toss the slimming diets out the window – you'll lose plenty of weight just walking this route.

Fit, experienced walkers can cover the distance in two weeks, although you might want to add a few more days to spread the load, or for sightseeing. For a 14-day walk the following is an ideal itinerary:

Day	From	To	Miles/km
1	Padstow	Treyarnon	10.9/17.5
2	Treyarnon	Newquay	12.8/20.5
3	Newquay	Perranporth	10.9/17.5
4	Perranporth	Portreath	12.5/19.6
5	Portreath	St Ives	17.9/28.7
6	St Ives	Pendeen	13.9/22.5
7	Pendeen	Sennen Cove	9.3/14.6
8	Sennen Cove	Porthcurno	6.8/10.6
9	Porthcurno	Penzance	11.8/18.6
10	Penzance	Porthleven	13.9/22.4
11	Porthleven	Lizard	14/22.4
12	Lizard	Coverack	10.4/16.7
13	Coverack	Helford	13.6/21.4
14	Helford	Falmouth	9.3/14.8

Alternatives

A worthwhile shorter section is the stretch from St Ives to Lizard Point. It takes in some of Britain's finest coastline in just five days. You can also do single-day linear sections of the SWCP, or a circular day route, taking in a stretch of the main route. From about Easter to mid-September seasonal buses often link points convenient to the coast path.

When to Walk

The route can be walked at any time of the year, but the best period is from April to September. In winter, conditions underfoot can be very wet and muddy in places. Severe gales should be expected during winter.

Cornwall's main tourist season is Easter to the end of September, and some B&Bs and cafés close outside this time.

Maps

The OS Explorer 1:25,000 maps are by far the best maps for this section of the SWCP. They show contours and field boundaries that often adjoin the path and make navigation easier. The relevant maps are Nos 106 *Newquay & Padstow,* 104 *Redruth & St Agnes,* 102 *Land's End & Isles of Scilly* and 103 *The Lizard, Falmouth & Helston.*

Books

The very useful *South West Coast Path Guide,* produced every year by the SWCPA, features a route outline, accommodation lists, transport information, planning tips and even tide tables. For step-by-step details on the route, the SWCPA produces a series of *Path Description* leaflets. Both the guide and leaflets are available from the **SWCPA administrator** (☎ 01752-896237; info@swcp.org.uk; Bowker House, Lee Mill Bridge, Ivybridge, Devon PL21 9EF).

The official National Trail Guide is the *South West Coast Path – Padstow to Falmouth* by John Macadam. Also recommended is *Cornwall Coast Path* by Edith Schofield (updated by Jim Manthorpe), covering the route from Bude to Padstow and on to Falmouth, with thorough text and very detailed line maps that are hand-drawn and include useful details on difficult junctions and sections of the route. It also covers useful sleeping and eating options.

The National Trust publishes an excellent series of *Coast of Cornwall* leaflets, giving fascinating details about parts of the walk that traverse National Trust property; they're available from tourist offices. Those of particular relevance to the Cornwall coast route are Nos 8 to 16.

Accommodation

In Cornwall, most B&Bs have only double rooms. For single accommodation in a double room, it is best to check ahead on price.

Information Sources

See the walk description for tourist offices on or near the route. The website of the indomitable **SWCPA** (www.swcp.org.uk) is full of information about all aspects of the route, and even includes a photo 'tour' of the entire trail.

The official national trails website for the SWCP is www.nationaltrail.co.uk/south westcoastpath. It offers some excellent general information and regular updates, as well as accommodation and other relevant websites.

Baggage & Pick-up Services

Several B&Bs along the route will arrange baggage transport to your next destination, usually for around £6 to £10. Within reason, some establishments will pick up and deliver walkers from and to a convenient point on the coast path. Ask about these services when you book.

NEAREST TOWNS
Padstow
pop 2450

The old fishing port of Padstow is located on the west bank of the broad, sandy expanse of the Camel Estuary. Fishing still plays a part in the town's vibrant, colourful life, although tourism is now a major industry, enhanced by Padstow's picturesque harbour and narrow, wriggling streets and alleyways. The **tourist office** (☎ 01841-533449; www.padstowlive.com; North Quay) is very helpful and friendly, reflecting Padstow's popularity.

SLEEPING & EATING

The tourist office offers a useful book-a-bed-ahead scheme for coast-path walkers.

For a budget option, **Dennis Cove Camping** (☎ 01841-532349; www.denniscove.co.uk; sites for 2 £16) is on the south side of town, close to the river-side Camel Trail and cycleway.

Worthwhile B&Bs include **Woodlands Close** (☎ 01841-533109; john@stock65.freeserve.co.uk; Treator; d £50), located just over 800m from the coast path; **Hemingford House** (☎ 01841-532806; www.padstow-bb.co.uk; 21 Grenville St; d from £60), where the owner has good information on walking; and the charming **Kellacott**

(☎ 01841-532851; shaunrevely@compuserve.com; 29 Church St; s/d £30/50).

Padstow is high in the culinary firmament thanks to the stellar reputation of celebrity chef Rick Stein, whose **Seafood Restaurant** (☎ 01841-532700; Riverside; meals £40-85) offers equally starry fare at starry prices. There are numerous other fine eating places around the town as well as plenty of snackeries.

GETTING THERE & AWAY

The nearest train station to Padstow is Bodmin Parkway, from where buses go to Padstow (55 minutes, 14 services Monday to Saturday, five Sunday). **National Express** (☎ 08705 808080; www.nationalexpress.com) has regular coach services from London and other parts of the country to Wadebridge (seven hours); local buses connect from Wadebridge to Padstow (25 minutes, nine daily Monday to Saturday, five on Sunday).

If travelling by car, Padstow is reached by following the A389 west from the A30 at Bodmin, bypassing Wadebridge on the A39, and then taking the A389 once more.

Cornwall County Council's (☎ 01872-322003; www.cornwall.gov.uk/buses) summer and winter bus timetables also contain very useful river ferry information. Copies of this and a *Public Transport: Map & Frequency* guide can be had from local bus stations and tourist offices, or direct from the council.

Falmouth
pop 28,800

Friendly, bustling Falmouth has a formidable history, not least because its huge

---

WARNINGS

Never assume at an unsigned junction that the path closest to the sea is the one to follow. Old mining tracks, livestock trails and paths used by sea anglers and others often lead seaward and into sometimes-dangerous ground.

There are three river crossings encountered on this section of the South West Coast Path (SWCP). Some can be crossed by stepping stones or by wading. Others are crossed by ferries, which may only run at high tide. Local shops stock current tide tables. Wading across rivers at low tide can save a lot of mileage but do so only when conditions are right; in the wrong conditions it can be fatal. Tides do not just rise and fall; they flood, and can be very fast and dangerous. They also vary substantially from day to day throughout the cycle of neap (low) tides and spring (high) tides. Check locally.

Many beaches shelve suddenly and have strong currents. Flags mark safe places to swim and lifeguards are sometimes on duty. If in doubt, stay out.

There is little shade on the SWCP, so in hot weather make sure you carry enough drinking water. Keep well in from cliff edges in high winds.

estuary: the Carrack Roads is the world's third-largest natural harbour. Ship repairs still go on at Falmouth Docks and the town is the venue for the splendid **National Maritime Centre** (☎ 01326-313388; www.nmmc .co.uk; Discovery Quay; adult/child £7/5), a celebration of Britain's seagoing heritage. Falmouth's helpful **tourist office** (☎ 01326-312300; Killigrew St) has masses of local information.

SLEEPING & EATING
A good budget bet, just off the southern seafront, is **Falmouth Lodge Backpackers** (☎ 01326-319996; www.falmouthbackpackers.co.uk; 9 Gyllyngvase Tce; dm/s/d £15/19/34).

Good-value B&Bs include **Castle Crest** (☎ 01326-313572; www.cornwall-online.co.uk/castle -crest; 23 Castle Dr; s/d £27/54), with views across Falmouth Bay.

Nearer the centre is the comfy **Ivanhoe** (☎ 01326-319083; www.ivanhoe-guesthouse.co.uk; 7 Melvill Rd; s/d £24/54); **Melvill House** (☎ 01326-316645; melvillehouse@btconnect.com; 52 Melvill Rd; d from £54); and the walker-friendly **Rosemary** (☎ 01326-314669; www.rosemaryhotel.co.uk; 22 Gyllyngvase Tce; d from £64).

For food, Falmouth's main drag is awash with decent eateries and pubs, one of the best being the colourful and central **Kings Head** (☎ 01326 319469; Church St; meals £4-10; ☺ lunch & dinner) pub.

GETTING THERE & AWAY
Falmouth is linked by rail branch line to Truro's mainline station (20 minutes, hourly Monday to Saturday). Regular buses run between Truro and Falmouth (45 minutes, five daily Monday to Saturday). For something completely different, ferries operate between Truro and Falmouth (one hour five daily Monday to Saturday May to September) on the scenic Truro River.

THE WALK
Day 1: Padstow to Treyarnon
4–6 hours, 10.9 miles (17.5km)
This stage is a fairly easy introduction, but also a taster for the general robustness of the path to come.

The route leaves Padstow harbour near the tourist office on North Quay and winds up to the headland of St Saviour's Point, where there is a granite war memorial. Descend to St George's Cove and Hawker's Cove then climb to the circular Pepperpot

Tower, a navigational 'day mark' on **Stepper Point**, from where there are superb views.

Next comes Butter Hole Cove and Gunver Head, with views of the rocky offshore stacks of the Merope Islands. On the grassy slopes just inland from the coast path at Roundhole Point is the spectacular **Round Hole**, a gaping void caused by the collapse of the upper roof of a sea cave. It is well away from the path, but be careful if you approach its rim. The main path leads securely downhill to Trevone car park and a nearby **café**.

Just inland at Trevone is the **Well Parc Hotel** (☎ 01841-520318; www.wellparc.co.uk; meals £6-11; ☺ lunch & dinner; ◻) From Trevone the trail follows the coastline round to the beach at Harlyn Bay, where you can camp at the well-run **Higher Harlyn Caravan Park** (☎ 01841-520022; pbharlyn@aol.com; sites for 2 £16) or get B&B at the handy **Harlyn Inn** (☎ 01841-520207; www .harlyn-inn.com; s/d £42/64).

From Harlyn the path continues to Trevose Head lighthouse and then sniffs its way round Stinking Cove (odour-free in fact) before turning south above the surfing beach of Constantine Bay to reach Treyarnon.

TREYARNON
At this little beachside village the **YHA hostel** (☎ 0870 770 6076; www.yha.org.uk; Tregonnan; dm £16) is the best bet, or there's camping at the **Treyarnon Bay Caravan and Camping Park** (☎ 01841-520681; www.treyarnonbay.co.uk; sites for 2 £12). There is a beach-side **café** as well.

Day 2: Treyarnon to Newquay
5–7 hours, 12.8 miles (20.5km)
This is a moderately tough day's walking, but always with superb views, bracing air and constant interest.

From Treyarnon Bay the trail follows a series of headlands to Porthcothan and then makes a short, steep crossing of Porth Mear valley before rising to the cliff top again to reach **Park Head**. About 800m further on you reach the cliff top above the spectacular **Bedruthan Steps**, a series of rock stacks on the beach, a popular tourist attraction since Victorian times. On the flat cliff top there is a car park, toilets and a National Trust shop and **café**. There are good viewpoints from where you can see the rock formations. These include Queen Bess Rock, which, before its royal head wore away, was said to resemble the Tudor Elizabeth I – who otherwise kept her head, in every way.

The SWCP continues along the cliff top to Mawgan Porth, where the **Merrymoor Inn** (☎ 01637-860258; www.merrymoorinn.com; d £50) has decent accommodation and also does filling bar meals.

From here the trail heads south for 2 miles along the cliff top above the famous surfing beach of Watergate Bay. At the end of the beach the path makes a small sidestep across the neck of Trevelgue Head, where there are the extensive remains of a prehistoric cliff **castle**. The SWCP continues round St Columb Porth Beach and along the cliff

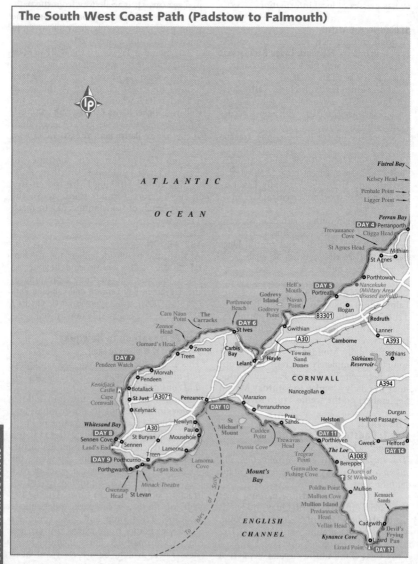

The South West Coast Path (Padstow to Falmouth)

edge until it joins Lusty Glaze Rd and then enters brash, breezy, lusty and often glazed, but always bountiful, Newquay.

NEWQUAY
pop 19,570

Newquay, major holiday resort and Surf Centre UK, is a colourful culture shock

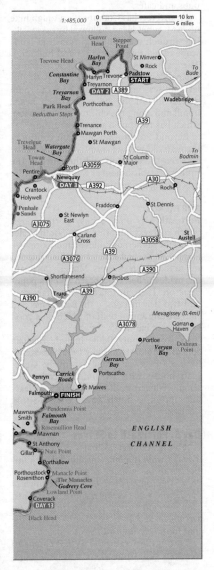

after miles of fairly remote coast walking. Its pedigree is pure Old Cornwall, however. Once known as Porth Lystry, the 'boat beach', it acquired a 'new quay' or harbour in the 15th century to cope with pilchard fishing and the export of copper and china clay. The biggest and most accessible beaches in Cornwall made it inevitable that Newquay would become the major resort that it is today. Embrace it for what it is.

There is a huge choice of B&Bs, although you'll still need to book ahead in summer – the **tourist office** (☎ 01637-854020; www.newquay .co.uk; Marcus Hill), in the council offices, can advise.

There's camping at well-equipped **Trenance Caravan & Chalet Park** (☎ 01637-873447; www.trenanceholidaypark.co.uk; Edgcumbe Ave; sites for 2 £14), and budget walkers can head for **Newquay International Backpackers** (☎ 01637-879366; www.backpackers.co.uk/newquay; 73 Tower Rd; dm £17) or **Fistral Backpackers** (☎ 01637-873146; www.fis tralbackpackers.co.uk; 18 Headland Rd; dm/d £16/34).

Newquay is crowded with eating places, many of them fast-food and budget. For chow with the stars try **Fifteen** (☎ 01637-86100; Watergate Beach; set-menu lunch £24, dinner around £50), opened in 2006 by celebrity chef Jamie Oliver.

Day 3: Newquay to Perranporth
4–6 hours, 10.9 miles (17.5km)

A tough day's walking begins with a crossing of the River Gannel, where the tide and the time of year decree how far upstream you have to go. Plan your day carefully.

Leave the bright lights of Newquay behind and follow the main road to the harbour. From here the SWCP goes up steps and on round Towan Head and above Fistral Beach, another major surfing venue, to reach the suburb of Pentire. Ahead lies the tidal estuary of the River Gannel. There are several options for crossing here. Consult tide tables carefully and seek local advice. The most seaward crossing is at Fern Pit, where there is a **café** and a footbridge that can be used at low tide only. At high tide there is a **ferry** (☎ 01637-873181), running between 10am and 6pm from late May to mid-September. When the café is closed both footbridge and ferry are not available. The 'official' public right of way crossing of the Gannel is about 800m upstream from

Fern Pit. Here, off Trevean Way, another footbridge, available at low tide all year, leads to Penpol on the south side of the river. At high tide there is a **ferry** (☎ 01637-873181) here; operating times are as for the Fern Pit ferry. If none of the above options is available, the alternative is a detour inland by road that adds about 4 miles to your journey and is not much fun. Think tidal.

Once across the estuary, pass by a National Trust car park, where there are toilets and a seasonal **café**, and then stroll across the grassy Rushy Green with its seaward sand dunes above the attractive Crantock Beach. The path then twirls its way round Pentire Point West and the lovely sea inlet of Porth Joke, where the slopes are swathed with vivid wildflowers in early summer.

The trail continues southwards past the little beach resort of Holywell, where there are toilets, cafés and shops. It then climbs to Penhale Point and skirts the military establishment of Penhale Camp – keep a careful check on signposting here – and then runs between the long expanse of Perran Beach and the inland Penhale Sands.

PERRANPORTH

A very big beach is Perranporth's very big asset. Otherwise it's a small resort, but with food stores, tourist shops, cafés and very big numbers of happy holidaymakers in summer.

At Droskyn Point, west of the village centre, the **YHA hostel** (☎ 0870 770 5994; perranporth@yha .org.uk; dm £14) is in a fabulous position, as befits a former coastguard station.

Walker-friendly B&Bs include **Chy an Kerensa** (☎ 01872-572470; wendychy@aol.com; Cliff Rd; s/d £28/55) and **Cliffside Hotel** (☎ 01872-573297; www.cliffsideperranporth.co.uk; Cliff Rd; d £60), both by the path and with comfy rooms and great views.

For a big choice of bar food and meals the **Watering Hole** (☎ 01872-572888; meals £8-13; ☺ lunch & dinner) is right on the beach.

Day 4: Perranporth to Portreath
5–7 hours, 12.5 miles (19.6km)
This stretch combines fairly easy walking along well-used cliff-top paths with stiffer sections where the trail dips into valleys. The final few miles to Portreath can be tiring.

From the Perranporth YHA Hostel at Droskyn Point, follow the signposted cliff

path that leads through old mine workings and quarried ground at **Cligga Head**.

The SWCP switchbacks through Trevellas Coombe and then into Trevaunance Cove, where there is a good **pub** and several B&Bs. Just inland is **St Agnes**, which has some attractive old houses and miners' cottages, a free museum and B&Bs, shops, pubs and cafés.

From Trevellas Coombe it's a tough hike up to St Agnes Head, followed by easy walking through a fascinating industrial landscape of old mine workings and buildings. The path then descends to the beach of Chapel Porth, where there is a car park, toilets and seasonal **café**. From here the route diverts inland for 200m and then heads uphill and along the cliff top to **Porthtowan**, which has two pubs, a café and a shop.

Beyond Porthtowan, the path continues through old mining country and then runs between the cliff top and the fence of the military establishment at Nancekuke before descending to Portreath.

PORTREATH

Portreath was once a busy port through which coal was imported from South Wales to fuel the numerous mines of mid-Cornwall. Copper ore from the mines was then shipped out to the Welsh smelters. Modern Portreath has made the best of its beach and is a popular resort. There are toilets, shops, a takeaway and two decent pubs – the **Basset Arms** and the **Portreath Arms** – both of which do a good selection of bar meals.

Walker-friendly B&Bs include **Fountain Springs** (☎ 01209-842650; www.fountainsprings.co.uk; Glenfeadon House; s/d £35/56), a lovely Georgian house with balconied facades; it's about 400m from the trail. Another pleasant option is **Sandy Acres** (☎ 01209-843608; j.klineberg@virgin.net; Green Lane; d from £50).

Day 5: Portreath to St Ives
8–10 hours, 17.9 miles (28.7km)
Today's walk is a long one, but after an initial climb the walking is generally flat and easy. The route passes through the town of Hayle where an overnight stop can be made. However, after some road walking, the next section to St Ives is not overly demanding and from Lelant onwards is scenic.

Leaving Portreath, the SWCP climbs to Western Hill, from where it runs through the flat heathland of Carvannel Downs and Reskajeage Downs, with fine views out to sea. The B3301 runs close to the cliff tops here, and at Hell's Mouth, a dramatic cleft in the vast slate cliffs, the path and road nudge each other on the edge of the gulf. There is a small road-side **café** here, mainly open in summer and at weekends. The path then heads away from the road to Navax Point and Godrevy Point, with its offshore lighthouse, inspiration for Virginia Woolf's novel *To the Lighthouse*.

The SWCP skirts the picturesque village of Gwithian, with its handsome old church and several thatched buildings. Waymarks lead for a tough 3-mile slog through Towans Sand Dunes, although at low tide you can walk on the beach.

At the end of the beach the route swings inland and follows roads for a couple of miles through the town of Hayle. Decent B&B options in Hayle include **Mrs Cooper** (☎ 01736-752855; 54 Penpol Tce; d from £50) and **Penpol Bed & Breakfast** (☎ 01736-754484; 34 Penpol Tce; d £50).

From Hayle's outskirts the route follows roads to Lelant village, from where a lane leads to Lelant church and then across a golf course to reach the coast. The trail runs beside the St Ives branch-line railway above Porthkidney Sands and above low, wooded cliffs to Carbis Bay and, finally, St Ives.

ST IVES
pop 9870
St Ives is one of the West Country's most appealing resorts. The harbour area of Down'long is a warren of narrow, cobbled streets and alleyways that wriggle to and fro past flower-bedecked courtyards and always

seem to lead to the broad harbour, where small fishing boats still work from the granite arm of Smeaton's Pier. The town also boasts two major beaches of silken sand: the sheltered Porthminster and the friskier surfing beach of Porthmeor on the north side of town. As if all this was not enough, art has taken a grip of St Ives in a big way, as exemplified by the bone-white, neoclassical façade of the **Tate St Ives** (☎ 01736-796226; www.tate.org.uk/stives; adult £6; ☺ 10am-5.30pm daily Mar-Oct, to 4.30pm Tue-Sun Nov-Mar) gallery above Porthmeor Beach.

During July and August the town is packed and prices can be higher here than in less-favoured resorts. The helpful **tourist office** (☎ 01736-796297) is in the Guildhall in the town centre.

For campers there's the excellent **Ayr Holiday Park** (☎ 01736-795855; www.ayrholidaypark.co.uk; sites for 2 £15) about 800m uphill from Porthmeor Beach and with great views.

Good sleeping options are the bright and friendly **Gowerton** (☎ 01736-796805; www.gowerton guesthouse.co.uk; 6 Sea View Pl; d £60), in a great position overlooking the harbour near the old quay; **Carlyon Guest House** (☎ 01736-795317; www.carlyon-stives.co.uk; The Terrace; d £60); and the lovely **Tamarisk** (☎ 01736-797201; www.tamarisk-bb .co.uk; Burthallan Lane; d from £50).

For harbour-side tradition the **Sloop Inn** (☎ 01736-796584; www.sloop-inn.co.uk; s/d £64/92, mains £5-10; ☺ breakfast, lunch & dinner) has comfy rooms and offers a range of food, from sandwiches and baguettes to meals.

Also near the harbour, in the old part of town, is the flower-heavy **Grey Mullet** (☎ 01736-796635; www.touristnetuk.com/sw/greymullet; 2 Bunkers Hill; s/d £25/56).

AS I WAS GOING TO THE WRONG ST IVES...

The famous song, *'As I was going to St. Ives, I met a man with seven wives'*, refers to St Ives in Cambridgeshire and not the Cornish St Ives. The two towns are often confused. There are apocryphal stories of delivery drivers from London and the north arriving at St Ives, Cornwall, only to discover they had come to the wrong town. Some never left...

St Ives owes its name to the Christian Irishwoman, Ia, who is said to have sailed across the Irish Sea in the 5th or 6th century on an ivy leaf, a fanciful tale that may be based on the fact that the substantial coracle-style vessels used at the time had hulls of interleaved hides. Ia built a chapel and then converted the neighbouring Romano-British ravers to Christianity. After her death, the village that developed round her chapel became known as Porth Ia and then Sancte Ye and then St Ives.

Other Cornish saints did the trip on similar apocryphal craft: St Piran zipped across on a millstone; St Newquay (had there been one) would surely have made it on a surfboard.

St Ives harbour-side is well stocked with fast-food outlets and snack bars, while there are numerous restaurants scattered throughout the adjoining streets.

Day 6: St Ives to Pendeen
7–9 hours, 13.9 miles (22.5km)

This is one of the most scenic and rugged sections of the SWCP, though it has no handy refreshment points. It's worth considering splitting the route by stopping overnight at Zennor or Treen, both about 800m inland, and both with sleeping and eating options. The more leisurely pace of this option gives you extra time to enjoy the unsurpassed cliff scenery, bird-watching and wildflower spotting. Take plenty of water and some food.

From above Porthmeor Beach, keep left of the toilet block in the small car park and continue to Man's Head, where the wilder coast begins. The trail now winds its way delightfully along the top of jet-black greenstone cliffs, with steep dips into the coves that slice into the land and with some tough uphill sections. A steep climb leads to dramatic Zennor Head, from where a path and narrow lane lead 800m inland to Zennor village.

If you want to break at this stage (6.5 miles from St Ives), the **Old Chapel Backpackers** (☎ 01736-798313; zennorbackpackers@btinternet.com; Zennor; camp sites for 2 £9, dm £15) also has a café serving breakfast, snacks and lunches. Just up the road is the friendly farmhouse B&B of **Trewey Farm** (☎ 01736-796936; d £56). The nearby **Tinners Arms** (☼ lunch & dinner) pub does excellent bar meals.

From Zennor Head the SWCP continues along the cliff top to the knuckle-like Gurnard's Head, once the site of an Iron Age promontory fort. Another potential overnight stop is the hamlet of Treen, about 800m inland from Gurnard's Head. A handy B&B is **Treen Farm** (☎ 01736-796932; d from £50). About 100m away, up on the main road, is the **Gurnard's Head Hotel** (☎ 01736-796928; www.gurnardshead.co.uk; s/d £50/83, dinner mains £9-16; ☼ lunch & dinner), which has bright, cheerful décor to go with comfy rooms and great food.

Beyond Gurnard's Head the path drops into lonely Porthmeor Cove, from where there is some steep uphill walking to the magnificent Bosigran headland with its west-facing cliffs that plunge 300ft into Porth-

moina Cove. There's a steep descent and ascent across the slopes of Porthmoina Cove, after which the trail winds along the lonely cliffs of Morvah and then passes above Portheras Beach to reach the **lighthouse** at the headland of Pendeen Watch. From here, lanes lead 1 mile inland to Pendeen village.

PENDEEN

Decent B&B options include the **Radjel Inn** (☎ 01736-788446; d £50, meals around £12; ☼ lunch & dinner). The nearby **North Inn** (☎ 01736-788417; ernestjohncoak@aol.com; camp sites for 2 £6, d £60, bar meals £6-10; ☼ lunch & dinner), a popular real-ale bar, does B&B in an adjoining bungalow-style building.

Pendeen has a well-stocked village shop with a fish and chip shop next door.

Day 7: Pendeen to Sennen Cove
4–5 hours, 9.3 miles (14.6km)

Today's walk leads south towards Land's End, first through the heartland of mineral mining and along the edge of great cliffs to Cape Cornwall, and then dropping closer to sea level for the final section to Sennen's glorious golden beaches.

From Pendeen Watch the SWCP follows the cliff top through dramatic mine ruins. Just inland is **Geevor Tin Mine** (☎ 01736-788662; www.geevor.com; adult/child £8/5; ☼ 9am-5pm Sun-Fri), which closed as a working mine in 1990, the last coastal tin mine to do so. It is now an excellent heritage centre and is well worth a visit. Further south is Levant Mine and **Engine House**, where a refurbished beam engine, used for pumping water from deep mines, can be seen. Next come the twin engine houses of **Crowns Mine**, perched on top of dramatic cliffs. From these buildings a wagon incline once led into a tunnel mouth that gave access to miles of undersea workings. Close to the path is an arsenic labyrinth (see the boxed text, opposite).

Inland from the trail is Botallack village, which has eating and sleeping options if required. There's an excellent camp site about 200m from Botallack at **Trevaylor Touring Park** (☎ 01736-787016; www.trevaylor.com; sites for 2 £12; ☼ Mar-Nov). On the northern edge of Botallack is the lovely old farmhouse of **Manor Farm** (☎ 01736-788525; s/d £40/56). In Botallack is the **Queen's Arms** (☼ lunch) pub.

Beyond Botallack is the headland of **Kenidjack Castle**, the site of yet another Iron

Age promontory settlement. The path descends steeply into the Kenidjack or Tregeseal Valley, an area that is crammed with more mining ruins. In the valley bottom the path passes another arsenic labyrinth and then climbs steeply to cross the neck of the shapely Cape Cornwall.

From the Cape car park, the SWCP passes Carn Gloose and Ballowal Barrow, a Bronze Age entrance grave that is very well preserved through having been buried beneath mine waste for many years. From here a road leads for 1 mile to the town of St Just, where there are several B&Bs, pubs and shops, including a supermarket and a post office. A number of pubs in St Just offer bar meals in the £5 to £10 range. **Wellington Hotel** (☎ 01736-787319; Market Sq) is a good choice and there's also a popular **fish and chip shop** (Market Sq). The **Star Inn** (☎ 01736-788767; Fore St) is a great pub that often has folk music sessions and does good bar meals.

Beyond Ballowal the SWCP dips down into Cot Valley. From the valley head, the useful **Land's End YHA Hostel** (☎ 0870 770 5906; www.yha.org.uk; Letcha Vean, St Just; camp sites for 2 £7, dm £14) is only about 200m away.

The route continues easily from Cot Valley along the cliffs. It descends gradually to sea level and reaches the major surf beach of **Gwenver** and the adjoining **Whitesand Bay** beach. Both beaches have potentially dangerous currents, Gwenver especially. Always heed lifeguard advice. At the end of Whitesand Bay beach is the seafront village of Sennen Cove.

SENNEN COVE

This is one of the area's most popular small resorts, overwhelmed in summer but with its charm intact. It should not be confused with Sennen village, a less-cohesive settlement on the high ground above, and about 800m from the Cove by a steep road.

There's B&B at the friendly **Myrtle Cottage** (☎ 01736-871698; Old Coastguard Row; s/d £50/58). An excellent overnight choice is to continue through Sennen Cove and then take the path leading inland from just beyond the final car park to **Treeve Moor House** (☎ 01736-871284; www.firstandlastcottages.co.uk; s/d £40/60) for peaceful, charming rooms and a friendly welcome.

Uphill, about 1 mile from the Cove and on the A30, is the bright and welcoming **Whitesands Lodge** (☎ 01736-871776; www.white

sandshotel.co.uk; dm/d £18/50), incorporating the attractive **Whitesands Hotel** (☎ 01736-871776; s £40, d £60-95, meals £10-20; ☺ breakfast, lunch & dinner), which has a stylish restaurant.

There are several cafés and pubs in Sennen Cove, including the **Old Success Inn** (☎ 01736-871232), which does bar meals.

Day 8: Sennen Cove to Porthcurno
3–3½ hours, 6.8 miles (10.6km)

Today you pass a major milestone – Land's End, from where the path leads above beautiful bays and across magnificent headlands with towering granite cliffs that shine like gold in the sun. There are a couple of superb beaches as well, and in spring and early summer there's the bonus of swathes of golden daffodils and a glorious palette of wildflowers.

From Sennen Cove it's an easy jaunt along the cliff tops to **Land's End**, where the Land's End complex engulfs the mainly carborne crowds with all the grinding charm of 'themed' tourism. There are separate entrance fees to the various enclosed attractions at Land's End and there are several ticketing systems. There is no charge at all for simply walking about the headland, or entering the hotel bar and the various retail outlets. You do not have to pay the entrance fee by reaching the headland via the coastal footpath. Embrace it all for what it is, but do not expect to be at one with the wilderness here.

Staying at the comfortable **Land's End Hotel** (☎ 01736-871844; www.landsendhotel.co.uk; s/d £77/134, 3-course meal £20; ☺ dinner) gives you the chance to stroll around the headland in the evening after the crowds have gone. You can eat here, or in the nearby **Trenwith Arms** (☺ lunch & dinner).

Beyond Land's End, where casual strollers steadily dwindle, the well-marked coast path leads along the airy cliff tops above glittering seas. After about 3 miles the path climbs steeply to Gwennap Head and then down to tiny Porthgwarra Cove, where there is a small seasonal **café** and toilets. Another mile or so leads to **St Levan's holy well** above the lovely Porth Chapel beach, from where a path leads inland for about 200m to the delightful and secluded **Grey Gables** (☎ 01736-810421; d £62). Nearby is the lovely granite **church of St Levan**. From above Porth Chapel beach it's an 800m climb to the famous **Minack Theatre** (see the boxed text, below). From the theatre entrance, very steep steps and pathways descend directly to Porthcurno. The alternative is to walk by road from the theatre.

PORTHCURNO

The village of Porthcurno is a straggle of buildings running up a narrow valley from one of the finest beaches in Cornwall. Porthcurno Bay is lined with fine shell sand, golden and silky, and the waters of the bay are an Aegean blue in the summer sun. The beach shelves quickly in places so heed the lifeguard advice. The eastern side of the bay is enclosed by the stunning

granite headland of Treryn Dinas, known popularly as Logan Rock. Porthcurno's other famous feature is the **Porthcurno Telegraph Museum** (☎ 01736-810966; www.porthcurno .org.uk; adult/child £5/3), contained within underground WWII bunkers and detailing Porthcurno's remarkable history as a cable station serving the world through undersea cables that run out beneath the beach.

There's a **café** and pub close to the beach and places doing B&B include the **Wearhouse** (☎ 01736-810129; wearsue@aol.com; d £50) and the very welcoming **Seaview House** (☎ 01736-810638; www.seaviewhouseporthcurno.com; s/d £30/66, dinner £11-15; ☐), which has excellent evening meals.

Day 9: Porthcurno to Penzance

6–8 hours, 11.8 miles (18.6km)

This day's walk is mixed, with some fairly easy sections to alleviate an otherwise tiring session. All along the route the views are superb.

From Porthcurno a steep climb leads to the cliff top and in less than 1 mile passes a diversion path that leads off seaward between the overgrown banks of Iron Age defences and onto Logan Rock.

Keep to the main path, negotiating some steep ups and downs through magnificent granite cliff scenery until the trail passes above a trim, white lighthouse below the dramatic cliffs of Tater du. The jet-black cliffs here are composed of black-hued greenstone, a cool contrast to all that golden granite. At Lamorna Cove there is a **café** serving snacks. The best accommodation is about 1 mile inland at **Castallack Farm** (☎ 01736-731969; www.castallackfarm.co.uk; s/d £40/52). About 800m uphill from the cove is the **Wink Inn** (☺ lunch & dinner), with bar meals.

THE MINACK THEATRE

The **Minack Theatre** (☎ 01736-810181; www.minack.com; adult £6-8, child £3-4) is an open-air theatre built into the cliffs – one of the world's most spectacular settings. The audience sits on steep, curved rows of seats, while the actors' backdrop is the view across the sea. In summer, performances have often been disrupted by a fabulous 'Dance of the Dolphins' in mid-bay. Even the actors take a break to watch these beautiful creatures leap and fly across the water. The theatre was built in the 1930s by the indomitable Rowena Cade, who, assisted by dedicated locals, did much of the construction. She was still mixing concrete until the year of her death in 1983. There are shows at the theatre most evenings from late May to late September; you can contact the theatre or a local tourist office for details. If the weather is kind, it's paradise; but bring a cushion for the hard seats, wine for sunny evenings and hot chocolate for when the Cornish mist steals in.

After Penzer Point you reach the edge of Mousehole (pronounced 'mowz'l'), an archetypal Cornish fishing village with granite houses rising in tiers from the walled harbour. There are several pubs, hotels and restaurants – the **Ship Inn** (☎ 01736-731234; s/d £40/65, mains £6-12; ☽ lunch & dinner) does good bar meals. Like St Ives, Mousehole is irresistible to visitors and artists.

The SWCP from Mousehole to Newlyn mostly follows the road. Newlyn is still a major fishing port, in spite of the decline of the industry generally, and there is a robust sense of life around the boat-crammed harbour. It's a pleasant seashore walk from here to join Penzance's splendid promenade.

PENZANCE
pop 20,260

The large town of Penzance spreads along the western side of Mount's Bay. It's a cheerful, bustling place and worth exploring, especially the older part of town around **Chapel St.** Unmissable are the colourful facade of the **Egyptian House** and the **statue of Humphry Davy**, the Penzance-born chemist and scientist who invented the miners' safety lamp – and discovered laughing gas along the way. Other places to visit include **Penlee House Gallery & Museum** (☎ 01736-363625; www.penleehouse.org.uk; adult/child £3/free, Sat free; ☽ 10am-5pm Mon-Sat Easter-Sep, 10.30am-4.30pm Oct-Easter), which has a superb collection of Newlyn School paintings as well as displays on the area's history. Penzance's **tourist office** (☎ 01736-362207; Station Rd) is right by the bus and railway stations.

The **YHA hostel** (☎ 0870 770 5992; www.yha.org.uk; camp sites for 2 £7, dm £16) is in an 18th-century mansion on the town's outskirts.

Penzance Backpackers (☎ 01736-363836; www.pzbackpack.com; Alexandra Rd; dm/d £13/28), also called the Blue Dolphin, is about 200m up from the promenade.

Penzance has a great many B&Bs and hotels, including the **Pendennis Hotel** (☎ 01736-363823; Alexandra Rd; s/d from £23/25), a reasonable, cheap option.

Just up from the promenade is **Kimberley House** (☎ 01736-362727; www.kimberleyhousepenzance.co.uk; 10 Morrab Rd; s £25-30, d £60), opposite the Penlee House Gallery.

Walker-friendly places include **Woodstock Guesthouse** (☎ 01736-369049; www.woodstockguesthouse.co.uk; 29 Morrab Rd; d £44-64) and **Warwick**

House Hotel (☎ 01736-363881; www.warwickhousepenzance.co.uk; 17 Regent Tce; s/d £45/76).

The centuries-old **Turk's Head** (☎ 01736-363093; Chapel St; ☽ lunch & dinner) pub serves good pub meals, while nearby **Bar Coco's** (☎ 01736-350222; 13 Chapel St; tapas £2-5; ☽ breakfast, lunch & dinner Mon-Sat) serves tapas and cappuccinos. **Archie Brown's** (☎ 01736-362828; Bread St; breakfast from £3, mains £4-7; ☽ 9.30am-5pm Mon-Sat) is a colourful vegetarian and vegan café. It's located above a health food shop off Causewayhead.

Day 10: Penzance to Porthleven
5–7 hours, 13.9 miles (22.4km)

Today is a fairly easy walk with a few steep sections towards the end. It skirts round Mount's Bay, with the dramatic island of St Michael's Mount nearly always in view. The cliffs here are much lower than further west.

Leave Penzance by following the path from opposite the exit to the large harbour-side car park. The trail leads between the railway line and a long stretch of beach, where there is very safe bathing, to Marazion, the oldest chartered town in Cornwall. The name Marazion has no connection to Judaism, but derives from the Cornish name of a medieval market: Marghas Byghan (Small Market).

Just offshore is the spectacular, tree-girt island of St Michael's Mount, with its handsome castle looking like an extension of the rock itself.

You walk along the road through Marazion before striking down to the coast once more. Easy walking then leads past Cudden Point to **Prussia Cove**, named after a notorious, but much admired, 18th-century smuggler, John Carter, who during childhood games styled himself the King of Prussia, after Frederick the Great.

The SWCP rounds Hoe Point, skirts the lovely beach of **Praa Sands** and then climbs onto rugged cliffs and past the remains of the Wheal Prosper and Wheal Trewavas mines. Beyond here, the way winds safely round the edge of impressive, but fairly unstable, cliffs to reach Porthleven.

PORTHLEVEN

The dark stonework and solid harbour walls of this old fishing and boat-building village give it a slightly stern look, but Porthleven is a charming place with several pubs and shops dotted around the harbour.

There's a walker-friendly welcome at the cosy **Seefar** (☎ 01326-573778; www.seefar.co.uk; Peverell Tce; s/d £24/54), while nearby **An Mordros** (☎ 01326-562236; www.anmordroshotel.com; Peverell Tce; d £58) has more hotel-style surroundings.

The cheerful **Nauti but Ice** (snacks £4-6) café on the eastern harbour side offers delicious snacks, including tasty crab rolls.

Two pubs that do decent bar meals are the **Ship Inn**, on the way into the village, and the **Atlantic Inn**, on the route out.

Day 11: Porthleven to Lizard
5–7 hours, 14 miles (22.4km)
The first part of today's walk is generally easy going along a stretch of coast that becomes increasingly scenic. The final section can be tiring.

Leaving Porthleven, follow Loe Bar Rd and Mounts Rd from the far end of the harbour. Very soon you pass the **Loe**, Cornwall's largest natural body of freshwater, once the estuary of the River Cober and now separated from the sea by the shingle bank of Loe Bar. *Swimming anywhere along the shore between Porthleven and here should never be attempted.*

The SWCP passes Gunwalloe Fishing Cove and then continues round Halzephron Cliff to Dollar Cove, where the little **church of St Winwallo**, with a separate tower of an older church, stands in an atmospheric position. The trail then climbs up to and alongside the Towans golf course.

South of Poldhu Point the route passes the **Marconi Monument**, which commemorates the first transatlantic telegraphic communication of 1901. From here you drop to Polurrian Cove, then up and over to the atmospheric Mullion Cove, where there are toilets and a seasonal **café**. The village of Mullion, with shops and an ATM in the Spar supermarket, is 1¼ miles uphill. Places to stay include the handy **Criggan Mill** (☎ 01326-240496; www.crigganmill.co.uk; s/d £35/60, dinner £10), which has pleasant chalet accommodation and also does an evening meal by prior arrangement. The delightful **Trenance Farm Cottages** (☎ 01326-240639; www.trenancefarmholidays.co.uk; s/d £34/58; 🐾) is about 800m inland.

Exhilarating cliff-top walking leads to Kynance Cove, where the fascinating multi-coloured serpentine rock has been attracting tourists since the 18th century. The offshore rock stacks have names such as Asparagus Island, Sugarloaf Rock, the Bellows and the Bishop.

On the cliff top there are toilets and a **café** at the car park. From Kynance the SWCP leads along the edge of dark, convoluted cliffs to Lizard Point, Britain's most southerly headland, famous for its mild climate, complex geology and associated unusual flora. The nearby **Lizard Lighthouse** (☎ 01326-290202; adult/child £2/1; ⏱ noon-5pm Sun-Thu Apr-Oct) has a collection of interesting artefacts. There are two **cafés** where the path reaches the point.

LIZARD
Just below the lighthouse is the handsome **Lizard YHA Hostel** (☎ 0870 770 6120; www.yha .org.uk; Lizard Point; dm from £16), a former 19th-century hotel, now owned by the National Trust and in a superb position. Rooms are family-size.

In Lizard village, 0.75 miles inland, is the homely **Bay View Cottage** (☎ 01326-290369; Cross Common; d £46) or you could pamper yourself at the **Housel Bay Hotel** (☎ 01326-290417; www .houselbay.com; s £45, d £110-140), Britain's most southerly hotel, with beautiful gardens overlooking a stunning vista of cliffs and sea. The trail passes right by the garden entrance.

In Lizard Village there are several cafés and a decent pub doing bar meals.

Day 12: Lizard to Coverack
4–6 hours, 10.4 miles (16.7km)
This is another spectacular day along the cliffs. The trail begins quite easily for the first few miles, but after Cadgwith it gets tougher.

Just before Cadgwith you'll pass the **Devil's Frying Pan**, a vast crater caused by the sea undermining the roof of a cave. Cadgwith's cottages, many of them thatched, are crammed into a steep-sided, narrow valley. Fishing boats still launch from the tiny beach. The **Cadgwith Cove Inn** (sandwiches around £6), or the attached tearooms in a former pilchard cellar, is usually guaranteed to have tasty crab sandwiches on offer.

Past Caerleon Cove and the substantial ruins of an old serpentine works, the path leads to **Kennack Sands**, popular with families in summer. A final set of steep ups and downs over the headlands of Beagles Point, Pedn Boar, Black Head and Chynhalls Point brings you to Coverack.

COVERACK

The charming old fishing port of Coverack is a good place to overnight. At the **YHA hostel** (☎ 0870 770 5780; www.yha.org.uk; Parc Behan, School Hill; camp sites for 2 £14, dm/d £14/40) you can camp beneath apple trees.

On the approach to Coverack is an excellent path-side B&B, **Porthbeer** (☎ 01326-280680; www.porthbeer.fsnet.co.uk; Chynhalls Point; d £56), with lovely, spacious rooms and great views.

In Coverack itself, **Fernleigh** (☎ 01326-280626; Chymbloth Way; d £50) is a handy stopover.

The **Paris Hotel** (☺ lunch &dinner) by the harbour has a lively bar that does decent pub grub. Just along the road is the popular **Archie's Loft** (sandwiches from £2.50), offering toasties and the famous, and delicious, Roskilly's ice cream.

Day 13: Coverack to Helford
5–7 hours, 13.6 miles (21.4km)
This is a moderately easy day, following the coast for much of the way and mixing scenic views with the ragged scars of quarrying.

From Coverack take the road past the beach and keep straight on past the houses to fields, keeping to the path closest to the sea; this runs to Lowland Point. From here the route winds through the sizeable gulf of **Dean Quarries**, where some gabbro rock is still extracted and loaded on to coasting vessels at the pier. Red flags indicate times when blasting takes place. A hooter sounds when a big bang is imminent. Relax; read a book.

The clearly signed route through the quarries should be followed exactly. It's a fascinating little journey through desolation that leads to the pleasant beach of Godrevy Cove, where the trail turns inland to Rosenithon and Porthoustock.

Take the road for the official route to Porthallow, where you meet the coast again and an excellent pub, the **Five Pilchards**, which offers tasty bar meals right on the beach.

The SWCP then continues to Nare Head and Nare Point, with fine views of the mouth of the River Helford. At Gillan Creek you can cross an hour either side of low water of spring tides, but there may still be a fair depth of water during neap tides. There is a line of partial stepping stones at a narrow, low-tide crossing place, but these can be very slippery. The official, dry-shod route adds 2 miles and goes inland by road round the head of the creek and returns to the coast for a final wooded stretch leading to Helford.

HELFORD

Pretty, popular and very populated in summer, Helford and its tree-lined, boat-bobbing river is always a delight. Accommodation options are sparse along the Helford River, where exclusive second homes and holiday cottages tend to dominate the market.

The excellent **Landrivick Farm** (☎ 01326-231686; d from £64) offers very friendly and comfortable service, with evening meals by arrangement. The farm is about halfway between Helford and Manaccan, about a 0.75-mile walk from Helford; it offers a pick-up from Helford if required. Helford's thatched **Shipwright's Arms** is a busy pub serving bar meals. You could also head for Manaccan's **New Inn** for similar fare.

Day 14: Helford to Falmouth
4–5 hours, 9.3 miles (14.8km)
The last lap is a relaxed stroll, although still with the occasional rise and fall for the foot-weary.

First catch your ferry. The little, businesslike ferries from Helford Point across the river to Helford Passage are operated by **Helford River Boats** (☎ 01326-250770; www.helford-river-boats.co.uk). They run on demand between 9am and 5pm April through October. There is some suspension of service at very low tides, so check first. Out of season, you're faced with a 13-mile detour inland via Gweek, at the head of the Helford River. Or you can succumb and catch a bus to Helston (four daily, two on Sunday) and then to Falmouth.

If you've caught your ferry, follow the SWCP from the north shore of the Helford River through Durgan, where an 800m inland detour leads to **Glendurgan Gardens** (☎ 01326-250906; Mawnan Smith; adult/child £5/3; ☺ 10.30am-5.30pm Tue-Sat & bank holiday Mon), an extravaganza of exotic shrubs, flowers and plants.

You then toddle effortlessly round Rosemullion Head and on to Maenporth and Pennance Point to reach journey's end at Falmouth.

MORE LONG-DISTANCE WALKS

SHAKESPEARE'S WAY

A relatively new arrival to Britain's collection of long-distance paths is Shakespeare's Way, named for Britain's best-known playwright. This route goes from Stratford-upon-Avon (Shakespeare's birthplace) to London, to finish at Shakespeare's Globe, the Elizabethan-style theatre on the banks of the Thames – a distance of 146 miles (235km). The route links some of Britain's other well-known tourist destinations – Blenheim Palace, the Cotswolds, Oxford and, er, Heathrow Airport. Walkers are encouraged to raise funds through sponsorship for a local charity: Stratford-upon-Avon's Shakespeare Hospice. For more details see www.shakespearsway.org.

MACMILLAN WAY

Another worthy walk – connected to the charity Macmillan Cancer Relief – and a delightfully varied and nonstrenuous route, running diagonally across the country from Boston on the Lincolnshire coast to Abbotsbury on the south coast near Weymouth. The total distance is 290 miles (467km), passing through the flat Fens, the rolling Cotswolds and the tranquil farmland of Dorset. The route is waymarked and many people do week-long sections (of around 90 miles to 100 miles) over three separate trips. For more details see www.macmillanway.org.

ACROSS SOUTHERN ENGLAND

If you're a real mile-eater, it's possible to join up several existing long paths to trace a very long route right across southern England.

In the Wessex chapter we describe the western section of the Ridgeway (p83). This ends at Goring, where you could join the eastern section of the Thames Path (p64), leading all the way to London to make a very varied nine- or 10-day walk through southern England.

For something even longer you could start walking at Avonmouth, a port town on the Severn Estuary near Bristol, and follow a path called the Avon Walkway through Bristol to Bath, then join the Kennet & Avon Canal (p80) as far as Pewsey, where you branch north to Avebury to join the Ridgeway and then the Thames Path all the way to London.

Another really long walk across the region starts on the South Devon coast at Lyme Regis and follows the Wessex Ridgeway path (p96) north to Avebury. Here, you could join the Ridgeway across the North Wessex Downs and the Chiltern Hills to its official end at Ivinghoe Beacon. This in turn is the start of the Icknield Way, which in turn links to the Peddars Way. Although only for the serious walker, this 370-mile (595km) epic is an ideal way to follow Neolithic, Roman and medieval footprints all the way across southern England, from the Channel to the North Sea – and it could easily fill a month of your holiday.

Northern England

CHRIS MELLOR

Northern England

0 ━━━━━ 50 km
0 ━━━━━ 30 miles

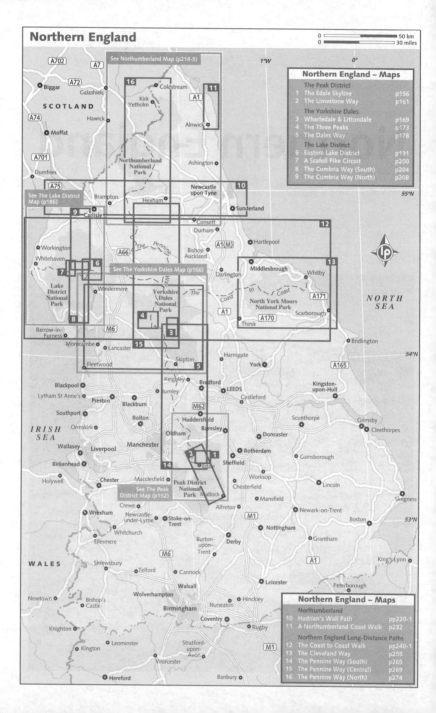

Northern England – Maps

The Peak District	
1 The Edale Skyline	p156
2 The Limestone Way	p161
The Yorkshire Dales	
3 Wharfedale & Littondale	p169
4 The Three Peaks	p173
5 The Dales Way	p178
The Lake District	
6 Eastern Lake District	p191
7 A Scafell Pike Circuit	p200
8 The Cumbria Way (South)	p204
9 The Cumbria Way (North)	p208

Northern England – Maps

Northumberland	
10 Hadrian's Wall Path	pp220-1
11 A Northumberland Coast Walk	p232
Northern England Long-Distance Paths	
12 The Coast to Coast Walk	pp240-1
13 The Cleveland Way	p255
14 The Pennine Way (South)	p265
15 The Pennine Way (Central)	p269
16 The Pennine Way (North)	p274

The Peak District

The first thing you notice about the Peak District – despite its name – is a distinct lack of pointed mountain tops. The word 'peak' actually comes from *peac*, an Old English term for any mound or hill, and while the area has very few soaring summits there are indeed plenty of hills, making the Peak District one of the most popular walking areas in northern England. And deservedly so: access is easy, facilities are good and there's a huge choice of routes of all lengths and standards through a variety of landscapes.

Much of the area is contained within the Peak District National Park – Britain's oldest and largest park – divided by geology into two distinct sections. The Dark Peak in the north is mostly high, wild, rolling moorland covered in rough grass, heather or peat bog, sliced by gullies known as 'groughs' and dotted with rocky outcrops of grey gritstone (a hard, coarse-grained sandstone), many eroded by the weather into unusual shapes. In sharp contrast, the White Peak in the south is a lower, 'friendlier' and less-imposing landscape of pale limestone and fertile farmland, with tranquil grassy dales and wooded valleys running between the pasture-covered hills.

In this chapter we describe two routes, one in the Dark Peak and one in the White Peak, as top-class samples of what the area has to offer. Use them as tasters, then go on to explore for yourself. Some pointers for further walks are given on p163, but wherever you go in the Peak, you won't be disappointed.

HIGHLIGHTS

- Gazing at views on both sides from the ridge near **Hollins Cross** (p157) on the Edale Skyline
- Enjoying the White Peak landscape of neat fields and dry-stone walls on the **Limestone Way** (p158)
- Following the idyllic river past the ancient village of **Youlgreave** (p162)
- Avoiding the peat bogs and striding through the heather on the **Kinder Plateau** (p157), gateway to the Pennines

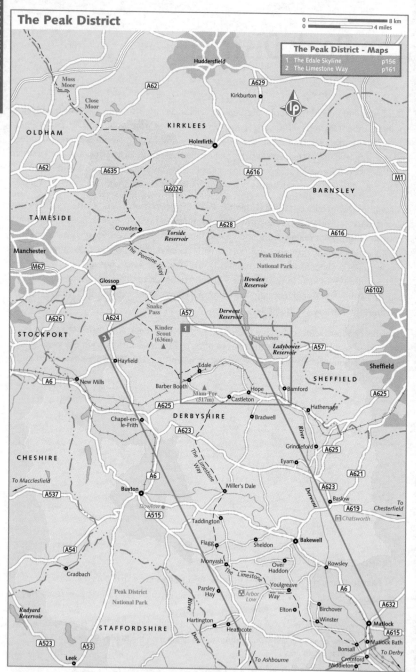

The Peak District

The Peak District - Maps		
1	The Edale Skyline	p156
2	The Limestone Way	p161

INFORMATION
When to Walk
The Dark Peak can be explored at any time of year, although in winter the weather on the upland areas can switch from balmy to arctic in less than an hour, making walking a serious business. Even in summer, mist and rain on the featureless, plateau-like moors can quickly turn an easy day out into an epic adventure – so be prepared. Walking in the White Peak is far less hazardous.

Maps
For the whole area on one sheet, get the Ordnance Survey (OS) Touring 1:100,000 map No 4 *Peak District & Derbyshire*. For more detail, you can use OS Landranger 1:50,000 maps No 110 *Sheffield & Huddersfield* and 119 *Buxton & Matlock,* but these are still not really detailed enough for walking. Much better are the OS Explorer 1:25,000 maps No 1 *The Peak District – Dark Peak Area* and 24 *White Peak Area,* or Harvey Maps Superwalker 1:25,000 *Dark Peak.*

Books
The Peak District is a popular walking area and very well covered by numerous guidebooks. An excellent choice is *Peak District Northern & Western Moors* and *Peak District Eastern Moors & the South*, both by local expert Roly Smith, with a good range of walks, colour maps and photos, and new information to take account of recent 'freedom to roam' legislation (see the boxed text, p448). In the same series are *The Pennine Divide* and *South Pennines & Bronte Moors*, both by Andrew Bibby, covering the hills and moors neighbouring the Peak District. All four books are endorsed by the Ramblers' Association.

Also with a good selection of walks of varying lengths and standards is the *Peak District Pathfinder Guide*. Highly recommended is *Walks from the Hope Valley*

Line, detailing routes from stations along the railway running through the park. For background, or maybe a souvenir of your visit, *The Peak District Official National Park Guide* is highly recommended – lavish and stylish but inexpensive – with text by Roly Smith and beautiful photos by Ray Manley.

Guided Walks
National park rangers organise an excellent series of guided walks throughout the year. They're free of charge (although you might need to reserve a place) and range from gentle strolls to strenuous all-dayers. For more information, see the *Peak District* newspaper (see below) or enquire at tourist offices.

Information Sources
There are many tourist offices in and around the Peak District; larger ones include **Bakewell** (☎ 01629-813227; bakewell@peakdistrict-npa .gov.uk), **Buxton** (☎ 01298-25106; www.highpeak.gov .uk) and **Matlock** (☎ 01629-583388; matlockinfo@derby shiredales.gov.uk). Others are detailed in the individual walk descriptions.

For online information about the whole area, start with the official sites www.peak district.org and www.visitpeakdistrict.com. For more tourism information, places to stay, local attractions and so on, try www .peakdistrict-nationalpark.com, www.peak districtonline.co.uk and www.derbyshire -peakdistrict.co.uk.

At tourist offices, shops and hotels you can pick up *Peak District*, a free newspaper produced annually by the national park authority, full of tourist and background information, with a full list of guided walks and other local events.

Tourist offices and many newsagents also sell the *Peak District Bus & Train Timetable;* as well as containing public transport details, this booklet lists places of interest, market days, local services and places for

---

BIG IN JAPAN

Surrounded by large cities such as Manchester and Sheffield, the Peak District is particularly popular over weekends and holidays when oxygen-starved urbanites invade its quiet serenity in pursuit of walking and other outdoor activities. Records show that the Peak District is visited by around 22 million people each year, putting the park among the busiest in the world, right up there with another well-known peak: Mt Fuji in Japan.

bicycle hire – especially useful if you're spending a few days in the area – plus a map showing all bus routes and long paths in the area, including the Limestone Way.

GETTING AROUND

Very few other national parks have such handy public transport access, with two services of particular use to walkers in the Peak District. The **TransPeak** (www.transpeak .co.uk) bus service crosses the area several times daily between Derby and Manchester via Matlock, Bakewell and Buxton and many smaller villages – plus some bus stops right out in the wilds. The Hope Valley Railway runs between Sheffield and Manchester through the heart of the Peak District, with trains at least every two hours, stopping at several rural train stations where you can walk off the platform and straight into the hills. For more information, pick up the *Peak District Bus & Train Timetable* (see p153), or use the national travel information lines and websites summarised in the boxed text on p456.

GATEWAYS

The main gateways for the Peak District are the cities of Derby, Sheffield and Manchester, all with good coach and train links to the rest of the country, and easily reached by car. From here you can reach several towns within the park (such as Bakewell or Buxton) that make good jumping-off points, plus the towns and villages nearest the start of the routes we describe.

between the gritstone Dark Peak and the limestone White Peak. To the north lies heather-covered moor, to the south the hills are covered in a patchwork of fields. This walk gives a taste of both landscapes.

The Edale Valley is enclosed and lightly populated, flanked on its southern side by a steep, grassy ridge and to the north by the notoriously boggy expanse of Edale Moor, commonly called Kinder Scout, the Kinder Plateau, or just plain Kinder. The quiet village of Edale, at the western end of its namesake valley, is most famous for walkers as the start of the Pennine Way (p261).

The Hope Valley is broad and contains several villages, including Hope itself and Castleton, a tourist honey pot famous for its nearby show caves. Another feature is the cement factory, its chimneys incongruously billowing smoke amid this lush and tranquil scene. Aesthetically it's an eyesore but economically it's a lifeline and a reminder that the Peak is a living, working park.

PLANNING

OK, we'll come clean. The route we describe here isn't the real Edale Skyline. The *real* Edale Skyline is a much longer outing, circling the entire Edale Valley. We're suggesting a shorter version here that misses none of panoramic views over the Derbyshire hills but does avoid some of the longer, wilder, boggier sections of the full walk.

Having said that, paths can be very muddy after rain, although they are well defined. There are few signposts, so the ability to use a map and compass is crucial, as weather conditions can change very rapidly. Don't let that put you off though; in the right conditions this route is a beauty,

THE EDALE SKYLINE

Duration	5¼–7½ hours
Distance	11 miles (17.5km)
Difficulty	moderate
Start/Finish	Hope (opposite)
Transport	bus, train
Summary A circular walk on hills and ridges, across open moor and farmland, mostly on good paths with marvellous views.	

The Edale Skyline route is a classic Peak District walk and a perfect introduction to the park. Keeping mainly to high ground, you make a circuit of the Edale Valley with views across the nearby Hope Valley from the ridge that marks the natural boundary and enthusiastic walkers will find it a very satisfying excursion.

The route starts and ends in Hope, and we describe the circular route in an anti-clockwise direction, so you can complete two-thirds of the distance before having a relaxed lunch in Edale village. If your timing is different you can easily do it the other way around. To include time for lunch or other long stops, you should allow seven to eight hours in total.

Alternatives

We describe a circuit from Hope village; an alternative start/finish point is Edale village. For a shorter walk you can do the route as described from Hope to Edale (6.5 miles) then get the train back to Hope.

If you're feeling strong, the full (20 miles) Edale Skyline route misses Edale village and continues round the western end of the valley, over Brown Knoll, Rushup Edge and Mam Tor – a wonderful outing for fine a summer day.

Maps

For the Edale Skyline you will need either the OS Explorer 1:25,000 map No 1 *The Peak District – Dark Peak Area* or the Harvey Superwalker 1:25,000 map *Dark Peak*.

Information Sources

The tourist office and national park centre at Edale, the **Moorland Centre** (☎ 01433-670207) is the best source of information on all aspects of the area, including accommodation, food, transport and weather forecasts. Useful websites are www.peakdistrict.org, www.visitpeakdistrict.com and www.edale-valley.co.uk.

NEAREST TOWN
Hope

This route starts and ends at the village of Hope, but the village of Edale (p263) is another possible start/finish point – and has more accommodation options.

SLEEPING & EATING

Campers can head for **Laneside Caravan Park** (☎ 01433-620215; www.lanesidecaravanpark.co.uk; sites for 2 £8-10), a well-organised and well-equipped site just on the eastern edge of the village.

In the centre of the village, the **Woodroffe Arms** (☎ 01433-620351; Castleton Rd; d £50, mains £7-

9; ☾ lunch daily, dinner Tue-Sat) is a friendly pub that welcomes walkers.

A long-standing favourite is **Woodbine B&B** (☎ 07778-113882; 18 Castleton Rd; s/d £25/50; ☾ café breakfast & lunch), attached to the equally popular Woodbine Cafe, serving meals and teas for walkers, cyclists and cavers, with a sumptuous selection of homemade cakes and a roaring open fire on cold days. This is also a hang-out for paragliders; the café has a direct radio link with a weather gauge on Rushup Edge, so the flyers can see if it's worth leaving their table.

Just a few doors away, **Courtyard Cafe** (snacks £2-3, mains £4-6; ☾ to 6pm, later in summer) has a sunny conservatory and garden, while **M & B Pizzas** (mains £4-8; ☾ 6-10pm Wed-Sun) is an unexpected little takeaway, serving burgers as well as margaritas and all the regulars – perfect if you're camping and don't feel like getting the stove out.

There are more accommodation choices on Edale Rd, leading north out of the village, including **Mill Farm** (☎ 01433-621181; millfarmhopevalley@hotmail.com; s/d £30/50), a picture-postcard cottage with lovely garden, and **Chapman Farm** (☎ 01433-620297; s/d £30/50), with just two guestrooms.

Also on Edale Rd is a walkers' favourite pub, the **Cheshire Cheese** (☎ 01433-620381; www.sallydog.co.uk/cheshirecheese; d £75, mains £5-7; ☾ lunch & dinner), with comfortable B&B, a traditional, no-frills bar, a good range of beer and a selection of filling meals.

Further up the road, about 1 mile outside the village, perennially recommended **Underleigh House** (☎ 01433-621372; www.underleighhouse.co.uk; d from £65) is friendly and good quality.

For food on the walk, Hope has a **Spar** (☾ daily) shop and a deli-bakery, both selling picnic ingredients.

GETTING THERE & AWAY

Hope is very well served by frequent buses from Sheffield, which go on to Castleton, but your best option is the frequent and convenient train service on the Hope Valley railway line between Sheffield (25 minutes) and Manchester (40 minutes), stopping at Hope and Edale train stations – among others – about 10 times per day (slightly less on Sunday). Make sure you get the stopping train though – otherwise you'll see the Peak at high speed from the Trans

Pennine Express! Timetables are available from local tourist offices or online at www .nationalrail.co.uk.

THE WALK
Hope to Win Hill
45 minutes–1 hour, 1.5 miles (2.4km)

Leave Hope village by going north along Edale Rd from the T-junction opposite the church. Continue for 300m, fork right onto a lane and follow this until you pass under a railway bridge. Turn immediately right onto a track that leads you uphill to Twitchill Farm. (Now holiday cottages, the farm is an attractive sight but also a reflection of recent developments in countryside economy – tourism makes more money than farming.)

Go through the farmyard and then through a gate into steep fields, where a path leads diagonally up to a junction of paths on the ridge crest. Turn right and walk for about 700m to reach the summit of **Win Hill** (462m).

Stop to enjoy the views here and look west across to Lose Hill. Local legend has it that the names derive from a battle many centuries ago when the victorious and the vanquished sides retired to a hill each.

While you are resting, beware of the greedy (and fearless) sheep who try to snatch your sandwiches.

Win Hill to Edale
2½–3½ hours, 5 miles (8km)

Retrace your steps to the junction of paths and continue straight on (northwest) along the broad ridge crest. Up here you really get the feeling of being near the sky, as panoramic views and a fresh breeze blow away the cobwebs in mind and body. Another path (a former Roman road) joins from the left, but keep going along the main ridge, with a plantation now on your right, to reach **Hope Cross** – an old stone marker built in 1737 and showing routes to Hope, Edale, Glossop and Sheffield.

Go through a gate and continue for about 300m to another gate. Here a signpost to Edale sends you left down a track into the small, steep-sided valley of Jaggers Clough. If it's been windy on the ridge, you can get

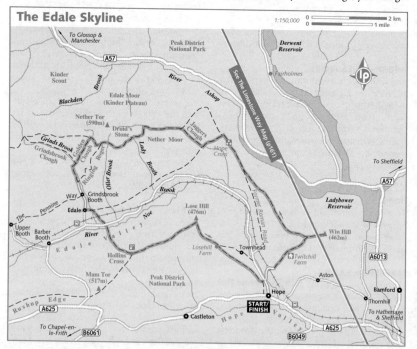

The Edale Skyline

a bit of peace down here and even listen to the birds. At weekends, though, your peace may be disturbed by the squealing brakes of descending mountain bikes.

At the bottom of the valley, wade the stream – in summer it's very shallow – or hop from rock to rock, then continue uphill on the track leading towards Edale for about 50m until it bends sharply to the left. Don't follow the track but carry straight on along an overgrown path leading up **Jaggers Clough** itself. This path is not signposted and easy to miss, so take care.

Assuming the Jaggers Clough path is passable (see the Warning box, right), continue up this delightful valley past miniature waterfalls, crystal-clear pools and clumps of hardy rowan trees. Look back, too, for great views of Win Hill and your route so far. The path crosses the stream a few times. Sometimes it's so narrow you have to use the stream, climbing up the rocks or skirting along the edge. Just before the top it becomes quite steep and rocky.

When the gradient eases you meet a good path running along the southeastern edge of the **Kinder Plateau**. Turn left (southwest) and follow the path – it soon swings in a more westerly direction – for about 1.5 miles. This is a great bit of the walk, with stunning views down to your left (south) over the Edale valley across to the ridge between Mam Tor and Lose Hill, your route this afternoon. You'll also pass a few rocky gritstone outcrops – so characteristic of the Dark Peak moorland – such as the fancifully titled Druid's Stone.

When you reach the top of a ridge called Ringing Roger (another delightful name), a path leads down towards Edale village, but it's more enjoyable to continue on the high ground a little further, around the edge of a beautiful valley called **Golden Clough**. Near the top of this valley, there's a junction of paths; take the path leading straight down Golden Clough. Near a plantation this meets another path coming down Grindsbrook Clough. If the weather is fine, and time's on your side at the top of Golden Clough, you could also continue along the edge of the Kinder Plateau for another mile and then come down Grindsbrook Clough itself. Either way, the paths all lead downhill, finishing with a gentle, pleasant stroll through the trees, across a footbridge and

> **WARNING**
>
> In spring or autumn, after rain, the stream through Jaggers Clough may overflow and block the path. In winter it may also be icy and dangerous. To avoid this section, either retrace your steps to the signpost near Hope Cross and continue north then west on clear paths round the head of the valley, or take the direct low-level path to Edale.

into Grindsbrook Booth, the northern end of Edale village.

Nearby is a famous pub called the **Old Nag's Head** (☎ 01433-670291; self-catering cottage £60, mains £10-15; ☻ lunch & dinner), and about 1 mile down the road, near the train station, is another pub officially called the **Rambler Country House** (☎ 01433-670268; www.theramblerinn .co.uk; s/d £36/72, mains £10; ☻ lunch & dinner) but known to all as the Rambler Inn. Both pubs offer bar food and are worth visiting for lunch, although at both places the menu is surprisingly dreary and the atmosphere disappointing. As an alternative, try the basic **café** at the train station, which is popular with walkers, serving hot drinks, snacks and meals – mostly with chips. For more information on places to eat or accommodation in Edale, see p263.

Edale to Hope
2–3 hours, 4.5 miles (7km)

Edale's lovely old church is about halfway along the road that runs through the village, around 250m beyond the Old Nag's Head. Opposite the church is an old cemetery. Look for the signpost and follow the footpath through the cemetery then across fields, skirting the camp site by the tourist office, to go under a railway bridge and then meet the road that runs along the Edale Valley. Go straight across and onto a good farm track leading steeply uphill to meet a path that then leads even more steeply up to the ridge between Mam Tor and Lose Hill.

You reach the ridge crest at a point called **Hollins Cross**. Pause to savour the view over the next valley, with the village of Castleton below. To the southwest you can make out the collapsed sides of Mam Tor. If conditions are right, the sky will be full of paragliders taking advantage of the wind above the appropriately named Rushup Edge.

WELL DRESSED

Unique to the Peak District is the custom of decorating wells or springs in thanksgiving for a local supply of water. The practice may have started in pre-Christian times, and seems to have died out by the early 17th century, to be revived by the inhabitants of Tissington in gratitude for their supply of pure water, which they believed protected them from the Great Plague of 1665.

Each year about 20 village wells are 'dressed' with large, colourful pictures depicting scenes from the Bible, local history and events, or tackling more modern issues such as rainforest protection.

The pictures are produced by spreading a thin layer of clay over a wooden frame, then outlining the design with bark and filling in the colours with an intricate mosaic of flower petals and leaves. And in these conservation-minded days, the traditional practice of using slow-growing mosses and lichens as colour is beginning to decline, with seeds, acorn cups and coloured stones creating a textured background instead.

Well dressing takes place in Peak District villages from May to mid-September, with June and July being the main months. Tourist offices have a list of when village well dressings will be displayed. Wirksworth, Eyam and Youlgreave are three villages particularly renowned for this tradition.

From Hollins Cross head east along the ridge path. This is another highlight section of the route, with excellent views down in both directions. You can clearly see the difference between the Dark Peak and the White Peak as you stroll along their dividing line.

It will take you about 30 minutes to reach the summit of **Lose Hill** (476m) for a final look at the panorama before descending. You meet a low path from Hollins Cross at a stile. Cross the stile and continue descending, with a wall on your left, to Losehill Farm. After the farm the path divides. The left branch (straight on) is an alternative route to Hope via Townhead, Edale Rd and the Cheshire Cheese pub. The right branch is the main route, going over another stile and then heading through fields directly to Hope, the Woodbine Cafe and the cream tea that you've been waiting for all day.

THE LIMESTONE WAY

Duration	2 days
Distance	26 miles (42km)
Difficulty	easy–moderate
Start	Matlock (opposite)
Finish	Castleton (p160)
Transport	bus, train

Summary A long but easy-going route on paths, tracks and lanes, winding through valleys and farmland, neatly avoiding busy areas.

The limestone country of the White Peak is characterised by steep-sided dales cloaked in ash woodland, while the higher land is covered by narrow fields edged with ancient dry-stone walls. In spring especially, many of the fields are bathed in the colour of wildflowers, while down in the dales rare orchids thrive. This scenic area, popular with tourists for more than a century (Victorian sightseers compared the area – with just a tad of imagination – to Switzerland), is perfect for easy walking.

With beauty comes a downside – some areas can get crowded at weekends. The Limestone Way deliberately avoids the honey pots and is ideal if you want an undisturbed taste of Derbyshire's White Peak landscape. You'll also get a glimpse of history, as the first part of the Limestone Way winds through an area that, centuries ago, was a centre for small-scale lead mining – the route follows tracks once used by generations of lead miners.

PLANNING

The Limestone Way was originally designed as a route through the White Peak from Matlock to Castleton in the Hope Valley – where White gives way to Dark. More recently, the route was altered slightly to pass west of Matlock, then extended southwards to Rocester, a village north of Uttoxeter, where it links with another route called the Staffordshire Way (p278). Our description, however, follows the original route, which can be walked in either direction but is described here south to north. Signposting and waymarks (sporting a Derby ram logo) are sporadic, and the whole area is crisscrossed with a network of other paths, so carrying a map is essential. We have described the route as a two-day walk but in summer keen walkers can polish it off in one go.

Day	From	To	Miles/km
1	Matlock	Monyash	13.5/21.8
2	Monyash	Castleton	12.5/20.2

Alternatives

The Limestone Way is never far from a bus route, so there are many options for doing just part of the walk before returning to your start point. On top of this, the White Peak is covered with footpaths, so endless opportunities exist for shorter circuits incorporating parts of the Way.

If you want to tackle something longer, you could do the route north to south, from Castleton via Bonsall (near Matlock) all the way to Rocester, a total distance of 46 miles.

Maps & Books

Most of the Limestone Way is marked on the OS Explorer 1:25,000 map No 24 *The Peak District – White Peak Area*. Castleton and the final 2.5 miles of the route are on map No 1 *Dark Peak Area*

Derbyshire Dales District Council publishes two leaflets – *The Limestone Way, Castleton to Matlock* and *The Limestone Way, Matlock to Rocester* – both in a north-to-south direction with strip maps and useful background information, available (free) from local tourist offices.

For more detail, *The Limestone Way* by R and E Haydock and B and D Allen covers both directions, with several circular walks based on the route, although this book was published in 1997 and copies are hard to find.

NEAREST TOWNS
Matlock & Matlock Bath

The country town of Matlock is easy to reach by public transport, and has banks, shops and several B&Bs. Matlock Bath is a large village about 2 miles from Matlock, decked out somewhat bizarrely as a seaside town, complete with promenade, gift shops,

cable car and discarded fish-and-chip wrappers. Other attractions include the famous evening 'illuminations' – multicoloured lights all along South Pde and North Pde (together forming the main street) and an impressive flotilla of decorated boats on the river – delighting the crowds at weekends from late August to late October. The **Matlock Bath tourist office** (☎ 01629-55082; matlockbath info@derbyshiredales.gov.uk) can advise on accommodation, public transport, local events and other walking options in the area.

SLEEPING & EATING

Options in Matlock include central **Riverbank Guesthouse** (☎ 01629-582593; Derwent Ave; d from £60), at the end of Old Englishe Rd, off Dale Rd. (There are a couple of other B&Bs nearby on Dale Rd itself.)

Also good are **Glendon** (☎ 01629-584732; Knowleston Pl; d from £50) and the friendly, well-organised and highly decorated **Sheriff Lodge** (☎ 01629-760760; www.sherifflodge.co.uk; Dimple Rd; s/d from £44/65), up on the hill a short distance from the centre.

A little out of the centre in the other direction, the **Boat House Inn** (☎ 01629-583776; www.boathousematlock.co.uk; 110 Dale Rd; d from £40) has good no-frills rooms, plus good no-fuss food and good no-fizz beer.

About halfway between Matlock and Matlock Bath, the **Flrs** (☎ 01629-502426; 180 Dale Rd; d from £48) is another walker-friendly place (and if it's full, there are two more B&Bs nearby).

In Matlock Bath, on the main street are two good-quality B&Bs: **Fountain Villa** (☎ 01629-56195; www.fountainvilla.co.uk; 86 North Pde; s/d from £35/50); and **Ashdale Guest House** (☎ 01629-57826; www.ashdaleguesthouse.co.uk; 92 North Pde; s/d from £35/60).

For food in Matlock, the **Crown** (Crown Sq) is a popular pub with good-value drinks and bar food. Other good pubs include the **Thorn Tree** (Jackson Rd), off Bank Rd.

For something more stylish, the **Strand** (☎ 01629-584444; www.thestrandrestaurant.com; Dale Rd; mains £15; ⊙ lunch &dinner) is a French-inspired bistro and café-bar.

Matlock has lots of takeaway options around Crown Sq and along Dale Rd, offering pizzas, kebabs, Chinese or Indian.

Neighbouring Matlock Bath has a string of cafés, takeaways and restaurants. Some of the pubs do food too; our favourites include the **Princess Victoria** (South Pde), with good beer, and the **Fishpond** (South Pde), centre of the local live-music scene.

GETTING THERE & AWAY

From Derby at least 10 local buses and around five trains per day run to Matlock (40 minutes), via Matlock Bath.

If you need to cut the route short, you can jump on the **TransPeak** (www.transpeak.co.uk) bus where the Limestone Way crosses the A6 near Taddington. This bus runs north to Buxton (15 minutes) and Manchester (1½ hours) or south to Matlock (35 minutes) and Derby (1½ hours).

Castleton

The village of Castleton was established more than 900 years ago, after William Peveril, illegitimate son of William the Conqueror, was made Steward of the Royal Forest of the Peak in 1080. He built a castle on a rock bastion above the valley, and the village grew up beneath it. Henry II added more defences in 1176 and used the castle as a hunting lodge, but despite these regal connections, Castleton never became important. Its present status as a tourist honey pot is derived from the nearby show caves (source of Blue John, a semiprecious mineral) 'explored' by several thousand visitors each year. If you come here in high summer, it'll seem like several million – but at least there's a good choice of places to stay. The **tourist office** (☎ 01433-620679) has information on accommodation, public transport, local events and other walking options in the area. For more local information, websites

include www.derbyshireguide.co.uk/travel/castleton.htm.

SLEEPING & EATING

Overlooking the village square, **Castleton YHA Hostel** (☎ 0870 770 5758; castleton@yha.org.uk; Castle St; dm £14; 🖳) is a large old building with friendly staff who know the area well.

Among many walker-friendly B&Bs, long-standing favourites include **Bargate Cottage** (☎ 01433-620201; www.bargatecottage.co.uk; Market Pl; d £55), very close to the end of the Limestone Way, and **Rambler's Rest** (☎ 01433-620125; www.ramblersrest-castleton.co.uk; Millbridge; s/d from £25/40), with a range of rooms, including one with a jacuzzi – ideal if you've had a hard day's walking. Also good and central is **Cryer House** (☎ 01433-620244; fleeskel@aol.com; Castle St; s/d £25/50), with welcoming hosts.

On the main road towards Hope is the historic **Peaks Inn** (☎ 01433-620247; www.peaks-inn .co.uk; How Lane; d from £75), now mixing old and new following a recent renovation, and **Ye Olde Cheshire Cheese Inn** (☎ 01433-620330; www .cheshirecheeseinn.co.uk; How Lane; d from £65), where stylish B&B apartments contrast with the traditional bar.

Castleton also has several good pubs, all doing meals and most doing accommodation too. The **George** (☎ 01433-620238; Castle St; 😊 lunch & dinner), next door to the YHA hostel, is a first port of call for many walkers, with good beer and home-cooked food.

Nearby, the **Castle Inn** (☎ 01433-620578; www .innkeeperslodge.com/castleton; Castle St; d from £60, meals £7-10; 😊 lunch & dinner) is a larger place with several en suite rooms and good-value meals served to 10pm.

PEAK DISTRICT RARITIES

Before the onslaught of modern intensive farming methods, the fields of the White Peak were multicoloured with some of the most flower-rich grassland in Britain. Commonplace plants mingled with rarer species and harboured a wonderful array of invertebrates that, in turn, attracted many birds. Although chemical fertilisers and uniform rye-grass have done away with much of this, in spring and summer many dales are still full of flowers specially adapted to living on the thin limestone soil.

One of these flowers is Jacob's ladder, found almost exclusively in the dales of the White Peak, with large blue petals and ladder-like leaves. Also rare, and especially enchanting, are orchids. Most flower in April and May but their numbers are small thanks to generations of collectors flouting the law against picking these flowers – and despite the fact that orchids need their own special soil fungi to grow, so won't germinate in people's gardens. As people are marginally better informed these days, you should see a few orchids if you walk here at the right time. Needless to say, the orchids should be left in peace.

As befits a major tourist spot, Castleton also has many cafés and tearooms. Try award-winning **Rose Cottage**, on the main street, or walker-friendly **Three Roofs** near the car park. **Peveril Shop**, opposite the bus stop, does hot snacks and excellent-value sandwiches to take away – ideal if your transport is just about to leave!

GETTING THERE & AWAY

From Castleton, buses go to Bakewell (50 minutes, three times per day), from where you can get another bus to Matlock or on to Derby. From Castleton, buses also go to Sheffield (1¼ hours, at least 10 per day) via Hope, where you can switch to the train and reach either Manchester or Sheffield, but make sure you tell the driver you want the station (about 1 mile beyond the village centre). On summer weekends there's a regular shuttle bus between Castleton and Hope train station (15 minutes), tying in with train departure and arrival times.

THE WALK
Day 1: Matlock to Monyash
6½–9 hours, 13.5 miles (21.8km)

From the car park near Matlock's train station go up Snitterton Rd. After 50m turn left onto a path on a bridge over the railway line. The path goes steeply uphill, crossing many fields. When you stop to catch your breath, look back over Matlock and the Derwent Valley, with High Tor and Riber Castle (actually a Victorian sham) behind.

Pass to the right of Masson Lees Farm, then bear right along the edges of fields skirting **Masson Hill**, known locally as the 'first hill of the Pennines' as it's the chain's southernmost hill over 1000ft. Follow a narrow track to a junction where a left turn leads down a steep path to the stone market cross at the village of Bonsall.

Keep the **King's Head** pub on your left, cross the village main street and follow the Way as it climbs a few steps between walls, then crosses a field to reach Upper Town. The path meets a lane. Go straight on for about 200m to the next road junction, where you go through a gate and follow the Way across a field. Take care by the small barn; ignore the clear path going straight on and make sure you keep left – the Way is the less-obvious path alongside the wall.

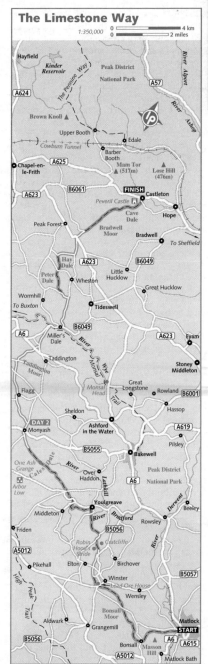

The Limestone Way

This leads you to a track called Moorlands Lane, across the fields of Bonsall Moor. The Way crosses more fields and a few lanes and tracks before swinging more westerly. Just past an outcrop called Luntor Rocks, keep left and stick to the track that runs along the hillside above the village of Winster. You may want to rest on the organic-looking bench made from wooden poles and strips of lead – a reminder of the industry that once thrived here.

The track meets a main road near the **Lead Ore House** – another relic from mining days (the history of this old building is explained on a plaque). From here you follow another track (a former packhorse route known locally as the Portway, which in turn followed an even older trade route dating from prehistoric times) to meet the main street running through Elton on the eastern edge of the village.

If it's time to refuel, detour left (west) into the village to reach **Elton Cafe** (⊙ Sat & Sun, Sun only in winter) serving homemade soup, things with chips and a selection of cakes, making it a favourite for cyclists and walkers.

If you can resist the lure of cholesterol, continue north on Dudwood Lane. At the bottom of the hill, just before meeting a main road, cross a stile on the left and follow the Way between the prominent gritstone outcrops of Cratcliffe (on the right) and **Robin Hood's Stride** (on the left). This is a popular picnic site and a playground for local rock climbers. Robin Hood may well have been here, as in medieval times Sherwood Forest – the legendary brigand's traditional home – covered much of Derbyshire too and the nearby valleys may have been ideal for a spot of robbery and wealth redistribution. (Incidentally, Robin Hood's trusty lieutenant, Little John, is buried at Hathersage, about 4 miles east of Castleton – the end of the Limestone Way.)

Beyond Robin Hood's Stride, go through a gap in the wall and cross two fields to reach a lane where you turn right. After 300m go left on a path through a nice patch of woodland, then down to a gate in a small valley, where the route turns sharp right. Continue over fields, mostly downhill, to meet a lane on the outskirts of the traditional White Peak village of **Youlgreave**. Turn right onto this lane, cross over a bridge and then go immediately left

along a path running through beautiful water meadows beside the River Bradford. After about 500m you cross a footbridge to the south bank. To the north (up the hill) is the centre of Youlgreave, where the **George Hotel** (☎ 01629-636292) welcomes walkers with no-frills surrounds, good beer and bar food. If you want to break the walk early, it also does B&B.

The Way runs beside another beautiful stretch of river, with small weirs and pools, then crosses over an arched bridge and zigzags up to a road. Go right for 500m, left over a stile, up an unclear path to another road, left along this road for 100m, then right through a squeeze gate. Continue diagonally uphill across fields and through a car park and picnic site to reach a minor road called Moor Lane.

Go left along Moor Lane to meet another road, where you go straight on, leaving the roads behind and back into fields again. The Way goes over several stiles and gates to skirt Calling Low Farm and drop steeply down into **Cales Dale** (part of Lathkill Dale National Nature Reserve) and then just as steeply up the other side.

After a few more fields you reach **One Ash Grange**, an old farm used in medieval times by the monks of Roche Abbey in Yorkshire as a penitentiary for rebellious brethren. Look out for the monks' former cold store and pigsties on the right of the path. The Way leads across more fields, eventually to meet a track between old stone walls, which takes you down to Monyash.

MONYASH

In the quiet village of Monyash, B&Bs include walker-friendly **Sheldon House** (☎ 01629-813067; www.sheldoncottages.co.uk; Chapel St; s/d £45/60), only taking guests for two consecutive nights, and friendly, award-winning **Rowson House Farm** (☎ 01629-813521; www.rowsonhousefarm .com; camp sites for 2 £5-16, s/d £25/50; 🖳), a working farm on the edge of the village, also offering camping at the attached Lathkilldale Campsite. For more accommodation ideas see www.monyash.info.

The only pub in the village is the historic **Bull's Head** (☎ 01629-812372; s/d £30/45, mains £8-10; ⊙ lunch & dinner), with B&B in large rooms and a range of bar meals. This place can get busy at weekends, but there's outside seating too.

Monyash also has the Village Store and the **Old Smithy Café** (☎ 01629-810190; www.old smithymonyash.piczo.com), another long-time walker favourite, serving up all the usual stuff – teas, cakes, sandwiches, pies and chips – and on Saturday evenings the café transmogrifies into a bistro.

Day 2: Monyash to Castleton
5½–7 hours, 12.5 miles (20.2km)

Leave Monyash heading north along the lane past the **Pinfold** (where stray animals were once kept until their owner paid a fine and collected them) then left along a walled track by Dale House Farm. This leads across fields to the village of Flagg.

Beyond Flagg, leave the fields and keep to lanes and tracks for several miles. Where the Way crosses the busy A6 near Taddington, there's refreshment and accommodation at the **Waterloo Inn** (☎ 01298-85230; d £65, mains £7-9; ✐ lunch & dinner); it also offers sandwiches and bar snacks for around £4, plus tea and coffee and a nice garden. Nearby is a **YHA camping barn** (☎ 0870 770 8868; dm £6).

The trail eventually leads down to the steep-sided valley of **Miller's Dale** and the village of the same name. Overhead, two large viaducts straddle the gap; they carried the railway between Manchester and Derby before short-sighted closures in the 1960s forced trains off the rails. It's hard to believe this sleepy settlement used to have a busy train station with constant traffic and five platforms. Today one viaduct carries the Monsal Trail – see p164 – and there's information (and loos) at the old station.

Go eastwards along the Miller's Dale main street, under the viaducts and past the church, before taking a minor road on the left up a hill (opposite the **Angler's Rest** pub). After 100m turn sharp left on a rough track, go up through the yard of Monks-dale Farm and then follow the Way north-wards. To the left (west) the fields drop into Monk's Dale. The track leads you across a high area of fields to meet a lane at Monk's Dale House. Go left and down the hill, then right over a stile to thankfully regain paths leading northwards up **Peter Dale** and **Hay Dale**, a pair of delightful limestone valleys particularly famous for their wild orchids (see the boxed text, p160).

Beyond Hay Dale you reach a lane. Turn left here to reach a main road (A623). Go left, then quickly right through a gate to follow tracks and paths over many stiles (tiring now as you reach the end of the walk) across the upland pasture of Bradwell Moor. Follow the path downhill into rocky **Cave Dale**, where you can almost imagine the cavern system before it collapsed to form this steep-sided valley.

This dale leads beneath the ramparts of **Peveril Castle**, through a narrow gap in the rocks and into the heart of Castleton. Turn left along Bargate to reach the village square.

If you're not staying the night, go through the square to the main road, then turn right and continue round some sharp corners to reach the bus stop. If you're not in such a rush, nearby are several pubs and cafés where you can celebrate your completion of the Limestone Way with a pot of tea or a pint of beer.

MORE WALKS

We have described two walks in this chapter to represent the different landscapes of the Peak District, but of course there are many more walking possibilities.

NORTHERN PEAK DISTRICT

The northern part of the Peak District is called the Dark Peak, where the moors are high, wild and frequently featureless, a map and compass absolutely essential, and the walking rather specialised. Sinking to your knees in wet peat may not be every-one's ideal day out, but the caste of walkers known as 'bog-trotters' simply love it, with 'old Kinder Scout,' and the moors therea-bout' offering endless possibilities.

A good Dark Peak introduction is the 13-mile (21km) circuit of Edale Moor, commonly called Kinder Scout, the Kinder Plateau or just plain Kinder, starting and finishing at the village of Edale. If you want to experience the high moor but prefer the comfort of a good path across the peat, the first day of the Pennine Way (see p264) is a rewarding walk from Edale over to Crowden.

Fit and experienced mile-eaters could try the 40-mile (64km) Derwent Watershed Walk, a tough challenge usually taking two days (although some heroes do it in one go), but a wonderful outing across the very best of the Dark Peak. The route goes from Yorkshire Bridge near Bamford, up Win Hill, along the ridge from Lose Hill to Mam Tor, round the head of the Edale Valley to Kinder Low, Kinder Downfall and Mill Hill, then across the A57 to Bleaklow Head, Bleaklow Stones, Howden Moor and back south to where you started via Back Tor, Strines Edge and Stanage Edge.

For a much less daunting taste of the Dark Peak, you could head for Fairholmes (consisting of a car park, national park centre, bike-hire outlet and café), between the Derwent and Ladybower Reservoirs, and quite easily reached by bus from Sheffield or Castleton, especially at weekends. A good circular walk takes you along the east side of Derwent Reservoir and up Abbey Brook onto the moors. The route then follows the ridge south over Back Tor and along Derwent Edge, past rocky outcrops with great names such as Cakes of Bread and Wheel Stones, ending back at Ladybower Reservoir.

CENTRAL PEAK DISTRICT

A good base for walking in the central area is the town of Bakewell, surrounded by a network of footpaths, and with hotels, B&Bs, a YHA hostel, shops, restaurants, cafés and pubs (as well as several bakeries selling world-famous Bakewell puddings), plus a good tourist office. The town also has good bus links to Buxton and Matlock, with onward connections to Manchester and Derby respectively.

An excellent (and mostly flat) one-day option from Bakewell is the Monsal Trail, the route of an old railway line that winds westwards through the heart of the central Peak District all the way to Buxton. The route includes the impressive viaduct at Monsal Head, and delightful river-side paths along Miller's Dale and Chee Dale. From Buxton you can get a bus back to Bakewell or simply stay the night (Buxton has some interesting sights and a good choice of places to stay). To save clock watching, you could get an early bus to Buxton, have a look around and then walk

back to Bakewell. The 13 miles (21km) will take about five to six hours of walking; with stops it'll be seven to eight hours.

A shorter option from Bakewell is to head eastwards along the Monsal Trail and continue along tracks and paths to the village of Rowsley, or over the hill to the famous stately home of Chatsworth.

South from Bakewell takes you to the village of Over Haddon and into the wonderful and classic limestone valley of Lathkill Dale, protected as a nature reserve.

Further south, routes also using longgone railway lines include the Tissington Trail (13 miles) between Ashbourne and Parsley Hay, and the High Peak Trail (17.5 miles) from Dowlow, near Buxton, all the way to Cromford, near Matlock. Both trails provide effortless walking through the heart of the Peak District.

For something equally linear, but with more views and gradients thrown in, from Bakewell you could also head for Baslow, either by foot on rights of way through the fields and Chatsworth Estate, or on the bus that goes towards Chesterfield. From Baslow you can follow the famous Derbyshire Edges – a line of gritstone cliffs and a classic Peak District feature, brought to worldwide attention in 2006 when the heroine of the *Pride & Prejudice* movie comes here to stare forlornly into space. A classic 'edge-walk' takes you north along Baslow Edge, Curbar Edge and Froggatt Edge, finishing down in Grindleford, which has a classic walkers' café and a train station on the Hope Valley railway line. This walk is 5 miles (8km).

If you want to stretch the walk, or start from Grindleford, you can go up through the woods around Padley Gorge, past the ancient hillfort of Carl Wark, over Higger Tor and across to the highest and longest of the edges – Stanage Edge. This is most easily done as an out-and-back route but if you want to keep going, footpaths lead eventually all the way to the A57, where you can pick up a bus to Castleton, Manchester or Sheffield. That's a long day-walk but an excellent Peak District outing on a fine summer day.

The Yorkshire Dales

The Yorkshire Dales is an area of valleys and hills roughly in the centre of northern England. Some of the so-called hills are fairly mountainous, with steep sides, exposed cliffs and peaks over 600m, but most are lower, smoother and less foreboding – making the Yorkshire Dales ideal for walkers. It's one of the most popular walking areas in England.

Added to this natural landscape are human influences. Centuries of habitation has given the area a legacy of ancient settlements, lonely farms, neat fields, classic limestone walls and isolated field barns, plus – it has to be said – the occasional modern eyesore quarry. There is no great wilderness here, but for many people that is the Yorkshire Dales' most important attraction.

The Yorkshire Dales are surrounded on three sides by other mountain areas. To the north extends the Pennine chain, to the west are the rugged fells of the Lake District and to the east lie the rolling North York Moors. South of the Dales are the great conurbations of Bradford and Leeds, looking close on the map but surprisingly distant when you're on open high ground or wandering through quiet valleys.

Much of the area lies within the boundaries of the Yorkshire Dales National Park, although just to keep you on your toes, some parts lie outside the county of Yorkshire (a county so large it's now actually split into four counties – North, South and West Yorkshire, and the East Riding of Yorkshire). Visiting the outer edges of the Yorkshire Dales, you may stray into the counties of Lancashire, Cumbria or possibly County Durham. Passports are not required for re-entry, although some proud Yorkshire folk may think they should be!

HIGHLIGHTS

- Wandering along the banks of the delightful **River Wharfe** (p168)
- Enjoying a post-walk pint in the delightful pubs of **Littondale** and **Wharfedale** (p168)
- Striding over the moorland between Wharfedale and Dentdale on the **Dales Way** (p174)
- Marvelling at the Victorian engineering of **Ribblehead Viaduct** (p173)
- Reaching the summit of **Pen-y-ghent** (p172) on the Three Peaks walk; one down, two to go

The Yorkshire Dales

THE YORKSHIRE DALES

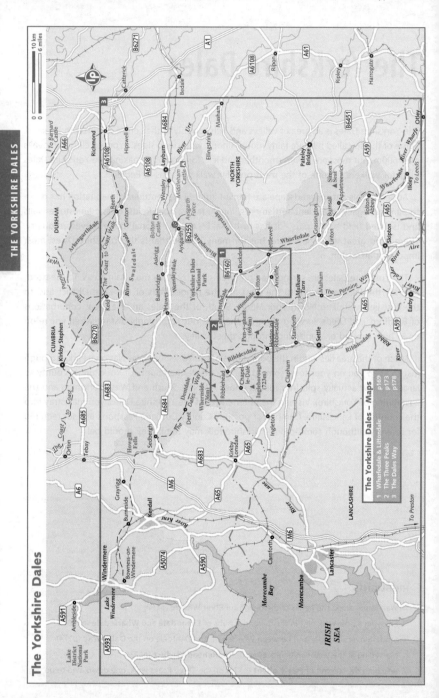

The Yorkshire Dales – Maps

1	Wharfedale & Littondale	p169
2	The Three Peaks	p173
3	The Dales Way	p178

INFORMATION
When to Walk
You can walk in the Yorkshire Dales in any season. One of the area's many great attractions is its year-round suitability. Having said that, in winter, although the valleys are relatively benign, there can be days of wind, rain and snow, so you'll need proper gear and map-reading skills if you go up on the high hills. Summer can be busy, making spring or autumn best for a combination of fair weather and a good chance of enjoying some solitude.

Maps
For a map of the whole Yorkshire Dales region, you can't do better than Harvey Maps' 1:100,000 *Yorkshire Dales Visitor Map*, with the whole park on one sheet, plus useful local information. Harvey also produces an excellent series of 1:40,000 *Yorkshire Dales Outdoor Maps* – great for walking – split into *North, South, East* and *West* sheets. The whole set is also available as a spiral-bound *Yorkshire Dales National Park Atlas*.

The Yorkshire Dales National Park is also covered mostly by Ordnance Survey (OS) Landranger 1:50,000 maps No 98 *Wensleydale & Upper Wharfedale* and 99 *Northallerton & Ripon*. For more detail, the park is also covered by OS Explorer 1:25,000 maps No 2 *Yorkshire Dales – South & West* and 30 *Yorkshire Dales – Northern & Central* areas, plus map No 19 *Howgill Fells and Upper Eden Valley*.

Books
General walking guidebooks covering this area include the excellent *Wharfedale & Nidderdale* and *Wensleydale & Swaledale*, both by Andrew Bibby. Between them, they cover the southern and northern parts of the Yorkshire Dales, with colour maps and photos and new information to take account of recent 'freedom to roam' legislation (see p448), endorsed by the Ramblers' Association. In the same series is *The Three Peaks & Howgill Fells* by Sheila Parker, covering the western part of the park. If you want it all in one book, the handy *Walk the Yorkshire Dales* covers a wide range of routes with OS map extracts, colour photos and GPS information. Other options include the *Yorkshire Dales* Pathfinder Guide and the inspirational *Yorkshire Dales, Moors & Fells* by local enthusiast Paul Hannon, describing 40 walks of various distances, with maps and beautiful colour pictures.

Guided Walks
The national park rangers and some local organisations organise guided walks in various parts of the Yorkshire Dales with different distances and themes (wildlife, archaeology, local legends etc). Guided walks are also organised by the Settle-Carlisle Railway (see the boxed text, p174); all start and end at stations along the line. Tourist offices have leaflets with all the details.

Information Sources
There are many tourist offices in and around the Yorkshire Dales, all selling walking maps and books, and providing information on places to stay and public transport. Most also provide the latest weather reports. Useful tourist offices for visitors are at **Ilkley** (☎ 01943-602319; www.visitilkley.com), opposite the bus and train stations, and **Grassington** (☎ 01756-752774; grassington@ytbtic.co.uk), in the car park on the edge of the village. Others include **Malham** (☎ 01729-830363; malham@ytbtic.co.uk), **Hawes** (☎ 01969-667450; hawes@ytbtic.co.uk), **Settle** (☎ 01729-825192; settle@ytbtic.co.uk) and

---

YORKSHIRE PRIDE

Perhaps surprisingly, there has long been a connection between the rural Yorkshire Dales and the industrial cities of Burnley, Bradford and Leeds lying just to the south. In the early 20th century, and particularly since the end of WWI, factory workers from the cities would escape to the Dales on Sunday for a breath of fresh air and a break from the drudgery of the 'dark satanic mills'.

It's still something like that today. Every summer weekend the area's population probably doubles as visitors from the nearby cities and further afield come to walk, cycle, cave, rock climb, fish or just tour by car or coach. Despite, or perhaps because of, the influx of visitors, the people of Yorkshire are especially proud of their landscape and heritage, and seem to have the strongest 'national identity' of any part of England.

Richmond (☎ 01748-850252; richmond@ytbtic.co.uk). On the edge of the Dales, in Cumbria, **Sedbergh tourist office** (☎ 01539-620125; www.sedbergh .org.uk) is also handy.

General tourist websites coving the whole area include www.yorkshiredales.org, while the official national park site is www.york shiredales.org.uk. For walking information see www.daleswalks.co.uk.

For information about events, transport and accommodation, check the *Visitor,* a free newspaper produced by the Yorkshire Dales National Park Authority.

GETTING AROUND

For walkers in the Yorkshire Dales, the most useful public transport service is the famous **Settle-Carlisle Railway** (www.settle-carlisle .co.uk), running through the western section of the park and stopping at several rural stations, providing easy access to many areas that would otherwise be hard to reach with a car. It also means you can walk in one direction, finish at a station, then catch a train back to your starting point. For more details on the line see the boxed text, p174. A leaflet describing walking routes from train stations is available from tourist offices.

Tied in with the trains on the Settle-Carlisle Railway are a series of bus services aimed specifically at tourists; for example, a bus runs from Settle train station to Malham and Grassington (both popular walking centres). For more details contact local tourist offices, phone **Traveline** (☎ 0870 608 2608), or check www.yorkshiretravel.net or www.traveldales.org.uk.

GATEWAYS

To reach the Yorkshire Dales, the main gateway towns are Skipton in the south (most easily reached via Leeds and Ilkley), Kendal in the northwest and Richmond in the northeast. They all have good coach links with other parts of Britain. Ilkley,

Skipton and Kendal are also on the railway network.

WHARFEDALE & LITTONDALE	
Duration	5–6 hours
Distance	13 miles (21km)
Difficulty	easy–moderate
Start/Finish	Kettlewell (opposite)
Transport	bus
Summary A fantastic circular walk through classic Dales scenery; hilly, but not too strenuous.	

This walk makes a perfect introduction to the Yorkshire Dales, following two contrasting valleys. Wharfedale, cut by the River Wharfe, is one of the largest and best-known dales in Yorkshire. In contrast, the valley of Littondale, home to the River Skirfare, is small and hardly known. This walk takes in both dales, linking them by paths across higher ground with fine views of the surrounding landscape. This is the kind of walk to be done slowly, maybe with a picnic or pub lunch halfway, so as to properly absorb the Yorkshire Dales scenery and atmosphere along the way.

PLANNING

We describe this circular route starting and ending in the village of Kettlewell, although you might want to do it from Litton. We describe it clockwise, but it can be followed in either direction. You should allow an extra hour or two for stops.

Maps

This route is on the OS Landranger 1:50,000 map No 98 *Wensleydale & Upper Wharfedale.* For more detail, see OS Explorer 1:25,000 map No 30 *Yorkshire Dales – Northern & Central areas,* although a tiny section of the route (through the village of Arncliffe) is just off the southern edge of the map.

NATIONAL PARK REALITIES

The Yorkshire Dales National Park covers around 680 sq miles (1770 sq km). Like all national parks in England and Wales, this is not state land. The park is made up of many privately owned farms and estates, administered by the national park authority. It's important to realise that this is very much a *working* park, not an environment preserved in aspic. More than 60,000 people live here, many engaged in farming and (more controversially) quarrying – and an increasing number in tourism-related jobs.

Information Sources

The nearest tourist office to the start of the walk is at **Grassington** (☎ 01756-752774; grassington@ytbtic.co.uk). You can also visit www.kettlewell.info.

NEAREST TOWN
Kettlewell

Kettlewell is a popular walking base with several places to sleep and eat. Scenic and traditional, Kettlewell was the set for popular Brit-flick *Calendar Girls,* so the village attracts movie fans as well as outdoor types.

SLEEPING & EATING

For those on a budget, there's simple camping at **Fold Farm** (☎ 01756-760886; sites for 2 £6) and good-value accommodation at **Kettlewell YHA Hostel** (☎ 01756-760232; www.yha.org.uk; dm £14).

B&Bs include walker-friendly **Lynburn** (☎ 01756-760803; lorna@lthornborrow.fsnet.co.uk; d £46-54) and **Littlebeck** (☎ 01756-760378; www.little-beck.co.uk; d £60).

On the main street, there's luxurious 'four-poster B&B' at **Cottage Tearoom** (☎ 01756-760405; d midweek/weekend £47/53) plus breakfasts, snacks, drinks and dinners from around £7. There's also **Zarina's Tea Room** in the village centre.

For drinks of a different sort, pubs include the **Bluebell** (bar meals around £7) and the **Racehorses** (bar meals around £7) – the latter has a nice river-side beer garden. Kettlewell also has a small general store.

There are more places to stay in the nearby villages of Buckden and Hubberholme (p179).

GETTING THERE & AWAY

There are several buses each day from the gateways of Leeds, Ilkley and Skipton to Grassington, from where you can get a local bus to Kettlewell (20 minutes). Services on weekdays during school holidays can be limited but on summer weekends there are extra services. The nearest train stations are at Skipton (from where you get a bus to Grassington) and Settle.

THE WALK
Kettlewell to Arncliffe
1–1½ hours, 2.5 miles (4km)

From the centre of Kettlewell go southwest along the main road, across the bridge over

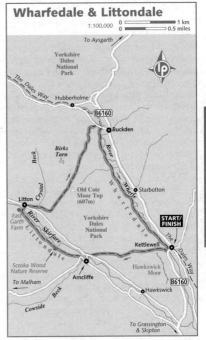

the River Wharfe. From the west side of the bridge, where the road bends to the left, take a wide track on the right, aiming uphill away from the river-side path. Go through a gate and almost immediately branch left again, onto a footpath signposted 'Arncliffe'. Keep heading up the fell (remembering to look behind at the fine views of Wharfedale), through a steep section of limestone cliffs and then over a few stiles as you cross the broad ridge between the two valleys.

As the path begins to descend into Littondale, you go through fields then over a stile and steeply down through woodland to reach the pretty little settlement of **Arncliffe**. Go straight across the lane and through a small gate opposite, turning right (north-west) alongside the River Skirfare, with the church on the opposite bank.

Arncliffe to Litton
1 hour, 2.5 miles (4km)

Follow the river-side path to reach a bridge. Cross this over the river, carry straight on and then turn right (signed 'bridleway') in front of Smithy Cottage and some barns. After a few minutes you meet the lane again and turn right, following it over another bridge. Where this lane bends left (towards Malham), go straight on along a track signposted to Litton and Halton Gill. Leave the track by a small gate, into fields and follow the path along the level valley floor, through meadows and over several stiles. You pass through **Scoska Wood National Nature Reserve**, the largest ash and rowan woods remaining in the Yorkshire Dales. Only lightly grazed by cows, in spring and summer a profusion of wildflowers flourishes here.

The path keeps to the southwest side of the river all the way to East Garth Farm, where you go right to meet a track over the river. Turn left on the far side, look for the bridleway signs and follow the track round a few bends to meet a lane opposite the **Queens Arms Inn** (☎ 01756-770208; www.yorkshirenet.co.uk/stayat/queensarms; d £75; ☷ Tue-Sun & Mon bank holidays), where lunch may beckon; it might even tempt you to stay the night and do the walk from here. This pub serves up snacks and good bar food (including homemade pies from £7), with a log fire when it's cold and a garden for when it's sunny. The pub is also a microbrewery and its Litton Ale is recommended. There are reductions on the B&B rate in winter. There's also a 'walkers room', sleeping up to six people for £75, plus £20 per additional person.

Litton to Buckden
1½–2 hours, 4 miles (6.5km)

With your back to the pub door, go left and uphill along a lane signposted 'Bridleway – Buckden'. The lane crosses a farmyard then becomes a track, dropping briefly into the pretty little valley of **Crystal Beck**, then climbs steadily up. Look back to see a patchwork of Dales fields, with the bulk of Pen-y-ghent and Plover Hill looming beyond. Keep your eyes on the route, though; as you climb out of the valley, the track becomes less distinct where it cuts back to the left to follow a stone wall steeply uphill. Keep the wall to your left.

After about 1.5 miles, where the gradient starts to ease, make sure you bear left through a gate to reach the broad top of the fell, marked by a new pathway of stone flagstones to guide you across the peaty ground. As you cross the ridge there's a trig point about 200m to the right. Unfortunately the top is too broad to allow views down into both valleys, but as you start descending into Wharfedale you can see the villages of Buckden and Starbotton and the edge of Kettlewell. The hills beyond include Buckden Pike.

The path down to Buckden follows further stretches of flagstones across boggy patches. At the end of the flags, the path is indistinct in places but there are a few blue-topped marker posts to keep you in line.

As you approach a line of woodland, the path meets a track (signposted 'Bridleway') that winds down around the edge of the wood and through fields near a farm, eventually meeting the lane just west of Buckden. Turn right and walk along the lane for 500m to reach the bridge over the River Wharfe. If you need refreshment, go over the bridge into Buckden village (p179).

Buckden to Kettlewell
1½ hours, 4 miles (6.5km)

If you're skipping the delights of Buckden, before crossing the bridge turn right over a stile and onto a river-side path heading southeast. You are now on the Dales Way, although heading against the direction most long-distance walkers take.

Keep to this flat and very pleasant path as it winds through a few patches of woodland, meadows and fields, past stone walls and classic Dales field barns, and over a rather tiring number of stiles, all the way back to Kettlewell. In summer there's sometimes an ice-cream stall near the bridge. Otherwise the teashops or pubs in Kettlewell will provide any required end-of-walk sustenance.

THE THREE PEAKS

Duration	9–12 hours
Distance	25 miles (40km)
Difficulty	demanding
Start/Finish	Horton in Ribblesdale (p270)
Transport	bus, train

Summary A classic walk, long and challenging through high Dales country, with some sections of lower farmland for respite.

The three highest peaks in the Yorkshire Dales are Whernside (736m), Ingleborough (723m) and Pen-y-ghent (694m) – the main points of this long, circular route, which has been a classic walk for many years. We mean *many* years: the first recorded completion was in 1887. Since then, thousands of walkers have done the circuit, traditionally aiming to complete the whole route in less than 12 hours. Some keen walkers knock it off in six hours or less. Even faster are the fell runners in the annual Three Peaks Race, who do it in about 2½ hours. If you're looking for a tough challenge, this might be one for you. If you like to actually enjoy your walking, doing a section of this route is perfectly feasible and still highly recommended.

PLANNING

This circular route can be followed in either direction; we describe it anticlockwise. The traditional start/finish is the village of Horton in Ribblesdale (usually shortened to Horton). Another possible start is Ribblehead, if only to avoid the crowds that clog Horton on summer weekends. In recent years 'doing the Three Peaks' has become particularly popular with groups on sponsored walks raising money for charity, and things can get especially crowded if you happen to hit one of these days.

Wherever you start, paths are mostly clear. There are some very boggy sections, although many (but not all) of the worst bits are crossed by wooden boards or stone slabs, to protect the fragile environment as well as prevent walkers getting mired. There are some signposts, but the route itself is not specifically waymarked, so map and compass knowledge is essential.

The official total distance is 25 miles, but with all the ups and downs, and twists and turns, it's better to reckon on 26 miles. The route involves over 1500m of ascent, so this is no stroll in the park. With lunch and other stops, you should be able to do it in less than 12 hours.

Alternatives

If 25 miles is too far, you can still enjoy a walk in this area by doing just one or two of the peaks. Pen-y-ghent and Ingleborough can be reached from Horton, while Whernside and Ingleborough can be reached from Ribblehead. All are fine walks in their own right, with circular routes of between 5.5 miles and 12 miles possible.

The railway opens up more options. For example, from Horton you can walk via Pen-y-ghent or Ingleborough and Whernside to Ribblehead, then catch the train back to Horton.

Maps & Books

The whole Three Peaks route is on the OS Landranger 1:50,000 map No 98 *Wensleydale & Upper Wharfedale*. For more detail use OS Explorer 1:25,000 map No 2 *Yorkshire Dales – South & West* or Harvey Maps' 1:40,000 *Dales West*.

Specific coverage of the route includes *The Three Peaks Map & Guide* by Arthur Gemmell, a handy little booklet that also describes other routes in the area, plus background on geology and history. Other guidebooks on the Three Peaks area include very nicely produced *Three Peaks & Howgill Fells* by Sheila Parker, with colour maps and photos and new information to take account of recent 'freedom to roam' legislation (see p448), endorsed by the Ramblers' Association. Others include *Walks in the Three Peaks Country* by Paul Hannon and *Settle & the Three Peaks* by Mick North.

Information Sources

The **Horton tourist office** (☎ 01729-860333; horton@ytbtic.co.uk) is in the Pen-y-ghent Café. In between pouring mugs of tea, the friendly staff can advise on routes, and recommend maps, guides (on sale in the café) and local accommodation. A website dedicated to the route is www.3peakswalks.co.uk.

YORKSHIRE HYPE

A local ditty reads 'Whernside, Ingleborough and Pen-y-ghent – the highest hills twixt Tweed and Trent'. The River Trent is in Nottinghamshire and the Tweed is on the Scottish border – an impressive 100 miles or more in each direction. But hold on there. Some walkers point out that the Lake District (and Scafell Pike – England's highest mountain) is only about 40 miles away, and so the rhyme is a little misleading. Although Yorkshire people are known to be proud of their county, this might be just a tad too much hype!

GETTING TO/FROM THE WALK

Buses run from the gateway town of Skipton to Settle during the day (45 minutes, hourly on weekdays, five buses each way on Sunday), but between Settle and Horton (20 minutes) there's a single bus that runs only on school days. So, by far the best way to reach Horton or Ribblehead is on the trains that run between Leeds (one hour to Horton) and Carlisle (1½ hours to Horton) via Skipton (30 minutes from Horton) and Settle (10 minutes from Horton). This is the famous **Settle-Carlisle Railway** (www.settle -carlisle.co.uk) – see the boxed text on p174 for railway details. From May to September at least six trains run daily in each direction (five on Sunday).

If you're driving, note that the car park in the village often fills at weekends. The tourist office will direct you to alternative parking places. Cars left on verges or in gateways may be towed away by farmers with powerful tractors…

THE WALK
Horton in Ribblesdale to Pen-y-ghent
1½ hours, 2.5 miles (4km)

Leave Horton southwards, along the main street past the church. Cross over the stream and turn left into a lane heading uphill to a farm at Brackenbottom. From here a path leads straight up the hillside, over several stiles, to the southern shoulder of Pen-y-ghent. You can't miss the great bulk of this mountain looming ahead. The cliffs look steep as you approach – and they are – but the path winds its way up between the worst bits, to flatten out for the final few step that take you to **Pen-y-Ghent summit** (694m). At the trig point, take a few moments to enjoy the view – hopefully the walk's other two peaks will be clearly visible.

Pen-y-ghent to Ribblehead
3 hours, 7.5 miles (12km)

Cross the ladder stile over the wall running across the summit plateau, and drop downhill to the northwest. Horton is down to your left. You'll also see the great hole of Hull Pot. Even more obvious is the Pennine Way coming up to meet you. Don't take the Pennine Way back to Horton but continue northwest. (In wet weather your route is likely to be blocked by Hull Pot Beck, in which case *do* follow the Pennine Way towards Horton to meet a track going up the west side of the beck. This will lead you back onto the path described above.)

The path drops gradually down and continues along the valley, over several streams and bogs, to finally meet a dirt track near a house called Old Ing. From here you keep going downhill through fields to cross the River Ribble on a bridge to reach Lodge Hall Farm. Follow the farm lane to the main road (B6479) then walk along the side of this road – busy in summer, so take care – north to Ribblehead.

WALKERS' SAFETY SERVICE

Every weekend (and on some weekdays by prior arrangement) the helpful people at the Pen-y-ghent Café in Horton run a safety service – aimed specifically at individuals or small groups rather than the larger groups on organised sponsored walks. This service is free, and run by the café staff on a voluntary basis.

Here's how it works: you complete a card with your name and details, get the time punched onto it by the old factory clock in the café and leave the card. (If you want to get away in the morning before the café opens, there's an early-bird service – see the notice on the café porch for details.) When you finish the circuit you clock in so the staff know you're safely back.

The café closes at 6pm, but the staff wait around to check everybody gets back. If you've clocked out and don't manage to get back to Horton, it is *essential* that you phone the café to advise that you're OK. Otherwise staff will report you missing and that wastes the time and resources of the police and mountain-rescue team.

Although the clock-in service is a safety device (and not designed as 'part of the fun' for big groups on a day out), if you fulfil the requirements and complete the circuit in less than 12 hours you may get invited to join the Three Peaks Club – this means a certificate and a badge – issued by the café for a small fee. Note, however, that this is not a race. All you have to do is finish inside 12 hours – you don't get extra points for shorter times.

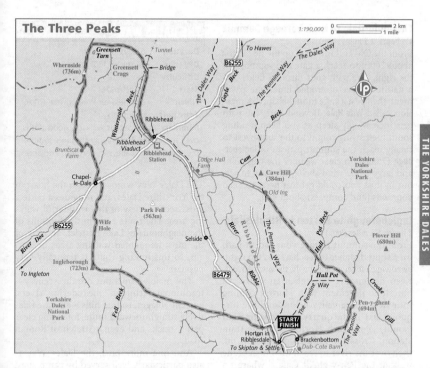

The Three Peaks

An alternative start and finish for this route, as well as a staging post, Ribblehead is about 6 miles northwest of Horton by road. For B&B, bunkhouse accommodation, something to eat or just a pint of beer, head for the **Station Inn** (☎ 01524-241274; www .thestationinn.net; dm/s/d £9/32/50, meals £8-11). The bar serves sandwiches, giant filled Yorkshire puddings and meals like steak-and-ale pie, and is usually full with a mixed crowd of locals and visiting walkers, bikers, cavers and train spotters. If you want to keep moving, near the road junction a **tea van** may be parked (summer and weekends only).

Ribblehead to Whernside
2 hours, 4.5 miles (7km)
From east of Station Inn, a dirt road leads northwest towards the **Ribblehead Viaduct**. When the Settle-Carlisle Railway was threatened with closure in the 1970s, this viaduct became the symbol of the fight to keep the line open. The success of that campaign is commemorated by a plaque showing a Victorian navvy and a modern railway engineer 'shaking hands across the century'.

Do not go beneath the viaduct but go up hill on the path running next to the railway as it curves round to the northeast, to take a small bridge across the line – also carrying Force Gill stream, so marked 'aqueduct' on OS maps. Continue upwards to the north of lonely (and lovely) **Greensett Tarn**.

The path eventually reaches a wall running along the ridge and leads all the way to the trig point marking the summit of **Whernside** (736m). The path is to the east of the wall and the trig point is to the west – so take care in mist.

Whernside to Chapel-le-Dale
1 hour, 3.5 miles (5.5km)
From Whernside follow the path southwest down the ridge for about 1.5 miles before branching left (south) and heading steeply down the hillside and into fields to reach Bruntscar Farm. From here a track then a lane leads directly to the B6255, about 500m north of the small village of Chapel-le-Dale. Almost opposite the point where the lane meets the main road is the popular **Old Hill Inn** – ideal if you need a meal or drink.

Chapel-le-Dale to Ingleborough Summit
1½ hours, 2.5 miles (4km)

From the Old Hill Inn head up the B6255 for about 200m to reach a gate and signpost on the right. The path goes through fields and a nature reserve of eroded limestone pavement, then past a large funnel-shaped depression called **Wife Hole**. Beyond here, the path gets increasingly steep as you keep heading south then swing round to the southwest to finally reach the summit plateau of **Ingleborough** (723m). In clear weather the trig point and large stone wind shelter are easy to see, but in mist you could get lost here, so keep your wits (and compass) about you.

Ingleborough to Horton in Ribblesdale
2 hours, 5.5 miles (9km)

From the summit retrace your ascent path for a short distance to reach a fork. Go right, heading east on a clear path, then southeast. Keep descending through a large area of limestone pavement with Horton coming into view in the valley below, and the turquoise lake in the quarry over to your right (south). You reach Horton near the train station. Cross the railway, go straight on, then over the river to reach the finish of the walk at the Pen-y-ghent Café – where no doubt you'll deserve several mugs of tea.

THE DALES WAY

Duration	6 days
Distance	84 miles (135km)
Difficulty	moderate
Start	Ilkley (p176)
Finish	Bowness-on-Windermere (p176)
Transport	bus, train

Summary An excellent walk on good paths, over some hills, but mainly through some of the most scenic valleys in northern England.

The Dales Way winds through the heart of the Yorkshire Dales, and provides a perfect cross-section view of this wonderful walking area. The route ends in the foothills of the neighbouring Lake District, another of the most frequented walking areas in Britain, so this linking route is naturally very popular.

The major attractions are the scenery – traditional farmland, meandering rivers, ancient villages, rolling hills – and the relatively straightforward route, following clear paths, tracks and even a stretch of Roman road.

And one more plus: the Dales Way is also particularly well served by camp sites, hostels, B&Bs and village shops, plus a great

THE SETTLE-CARLISLE RAILWAY

One of the greatest engineering achievements of the Victorian era, the **Settle-Carlisle Railway** (www.settle-carlisle.co.uk) takes passengers across some of the most scenic countryside in England. The line was created by the Midland Railway Company at the end of the 19th century; legend has it that the company chairman looked at a map of Yorkshire, saw the big gap that was the Dales and drew a line across it with a pencil, saying, 'That's where I'll have my railway'.

The chairman hadn't realised there were quite so many hills and valleys to cross, and the line took 6000 men known as navigators (or 'navvies') more than seven years to build. It cost over £3.5 million (a vast sum in those days) and 100 lives (an even greater cost) due to accidents and appalling conditions in the workers' camps.

It was the last major railway to be built using pick and shovel by gangs of navvies, and involved some amazing work. The Ribblehead Viaduct has 24 arches, the tallest almost 50m high, and the viaducts at Dent Head and Arten Gill are almost as impressive. The longest tunnel is under Blea Moor and is over 1 mile long. Altogether there are 325 bridges, 21 viaducts and 14 tunnels.

In the 1970s British Rail decided the expense of repairing the line was unjustifiable and the line was threatened with closure, but the ensuing public outcry ensured its survival. Today, passenger trains between Leeds and Carlisle run along the line at least six times daily, and it's also used by freight trains carrying coal and stone. During summer there are occasionally steam-hauled trains on the route but normally there are simply two-carriage diesels. Nevertheless, the views from the windows are amazing, and the railway is still one of the best ways for walkers to get to the heart of the Dales. For more details about the line's history, background and timetables see the website.

many comfortable cafés, teashops and pubs. If you stopped in them all you'd never make it to Windermere.

PLANNING

The Dales Way can be walked in either direction but we recommend going southeast to northwest. It's better to leave Ilkley than to arrive, and Lake Windermere makes a very precise and satisfying finish.

The official length of 84 miles is measured on the map, so it's a bit more with all the ups and downs, and most people take six days to cover the route. Many also start at a weekend, meaning a 'bulge' goes along the trail, sometimes filling all B&B options in the villages at the end of each day. To avoid this, try to start the route midweek. We suggest the following stages as most convenient:

Day	From	To	Miles/km
1	Ilkley	Grassington	17/27.5
2	Grassington	Buckden	11/17.5
3	Buckden	Dentdale	16/25.5
4	Dentdale	Sedbergh	13/21
5	Sedbergh	Burneside	17/27.5
6	Burneside	Bowness-on-Windermere	10/16

Alternatives

If you're a fast walker you could do the Way in five days but it would be a shame to rush. So, if your time is limited, start at Bolton Abbey and end at Sedbergh, a four-day trip covering the best bit of the route. If you really want to saunter, the route can be done in seven or eight days, splitting Day 1 at Burnsall and Day 3 at Cam Houses, for example.

As with all long-distance paths (LDPs), you can do just a single-day linear section of the Dales Way or a circular route taking in a stretch of the main path. Publications suggesting other routes are listed on right.

Maps

Despite its popularity, the Dales Way is not well waymarked throughout, so you'll need a map and you'll have to keep an eye on it to avoid following other footpaths that branch off the route.

For the whole route on one map, you can't do better than Harvey Maps' *Dales Way* 1:40,000 strip map. If you want to explore the Dales beyond the strip, then you'll need more sheets. In the Harvey *Yorkshire Dales* 1:40,000 series this means the *East, South* and *West* sheets.

If you prefer OS Landranger 1:50,000 maps, the Dales Way is mostly on maps No 98 *Wensleydale & Upper Wharfedale* and 99 *Northallerton & Ripon*, with the start of the route on No 104 *Leeds & Bradford* and the end on No 97 *Kendal & Morecambe*.

For more detail, the southern and central parts (except the first few miles out of Ilkley) are also shown on the OS Explorer 1:25,000 maps No 2 *Yorkshire Dales – South & West* and 30 *Yorkshire Dales – Northern & Central*. The section of the route north of Dent is on maps No 19 *Howgill Fells* and 7 *The English Lakes – South Eastern*.

Books

The book that started it all is *Dales Way* by Colin Speakman, first published in 1970 and since gone through many editions. *Dales Way Route Guide* by Colin Speakman and Arthur Gemmell is another long-standing, very handy and inexpensive booklet, with details of the main route plus several circular day walks taking in sections of the Way. The *Dales Way Companion* by Paul Hannon is lovingly handcrafted in the Wainwright tradition, combining pen-and-ink text and illustrations, plus just enough background information to entertain without distraction. These three books have hand-drawn maps but they should still be used with a proper survey map. Other route guides include *The Dales Way* by Terry Marsh and *The Dales Way* by Anthony Burton, containing extracts from the OS 1:25,000 maps.

The exceedingly useful *Dales Way Handbook,* published annually by the Dales Way Association (and available by post), contains accommodation listings, public transport details and other essential information. It's also available in most tourist offices.

Information Sources

See the walk description for tourist offices on or near the route. Also near the Dales Way, and handy for information on the area surrounding the northern part of the route, is Kendal, which has a **tourist office** (☎ 01539-725758; www.lakelandgateway.info).

The website of the **Dales Way Association** (www.dalesway.org.uk) is full of information, including latest updates to the route, new guidebooks and places to stay. Membership of the association includes the handbook (see p175), and in this way you can support the people who support the route.

Baggage Services

Baggage-carrying services are listed on p437.

NEAREST TOWNS

Ilkley

At the start of the route, Ilkley was originally established as a village on a packhorse route across the Yorkshire Dales, then grew into a wealthy market centre in the Middle Ages, with much of the trade based on wool. Today, Ilkley still exudes an air of quiet comfort, with hanging baskets and antique shops, the ever-reliable indicators of well-to-do towns, much in evidence. The **tourist office** (☎ 01943-602319; www.visitilkley.com) is opposite the bus and train stations.

SLEEPING & EATING

There are many B&Bs in town and those welcoming walkers include **Archway Cottage** (☎ 01943-603399; thegreens@archcottage.fsnet.co.uk; 24 Skipton Rd; d from £50); **1 Tivoli Place** (☎ 01943-600328; www.tivoliplace.co.uk; d from £70); **63 Skipton Rd** (☎ 01943-817542; d from £70); and the **Riverside Hotel** (☎ 01943-607338; www.ilkley-riversidehotel.com; s/d £45/65), in a quiet setting very near the start of the route, also with a bar and restaurant.

Ilkley has a good selection of places to eat, including the famously genteel **Betty's Cafe** and several pleasant pubs.

GETTING THERE & AWAY

Ilkley is served by frequent buses from Leeds (one hour) and Skipton (30 minutes), both easily reached from anywhere in the country by National Express coach. By train, the nearest mainline station to the start of the walk is Leeds, linked to London and the rest of the country by fast and regular services. From Leeds, local commuter trains run to Ilkley (30 minutes) at least once an hour.

Bowness-on-Windermere & Windermere

The Dales Way ends at the small town of Bowness-on-Windermere, only 1.5 miles from the larger town of Windermere itself, although the two places pretty much merge. As the name implies, Bowness-

on-Windermere sits on the shores of Lake Windermere, on the eastern edge of the Lake District. There's a **tourist office** (☎ 015394-46499; windermeretic@southlakeland.gov .uk) in Windermere.

SLEEPING & EATING

When it comes to accommodation, if any house in Bowness or Windermere doesn't do B&B, it's probably abandoned. Or at least that's how it seems in this busy tourist honey pot. Having said that, in high season you may still have to do a bit of phoning around to find a bed for the night. Another point to remember is that many B&Bs here don't really cater for passing walkers but prefer to take tourists for a number of nights.

The more walker-friendly places include the **Fairfield** (☎ 015394-46565; www.the-fairfield .co.uk; Brantfell Rd; d £74), a smart and comfortable place – to your left as you come down the road at the end of the route – with discounts for stays of two or more nights and in the quieter months, and the nearby **Blenheim Lodge** (☎ 01539-443440; blenheimlodge@supanet.com; d £32-50).

Good-quality **Belsfield House** (☎ 01539-445823; www.belsfieldhouse.co.uk; 4 Kendal Rd; d from £50) is very near the end of Brantfell Rd; guests can use the sauna, massage and jacuzzi facilities free of charge at a nearby hotel leisure centre – ideal for reviving tired legs after the walk!

Also good is **Lingwood Lodge** (☎ 01539-444680; www.lingwoodlodge.co.uk; Birkett Hill; d £70), about 800m south of the pier.

Just off the Dales Way, near Matson Ground, about 1 mile before you reach Bowness, a good choice is **Gillthwaite Rigg** (☎ 01539-44621; Lickbarrow Rd; d £60). The friendly people here will pick you up from the end of the route and run you back into town, if required, for an evening meal. If you have your own car, they also offer long-term parking, so you can leave it here while you're walking the Dales Way.

If you want a real blowout at the end of your walk, try the **Old England Hotel** (☎ central reservations 0870 400 8130; www.macdonald-hotels.co.uk /oldengland), overlooking the lake. B&B ranges from £39 per person midweek in winter to about £85 on summer weekends. Take your boots off before checking in, though!

A favourite pub in the same part of town is the **Hole in't Wall** (a reminder of all those squeeze gates you've pushed through on the

Dales Way!), with good beer, lively atmosphere, bar food and music some evenings. There are other good pubs on the nearby streets, most doing food. For other eating options, Bowness and Windermere have more teashops, cafés and takeaways than you can shake a stick at, not to mention a batch of classy restaurants. Stroll around for 10 minutes and you'll soon find a place to suit your taste buds and budget.

GETTING THERE & AWAY
In the summer, local buses run between Bowness-on-Windermere and Windermere, from where buses go to all parts of the Lake District and other places in the north of England, while National Express coaches go to all parts of the country. From Windermere there are hourly trains to Kendal (15 minutes), on a main line, from where you can reach the rest of the country. (For more details on transport away from Windermere to other parts of the Lakes, see p188)

THE WALK
Day 1: Ilkley to Grassington
6–8 hours, 17 miles (27.5km)
This is a long day and can be a hard introduction to the route. It can be busy too, especially around Bolton Abbey on summer weekends. If you're fully kitted out with boots and backpack, you'll feel a bit silly surrounded by people in beachwear, kids in pushchairs and grannies on Zimmer frames. Nevertheless, this is a really beautiful bit of the valley. Try to do it on a weekday.

From the centre of Ilkley go to the 'new' bridge (built in 1904) over the River Wharfe. Don't cross this bridge but go left down some steps and along the river to reach the Old Bridge, the official start, marked by a single Dales Way signpost.

Continue along the south bank of the Wharfe, then follow the path away from

the river, through woodland, past a tennis club and then across flat meadows to enter more woodland next to the river once again. Although the main road is nearby, it's surprisingly quiet – the sound of traffic is not enough to drown out the birdsong.

The Way winds around the backstreets of the village of Addingham, then follows the river bank closely for 1.5 miles to suddenly pop out on the busy and narrow B6160. The Way used to follow this road but thankfully a new route leads to the driveway of Lobwood House then through the fields, parallel to the road but separated from the traffic by a wall. Not quite far enough, though, as there's still a nasty little section along the edge of the road before you branch off onto a path back to the river.

Follow the river-side path, under another main road (the A59) then past old Bolton Bridge and across fields, following signposts to Bolton Abbey. Keep near the river to bypass the village of Bolton Abbey. Just beyond here are the ruins of **Bolton Priory** – see the boxed text, below.

Near the priory you cross the stepping stones (or the nearby footbridge) to the east bank of the river and head north. A short distance along you could divert across another footbridge to reach the **Cavendish Pavilion**, selling drinks, meals, snacks, ice creams and postcards. The route continues through delightful woods above a narrow gorge called the **Strid** (there's a tearoom at the nearby car park), to reach Barden Bridge.

Follow the river through farmland, passing close to the village of Appletreewick – with a couple of pubs that get very crowded on summer weekends. Less frenetic is Burnsall, about 2 miles upstream, where excellent food and accommodation is available at the **Red Lion Hotel** (☎ 01756-720204; d £125). It's just a few more easy miles, through fields and patches of woodland, to Grassington.

BOLTON PRIORY

Bolton Priory is often mistakenly called Bolton Abbey (but that's the name of the village). The priory was built in the 12th century by Augustinian monks. During the dissolution of the monasteries under Henry VIII in 1539 all but the nave of the priory was destroyed. The surviving nave has now been converted into the parish church. The spectacle of these grand ruins in such beautiful surroundings has inspired poets and painters such as Wordsworth and Turner. The priory is open to visitors every day and contributions towards the upkeep are always welcomed.

THE YORKSHIRE DALES

The Dales Way

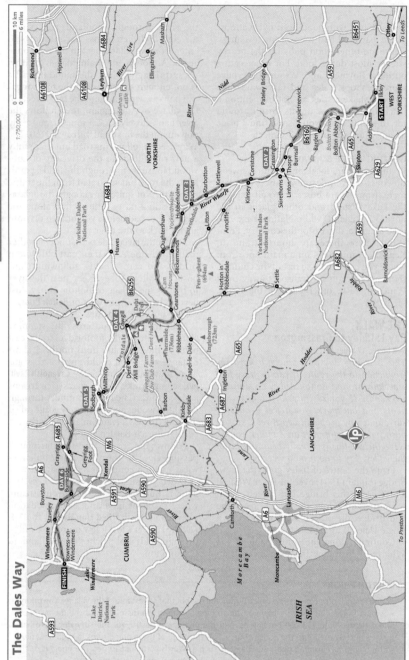

GRASSINGTON

The very attractive village of Grassington was once a lead-mining centre but today the major industry is tourism, with several pubs, cafés and craft shops, a small supermarket, a bank, an outdoor gear shop and heavy crowds on summer weekends. If you've arrived with time to spare, the Mining Museum is worth a visit. The **tourist office** (☎ 01756-752774; grassington@ytbtic.co.uk) is in the car park on the edge of the village.

Campers can go to **Wood Nook Caravan Park** (☎ 01756-752412; Skirethorns; sites for 2 £10), about 1 mile west of Grassington, a good place with hot showers and shop.

Walker-friendly B&Bs include **Lythe End** (☎ 01756-753196; Wood Lane; d £25). At the upper end of the main street are **Craven Cottage** (☎ 01756-752205; cullingford44@aol.com; d from £50) and **Grove House** (☎ 01756-753364; www.grovehousegrassington.net; d from £60).

A little out of the village centre are **Raines Close** (☎ 01756-752678; www.rainesclose.co.uk; Station Rd; s/d £32/50) and **Springroyd House** (☎ 01756-752473; www.springroydhouse.co.uk; Station Rd; d from £46). A smarter option is the **Grassington House Hotel** (☎ 01756-752406; Market Sq; s/d £44/76), with good meals and comfortable en suite rooms.

Of the pubs in the village, our favourite is the **Foresters Arms** (☎ 01756-752349; www.forestersarmsgrassington.co.uk), an old coaching inn on the main street, serving good beer and no-nonsense bar meals. Other pubs (also with food and accommodation) include the **Black Horse** (☎ 01756-752770; www.blackhorsehotelgrassington.co.uk) and the **Devonshire Hotel** (☎ 01756-752525; www.thedevonshirehotel.co.uk), both in the centre of the village.

Away from the pubs, Grassington's best eating option is **Number Forty-seven** (☎ 01756-752069; ☽ lunch & dinner), a delightful little restaurant at the upper end of the main street.

Day 2: Grassington to Buckden
4–5 hours, 11 miles (17.5km)

Today you continue up Wharfedale, but leave the valley floor to cross grassy fields and some beautiful sections of limestone pavement. The route also winds through several picturesque villages, most with lunch or overnight possibilities.

From the centre of Grassington go up the main street, left into Chapel St, turn right and go up a lane. Follow the waymarks across fields in a westerly direction, before swinging north again, high above the valley. The route passes through an old lead-mining area, and there are some entrances and shafts dotted about – so take great care if you lose the path in mist.

About 2.5 miles from Grassington, the Way crosses Bycliffe Road, an old packhorse route and now a bridleway used by mountain bikers. On the other side of the valley is Kilnsey Crag, a rock climbers' test piece. All activities catered for here!

The route drops to meet a lane about 1 mile south of the pretty little village of Kettlewell then soon branches off right (north). If the lane is quiet you might as well head straight into **Kettlewell** – an ideal lunch stop with pubs and tearooms, plus a shop and a post office. If you want to overnight here, details are given on p169.

Beyond Kettlewell the path follows the river, sometimes near the bank, sometimes a few fields away from it, but all the time through classic Dales scenery of stiles, drystone walls, ancient barns and a few patches of woodland, to reach Buckden.

BUCKDEN & HUBBERHOLME

The small and scenic village of Buckden has several walker-friendly B&Bs, including **West Winds Cottage** (☎ 01756-760883; d from £40), which is also a tearoom; **Birks View** (☎ 01756-760873; d from £44), next to the shop; and **Romany Cottage** (☎ 01756-760365; www.romanycottage.co.uk; s/d £27/44), also offering guided walks in the area. On the outskirts of the village is lovely old **Hartrigg House** (☎ 01756-760443; www.hartrigghouse.co.uk; d £60), originally built about 120 years ago as the station hotel – a little ambitious at the time, as the railway never arrived.

The village shop stocks enough for lunch or overnight if you're camping. Attached is the friendly **Buckden Village Restaurant** (lunch around £6, dinner £8-11; ☽ to 8pm Thu-Tue in summer). For evening food and refreshment, there's the **Buck Inn** (☎ 01756-760228; www.thebuckinn.com; mains from £8).

Less than 2 miles upstream from Buckden is the even smaller village of Hubberholme, where you'll find the highly rated **George Inn** (☎ 01756-760223; www.thegeorge-inn.co.uk; d £60), with good beer and excellent bar meals; walker-friendly **Church Farm** (☎ 01756-760240; gillhuck@hubberholme.fsnet.co.uk; d £44); and **Kirkgill Manor** (☎ 01756-760800; d from £58).

Day 3: Buckden to Dentdale

7–9 hours, 16 miles (25.5km)

This is a long day and potentially the most serious stage of the whole route. There are no shops or cafés for lunch on this section – in fact there's not much at all, except wonderful, wild, open hills, big views and the sound of the breeze.

After Hubberholme (where the ancient **church** is well worth a look around), the valley is called Langstrothdale but the river is still the Wharfe, getting more stream-like as it nears its source. The path passes through the lonely farmsteads of Yockenthwaite and Deepdale, then at Beckermonds you take a lane north towards Hawes. Just after the hamlet of Oughtershaw the Way branches off to the left (westwards) and into the fields again. The names of these dispersed farmsteads – and many other local names – are derived from the period when the Yorkshire Dales were inhabited by Vikings. Even words like 'fell' and 'dale' are Nordic in origin.

Meanwhile, back in the present, the valley gets broader and the landscape more exposed. When the wind blows up here you really know about it and, even on calm days, there's a great feeling of remote emptiness.

The route passes **Swarthghyll Farm** (☎ 01756-760466; www.swarthghyll-farm.co.uk; d £40). It's a long way to the pub for dinner, so the owners provide a food package (£6) for you to cook yourself, and also do packed lunches for the next day.

The route keeps going up gradually to pass the remote farmstead of Cam Houses (also called Camm Farm), up the hill, through the northern corner of Cam Woods, across a farm track, then diagonally up a final slope to a cairn. Here you meet the **Cam High Road**, part of an old Roman road, where you turn southwest. You can put the map away for a while and stride out like a centurion, taking in the splendid panoramas of Ingleborough and Whernside – two of the highest peaks in the Yorkshire Dales – away to the left. This section of the route is also part of the Pennine Way and you may see other long-distance walkers, mostly heading in the opposite direction on their way to Kirk Yetholm in Scotland.

At a second cairn the Pennine Way branches off left but you keep straight on, descending on the track to meet the B6255

at Gearstones. If you need sustenance or a bed, 1.5 miles to the west is Ribblehead and the Station Inn (see p173). If you're leaving the Dales Way here, the station is on the railway south to Settle and north to Carlisle. For details see the boxed text on p174.

If you're staying on the Dales Way, turn left and follow the road for 100m, then go up the first farm track on the right (signposted 'Dent Head'), past Winshaw House. From here the path leads through fields and the moorland edge to a lane. Turn left and follow the lane downhill into the top of Dentdale valley, under the arches of **Dent Head railway viaduct** – a fine example of Victorian engineering that comes as quite a surprise in this quiet rural area. The Way continues along the lane; traffic is light but take care.

DENTDALE

The route descends along Dentdale, and passes some accommodation options strung along the valley. In the tiny settlement of Cow Dub, the longstanding and near-legendary **Sportsman's Inn** (☎ 015396-25282; www.thesportsmansinn.com; d £54) has comfortable rooms, log fires, fine beers and good bar food every day, and provides a real welcome for Dales Way walkers.

Another 800m brings you to the equally walker-friendly **River View** (☎ 015396-25592; RiverView@btinternet.com; Cowgill; d from £50), near Lea Yeat Bridge.

Camping is possible at **Cow Dub Farm** (☎ 015396-25278; sites for 2 £5), next to the Sportsman's Inn, and at **Ewegales Farm** (☎ 015396-25440; sites for 2 £8), further down the valley.

There are more B&Bs a few miles along the valley (see the Day 4 description, below) and others in Dent village; some will pick you up from here if you arrange it in advance.

If you're leaving the route here, Dent train station is nearby – at the top of a very steep hill north of Cowgill. Trains head north to Carlisle or south to Settle and Leeds.

Day 4: Dentdale to Sedbergh

5–6 hours, 13 miles (21km)

This is a fairly easy day as the Way meanders through fields and woodland. The scenery is once again classic Yorkshire Dales (even though you're now in Cumbria).

From Cowgill the Dales Way winds down Dentdale, first on the south side of the valley, but crossing and re-crossing on a couple of occasions. At Mill Bridge (about 2 miles from Cowgill) there's a range of accommodation options at **Whernside Manor** (☎ 015396-25213; camp sites for 2 £6, bunkhouse £8, B&B d £60), though we found this place doesn't exactly ooze welcome. Next door, homely and friendly **Smithy Fold** (☎ 015396-25368; www.smithy fold.co.uk; d £40, dinner £13) offers comfortable B&B, and dinner by prior arrangement.

From Mill Bridge you follow a delightful path beside the River Dee to the large village of **Dent** – an interesting place to look around, with narrow, cobbled streets and a fine old church, and a **shop** (☻ daily) for supplies. For lunch there are a couple of teashops, plus two good pubs, also doing accommodation: the **George & Dragon** (☎ 015396-25256; www.the georgeanddragondent.co.uk; d weekdays/weekends £59/75) and the **Sun Inn** (☎ 015396-25208; d from £37). With several B&Bs in and around the village, Dent is also an overnight possibility.

From Dent return to the River Dee and continue following the Dales Way along a beautiful section of river bank on paths through fields. Near a point called Ellers the path meets the quiet lane along the south side of the valley and follows this to Brackensgill, where you turn right onto a track and the river is crossed on a new footbridge (older maps still show 'ford' here). The track meets the larger road running along the north side of the valley. You go almost straight across here and uphill on another track, going left, then left again past Gap Wood, where the gradient eases. There's one final hill, with fine views from the summit, before dropping through the village of Millthrop into the town of Sedbergh.

SEDBERGH

The busy old market town of Sedbergh promotes itself as 'England's Booktown' and this certainly is a good place to stock up on reading material. The town also has food stores, banks, pubs, a couple of outdoor gear shops and a **tourist office** (☎ 01539-620125; www .sedbergh.org.uk), which is, perhaps not surprisingly, in a bookshop on the main street.

The most convenient place for camping is **Pinfold Caravan Site** (☎ 015396-20576; sites for 2 £10), on the east side of town, with plenty of facilities, including a laundrette.

The well-equipped **Catholes Bunkhouse** (☎ 015396-20334; dm £6) is just off the Dales Way, before Sedbergh, and is best reached by turning off at Millthrop.

Walker-friendly B&Bs in Sedbergh include **Holmecroft** (☎ 015396-20754; www.holmecroft bandb.co.uk; Station Rd; d £46) and **Wheelwright Cottage** (☎ 015396-20251; 15 Back Lane; s/d £25/44).

Of the pubs in town offering B&B, the characterful **Dalesman Country Inn** (☎ 015396-21183; www.thedalesman.co.uk; Main St; s/d £30/60) serves fine beer and bar food. Also worth a try is the **Bull Hotel** (☎ 015396-20264; Main St; s/d £30/60; ☻ lunch & dinner), while the **Red Lion** is a traditional pub with very friendly and helpful staff.

For tomorrow's picnic, stock up from the good range of home baking at **Ellie's Bakery & Tearoom**.

Day 5: Sedbergh to Burneside
6–8 hours, 17 miles (27.5km)

This is a day of transition. The Way leaves the Yorkshire Dales and passes through the gently rolling landscape of the Eden Valley. You need to keep an especially good eye on the map here, as you encounter farmyards, old lanes and a great number of stiles and gates. There's no place to buy lunch, so bring a picnic.

The route leaves Sedbergh along the River Rawthey, which flows into the beautiful River Lune. This is followed through fields and meadows (and, at Hole House, almost through someone's kitchen!) for several miles. All morning the velvety humps of the Howgill Fells dominate the scene to your right (east) and the route is crossed by several splendid viaducts belonging to a disused railway, seemingly out of scale for what was a fairly minor branch line.

The handsome **Crook of Lune Bridge** is a good place for a rest, and maybe an early lunch and a spot of reflection over the last few days of walking, as the river marks the boundary of the national park. Go over the bridge and bid farewell to the Dales. After another 2 miles, the next bridge is quite a contrast – over the thundering traffic on the M6 motorway – but you soon enter farmland once again. A little further along you join a lane to cross a major railway line.

The Way continues through the small settlement of Grayrigg Foot (1 mile west of the slightly larger village of Grayrigg), where it crosses the A685 running south to Kendal, then continues through more sleepy farmland. If you're thinking about stopping for the night, there's B&B or a place to pitch your tent at **High Barn** (☎ 01539-824625; www .highbarn.info; sites for 2 £6, d £32, dinner £13) in the hamlet of Shaw End, about 1 mile beyond Grayrigg Foot, near Pattern Bridge.

Beyond here you pass the small lake of **Black Moss Tarn**, then it's another 3 miles or so of potentially complicated walking (you'll definitely need your map) along lanes, paths and farm tracks to finally reach Burneside.

BURNESIDE

On the edge of the Lake District, and overshadowed by the nearby honey-pot town of Kendal, the large village of Burneside sees few visitors. It may be the better for that. There's a shop, post office, and (for those wanting to leave the Dales Way) a train station.

Campers can go to the simple site at **Burnside Hall Farm** (sites for 2 £6), just before Burneside as you come in from the east.

On the main street, the **Jolly Anglers Inn** (☎ 01539-732552; s/d £38/56; ☯ dinner except Monday in winter) is a friendly village local. Next door, the **Jolly Fryer** (☯ dinner Tue, Thu & Fri) serves fish and chips to take away in the evening, plus a few lunchtimes.

In the next village of Bowston (also on the Dales Way), B&B is available at **Hillcrest** (☎ 01539-821489; d £56); with notice the friendly landlady will cook you an evening meal for around £18, including a bottle of wine.

If these places are all full, some B&Bs in Kendal will come and pick you up. These include friendly and historic **Bridge House** (☎ 01539-722041; www.bridgehouse-kendal.co.uk; Castle St; s/d £30/52). Guests are also offered complimentary Kendal Mint Cake – a locally made, sugar-based, traditional energy food, vital fuel for generations of British walkers and mountaineers.

Day 6: Burneside to Bowness-on-Windermere

3–4 hours, 10 miles (16km)
This final day is pleasingly easy, alongside rivers and through rolling farmland. Waymarking is generally good but there are still a few tricky bits. Rather than stopping en route, plan for a late lunch at Bowness-on-Windermere.

From Burneside the Way follows the River Kent for about 3.5 miles – a very enjoyable stretch of walking to get you in the mood for your first steps in the Lake District. The route passes just south of Staveley village, crossing a road, under a railway and then over the busy A591 between Kendal and Windermere on a small road bridge. If it's time for coffee, head into Staveley to find **Wilf's Café** (☎ 01539-822329; www.wilfs-cafe .co.uk), a very popular spot for walkers and cyclists, on a small industrial estate near Wheelbase Cycle Shop.

Beyond Stavely, there's a short section of walking along a lane and then the Way once again crosses peaceful farmland and some high ground near Hag End Farm, where a wide vista of Lake District mountains suddenly opens out before you. It's a wonderful sight but don't try to admire it while you're walking – stop and do it properly! – as on these last few miles the route ducks and dives through gardens and narrow farm lanes, with several paths branching off the main route, and it would be a shame to get lost so close to the end.

Although you can see the mountains of the Lake District, thus far there's been no view of Windermere, but on **Brant Fell**, just 1 mile or so before the finish, you're treated to the first view of the lake. Below this lookout is a slate bench with a plaque marking the official end of the Dales Way. You may want to sit down and celebrate, or you may decide it's more pleasing to continue down the path to Brantfell Rd, which then leads to the centre of Bowness-on-Windermere – a busy tourist town that can be quite a shock after days of near-solitude in the Dales.

Keep going downhill, past the pubs and cafés and souvenir shops, to the lake shore, where you can reach the water between crowds of holidaymakers and boats moored at the pier, and dip your toe in the lake to ceremoniously mark the end of your Dales Way walk. You can then enjoy a well-earned cup of tea or ice cream at one of the nearby snack bars overlooking the shore.

This goodbye to the Dales Way is also hello to the Lake District. For more details on this area, see p185.

MORE WALKS

In this chapter we have described a classic peak route, a less-demanding circuit through two valleys, and a wonderful long-distance route through the heart of the Dales. But there are many more opportunities for walking here; the following pointers describe areas roughly south to north.

THE SOUTHERN DALES

A great place to base yourself in this area is the village of Malham (p268). It's on the Pennine Way, and there's plenty of accommodation, and easy access by bus. Malham can get very busy, however, so is best avoided at weekends and during holidays. The surrounding area is a geologist's paradise – you can visit the precipitous cliff of Malham Cove, the remains of an ancient waterfall topped by an area of classic limestone pavement complete with numerous clints and grikes (sections of rock between narrow fissures). Nearby are picturesque Malham Tarn and the waterfall of Gordale Scar, and these can all be linked on an excellent 8-mile (13km) walk.

East of the River Wharfe, the hills of the Dales are quieter. A good circuit goes from Bolton Abbey, northwards for a short distance along the river's east bank before climbing up through an area marked 'The Valley of Desolation' on OS maps (although it's very pleasant in reality) to reach the wide, flat moorland of Barden Fell and the impressive summit of Simon's Seat, with great views over lower Wharfedale and the surrounding area.

THE WESTERN DALES

In the western part of the Dales, the small town of Ingleton makes a good base; it's quite easy to reach and has several places to stay. In the area to the north, the valleys of the Rivers Twist and Doe are popular, but the stunning scenery attracts many visitors, so come at a quiet time of year if you can. The nearby village of Clapham is easy also to reach – there's a train station 1.5 miles away. From here you can walk to the large and impressive Ingleborough Caves and continue on to the high ground, even to the summit of Ingleborough itself – one of the famous Three Peaks.

Northwest of Ingleton is Ribblehead, easily reached on the Settle-Carlisle Railway. As well as Ingleborough and Whernside (described in the Three Peaks walk, p170), many other areas can be reached from here. If you have an interest in history, you can go a few miles north of Ribblehead and walk part of the Roman route known as the Cam High Road. For a great day walk you can stride out along this ancient route all the way (12 miles) across the moors from Ribblehead to Bainbridge in Wensleydale.

THE HOWGILLS

In the western reaches of the Yorkshire Dales National Park, within sight of the Lake District, is a group of very impressive, though often ignored, hills called the Howgill Fells. They're big, rounded and compact, sometimes likened to a group of squatting elephants, with some good walk options. The best base for exploring these hills is the town of Sedbergh (p181), from where a hike over Calders to a summit called the Calf is an excellent introduction to the Howgills. Take care though, as there are not many paths and the tops are featureless, making navigation a serious test in bad weather. But the walking underfoot is easy and the hills are not crowded, with unsurpassed 360-degree views of the Lake District to the west, the Yorkshire Dales to the east and south, and the Pennines to the north.

THE NORTHERN DALES

The main valley in the northern part of the Dales is Wensleydale, famous worldwide for its cheese, and with plenty of walking opportunities on the wild fells to the north and south. The town of Hawes (p270) makes an excellent base, with several places to stay. Other possible bases, further to the east, are the villages of Askrigg and Aysgarth – handy for a visit to the spectacular Aysgarth Force waterfall.

Finally, don't forget Swaledale, a relatively remote but beautiful valley in the far north of the national park. A route along the length of this valley forms part of the Coast to Coast Walk (p237), but there are many circular day-walk options. Good bases include the small town of Reeth (p247) and historic Richmond (p248), a gateway town just beyond the far north-eastern tip of the park.

HERRIOT WAY

Perhaps one of the best ways of exploring the northern Dales is to follow the four-day, 53-mile (85km) Herriot Way, named for James Herriot, who wrote many popular books about his work as a vet in the farms of this area. The circular route links Hawes, Aysgarth, Reeth and Keld, thus combining two days of valley walking with two days of fell walking – a perfect Dales outing for a long weekend. For more details see www .herriotway.co.uk.

THE INN WAY

The Inn Way through the Yorkshire Dales is a 76-mile (122km) circuit starting (and finishing) at Grassington (p179). The walk goes via Wharfedale and Littondale to Buckden, then through Langstrothdale and Raydale to Askrigg in Wensleydale, and along Swaledale to Reeth, before turning south through Apedale, Bishopdale, Walden, Coverdale and Kettlewell. The route is described in *The Inn Way to the Yorkshire Dales* by Mark Reid – one of several guidebooks in a series combining great country walks with great country pubs. For more details see www.innway.co.uk.

The Lake District

If anywhere is the heart and soul of walking in England, it's the Lake District – a wonderful area of high mountains, deep valleys and, of course, beautiful lakes. Why is it so popular? There may be a historic reason; this is where William Wordsworth and other 19th-century romantic writers were among the first people to take up walking for pleasure. But it's probably a matter of aesthetics. Whereas some other parts of England have rounded hills and moors, the Lake District has proper peaks – high, wild and rugged – or, as one fan put it, 'mountains with knobs on'.

Here in the Lake District, the choice of one-day walking routes is endless. There are hundreds of high walks, peak walks, ridge walks, valley walks and (naturally) lake walks. Even a list of classics would run to several pages, so picking just a few routes to represent the whole area is particularly hard, but we've made a brave attempt and selected a batch to include the area's best-known and best-loved mountains, such as Scafell Pike, Fairfield and Helvellyn. If your time is short, some routes can be done from the same base, so you won't have to move camp every night.

Also in this chapter we describe the Cumbria Way – a mainly lowland long-distance path (LDP) through the heart of the Lake District, dipping in and out of moorland, farmland and woodland, and taking in the shorelines of lovely Lake Coniston, Elterwater and Derwent Water. But whether you go high or low, after a week or two here you'll just have to agree that the Lake District is something special.

HIGHLIGHTS

- Wandering in Wordsworth's footsteps on the **Fairfield Horseshoe** (p189)
- Following the ancient Roman road over the summit of **High Street** (p197)
- Reaching the summit of **Scafell Pike** (p200) on a clear day – Scotland seems so close…
- Completing the central days on the **Cumbria Way** (p203); Coniston to Ullswater, lake to lake

THE LAKE DISTRICT

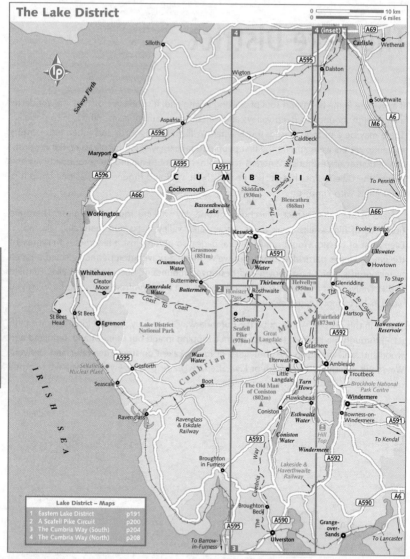

Lake District – Maps	
1 Eastern Lake District	p191
2 A Scafell Pike Circuit	p200
3 The Cumbria Way (South)	p204
4 The Cumbria Way (North)	p208

INFORMATION

The Lake District (often called 'Lakeland' or simply 'the Lakes' – but never 'the Lakes District') has an irresistible attraction to walkers. They may moan about crowded footpaths and notoriously unpredictable weather, but many return year after year. And as well as the walkers, several million other visitors come each year for fishing, sailing, mountain biking or to simply tour the area in cars and coaches. Over the years, various plans have been mooted to restrict the number of vehicles, but none have really been successful, so if you're on the roads during summer be prepared for a mighty crush – another reason to take to the hills on foot!

Most of the landscape is contained within the Lake District National Park. Like all national parks in England and Wales, this is not public land. It's made up of many privately owned farms and estates, and includes many villages and even a few towns – this is a living, *working* park. Some local people are employed in farming but many more depend on tourism for their income and welcome the annual influx.

Maps

All but the very outer reaches of the Lake District are covered by four Ordnance Survey (OS) Landranger 1:50,000 maps: Nos 85 *Carlisle & Solway Firth,* 89 *West Cumbria,* 90 *Penrith & Keswick* and 96 *Barrow-in-Furness & South Lakeland.*

If you want greater detail, there are the OS Explorer 1:25,000 maps titled *The English Lakes:* No 4 *North Western Area,* No 5 *North Eastern Area,* No 6 *South Western Area* and No 7 *South Eastern Area.* Harvey Maps' excellent Superwalker 1:25,000 series covers the whole Lake District in six maps: *Central, North, East, West, Southwest* and *Southeast.*

If you want to carry just one map, recommended for most walks is the British Mountaineering Council's (BMC) excellent and award-winning 1:40,000 *Lake District* map.

For maps covering individual routes, see the Planning sections of each walk.

Books

If you piled up all the Lake District walking guidebooks available, there'd be another mountain to scale, so here are some of our favourite titles. Specific books for the routes described are listed in the relevant sections.

The classic series *A Pictorial Guide to the Lakeland Fells* by Alfred Wainwright is a set of seven pocket-sized volumes – *Eastern Fells, Western Fells, Central Fells* and so on (see also the boxed text, p188). For an overview, get *The Best of Wainwright* by Hunter Davies, describing 18 mountains lovingly selected from the original *Pictorial Guides* series, with handy little introductory sections giving a wider perspective.

Modern guidebooks include the *Rambler's Guide to the Lake District* published by Collins; it's a selection of 30 walks with illustrations, Harvey map extracts and an endorsement from the Ramblers' Association. The *Lake District Walks* and *More Lake District Walks* Pathfinder Guides, published by Jarrold, describe routes from a few miles to all-day treks, with extracts from relevant OS 1:25,000 maps.

The excellent spiral-bound guidebooks *Walk the Lake District, North* by Vivienne Crow and *Walk the Lake District, South* by Charles David, published by Discovery Walking Guides, cover a wide range of short and long routes across the entire region with OS map extracts, colour photos, handy tips and GPS information.

For a more relaxing option, there's a choice of guidebooks covering easier routes, with titles such as *Short Walks in the Lake District, Lake District Walking on the Level* and even *All-Terrain Buggy Walks.* Also good are titles such as *Pub Walks in the Lake District* (circular walks including a pub stop for lunch) and *Teashop Walks* (you can guess the concept). To make use of bus 555 (see Getting Around, p188) get the handy *55 555 Walks* by Robert Swain.

The Lakes scenery naturally inspires a whole stack of picture books too. Start with the splendid photos and fascinating background information in *The Lake District,* the official national park guide by Terry Marsh and Jon Sparks. Others include *The English Lakes* by Rob Talbot and Robin Whiteman, and *The Lake District* by Colin Baxter. A beautiful, informative and bargain-priced book is *Flora of the Fells* by Martin Varley, with proceeds going to the Friends of the Lake District (see www.fld.org.uk and www.floraofthefells.com).

Guided Walks

National park rangers organise a series of guided walks throughout the year – details are available from tourist offices. If these don't suit, the Lake District abounds with private mountain guides who can show you around on foot or arrange more energetic activities such as rock climbing. Most advertise in tourist offices, hostels and outdoor gear shops.

Information Sources

For general tourist information on central Cumbria and the Lake District, the main **tourist office** (☎ 015394-46499; www.lakelandgateway.info) is in Windermere, next to the train station. There are many other tourist offices in the region – those near specific walks are mentioned in the route descriptions.

The main national park website is www .lake-district.gov.uk. For general tourist information on the whole of Cumbria and the Lake District, see www.cumbria-the-lake -district.co.uk and www.golakes.co.uk. Especially good for walkers are www.lakedistrict outdoors.co.uk/walking.htm and www.lake districtwalks.com. Specific area websites are listed in the individual walk sections.

At tourist offices, hotels and shops you can pick up *Out & About*, a freebie newspaper produced by the national park authority, full of useful tourist information, background articles and advertisements for places to stay and things to do.

GETTING AROUND

A very handy bus for walkers is Stagecoach Cumbria's Lakeslink service (bus 555), running through the heart of the Lake District at least 10 times daily between Keswick and Kendal, via Grasmere, Ambleside and Windermere, extending north to/from Carlisle three times per day and south to/from Lancaster about six times per day.

For more details on this and all routes in the Lake District, see *Lakes Rider*, a very useful booklet available free from tourist offices. It covers boats and trains too.

IN THE FOOTSTEPS OF WAINWRIGHT

The Lake District is traditionally divided into several smaller areas – the Central Fells, the Northern Fells, the Eastern Fells and so on. These high areas are separated by large valleys and also based on divisions used by the iconic walker-writer Alfred Wainwright in his seven-volume *Pictorial Guide to the Lakeland Fells*. First published in the 1950s and 1960s, Wainwright's books have inspired countless walkers ever since.

Wainwright (or AW as he's universally known) combined a romantic devotion to wilderness and solitude with a scientific attention to detail – and an occasional dry wit – to produce unique, hand-crafted text, maps and illustrations. For walkers today, the original books are great for inspiration but need to be read alongside a modern map, as little details like following rights of way were less of an issue in AW's day.

Now published by Frances Lincoln, Wainwright's *Pictorial Guide* series is currently being lovingly revised and completely updated by author Chris Jesty; the second edition of the *Eastern Fells* was published in 2005 – a mere half-century after the first edition – and others will be produced in coming years.

As well as his guides to the Lakeland Fells, AW also wrote several other books for walkers. *A Coast to Coast Walk* was published in 1973 and has since inspired many thousands of walkers to cross the country on foot. The route, while not a national trail (yet), is one of the most popular long-distance routes in Britain. AW was careful to call his creation *A Coast to Coast Walk*, implying that it was only one of many options. However, most people doing Wainwright's route call it *The* Coast to Coast and follow the description very closely.

Wainwright's other long-distance classic is *The Pennine Way Companion*. It's fun, part of Pennine Way tradition and characteristically idiosyncratic – you have to read it backwards and follow the text *up* the page to stay in sync with the maps, which are designed to be followed south to north. As with all Wainwright guides, the text is (neatly) hand-printed and the intricate maps show every stile, gate and cow pat along the way – wonderful if you're on track, but useless once you're five steps off it. The original is now out of print and secondhand copies are collectors' items, so you'll be lucky to find one.

Many years ago, walkers who'd completed the whole Pennine Way in one go used to get a free drink in the bar of the hotel at Kirk Yetholm – on AW's tab. These days the hotel sometimes revives the tradition with sponsorship from a local brewery, so it's always worth asking – if you're a genuine Pennine Way walker of course!

AW is remembered today by the work of the **Wainwright Society** (www.wainwright.org.uk) and by walkers' attempts to bag 'The Wainwrights' – all 214 Lakeland Fells named in the famous seven guidebooks.

VOLCANIC LEGACY

The Lake District is the remains of an old volcano, with the high ground roughly in the centre, from where long ridges radiate like the spokes of a wheel. Between the ridges are valleys, many containing the lakes that give the area its distinctive scenery (and name). Roads lead up to the end of several valleys but few go right across the central part of the national park, meaning the high ground remains relatively remote and can only be reached on foot.

The YHA shuttle bus runs from Windermere train station to the YHA hostels at Windermere, Ambleside, Elterwater, Grasmere, Keswick and Patterdale, seven times daily Easter to October. Phone **Ambleside YHA Hostel** (☎ 0870 770 5672) for details.

For general information on public transport throughout the Lake District, use **Traveline** (☎ 0870 608 2608; www.traveline.org.uk) or check www.travelcumbria.co.uk.

GATEWAYS

The Lake District's main gateway cities and towns are Kendal, Windermere, Penrith, Keswick (p205) and Carlisle (p203), which all have good coach links to the rest of Britain, and are easy to reach by car.

The main railway line between London and Scotland goes through Kendal (with a branch off to Windermere) and Penrith (from where buses serve Keswick).

THE FAIRFIELD HORSESHOE

Duration	5–7 hours
Distance	10 miles (16km)
Difficulty	moderate
Start/Finish	Ambleside (p190)
Transport	bus

Summary A classic mountain circuit with fine, open walking and wonderful views. It's relatively straightforward in good weather, but potentially serious if conditions are bad.

Fairfield is the name of a large mountain close to the centre of the Lake District, and the Fairfield Horseshoe is a classic circuit, going up one ridge and down another on either side of a valley, with the summit of Fairfield at the highest point of the route where the two ridges meet. The Fairfield Horseshoe provides top-class walking over a rolling landscape, and is relatively straightforward in good weather. If this is your first visit to the Lakes, and you're not a complete beginner, we can't think of a finer introduction.

At 873m, Fairfield is one of the highest peaks in the area, along with neighbours Helvellyn (950m) and the wonderfully named Dollywaggon Pike (858m). When conditions are kind, the panoramic vistas are excellent. To the west you can see Scafell Pike – England's highest peak at 978m – and to the east sits the long ridge of High Street. The view south is dominated by the vast lake of Windermere, usually dotted with sailing boats that, from this distance, look like scattered confetti.

Often, however, you'll get no view at all. The weather on Fairfield can sometimes be awful with wind, rain and mist making a walk unpleasant and navigation skills necessary. As with anywhere in the Lakes, the conditions can change very quickly so, even if it looks fine, take warm, waterproof clothes, plus a map and compass that you know how to use.

PLANNING

The Fairfield Horseshoe is not a waymarked route, so you'll need a map. You can do the circuit in either direction, but we suggest going clockwise as this way the walk ends in the centre of Ambleside – full of reviving teashops and pubs. The distance is 10 miles, but you gain around 800m in height so the walking time is five to seven hours. Allowing for lunch and photo opportunities, your overall time will probably be around six to eight hours.

Maps & Books

If you're using OS Landranger 1:50,000 maps, the Fairfield Horseshoe is on No 90 *Penrith & Keswick*. With OS Explorer 1:25,000 maps you need No 7 *The English Lakes – South Eastern Area*, and a small but important section is on No 5 *North Eastern Area*. The whole route is on the 1:25,000 Harvey Map *Lakeland Central*, and on the BMC 1:40,000 *Lake District* map.

Wainwright's classic *Pictorial Guide to the Eastern Fells* includes a section on

THE LAKE DISTRICT

WILLIAM WORDSWORTH

The poet laureate of the Lake District is William Wordsworth, a leading figure in the English Romantic movement, and still one of Britain's best-known writers, even if it is only for a couple of lines about daffodils. A true son of the Lakes, Wordsworth was born in Cockermouth in 1770 and went to school at Hawkshead, near Ambleside. In 1799 he and fellow-scribe Samuel Coleridge enjoyed a tour of the Lake District, the inspiration for much of his writing. Later the same year, Wordsworth and his sister Dorothy moved into Dove Cottage in Grasmere. In 1802 Wordsworth married and, as his family and fame grew, Dove Cottage became increasingly crowded, so in 1808 the family moved to Allan Bank, then to the Old Parsonage in Grasmere and, finally, to Rydal Mount near Ambleside (passed on the Fairfield Horseshoe route), where he lived until his death.

Fairfield, and is good for further inspiration. Many of the other local route guides mentioned under Books (p187) suggest routes on or around Fairfield. Most of the shops selling outdoor clothing and equipment also sell maps and local guidebooks. **Wearing's Bookshop** (Lake Rd, Ambleside) has a particularly good stock.

NEAREST TOWN
Ambleside

Ambleside is a small but busy town and a very popular base for walkers. There are supermarkets, shops, banks (with ATMs), a laundrette, plenty of accommodation options and about a million outdoor gear shops to explore if there's too much rain on the hills. The large **tourist office** (☎ 015394-32582; www.lakelandgateway.info; ⊙ daily Apr-Oct, Fri & Sat Nov-Mar) in the town centre has very helpful staff and shelves full of maps and leaflets.

SLEEPING & EATING

The nearest camping ground is **Low Wray** (☎ 015394-32810; www.ntlakescampsites.org.uk; sites per person £4), 3 miles south of Ambleside on the western shore of Windermere. **Ambleside YHA Hostel** (☎ 0870 770 5672; ambleside@yha.org.uk; dm £20) is 1 mile south of the centre, overlooking the lake.

There are plenty of B&Bs in the centre of town. On Church St these include **3 Cambridge Villas** (☎ 015394-32307; d from £48), **Croyden House** (☎ 015394-32209; www.croydenhouseambleside .co.uk; s/d from £30/50), **Hillsdale** (☎ 015394-33174; www.hillsdaleambleside.co.uk; s/d from £30/60) and **Norwood House** (☎ 015394-33349; www.norwood house.net; d £55), the latter run by a member of the local mountain rescue team who is very knowledgeable about the surrounding area.

Lake Rd (the one towards Windermere) is another happy hotel hunting ground.

For food, Ambleside centre is full of cafés (most open from 8am or 9am until 5pm or 6pm, sometimes later in summer). Our favourites include **Apple Pie**, large, busy, bright and cheerful, with good food plus sandwiches to take away, and **Daisy's**, near the tourist office and popular with walkers.

For something more substantial, **Zeffirelli's Restaurant** (☎ 015394-33845; www.zeffirellis.com; Compston Rd; mains £7-9; ⊙ lunch & dinner), attached to the cinema, is a long-time favourite for pizza and pasta, also serving good coffee during the day and great live jazz in the evening. For traditional Lake District food and ambience, we like **Sheila's Cottage** (☎ 015394-33079; The Slack; mains £7-11; ⊙ lunch & dinner), in a narrow lane off the main street.

GETTING THERE & AWAY

Ambleside is easy to reach by bus from the towns of Windermere and Keswick, in turn both well served by National Express coaches from all parts of the country (Windermere also by train). The most useful service is Lakeslink bus 555 between Lancaster and Carlisle via Ambleside (see p188). There's also the Coniston Rambler bus 505, running eight times per day (less on Sunday and in winter) between Bowness and Coniston via Ambleside, Rydal, Grasmere and Hawkshead; and bus W1, which operates two or three times per hour between Windermere train station and Grasmere via Ambleside.

Your other option between Windermere and Ambleside (or any other town with a hostel in this part of the Lakes) is the YHA Shuttle Bus – see p188.

By car, the usual route into the Lake District from the south is through Windermere.

Ambleside is 5 miles north along the A591, although in summer it can take an hour or more to drive this bit due to traffic jams.

From the north you can approach Ambleside by the A591 from Keswick or the A592 from Penrith. This latter route goes over the Kirkstone Pass, the highest A-road in England. It is very dramatic but the road hasn't been widened much since horse-and-cart days, so it's also frequently jammed and best avoided in busy times.

THE WALK
Map below
Ambleside to Rydal
30–45 minutes, 1 mile (1.5km)
Leave Ambleside by walking alongside the busy A591 northwest towards Grasmere.

After about 800m the road crosses over a stream on a small bridge. Immediately after this, turn right through some gates onto a track signposted to Rydal Hall. Follow the main track through parkland, ignoring minor tracks branching off left and right, to reach the outbuildings of Rydal Hall. Go between the buildings and leave the grounds of Rydal Hall by a gateway to meet a steep lane leading up from the main road.

Rydal to Fairfield Summit
2½–3½ hours, 4 miles (6.5km)
Go right (north) up the steep lane, past an old house called **Rydal Mount**. This was the house of Lakeland laureate William Wordsworth (see opposite) until his death in

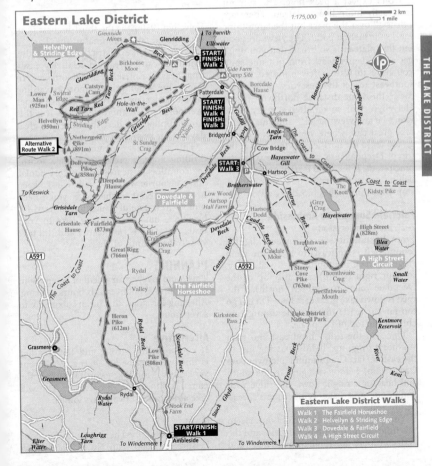

Eastern Lake District

1:175,000

Eastern Lake District Walks
Walk 1   The Fairfield Horseshoe
Walk 2   Helvellyn & Striding Edge
Walk 3   Dovedale & Fairfield
Walk 4   A High Street Circuit

THE LAKE DISTRICT

1850. Continue up the zigzags. Beyond the houses, at the top of the lane, go through a gate. The track goes straight on but you strike off left (northwest) on a path, steeply up over a few stiles and then up the ridge through open fell on a clear path, swinging round to the north to reach the first peak of the day, **Heron Pike** (612m).

From here the path undulates – although the ups are less steep than the first bit of the route – over a few more peaks, including **Great Rigg** (766m). The views to the left (west) are fabulous. Across the valley you can see the back of the Langdale Pikes, Bowfell and Scafell Pike. There's a final ascent to the top of the ridge and the broad summit of **Fairfield**.

Don't expect a peak here. The summit is actually more like a plateau. There are cairns all over the place but the largest one marks the highest point. The views are good but this plateau is so broad that you don't get a 360-degree view from just one spot; you have to walk a few hundred metres southeast to get the best view of Windermere, the same distance northwest to see Helvellyn, and so on. If it's misty there won't be any views at all – and you should take great care where you wander. Do not go too far to the northeast as the cliffs at the top of Deepdale are, as the name suggests, precipitous. If the wind is strong you can sit behind one of the dry-stone shelter walls to stop your sandwiches blowing away.

Fairfield Summit to Ambleside
2–2½ hours, 5 miles (8km)
From the summit retrace your steps slightly, tending left (southeast) to reach the main ridge between the top of the Rydal Valley, to your right (south), and the top of the Deepdale Valley, to your left (north). If the mist is down take great care here. Do not go too far left (east) towards the unforgiving cliffs at the top of Deepdale.

Once on the ridge, head east and then southeast to go up slightly, passing just to the east of Hart Crag summit and over **Dove Crag** (792m) before swinging to the south and heading straight down the ridge with Ambleside and Lake Windermere spread before you.

You pass **Low Pike** (508m) about 1½ to two hours from the top of Fairfield, and the path continues downhill, through fields and

over several stiles, to cross Scandale Beck at Low Sweden Bridge and pass Nook End Farm. From here a lane runs down into the centre of Ambleside, where cafés, teashops and pubs await.

HELVELLYN & STRIDING EDGE

Duration	5–6 hours
Distance	7.5 miles (12km)
Difficulty	moderate–demanding
Start/Finish	Glenridding (opposite)
Transport	bus

Summary A top-quality route up a classic Lakeland peak. The paths are clear but the gradients are steep, and one section requires the use of hands.

Helvellyn (950m) is the third-highest peak in England and dominates the Eastern Fells of the Lake District. Although this mountain can be reached relatively easily from near Grasmere via its smooth western slopes, the walking is far more rewarding (albeit harder) on the rugged eastern slopes overlooking the Patterdale Valley. It is this harder option we describe here – a great day out for keen walkers.

This route also includes a traverse of Striding Edge, a precipitous ridge adorning countless postcards and picture books, and a favourite walkers' challenge. To keep to the very crest of the ridge, you'll need nimble feet, careful hands and a head for heights – but if scrambling isn't to your taste, easier paths run nearby and still take you to the summit of Helvellyn.

PLANNING
This route involves an ascent of about 830m and requires about five to six hours' walking. Allowing for stops, this means about six to seven hours.

Alternative
If you're feeling strong and the weather is fine, we describe an alternative descent via Dollywaggon Pike (worth it just for the name) and the valley of Grisedale. This will take about one to two hours longer.

Maps
The route described here is on OS Outdoor Leisure 1:25,000 map No 5 *The English*

Lakes – North Eastern Area and on Harvey's Superwalker 1:25,000 map *Lakeland Central*.

Guided Walks

In summer there are about three guided walks per week, organised from the Ullswater tourist office (below) in Glenridding.

Information Sources

Good websites for local information include www.ullswater.com and www.visiteden.co.uk.

NEAREST TOWN
Glenridding

The busy village of Glenridding sits at the southern end of the long lake of Ullswater. It's a main centre for walking, with a gear shop, food shop, pub, cafés and several places to stay. The very efficient **Ullswater tourist office** (☎ 017684-82414; www.lake-district.gov .uk) offers stacks of information on Helvellyn and surrounding peaks, plus maps and guidebooks, local weather bulletins and an accommodation booking service.

SLEEPING & EATING

Campers can head for **Gillside** (☎ 017684-82346; www.gillsidecaravanandcampingsite.co.uk; sites for 2 £12, bunkhouse £8; 🕒 Mar-Oct), on the western edge of Glenridding. Nearby is **Helvellyn YHA Hostel** (☎ 0870 770 5862; helvellyn@yha .org.uk; dm £12), on the fellside in a sturdy old former mine building about 1 mile from the village. Also in the old mine area is **Swirral Barn** (☎ 01946-758198; www.lakelandcampingbarns .co.uk; dm £6), in a great position for heading out on the hills; advance reservations are essential.

Good walker-friendly B&Bs in Glenridding include **Beech House** (☎ 017684-82037; www .beechhouse.com; d £46), **Moss Crag** (☎ 017684-82500; www.mosscrag.co.uk; d £52) and **Fairlight Guesthouse** (☎ 017684-82397; www.fairlightguesthouse.com; d £48).

For more comfort, the **Glenridding Hotel** (☎ 017684-82228; www.bw-glenriddinghotel.co.uk; s/d £90/130; 🖳 🕹) has a residents' bar-lounge and sauna, plus lunches, flasks, maps and advice for walkers, and discounts if you stay for two nights or more. Downstairs is the lively **Ratcher's Bar** (bar food around £10; 🕒 lunch & dinner), open to all, with TV, a pool table and good bar food. For the same

food in quieter surrounds, there's **Ratcher's Restaurant** (🕒 lunch & dinner). Also in the hotel is **Kilners Coffee Shop** (🕒 9am-6pm; 🖳), with hot drinks and snacks.

Glenridding's only pub is the **Travellers Rest**, up the hill from the village centre. Bar food is served but this place gets very busy at weekends so you may need to fight for a table.

Also in the village is the **Glenridding Minimarket** (🕒 daily), selling sandwiches, cakes and groceries, plus a very impressive range of traditional bottled beers.

There are more places to stay and eat in the nearby village of Patterdale (p195).

GETTING THERE & AWAY

It's easier (but not essential) to approach Glenridding and Patterdale from Penrith – the major gateway for the north side of the Lake District, easily reached by train and National Express coach from all parts of Britain. From Penrith, bus 108 ('the Patterdale bus') runs five times daily (four on Sunday) to/from Glenridding and Patterdale. In summer (late May to early September) bus 208 ('the Ullswater Connexion') runs between Keswick and Glenridding and Patterdale five times daily on weekends and bank holidays.

From Windermere, bus 517 runs over the Kirkstone Pass and down to Patterdale and Glenridding three times per day at the weekend April to July and in October, then daily in August and September. Through the rest of the year there's no bus service this way.

For more public transport information, see p188.

By car, Glenridding and Patterdale are on the A592 between Windermere and Penrith. From Ambleside you can join the A592 at the top of the Kirkstone Pass by taking the steep, narrow minor road to the west labelled 'The Struggle' on the map, so give it a miss if there's 10 of you in a campervan.

THE WALK   Map p191
Glenridding to Hole-in-the-Wall

1½–2 hours, 2.5 miles (4km)

From the small row of shops in Glenridding village centre, keep Glenridding Beck to your right (with the tourist office on the other side of the stream) and follow the track signposted to Helvellyn. After Gillside Farm (10 minutes from Glenridding) turn left up a track (still signposted to Helvellyn). After 100m, a path to Grisedale goes off to the left – ignore this, and the path branching off to the right to Greenside Mines. After another 100m another track branches off right and goes through a gate in a wall marking the boundary of the open fell – follow this. Once through the gate the path divides; go left (right goes to Red Tarn), following the path uphill beside Mires Beck.

The clear path now climbs steadily, with a few large zigzags, to reach a ridge top at a point marked on the OS map as **Hole-in-the-Wall**. From here you get a great view of the rest of the route: Helvellyn at the head of the valley, overlooking Red Tarn; with Striding Edge to the left (south) side and the pointed peak of Catstye Cam to the right.

Hole-in-the-Wall to Helvellyn Summit
1½–2 hours, 1 mile (1.5km)
Continue following the clear path uphill. After about 300m the ridge narrows to about 2m in width and you're on the jagged teeth of **Striding Edge**, with precipitous slopes on either side. You'll need to use your hands in places and less experienced walkers may feel decidedly vulnerable. However, much of the exposed area is optional; there are paths on the right (north) side of the ridge that avoid some of the most vertiginous sections. Note that at the end of the ridge there is a 2m vertical rock face to descend, which definitely requires the use of all hands and feet.

From the end of Striding Edge the path climbs steeply through rough ground, strewn with loose rocks, to the summit of **Helvellyn**. As with Fairfield, there is no lofty pinnacle here but a wide summit plateau – so wide, in fact, that in 1926 someone managed to land a plane on it; the spot is marked by a plaque. Near the centre of the plateau is a cross-shaped wind shelter, but the highest point is marked by a trig point 100m further on.

The views from the summit of Helvellyn, if the weather is clear, are tremendous. To the west loom the great peaks around Scafell Pike, while to the east the broad summit ridge of High Street can be seen. Both of these mountains are described later in this chapter – see p197 and p196 respectively – and looking at them from here should provide plenty of inspiration!

Helvellyn Summit to Glenridding via Swirral Edge
2 hours, 4 miles (6.5km)
The usual descent from Helvellyn is via Catstye Cam. From the summit trig point, walk 100m northwest and then descend to the right (east), following another dramatic narrow ridge called **Swirral Edge**. Great care is needed to locate the correct place – in bad weather a wrong move can be potentially fatal. Scramble down the crest of the ridge until, after about 200m, the steepness eases. From this point you can divert up to the dramatic summit of Catstye Cam itself or continue descending the ridge, passing north of Red Tarn, then swinging northeast round the base of Catstye Cam, following the stream from Red Tarn (called, not surprisingly, Red Tarn Beck). Follow this down to meet Glenridding Beck and continue along the south side. The route passes old lead mines at Greenside (to reach the YHA hostel, cross the footbridge above the weir) and continues on the southern slopes of Glenridding Valley. Keep to the path beside the wall to meet your outward path and retrace the last mile or so back to Glenridding.

ALTERNATIVE ROUTE: HELVELLYN SUMMIT TO GLENRIDDING, VIA DOLLYWAGGON PIKE
3–4 hours, 5.5 miles (9km)
From Helvellyn summit aim southwards – along one of the finest broad ridges in the whole of the Lake District – with the smooth slopes of the Thirlmere Valley to your right (west) and steep cliffs falling away to your left (east). The views from here are even better than from the summit.

The path skirts the summit of Nethermost Pike (891m) – it's littered with a jumble of small rocks but you might want to bag it anyway – and then heads for the summit of **Dollywaggon Pike** (858m), although again you have to branch off the path if you actually want to reach the summit.

The path then zigzags steeply down to little **Grisedale Tarn**. Just before the stepping stones over the stream (Grisedale Beck), the path curves away to the northeast and leads all the way down the Grisedale Valley, keeping north of the beck. Near the end of the valley, paths branch off left round the hillside to reach Gillside (if you're camping) and lead down to the pubs, cafés and other delights of Glenridding.

DOVEDALE & FAIRFIELD

Duration	5–7 hours
Distance	7.5 miles (12km)
Difficulty	moderate–demanding
Start	Cow Bridge
Finish	Patterdale (p196)
Transport	bus

Summary A hard but varied and very rewarding walk. Some ascents are very steep. It's a difficult route in bad weather.

The well-known Lake District mountain of Fairfield (873m) lies to the north of the town of Ambleside and to the west of the large Patterdale Valley. The most popular route up to the top is the Fairfield Horseshoe (p189), which is also probably the least serious approach. The ascent of Fairfield from Patterdale is very different; it leads initially through farms and woodland in the picturesque Dovedale Valley (not to be confused with the famous valley of the same name in the Peak District), then forces its way up a craggy fellside before finally reaching Fairfield summit via open tops and a dramatic ridge. The return is via St Sunday Crag, another splendid long ridge. This route is undeniably harder than the Fairfield Horseshoe, but it's a gem of a walk and well recommended.

PLANNING

This route starts at Cow Bridge, near the northern end of a small lake called Brotherswater (1.5 miles south of Patterdale), where the main road (the A592 between Windermere and Penrith) crosses the river running between Brotherswater and Ullswater.

The route can be followed in either direction but it's better to walk on the main road earlier in the day (when the traffic is quieter). Also, going up Dovedale is better than coming down, and finishing on St Sunday Crag leads you straight back to Patterdale.

The route includes at least 700m of ascent, so will take an absolute minimum of five hours to walk, and probably nearer to seven for most people. In reality, with stops, lunch and so on, you should allow at least eight hours. And don't forget the 1.5 miles along the road between Patterdale and Cow Bridge to get to the starting point of the walk. Your total day out will probably be nearer nine hours.

For details on guided walks and maps, see p192).

NEAREST TOWN
Patterdale

The village of Patterdale sits just beyond the southern end of Ullswater. It's smaller and quieter than nearby Glenridding (p193), with just a few places to stay and eat.

SLEEPING & EATING

Campers should head for **Side Farm** (☎ 017684-82337; sites for 2 £12), on the eastern side of the valley next to Ullswater. There's also a café at the farmhouse, serving breakfast and snacks.

In the village itself, **Patterdale YHA Hostel** (☎ 0870 770 5986; patterdale@yha.org.uk; dm £14) is very comfortable.

B&Bs include small and welcoming **Grisedale Lodge** (☎ 017684-82084; d £48) and **Glebe House** (☎ 017684-82339; d £50) with en suite rooms.

About 1 mile south of the village, walker-friendly **Greenbank Farm** (☎ 017684-82292; per person £19-26) also serves evening meals for £9 and packed lunches.

About 400m northeast of the village, and neatly combining historic ambience with modern style and facilities, **Wordsworth Cottage** (☎ 017684-82084; www.wordsworthcottage.co.uk; d £56) is in a great location.

White Lion Inn (☎ 017684-82214; d £60) is Patterdale's only pub, with comfortable B&B in en suite rooms and good bar meals. For food and other supplies (including packed lunches), Patterdale also has a great little **shop** at the post office.

There are more places to stay and eat in the busy village of Glenridding about 1 mile along the main road. You can walk between the two villages on footpaths that are cut through woods on either side of the road for much of the way, keeping you a safe distance from the traffic.

THE LAKE DISTRICT

GETTING THERE & AWAY
Details on reaching Patterdale are as for Glenridding (see p193).

GETTING TO/FROM THE WALK
From Patterdale, the best way to reach Cow Bridge is to walk for 1.5 miles along the side of the road. It's quite busy, so take care.

THE WALK
Map p191
Cow Bridge to Fairfield Summit
3–4 hours, 4 miles (6.5km)
Near Cow Bridge, on the west side of the A592, is a small car park. Go through the gate at the back of the car park and take the rough vehicle track along the western shore of the small lake, Brotherswater. After 1 mile or so you pass **Hartsop Hall Farm**, a venerable old building dating from the 16th century. Here the path goes uphill beside a wall, through some old oak woodland, and then runs alongside a stream to open hillsides beneath the imposing cliff of **Dove Crag**, at the head of the valley.

The path then climbs steeply to the right of the crag and then 'round the back' to reach the top. Time for a breather and a look back down the valley the way you've just come.

From Dove Crag, follow the ridge top northwest for 800m to **Hart Crag**. You're on the traditional Fairfield Horseshoe route now, so you'll see more people, but you can feel smug because you walked here the hard way. One last little ascent takes you up to the summit of **Fairfield**.

Fairfield Summit to Patterdale
2–3 hours, 3.5 miles (5.5km)
From the summit of Fairfield head north over the minor summit of Cofa Pike, then descend about 200m to the broad pass of **Deepdale Hause**. To your right the ground drops very steeply into Deepdale, while to the left (west) you can see the steep side of Dollywaggon Pike, with Grisedale Tarn at its foot and the broad, flat top of Helvellyn behind.

From Deepdale Hause the path climbs to the top of St Sunday Crag (you'll be glad to know it's not as steep as the descent from Fairfield) and then follows the crest of the ridge – a very enjoyable section of gradual downhill giving you time to enjoy the views.

Near the end of the ridge, the path keeps to the left (north) and then drops quite steeply, offering excellent views along Ullswater. There's a nice final section, heading through a small patch of wooded farmland before you meet the lane leading down to Patterdale.

A HIGH STREET CIRCUIT	
Duration	6–8 hours
Distance	12.5 miles (20km)
Difficulty	moderate
Start/Finish	Patterdale (p195)
Transport	bus
Summary A long day out in the mountains, with excellent views and generally easy paths.	

High Street (828m) is an unusual title for a mountain but it gets its name from a Roman road that once ran across the broad, flat summit ridge. Since the days of the legionnaires this route has been tramped by shepherds, farmers, travellers, traders, horses, hillwalkers and fell-runners, not to mention a lot of sheep, so a day out on this mountain has a historic feel, as well as spectacular views.

A walk along High Street is particularly satisfying because, once you've gained height initially, you stay fairly level for most of the day, to enjoy the wide open scenery with only a few steep ascents and descents.

This circuit is long, but route conditions are not especially difficult. Thick mists are not uncommon though, and the wind can really pick up speed over the summit, so you must be properly prepared.

PLANNING
This route starts and ends at Patterdale. The circuit can be followed in either direction, but clockwise is more pleasant as the ascent is more gradual. There's at least 800m of ascent so, allowing for stops, most walkers will take between seven and 10 hours to do this route.

Maps
The route described here is on OS Explorer 1:25,000 map No 5 *The English Lakes –*

North Eastern Area and on Harvey's Super-walker 1:25,000 *Lakeland Central* map.

Information Sources

The **Ullswater tourist office** (☎ 017684-82414; www.lake-district.gov.uk) in Glenridding is the nearest information source.

THE WALK
Patterdale to High Street Summit
Map p191

3–4 hours, 5.5 miles (9km)

From the main road that runs through Patterdale, about 50m northwest of the primary school, follow a track that leads east to Side Farm camp site.

Go past the farmhouse (with a **café**) and turn right along a track. About 250m from the farm, go through a gate and turn sharp left up a path.

The path climbs steeply across the open fellside to a gap called Boredale Hause, then keeps aiming southeast, past pretty little **Angle Tarn**, to finally skirt the summit of a small peak called the Knott. This section between Patterdale and the Knott follows the route of the Coast to Coast Walk (see p237) and you'll inevitably see more walkers than usual along here.

About 500m south of the Knott, the Coast to Coasters turn left (heading for Kidsty Pike and distant Shap), but our path continues southwards along the broad ridge, parallel to the route of the old Roman road, close to a dry-stone wall that runs across the mountain. This eventually takes you to the trig point that marks the summit of **High Street**, where it will be time to unpack the sandwiches, sit down for a rest and try to guess what all those distant mountains are called.

High Street Summit to Patterdale

3–4 hours, 7 miles (11.5km)

Leave High Street summit and continue southwards for 1 mile or so along the broad ridge until it swings west to reach **Thornthwaite Crag**, marked by a huge dry-stone pillar, labelled as a 'beacon' on the OS map.

From Thornthwaite Crag the main path descends steeply to a pass called Threshthwaite Mouth. (If time is short, you can go north from here, down into Threshthwaite Cove and along Pasture Beck to Hartsop.) Our route continues west from the pass,

climbing steeply to reach **Stony Cove Pike** (763m). From this summit, paths are not clear but you need to aim northwest, keeping to the west side of a dry-stone wall that runs along the ridge towards a small peak called Hartsop Dodd.

Take one last look at the view, because now it's time to start descending. A steep path zigzags down to a bridge over Pasture Beck and into the tranquil little village of Hartsop, with its old stone houses tucked away behind solid walls and neat gardens. **Hartsop** means 'valley of the deer' but you're unlikely to see any here these days.

Follow the lane down through Hartsop. Just before the main road, turn right into a small lane, which soon becomes a track and then a path, and leads you past the farms of Beckstones and Crookabeck, and then finally into Patterdale.

A SCAFELL PIKE CIRCUIT

Duration	5–6½ hours
Distance	8.5 miles (13.5km)
Difficulty	moderate–demanding
Start/Finish	Seathwaite (p198)
Transport	bus

Summary The hardest and most serious walk described in this chapter, but with the right conditions it's one of the finest and most rewarding.

The tall and airy mountain of Scafell Pike (978m) dominates the Lake District's Southern and Western Fells. It is also the highest peak in England and a natural magnet for keen walkers.

There are several routes up Scafell Pike, including those from the surrounding valleys of Langdale, Eskdale and Wasdale. We've chosen one from Borrowdale simply because we think it's the best. It's hard too, plunging right into the heart of the high Lake District's rugged and dramatic scenery that seems, at times, to engulf you. Once you get to the summit, though, any struggle is repaid as the top of Scafell Pike provides some of the finest views you could wish for.

Before setting out, take stock. In these wild and steep-sided fells, paths are steeper, the ground rougher and routes more circuitous than elsewhere in the Lakes. Weather conditions can also change quickly, so there's far less room for error if the mist comes down and you have to rely on your map and compass to get home.

PLANNING

You could do the route in either direction but we have described it anticlockwise. The route is not waymarked and there are very few signposts, so you need to be competent with a map and compass.

Measured on the map, the distance is 8.5 miles. It doesn't seem far but, with one or two hours for lunch, photos and map reading added on, it will take around to seven to nine hours. On top of this you may have to allow more time for getting to the start from wherever you stay (eg Seatoller or Rosthwaite).

Alternative

If you have the time and energy, and the weather is kind, you can extend this walk by taking an alternative finish back to Stonethwaite via a peak called Glaramara (see p200). This extends the circuit by about 800m and adds an extra hour of walking.

When to Walk

The route we describe is long and should only be considered in spring, summer or autumn. In winter the days are too short to do it comfortably, while weather and ground conditions may make it dangerous for inexperienced walkers.

At any time of year, if the weather does turn bad while you're out, there are a number of short cuts and diversions that avoid the highest and potentially most dangerous section of this route.

Maps

The Scafell Pike route described here is on the OS Landranger 1:50,000 map No 90 *Penrith & Keswick*. For more detail (highly recommended for this route), you'll need OS Explorer 1:25,000 maps No 4 *The English Lakes – North Western Area* and 6 *South Western Area*. Much handier is Harvey Maps' Superwalker 1:25,000 *Lakeland West*, with the whole route on one sheet, including an enlargement of the Scafell Pike area.

Information Sources

The nearest tourist office is in **Keswick** (☎ 017687-72645; www.keswick.org), where the friendly staff can help with local accommodation and transport enquiries.

NEAREST TOWN

This walk starts at the head of the valley of Borrowdale, where the 'nearest town' is a collection of neighbouring hamlets: Seatoller, Seathwaite, Rosthwaite, Longthwaite and Stonethwaite (surely enough thwaites for anyone), listed here in order of distance from the start of the walk. This is a very popular walking area, so there's a wide choice of accommodation for all budgets.

Seathwaite

This former settlement is now reduced to lonely **Seathwaite Farm** (☎ 017687-77394; camp sites for 2 £6) with hot showers, a scruffy camping barn and a very good café (summer only). Seathwaite also has a phone box.

About 2 miles west of Seathwaite, via Seatoller and up a very steep hill, is **Honister Hause YHA Hostel** (☎ 0870 770 5870; honister@yha .org.uk; dm £12), a former quarry workers' building in a spectacular setting atop the pass between Borrowdale and the neighbouring Buttermere Valley.

Seatoller

The little settlement of Seatoller is about 1.5 miles from Seathwaite on the 'main road' (the lane that runs along the valley and up to Honister). There's good camping and B&B at **Seatoller Farm** (☎ 017687-77232; www.seatollerfarm.co.uk; sites for 2 £9, d £52), while the charming and walker-friendly **Seatoller House** (☎ 017687-77218; www .seatollerhouse.co.uk; B&B per person £42) charges £52 per person for bed, breakfast and a four-course dinner, including homemade truffles. Just outside the village, to the east, **Glaramara** (☎ 017687-77222; www.glaramara.co.uk; d £50) is a large old country house now converted to a walking and activity centre.

For drinks, snacks or meals in the daytime or evening, the **Yew Tree** (☎ 017687-77634; ⏰ 11am-late Tue-Sun, daily in summer school holidays, mid-Feb–mid-Nov) is a stylish and welcoming café-bar-restaurant with low ceilings and some garden seating. It also sells outdoor gear.

Longthwaite

In Longthwaite, 1 mile northeast of Seatoller, **Borrowdale YHA Hostel** (☎ 0870 770 5706;

borrowdale@yha.org.uk; dm £15.50) is a long house nestling under the wooded hillside. There's B&B at **Gillercombe** (☎ 01768-777602; d £50) and the friendly people here also run nearby **Chapel Farm Campsite** (sites for 2 £10).

Stonethwaite

The hamlet of Stonethwaite is about 1 mile east of Seatoller, off the main road. B&Bs include **6 Chapel Howe** (☎ 01768-777649; rcjedmondson@aol.com; d £43), in a small row of modern houses; and the more cottage-like **Knotts View** (☎ 01768-777604; d £52), also offering dinner for £9.

At the end of the lane, the **Langstrath Hotel** (☎ 01768-777239; www.thelangstrath.com; d £60-70) supplies comfortable B&B, and has good beer and meals in the bar. It also offers packed lunches and evening meals to order.

Simple camping is available at **Stonethwaite Farm** (sites for 2 £6), and teas and snacks during the day are served up at the **Peathouse Café**.

Rosthwaite

In Rosthwaite, 2 miles northeast of Seatoller, your best bargain choice is the splendidly titled **Dinah Hoggus Camping Barn** (☎ 01946-758198; www.lakelandcampingbarns.co.uk; dm £6); bookings are essential.

Walker-friendly B&Bs include goodvalue **Nook Farm** (☎ 01768-777677; d £48-54) and **Yew Tree Farm** (☎ 01768-777675; www.borrowdaleyewtreefarm.co.uk; d £60), in a lovely position overlooking the valley. Nearby, the **Flock-In Tearoom** offers 'drinks if you're flock-in thirsty and food if you're flock-in famished', with big mugs and hearty portions.

On the main road, the **Royal Oak Hotel** (☎ 01768-777214; www.royaloakhotel.co.uk; dinner, bed & breakfast per person £47, mains around £7) serves good, hearty pub food in the back bar. Nearby, the **Scafell Hotel** (☎ 01768-777208; www.scafell.co.uk; d £100) offers 'Fell Break Weekends', combining fine food and comfortable accommodation with guided walks.

For supplies on the hills, Rosthwaite has a small but well-stocked village **shop**.

GETTING THERE & AWAY

Seatoller and the other settlements at the head of Borrowdale are easily reached by bus from Keswick – the main gateway town for the northern Lake District, and well served by National Express coaches from all parts of the country, as well as by buses from other nearby towns. (For more details on Keswick, see p206.)

Between Keswick and Seatoller, bus 79 ('the Borrowdale Rambler') runs around 10 times daily Monday to Saturday (with extra services in August) and seven times on Sundays and bank holidays.

For more public transport information, see p188.

By car, Seathwaite is 1.5 miles from the village of Seatoller, which is about 8 miles south of Keswick. Parking at Seathwaite and Seatoller is limited, so you should consider taking a bus from Keswick.

THE WALK
Seathwaite to Scafell Pike
2½–3½ hours, 4 miles (6.5km)

This route description starts in Seathwaite. Obviously, if you're staying at Seatoller or one of the other nearby settlements, you need to walk here along the lane.

In Seathwaite, go through the farmyard and past the café. Follow the bridleway to Stockley Bridge, then directly up the valley of Styhead Gill to pass small Styhead Tarn and reach **Styhead Pass**.

The route so far has been following the ancient packhorse route into Wasdale. In the days before road transport (and before walking became a leisure activity), packhorses carried goods across the mountains of the Lake District. Styhead Pass was one of the busiest routes and a major junction for traders heading between the western, northern and southern parts of the area. Today you won't see any horses – just walkers and a large wooden box marked 'Mountain Rescue First Aid Kit'.

From Styhead Pass take the path branching to the left (southeast). About 300m from the rescue kit another path branches off right (southwest then south). This path is called the **Corridor Route** and it leads – always heading roughly southwest – through a complex landscape of shattered rocks surrounding the high peaks. Go above the southern end of a large and deep gully called **Piers Gill** and shortly afterwards the path becomes indistinct, eventually fizzling out completely as you reach the rocky outcrops below the summit. Keep going up (you need to take very great care here if the mist is down);

eventually the gradient eases and you reach the summit of **Scafell Pike**.

After the broad summits on some other mountains (like Fairfield and Helvellyn), this one feels like a real mountaintop. A trig point and large cairn mark the highest point in England. You'll also find several rock shelters dotted around – most welcome when the weather is bad. When conditions are good you'll get spectacular views over the whole Lake District: northeast across your route, over Derwent Water and Keswick with Skiddaw beyond; southeast to Crinkle Crags and Bowfell, with a glimpse of Windermere; northwest to Great Gable and Buttermere; and lots more. On a clear day you see the coast (and Sellafield Nuclear Power Station) and if you're lucky you'll see the Isle of Man rising from the sea, looking like it's a mere hop away. If you're extra-specially blessed, the coasts of Ireland and Scotland will also be visible. That's three countries from one mountaintop, four if you count the independent Isle of Man, five if you count the kingdom of Heaven. And why not? On this peak, you could be close.

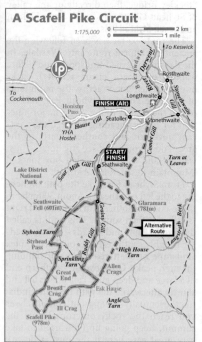

Scafell Pike to Esk Hause
1 hour, 1.5 miles (2.5km)

But enough philosophy. It's time to move on. From the summit aim northeast, but take care, especially when the weather is bad, as the route is not obvious across the rocks. A path descends steeply on a rocky ridge, with cliffs and buttresses on either side, to reach a small pass between Scafell Pike and its neighbour Broad Crag. The path climbs up again, passing to the right (east) of the summit of Broad Crag and north of another neighbouring peak called Ill Crag.

The path curves down and to the right (east) below another peak called Great End to finally reach a pass and junction of paths called **Esk Hause**, where there's a cross-shaped wind shelter. (For peak-baggers it's possible to go on a quick detour up and down **Great End** for some more wonderful views. On long summer days this will be quite easy, but adds about 45 minutes onto your time.)

Esk Hause to Seathwaite
1½–2 hours, 3 miles (5km)

From Esk Hause take the path west towards the little lake of Sprinkling Tarn. After about 500m, before you reach the tarn, a path on the right (north) goes down beside a stream called Ruddy Gill, becoming Grains Gill a bit further down. At Stockley Bridge you'll meet the bridleway you came up on, and from here you simply retrace your steps to Seathwaite.

ALTERNATIVE ROUTE: SEATHWAITE VIA GLARAMARA
2½–3 hours, 3.5 miles (5.5km)

From Esk Hause, this is a longer, harder and much more enjoyable return route to Seathwaite. Aim northeast, over the top of a small peak called Allen Crags and then along a broad ridge with several ups and downs, to reach the fine summit of **Glaramara** (781m). Beyond the summit the path divides: left (northwest) takes you steeply down the fell-side to Seathwaite and the finish.

(If you're staying at Seatoller or Rosthwaite, you could continue heading north from Glaramara along the ridge, descending through pleasant woodland on the lower section to finally reach Strands Bridge on the main road.)

THE CUMBRIA WAY

Duration	5 days
Distance	68 miles (109.5km)
Difficulty	moderate
Start	Ulverston (p202)
Finish	Carlisle (p203)
Transport	bus, train

Summary An excellent route through the heart of the Lake District, keeping mostly to valleys but with a few high and potentially serious sections.

Although apparently steeped in tradition, the county of Cumbria is a new entity, created in the 1970s by joining the old shires of Westmorland and Cumberland, with some parts of Lancashire and Yorkshire's West Riding thrown in for good measure. For most visitors 'Cumbria' and the 'Lake District' are synonymous, although locals are often at pains to point out that there's more to their county than *just* lakes, and so the Cumbria Way presents a true cross section of all the area has to offer. It starts in southern Cumbria, winds through the heart of the Lake District, and ends in northern Cumbria, rewarding walkers with top-quality mountain views – but it's essentially a valley walk and doesn't cross any summits, making it ideal for less hardy types.

The scenery of the Lake District is the main draw of course. Outside the national park boundary, the other parts of Cumbria are perhaps not quite as stunning as the high mountain areas, but they're scenic nonetheless and far less crowded, so you're assured of some days of solitude as well as breathtaking views.

PLANNING
The Cumbria Way can be followed in either direction, but we recommend starting in Ulverston and going north to Carlisle. This way you should have most of the wind behind you (although don't bank on it).

The Cumbria Way is 68 miles long. That's measured on the map, so with the ups and downs it's probably 70 miles or more. Although it's mostly a low-level route, it goes near several tempting mountaintops so the possibilities for diversions are numerous, but these will of course add to your mileage (and time).

Many people take five days to cover the Cumbria Way and we have divided the walk accordingly:

Day	From	To	Miles/km
1	Ulverston	Coniston	15/24
2	Coniston	Great Langdale	11/17.5
3	Great Langdale	Keswick	15/24
4	Keswick	Caldbeck	13/21
5	Caldbeck	Carlisle	14/22.5

Note that the hours given for each stage in the route description are walking times only. You should allow an extra couple of hours for rests, photos, lunch stops and so on.

Alternatives
If you're a fast walker, you could possibly do the whole route in four days. If you're simply pushed for time you could consider cutting the last day. If you only have a couple of days to spare, we recommend all or any of Days 2, 3 and 4.

Relaxed walkers could easily take six days, with breaks at Coniston, Elterwater, Borrowdale, Keswick, Caldbeck and Carlisle. With more days you could branch off the Way for some high-level add-ons. For example, you could stay at Borrowdale for two nights and bag Scafell Pike on the day in between – see p197.

As with all LDPs, you don't have to do the whole thing. Many sections of the route can be incorporated into shorter one-day circuits.

When to Walk
You can do this route at any time of year, although in spring, summer and autumn there's more chance of better weather, and in winter the high sections may be blocked by snow. Many people start on a Saturday or Sunday, meaning a 'bulge' travels along the route. Nice and sociable, but on Thursday or Friday everyone reaches Caldbeck, where B&Bs are in short supply. It's worth starting on a weekday if you can.

Maps
A good map is essential for this route as there are very few specific Cumbria Way signposts or waymarks. The *Cumbria Way* strip map by Harvey is excellent and highly recommended.

If you want more detail (or want to know what's beyond the strip), you'll need Harvey Maps' 1:25,000 Superwalker sheets *South-West, South-East, Central* and *North Lakeland* – although the first and last sections of the Cumbria Way are not covered by these maps.

If you go for OS maps, the Cumbria Way is covered by Landranger 1:50,000 maps No 96 *Barrow-in-Furness & South Lakeland,* 90 *Penrith & Keswick* and 85 *Carlisle & Solway Firth.* For more detail, you'll need OS Explorer 1:25,000 maps No 4 *The English Lakes – North Western Area,* 5 *North Eastern Area,* 6 *South Western Area* and 7 *South Eastern Area.* Note that only a small bit of the route is on map No 6, and No 5 doesn't quite stretch as far as Carlisle.

Books

A detailed guidebook for the Cumbria Way is not essential but can be very handy. The guidebook that originally created this route, *The Cumbria Way* by John Trevelyan, is out of print but still available in some local shops and tourist offices. More recent alternatives include *The Cumbria Way* by Phillip Dubock, with lovingly hand-crafted Wainwright-style maps and instructions, and *The Cumbria Way* by Anthony Burton, with very detailed route descriptions and extracts from OS 1:25,000 maps.

Guided Walks

Many of the tour companies listed in the boxed text on p26 organise walking holidays on the Cumbria Way.

Information Sources

For specific information along the Cumbria Way, the local tourist offices are in **Ulverston** (☎ 01229-587120; www.ulverston.net), **Coniston** (☎ 015394-41533; www.conistontic.org), **Keswick** (☎ 017687-72645; www.keswick.org) and **Carlisle** (☎ 01228-625600; www.carlisle.gov.uk). From all of these, and other tourist offices in the Lake District, you can pick up the *Cumbria Way* information leaflet, with details on the route and places of interest, town plans of Ulverston and Carlisle, useful phone numbers and so on. You can also use the leaflet as your Cumbria Way 'passport' – getting it stamped at various points along the way.

Ulverston tourist office has friendly staff and, for a small charge, offers a booking service for B&Bs along the Cumbria Way.

Baggage Services

For baggage-carrying services, see p437.

NEAREST TOWNS

The start and end of the walk are at the Cumbrian market town of Ulverston and the large city of Carlisle – the latter is in Cumbria but has a feel of places further north.

Ulverston

At the start of the route, Ulverston is not a typical Lake District town. Its cobbled streets have yet to be lined with gift emporiums and other tourist paraphernalia. There are shops, a supermarket and lots of pubs – some get lively on Thursday (market day) and at the weekend. Somewhat bizarrely, there's a **Laurel & Hardy Museum** (☎ 01229-582292; www.laurel-and-hardy-museum.co.uk; admission £2.50; ⏰ 10am-4pm Feb-Dec) in Ulverston – Stan was born here in 1890 – which is worth a short visit before you set off, especially if it's raining and you need cheering up a little.

SLEEPING & EATING

The nearest camp site to town is **Bardsea Leisure Park** (☎ 01229-584712; sites for 2 £10) on the outskirts of town; it's mainly for caravans but walkers are welcome. If you prefer a roof over your head, **Walkers Hostel** (☎ 01229-585588; www.walkershostel .co.uk; dm/d £14/28), on the edge of town as you come in from the east, is a recommended budget option. Facilities include free tea, coffee and toast, a nice lounge with lots of books, a garden, and evening meals for £10. The owners can advise on the Cumbria Way and other routes in the area. They also offer long-term parking for guests.

B&Bs catering for walkers include **Orchard House** (☎ 01229-586771; www.orchardhouseulverston .co.uk; Hazelcroft Gdns; d £52-64), near the train station; **Town House** (☎ 01229-580172; townhouse@tiscali .co.uk; d £50), a beautiful Georgian residence in the centre of town; and **Church Walk House** (☎ 01229-582211; churchwalk@mchadderton.freeserve .co.uk; d from £70), very near the Gill and the start of the walk.

For food in the evening there are a couple of fish and chip shops in and around the centre, while both the **Rose & Crown** (King St) and the **Farmers Arms** on the marketplace do good pub food at reasonable prices.

For slightly more stylish eating and drinking, **Laurels Bistro** (☎ 01229-583961; ☻ dinner) is recommended. Or try **Amigos** (☎ 01229-587616; ☻ dinner), a lively Mexican restaurant opposite the tourist office.

GETTING THERE & AWAY

Ulverston is easily reached by bus from the central Lake District gateway Windermere, itself linked by train and National Express coach to most parts of the country. From Windermere, local buses run to Barrow-in-Furness via Ulverston about six times per day. There are also National Express coaches direct to Barrow-in-Furness via Ulverston.

Ulverston is also on the Cumbria Coast railway line between Lancaster and Carlisle – both of which can be easily reached by train from all parts of Britain. The local train service runs every few hours Monday to Saturday, less often on Sunday.

Carlisle

At the end of the route, Carlisle is the capital of north Cumbria, with all the facilities you'd expect of a city and a surprisingly pleasant atmosphere. Historically it's fascinating, with a famous red-stone **cathedral** and dramatic **castle**. The **Tullie House Museum** (p218) is one of the best in Britain.

SLEEPING & EATING

As well as marking the end of the Cumbria Way, Carlisle is also on the Hadrian's Wall Path National Trail. For accommodation details, see p227.

GETTING THERE & AWAY

Carlisle is well served by National Express coaches to many parts of Britain. If you're heading south, or plan more Lake District adventures, the 555 Lakeslink service runs between Carlisle and Lancaster, via Keswick, Ambleside and Windermere (from where a local bus runs to Ulverston, if you need to return to the start).

Carlisle also has frequent rail links with most parts of the country, including main-line services to London and Scotland, and the Cumbria Coast line back to Ulverston.

THE WALK
Day 1: Ulverston to Coniston
6–7 hours, 15 miles (24km)

This first day is quite long, but undulating rather than steep, and not too hard. Keep a close eye on your map, as the walk is a bit complex and not well signposted, and prepare for a full day out – there are no pubs or cafés en route for lunch. As you head north, the landscape changes from rolling farmland to rugged fells – a taste of greater things to come.

The start of the Way is in the corner of an open area (used as a car park) called the Gill, on the northern side of town, marked by an impressive steel Cumbria Way sculpture. There are also some public toilets – handy if you've just got off the bus and need to change into walking gear.

From the sculpture follow a footpath uphill, keeping close to the stream on your left. After five minutes go left across the stream on a small bridge and up another path to meet a lane. Don't cross the lane, but go sharply right instead, through a very narrow gap in the wall called a 'squeeze gate' – the first of many you'll encounter on this route – and then across the fields towards Old Hall Farm.

From here the Way is mostly straightforward, winding through more fields and farmyards. Places where you need to keep a particular eye on the map include the village of Broughton Beck (take a small 'no through road' and, just *before* the stream, turn left along a path) and near a large farm called Keldray (the Way goes left of the farmhouse then diagonally left and uphill to reach Gawthwaite).

Once past Gawthwaite, you enter Lake District National Park. This means a few more signposts and neater stiles, and after a few miles there's a slightly rougher edge to the landscape as you walk through the craggy moorland of **Torver Common**. Go past picturesque Beacon Tarn (take care in mist as there's a bewildering choice of paths in this area) before dropping to cross the A5084 and reach the shores of **Coniston Water**, the first of several major lakes you'll encounter on this walk.

The final section of today's stage follows a path through delightful lake-side woodland, with the glistening water just beyond your boots, and the forested fells leading up to

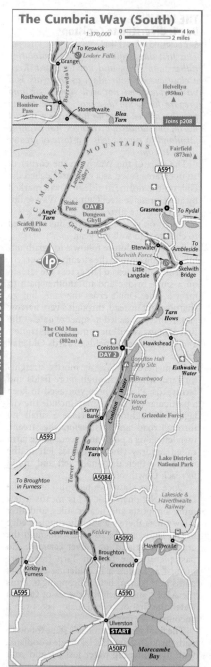

Grizedale on the other side of the lake forming a backdrop. You return to civilisation on the outskirts of Coniston, where a path leads to the road linking the town and the jetty.

CONISTON

The small town of Coniston has a manicured look, but the surrounding craggy hills give it an authentic edge. Attractions include the combined **John Ruskin Museum** (☎ 015394-41164; www.ruskinmuseum.com; ⏰ 10am-5pm Mar-Nov) and Donald Campbell Museum, commemorating the world speed records attempted on the lake in the 1960s (see opposite for infromation about Ruskin). On the main street are the supermarket, post office, bank, cafés and several shops selling walking gear, maps and books.

The nearest camp site is **Coniston Hall** (☎ 015394-41223; sites for 2 £9), about 1 mile south of town beside the lake – very convenient as the Cumbria Way passes right through the site (but it's closed in winter).

Holly How YHA Hostel (☎ 0870 770 5770; conistonhh@yha.org.uk; dm £14) is an old country house on the town's north edge. Lonely **Coppermines YHA Hostel** (☎ 0870 770 5772; coppermines@yha.org.uk; dm £12) is just over 1 mile away, spectacularly set in the foothills.

B&Bs that welcome walkers include **Lakeland House** (☎ 015394-41303; www.lakelandhouse.com; Tilberthwaite Ave; s/d £20/40), **Beech Tree** (☎ 015394-41717; Yewdale Rd; d from £36) and **Oaklands** (☎ 015394-41245; d £56).

Of the pubs in town, the recently renovated **Crown Hotel** (☎ 015394-41243; www.crown-hotel-coniston.com; d £80) is good, although the **Black Bull Hotel** (☎ 015394-41335; www.conistonbrewery.com; d £90) is our favourite, with excellent beer, good food and charm that's not too olde-worlde.

Other options for accommodation, food or drinks are the **Yewdale Hotel** (☎ 015394-41280;

BOATING CONISTON

If you want to save a few steps on Day 1, or you just enjoy boating, the **Coniston Launch** (☎ 01539-436216; www.conistonlaunch.co.uk) stops at Torver Wood jetty (about 2 miles before Coniston town) about six times daily from 11am to 5pm, during summer. For £3 you can cruise along to Coniston jetty, via the Brantwood jetty.

www.yewdalehotel.com; d from £85) and the **Sun Hotel** (☎ 015394-41248; www.thesunconiston.com; d £80, mains £7-10), up the hill off the main street.

JOHN RUSKIN

John Ruskin (1819–1900), the poet, writer, painter, philosopher, conservationist, social reformer and visionary, was a major influential figure of the 19th century. He lived in a house called Brantwood, on the east side of Coniston Water, from 1872 until his death. The John Ruskin Museum in Coniston village covers some aspects of his life and work, and also includes exhibits relating to the lake and surrounding landscape. If you've got time before striding on to Langdale, you can reach Brantwood by public boat from Coniston village.

Day 2: Coniston to Great Langdale
5–6 hours, 11 miles (17.5km)
This day is a wonderful mix of farmland, woodland, hills and river plains, leading to the end of Great Langdale, a large valley penetrating into the heart of the high Lake District. Steep sections are rare, with just a few short, sharp shocks at the end of the day.

The Way leaves from the east side of Coniston and can be tricky to find. From the tourist office take Tilberthwaite Ave (towards Hawkshead) for 400m, go left (signposted to Ambleside) past the football field on the right, to reach a small, old stone bridge on the right. Go over this bridge and immediately left (not through the gate) over a stile to reach a path leading uphill through meadows and into woodland.

From here the Way is clear, past Low Yewdale Farm and Tarn Hows Cottages, then up a lane to reach little **Tarn Hows**. Go west of the tarn, then along a track to meet and cross the A593 main road.

After a short stretch near the road, the peaceful woodland theme continues as you follow lanes and paths, mostly downhill (with a possible diversion to view **Skelwith Force** – an impressive waterfall when the river is high) to Skelwith Bridge, where the Way goes through the yard of a slate factory. In the factory showroom (you'd be surprised how many things can be made from slate) is a **restaurant** with good home-made food at reasonable prices. Nearby, the

Talbot pub serves sandwiches and bar meals from £4.

Beyond Skelwith Bridge, the Way follows the north bank of the river upstream to **Elterwater**, a beautiful little lake. From here you get a fine view up Great Langdale, with rising fells on either side and the curiously conical Langdale Pikes dominating the end of the valley.

Follow the path close to Great Langdale Beck to arrive at **Elterwater** village, a good spot for a late lunch or an early overnight stop. The **Britannia Inn** (☎ 015394-37210; www .britinn.co.uk; d around £50) does B&B and good bar meals. Charming **Elterwater YHA Hostel** (☎ 0870 770 5816; elterwater@yha.org.uk; dm £12) is in a former farmhouse nearby. The village also has several other essentials – shop, post office, telephone, public toilet and bowling green.

Beyond Elterwater, the Way continues along the valley of Great Langdale.

GREAT LANGDALE
Near the head of the valley, campers can pitch at the **National Trust camp site** (☎ 01539-437668; www.ntlakescampsites.org.uk; sites for 2 £9); it's often busy but is in a lovely location. Nearby, the **Old Dungeon Ghyll Hotel** (☎ 01539-437272; www.odg.co.uk; d from £96) is a Lake District legend with a great atmosphere and a long-standing welcome for walkers. Next door is the no-frills **Hiker's Bar**, with stone floor, big fire, good beer and large helpings of food from about £5. Less than 1 mile down the valley, the **New Dungeon Ghyll Hotel** (☎ 01539-437213; www.dungeon-ghyll.com; d from £100, mains £10) does good-quality B&B, bar snacks and meals. Next door, the lively **Sticklebarn** (☎ 01539-437356; sticklebarn@aol.com; dm £10, mains £8; ☙ breakfast & dinner) has a spartan bunkhouse; there are no cooking facilities.

Day 3: Great Langdale to Keswick
6–8 hours, 15 miles (24km)
Until this point the route has mostly followed valleys, but today takes you into (and over) the fells proper. This is a hard stage, as you get a taste of the Lake District's splendid ruggedness before the Way returns to valleys once again.

Today's walk starts at the head of Great Langdale, where this valley splits into two branches. Take the right (north) branch, a valley called Mickleden, with the towering buttresses of Langdale Pikes on your right. At the end of Mickleden there's a fork in the path. Go right and up fairly steeply to **Stake Pass**. From the top you can see back down Mickleden, with a range of wonderfully named peaks spread out behind – Pike of Blisco, Crinkle Crags, Bowfell – and on the other side the pointed top of the Pike of Stickle can also be seen.

All views briefly disappear as you cross the top of the pass, winding through grassy mounds and past the cairn that marks the highest point on this day's walk (about 480m). In misty conditions, make sure you take a compass bearing at the top of Stake Pass to ensure you get the correct path down into the quiet and narrow valley of Langstrath. Many people go wrong and arrive at Angle Tarn!

The path drops into Langstrath and this runs into another (larger) valley called Borrowdale. Here the Cumbria Way crosses the Coast to Coast Walk, so you may see many fellow walkers heading in the opposite direction.

If it's time for a break, there's a welcome **café** in the tiny settlement of Stonethwaite, just west of the Way. There's also an inn and some B&Bs, with more options in nearby Rosthwaite, making this a possible overnight stop; for details see p199.

From Stonethwaite, the Way continues to Rosthwaite and then keeps fairly close to the River Derwent (one of many rivers in Britain with this name, so don't be confused) to reach the west bank of **Derwent Water** – one of the most scenic lakes in Cumbria. Make the most of the views because beyond Victoria Bay the Way leaves the lake and passes through woodland. Look out for **bears** among the trees – but don't worry, they're only big sculptures skilfully

---

BOATING DERWENT WATER

If you want to cut the last few miles of Day 3, the **Keswick Launch** (☎ 017687-72263; www .keswick-launch.co.uk) passenger boat circumnavigates the lake (clockwise hourly in summer) via several jetties, including Hawse End and Nichol End (just before the route goes through Pontinscale). Cruising into Keswick is a splendid way to end the day's walk.

---

cut by chainsaw from local logs and sold at a nearby workshop. Beyond the woods, the Way goes through Pontinscale, from where you follow clear paths into Keswick.

KESWICK

The town of Keswick is the hub of the northern Lake District and often very busy, but it has been a market centre for centuries and on the tourist map for over 100 years, so it easily copes with the crowds. The **tourist office** (☎ 01768-772645) is in the central market square. Keswick also has plenty of food stores, banks, a laundrette and main post office, plus several outdoor gear shops.

Keswick Camping & Caravanning Club Site (☎ 01768-772392; sites for 2 £12) has nice backpacker pitches. Cheap places to stay include the central **YHA hostel** (☎ 0870 770 5894; keswick@yha.org.uk; dm £17.50) and **Catbells Barn** (☎ 01946-758198; www.lakelandcampingbarns.co.uk; dm £6) at Skelgill, about 3 miles southwest of Keswick, less than 1 mile off the Cumbria Way route; advance booking is essential.

For excellent-value, no-frills B&B, you can't go wrong at **Bridgedale Guesthouse** (☎ 01768-773914; helen.taylor4@btconnect.com; Main St; s/d £14/28), around the corner from the main bus stop. The room price is bed-only; add £2 for a light breakfast or £4 for the works (including vegetarian options). If you need to make an early start, breakfast is served from 7.15am. There's a drying room, and the attached tearoom provides snacks or lunches. The friendly and laid-back owner can advise on local places for dinner.

The main cluster of B&Bs is just southeast of the town centre in the area around Southey and Blencathra Sts. On Eskin St, several places cater for walkers, including the very welcoming and well-equipped **Allerdale House** (☎ 01768-773891; www.allerdale-house .co.uk; d £56; 🖳) and friendly **Clarence House** (☎ 01768-773186; www.clarencehousekeswick.co.uk; d £56). Crosthwaite Rd, north of the town centre, has another row of B&Bs.

If you want to reduce tomorrow's mileage, **Spooney Green** (☎ 01768-772601; spooneygreen@beeb .net; d £60) offers very comfortable B&B in a former farmhouse on the northern side of town, just beyond the footbridge over the A66 bypass at the foot of the path up to Skiddaw.

For something to eat, there's a huge choice of cafés and teashops in Keswick.

THE WRITING WAS ON THE WALL David Else

By geological good fortune, the rock around Keswick happens to contain the finest graphite in the world. This is ideal for making pencils, and a pencil industry has existed here since the 15th century. The 160-year-old factory of the Cumberland Pencil Company is in the centre of Keswick, also home to the Cumberland Pencil Museum and – wait for it – the world's largest pencil shop. For more details see www.pencils.co.uk.

It may not be fascinating for everyone, but I'll admit to a special fondness for this place. I have a vivid childhood memory of a set of colouring pencils. On the lid was written *Lakeland by Cumberland* below a hand-drawn illustration of a range of mountains. I lived then in the south of England and had never seen a real mountain. What struck me about the illustration was that the mountains were not green but shaded in purple. This image (and the pencil box) stayed with me for a long time. For many years I wanted to go to Lakeland by Cumberland, which I assumed was a place in the north, to see those amazing purple mountains.

Maybe the pencil set planted subliminal seeds that got me into walking. These days I understand about artistic licence but still find Lake District mountains constantly attractive – even if they are mainly green – and I even find obscure museums quite interesting.

Our favourite is the **Lakeland Pedlar** (☎ 01768-774492; www.lakelandpedlar.co.uk; Bell Close; ☺ 9am-5pm; 💻), off the main street near the car park, with tasty wholefood/veggie snacks and lunches, plus a bike shop.

Greensleeves Restaurant (St John's St; mains from £6; ☺ lunch & dinner) has good-value meat and veggie dishes, while the **Square Orange Café-Bar** (St John's St; ☺ breakfast, lunch & dinner) does healthy breakfasts, light lunches and evening meals.

Of the pubs in town, the **Dog & Gun** (Lake Rd) does good food and is justifiably popular, though often crowded. The **Oddfellows Arms** (Market Sq) and the **George Hotel** (St John's St) are also recommended.

Day 4: Keswick to Caldbeck
5–6 hours, 13 miles (21km)

This day is not especially long, but it's the most serious on the route, as it crosses the open moorland of Skiddaw, where you're further from civilisation than at any other point on the Way. This has benefits – a splendid feeling of space and airy isolation. But it also has its dangers – paths are not always clear and mist is a frequent possibility. You definitely need to know how to use your map and compass here. If the clouds are low or you're not feeling intrepid, you can take an alternative low-level route to the west of the main route, following clear tracks and quiet lanes.

From Keswick town centre take Station Rd across the bridge near the YHA hostel. When this road bears right, take a path straight on, past a swimming pool, to meet Brundholme Rd. Turn left, ignore a lane coming in from the right, then take a rough track on the right, uphill and over the A66 bypass on a footbridge. This goes up through a pine plantation to meet the end of a lane that comes from Applethwaite.

From here the Way strides out across the open fells, ignoring the well-worn route up Skiddaw and taking instead a quieter path along the steep side of Glenderaterra Valley. At remote **Skiddaw House**, the alternative low-level route branches off northwest towards Bassenthwaite. The main route heads northeast then up beside Grainsgill Beck before going steeply up the valley side away from the beck to reach **Lingy Hut** – a handy landmark and potentially life-saving mountain shelter.

Beyond the hut, head east of north on a faint path to the summit of **High Pike** (658m; the highest point on the Cumbria Way), marked by a cairn and a slate bench. This is an ideal place to rest and admire the view north to the Cheviot Hills and the silvery tongue of the Solway Firth, marking the border between England and Scotland. Below the view point, the wild fells drop steeply and suddenly to farmland. The Lake District ends here, almost as if cut by a knife.

To leave the summit of High Pike use your compass to take a bearing on the hamlet of Nether Row, then drop to meet farm tracks, lanes and a short section of path that leads you into the village of Caldbeck.

THE LAKE DISTRICT

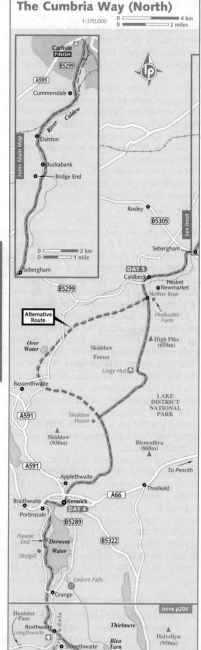

The Cumbria Way (North)

CALDBECK

The peaceful village of Caldbeck nestles below the fells. In the churchyard is the **grave of John Peel**, the famous huntsman immortalised in song. There's no tourist office, but www.caldbeckvillage.co.uk gives all the information you need. Facilities on the ground include a village store, a museum and some other interesting little shops at Priests Mill, near the church.

Hudscales Barn (☎ 01697-478637; www.lakeland campingbarns.co.uk; Hudscales Farm; camp sites for 2 £6; dm £6), just under 1 mile east of Nether Row, is an excellent budget option and the people who run it are very friendly. Whether you're in the barn or a tent, hearty breakfasts (prebooked, please) cost £6. To get here, take the footpath from Nether Row straight to the farm. Don't follow the signposts as they take you a long way round on lanes and farm tracks.

B&Bs in and around Caldbeck include the **Briars** (☎ 01697-478633; d £50), frequently recommended by walkers, and **Swaledale Watch** (☎ 01697-478409; www.swaledale-watch.co.uk; s/d from £25/50), a working farm about 1 mile from the village offering great views and friendly service.

The **Oddfellows Arms** (☎ 01697-478227; www .oddfellows-caldbeck.co.uk; d from £60, mains £7-10) is a friendly inn with good beers and tasty evening meals to set you up for tomorrow's final stage.

Day 5: Caldbeck to Carlisle
5–6 hours; 14 miles (22.5km)

After the long upland sections, this final day looks deceptively easy on the map. But it's circuitous, with a more-than-generous helping of stiles and gates, and surprisingly tiring. There are also some sections that are not exactly scenic, so it's tempting to cut this day completely. If you're short of time and weighing up this day against an extra one in the high fells then we'd definitely recommend the latter. But this is the Cumbria Way, not the Lakes Way, and this final bit of the route shows you parts of the county rarely seen by visitors.

To leave Caldbeck, the Way takes a residential road along the north bank of the river, past Briars B&B. This road soon becomes a track, which you follow through fields into woodland and pine plantation. There's a maze of paths and tracks here;

don't be tempted to go too close to the river but go left at two forks, gradually uphill, then level through more fields to re-enter woodland on a wide track used by forestry vehicles. About 2 miles out from Caldbeck, a path branches off this track to the right, marked by a small stone cairn, and goes steeply down to meet the river.

The Way now follows the river (rarely more than a few hundred metres from it), using faint paths, clear tracks and some sections of busy lane through farmland. At the village of Bridge End, the **pub** has food and the nearby garage has a small **shop** (closed Sun), and the Way crosses to the east side of the river, through Buckabank, then back to the west side over a white footbridge (built in 1999 to replace its predecessor, washed away in a flood) into the small town of Dalston.

From Dalston, the Cumbria Way follows the Caldew Cycleway (a well-surfaced cycle-footpath), keeping west of the river, for the last few miles into the outskirts of Carlisle. The final section (from about 1 mile beyond Cummersdale) is rather untidy and poorly waymarked, following a footpath along the west side of the river, then ducking and diving round some suburban streets. Follow a former railway, now called the Caldew River Trail, under a road bridge, over a metal viaduct and along the back of some retail units, before finally going alongside a road up a ramp and over a footbridge across the main road to end at **Carlisle Castle** (see the boxed text, below).

For a neater finish to the walk, take the following alternative route: about 1 mile beyond Cummersdale, just after a weir and a pub called the **Bay**, cross the footbridge to the east bank of the river and walk along a street called Boustead Grassing, with houses on your right and the river still down to your left.

Pass between two large gas-tank towers to meet a main road at a mini-roundabout near the **Cumberland Wrestlers** pub. Turn left along the main road, then swing right over a railway bridge. Take the third left, leading to a pedestrian shopping street, where you'll see the old town hall (now the tourist office) and the famous **Carlisle Cross**, a fitting and welcome end to your walk along the Cumbria Way. For a more historical flourish, it's a short walk to Carlisle Cathedral and the castle.

CARLISLE BORDERLANDS

The city of Carlisle has a long and turbulent history. The Romans first built a military station here, probably on the site of a Celtic camp. Later, Hadrian's Wall was built nearby and Carlisle became an administrative centre (see the Hadrian's Wall Path, p227) on the border between the Roman Empire and the land of the 'barbarian' Picts. Even the mighty Roman army was hard-pressed to maintain control, however, and the Picts ransacked Carlisle in AD 181 and 367.

The town survived into Saxon times, and the Picts had been superseded by the Scots, but Carlisle was still under constant pressure from the folk across the border, and just for good measure was also sacked by Danish Vikings in 875.

The Normans seized the town in 1092 and began construction of the castle and town walls, although the Scots regained control between 1136 and 1157. Around 150 years later the city withstood a siege by the army of the famous hero William Wallace during the Scottish War of Independence.

From the late 13th to the mid-16th century, under the constantly shifting powers of English and Scottish forces, this area was called the 'Debatable Lands', and was effectively ungoverned and ungovernable. The local warlords and their ruthless armies were known as *reivers*, appropriately remembered in the modern word 'bereaved'. Carlisle was in the middle of this unstable territory, and the city's walls and the great gates that slammed shut every night served a very real purpose.

Today, you can visit **Carlisle Castle** (01228-591922; www.english-heritage.org.uk; adult/child £4/2; 9.30am-5pm Apr-Sep, 10am-4pm Oct-Mar) and get a real feel for Carlisle's turbulent history as you follow a maze of chambers and passages, shiver through the dungeons then stride out along the ramparts.

MORE WALKS

In this chapter we have described the high-profile mountains of Fairfield, Helvellyn, High Street and Scafell Pike, and a long route through the national park keeping mainly to the valleys. Of course, these mountains and valleys are just a taste of the Lake District and there are many more opportunities. This section outlines some of our favourites. With a map and a sense of adventure (and, ideally, a sense of direction) you can go off and explore this wonderful part of Britain on your own.

MOUNTAIN WALKS

Starting with the highest peaks, in the Scafell Pike area are several mountains that make excellent days out for experienced walkers. To the north is Great Gable, with scree-ridden sides that always look so sheer, while to the east lies the impressive peak of Bowfell, at the head of the Great Langdale Valley. Great Gable can be approached from Seatoller (p198) and Bowfell can be approached from Langdale (p205).

Great Gable can also be reached from Wasdale, one of the Lake District's more remote and hard-to-reach valleys. Wasdale also makes an excellent gateway to the Western Fells, which are usually much quieter than the popular central parts of the Lakes and worthy of a few days' exploration if you have the time, skills and inclination.

A good base is Wasdale Head, at the eastern end of Wasdale, where the **Wasdale Head Inn** (www.wasdaleheadinn.co.uk), with B&B, camping, good beer and food, has been a popular base for walkers and mountaineers for almost a century; early photos in the bar show leading climbers of the day limbering up on the inn's stable wall! For more details on the Wasdale area, including walking options (and the pub), see the pub website.

In the Eastern Fells are the peaks of Great Dodd and Stybarrow Dodd. These can be approached from the east from Patterdale (p195) or Glenridding (p193) or from the west from the settlement of Legburthwaite in the Thirlmere Valley. Probably the most pleasing way to bag these summits is as part of a spectacular ridge walk, along the 'Backbone of the Eastern Fells' between Clough Head (southeast of Keswick) and Grisedale

Tarn (north of Grasmere), also taking in Helvellyn and Dollywaggon Pike. You can even continue southwards and do Fairfield as well, to finish at Ambleside (where a bus takes you back to your starting point). The top-class route can also be done south to north, but either way it's long and potentially serious – perfect for the fine days of summer.

LOWLAND WALKS

There are many other high peaks in the Lake District to explore but, if the weather is bad or you just want to stay on flatter ground for a while, there's also a whole set of valley, woodland and lake-side walks.

The Cumbria Way (p201) winds through the Lake District via Coniston, Elterwater, Great Langdale, Borrowdale and Derwent Water, skilfully keeping to low ground for much of the way. Any of the stages of this route can be followed as a day walk or used as part of a circular route if you base yourself at, say, Coniston, Elterwater, Keswick or anywhere in the Langdale or Borrowdale valleys.

Other places for short or flat walks include the west bank of Lake Windermere. If you're staying in Bowness-on-Windermere you can take the ferry across the lake and follow the shore northwards on paths and tracks through woodland. You can either continue northwards to Ambleside (from where you can return to Windermere by bus or lake steamer) or you could return through the woods on the higher ground slightly further to the west. A small hill called Letterbarrow has surprisingly good views. Alternatively, base yourself in Hawkshead. Nearby, a place for easy walks is Grizedale Forest, with a good network of marked routes, including a Sculpture Trail, taking you past many large and imaginative outdoor works of art.

TARN WALKS

In between the large lakes in the valleys and the high peaks of the fells lie the many tarns (small upland lakes and ponds) that are so characteristic of the Lake District scenery. Many people include a tarn or two during their walk as it gives the satisfaction of a definite point to aim for (and is usually nice for a picnic). One outdoor magazine has even suggested that 'tarn bagging' might become as popular as 'peak bagging'. All the Wainwright Pictorial Guides include coverage of tarns, and for more modern guidance you could get *The Tarns of Lakeland* by J and A Nuttal.

BOAT WALKS

Tying in your walk with a ride on a lake steamboat is always an enjoyable way to travel – see the boxed texts on p204 and p206 for information on Coniston and Derwent Water boats. As well as these, and the Windermere ferry (opposite), there's a boat service on Ullswater between Glenridding and Pooley Bridge via Howtown. A good walk from Glenridding goes round or over Place Fell to Howtown, from where you can return on the steamer to Glenridding. The tourist offices have boat timetables or you can visit www.ullswater-steamers .co.uk. This is an ideal lower-level option if you're based at Glenridding for the Helvellyn & Striding Edge and High Street Circuit routes.

LONG-DISTANCE PATHS

Apart from the Cumbria Way and the Coast to Coast Walk (p237), several other LDPs go through the Lake District. Even if you don't have the time or inclination to do them end-to-end, you can follow a section for a day or two, or even for a few hours, tying in with a circular walk.

The Cumberland Way

Whereas the Cumbria Way crosses the Lake District north to south, the 80-mile (128km) Cumberland Way goes west to east. It starts at Ravenglass and goes mainly via valleys through Wasdale, Black Sail Pass, Buttermere, Keswick and near Penrith to finish at Appleby-in-Westmorland. At the finish there's a very handy train station on the Settle–Carlisle railway to take you onwards to Northumberland or the Yorkshire Dales. The route is described in *The Cumberland Way* by Paul Hannon.

The Wainwright Memorial Walk

Another one for Wainwright fans! This is a 102 mile (163km) comprehensive tour of the finest mountains in the Lake District, based on a route taken by AW himself over a long weekend in 1931. It has been split into 11 daily stages for today's softie walker. The route is described in *The Wainwright Memorial Walk,* including maps and text from Wainwright's famous Pictorial Guides.

THE LAKE DISTRICT

Northumberland

Taking its name from the Anglo-Saxon kingdom of Northumbria (the land north of the River Humber), Northumberland is one of the largest and wildest of England's counties. The vast and starkly beautiful Cheviot Hills – the northern part of the Pennines – make up much of the western part of the county, now protected as Northumberland National Park.

The eastern side of the county is marked by the equally beautiful (and, some would say, equally stark) Northumberland coast, also justifiably protected as an Area of Outstanding Natural Beauty (AONB). These wide stretches of sand are rarely crowded, leaving a wild and windswept shore relatively untouched for walkers to enjoy.

Perhaps the most striking feature of the coast and the hills of Northumberland is the number of castles and battlefield sites, providing vivid reminders of long and bloody struggles between the English and Scots, and between powerful barons and the Crown. In the south of the county are older remains of even earlier battles from the time of Roman occupation – villas and forts, plus of course Hadrian's Wall, one of Britain's best-known ancient monuments, now a World Heritage Site.

In this chapter we describe a wonderful seven-day walk along the southern edge of the national park following Hadrian's Wall, leading into neighbouring Cumbria, plus a shorter walk along the coast, taking in empty sands, fishing villages and two dramatic castles overlooking the sea. The hills and beaches of Northumberland may be wild and empty, but that's their very attraction, and a visit here is unlikely to disappoint fans of the outdoors.

NORTHUMBERLAND

HIGHLIGHTS

- Following the River Tyne through the reborn centre of **Newcastle upon Tyne** (p217)
- Admiring the ramparts, forts and castles of **Hadrian's Wall** (opposite)
- Feeling small in the wild and empty big-sky landscape of the **Cheviot Hills** (p233)
- Discovering northern Cumbria's **Solway Firth** (p229) – a forgotten corner of England
- Enjoying empty sands and sea air along the **Northumberland coast** (p229)

INFORMATION

Maps

Northumberland is a big county covered by several Ordnance Survey (OS) Landranger 1:50,000 maps. Those most useful to walkers include Nos 74 *Kelso & Coldstream,* 75 *Berwick-upon-Tweed,* 79 *Harwick & Eskdale,* 80 *Cheviot Hills & Kielder Water* and 86 *Haltwhistle & Brampton.*

For more detail, Harvey Maps produces the very useful 1:40,000 *Cheviot Hills.* Other detailed maps for the individual walks in this chapter are listed in the route descriptions.

Books

General walking guidebooks on the whole of Northumberland include *Best Walks in Northumberland* by Frank Duerden. The *Northumbria Walks* Pathfinder Guide, published by Jarrold, also has a good selection of routes of varying lengths, combined with extracts from OS maps. *The Inn Way to Northumberland* by Mark Reid describes a circular route broken into stages you can do as day walks combing excellent footpaths and traditional pubs. For beverages of a different sort, try *Best Teashop Walks in Northumbria* by Stephen Rickerby.

Guided Walks

Guided walks (ranging in length from a few hours to all day) are organised by rangers within Northumberland National Park and by guides or historians along Hadrian's Wall. You can get details from tourist offices or the national park website (www.nnpa.org.uk).

Information Sources

For general information, there are many tourist offices in Northumberland; those most useful for the walks described in this chapter are listed in the relevant sections.

Online, you can also check www.visitnorthumbria.com and www.ntb.org.uk. For specific information on Northumberland National Park, the park website, www.nnpa.org.uk, has a particularly good walking section.

GATEWAYS

To reach Northumberland from other parts of Britain, the main gateway cities and towns are Newcastle upon Tyne, Carlisle, Alnwick and Berwick-upon-Tweed. All have good train and coach links with other parts of Britain.

Trains and buses run between all these major towns, through the national park and via several places recommended as walking bases. For details see p458 and p456.

HADRIAN'S WALL PATH

Duration	7 days
Distance	84 miles (135km)
Difficulty	moderate
Start	Wallsend
Finish	Bowness-on-Solway (p218)
Nearest Town	Newcastle upon Tyne (p217)
Transport	bus, train
Summary A fascinating walk through history – clear and easy to follow, strenuous in parts, with many sites of interest along the way.	

Hadrian's Wall is one of the finest and most dramatic historic monuments in Britain. It was built by the Romans in the early centuries of the 1st millennium, and crosses a neck of northern England, virtually from coast to coast, for about 75 miles between the modern-day cities of Newcastle upon Tyne and Carlisle.

An amazingly impressive feat of military engineering, Hadrian's Wall effectively marked the outer limit of the great Roman Empire that stretched across much of Europe and into North Africa (see the boxed text, p216). Today, despite the passing of almost 2000 years, various sections of the wall remain visible; some parts are in a poor state of preservation, but others have survived the ages remarkably well and are a fascinating sight.

In recognition of the area's important archaeology, culture and landscape, Unesco – the UN cultural body – incorporated Hadrian's Wall into a new pan-European World Heritage Site in 2005, together with a similar Roman fortification in Germany called the Limes. The wall's official (and slightly cumbersome) title is now Frontiers of the Roman Empire World Heritage Site: Hadrian's Wall. It is anticipated that the Antonine Wall in Scotland will be added to this site.

Raising the monument to global status was not without controversy, as some local farmers and landowners resisted

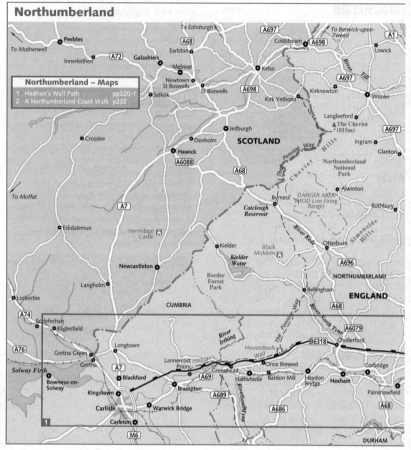

Northumberland

wide-ranging plans for conservation and development, but despite this latter-day battle between the wall's guardians and the restless natives thereabouts, the best way to experience Hadrian's legacy is to walk its length, striding out in the shadow of the ramparts, Roman-soldier-style.

The Hadrian's Wall Path National Trail is a waymarked long-distance path (LDP) that was finally established in 2003, crossing the country from appropriately named Wallsend (known as Segedunum by the Romans) in the east to Bowness-on-Solway (Maia) in the west. Much of the route goes through the magnificent scenery of Northumberland National Park, taking in turrets, temples and forts from the Roman era, including top-class Housesteads and Vindolanda, and some excellent museums. Also nearby are several historical sites from other ages, including Thirlwall Castle and Lannercost Priory – although even these medieval structures have a link to the wall, as they were constructed from recycled Roman masonry.

By 'marching in the footsteps of bygone shadows' (as the route is described in one local guidebook), it's easy to enjoy Hadrian's Wall and its unique atmosphere. You can look out across the austere landscape, unchanged for millennia – except for the addition of a few farmhouses and the lack of rebellious tribes – just as the centurions must have done all those years ago.

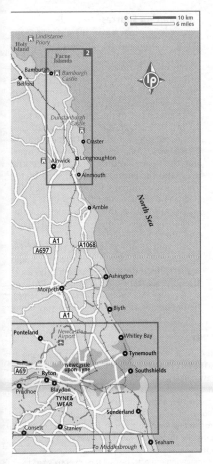

Day	From	To	Miles/km
1	Wallsend	Heddon	15/25
2	Heddon	Chollerford	15/25
3	Chollerford	Once Brewed	12/19
4	Once Brewed	Gilsland	8/13
5	Gilsland	Walton	8/13
6	Walton	Carlisle	11/17
7	Carlisle	Bowness-on-Solway	15/25

As with all LDPs in Britain, you don't have to do the whole route. You can follow it for just a day or two, or enjoy a circular day walk taking in a stretch of the main route. If you only have a few days to spare, we recommend following the central sections between Chollerford and Gilsland (Days 3 and 4), where the wall itself is most visible and dramatic.

Maps

The *Hadrian's Wall* strip map, published by Harvey Maps, is an excellent companion, showing the route at 1:40,000 scale with several detailed inset maps to make things even clearer, plus some very useful background information.

If you want to get beyond the strip, from east to west you'll need OS Explorer 1:25,000 maps No 316 *Newcastle*, 43 *Hadrian's Wall*, 315 *Carlisle* and 314 *Solway*.

Books

The official National Trail Guide is *Hadrian's Wall Path* by Anthony Burton, covering the route east to west. Other guides include *Hadrian's Wall Path* by Mark Richards, describing the route in both directions, and *Hadrian's Wall Path* by Henry Stedman, published by Trailblazer, full of information and using walker-specific hand-drawn line maps.

The prolific Mark Richards has also written *Wall Country Walks*, with suggested routes along and around the wall, and *The Roman Ring*, describing two walking routes north and south of the wall, providing year-round alternatives to the national trail itself, and helping reduce the erosion in the wet winter months.

Look out too for *Walking around Hadrian's Wall*, a series of 'walk packs' each containing around 10 leaflets describing different walks between 3 and 8 miles long in the areas along and around Hadrian's

PLANNING

The Hadrian's Wall Path National Trail can be walked in any direction, but history dictates a westbound route. The wall was built from east to west, the milecastles and turrets are numbered from east to west and most detailed guidebooks to the wall also proceed this way. We have gone with the flow.

If you're a real mile-eater, you could cover the route we describe here in five or six days, but you wouldn't be leaving yourself much time to see the historic sites along the way. If you're a history fan, then doing the walk in eight to 10 days would be better. The daily stages that we suggest are as follows:

Wall. These include: *Walks around Newcastle*, focusing on the area around the eastern end of the trail; *Walks in Northumberland, from Oxen to Opencast*, with wide coverage of the central area of Hadrian's Wall; *Walks in East Cumbria* and *Walks on the Solway Coast*, covering the area around the western end of the trail; and *Tyne Valley Train Trails*, listing walks to and around the wall from stations on the railway line between Carlisle and Newcastle.

The East Cumbria Countryside Project and the Solway AONB publish a range of excellent local walk guides in the area around the trail in Cumbria, available from tourist offices.

A little background reading will help to unravel the wall and its landscape. The excellent illustrated *Hadrian's Wall* by David Breeze (published by English Heritage) covers the wall itself, plus associated earthworks, forts, roads and other infrastructure. For more thorough detail see *Hadrian's Wall* by David Breeze and Brian Dobson (Penguin).

Information Sources

For a comprehensive insight into the national trail and its landscape, with accommodation listings, frequently asked questions and up-to-date news, go to the official website: www.nationaltrail.co.uk /hadrianswall. For general tourism matters see www.hadrianswallcountry.org.

At either end of the trail, there are tourist offices in **Newcastle** (☎ 0191-277 8000; www .visitnewcastlegateshead.com) and **Carlisle** (☎ 01228-625600; www.historic-carlisle.org.uk), each covering their surrounding area. The central area, and the entire wall, is covered by the Haltwhistle tourist office, also called the **Hadrian's Wall Information Line** (☎ 01434-322002; info@hadrians-wall.org); this office stocks a comprehensive selection of books and maps, and offers a mail-order service.

All tourist offices stock a range of inspirational and informative brochures and leaflets, including the exceedingly user-friendly *Hadrian's Wall Country Walking & Cycling Accommodation Guide* (free), listing a wide range of places to stay along

---

HADRIAN'S WALL – BACKGROUND & HISTORY

The Romans occupied and dominated Britain for about 350 years from AD 44, but the island remained a constant headache for the invaders. The Pict peoples of the north (today's Scotland) constantly rebelled against the Romans, and vast military expenditure was required to ensure the safe exploitation of the mineral-rich territories.

Eventually the costs could not be justified – about 10% of the empire's entire army was committed in Britain, probably the least important colony – so in AD 122 the Emperor Hadrian decided that rather than conquer the Picts he'd settle for simply keeping them at bay. Accordingly he ordered a great wall to be built across the country. To the south would be civilisation and the Roman Empire; to the north would be the savages.

His plan became the Roman Empire's greatest engineering project. The wall took over six years to build, with some evidence suggesting work continued for almost 10 years, from AD 122 to 132.

The wall followed the course of an already-established coast-to-coast military road, the Stanegate, and incorporated the north-facing cliffs of the Whin Sill, a geological feature that also crossed the country at this point, providing extra natural defences.

The wall is 80 Roman miles long (about 75 modern miles or 120km) and follows a standard pattern for its entire length: at every Roman mile there was a milecastle, and in between every two milecastles were two turrets. Later historians allocated numbers to these defences, starting with Milecastle 0 at Wallsend (now a suburb of Newcastle upon Tyne) and ending with Milecastle 80 at Bowness-on-Solway, west of Carlisle. The intermediate turrets are tagged A and B, so Milecastle 37 is followed by Turret 37A, Turret 37B and then Milecastle 38.

After the wall's completion it was decided that larger forts were also necessary and 16 of these were built. The prime remaining forts include Vercovicium and Banna (more commonly known today by their English names: Housesteads and Birdoswald). In addition there are several other forts that predate the wall and stand some distance behind it, including Vindolanda (Chesterholm).

The wall also followed a standard pattern in cross section. It was intended to be about 10ft (about 3m) wide at the base and somewhere between 12ft (roughly 4m) and 20ft (6m) high,

the route and also containing some general tourist information.

Also useful is the small but comprehensive *Essential Guide to Hadrian's Wall Path*, covering the entire route with details of things to see, bus and taxi information, useful phone numbers and so on.

Baggage Services

The **Walkers' Baggage Transfer Company** (☎ 0870 990 5549; www.walkersbags.co.uk) is a Brampton-based firm covering the entire Hadrian's Wall route, charging £5 per bag per transfer. Other baggage services are listed on p437.

NEAREST TOWNS

The 'nearest towns' to the start and finish of the Hadrian's Wall Path are the large city of Newcastle upon Tyne at the route's eastern end, and the tiny village of Bowness-on-Solway in the west.

Newcastle upon Tyne

Dominating the northeast of England, Newcastle upon Tyne (often shortened to simply Newcastle) – along with the neighbouring cities Gateshead and Sunderland – is one of the largest urban areas in the country. Formerly a major shipbuilding centre, the region hit hard times in the 1980s and 1990s, but is now enjoying a cultural and architectural renaissance, making the inhabitants of Newcastle – known as Geordies – as proud of their city as they have ever been.

SLEEPING & EATING

As befitting a major city, there's a wide choice of places to stay. In the centre, budget choices include **Newcastle YHA Hostel** (☎ 0870 770 5972; www.yha.org.uk; dm £18) in the suburb of Jesmond, and the more central and lively **Albatross Backpackers** (☎ 0191-233 1330; www.albatrossnewcastle.co.uk; dm from £17, d £45).

Very near the start of the trail in Wallsend are two useful walker-friendly options: **Hadrian Lodge Hotel** (☎ 0191-262 7733; www.hadrianlodgehotel.co.uk; s/d £41/59) and the highly decorated **Imperial Guesthouse** (☎ 0191-236 9808; www.imperialguesthouse.co.uk; s/d from £33/60).

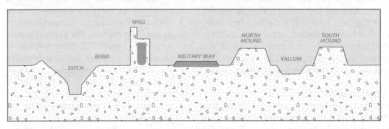

although budgetary constraints later forced parts to be built with a narrower 8ft (2.5m) width. Immediately to the north a protective ditch was dug, except where the wall runs along the top of the Whin Sill cliffs. To the south of the wall is a wider ditch known as the vallum, with embankments on each side. This sometimes runs close to the wall, and sometimes some distance away. In many places where all traces of the wall itself have disappeared (it made a fine source of stone for later generations), the ditch or the vallum still remains as clear as ever. Wall walkers soon develop a keen eye for signs of these irregularities in the landscape.

After completion, the wall brought stability to this area of Britain and settlements sprung up around the forts. Over the following centuries the garrisons steadily became more British and less Roman. Meanwhile, the remote outposts were gradually forgotten by Rome, which was busy fighting fires closer to home. Pay came less frequently and farming began to replace soldiery as a source of income. It's generally accepted that Britain was abandoned by Rome around 410 and the wall and its settlements went into steady decline. Population numbers fell, and the border zone between Scotland and England became unstable and dangerous, a bitterly contested battlefield known as the 'Debatable Lands' until the start of the 17th century, when unification of the two countries finally brought fighting to a stop. There can be few bloodier frontiers on the planet; certainly few where the struggles continued for 1500 years.

WALL

NORTH MOUND

SOUTH MOUND

BERM   MILITARY WAY   VALLUM

DITCH

NORTHUMBERLAND

DIGGING THE WALL

Your walk along Hadrian's Wall will be further enhanced by getting some archaeological and historical background at the fascinating museums near the start and finish of the route.

In Newcastle, the **Museum of Antiquities** (☎ 0191-222 7849; www.ncl.ac.uk/antiquities; The Quadrangle, University of Newcastle upon Tyne; admission free; 10am-5pm Mon-Sat) contains many items found along the wall and a reconstruction of a Roman temple. One of the most interesting exhibits is a model of Hadrian's Wall at a scale of 6 inches to 1 mile, neatly reducing the whole walk to 36ft (about 10m).

Segedunum Roman Fort (☎ 0191-236 9347; www.twmuseums.org.uk; adult/child £4/free; 10am-5pm Apr-Oct, 10am-3pm Nov-Mar), at the start of the trail in Wallsend, is well worth a visit before you start walking. The museum gives a deep insight on Roman life, and a highlight is the observation tower overlooking the ruined fort and the more recent remains of the nearby shipyards along the River Tyne.

In Carlisle the award-winning **Tullie House Museum** (☎ 01228-534781; www.tulliehouse.co.uk; Castle St; adult/child £5/3; 10am-5pm Mon-Sat Apr-Oct, 10am-4pm Mon-Sat Nov-Mar, slightly shorter hr Sun) has a good Roman collection, including a reconstructed section of the wall. It also has exhibits from the 1000-year period of clan warfare and general unrest after the Romans pulled out, when the border country between England and Scotland became 'the Debatable Lands'.

In the city centre, **Premier Travel Inn** (☎ 0870 990 6530; www.premiertravelinn.com; d £63) is a modern chain hotel, on the Quayside near the historic Tyne bridges, a mere step from the national trail. Breakfast is an extra £5.

Instead of staying in Newcastle, some trail walkers stay two nights in Heddon (the end of Day 1; p221) and come into Newcastle by bus in the morning, then walk back. Others stay two nights in Newcastle and do it the other way around.

GETTING THERE & AWAY

Getting to Newcastle upon Tyne is very easy. This major city is served by train and National Express coach from all parts of Britain.

Bowness-on-Solway

The little village of Bowness-on-Solway sits on the ruins of Hadrian's Milecastle 80 – although the only visible evidence is the large number of Roman bricks used in more recently constructed houses and barns. Around this village, and in nearby Port Carlisle, look out for reminders from another historic period: nets on wide cross-like frames used by locals for *haaf-netting*, a style of fishing unique to the area that was introduced by Vikings a millennium ago.

SLEEPING & EATING

The nearest campground is at **Chapel Side** (☎ 016973-51400; sites per person £5), 2 miles away in Port Carlisle. In Bowness itself, accom-

modation includes the inevitably titled **Wallsend Guesthouse** (☎ 016973-51055; www.wallsend.net; s/d £40/60) in the former village rectory, offering a lift service back to Carlisle and long-term car parking.

On the main street, **Old Chapel** (☎ 016973-51126; www.oldchapelbownessonsolway.com; B&B per person £20) offers very comfortable, no-frills B&B; there's a self-catering kitchen and the price includes a light breakfast and packed lunch for the following day. In Port Carlisle, friendly and flexible **Hesket House** (☎ 016973-51876; heskethouse@onetel.com; r per person from £25) is a lovely old farmhouse built partly with Roman masonry, with singles, doubles and family/group rooms.

For food and drink there are two pubs; the friendly and refreshingly no-frills **King's Arms**

PASSPORT TO SUCCESS

The Hadrian's Wall National Trail Passport is obtainable (free) from most sites and tourist offices along the wall. As you walk the wall, the passport is stamped at checkpoints along the way. The passport season runs from 1 May to 31 October. A full set of six stamps entitles you to buy an exclusive souvenir badge and certificate. This scheme is immensely popular, with about half of all long-distance wall walkers judiciously collecting stamps and sending off for the badge and certificate.

on Bowness-on-Solway's main street, or the welcoming **Hope & Anchor** in Port Carlisle.

GETTING THERE & AWAY

Leaving Bowness-on-Solway by public transport means heading for Carlisle, about 15 miles to the east, from where you can get to anywhere in Britain by train or National Express coach. Your choice is pretty much limited to bus 93, running about six times between Bowness-on-Solway and Carlisle every day except Sunday. If you need to get back to the start (or another point along the wall) you can use the Hadrian's Wall Bus (bus AD 122); see below. Your other option back to the start is a train (there are several each day) between Carlisle and Newcastle along the Tyne Valley line.

GETTING TO/FROM THE WALK

From Newcastle's main train station in the city centre the quickest and easiest way to get to the start of the trail at Wallsend is by Metro (the city's urban train network), changing at Monument station. Have change ready to pay at the ticket vending machine.

For reaching points along the trail, from the end of May to the end of September, the seasonal Hadrian's Wall Bus (AD 122) cruises the roads parallel to the wall. There are actually two routes: from Carlisle eastwards, stopping at all the important places, such as Brampton, Birdoswald, Greenhead, Once Brewed, Vindolanda and Housesteads; and from Newcastle westwards, with the two routes overlapping in the central (and busiest) part of the wall.

The Hadrian's Wall Bus runs about five times per day in each direction, making it

easy to get back to your starting point each day if you don't want to carry a heavy pack, or if you're just doing day walks. Note however that drivers will pick up and drop off only at official bus stops.

Fares on the Hadrian's Wall Bus are very reasonable – no more than a pound or two for each stage of the trail. An all-day unlimited travel ticket is also available. You can get a timetable (also containing two-for-the-price-of-one vouchers to various historical sites along the wall) from local tourist offices, or check details at www.hadrians-wall.org.

Alternatively, bus 685 runs several times a day (three times on Sunday) throughout the year between Carlisle and Newcastle, on a route close to the wall or a few miles south, via Heddon, Hexham, Greenhead, Bardon Mill, Haltwhistle and Brampton. If you're heading for Once Brewed, get off bus 685 at Hexham or Haltwhistle then catch the Hadrian's Wall bus AD 122, or get off at Bardon Mill and walk (or taxi) the 2.5 miles.

And finally, there are several trains each day between Carlisle and Newcastle along the Tyne Valley line, stopping at Brampton (the train station is about 2 miles southeast of the town), Wylam, Haltwhistle and Bardon Mill – all within a few miles walk or taxi ride from the trail.

THE WALK
Day 1: Wallsend to Heddon-on-the-Wall
5–7 hours, 15 miles (25km)

Today's walk, though very urban in character, is almost traffic-free and never very far from the historic River Tyne, following a combination of landscaped disused railway lines and river-side promenades out to the edge of the city and the start of the countryside. There's only a couple of steep gradients, the longest being a haul into Heddon-on-the-Wall at the end of the day.

NORTHUMBERLAND

Hadrian's Wall Path

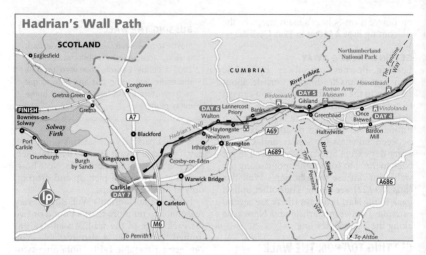

The Hadrian's Wall Path starts (or ends) appropriately at Wallsend, a former town with a proud history of mining and shipbuilding, today a suburb of Newcastle upon Tyne. Wallsend is also proud of its Roman heritage; the metro station, only two minutes' walk from the start of the trail, is unique in the world in having its signs in English and Latin.

Near the metro station is a **supermarket**, so you can fill up with *bait* (local slang for snack or packed lunch) before setting off. There's also a good **café** at Segedunum Roman Fort – well worth looking around; in addition to that, it's passport-stamping station No 1.

From the official start of the national trail at Segedunum Roman Fort, follow signs down to the former railway, now a cycle and footpath called Hadrian's Way, aim southwest and begin your march. (For most of this first stage the signs say Hadrian's Way, but be assured this is also the Hadrian's Wall Path – indicated by the usual acorn waymarks.) It has to be said that after leaving Segedunum you won't see much more of the wall today. The attraction instead is the **River Tyne**, still very much a working river despite an industrial decline in recent years. The Hadrian's Way path leads through (frankly unattractive) suburbs away from the river, then after about 2 miles drops down a river-side path called Walker Promenade. You're very close to the city centre but you wouldn't think so, with just the occasional dog-walker and perhaps a cormorant or two for company. At low tide, look for the limbs of a Victorian wherry stretching out of the shore sands where it has lain abandoned since the end of its working life.

The route passes the tall, white Spillers flour mill, and by far the most interesting and attractive section of today's route begins. As you follow the river around a bend, the **Gateshead Millennium Bridge** comes into view with its large, delicate arch framing the other famous Tyne bridges. Ocean-going ships no longer dock along the quaysides, and the area has been transformed in recent years into a cultural centre, the latest addition being the bulbous glass Sage music venue on the Gateshead side. The bridge also marks the halfway point on today's stage, so it may be time to find a river-side bench and enjoy the view with your *bait*. Alternatively, along the embankment are numerous coffee bars, cafés and pubs. Our favourite pub was the **Quayside**, with good-priced food and drink, plus outside tables overlooking the river.

With lunch and the bridges behind you, carry on along the river-side embankment. Plenty of information boards explain the local history of this area. Look out for the long wooden structure of **Dunstan Staithes** on the south bank of the river, a monument to the coal era where *chaldrons* (wagons) of coal were once loaded onto *colliers* (coal-carrying ships) for export.

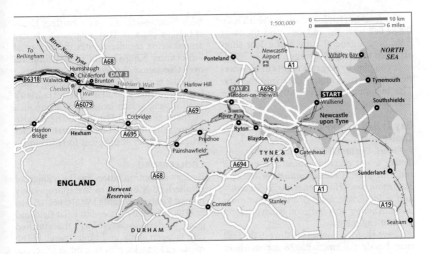

A little further and the trail leaves the river, following first the Scotswood Rd, immortalised in the Geordie folksong 'Blaydon Races' but now a busy urban highway, and then another former railway turned cycle and footpath. After a mile or two the trail passes through some patches of green and a footbridge takes you over the busy A1 dual-carriageway. You then go through the suburb of Leamington, where the good **café** at the glass-fronted community centre, right next to the trail, enthusiastically welcomes walkers. Next comes the outer suburb of Newburn; shortly after passing the **Boathouse** pub you reach the car park, public loos and information centre marking the start of Tyne Riverside Country Park. If you need sustenance or accommodation, the **Keelman** (☎ 0191-267 1689; www.biglampbrewers.co.uk; s/d £39/52) is highly recommended for its food, own-brewed beer and comfortable rooms.

From Newburn, the trail finally leaves the urban flavour behind and runs along a short stretch of peaceful river-side path. About 12 miles from Wallsend, the path heads away from the river and across the **Wylam Waggonway**, only 800m from the birthplace cottage of train pioneer George Stephenson. The earliest locomotives were trialled along the waggonway, now an important relic of railway archaeology. Finally, cross the Close House golf course and the promised long haul uphill takes you into Heddon-on-the-Wall.

HEDDON-ON-THE-WALL

In the little town of Heddon, places to stay include the very friendly **Houghton North Farm** (☎ 01661-854364; www.hadrianswallaccommodation .com; dm £22), an excellent independent hostel with four-berth bunk rooms and good facilities; a light breakfast is included in the rate. There's also **Ramblers Repose** (☎ 01661-852419; 8 Killibrigs; s/d from £35/45), a small house in a modern housing estate with good views over the surrounding countryside.

NORTHUMBERLAND

TOP TIPS

Before setting out on your walk – short or long – read the Hadrian's Wall Path National Trail Conservation Tips attached to stiles and gates along the route. These have been produced to inform walkers about ways they can help look after the World Heritage Site. It is all about spreading the visitor load and protecting the grass, because the grass is the best way to protect the soil, which in turn is the best way to protect still-buried archaeological artefacts. The tips ask that people help avoid the emergence of worn lines, simply by walking side-by-side instead of in single file, quite the opposite to the advice given to walkers in places such as the Lake District, where a narrow eroded line is better than a wide eroded line.

For food in Heddon, there is the friendly **Dingle Dell** tearoom and deli, and the **Swan** pub, plus a general store and a **Spar** shop attached to the Shell garage.

If you plan to stay two nights in Newcastle, bus 685 runs hourly back into the city. The bus stop is conveniently next to the Three Tuns pub.

Day 2: Heddon-on-the-Wall to Chollerford
5–7 hours, 15 miles (25km)
Today is not everyone's idea of a national trail; the path is mostly within earshot of a busy main road. However, it has its rewards – and a landscape feast is only a few miles away! Another plus is a good batch of places to eat along the way.

Leave Heddon aiming northwest; the trail runs beside the main B6138 for much of today. To take your mind off the traffic, tune your eye into the Roman landscape; there are plenty of clues, and it adds depth to your journey when you know the meaning of those lumps and bumps in the fields.

Briefly, as well as the wall itself, the military structure included a defensive ditch on the north side, while on the south side was a road, known today as the Military Way, then a double bank and ditch called the vallum. (See also the boxed text, p216.) It's these earthworks that are mostly visible today – look for slight changes in the level of the fields, they will become more obvious as time passes – as, for about 20 miles beyond Heddon, Hadrian's Wall is out of sight *beneath* today's B6318, constructed on the orders of General Wade following the Jacobite uprising of 1745. It clearly made a good foundation; as you step into the first field west of Heddon, look along this stretch for the occasional piece of Roman masonry still supporting the modern road.

About 4 miles from Heddon, you pass Whittledene Reservoir Nature Reserve, and a bird hide kindly provided by Northumbria Water. It's a good place for a rest, although the cosy **Robin Hood Inn** (passport station No 2) and excellent **Vallum Farm Café** are only 1 mile further. Your next refuelling points are the **Errington Arms** (✿ closed Mon) and nearby **Shop on the Wall Café**, on the junction with the A68 at the 10-mile mark.

Around 13 miles from Heddon friendly **St Oswald's Farm Café** (✿ closed Mon) also offers

B&B. Nearby is the site of the Battle of Heavenfield, a place of holy pilgrimage, where an oak cross commemorates the victory of 7th-century King Oswald of Northumbria over Cadwallon of Gwynedd.

At the end of the day, approaching Chollerford, you get your first sight of Hadrian's Wall – well, a 25m length – at an English Heritage site called **Planetrees**. There's also a minor diversion to **Brunton Turret**, another relic and a taste of the great forts to come.

CHOLLERFORD
Budget accommodation in the village of Chollerford is limited to the appropriately named **Riverside Campsite** (✿ 01434-681325; sites for 2 £10), a friendly place with a flat field and good modern shower block; the attached café is open daily and offers good filling meals and snacks, plus free internet access. Nearby is the large, comfortable and well-appointed **George Hotel** (✿ 01434-681611; www .swallow-hotels.com/hotels/george-hotel-chollerford; d from £100-150) with beautiful gardens overlooking the River North Tyne. Rates vary according to the season, and bargains can be had at quiet times.

Just to the north of Chollerford, in the larger village of Humshaugh, the **Crown Inn** (✿ 01434-681231; www.crowninnhumshaugh.co.uk; d £55) offers comfortable B&B and substantial evening meals. You can stock up on lunch stuff at the delightfully old-fashioned **post office shop**.

About 1 mile southeast of Chollerford, in the tiny settlement of Wall, **Hadrian Hotel** (✿ 01434-681232; www.hadrianhotel.com; d with/without bathroom £65/58) has a consistently good reputation for food and accommodation. About 2 miles west of Chollerford, just north of the trail, everything a weary walker could want is provided at friendly and welcoming **Greencarts Farm** (✿ 01434-681320; www .greencarts.co.uk; camp sites for 2 £10, camping barn £10, bunkhouse £20, B&B s/d £30/50); as well as a range of rooms and optional evening meals, there's a laundry and drying room.

Day 3: Chollerford to Once Brewed
4–5 hours, 12 miles (19km)
For history fans the wait is over, as Hadrian's Wall proper is a major feature of this stage, with the impressive vallum and ditch more than just a sideshow. Walkers too will love this day; the trail is now in Northumberland

---

RESPECT

The Hadrian's Wall National Trail Officer, along with several organisations representing walkers, archaeologists, farmers, traders and other local inhabitants, has developed the following Code of Respect for visitors. Please abide by its principles:

▪ Avoid walking *on* the wall; you may cause it to collapse

▪ Keep to signed paths at all times

▪ Respect private land and livestock

▪ Keep dogs under close control

▪ Visit organised sites (forts, museums etc) as these can handle larger visitor numbers

▪ Use local shops, restaurants and other facilities

▪ Take public transport where possible

▪ Consider circular walks instead of an out-and-back along the wall; this reduces path damage, especially in winter months when the ground is waterlogged

Note that all the land next to the wall and in the surrounding area is privately owned. Some of it is owned by the National Trust and open to the public. You are not allowed to cross enclosed or cultivated land, apart from on legal rights of way. If in doubt, keep to paths, follow signs, and use only stiles or gates to cross walls and fences, and you should be OK.

National Park, becoming more elevated and bumpy as the day progresses. If there has to be a downside, there are no cafés or pubs for lunch directly en route (not even a water tap), so carry all the bait you need.

From the roundabout at Chollerford take the pavement alongside the road towards Housesteads, soon calling into **Chesters Roman Fort** (an English Heritage site) to collect your third passport stamp. Chesters was the home of John Clayton, pre-eminent among the originators of the conservation movement; in the mid-19th century he bought up several miles of Hadrian's Wall, including Housesteads Fort, with the specific aim of preserving it.

The trail beside the road heads uphill to the settlement of Walwick, turning right along a narrow road. Follow this for about 300m, then take the stile on the left and follow paths across mostly pasture fields for a few miles, passing a remnant of the wall at Black Carts, to reach a notable bend in the trail (and the nearby road) called **Limestone Corner**. It's tempting to imagine a Roman auxiliary looking for his *bait* box, accidentally lost down one of the cracks in the rock. Make sure you hang onto yours.

The trail remains on the easy-going level for about 4 miles, crossing and recrossing the B6318 near the Mithraic temple at Brocl-titia (where followers of Mithras still leave offerings on the altar). Soon after this, you get your first proper views of the **Whin Sill**, the rocky ridge with a sharp north face – almost a cliff in some places – that crosses England at this point. Hadrian's Wall was built along the top of this cliff wherever possible, taking full advantage of the natural defences.

You pass a fine section of buried wall, then the remains of Milecastle 33, Turret 33B, Milecastle 34 and Turret 34A, and finally gain the crest of the Whin Sill at **Sewingshields Crags** – a grand view point, well worth a pause to take in the impressive scenery and tangible sense of history. If you really want to linger, nearby is the **Old Repeater Station** (☎ 01434-688668; www.hadrians -wall-bedandbreakfast.co.uk; d with/without bathroom £50/45) with clean and tidy accommodation and a very friendly café; evening meals and drinks are also available.

From here it's 2 miles of energetic walking along the Whin Sill switchback to **Housesteads Fort** (see the boxed text, p225). If you need food, there's a refreshment kiosk in the car park near the main entrance to the fort.

From Housesteads, continue west along this finest section of the wall, with superb views to the north and along the wall in both directions. Don't forget to look back as well as forward: the view of the wall from Housesteads Crags and Milecastle 37 is superb.

A mile beyond Housesteads, the Pennine Way joins the wall and shares the route for the next 8 miles, so you may see fellow long-distance walkers going in the other direction.

The trail drops down to Milking Gap, then up and over the dramatic cliffs of Highshield and Peel Crags, past the much-photographed tree in **Sycamore Gap** (a stretch of wall that featured in the movie *Robin Hood, Prince of Thieves,* even though the characters were supposedly walking from Dover to Nottingham) and Milecastle 39 to reach Turret 39A, with yet more superb views. Before the next milecastle a lane crosses the trail; take this southwards down to Once Brewed.

ONCE BREWED

The tiny settlement of Once Brewed, on the B6318 northeast of Haltwhistle, consists of only three or four buildings. One of these is the excellent **Once Brewed tourist office** (☎ 01434-344396; tic.oncebrewed@nnpa.org.uk; ☺ closed winter). The **Northumberland National Park Centre** (☎ 01434-344396; www.northumberland-national-park.org.uk; 🖳) has helpful staff who can make accommodation bookings and provide all manner of tourist information. It also sells refreshments and has free internet access.

About 500m west along the main road, campers can pitch their tents at **Winshields Farm** (☎ 01434-344243; camping barn £6, sites for 2 £10). Next to the tourist office is the large, modern and friendly **Once Brewed YHA** (☎ 01434-344360; www.yha.org.uk; dm £15, d with shared bathroom £35), which also serves two-course evening meals to nonguests. About 800m east of the tourist office, in East Twice Brewed, there's friendly, basic B&B at the **Craws Nest** (☎ 01434-344348; s/d with shared bathroom £24/48), while in West Twice Brewed (about the same distance west) is the well-run and pleasant **Vallum Lodge** (☎ 01434-344248; www.vallum-lodge.co.uk; s/d £50/66; 🖳).

Around 1 mile north of Once Brewed, **Saughy Rigg Farm** (☎ 01434-344120; www.saughyrigg.co.uk; s/d £35/70, dinner £15) provides good accommodation and serves a four-course evening meal. Your only other option for dinner or a drink is the **Twice Brewed Inn**

(☎ 01434-344534; www.twicebrewedinn.co.uk; s/d with shared bathroom £28/48, d from £60; ☺ breakfast, lunch & dinner; 🖳), back on the main road. Despite the fairy lights around the bar and the friendly staff, it's less than sparkling.

If you can't find a place to stay around Once Brewed, the market town of Haltwhistle (about 4 miles to the southwest) has more options, and makes a good base if you want to linger longer, with neat transport connections, banks, shops, cafés, pubs and a wide selection of places to stay and eat. Haltwhistle claims to be at the centre of Britain; a signpost on the main street points to the far (and equidistant) corners of the land. The tourist office can provide details, and local taxi firms can ferry you to and from the wall for a few pounds each way.

Day 4: Once Brewed to Gilsland
3–4 hours, 8 miles (13km)

Today's stage is short, to allow time to visit historic sites and museums along this excellently preserved section of the wall – and to recover from several steep climbs along the switchback of the Whin Sill. Today also has three possible food stops.

From Once Brewed, cross the B6318 and walk up the lane to reach the trail near the site of Turret 39B. From here head west, following the route as it strides over the impressive **Winshields Crags** – at 375m the highest point along the wall.

The trail crosses two minor roads and continues on to the remains of **Aesica Fort** (also Milecastle 43), now partly occupied by a farmhouse called Great Chesters.

The next section of the trail is particularly fine as the wall roller coasts up and down a row of cliffs called the **Nine Nicks of Thirlwall** (from 'nick', an old English word for 'cut', referring to the gaps between the cliffs). Today, only six cliffs remain, the rest having been quarried away, but who's to quibble? Then, just past Turret 45A, the Roman remains end abruptly at **Walltown** – a former quarry, now a nature reserve, with a sculpture park, visitors centre, public toilets and a friendly little refreshment kiosk.

Just beyond Walltown, there's no sign of Magnis Fort, which once stood here, but instead the **Carvoran Roman Army Museum** (☎ 016977-47485; www.vindolanda.com; adult/child £4/3, combined ticket with Vindolanda £7/4; ☺ 10am-5pm mid-Feb–mid-Nov, 10am-6pm Apr-Sep) gives an excellent impression of life on the wall for the troops. There's a café inside the museum, but you have to be a paid-up museum visitor to use it. Popping in just to buy food is not permitted.

Go back to the lane and turn left to pick up the route of the path along the wall, which drops down rather circuitously to Thirlwall Castle Farm and charming **Holmhead Guesthouse** (☎ 016977-47402; www.bandbhadrianswall.com; s/d £43/66), steeped in history, standing *on* the wall and reusing the Roman stonework (note the Latin inscriptions on the kitchen wall). Nearby are the ruins of **Thirlwall Castle** (built with more recycled Roman masonry) from where you cross a field, a river and the railway to reach the Greenhead–Gilsland road.

Turn right (not straight on, that's the southbound Pennine Way) and follow the road for a short distance. Ignore the road to the golf course and Wall End Farm, then take a path up some steps on your left, crossing fields, stiles and a small footbridge, running parallel to the wall mound. Continue west across fields, past Chapel House Farm, then through its next-door-neighbour's garden (look out for Dennis the Menace and friends) and towards a lane on the edge of Gilsland. Go straight on, through another garden (aren't rights of way amazing?) and

a few more fields to reach another lane near a shed decorated with a Roman shield. Go right, and down the lane to reach the **Samson Inn** (☎ 016977-47220; d £50), a friendly local pub with good beer, bar food and bedrooms. Go left, and up the lane to reach **Bordersyde** (☎ 016977-47613; bookings@bordersyde.co.uk; d £50), offering B&B at weekends only when we passed through, although with plans to expand to weekdays soon; the friendly people here can also advise on camping.

The trail leads on past the very fine **Poltross Burn Milecastle** (No 48), wedged incongruously up against the railway embankment. The burn (stream) itself is the border between Northumberland and Cumbria. The trail runs next to the railway, then crosses the lines and skirts the primary school to meet a main road on the western edge of Gilsland.

GILSLAND & GREENHEAD

In Gilsland, walker-friendly B&Bs include the long-standing and popular **Howard House** (☎ 016977-47285; s/d from £30/55), on the northwest side of the village. Slightly to the west, on the road towards Birdoswald, is friendly and welcoming **Brookside Villa** (☎ 016977-47300; www.brooksidevilla.com; d £60). There's also the **Hill on the Wall** (☎ 016977-47214; d £60), a large house with a tranquil atmosphere.

HOUSESTEADS & VINDOLANDA FORTS

Housesteads Fort (☎ 01434-344363; adult/child £4/2; ✆ 10am-6pm Apr-Sep, to 4pm Oct-Mar), correctly but rarely called Vercovicium, is without doubt the finest fort along the wall. It's well preserved and certainly has the most impressive location, perched atop the Whin Sill ridge. The long stretches of wall leading to it from either direction add to the grandeur and sense of history. A prime attraction is the fort's huge flushing latrine, but there's a host of other structures, including the hospital and four fine gateways.

At **Vindolanda** (☎ 01434-344277; www.vindolanda.com; adult/child £5/3; ✆ 10am-5pm mid-Feb–mid-Nov, to 6pm Apr-Sep), still occasionally known by its English name of Chesterholm, you can see the impressive remains of walls and buildings spread over a wide area. There are also reconstructions of a stone turret, an earlier wooden turret and houses from the Roman-British period. Most interesting is the museum, which contains pristine pottery, some early travel gadgets (including a portable comb and a midge net) and some extraordinary written records – the Roman equivalent of stray memos that escaped the office shredder. The evocative fragments include a birthday-party invitation to the commander's wife, an officer's complaint that his men didn't have enough beer, a soldier's mention of the 'wretched British', a note accompanying a parent's present of warm socks and underpants, and a child's piece of school work with the teacher's acidic comment: 'sloppy'.

If you plan to visit the Roman Army Museum at Carvoran (opposite) – passed on Day 4 of this route – a combined ticket for this and Vindolanda costs £7/5. Vindolanda entry days and times are variable; phone or check the website for details.

Bang on the trail and steeped in history, **Willowford Farm** (☎ 016977-47962; www.willowford .co.uk; d/f £60/80) is another very friendly place; evening meals are available. Gilsland also has a **post office shop** and the **Bridge Inn** for evening drinks and food.

In nearby Greenhead, there's budget accommodation at **Greenhead YHA Hostel** (☎ 0870 770 5842; greenhead@yha.org.uk; dm £14), while campers can head for small-n-neat **Roam-n-Rest Caravan Park** (☎ 016977-47213; sites for 2 £4). The freshly modernised **Greenhead Hotel** (☎ 016977-47411; d £60) offers good food and beer and a friendly welcome to walkers, while the **Olde Forge Tearoom** serves snacks and meals from lunchtime to 5pm, sometimes later in the summer.

Day 5: Gilsland to Walton
3–4 hours, 8 miles (13km)
Today's stage is your last chance to see the masonry sections of the wall, so savour it while you can, but on the upside the terrain is gentle and on a clear day you will get your first views into Scotland. There are two food stops on this stage.

From the outskirts of Gilsland, the trail follows a well-preserved section of the wall down to **Willowford Farm** (with accommodation; see above). In days gone by the wall was seen as a handy source of construction material, and locals simply used the Roman stonework to build their own farms and houses. Willowford Farm was no exception: a plaque indicates a Roman inscription on a brick that now forms part of a barn.

From the farm another stretch of wall leads down past Turret 48B to the remains of a large bridge built by Roman engineers across the River Irthing. The river has since shifted its course and today there's a modern and award-winning footbridge to take you to the north bank.

Beyond the footbridge a stiff uphill section takes you to Milecastle 49 and then to Banna Fort, more commonly known by its English name, **Birdoswald** (☎ 016977-47602; adult/child £4/2; ⏰ 10am-5pm Apr-Sep, 10am-4pm Mar & Oct). The fort is also passport station No 4, and has a wonderful café and an interesting little museum, displaying numerous fascinating finds and a reproduction of a section of the wall as it would have looked, complete with watchtower and guards. (There is also a life-size statue of

Tony Wilmott, the archaeologist who, in the 1990s, excavated part of the fort.) If the weather's fine, head for the picnic area at the southern edge of the fort, with good views over the River Irthing valley. If you're tempted to stay longer, **Birdoswald YHA Hostel** (☎ 0870 770 6124; birdoswald@yha.org.uk; dm £15) has good facilities, and must be one of the most atmospheric places to spend a night along the wall.

Leaving Birdoswald, take the path signed from the road into the restored Victorian orchard, leaving it via a kissing gate into a large pasture field, bearing right towards Hadrian's Wall. The next 4 miles are all easy-going, and the route is simple to follow. For now at least, the landscape and atmosphere remain as upland, although this is about to change.

From the hamlet of Banks there is a short stretch along a quiet road passing the last existing, as well as the tallest, piece of the wall – so it may be time to reflect on the route so far as you continue past Hare Hill Farm and across several fields. This is a pretty section and the trail is clear, with the buried wall remains to your right, but it's well worth pausing to take in the 360-degree views from the summit of Craggle Hill. On a clear day you can see your ultimate destination, the Solway coast, as well as the north Pennines, the Galloway Hills and even the mountain outline of the Lake District. Another day, another walk…

But it's time to refocus on Hadrian's route, as you drop steeply to Haytongate and the oasis of a self-service **refreshment point** situated in a garden shed. While you're sipping your tea, read the many 'thank you' notes pinned to the wall by grateful customers.

The trail ahead presents only a couple of minor bumps, mere excuses for hills. You're well into Cumbria now – notice how much longer the grass is here, and the temperature is likely to be warmer than yesterday's stride across the high Whin Sill. The rest of today's walk meanders through fields, almost always accompanied by the wall in the form of a mound or ditch, and takes you into Walton.

WALTON & BRAMPTON
The village of Walton has only one amenity: the **Centurion Inn** (☎ 016977-2438; d from £50), offering good B&B, and well worth the walk

for its good beer, fine food and a garden just perfect for relaxing in if you've been lucky with the weather and had a hot day.

About 800m west of Walton, and right on the trail, there's a range of accommodation at **Sandysike Farm** (☎ 016977-2330; camp sites per person £5, bunkhouse £15, B&B per person from £25).

Your other accommodation options are all in Brampton, a 3-mile walk south, although some B&Bs offer a drop-off and pick-up, with the **Centurion Inn** making the perfect rendezvous...

The small town of Brampton has an old market square surrounded by shops, banks, some historic buildings and several pubs (most doing food), plus Chinese, Indian, pizza and fish takeaways.

Campers can pitch at the neat and low-key **Irthing Vale Caravan Park** (☎ 016977-3600; sites for 2 £10) on the outskirts of town. Other places to stay include peaceful and walker-friendly **Oval House** (☎ 016977-2106; www.oval house.demon.co.uk; s/d £35/60) and the delightfully old-fashioned **Oakwood Park Hotel** (☎ 016977-2436; s/d £35/56) in its own grounds on the northern edge of Brampton.

For more accommodation ideas contact the tourist offices in **Brampton** (☎ 016977-3433) or **Carlisle** (☎ 01228-625600; www .historic-carlisle.org.uk).

Day 6: Walton to Carlisle
4–5 hours, 11 miles (17km)
If there is such a thing as a rest while still on the hoof then today is it. The uplands are behind you and this stage is a level, easy-going walk, mostly through fields. Lunch stops are limited, so plan the route, or bring sandwiches.

From Walton, the sign on the wall of the Centurion Inn points the way out of the village towards Sandysike Farm, from where the trail leads to Swainsteads and down through a field, with the remains of the Roman ditch to your left, towards the Cam Beck footbridge. Look out for king-fishers here.

The next mile passes through pasture, skirting three farms. You're still faithfully following the wall and ditch, and you should by now be expert at recognising its course in the hedgerows – after almost two millennia Hadrian's Wall still serves to define the boundaries of land ownership hereabouts.

Pass through quiet Newtown (like many settlements in this area, part of the Carlisle commuter belt), where **Newtown Farm** (☎ 016977-2768; susangraice@tiscali.co.uk; d £50) is another possible overnight option, and then continue following the well-waymarked trail over fields and across a road at Old-wall. About 1 mile off the route is Carlisle airport, where plane fans will enjoy Solway Aviation Museum (there's also a **café** at the terminal building).

Keep on the straight-as-a-die route alongside several fields, past Bleatarn (pronounced Blè-trun), joining a minor road sitting on top of the wall, then turning left down Sandy Lane and into Crosby, where the sturdy old **Stag Inn** provides excellent drinks (tea, coffee or beer) and food.

The trail leads down a short stretch of road, then through a kissing gate onto the bank of the River Eden. After about 350m, aim away from the river to reach a foot-bridge across a tributary stream, then rejoin the main river-bank path before cutting across to Linstock village.

A short stretch of minor road leads over the M6 motorway then onto a footpath-cycleway beside the road into Rickerby Park on the edge of Carlisle itself. The last mile or so is parkland, crossing the River Eden over the Memorial Bridge before a river-side walk takes you to Sands Sports Centre, just before the main road bridge over the river. Look out for the statue of the cormorant – maybe the first you've seen since leaving the Tyne. The centre's **café** is passport station No 5 and this is a convenient place to leave the trail and go into Carlisle.

CARLISLE
As one of the larger cities in northern England, there is ample scope for accommodation in Carlisle. There's also some rich history, including the dramatic red-stoned **castle**, the stunning **cathedral** (both built with, you guessed it, reused Roman masonry) and the award-winning **Tullie House Museum** (see the boxed text, p218). For more history see the boxed text, p209.

Campers will have to keep on walking; the nearest useful site is **West View** (☎ 01228-526336; sites for 2 £10), a friendly, low-key place, 3 miles beyond Carlisle and about 1 mile off the trail near Grinsdale. The best budget option is **Carlisle YHA Hostel** (☎ 0870 770 5752; www.yha.org.uk; s £18), part of the university residences in a central position next to the castle, with single rooms in flats.

For B&B, there's a handy cluster along Victoria Pl, conveniently positioned between the trail and the city centre, including **Abberley House** (☎ 01228-521645; www.abberley house.co.uk; 33 Victoria Pl; s/d £35/55), **Brooklyn House** (☎ 01228-590002; 42 Victoria Pl; d £50) and **Cartref Guesthouse** (☎ 01228-522077; 44 Victoria Pl; d £50).

On nearby Warwick Rd, options include **Ivy House** (☎ 01228-530432; 101 Warwick Rd; d £44), **Cornerways Guesthouse** (☎ 01228-521733; www .cornerwaysbandb.co.uk; 107 Warwick Rd; s/d £35/60) and **Craighead** (☎ 01228-596767; 6 Hartington Pl; d £48), just off Warwick Rd. If you're stying here, Victoria Pl and Warwick Rd are most easily reached by leaving the trail on a footpath about 300m after leaving the Memorial Bridge.

On the west side of the city, in the suburb of Newtown, **Vallum House Hotel** (☎ 01228-521860; 75 Burgh Rd) is another walker-friendly option.

For food, the centre of Carlisle is teeming with options, from takeaways and pubs to café-bars and restaurants. For unusual surroundings try the **Priory Kitchen** in the old vaults of the ruined cathedral. For an evening meal, a quick stroll and perusal of the menus will soon find something to suit your taste and budget.

Day 7: Carlisle to Bowness-on-Solway
5–7 hours, 15 miles (25km)
This final stage is fairly long, but is mostly at sea level so the going is easy. The landscape changes once again and this little-known corner of England, peering out across the Solway Firth into Scotland, presents itself as special without making any kind of fuss. Typically Cumbrian, some might say…

Today's stage starts at the Sands Sports Centre, next to the River Eden. Information boards tell the history of 'the Sands', which is a former island, and also indicate the start of the Cumbria Coastal Way, another LDP. For much of this day, the Hadrian's Wall Path follows the route of the Cumbria Coastal Way and you will see waymarks for both.

Keeping the river on your right, go under the road bridge that also crosses the river, and continue through Bitts Park, crossing

the tributary River Caldew, then past the athletics stadium and along the river-side path. The trail goes under two rather unsavoury concrete railway bridges then, about 800m later, under an older and more graceful (though now disused) viaduct, finally leaving the remnants of the city behind as it ascends a flight of timber steps and continues through fields along the bank of the Eden. There are steep drops where the path crosses a handful of steep-sided ghyls (little valleys) entering the main river, but apart from that the going is easy.

At Grinsdale the trail leaves the river, then (still on the line of the wall) passes through fields to Kirkandrews and along another stretch of river side to Beaumont, before aiming west through farmland to meet the main road just east of Burgh by Sands (pronounced – presumably to confuse tourists – Bruff by Sands). The trail follows the pavement beside the road through this long linear village, where **Greyhound Inn** is a very good lunch option – with an inviting garden just perfect for sunny days.

Beyond Burgh, at Dykesfield, you may be surprised to see a coastguard station, but it's here for a very good reason: the next 2 miles are at sea level, the nearby river is tidal and the road periodically floods. It's important to check the tide predictions on the notice board before continuing – then it won't be you who needs the lifeboat.

A few flat miles beside the road brings you to Drumburgh (pronounced, naturally, Drum-bruff). There's a self-service refreshment point at **Grange Farm** that trail walkers are delighted to find, with drinks, snacks, and somewhere to sit and rest.

From here, you head southwest along the rough road towards Drumburgh Moss National Nature Reserve, turning right for Walker House Farm then over a small footbridge and through fields to Glasson village, where the **Highland Laddie** pub – a reference to the neighbours on the other side of the river – is another possible refreshment option with food and drink every day (except Tuesday). Opposite the pub, follow the track (which is constructed on top of the Roman vallum) to reach **Glendale Holiday Park**, where the shop may be a handy place to resupply for the last few miles of walking.

SOLWAY TIDES

The Solway Firth has a capricious edge – the land is flat, tides can be high, storms can brew up at any time of year, and parts of the trail (Dykesfield to Drumburgh, Port Carlisle to Bowness-on-Solway) may flood – so it's important to check the tide predictions before you set out on the final stage of the trail.

For checking on the spot, see the information panels beside the road at Dykesfield and Bowness. You need to know the times of high tides of 9m and above, as that's when you may find water lapping round your ankles (or higher!).

For a longer forecast go to www.ukho.gov.uk and select the port of Silloth, about 10 miles down the coast from Bowness. Once you've found the high tide times at Silloth, add one hour in winter time (Greenwich Mean Time) and two hours in British Summer Time to get the time of high tide on the affected parts of the trail. For an hour either side of high tide you should avoid walking this section.

Do bear in mind that the tide tables give predictions only and that many conditions (such as wind speed and atmospheric pressure) can influence the likelihood of the Solway marshes flooding. The water can and does rise very quickly. You have been warned!

The trail runs next to the road, past Kirkland Farm and **Chapel Side Campsite** (☎ 016973-51400; sites for 2 £5), then takes you into **Port Carlisle**. This sleepy village was once an important harbour, as the crumbling masonry testifies. Centuries ago, ships docked here, from where barges carried their cargo into the city of Carlisle.

The trail crosses the now-silted-up canal basin; it was replaced in the 19th century by the railway, only for that to disappear into distant memory too, remembered now by some old photos on the wall of the **Hope & Anchor** pub, just off the trail, a friendly place with good beer and food (except some Mondays).

The final leg of the trail follows the edge of the marshes, alongside the road then *on* the road into the town of Bowness-on-Solway. There's little to indicate the exact position of the Roman fort of Maia that stood here at the end of Hadrian's Wall, but many of the modern roads follow the original Roman layout.

Enter the village, pass a few houses, then turn off the main street to reach, at the **Banks**, a restored Edwardian promenade and lovingly maintained natural garden with a Romanesque shelter, plenty of on-site information boards, a lovely view over the river, and the final passport stamping station (there is another in the nearby King's Arms pub). Best of all, it is somewhere peaceful to sit down and rest, and reflect on your walk through history over the past seven days.

A NORTHUMBERLAND COAST WALK

Duration	5–6½ hours
Distance	13 miles (21km)
Difficulty	easy
Start	Bamburgh (p230)
Finish	Craster (p231)
Transport	bus

Summary A beautiful coastal route via pretty fishing villages and imposing medieval castles. The walk isn't too strenuous, although if a cold wind is blowing off the sea it can be tiring.

The Northumberland coast has some of the longest and sandiest beaches in Britain, but you won't find busy seaside resorts or the bucket-and-spade brigade here. The reason for this is the weather – probably one day in three the coast is shrouded by a sea mist, known locally as a 'fret', so the sun and fun seekers go elsewhere, leaving the beautiful, wild and windswept shore relatively untouched for walkers to enjoy.

It's not completely deserted, of course. Along the coast are some small fishing villages (many with good pubs), a small port town, plus a few charming hotels and low-key camp sites. Also here are several bird reserves and two of the county's most spectacular castles: Bamburgh and Dunstanburgh. Not surprisingly, this area has been declared the Northumberland Heritage Coast and is protected as an AONB.

Even if you're not especially into bird life, you'll be impressed here. The cliffs, rocks, islets, pools and beaches are home to cormorants, shags, kittywakes, fulmars, terns, gulls and guillemots. You are also likely to see seals bobbing about in the waves.

This walk takes in the finest section of the Northumberland coast and neatly links the castles of Bamburgh and Dunstanburgh. From the small port of Seahouses, about one-third of the way along the route, the offshore Farne Islands – world-famous for their sea-bird colonies – can be reached by boat. So with a full day at your disposal you could combine walking, boating and birding.

PLANNING

This linear route could be done in either direction, but we describe it north to south. The total distance by coastal footpath between Bamburgh and Craster is 13 miles, but this can sometimes be a bit shorter if you walk on the firm sand of the beach (only possible at low tide). Paths are mostly in good condition, but you should allow extra time for looking around castles, lunch, swimming and bird-spotting.

Alternatives

Good local transport along the coast gives various options for reducing the distance without missing the highlights. For example, you could walk from Bamburgh to Seahouses, then go by bus to Embleton and walk the final stretch to Craster, reducing the walking distance to about 6 miles.

You could also extend this walk by continuing south from Craster to Alnmouth, adding another 7 miles (11km) and three to 3½ hours, bringing the total walk up to 20 miles (32km) and eight to 10 hours. This is possible for fit walkers on a long and fine summer's day, but could also be spread over two days (see p233).

Maps & Books

The walk described here is covered on OS Landranger 1:50,000 maps No 75 *Berwick-upon-Tweed* and 81 *Alnwick & Morpeck*. Books on the area include *The Northumberland Coastline* by Ian Smith, describing the coast from the Scottish border to Newcastle upon Tyne, with Wainwright-style text and hand-drawn maps. Most useful is the *Exploring the Northumberland Coast* pack of six leaflets published by Northumberland Countryside Service, covering areas such as

Bamber, Craster and Alnmouth, with colour illustrations and notes on history and wildlife. All maps and books are available from local tourist offices.

Guided Walks

The National Trust organises walks on the Northumberland coast about twice a month. They're free, and you can get details from local tourist offices.

Information Sources

Local tourist offices covering the coast and hinterland are at **Alnwick** (☎ 01665-510665; www.alnwick.gov.uk) and **Berwick-upon-Tweed** (☎ 01289-330733; www.berwick-upon-tweed.gov.uk/guide), both open all year. On the route, there are small tourist offices at **Seahouses** (☎ 01665-720884; www.seahouses.org; ☒ closed winter) and **Craster** (☎ 01665-576007; ☒ daily in summer, Sat & Sun only in winter). All stock walking leaflets, books and maps, and can advise on bus timetables.

NEAREST TOWNS
Bamburgh

The route starts at the village of Bamburgh, just inland from the beach and overlooked by the giant walls of famous Bamburgh Castle (see the boxed text opposite).

SLEEPING & EATING

There are several B&Bs and hotels on the wide square called Front St, including the **Greenhouse** (☎ 01668-214513; d £56), also a good restaurant and tearoom. Other options are **Hillcrest House** (☎ 01668-214639; www.hillcrest-bamburgh.co.uk; Lucker Rd; d £60) and **Glenander** (☎ 01668-214336; www.glenander.com; per person from £28). The smart **Victoria Hotel** (☎ 01668-214431; per person from £55) offers accommodation, a bar serving meals from around £7 and a brasserie serving main courses (£11 to £13). Another good hotel is **Lord Crewe** (☎ 01668-214243; www.lordcrewe.co.uk; d with/without bathroom from £88/76), also with bar and restaurant.

For food, apart from the pubs and hotels, **Blacketts Restaurant** (☎ 01688-214714; www.blackettsofbamburgh.co.uk; Lucker Rd) offers lunches from £6, dinner from £11, and breakfasts at weekends.

GETTING THERE & AWAY

The region's gateways of Newcastle upon Tyne, Berwick-upon-Tweed and Alnwick can all be reached from other parts of the

BAMBURGH CASTLE

Dominating the coast for miles around, and appearing to rise from the sea, **Bamburgh Castle** (☎ 01668-214515; www.bamburghcastle.com; adult/child £6/3; ⌚ 11am-5pm mid-Mar–Oct) is an undeniably impressive fortress. It stands on an outcrop of basalt that makes up part of the great Whin Sill, a natural barrier stretching across the county (where it forms part of the Hadrian's Wall defences; p223) and continuing east out to sea to create the Farne Islands. For obvious defensive reasons, this site has been occupied since prehistoric times. It is thought that both the ancient Britons and the Romans had forts here.

Move on a few years, and Bamburgh was the capital of the Anglo-Saxon kingdom of Northumbria from the 6th to 9th centuries, although the oldest part of the castle visible today is the 12th-century Norman keep, built in the reign of Henry II with walls more than 3m thick. Probably the most famous battle to take place here was during the War of the Roses in 1464, when Yorkist Edward IV defeated Lancastrian Henry VI.

Much later, at the end of the 19th century, the castle was bought by wealthy industrialist Lord Armstrong. He oversaw a major rebuild – just about everything you see today dates from this time or later – and the castle is still the home of his descendants. Tours of the castle take in various halls, the armoury and exhibitions of later weapons and machinery from Lord Armstrong's time. Views from the upper castle walls out to the islands and along the coast to Dunstanburgh provide inspiration for the walk to come.

country by National Express coach and train (the nearest station to Alnwick is about 1.5 miles west of Alnmouth).

Between Berwick and Newcastle, the exceedingly useful local bus service (buses 501 and 401) operates via Alnwick, Craster, Beadnell, Seahouses, Bamburgh and Belford five times per day in each direction (four on Sunday). This means you can base yourself somewhere for two nights, do the walk on the day in between and easily get back to your accommodation by bus. It might be best to catch the bus to the start of the route and walk back, so you have no worries about keeping time.

Craster

At the walk's end, the small and picturesque fishing village of Craster is about 1 mile south of Dunstanburgh Castle (see p233).

SLEEPING & EATING

Your options include camping at well-organised **Proctor's Stead** (☎ 01665-576613; www.proctorsstead.co.uk; sites for 2 £10). B&Bs include friendly **Stonecroft** (☎ 01665-576433; www.stonecroft.ntb.org.uk; d £48), just outside the village, and **Howick Scar Farmhouse** (☎ 01665-576665; www.howickscar.co.uk; d £44-48), a working farm overlooking fields running down to the sea.

Craster is particularly famous for its kipper (smoked fish) factory, but if you're peckish for other types of seafood, the crab sandwiches served at lunchtime in the **Jolly Fisherman** pub are pretty legendary too. There's a great view over the sea, good beer, and bar meals are served in the evening, although we found the service a touch indifferent. Your other eating options are the village **shop**, which sells picnic supplies, and **Robson's Restaurant & Coffee Lounge** (mains £5-8), connected to the kipper factory.

GETTING THERE & AWAY

The way to/from Craster by public transport is by buses 501 or 401, as outlined in the Bamburgh section (opposite).

THE WALK
Bamburgh to Beadnell
2–2½ hours, 5.5 miles (9km)

After looking around **Bamburgh Castle** (see the boxed text, above), go down to the beach, turn right and stride out southwards. To your right are large sand dunes and to your left is the sea, with the island of **Lindisfarne** (or Holy Island), topped by the castle-like priory, visible to the northwest. The Farne Islands are visible to the northeast. For the next hour or so you follow this beautiful section of beach and enjoy a wonderful feeling of space – unless you hit one of Northumberland's notoriously unpredictable sea mists, which will completely spoil your view.

A Northumberland Coast Walk

1:200,000

English dish. The harbour is interesting and usually busy, as this is where you find boats for the Farne Islands. Seahouses' tourist office (p230) can provide more details.

Work your way out of the northeast side of town, past the caravan park, round the golf course, along some strange parallel ridges and back onto the beach again (you may possibly be forced onto the road for a short distance to cross a small river that flows in here). These obstacles overcome, you can once again enjoy fine, open walking along the beach for another mile to **Beadnell**.

At the northern end of the village is a small **shop** selling hot drinks and takeaway snacks. From here follow the small road through the village, past holiday homes and fishermen's shacks, all the way to the harbour, where there's usually some activity involving fishing boats or scuba divers, and some interesting old lime kilns (a nearby plaque explains their history). Beadnell also has a camp site and a handful of B&Bs – useful if you're going all the way from Bamburgh to Alnmouth, and splitting the route over two days.

Beadnell to Craster
3–4 hours, 7.5 miles (12km)

From Beadnell Harbour, your route continues southwards round the wide curving beach of Beadnell Bay down to Snook Point, a spit of exposed rock sticking out into the sea. Beyond here is Newton Point. Our route does not go to the end of the point itself, but continues straight on, to the left (north and east) of an old coastguard station up on the hill, to meet a lane that goes down into the tiny fishing village of **Low Newton-by-the-Sea**, consisting of three rows of houses in a square, with the fourth side open to the sea so boats could be pulled up in bad weather. One of the houses is now the **Ship** pub, which does lunchtime food, including very good crab sandwiches. (Incidentally, the bay between Snook Point and Newton Point is called Football Hole. It seems a modern title, but the 1850 map on the wall of the pub shows it with this name, so it can't be that new.)

After enjoying a bite and a pint or two, it's time to keep on going down the beach round Embleton Bay. If you want a change from sand under your boots, a pleasant

On reaching the outskirts of **Seahouses**, it's easier to join the road for the last 800m into town. This is a strange place; half traditional fishing port, half tacky seaside town. It does have a good supply of cafés and takeaways selling fish and chips, though – and the fish seems fresh, so this is probably one of the better places to try the traditional

footpath runs through a National Trust nature reserve just back from the shore. Either way, the ruined tower of **Dunstanburgh Castle** (see the boxed text, below) looms large on the opposite headland – standing like a jagged tooth waiting to be pulled.

Your route takes you under the castle's remaining walls (the entrance is on the south side) and after a stroll around the ruin it's only 1 mile or so to the picturesque fishing village of Craster, and the end of this walk.

OPTIONAL EXTENSION: CRASTER TO ALNMOUTH

3–3½ hours, 7 miles (11.5km)

This optional extension from Craster turns the walk into quite a lengthy enterprise. With good weather, a following wind and a late lunch at Craster, the whole walk from Bamburgh to Alnmouth could be done in a day. Alternatively you can split it into two days, overnighting in Beadnell.

From Craster, continue south along the path that runs along the top of the cliffs overlooking the rocky, wave-cut platform. You can't miss the noisy groups of sea birds nesting on the cliffs. From Cullernose Point, you can either keep to the inland path or walk on the beach or over the rocks

---

DUNSTANBURGH CASTLE

Dating from the 14th century, **Dunstanburgh Castle** (EH; ☎ 01665-576231; adult/child £2.70/1.40; ☻ 10am-5pm Mon-Sun Apr-Sep, 10am-4pm Mon-Sun Oct, 10am-4pm Thu-Mon Nov-Mar) was built in a strategic position, protected to the north and east by the sea and to the west by the cliffs of the Whin Sill. On the vulnerable south side a large wall was constructed to complete the defences. The castle was originally built in the early 14th century by the Earl of Lancaster, a powerful baron opposed to the rule of King Edward II. It later became home to John of Gaunt and his son Henry IV and, like neighbouring Bamburgh, was a Lancastrian stronghold during the War of the Roses. Unlike Bamburgh though, the castle was abandoned in the 16th century and is now a ruin. Today the impressive gateway still survives, as well as a tower and some of the wall, and the castle is well worth a visit as you pass by on your walk.

---

past the outcrops of Longhoughton Steel and the small fishing village of Boulmer.

The route passes Seaton Point, a sandy beach and the Marden Rocks outcrop, and then passes a last stretch of beach to reach Alnmouth, set dramatically on a steep ridge overlooking the estuary of the River Aln – a striking finish to this walk along the coast.

MORE WALKS

Most walking opportunities in Northumberland (apart from the coast) are in Northumberland National Park, one of the largest yet least visited parks in the country and often billed as 'the loneliest park in England'. It covers 398 sq miles of high ground inland from the coastal plains, between Hadrian's Wall in the south and the Scottish border in the north. Only a few roads cross the park, and the landscape is characterised by high, windswept grassy hills cut by streams and valleys, almost empty of human habitation.

Multiday routes that cross this wild and remote area include the infamously tough Pennine Way (p261) and the increasingly popular St Cuthbert's Way (p427).

For day walkers there are several options. In the southern part of Northumberland, Hadrian's Wall is an ideal focus for easy strolls or something longer. (The guidebooks mentioned in the Hadrian's Wall section of this chapter on p215 provide plenty of ideas.) North of Otterburn is a military training area where access to the public is restricted – for more details, see the boxed text on p234.

CENTRAL NORTHUMBERLAND

For walks in the central part of Northumberland, and the centre of Northumberland National Park, a good place to base yourself is the small town of Bellingham. To get here, there are bus connections to/from Otterburn and Hexham, with connections to the gateway towns of Carlisle and Newcastle upon Tyne.

Bellingham (pronounced 'bellinjam') is surrounded by beautiful countryside and plenty of walking options. For a starter, you could follow a section of the Pennine Way that passes through Bellingham. You could even get here on foot by walking from Once Brewed, on Hadrian's Wall, about 18 miles south. For information on the town, including places to stay, see p224.

Another good base in central Northumberland is the charming town of Rothbury, easily reached in summer months by direct bus from Newcastle upon Tyne. The town offers relatively easy access to the Simonside Hills on the eastern side of the park. The hills have some of the widest views in Northumberland, from the Cheviots to the coast. The town also makes a good base for circular walks in the hills to the north (outside the park and not so 'wild' but still well worth a visit). For a place to stay, there are several B&Bs on and around the wide main street, plus teashops and a couple of nice pubs doing evening meals. Rothbury tourist office (☎ 01669-620887) can give information, and stocks books, maps and leaflets on walks in the surrounding area.

North of Bellingham and west of Rothbury, tiny Byrness also lies in splendid countryside, and is on the Pennine Way. Straddling a main road, access includes National Express coaches between Newcastle upon Tyne and Edinburgh. From Byrness, you can walk 15 miles along the Pennine Way to Bellingham, or (if properly equipped) you can head into the starkly beautiful Cheviot Hills – for details on the route and Byrness, see p275.

NORTHERN NORTHUMBERLAND

The best place to base yourself for walks in northern Northumberland, and the top end of Northumberland National Park, is the sturdy old market town of Wooler, with several good walker-friendly places to stay, plus shops, banks, cafés and pubs. This place is easy to reach by bus from the gateways of Newcastle upon Tyne, Berwick-upon-Tweed or Alnwick, and the **Berwick tourist office** (☎ 01668-282123; www.berwick-upon-tweed.gov .uk/guide) can provide more information on walking routes, accommodation and transport in the park and surrounding area.

There are several circular day walks possible in this area. You can walk up the quiet and beautiful Harthorpe Valley into the Cheviot foothills, and some walks even deeper into the heart of the park become viable if you tie in with the local postbus that goes up this valley to Langleeford. Hardy walkers go up the Harthorpe Valley and continue all the way to the summit of the Cheviot (815m), the highest point in the county and the remains of an ancient volcano.

For a real adventure, from the Cheviot summit you could follow the Pennine Way to Kirk Yetholm in Scotland, 14 miles away, but only consider this if you have enough time and the right equipment – the weather can be terrible up here, the area is not so well frequented and paths are

NORTHUMBERLAND'S TURBULENT HISTORY

A significant part of Northumberland National Park is used by the army as a training ground. This may seem strange to visitors from countries where national parks are carefully preserved areas virtually untouched by human interference, but it happens in Britain (where all national park land is privately owned) so while you're walking in this area you may hear the bangs and thuds of live ammunition carried on the wind from nearby valleys.

The involvement of the army here is not completely inappropriate, as this was once the most war-torn region of England. The Romans built Hadrian's Wall in an attempt to control rebellious tribes and, after they left, the region remained a contested zone between Scotland and England – home to warring clans and families led by ruthless warriors called reivers, from where we get the modern word 'bereaved'.

Few buildings from this time remain. Most families lived in simple structures of turf that could be quickly and cheaply built and just as quickly abandoned. A few larger farms were more solidly constructed and better fortified. Known as bastle-houses, one of the best remaining examples is at Black Middens, between Bellingham and Byrness, west of the Pennine Way.

Peace came in the 18th century, but coincided with new farming practices; large estates were created and the tenant farmers dispossessed. For today's walker on the high ground of Northumberland this leaves a landscape with no stone walls and only a few small isolated farms. Instead there's a bleak grandeur, wide horizons and vast skies...

often faint on the ground. There are more straightforward and less energetic options in the area north of the Harthorpe Valley and south of the road between Wooler and Kirknewton.

Also near Wooler is the Breamish Valley, with the village of Ingram at its eastern end, and a **National Park Visitor Centre** (☎ 01665-578890; www.northumberland-national-park .org.uk), with lots of information and leaflets on suggested local walks in the valley or up onto the high ground. Many of these take in the remains of Bronze Age settlements that once covered this area.

Northern England Long-Distance Paths

This chapter covers three of the longest, finest and most famous long-distance paths (LDPs) in Northern England. The Coast to Coast Walk and the Pennine Way are in this special chapter because they're too long to fit in any other chapter in this book, and the Cleveland Way is here simply because we love it. Between them, these classic routes cross several different parts of England, including the Lake District, Peak District, Yorkshire Dales, North York Moors and North Pennines, which are all famous walking areas in their own right, and described elsewhere in this book.

Following these routes will take you across high mountains, deep valleys, rolling moors and flat farmland. You can stroll alongside rivers and bound along breezy cliff tops overlooking the sea. There's no finer way to sample northern England's wonderfully varied landscape.

The Coast to Coast is one of the most popular LDPs in the country, thanks partly to the route being founded by the near-mythical Alfred Wainwright. The venerable Cleveland Way is quieter and adds dramatic ruined castles and abbeys to the scenic mix. And the Pennine Way is the grand-daddy of them all, the first LDP to be established, way back in the 1950s.

Of course, the Coast to Coast, Cleveland Way and Pennine Way are by no means the only LDPs in Northern England. Others described in this book are the Cumbria Way (p201) and the Dales Way (p174), and further ideas are given in the More Long-Distance Walks section on p277.

HIGHLIGHTS

- Slaking your thirst with a pint at the **Bay Hotel** (p252) after completing the Coast to Coast Walk
- Conquering a range of peaks in the Lake District National Park, including **Helvellyn** (p243)
- Ascending the 199 steps up the coastal cliffs to historic **Whitby Abbey** (p260)
- Marvelling at the natural amphitheatre of **Malham Cove** (p269) in the Yorkshire Dales National Park
- Striding in the footsteps of Roman centurions along **Hadrian's Wall** (p274)

THE COAST TO COAST WALK

Duration	12 days
Distance	191 miles (307.5km)
Difficulty	moderate–demanding
Start	St Bees (p239)
Finish	Robin Hood's Bay (p239)
Transport	train, bus

Summary The magnificent and varied scenery of the Lake District, the Yorkshire Dales and the North York Moors, plus the companionship of fellow walkers, make this England's classic cross-country route.

Traversing three spectacular national parks – the Lake District, Yorkshire Dales and North York Moors – the Coast to Coast Walk passes through some of England's finest landscape. Along it you'll encounter disbanded mines and railway lines, reminders of a once-flourishing industrial age; lonely inns on isolated hill tops; historic buildings in bustling market towns; the rugged windswept splendour of both coasts; dry-stone walls and barns; and grassy fields of sheep and cattle. Small wonder it's Britain's favourite LDP.

The prime attraction, however, of the Coast to Coast, a walk created by that notorious curmudgeon Alfred Wainwright (see the boxed text, p188), is the camaraderie shared with fellow walkers – people of all ages and many nationalities. Add in friendly local folk, particularly the owners of the B&Bs and pubs along the route, and you have a pretty-close-to-perfect way to discovering the wilderness, the space and the sheer beautiful bleakness of the mountains and moors of northern England.

Signposting and waymarking is often minimal or nonexistent, though you will see some 'Coast to Coast' signs (often shortened to 'C to C', or the like). You'll need to keep a close eye on your map to keep going in the right direction. Some sections include several miles of forestry tracks and sealed roads, which are, frankly, tedious at times. However, for the most part it's an inspiring journey though a slice of British geography, history and society.

HISTORY

The route, which isn't a national trail and has no official recognition, was first described in Alfred Wainwright's *A Coast to Coast Walk*, published in 1973. Wainwright had taken a year to carefully plan his route, but encouraged readers to make up their own Coast to Coast itineraries: 'There's no end to the possibilities for originality and initiative,' he wrote in the introduction. However, most people doing Wainwright's route call it *the* Coast to Coast, and follow his description very closely. Purists refuse to deviate even a few steps from Wainwright's incredibly precise instructions. Although the route has been realigned in some places (mainly so it now follows legal rights of way), it still keeps pretty much to the original and certainly follows it in spirit.

PLANNING

Most people walk the Coast to Coast from west to east, with the wind and sun behind them (mostly, anyway). Although this provides steep terrain at the start, you can tackle it while you're still fresh.

Wainwright's original itinerary covered 12 days. We've kept with tradition and split the route as follows:

Day	From	To	Miles/km
1	St Bees	Ennerdale Bridge	14/22.5
2	Ennerdale Bridge	Rosthwaite	15/24.5
3	Rosthwaite	Patterdale	17.5/28.5
4	Patterdale	Shap	16/26
5	Shap	Kirkby Stephen	21/34
6	Kirkby Stephen	Keld	13/21
7	Keld	Reeth	11/18
8	Reeth	Richmond	11/18
9	Richmond	Ingleby Cross	23/37
10	Ingleby Cross	Blakey	21/34
11	Blakey	Grosmont	13/21
12	Grosmont	Robin Hood's Bay	15.5/25

This is a demanding itinerary if completed in one go, particularly if you're not fit, or if you're camping and carrying your own gear. Most days have some serious ascents and descents.

Alternatives

The 12-day itinerary is achievable but is tough going, particularly if the weather turns nasty. Many people add a few extra overnight stops. Consider staying at Grasmere, to break up the Rosthwaite to Patterdale leg on Day 3. Days 4 and 5 could be turned into three days by staying a night each in Bampton and Orton, instead of at Shap. Another option is to break Day 9 at Danby Wiske, then continue to Ingleby Cross or Osmotherley the next day. Similarly, the distance from Ingleby Cross to Blakey can be broken at Clay Bank Top.

If you're short of time, some days could be combined but this would turn the walk into quite a march – although the whole route has been done as a run in around 39 hours! You're better off splitting the route and doing different sections at different times. Possible entry and exit points include Kirkby Stephen and Richmond, which are on or near major train lines.

When to Walk

Avoid starting the Coast to Coast on a weekend, which is when most walkers begin, aiming to do the walk within a two-week holiday. If you start midweek you'll have a bit more space on the hills. You'll also be out of sync with the 'bulge' of high demand for accommodation that follows these walkers along the route, and thus have more chance of finding a place to stay.

Maps

Harvey's 1:40,000 *Coast to Coast West* and *Coast to Coast East* strip maps are detailed enough and easy to follow. Their larger scale is preferable to that of the strip maps produced by Footprint Maps. There are two Ordnance Survey (OS) 1:27,777 *Coast to Coast* strip maps covering the whole route, but they're out of print so you'll have to hunt around in secondhand bookshops.

To cover the whole route using OS Landranger 1:50,000 maps you're going to need Nos 89 *West Cumbria*, 90 *Penrith & Keswick*, 91 *Appleby-in-Westmorland*, 92 *Barnard Castle & Richmond*, 93 *Middlesbrough*, 94 *Whitby & Esk Dale*, 98 *Wensleydale & Upper Wharfdale* and 99 *Northallerton & Ripon*.

For maximum detail the route is covered by (from west to east) OS Explorer 1:25,000 maps No 303 *Whitehaven & Workington*, 4 *The English Lakes – North Western Area*, 5 *The English Lakes – North Eastern Area*, 19 *Howgill Fells and Upper Eden Valley*, 30 *Yorkshire Dales – Northern & Central Areas*, 304 *Darlington & Richmond*, 26 *North York Moors – Western Area* and 27 *North York Moors – Eastern Area*.

Consider using a combination of strip and full maps of the Lake District, where the possibility of bad weather and the complicated route means you could need more coverage.

Books

Don't leave without the classic *A Coast to Coast Walk* by Alfred Wainwright. The revised edition, published in 2003, describes alternatives to Wainwright's route where it had strayed from public rights of way, although still faithfully keeping the original text.

Coast to Coast Path by Henry Stedman is an up-to-date (2006), dependable and practical addition to Trailblazer's British Walking Guide series. Its hand-drawn 1:20,000 strip maps are not always clear to follow, so you will also need proper maps.

Also revised in 2006 is *A Northern Coast to Coast Walk* by Terry Marsh, which has adjusted the original route in consultation with conservation officials, keeping to rights of way, avoiding eroded areas and reducing time spent walking on roads.

The Coast to Coast Walk by Paul Hannon describes the route in, at times, annoyingly archaic style. Like the Wainwright original, it has hand-drawn illustrations, but printed text, which makes it easier to read.

The Coast to Coast Accommodation Guide, a useful booklet produced by **Doreen Whitehead** (☎ 01748-886374; Butt House, Keld, North Yorkshire DL11 6LJ), is available by mail order for £4, including postage; overseas visitors can send a US$10 bill. It can also be downloaded free at www.coasttocoastguides .co.uk. Mrs Whitehead also offers accommodation in Keld (see p246).

Information Sources

See the walk description for tourist offices on or near the route – all provide information on local accommodation and services in their surrounding area.

The best source of online information is www.coast2coast.co.uk, run by Sherpa Van. Check out the message board and walker comments on the various places to stay along the route. Also useful is www.coast tocoastguides.co.uk, the website of Castle Hill Books in Richmond; it provides a free online advice service with answers from professional walking guides, sells the latest guidebooks and maps covering the route, and has Doreen Whitehead's accommodation list (see opposite) available free online – follow the 'Accommodation' link.

You'll also find a chat forum for long-distance walkers at www.uglysheep.co.uk, a website that mainly sells Coast to Coast merchandise.

Baggage Services

To make things easier, we recommend that you use a baggage-forwarding service, such as the **Coast to Coast Packhorse** (☎ 017683-71777; www.cumbria.com/packhorse; each transfer per bag £6). Other baggage-carrying services are listed on p437.

NEAREST TOWNS
St Bees

Bracketed by Sellafield nuclear power station to the south and Whitehaven chemical works to the north, it's easy to see why the windswept village of St Bees is generally overlooked by tourists. However, St Bees is not without its charms, boasting a pristine sweep of sand, the **St Bees Head RSPB Nature Reserve** (the only place in the country where black guillemot breed), the historic **Priory Church of St Bega** – St Bees' original name – and with the beautiful Lake District immediately to the east.

There's no tourist office in town, but for more visitor information you can consult www.stbees.org.uk.

SLEEPING & EATING

Near the train station, the very friendly Carole runs **Stonehouse Farm** (☎ 01946-822224; www.stonehousefarm.net; 133 Main St; camp sites for 2 £6, s £26-30, d £50; 🖳), a well-appointed B&B with camping in the back garden.

Further uphill is the classy **Fairladies Barn** (☎ 01946-822718; www.fairladiesbarn.co.uk; Main St; s £30-33, d £50).

The fanciest hotel is **Fleatham House** (☎ 01946-822341; www.fleathamhouse.com; High House Rd; s/d from £35/70, mains £15; 🕑 dinner Mon-Sat), which also has a smart restaurant serving gourmet meals.

Platform Nine (☎ 01946-822600; Old Railway Station; s/d £45/60, meals £5-15; 🕑 lunch & dinner) also has three kitschly decorated rooms, but is principally a restaurant where, three nights a week, a Thai chef is brought in to spice up the menu; it also does takeaway sandwiches.

You can get sandwiches from **Hartley's Tearoom** (☎ 01946-822600; Beach Rd), which also serves delicious locally made ice cream. Otherwise there are several pubs, the pick of which are the **Queens Hotel** (☎ 01946-822287; Main St; 🕑 lunch & dinner), which scores for its cosy ambiance, pleasant garden and choice of more than 100 whiskies; and the **Manor House** (☎ 01946-822425; Main St; 🕑 dinner), with its Coast to Coast bar – as good a place as any for a drink to start off your walk. Both have accommodation if you can't find anywhere else to stay.

GETTING THERE & AWAY

St Bees is on the **Northern Rail** (www.northernrail .org) Cumbrian Coast line between Carlisle (1¼ hours) and Barrow-in-Furness (one hour), with regular trains throughout the day. **Stagecoach** (www.stagecoachbus.com) runs sporadic buses from Whitehaven to St Bees (25 minutes, five a day Monday to Friday). By car, the town is reached from the M6 at Penrith, taking the A66 to Cockermouth, the A5086 to Egremont and from there along a small country road.

Robin Hood's Bay

Romantics may be disappointed to find out that the link between Robin Hood's Bay and the heroic outlaw is only legendary, and extremely tenuous. Nevertheless, while roaming the steep and narrow cobbled lanes, with miniature cottages and tiny gardens glued to the steep slopes of the bay, there is nothing to stop you from imagining the bustling fishing community of earlier centuries – a haven for smugglers, shipwrecked sailors and, of course, heroic outlaws.

SLEEPING & EATING

The best place for camping walkers is **Hooks House Farm** (☎ 01947-880283; sites for 2 £10), about 800m outside of town on the main road towards Whitby. You can also head inland along the disused rail trail toward Fylingthorpe and **Middlewood Farm** (☎ 01947-880414; sites for 2 £10; 🕑 mid-Feb–mid-Jan).

The nearest YHA hostels are at Whitby (p260), to the north, and at the delightfully named Boggle Hole (p260), to the south.

On the outskirts of town, just as you come off the cliffs, **Meadowfield** (☎ 01947-880564; s/d £20/40), on Mount Pleasant North, is a recommended B&B.

In the heart of the village is the quaint and secluded **Orchard House** (☎ 01947-880912; d from £60).

Also recommended is the **White Owl Guesthouse** (☎ 01947-880879; s/d from £25/50).

The **Bay Hotel** (☎ 01947-880278; r from £50), overlooking the slipway, has a popular walkers' bar.

Back up the hill, and more upmarket, is the **Victoria Hotel** (☎ 01947-880205; r from £74, mains £6-8), with great sea views and good bar food, including vegetarian, and a restaurant serving à la carte.

GETTING THERE & AWAY
Arriva (www.arriva.co.uk) bus No 93 travels several times daily to Robin Hood's Bay from Whitby (20 minutes) and Scarborough (30min).

THE WALK
Day 1: St Bees to Ennerdale Bridge
6–7 hours, 14 miles (22.5km)
The first day introduces the contrasts and variety to come. From the foaming Irish Sea breaking below the sheer cliffs of St Bees you cross industrial and agricultural plains, patches of forest, quiet valleys and some high ground with panoramic views.

It's your choice whether you pick up a pebble or dip your toe into the water at St Bees beach – a ritual to repeat at Robin Hood's Bay. That done, head to the northern end of the concrete promenade, climbing the cliff path that leads to St Bees Head

and Fleswick Bay. 'C to C' signposts and yellow arrows are easy to follow until Bell House Farm.

Continue past the farm, go through a gate and follow the right-hand path. At a fork, go left, down the field, underneath the railway line and immediately left to zigzag through several fields (and under another railway, now dismantled and converted into a cycle path), passing through the villages of Moor Row and Cleator – the former has **Jasmine House B&B and Tea Garden** (www.jasminehousebandb.com; s/d from £28/48, sandwich & drink around £5), a pleasant and friendly place to pause for lunch.

The route continues through fields then follows a forestry track uphill. Look for a sign on the left to 'Dent Fell'; here you exchange, with a sigh of relief, the hard track for a soft, grassy path to the summit of Dent Fell. The views from this peak make you feel like the journey really starts here. Behind is the glinting sea, the hazy, sinister silhouette of the nuclear reactors and the billowing clouds of the chemical works, while ahead rises the challenging skyline of the mountains of the Lake District.

After descending steeply through a patch of eerie, silent forest (make sure you take the route to the right after coming off the top of Dent Fell), you enter the enchanting limestone vale of Nannycatch Beck, where the gurgling of a stream replaces the howling of the wind. Keep a close eye on the map in this area as there are numerous path

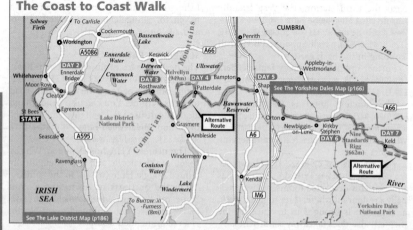

The Coast to Coast Walk

junctions; take a wrong turn and you could mistakenly head back towards Cleator. The path leaves the beck and meets a lane, which continues for about 1 mile to the main road and the village of Ennerdale Bridge.

ENNERDALE BRIDGE
This quiet and attractive village has no ATM or shop, so make sure you bring enough cash and supplies with you.

Low Cock How Farm (☎ 01946-861354; www.walk -rest-ride.co.uk; camp sites for 2 £8, s/d with shared bathroom £25/50) is about 1 mile south of the village; you'll pass it on the route.

Getting good reviews, but a couple of miles north of the village, is **Ennerdale View** (☎ 01946-862311; http://myweb.tiscali.co.uk/enner daleview; s with/without bathroom £33/20, d with/without bathroom £46/30).

In the village itself, B&B can be found at **Bridge End Cottage** (☎ 01946-861806; d with shared bathroom £36) and the **Cloggers** (☎ 01946-862487; d with shared bathroom £44).

Both the village pubs also do B&B, meals and packed lunches – order one the night before as there's nowhere else for food until you get to Seatoller near the end of Day 2. The smartly renovated **Fox & Hounds** (☎ 01946-861373; www.tp-inns .co.uk; s/d £45/70; ☻ lunch & dinner) is tops both for accommodation and food, while the friendly **Shepherds Arms Hotel** (☎ 01946-861249; shepherdsarms@btconnect.com; s/d £45/75, meals £9-12; ☻ lunch & dinner) serves afternoon tea and has a fine restaurant, with hearty meals.

WILD ENNERDALE
In what is something of an about-face for one of the major landowners in the Ennerdale Valley, the Forestry Commission, in line with its revised policy in other parts of the UK, is scaling back its operations and has joined with the National Trust and United Utilities to promote **Wild Ennerdale** (www .wildennerdale.co.uk). The project aims to use natural forces to help the valley develop into an unique wild place. Forestry is being cut back and wild cattle have been re-introduced into the valley – you'll see a sign at the end of Ennerdale Water warning you to watch out for the bull!

Day 2: Ennerdale Bridge to Rosthwaite
6–7 hours, 15 miles (24.5km)
The challenge of the Coast to Coast really begins with this long but enjoyable day, which starts with a pleasant section along Ennerdale Water, proceeding to the first serious summit to be conquered, and culminating with a descent into lovely Borrowdale.

Head east out of Ennerdale Bridge, following the signs to Ennerdale Water. After about 800m, the official route turns right onto a quiet lane that zigzags through a plantation to a rocky path along the south side of the lake. However, if you want to save a bit of time (particularly if you're aiming for either of the youth hostels further along the route on your first walking day)

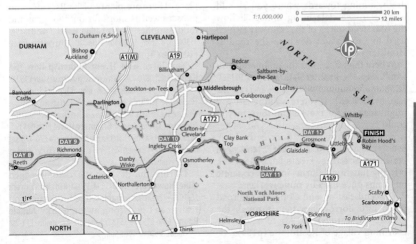

stay on the main road and then take the easier path along the north side of the lake, which joins up directly with the forestry path.

At the end of the lake, stiles lead to a footbridge across the River Liza and you go up the valley on the forestry path, passing first the outdoor activities operation **Low Gillerthwaite Field Centre** (☎ 01946-861229; www.carolclimb.co.uk), and then the recommended **Ennerdale YHA Hostel** (☎ 01946-861237; ennerdale@yha.org.uk; dm £12; ☺ Easter-Oct, Nov-Easter by advance booking). It does evening meals and can provide a packed lunch (£4.50).

Just past the hostel, a high-level option over Red Pike and Hay Stacks goes off left, but this is a long and very demanding route and requires mountain experience. The sensible low-level route follows 4 miles of flat and fairly boring forestry track along the valley to the fantastically isolated shepherd's bothy (cottage) that is **Black Sail YHA** (☎ 07711-108450; dm £12; ☺ Easter to Oct, Nov-Easter by advance booking). This is a good place to pause for lunch and a rest before heading steeply upwards beside Loft Beck (the route furthest to the west) to the top of the fell.

The view from the summit across to Buttermere is wonderful, but read your map carefully from here to make sure you're heading in the right direction, particularly if the weather is bad (if you're in cloud you'll need your compass or GPS). The route contours below a peak called Brandreth, aiming towards where you should be able to see slate being mined. Follow the old, steep tracks of the tramway (which used to carry slate) down to the road at Honister Pass.

Where the track joins the main road you won't miss the **Honister Slate Mine** (☎ 017687-77230; www.honister-slate-mine.co.uk; Honister Pass; tour adult/child £9.50/4.50). If you're walking fast you might make it for the 3.30pm tour, or you could pop in for refreshments as you shelter from the elements. Next door is the basic **Honister Hause YHA** (☎ 0870 770 5870; honister@yha .org.uk; Seatoller; dm £12; ☺ Easter-Oct, Sat & Sun Nov), offering functional dorms in grey, concrete buildings once used by mine workers.

Descend east on and alongside the road down into Borrowdale, then through the hamlet of Seatoller (p198) to reach the charming village of Rosthwaite (p199).

Day 3: Rosthwaite to Patterdale
8–10 hours, 17.5 miles (28.5km)
This is a very long, hard and potentially serious day through the heart of the Lake District, during which you make two major ascents and descents. Many walkers opt to break the section into two days by staying at Grasmere, making it easier and much more fulfilling, with time to enjoy the wonderful scenery.

From Rosthwaite go up the road towards Keswick for 50m then turn right (east) down a stony lane towards Hazel Bank Hotel. Go over a bridge and turn immediately right onto a track. This runs uphill along the northern side of Stonethwaite Beck, past the imposing **Eagle Crag** (marking the junction with Langstrath Beck) and gradually ascends Greenup Gill to Lining Crag. Take great care here as there's a confusing maze of paths and cairns. Use your compass or GPS to take a bearing and head southeast to reach the pass through **Greenup Edge**.

The usual descent is via Far Easedale Gill, which leads you down through a fell called Grasmere Common. In fair weather, if you have the time, the high-level option via Gibson Knott and Helm Crag is a wonderful alternative; it makes use of the height already gained and is not strenuous. The paths rejoin about 1.5 miles outside **Grasmere**.

Thanks to its Wordsworth connection (see the boxed text, p190) the beautifully situated village of Grasmere is a popular place. There are plenty of B&Bs, cafés and pubs, as well as shops for outdoor gear and food supplies. **Dales Lodge Hotel** (☎ 015394-35300; s/d from £75/110) has a tourist office (10am to 4pm).

The large and lively **Butharlyp How YHA Hostel** (☎ 0870 770 5836; www.yha.org.uk; dm £15.50; ☺ Feb-Nov, weekends Dec & Jan; 🖳) is just off Easedale Rd in a converted Victorian house; the restaurant is licensed and good value. Nearby, the chintzy **Grasmere Hotel** (☎ 015394-35277; www.grasmerehotel.co.uk; Broadgate; d £70-110, set dinner £20, ☺ dinner) offers more luxury and a posh restaurant.

During the day try the chrome-edged **Miller Howe Café** (☎ 015394-35234; Red Lion Sq; mains £6-10; ☺ breakfast & lunch), while for dinner you really can't go wrong at the quirky **Jumble Room** (☎ 015394-35188; Langdale Rd; mains £11-20; ☺ lunch & dinner Wed-Sun).

To skip Grasmere follow the Coast to Coast path as it turns left (north) before the village, near the **Thorney How YHA Hostel** (☎ 0870 770 5836; www.yha.org.uk; dm £13; ☺ Apr-Oct); this lovely little hostel was the first one purchased by the YHA, way back in 1931.

The route then crosses the main road at Mill Bridge. Here, **High Broadrayne Farm & Grasmere Hostel** (☎ 015394-35055; www.grasmere hostel.co.uk; dm £15.50; ☐) is a great little independent hostel, boasting a 'Nordic sauna' and a luxurious lounge lit by skylights and a round picture window. Wonderful views, plus the friendly and helpful management, make it one of the finest hostels along the whole route.

Nearby, the **Travellers Rest Inn** (☎ 015394-35604; www.lakedistrictinns.co.uk; d weekdays/weekends £84/104; mains from £8-14; ☺ lunch & dinner) is a 16th-century pub with all the trappings of a quintessential Lakeland inn, including slate-fronted fireplaces, oak-beamed ceilings and a bevy of real ales.

Continuing on, you ascend to Grisedale Hause, with the picturesque little **Grisedale Tarn** just beyond. From here the low-level option leads you down the valley of Grisedale, which is like a dream brought to life: meadows teeming with wildflowers, a melodious stream cutting a silvery trail along the foot of the fellside and lonely barns hiding secrets of days gone by. It's plain sailing now into the village of Patterdale (p195), just southeast of Ullswater.

ALTERNATIVE ROUTES: HIGH-LEVEL PATHS FROM GRISEDALE TARN

If you broke this day at Grasmere you may be ready to consider a high-level alternative. From Grisedale Tarn walk up to Deepdale Hause (just north of Fairfield summit) and then over St Sunday Crag, with great views of Ullswater as you descend into Patterdale. This 4-mile route should take around two hours.

If you're feeling really fit, from Grisedale Tarn you could go up the path to Dollywaggon Pike and then to Helvellyn, descending via Striding Edge and Glenridding (p193), still with enough energy left to saunter into Patterdale – allow about three hours to walk this 5-mile section, which is described (in reverse) on p192 and could be the highlight of your route, though it's very serious and not to be undertaken lightly.

Day 4: Patterdale to Shap
6–7 hours, 16 miles (26km)

This challenging section offers final, magnificent views over Ullswater and the Helvellyn ranges. Work through the pain of the climb, bid a wistful goodbye to the lovely Lakes and look forward to the prospect of a new, gentler landscape.

From Patterdale, south of the White Lion pub, turn east off the main road onto a small lane. Follow it to its end, where a wall marks the beginning of the open fell. Go through a gate and take the path that climbs diagonally up the fellside to Boredale Hause, from where you follow a glorious, airy path with wonderful views over the valley and surrounding mountains. Go to the north of **Angle Tarn** and skirt a peak called the Knott. Alternatively, you can divert briefly to the summit, where the views are excellent.

From the Knott, aim south beside a wall for about 300m, then turn left (northeast) at a junction of paths (straight on leads to a peak called High Street; see p196). Take great care here, especially in the mist. Even on clear days some walkers miss this path and end up on top of High Street by mistake. The path swings round to aim east, continues over **Kidsty Pike** (780m), the last Lakeland summit on this route, and then drops down to the southern end of the Haweswater reservoir. In bad weather precise compass bearings are called for so that you don't miss Kidsty Pike.

Once you reach Haweswater, there are a couple of choices. The official route, which hugs the northern bank of the reservoir to **Burbanks**, is rather rugged with long slogs through towering ferns and behind forests. Alternatively, you can reach the same point by heading around the southern end of Haweswater to join the road running up this side, providing good views of the lake, largely level walking and the chance to pause at the upmarket **Haweswater Hotel** (☎ 01931-713235; www.haweswaterhotel.com; s with/without bathroom £40/35, d with/without bathroom £90/70, 2-course dinner £20; ☺ lunch & dinner); the bar also serves food.

A third possibility is the high-level route, which goes from just before Kidsty Pike over High Raise and Wether Hill, down to Haweswater's northern end. This should only be attempted if you have plenty of time, good weather and map-reading skills.

From Burbanks the route continues east. If you're tired, or are cutting this day short, branch off here and walk 1.5 miles to the neighbouring villages of Bampton and Bampton Grange; in the latter the **Crown & Mitre** (☎ 01931-713225; www.freewebs.com/crown mitre; s/d £23/45) gets good recommendations.

If Shap is your aim, you will enjoy a lovely stroll via Haweswater Beck and the River Lowther. You will then pass the remains of 12th-century **Shap Abbey** before entering the village.

SHAP

Hugging the A6, Shap is not the most attractive village on the Coast to Coast, but it's well served by several good B&Bs and pubs. It also has a **New Balance Factory Shop** (☎ 01931-716333; Main St), which could be a lifesaver for any walkers suffering from poor footwear.

For more information on the village, check the community website at www .shapcumbria.co.uk.

You can camp at the **Bulls Head Inn** (☎ 01931-716678; www.bullsheadshap.co.uk; camp sites for 2 £10, mains £5-7; 🖳), use its ATM, and be fed pretty well.

At the north end of town, **New Ing Farm** (☎ 01931-716719; angela.parkinson@onetel.com; Main Rd; s/d with shared bathroom £25/50) is an excellent B&B, thoughtfully providing all manner of soothing foot products in the bathroom to pamper tired feet.

The unpretentious **Fell House** (☎ 01931-716343; fellhouse.shap@btopenworld.com; s/d £28/48) is well set up for walkers and serves evening meals; it's practically on the route, just south of the Kings Arms pub, which was being renovated at the time of research.

Traditional **Brookfield** (☎ 01931-716397; www.brookfieldshap.co.uk; s/d £30/55) also offers evening meals, a bar and a chatty host, while the **Hermitage** (☎ 01931-716671; jeanjackson _hermitage@btopenworld.com; s with shared bathroom £30, d £58) is a characterful old house, with wood panelling and a stained glass window.

The **Greyhound Hotel** (☎ 01931-716474; www .greyhoundshap.co.uk; Main St; s/d £38/66), in business as a coaching inn since 1680 (Bonnie Prince Charlie is said to have stopped the night in 1745), has a fine range of beers and serves great food, including a cooked breakfast with the requisite Cumberland sausage and black pudding.

Other options for food include **Shap Chippy** (☎ 01931-716388; 🕑 lunch & dinner Mon-Sat) opposite the Bulls Head, and the **Crown Inn** (☎ 01931-716229; 🕑 lunch & dinner), which has several vegetarian options.

Day 5: Shap to Kirkby Stephen
8 hours, 21 miles (34km)

After the exhilarating experience of crossing England's highest mountain region, this day will feel tame but will be a welcome respite from the windswept desolation of upland fells. Ancient stone circles and other prehistoric remains are welcome distractions along the way and a short detour from the route takes you to the charming village of Orton for lunch.

The route leaves Shap, turning off the A6 opposite the King's Arms Hotel and crossing the railway line, taking you straight to the M6 motorway – an unfortunate reminder of 'civilisation'. Cross the footbridge and make a quick escape to the moors.

Just past the secluded hamlet of Oddendale, slow down for **Oddendale Stone Circle**, a superb lookout, and get back in touch with the serenity of ancient sites that abound in this area. These include **Robin Hood's Grave**, about 2 miles further along the route, an ancient cairn that is highly unlikely to be the resting place of the legendary brigand.

From here the route drops down to the B6260, from where you can detour slightly into **Orton**. It's a quaint village, with a well-stocked shop, and it would be a shame to miss it, especially as you can get lunch or a great cup of tea and a freshly baked scone at **New Village Tea Rooms** (☎ 015396-24886), or sample the chocolate and cakes at **Kennedys** (☎ 015396-24781; www.kennedyschocolates.co.uk). It's also possible to stay at the **George Hotel** (☎ 015396-24225; www.georgehotel.net; s/d £28/50).

Returning to the route, you'll next pass **Sunbiggin Tarn**, a protected breeding ground for birds. Soon after, you're back on the road for 3 miles of dull walking. Along the way you could stop off at **Bents Farm** (☎ 01768-371760; www.bentscampingbarn.co.uk; dm £6), which offers dorm accommodation in a 17th-century shepherd's cottage, with a well-equipped kitchen. You'll need your own sleeping bag.

The route crosses a small river called Smardale Gill and goes over Smardale Fell. From Lime Kilne Hill, the views of the Eden

Valley to Nine Standards Rigg will help take your mind off your aching feet and whet your appetite for tomorrow's jaunt. Beyond here, it's a couple of miles to Kirkby Stephen.

KIRKBY STEPHEN

The bustling, amiable market town of Kirkby Stephen has long been a pit stop for travellers in the region. As the largest town on the route so far, it has plenty of facilities, including a **tourist office** (☎ 017683-71199; www.visiteden.co.uk; Market St) in the centre of town; a Co-op supermarket; a couple of banks with ATMs; a good outdoor gear store, **Eden Outdoor** (☎ 017683-72431; 42 Market St); and, most usefully, a self-serve **laundrette** (☻ 9am-8pm) behind the post office. Market day is Monday. There's even a **Holistic Health Centre** (☎ 017683-72482; www.holistic-health.co.uk; 37 North Rd; ☻ 9.30am-8pm Wed-Mon), offering remedial massage for weary walkers plus a sauna and Jacuzzi; a 30-minute leg-and-foot rub costs £20.

You can camp at **Pennine View Caravan Park** (☎ 017683-71717; Station Rd; camp sites for 2 £12), on the southern edge of the town.

There are plenty of B&Bs. **Fletcher House** (☎ 017683-71013; www.fletcherhousecumbria.co.uk; s/d £25/52; 🖳) is one of the best, with friendly owners, an award-winning garden and an above-average choice of breakfast items.

Other excellent choices include the delightful **Redmayne House** (☎ 017683-71441; Silver St; s/d with shared bathroom £22/44), with a large garden and a wooden-seat Victorian toilet that gets everyone talking; the **Old Croft House B&B** (☎ 017683-71638; www.oldcrofthouse.co.uk; Market St; s/d from £25/52, dinner £14), opposite the tourist office, which offers a set dinner open to nonguests who book; and the **Jolly Farmers** (☎ 017683-71063; www.thejollyfarmers.co.uk; 63 High St; s/d from £26/52), an efficient place that offers a couple of rooms with spa baths.

The **King's Arms Hotel** (☎ 017683-71378; www.kingsarmskirkbystephen.co.uk; Market St; s with/without bathroom £33/25, d with/without bathroom £53/45) is the upmarket choice, but the rooms are modern and have less character than the rest of the bar. Walkers sometimes can get discounts of up to 25%.

Kirkby's best pub, serving very decent bar meals, is the **Black Bull Hotel** (☎ 017683-71237; blackbull@kirkby38.fsnet.co.uk; 38 Market St; s/d £30/50; ☻ lunch & dinner), which also has accommodation.

There's no shortage of fish and chip shops and cafés but, oddly, many of the latter shut at 4pm – tough if you straggle into town late in the afternoon gagging for a cuppa. One place that doesn't is **Church Gallery** (☎ 017683-72395; 3-7 Market St), just behind the historic St Hedda's Church.

You could also try the smart **Mulberry Bush** (☎ 017683-71572; 35 Market St), which recently obtained a liquor license and so may start opening for dinner.

Make a booking if you wish to eat at the tiny **Old Forge** (☎ 017683-71832; 39 North Rd; meals £10-15; ☻ dinner Tue-Sun); its gourmet menu includes 'cock and bull' – chicken stuffed with beef in peppercorn sauce.

Day 6: Kirkby Stephen to Keld
6 hours, 13 miles (21km)

You saw them yesterday, atop the hill in the distance, and today you'll visit them: the enigmatic group of cairns known as the Nine Standards. This is a highlight of a great day's walking that takes you from the moorland of Lancashire into the picturesque landscape of the Yorkshire Dales via the Pennine watershed. Bring food, as you pass no cafés, and be sure to follow the assigned routes according to the time of year.

From Kirkby Stephen's marketplace head north, over picturesque **Frank's Bridge**, for a short but pleasant river-side stroll to the village of Hartley. From the main street take a path down to a footbridge, and then a lane that bears left uphill to Hartley Quarry. It's a stiff uphill push for a few miles as you enter the hills of the Yorkshire Dales. The lane ends at a fork; go left, through a gate and uphill over Hartley Fell.

The fragile moorland vegetation has been damaged by thousands of Coast to Coast boots here so, depending on the time of year, there are different routes to follow. From December to April, and in very bad weather, the Green Route avoids the summit, heading south instead, back downhill to join the B6270 for part of the way to Ney Gill. From May to November the Red and Blue Routes aim for **Nine Standards Rigg** (662m) – the highest you'll be for the rest of the walk – and its set of nine stone cairns.

The origin of the Nine Standards is a matter of imagination. Are they a stone army to ward off invaders or merely boundary markers? The choice is yours. One thing is certain: in good weather the views are magnificent – east to Swaledale, west to the Lake District, north to the Pennines and south to the long grassy ramp of Wild Boar Fell (reputedly the last place in the country where wild boar were hunted).

From the summit, head south briefly and, a short distance past the view indicator (dedicated to Lady Di's wedding), the Red and Blue Routes diverge. The Red Route, in operation from May to July, follows the original Wainwright way down to Ney Gill. The Blue Route, used from August to November, takes another path to the same place and is well marked by a series of regular posts.

All routes converge just before the farm of Ravenseat; from here the section along Whitsundale Beck is a delight. A final stretch of road takes you into the village of Keld – the halfway point.

KELD

There's not much to the tiny, unspoilt village of Keld, with few facilities for the traveller – except some public toilets. Sadly, there's no restaurant or pub to celebrate having walked this far; the pub was turned into a Methodist chapel years ago. So, apart from spiritual nourishment, you'll go hungry unless you book a meal at the hostel or your B&B. The Pennine Way also comes through here, so accommodation is at a premium.

Campers have two choices: **Park House** (☎ 01748-886549; parkhouse@btinternet.com; sites for 2 £8), near the bridge about 1 mile west of Keld, has friendly owners, showers, a cooking and drying area and a small shop selling provisions; while **Park Lodge Farm** (☎ 01748-886274; http://web.ukonline.co.uk/babrarukin; sites for 2 £7), in the village, always has plenty of room and hot showers. It also runs a café (9am to 6pm), where you can get drinks and light meals.

YHA's Keld Lodge was sold in 2006, and was due to reopen for bookings in April 2007 under new ownership; contact **Brigantes Walking Holidays & Baggage Couriers** (☎ 01729-830463; www.brigantesenglishwalks.com) for bookings.

There are only three B&Bs and all include the evening meal in their rates. The top pick is **Butt House** (☎ 01748-886374; butthouse@supanet .com; s/d £42/84), the comfy home of the legendary Mrs Whitehead – compiler of the *Coast to Coast Accommodation Guide* (see p238) – who is very welcoming and a fount

of knowledge on local history and society. She always offers choices for her evening meals, including vegetarian options.

East View Keld (☎ 01748-886776; www.keldholiday cottages.co.uk/holidaycottages/eastview.html; s/d with shared bathroom £37/74) is in a small house in the village, while **Greenlands** (☎ 01748-886576; greenlands@keld.uk.net; s/d £43/86), just over 800m south of Keld, on the road towards Thwaite, offers views over the valley.

In Thwaite, 3 miles away, the **Kearton Country Hotel** (☎ 01748-886277; www.keartoncountry hotel.co.uk; s/d £40/59, with breakfast £49/78) is a convivial place that also runs a teashop where you can get lunch.

Day 7: Keld to Reeth
5–6 hours, 11 miles (18km)

The main feature of today's walk is Swaledale – an enchanting, verdant valley winding a course through a backdrop of grey and austere moorlands. On the upper slopes you'll see industrial waste from the lead mines that flourished here 300 years ago. In mist and rain the surroundings will either fuel a romantic taste for mystery or simply turn your day into a tedious trot across bleak and barren nothingness. There is an alternative, shorter, route that follows the River Swale through the valley.

Leave Keld down a path to a footbridge over the Swale. This is a junction with the Pennine Way, where you might want to swap experiences with other long-distance walkers. From the footbridge the path takes you up to the top of Swinner Gill and then follows a wide dirt track to the steep-sided valley of Gunnerside Gill. Cross the gill and go up the other side, to pass through the ghostly **ruins of lead smelting mills**, where there are empty mine shafts, stark chimneys and mounds of debris. The ruins evoke the blood, sweat and tears of the men and women who toiled in the bowels of the earth for a meagre subsistence, and the names are evocative. You pass near Old Rake Hush and descend by Old Gang Beck to Surrender Bridge. Beyond here, the route winds through pleasantly green farmland into Reeth.

ALTERNATIVE ROUTE: ALONG THE RIVER SWALE
4–5 hours, 12 miles (19.3km)

If you're tired, or the weather is grim, this walk alongside the River Swale and through several pretty villages is a pleasurable alternative. Follow the Swale to Muker, where you could pause for refreshments at the convivial **Farmers Arms** (☎ 01748-886297; ☺ lunch & dinner) before continuing on to Gunnerside where the **Ghyllfoot Tearooms** (☎ 01748-886239; ☺ lunch) and another pub, the **King's Head** (☎ 01748-886261; ☺ lunch & dinner), also beckon invitingly! From here it's around a 4-mile stroll into Reeth. About halfway, you'll pass **Low Row Farm** (☎ 01748-884601; rwcclarkson@aol.com; sites for 2 £10, dm £6), which offers camping and a bunkhouse barn with kitchen.

REETH
The heart of Swaledale is the attractive, popular village of Reeth. Here you'll find a helpful **tourist office** (☎ 01748-884059), shops, cafés and some good pubs, all dotted around a large, sloping green. Friday is market day.

Orchard Park Caravan & Camping (☎ 01748-884475; sites for 2 £10) is in town but the owner is a bit gruff.

The closest hostel is **Grinton Lodge** (☎ 01748-884206; www.yha.org.uk; Grinton; dm £14), in a former hunting lodge, 1.5 miles south of Reeth.

The cheapest B&B is **Wayside** (☎ 01748-884176; www.tomclellworld.com; Fremington; s/d with shared bathroom £22/44), less than 1 mile east of Reeth; it's a small cosy place where the owners bake fresh bread for the hearty breakfast.

In Reeth itself, popular options include the walker-friendly **Walpardoe** (☎ 01748-884626; walpardoreeth@aol.com; Anvil Sq; s/d £35/38), a pretty cottage just off the square; and the often-recommended **Hackney House** (☎ 01748-

884302; hackneyhse@tinyworld.co.uk; s/d £25/48, 3-course dinner £15).

Cambridge House (☎ 01748-884633; www.cambridge-house-reeth.co.uk; Arkengarthdale Rd; s/d £30/60; 🖳) is one of the smarter B&Bs, while at the top end the choice is between the convivial **Arkleside Hotel** (☎ 01748-884200; www.arkleside hotel.co.uk; s/d from £62/92), which has lovely views across the valley from its garden; and the highly salubrious **Burgoyne Hotel** (☎ 01748-884292; www.theburgoyne.co.uk; The Green; s/d from £99/113, 4-course dinner £29), where you can also sample afternoon tea for £4.50.

As you come into the village, the **Reeth Bakery** (☎ 01748-884735; ☺ 10am-4pm Mon-Sat, 11am-5pm Sun) is worth pausing at for its freshly baked goods and selection of Swaledale goodies.

There's also the twee **Copper Kettle** (☎ 01748-884748; mains £7; ☺ lunch & dinner).

Best of all is **Overton House Café** (☎ 01748-884332; High Row; mains £10; ☺ lunch Wed-Mon, dinner Thu-Sat), which knocks up high-grade gourmet grub at very decent prices.

The **King's Arms** (☎ 01748-884259; www.thekings arms.com; High Row; s £30-50, d £60-100, mains around £10; ☺ lunch & dinner) has pleasant rooms, a roaring fire in the bar on cool evenings, fine ales and is recommended for its meals.

Next door, and also very good, is the **Black Bull** (☎ 01748-884213; www.theblackbullreeth .co.uk; High Row; s with/without bathroom £30/25, d with/without bathroom £60/50; ☺ lunch & dinner).

In Grinton the **Bridge Inn** (☎ 01748-884224; www.bridgeinngrinton.co.uk; s/d from £42/64, mains £10; ☺ lunch & dinner), a traditional pub with beams,

---

SWALEDALE MINERS

The Yorkshire Dales were formed during the ice age by glaciers cutting through the rocks and the mineralised faults, which revealed seams of lead beneath. Mining for lead probably began here as early as 1000 BC, but by the 17th and 18th centuries, lead mines dominated the scenery and the whole social fabric of the area. The miners either worked for themselves or were employed by companies in groups or 'gangs'.

The work was arduous, dangerous and very poorly paid. Child labour was common and diseases such as scarlet fever and typhoid were rife. When cheaper foreign ore was imported into Britain in the late 19th century, the mines of Swaledale began to close. Many miners, desperate for a livelihood, emigrated to Australia and America, while the Yorkshire mines and mills gave way to the farming communities found in the area today.

To gain a greater understanding of Swaledale's grim history, drop by the dusty little **Swaledale Museum** (☎ 01748-884118; www.swaledalemuseum.org; The Green; adult/child £3/free; ☺ 10.30am-5.30pm Wed-Sun Easter-Oct, Sun only Nov-Easter) in Reeth, or the delightful **Richmondshire Museum** (☎ 01748-825611; http://communigate.co.uk/ne/richmondshiremuseum; Ryders Wynd; adult/child £2/1; ☺ 10.30am-4.30pm Easter-Oct) in Richmond.

horsebrasses and a games room, has a wide range of beers and a decent restaurant.

Day 8: Reeth to Richmond
5 hours, 11 miles (18km)

This is a very pleasant day of sauntering through picturesque, sleepy villages, fields of cows, sheep and horses, and meadows and woodlands that – in spring and summer – explode with wildflowers. You'll have time at the end to rest up and explore historic Richmond, the largest town on the route.

From Reeth the route keeps north of the swirling River Swale, following lanes to **Marrick Priory**. The nearby woodlands were enjoyed by nuns in the 12th century. If the sun is shining and the birds singing, with carpets of bluebells and primulas covering the ground, heaven could certainly be within reach.

From Marrick village the route embarks on a waymarked journey, with fabulous views over rolling farmland. Three miles from Reeth, **Nun Cote Farm** (☎ 01748-884266; camp sites for 2 £7) serves teas, cakes and is famous for hot apple pie. It also has camping and will provide dinner and breakfast as well as a hot shower. Beyond the village of **Marske**, it's a stroll across to Applegarth Scar; here you'll pass **East Applegarth Farm** (☎ 01748-822940; rebekah.atkinson@virgin.net; sites for 2 £6, camping barn dm £6). Uphill from here you'll pass through shady Whitecliffe Wood, then go down a quiet lane with great views into Richmond.

RICHMOND
pop 8178

Tumbling down to the rushing River Swale, the cobbled streets and alleyways of Richmond, lined with elegant Georgian buildings and sturdy stone cottages, constitute one of England's most handsome market towns. For a panoramic view of the town and surrounding hills and dales, climb the ruined tower of **Richmond Castle** (☎ 01748-822493; admission £3.60; 10am-6pm Apr-Sep, to 4pm Oct-Mar), a massive Norman-era monument.

Just north of the central Trinity Church Sq (with market day on Saturday), you'll find the very helpful **tourist office** (☎ 01748-850252; richmond@ytbtic.co.uk; Friary Gardens, Victoria Rd), which sells guides and maps for the Coast to Coast, and can book accommodation and National Express tickets. You can access the

internet at the **public library** (☎ 01748-821935; closed Wed & Sun). The closest laundrette is near Catterick Garison; ask the tourist office for directions. For more local information see www.richmond.org.uk.

Castle Hill Books (☎ 01748-821111; 1 Castle Hill) specialises in books on the Coast to Coast, while camping and outdoor gear can be purchased from **Yeomans** (☎ 01748-821818; 6a Finkle St).

The nearest place for camping is **Village Farm** (☎ 01748-818326; Brompton-on-Swale; sites for 2 £10, camping barn dm £5), about 1 mile east of Richmond.

At the northern end of Richmond you'll find **Pottergate Guest House** (☎ 01748-823826; 4 Pottergate; s with shared bathroom £23, s/d £35/50), where the friendly owner will do your washing.

Two fine midrange B&B options are **Frenchgate Guesthouse** (☎ 01748-823421; 66 Frenchgate; s £30-55, d £70), with sweeping views across the Swale; and the **Old Brewery Guesthouse** (☎ 01748-822460; www.oldbreweryguesthouse .com; 29 The Green; s/d with shared bathroom £25/27; d £29-31), down the hill in a quiet location at the southern end of Richmond.

If you're after a treat, book into **Millgate House** (☎ 01748-823571; www.millgatehouse.com; Market Pl; d £85-95;). Behind an unassuming green door is an extraordinarily lovely guesthouse with the unexpected pleasure of a glorious garden, open to nonguests (10am-5pm). The charming owners are used to hosting walkers and several of the palatial rooms have fine river views across the Swale.

Eating options are plentiful. For fish and chips in reasonably classy surrounds try the restaurant atop **Barker's** (☎ 01748-825768; 18-19 Trinity Church Sq, Market Pl; meal £6; lunch & dinner).

Best for vegetarians is the bistro-like **New Frenchgate @ 29** (☎ 01748-824949; 29 Frenchgate; meals £7-12; lunch & dinner).

A Taste of Thailand (☎ 01748-829696; 15 King St; mains about £10; dinner) has an extensive menu of Thai favourites and a convenient BYO policy.

For all the gourmet works try the elegant **Frenchgate Restaurant & Hotel** (☎ 01748-822087; www.thefrenchgate.co.uk; 59-61 Frenchgate; s/d £58/98, 2-/3-course meal £24/28; lunch & dinner), where you can eat in a Georgian period dining room or, during summer, in the garden.

The pick of the pubs is the **Black Lion Hotel** (☎ 01748-823121; Finkle St; s/d £35/60, bar food £5, restaurant mains about £10; 🕒 lunch & dinner Tue-Sat), with cosy bars, low beams, good beer and food, plus B&B.

Day 9: Richmond to Ingleby Cross
8 hours, 23 miles (37km)

In comparison to the rest of the route, this monotonous walk across the flat and pastoral Vale of Mowbray is memorable mainly for encounters with cows, sheep and the free-range hens in the working farms along the way. It's easily doable in one go, but if you want to split the section in two, Danby Wiske offers several accommodation options. You can shorten the length, or skip it altogether by taking bus 55 to Northallerton and continuing on to Osmotherley.

Leave Richmond marketplace and cross Richmond Bridge for the south bank of the River Swale and a splendid view of the castle. Follow the course of the river, savouring sections of woodland and meadow, to just north of the small town of Catterick (home to a famous army base) and then cross back to the north side. From here you bid the Swale farewell and embark on a 2½-hour-long trot along country lanes.

Wainwright, denied a meal at the local pub, labelled the sleepy village of **Danby Wiske** 'a slough of despond'. You'll be happy to hear there have been improvements. The **White Swan Inn** (☎ 01609-770122; www.whiteswaninn.co.uk; s with/without bathroom £45/35, d with/without bathroom £65/56) now offers B&B, sandwiches for lunch (Saturday to Tuesday), and evening meal for around £10 if you book ahead. There are also several other pleasant places to stay, including the **Manor House** (☎ 01609-774662; m.sanders@firenet.uk.net; s/d £22/44); the **Old School** (☎ 01609-7742227; oldschooldanbywiske@yahoo.co.uk; s/d £25/50); and **Ashfield House** (☎ 01609-771628; jeannorris@btinternet.com; s/d £50/100; 🕒 lunch Mon-Sat), where the rates include breakfast, dinner and your laundry. Ashfield House also provides refreshments, making it a good place to aim for lunch.

Less than 1 mile east of Danby Wiske, at Oaktree Hill, those who prefer to feel earth instead of asphalt under their feet, can sigh with relief. The next few miles remain flat and fairly boring. As you approach the thundering A19 dual carriageway you'll pass **Longlands Farm** (☎ 01609-882925; longlandsfarm@oilman.net; s/d £20/40). The self-catering accommodation here is a comfy

mobile home with a nice view of the fields, but it's plagued by traffic noise.

If you need sustenance, there's a petrol station right next to where the route crosses the A19, with a small **shop** (☎ 01609-882720; 🕒 6am-10pm Mon-Fri, 7am-9pm Sat, 8am-9pm Sun) and a trucker's **café** (🕒 breakfast & lunch).

On the other side of the road, head through the small village of Ingleby Arncliffe to even smaller Ingleby Cross.

INGLEBY ARNCLIFFE & INGLEBY CROSS

In Ingleby Arncliffe B&Bs include the homely **Estavale** (☎ 01609-882302; jo.collinson@tiscali.co.uk; s/d £23/46) and the efficient and walker-friendly **Ingleside** (☎ 01609-882433; mauriceg@tinyworld.com; s/d £30/50).

A short walk downhill will bring you to Ingleby Cross where you'll find the **Blue Bell Inn** (☎ 01609-882272; www.the-blue-bell-inn.co.uk; camp sites for 2 £10, s £30, d £48-52, meals from £7; 🕒 lunch & dinner), a popular Coast to Coast watering hole, which does reasonable pub meals and offers a toilet and shower for its camping field.

If you have the energy, it's worth plodding a couple of miles off the route to the charming village of **Osmotherley** (p256), where there's a handful of very appealing places to stay and eat.

Day 10: Ingleby Cross to Blakey
8–9 hours, 21 miles (34km)

On this demanding, but very enjoyable rollercoaster stomp along easy paths you'll feel like one of the Grand Old Duke of York's 10,000 men. Up and down hill after hill you'll go, through leafy woodlands then across the spectacular North York Moors, the largest continuous area of heather moorland in England. In the middle of it all is a wonderful little café, the only chance you'll have to buy refreshments, so, if it's a hot day, make sure you pack plenty of water.

From Ingleby Cross head directly uphill through woodland to join the Cleveland Way (p252), which follows the edge of the North York Moors. Views to the north are dominated by the industrial chimneys of Middlesbrough, while to the south are the moors themselves, hiding secrets of a barren but engaging wilderness.

After a few miles the little valley of **Scugdale** provides a surprisingly lush interlude to the empty moors, with its delightful mixed woodlands, abundant wildflowers and twittering birds. Then it's upwards and onwards, crossing a lane that comes up from Carlton-in-Cleveland. At this point the well-landscaped **Lord Stones Café** (☎ 01642-778227; mains £2-6; ⏲ breakfast, lunch & dinner) is a welcome oasis if the weather's hot, and a refuge if it isn't.

It's up and down another hill before you reach another possibility of shade: the impressive collection of boulders known as the **Wainstones**. Dropping sharply downhill from here the path reaches **Clay Bank Top**, where the route crosses the B1257. If you've had enough walking for the day, this is a possible exit point from the route. There's a primitive camp site here; see p257 for details. There is accommodation in the hamlet of Urra, about 1 mile south, and at Great Broughton, 2.5 miles north. For details, see p257.

The next uphill push, you'll be delighted to hear, will be the last of the day. Once atop Urra Moor a broad track runs across appropriately named Round Hill. Just past here the path joins the route of the former Rosedale Ironstone Railway, which served mines in the area during the 19th century. At Bloworth Crossing you cross an ancient track called Westland Road and can still see old, wooden sleepers buried in the shale.

At this point, say goodbye to any fellow walkers who may be doing the Cleveland Way; they turn sharply north but you stay on the old railway for the next 5 miles, a fairly straightforward plod to the isolated hamlet of Blakey.

BLAKEY

The **Lion Inn** (☎ 01751-417320; www.lionblakey.co.uk; camp sites for 2 £5, s with/without bathroom £39/33, d with/without bathroom £62/50) has been the focal point of this lonely stretch of moors since the mid-16th century. It doesn't look much from the outside, but inside it's all low, wood-beamed ceilings, age-old stone walls and cosy nooks. Many walkers come to grief here, calling in for a quick drink or to shelter from the rain, then lingering in the warmth and comfort. Fortunately, the pub caters for such tardiness and offers B&B in small, pleasantly furnished rooms and a spacious camp site with showers in the pub.

Directly across the road, it's also possible to stay in the only other building up here, the very comfortable and stylish **High Blakey**

House (☎ 01751-417186; www.highblakeyhouse.co.uk; s with shared bathroom, d with/without bathroom £68/56); the friendly owner will make up packed lunches (£4) and several rooms have splendid views.

Day 11: Blakey to Grosmont
5–6 hours, 13 miles (21km)
This day's walk continues across heather-covered moor before joining an old horse track leading down to the Esk Valley. Your pace will quicken as you glimpse the North Sea, but slow down to enjoy the peerless views from what seems like the roof of England. Down in the verdant valley, the sparse beauty of the moor is replaced by lush woodland, culminating – if you time it right – with the arrival of a steam train at the historic station at Grosmont.

From Blakey walk north along the main road (left as you step out of the pub door). After about 1.5 miles a right turn brings you to an ancient stone called **White Cross** (also called 'Fat Betty' – you'll see why). Pause for a minute to enjoy panoramic views over a sea of endless moorland. You are now bound east, following lanes and tracks, skirting south of the head of Fryup Dale and then veering northeast to stride along the incredible, endless ridge of **Glaisdale Rigg**, with wonderful views into the valleys on either side, to finally reach the village of **Glaisdale**.

The village is quite spread out, from the shops and post office on the hill, down past the church to the pub and the train station in the valley.

There's a good choice of B&Bs at several of the farms in the Glaisdale valley, west of the village. (If you stay here, make sure you come down, south, off Glaisdale Rigg at the right place, without going into the village, otherwise it's a long tramp back along the road.) These include (from west to east) the small and quaint **Hollins Farm** (☎ 01947-897516; camp sites for 2 £6, s/d with shared bathroom £25/50); the excellent accommodation at **Red House Farm** (☎ 01947-897242; www.redhousefarm.com; s/d £30/60); and **Hart Hall Farm** (☎ 01947-897344; www.farmhousebandb.com; s/d with shared bathroom £22/44), another very friendly place.

At the top end of the village, B&Bs include **Sycamore Dell** (☎ 01947-897345; www.sycamoredell.co.uk; The Dale; s/d £25/50) and **Greenhowe** (☎ 01947-897907; Hall Lane; s/d £35/50). Further downhill is the appealing and friendly **Ashley House** (☎ 01947-897656; johncowan@ashleyhouse.fsnet.co.uk; s/d with shared bathroom £20/40).

Glaisdale's only pub and place to eat is the **Arncliffe Arms** (☎ 01947-897555; www.arncliffearms.co.uk; s/d £33/56; mains £5-10; ☾ lunch & dinner), which offers a good selection of dishes and B&B.

From the pub, head past the train station and, at the bottom of the hill, go under the railway bridge briefly to see the **Beggar's Bridge**, built in the 17th century and still standing proud – a beautiful witness to travelling days gone by. Retrace your steps back through the railway bridge, heading up into delightful Arncliffe Woods – half an hour of luscious indulgence and peaceful calm.

At the end of the woods a quiet lane carries you downhill, across the River Esk and into the pretty village of **Egton Bridge**. You'll first pass the pleasant, river-side **Horseshoe Hotel** (☎ 01947-895245; s/d with shared bathroom £50/60, mains £9-16; ☾ lunch & dinner) then, further on into the village, with a terrace overlooking the train station, the **Postgate** (☎ 01947-895241; s/d £49/69, mains £18; ☾ lunch & dinner). Either would be a pleasant place to rest and recuperate, with the Postgate having the edge in friendliness and range of dishes.

Opposite **St Hedda's Church**, follow an old toll road (note the toll charges written on a board hanging from the toll cottage midway along) for an easy one-hour stroll beside the River Esk into the village of Grosmont.

GROSMONT

Fans of the Harry Potter movies will recognise Grosmont's attractive, old-fashioned station. Even though Hollywood has come calling it hasn't ruined the robust charm of the village, most famous for its delightful **North Yorkshire Moors Railway** (☎ 01751-472508; www.northyorkshiremoorsrailway.com), complete with chuffing and puffing steam trains.

If you're camping, **Priory Farm** (☎ 01947-895324; sites for 2 £4) is on the route east of the village, with toilets and hot-water wash basins in the farmhouse.

For B&B a friendly choice is **Hazlewood House** (☎ 01947-895292; www.hazelwoodhouse.fsbusiness.co.uk; Front St; s/d £25/50, snacks £5), just downhill from the train station; it comes with a tearoom (10.30am-5.30pm), garden seating and good home baking.

The **Station Tavern** (☎ 01947-895060; www.tunnelinn.co.uk; s/d with shared bathroom £25/50) offers basic, good accommodation, friendly service and decent homemade bar food.

Grosmont House (☎ 01947-895539; www.grosmonthouse.co.uk; s with/without bathroom £35/28, d with/without bathroom £70/56; ☾ dinner) is tucked behind the train station. If you pay a little more you can stay in a room with a four-poster bed, and the dining room is open to nonresidents.

There's a Co-op supermarket in the village for self-catering.

For snacks and lunches, try the arty **Grosmont Gallery & Jazz Café** (☎ 01947-895007; www.grosmontgallery.com; Front St; ☾ 11am-5pm) and the old-fashioned **Signals Tearoom** (☾ 9.15am-4.30pm), on the platform at the station.

Day 12: Grosmont to Robin Hood's Bay
6–7 hours, 15.5 miles (25km)

Remember that lovely valley you climbed down into yesterday? Well, now it's time to climb back out! Take heart as, although this final day starts off with a stiff, uphill hike, that's soon replaced with more rugged moorland then sweet-smelling woodlands, ancient trees, rolling pastures and gurgling rivers, before you hit the coast. You'll rejoin the Cleveland Way for the ultimate cliff-top section, descending to join bands of holiday-makers in the picturesque fishing village of Robin Hood's Bay.

Out of Grosmont the route follows the road up to Sleights Moor, where you can avoid the tarmac briefly to cross to the busy A169. A short walk northeast along the road brings you to a grassy track, which joins a lane leading down to the peaceful village of **Littlebeck**.

From here the path follows the banks of May Beck into the beautiful **Little Beck Wood** – a last sylvan feast on the Coast to Coast. It harbours treasures such as the 18th-century **Hermitage**, hollowed out of a boulder, and **Falling Foss**, a waterfall that plunges 20m into a leafy ravine.

At May Bank car park (which has an ice-cream van in summer) you turn sharply up a sealed lane and leave the beauty of nature behind. A handful of miles further on you could pause for lunch at the **Hare & Hounds** (☎ 01947-880453) in Hawsker but you're so close to the coast at this point that the urge to continue is strong.

The route ends with a final hour of wonderful, cliff-top walking overlooking the sea, depositing you rather unceremoniously in the suburbs of Robin Hood's Bay. Keep going until you meet the main road and go left and downhill to descend the final stretch of steep cobbles to the water's edge at the slipway. Naturally, you'll want to dip your boot in the sea, or pick up another pebble, to mark the official end of your walk.

The **Bay Hotel** (☎ 01947-880278; meals £7) hosts Wainwrights Bar, where you can have a celebratory pint, sign the Coast to Coast log book and get yourself awarded with a certificate (£2.50). For further details about the town, see p239.

THE CLEVELAND WAY

Duration	9 days
Distance	109 miles (175.5km)
Difficulty	moderate
Start	Helmsley (opposite)
Finish	Filey (opposite)
Transport	bus, train

Summary This national trail roams the spectacular North York Moors, a national park full of grand views and picturesque ruins, before edging along the dramatic coastline.

The extreme beauty of the North York Moors – from high coastal cliffs to heather-covered moorlands, and a decadent share of crumbling ruins – is on full display along the Cleveland Way National Trail. A jagged horseshoe that mostly stays within the 550-sq-mile North York Moors National Park, the trail makes for a brilliant visual smorgasbord of this region.

The Cleveland Way is the second-oldest long-distance path in Britain. It skirts the western, northern and eastern edges of the North York Moors, with views galore and enough variation in terrain to keep your interest up. This is a landscape of wild and empty rolling hills cut by valleys that shelter woods, fields and small villages, plus abbey and castle ruins. The western and northern sides of the Moors are buttressed by steep hills and escarpments, while on the southern side, gradients are more gradual. On the eastern side is the North Sea coast, protected as heritage coast. The southern

part of the park, and the area just south of the Moors, is known as Ryedale.

This region is famous for its heather (see the boxed text, opposite) – the North York Moors constitute the largest continuous area of this hardy upland plant in England. A gift from the area's Bronze Age inhabitants, who cleared the forest and leached nutrients from the soil, the heather becomes a riot of purple from July to early September, and its vivid brownish-purple glow gives the park its characteristic appearance all year.

PLANNING

Traditionally the Cleveland Way is walked clockwise, so that the wind is predominantly behind you. Going the other way, foul weather on the North Sea can make the journey north up the coast rather more of a trial than it ought to be. Also, although generally good all along the route, the signposting is clearer for the clockwise walker.

Nine days is a comfortable amount of time for completing the walk; we've divided it as per the following table.

Day	From	To	Miles/km
1	Helmsley	Sutton Bank	10.5/17
2	Sutton Bank	Osmotherley	11.5/18.5
3	Osmotherley	Clay Bank Top	11/17.5
4	Clay Bank Top	Kildale	9/14.5
5	Kildale	Saltburn-by-the-Sea	15/24
6	Saltburn-by-the-Sea	Sandsend	17/27.5
7	Sandsend	Robin Hood's Bay	10/16
8	Robin Hood's Bay	Scarborough	14/22.5
9	Scarborough	Filey	11/17.5

Maps & Books

The official National Trail Guide, *The Cleveland Way* by Ian Sampson, is the best guide to the route, not least because it contains extracts from OS 1:25,000 maps. Except for the odd circumstance when you must leave the route in search of accommodation, this is a good stand-alone guide, although it doesn't have specific accommodation information. For that you need the indispensable *Cleveland Way National Trail Accommodation & Information Guide,* published annually and well worth the small price.

You can also buy a set of five OS Landranger 1:50,000 maps to cover the walk: Nos 93 *Middlesbrough,* 94 *Whitby & Esk*

HEATHER & GROUSE

The North York Moors have the largest expanse of heather moorland in England. Three types can be seen: ling is the most widespread, has a pinkish-purple flower and is most spectacular in late summer; bell heather is deep purple; and cross-leaved heather (or bog heather) prefers wet ground (unlike the first two) and tends to flower earlier. Wet and boggy areas also feature cotton grass, sphagnum moss and insect-eating sundew plants.

The moors have traditionally been managed to provide an ideal habitat for red grouse – a famous game bird. The shooting season lasts from the 'Glorious Twelfth' of August to 10 December. The heather is periodically burned, giving managed moorland a patchwork effect – the grouse nests in mature growth but feeds on the tender shoots of new growth.

Dale, 99 *Northallerton & Ripon*, 100 *Malton & Pickering* and 101 *Scarborough*.

The most manageable map you can get away with is Footprint's very handy strip map, *The Cleveland Way*, complete with trail notes and suggested stopover points.

Information Sources

Tourist offices in the area include Helmsley, Pickering, Scarborough and Whitby; for details see the route description. Accommodation and transport information is also available from the **Sutton Bank National Park Centre** (☎ 01845-597426; www.moors.uk.net).

Around the park are several information points, in shops or post offices, where you can get a more limited range of leaflets and information. You can also get information from the Cleveland Way's official website at www.nationaltrail.co.uk/clevelandway, and a new website devoted to North Sea Trail walks, www.northseatrail.co.uk.

Baggage Services

Baggage-carrying services are listed on p437.

NEAREST TOWNS
Helmsley
pop 1559

At the start of the route, Helmsley looks the way it sounds – pretty, prim and sophisticated. It thrives on tourism and has a number of worthwhile attractions, including the marketplace (Friday is market day) and the monument to local nobleman William, second Earl of Feversham, which stands at the start of the Cleveland Way. There's also **Helmsley Castle** (☎ 01439-770442; adult/child £4/2), run by English Heritage; **Duncombe Park** (☎ 01439-771115; adult/child £7/3), a large estate just west of the centre; and

Helmsley Walled Garden (adult/child £4/free). Try to visit either the castle or estate before striking out on your walk; they're passed by the trail, but you won't have time to do them both justice in a morning.

Helmsley **tourist office** (☎ 01439-770173) is on the west side of the marketplace.

SLEEPING & EATING

Accommodation and good food are plentiful. Recommended places to stay include the **Feathers Hotel** (☎ 01439-770275; 5-6 Market Pl; r from £60). There's also a **YHA hostel** (☎ 01439-770433; www.yha.org.uk; Carlton Lane; dm £12.50).

Gepetto's (☎ 01439-770479; 8 Bridge St; mains £6-12) serves fine Italian food. There are a couple of central supermarkets, and Hunter's, on the marketplace, is perfect for any picnic preparations.

GETTING THERE & AWAY

TransPennine (☎ 0845 678 6974; www.tpexpress.co.uk) trains go several times daily from London to York (two hours), from where you can catch a bus to Helmsley (25 minutes, frequent). There are links between Helmsley and other towns along the trail via **Cleveland Way Explorer bus services** (☎ 01845-597000; www.moors.uk.net/moorsbus), part of the summer Moorsbus network; tickets cost between £3 and £6.

By car from the A1, take the A61 northeast to Thirsk, continuing east on the A170 to Helmsley.

Filey

Filey began life as a fishing village and has a restful, beachside-holiday feel – just the thing after a good long walk. There's a compact town centre, a pretty church and a 5-mile-long beach. The **tourist office** (☎ 01723-518000; John St) has the scoop.

SLEEPING & EATING

Near the beach, **Downcliffe House** (☎ 01723-513310; r from £48) is expensive but worth it if you want to spoil yourself. Or try **Abbots Leigh Guest House** (☎ 01723-513334; 7 Rutland St; r from £24). The **Star** (Mitford St), on the way up to the train station, is a welcome pub at the end of the walk.

GETTING THERE & AWAY

Northern Rail (www.northernrail.org) trains go regularly from Filey to Hull (1¼ hours) and Scarborough (20 minutes, four daily), where you can change for York and further connecting services. By car, take the A165 southeast out of Scarborough and then the A1039.

THE WALK
Day 1: Helmsley to Sutton Bank
4–6 hours, 10.5 miles (17km)

The first day's walk is short on distance but long on history, with a gentle stroll through crops and plantations broken up by sites of archaeological interest.

Setting off from the monument in Helmsley, head northwest on the road towards Stokesley, leaving the church to your right. A few yards after the church you encounter the first Cleveland Way signpost, directing you to Rievaulx, 3 miles away. Follow the stony track as it rises out of Helmsley, through fields and woodland, and past Griff Lodge, where you get your first view of the Rye Valley, covered in a mantle of conifers. Just prior to entering the next patch of woodland at Quarry Bank, there's a short detour to the right, leading up to the remains of the medieval village of **Griff**, a field now consigned to grazing sheep, and crisscrossed by ancient earthworks. Once back on the trail, descend through Quarry Bank Wood past overgrown limestone scars to reach a minor road. Turn left and follow the road to the junction at pretty Rievaulx Bridge. A right turn here takes you up the road to **Rievaulx Abbey** and village (see the boxed text, right).

Return to the junction at Rievaulx Bridge to rejoin the trail. Cross the bridge and continue along the minor road past Ashberry Farm for 800m, where you turn right onto a track that follows a series of ponds towards the head of Nettle Dale. Watch out for adders basking on the banks

of the path. Follow signposts with care as you cross a stream on stepping stones and pass through a thicket to join a gravel track paralleling the stream up Nettle Dale. After negotiating this segment the track soon leaves Nettle Dale by way of a valley to the left, shortly turning right up a narrowing gully to emerge on the open plateau of the Hambleton Hills. A straight track leads into Cold Kirby.

Climb through the village, turning left after the last building on the left and following the track as it zigzags across fields to the edge of a plantation. At the plantation, turn right and take the track past the stables at Hambleton House, turning left at the driveway, which takes you through the woods to the A170 and the **Hambleton Inn** (☎ 01845-597202; mains £7-14), which has excellent meals; arrive early enough and you may nab one of the five free camp sites. Two doors up from the pub, **Cote Faw** (☎ 01845-597363; r from £19) offers B&B. While Sutton Bank is the official end of today's stage, accommodation is only available here or roughly 2.5 miles south at Kilburn.

If you decide to stop here but still have time to make an excursion to the White Horse of Kilburn chalk figure, drop the bags and enjoy an unfettered stroll via Sutton Bank.

From Hambleton Inn take the A170 west towards Sutton Bank, branching diagonally left at the road to the White Horse and following a straight path through trees to **Sutton Bank**, an expansive precipice from where you can catch a stunning sunset over the

---

RIEVAULX ABBEY

Rievaulx Abbey (☎ 01439-798228; adult/child £5/3; ⏰ 10am-6pm Apr-Sep, to 5pm Thu-Mon Oct, to 4pm Thu-Mon Nov-Mar) is in a beautiful setting that is at once pastoral and powerful. Henry VIII's dissolution of the monasteries in the 1530s doomed this site, the 'mother ship' of the Cistercian order; it is today the largest monastic ruin in Britain. From the entrance, follow the road up through Rievaulx village to the National Trust's elegant **Terrace and Temples** (☎ 01439-798228; adult/child £4/3; ⏰ 10.30am-6pm Mar-Sep, to 5pm Oct-Nov) property, which affords views of the abbey from above.

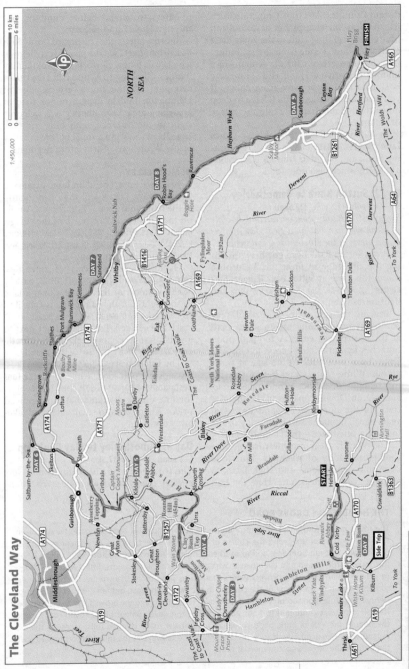

distant Pennines. At a trail T-junction, turn left to follow the escarpment past Roulston Scar and the gliding club to the **White Horse of Kilburn**, about 1 mile from the trail junction. Keep an eye out for the remains of a hillfort on outlying Hood Hill. The horse is singularly unimpressive from above. If you want a proper look you'll have to drop down the hill another mile into the village of Kilburn.

In Kilburn, B&B is available at **Church Farm** (☎ 01347-868318; s/d from £22/44), a working farm; and **Forresters Arms** (☎ 01347-868386; d from £62), which also does food.

Day 2: Sutton Bank to Osmotherley
5½–7½ hours, 11.5 miles (18.5km)

Today's stretch may seem barren and desolate in bleak weather, but on a clear day it offers grand views of the surrounding landscape.

From Sutton Bank head north, maintaining the cliff edge to meet the A170 once more, this time at **Sutton Bank National Park Centre** (☎ 01845-597426). A café serves tea and light refreshments.

Leaving the centre, the Cleveland Way continues north along an enclosed path at the escarpment edge. A footpath soon branches left, providing access to Gormire Lake. Turn your back to the lake at vertiginous White Mare Crag; before you lay the remains of a once-proud racecourse, Hambleton Down, considered the premier track in the north of England until 200 years ago. The name survives today in the form of a titled race – the Hambletonian.

The Way is clear northwards, past the geological oddity of **Windypits** (limestone caves and depressions) and High Barn, to a minor road at Sneck Yate. Here the trail re-enters woodland before climbing out through High Paradise Farm.

Shortly after the farmyard you join **Hambleton Street** (see the boxed text, below), which you follow north for approximately 5 miles, climbing to White Gill Head then dropping off the northwestern edge of Hambleton End to meet a minor road at a parking area. Osmotherley is a welcome sight in the distance, with only the Oak Dale Reservoirs and a small but steep valley below Whitehouse Farm left to negotiate.

OSMOTHERLEY

If you have time, spend an hour exploring Osmotherley. Locals will urge you to stop at the fabled old shop, Thompson's. A mile off the Cleveland Way, north of the village, **Mount Grace Priory** (☎ 01609-778132; adult/child £3/2; ☽ 10am-6pm Apr-Sep, to 5pm Oct, to 1pm Nov-Mar) is worth an excursion.

Osmotherley has plenty of amenities. **Cote Hill Caravan Park** (☎ 01609-883425; site for 2 from £5) is north of the village, down a lane to the right. On the same lane is **Cote Ghyll YHA Hostel** (☎ 01609-883575; www.yha.org.uk; dm from £11; ☽ Mar-Nov). For a B&B right next to a walking supply shop, seek out the **Osmotherley Walking Shop** (☎ 01609-883818; r from £25).

The **Golden Lion** (☎ 01609-883526; mains £8-14) has upscale pub food, while the **Three Tuns Restaurant** (☎ 01609-883301; mains £10-16) aims for fine dining at somewhat more refined prices. There are also small cafés and takeaway options.

Day 3: Osmotherley to Clay Bank Top
6–8 hours, 11 miles (17.5km)

This is a short but strenuous day's walk, more difficult than yesterday but more rewarding,

---

THE HAMBLETON DROVE ROAD

The route north from Sneck Yate (pronounced 'yat', an old local term for gate) takes you up onto the high moor, following the course of Hambleton Street, part of an ancient network of drove roads that ran from Scotland to southern England. All sorts of livestock were driven along this track: cattle, sheep and even geese, which were, by some accounts, fitted with felt 'shoes' to protect their feet! Early drovers were regarded as little more than rogues and vagabonds, something akin to the image of the cowboy in the American West, but later, under the reign of Henry I, the profession succumbed to government regulations and the drovers had to be licensed. Hambleton Street continued to flourish, even after the development of improved roads along the floor of the Vale of York, because, while these newer roads charged tolls, access to the old upland ways remained free. It took the coming of the railways in the mid-19th century to spell the end for the Street as a commercial route.

with views opening out to the north and east. There are a lot of steep climbs and descents, and the land can be quite exposed.

From Osmotherley set off north for a few hundred metres, turning left at Rueberry Lane. Follow the track as it meanders round the brow of a hill, passing Chapel Wood Farm and the detour to Mount Grace Priory. Requiring less effort to get to than the priory, **Lady's Chapel**, off to the right of the trail, is worth a peek.

The Cleveland Way joins the Coast to Coast Walk (p237) in this section then traverses Beacon Hill (with its fearsome array of radio masts) and Scarth Wood Moor, crossing a minor road into Clain Wood before dropping down to a road leading into Swainby. This village, 1 mile north of the trail, is a good place for lunch. The **Blacksmiths Arms** (☎ 01642-700303; Black Horse Lane; mains £5-8), with a large, adventurous menu, is a good bet. The **Black Horse** (☎ 01642-700436; 23 High St) also does lunches daily, and there's a village **shop** nearby.

Resuming on the trail, head southeast for about 800m before dropping out of the woods through fields to Scugdale Beck, crossed on a small road bridge. Climb the road past Hollin Hill Farm, over a road junction and by a phone box to start the ascent onto Round Hill. This is the first of four tough ridges for the day. The glider strip and facilities on **Carlton Moor** are still used, but only when winds are favourable. A steep drop off the eastern end of the moor lands you in the lush, wide saddle in front of Cringle Moor, where the trail crosses a lane coming up from the village of Carlton-in-Cleveland. The **Lord Stones Cafe** (☎ 01642-778227; mains £2-6; ☺ breakfast, lunch & dinner), a few yards southeast of the lane crossing (and easy to miss), makes a good tea break – it offers free camping to those using the café.

Cringle Moor, Broughton Bank (more commonly known as Cold Moor) and Hasty Bank lie ahead and, with them, further scars on the landscape, including a disused alum mine and jet workings. Jet, a carbonaceous substance, was tremendously popular during Victoria's reign (she wore it in mourning for her dead husband, Albert) but its role as a fashion accessory did not endure. Alum had a more solidly prosperous life as an important ingredient in the

dying of textiles and leathers. Alum mines also went the way of the dodo due to a technological innovation allowing for the derivation of alum from coal mines' waste materials. The focus of the day's final big ascent, up Hasty Bank, are the **Wain Stones**, giant blocks of a coarse, hard sandstone called gritstone, scattered about the hillside. A welcome final (but sharp) descent brings you to Clay Bank Top, where the trail crosses the B1257. There's a primitive **camp site** (sites for 2 £2; ☺ May-Oct) set in a meadow. The caretaker comes around in the evening to collect the fee. There are other accommodation options at Urra and Great Broughton.

URRA & GREAT BROUGHTON

To reach Urra, head south up the road from Clay Bank Top and turn left as signposted, or avoid the road by taking the footpath that leaves the trail a little beyond Clay Bank Top. In this tiny hamlet is **Maltkiln House** (☎ 01642-778216; s £18-25, d £37-45, dinner £10), definitely the most sensible option for accommodation and food, though you need to book ahead as it's a popular choice. It offers unpretentious luxury and a welcome evening meal in the convivial dining room.

Other options are in Great Broughton, 2.5 miles north of Clay Bank Top on the B1257 (although it's better to take footpaths from just west of the Wain Stones, before you reach Clay Bank Top). B&Bs include **Holme Farm** (☎ 01642-712345; 12 The Holme; r from £20), where, as with most other walker-friendly B&Bs in this town, the owner will drop you back at Clay Bank Top the next day. The **Jet Miners Inn** (☎ 01642-712427; camp sites for 2 £6), on the main street, does decent evening meals and welcomes campers and caravans.

Day 4: Clay Bank Top to Kildale
4–6 hours, 9 miles (14.5km)
A short day, and a welcome one given the earlier taxing terrain. Heather, grouse, ancient milestones and a disused incline railway are the discernible features overlying otherwise undistinguished country.

Beginning at Clay Bank Top, there's a steep approach up Carr Ridge to the gently rising summit of **Round Hill**, the highest point on the walk (454m). From the trig point an easy walk across featureless moorland merges with a disused railway and then doubles back dramatically at Bloworth Crossing, where traces of railway workers' dwellings exist. At this point the Coast to Coast Walk (p237) parts company and heads east.

Proceeding north you pass stones near Burton Howe that indicate this track was once a main route between Helmsley and Stokesley. The gentle descent continues after Tidy Brown Hill, to the point where you meet the Baysdale Abbey–Kildale road. Just over 1 mile along this minor road and you are down into the valley of Battersby, near the village of Kildale.

BATTERSBY & KILDALE

Places to stay in the Battersby valley include **Low Farm** (☎ 01642-722145; r from £20), the residence of Mr and Mrs Cook, who, in addition to running a B&B in their farmhouse, also tend **Kildale Camping Barn** (☎ 01642-722135; sites per person £5) at nearby Park Farm. Both places are less than 1 mile southwest of Kildale.

Another welcoming B&B choice is **Bankside Cottage** (☎ 01642-723259; d from £46). The cottage stands on the far side of Kildale from your approach, overlooking the village from the side of Coate Moor.

The 17th-century **Dudley Arms** (Ingleby Greenhow; mains £6-10), 2 miles beyond Park Farm, is worth the extra walk; it serves meals with massive portions. **Glebe Cottage** (☎ 01642-724470; Kildale; ☽ lunch) does evening meals by prior arrangement only.

Day 5: Kildale to Saltburn-by-the-Sea
7–10 hours, 15 miles (24km)

Today the trail gradually leaves its namesake hills behind and, after the landmark peak of Roseberry Topping, makes a beeline for the sea.

From Kildale, cross the nascent River Leven east of the road that leads to St Cuthbert's Church and the train station, then climb Coate Moor on a lane. At the top, cut left through the plantation to reach Captain Cook's Monument on Easby Moor summit, complete with rousing epitaph on the side of the 51ft-high **obelisk**. The hill here is sometimes used by paragliders as a launching point and its appeal is obvious; the slope drops sharply away to the southwest, with 5 miles of valley floor before Carlton Moor rises up to match Easby's elevation.

From Easby you nip down the hill into Gribdale, across a road and up the other side onto Great Ayton Moor. Next is the official 1-mile detour to the last challenging knoll of Roseberry Topping, a popular peak known as the 'Matterhorn of North Yorkshire' (unlike the original it has stone stairs built into its side). The ascent is tiring, but the views are rewarding.

From here it's worth dropping down to the **King's Head** (☎ 01642-722318; Newton Under Roseberry; s/d from £65/75, mains from £9), recently named B&B of the Year, for a meal and a look around.

The trail drops east off the Topping, then goes back up onto heather moorland, past a farm and into Guisborough Forest (pronounced 'giz-boruh'). Follow logging tracks for a few miles, past the junction with the Tees Link path. This section can be quite muddy and, despite signs prohibiting them, horses and mountain bikers add further to the mire.

The scenic low point of the day comes on the descent to Slapewath and the busy A171 Middlesbrough–Whitby road. Before the crossing, take care as the wooded hillside here is used by off-road motorcycles (you'll hear them coming). Once across the A171 turn left, following the right-hand side of the road 200m to the **Fox & Hounds** (☎ 01287-632964; s/d from £36/47, mains £6-12; ☽ lunch & dinner), off to the right. This pub, despite its godforsaken location, does hearty lunches and has comfortable rooms.

When leaving the pub be careful not to confuse the signs for Cleveland Street with those of the Cleveland Way. The Street is a different path. Instead, head northwest from the pub up a short rise leading to the end of a residential street. Turn right beyond the last driveway. A sharp climb round a quarry rim puts you back up onto higher ground and leads you mercifully away from the sound of traffic. The walk is easy from here as you cross fields to a farm and down Airy Hill Lane to Skelton Green, continuing in a straight line through encroaching suburbia and Skelton proper.

Cross the main road in Skelton and head downhill, turning right at Ullswater Dr then left at a T-junction. Go down to the end of the road and into a small subdivision on the right, which leads to fields and a path once more.

The approach to Saltburn-by-the-Sea diverts slightly from the course on the OS map to accommodate the recent Skelton–Brotton bypass, but it's a well-marked section. After an underpass, a descent through woods deposits you at Skelton Beck, at the foot of an impressive railway viaduct, which still carries freight. The sign warning of danger from falling bricks doesn't instil confidence, although the bridge certainly looks a sturdy construction. A footbridge leads you back up the other side of the valley; follow its steeply wooded banks into Saltburn-by-the-Sea (commonly called Saltburn).

SALTBURN-BY-THE-SEA

At Saltburn the trail meets the sea and sticks with it for the rest of the walk. There's a restored Victorian pier here that's worth seeing, especially because you can access it on the cliff lift, the world's oldest water-powered, funicular-style hill-side lift.

Campers should head for **Hazelgrove Caravan Park** (☎ 01287-622014; Milton St; sites for 2 £8; ❤ Mar–Oct). If you're travelling in pairs, try the **Spa Hotel** (☎ 01287-622544; Saltburn Bank; s/d/tr £40/50/62, mains £6-14), with good-value double rooms and views over the pier. The hotel has a restaurant and 24-hour bar and serves a buffet breakfast.

Alessi's (☎ 01287-625033; 10 Dundas St; mains £6-14) is straight out of Sicily, and a real find. The Ship, on the waterfront, is a great stop for a pint. There are also plenty of takeaway stores, as well as other useful services, including walking-supply shops.

Day 6: Saltburn-by-the-Sea to Sandsend

7½–10 hours, 17 miles (27.5km)
The trail from Saltburn hugs the coastline pretty closely all the way to Filey. You are now on some of the most unstable coastline in Britain. Watch your step in wet and windy conditions and stay well away from the cliff edge as landslips can occur without warning.

From Saltburn, route-finding is straightforward, but there are a few points where waymarks disagree with the OS map. Usually this is due to coastal erosion, which makes it necessary to divert sections of the trail on an annual basis; any major diversions are noted on the official trail website (www.nationaltrail.org.uk/clevelandway),

and it's not a bad idea to ask about alterations at tourist offices along the way.

Crossing the beach at Saltburn to reach the cliffs to the east you'll spot cobles (pronounced 'cobbles'), a local variety of fishing boat, and their attending tractors, which drag them up the sands from the sea. From here to Skinningrove the trail follows the marvellously engineered Saltburn–Whitby railway line, now only used as far as Boulby by goods trains.

Three miles along the cliff top from Saltburn, past the first of a series of Roman signal-station sites, used to warn of attacking fleets, and down a cliff scarred by industry, you arrive in Skinningrove. This is a curious village that, with the discovery of iron seams in the 1850s, grew from a quiet fishing cove to a crowded mining community. Today, Skinningrove's economic future lies very much in the hands of the steel mill overlooking the bay. The **Tom Leonard Museum** (☎ 01287-642877; ❤ 1-5pm Apr-Oct) up the hill shows what life was like for the miners.

A considerable climb sets you atop the high cliffs at Rockcliffe (more commonly known as Boulby Cliff), the highest point on the east coast at 213m. From here things get easier. If the chimneys at the potash mine to the right look tall, consider that the shafts over which the complex is built are a dozen times as deep, the deepest mines in Britain. They extend laterally as well, reaching 3 miles or more out to sea, with working temperatures exceeding 40°C.

Cut across Cowbar Nab and drop down into justifiably touristy **Staithes**, where you can grab a bite to eat at the **Cod & Lobster** (☎ 01947-840295; mains £5-12) on the seafront. Nearby, and also on the water, **Sea Drift** serves light meals all day.

Back up on the cliffs, continue by Port Mulgrave and unspoilt **Runswick Bay** (with its **Royal Hotel**), along the beach to a hidden inlet leading to winding steps that regain the cliff-top path to Kettleness. Only a few farms and houses remain here; in 1829 a landslip claimed the village. Pass the next Roman signal station at Goldsborough and cross fields. After a steep and muddy descent through trees you emerge just in front of the looming mouth of an abandoned rail tunnel. From here it's level walking along the disused railway line into Sandsend.

SANDSEND

This village has plenty of places to stay. **Sandfield House Farm** (☎ 01947-602660; Sandsend Rd; camp sites for 2 from £7; Apr-Oct) has a modern central building, hot showers, hairdryers and a laundry room, and many of its camp sites have a sea view.

Haven under the Hill (☎ 01947-893202; r from £25) is on the hill leading out of town. If you're lucky, a pot of freshly made tea will be brought to your room in the morning.

For a meal in the evening, try the **Hart Inn** (☎ 01947-893304; mains £6-12).

Day 7: Sandsend to Robin Hood's Bay

5–6½ hours, 10 miles (16km)

The shorter distance today should allow you to spend a bit of time in bustling, historic Whitby. But don't linger too long; late in the day, the coastline is undulating and tiring.

Start out on the uninspiring Whitby Rd, turning left at the golf course to meet the sea bluffs and the western suburbs of Whitby. Continue down to the harbour, past amusement arcades and the fish market, crossing the swing bridge to the old town, where countless nooks and crannies lead to tiny shops and pubs. The **Duke of York**, at the foot of the 199 steps to the abbey, is well placed for food. Up the steps, the foreboding dark stone of **Whitby Abbey** (☎ 01947-603568; adult/child £4/2; 10am-5pm Mar-Oct, to 4pm Thu-Mon Nov-Mar) surveys the town and coast. Its decline in the 16th century closely mirrors Rievaulx's later history (see the boxed text, p254). Next door is the **YHA hostel** (☎ 01947-602878; www.yha.org.uk; dm £12).

From the abbey entrance, turn away from Whitby to follow a minor road, turning left soon after at a Cleveland Way signpost. Head out of Whitby and watch for the exclamation mark of rock that is Saltwick Nab. Again, the integrity of the cliffs along this stretch is questionable; take care. A few miles' walk funnels you into the upper part of Robin Hood's Bay (p239).

Day 8: Robin Hood's Bay to Scarborough

7–9 hours, 14 miles (22.5km)

The character of the coastline changes today, most noticeably at Hayburne Wyke, a nature reserve and renowned beauty spot, where hardwood deciduous trees still flourish. This is a rare glimpse back to a time before settlement and industry hit North Yorkshire.

On leaving Robin Hood's Bay you have two options. At low tide you can walk the length of the wide beach to Boggle Hole, or you can follow the waymarked trail along the cliffs above the bay. **Boggle Hole YHA Hostel** (☎ 01947-880352; www.yha.org.uk; dm £14; Feb-Oct) is in an old mill facing a bay that once served as a smugglers' hideout; evening meals are available. At the far end of the wide, sweeping bay, climb through mixed woodland and scrub to Ravenscar. The National Trust has a small **visitor centre** (☎ 01723-870423; Mar-Aug) here. Go on to the road and turn left for **Raven Hall Country House Hotel** (bar snacks £6-12, carvery £17) where, if you're not feeling too scruffy, you can get some refreshment at the bar. **Foxcliffe Tearooms** (☎ 01723-871028; Station Rd) is a popular halt for teas or light lunches.

A pleasant 3.5-mile ramble straight along the cliff edge gets you to the 'pocket beach' at Hayburne Wyke, strewn with rounded stones. If you don't fancy a picnic lunch by the water, head up the wooded valley to **Hayburne Wyke Inn** (☎ 01723-870202; lunch from £5) for lunch in peaceful surroundings.

Beyond Hayburne Wyke the countryside opens out and affords a sweeping prospect over the last stage of the walk. On a clear day Flamborough Head, just north of Bridlington, is visible and, as you approach Scarborough, its castle shines like a beacon in the setting sun. If you're camping, down your pack at **Scalby Manor** (☎ 01723-366212; Field Lane; sites for 2 £9-12), just off to the right of the trail before you hit Scalby Mills.

SCARBOROUGH

pop 57,649

This bustling seaside resort offers a wide choice of accommodation. The **tourist office** (☎ 01723-373333; cnr Westborough & Northway) can help with your choice.

If you're on a tight budget, try the **Kerry Lee Hotel** (☎ 01273-363845; 60 Trafalgar Sq; r from £18). **Cliffside Hotel** (☎ 01723-361087; 79-81 Queen's Pde; r from £23, dinner £7.50) offers good views. Or splash out at the mint-green **Clifton Hotel** (☎ 0173-375691; Queen's Pde; s/d from £50/100).

The town centre offers a variety of restaurants and fast-food joints.

Day 9: Scarborough to Filey

5½–6½ hours, 11 miles (17.5km)

The final day is an easy cliff-top walk, a fittingly enjoyable end to the trail.

The first hour or so is spent getting clear of Scarborough. The route round the headland and along the beach to the Spa (a complex dating from the Victorian era, nestled beneath a steep, Italianate garden) is a bracing start that introduces you to the typical elements of a British resort town. You leave grand northerly hotels behind and pass the beach-front amusement arcades and the harbour, and finally climb past even grander hotels overlooking South Bay.

Beyond the Spa you come to the spot where, in 1993, the Holbeck House Hotel and the land on which it stood gave way and crumbled into the sea. Not many clues to its existence remain, but the disaster is a reminder of the coast's flighty geology.

The Way runs through fields and subdivisions to a view over the surfer's hangout of Cayton Sands. There's a **café** midway down the beach, which you can reach either by the beach or from the road above. Caravan parks give way to wheat fields on the breezy track to **Filey Brigg**. The seas around the Brigg are a favourite haunt of seals, who know when the salmon nets are out. If the tide is favourable you can make it out to the tip of the Brigg by descending steps on its south side. The area is a nature reserve and it's common to find sea creatures trapped in the many rock pools around the point.

Then it's back on the track, where one final mile brings you into Filey (p253). The official completion book, kept at the Filey Country Park Stores, provides an excellent opportunity for giving feedback on the route just completed.

THE PENNINE WAY

Duration	16 days
Distance	255 miles (411km)
Difficulty	moderate–demanding
Start	Edale (p263)
Finish	Kirk Yetholm (p263)
Transport	train, bus

Summary This classic national trail, along the central mountain spine of Britain, is long and challenging, but very rewarding. Thanks to increased paving along the route it's a less fearsome undertaking than it once was.

The grand-daddy of Britain's national trails follows a north–south line of mountains and upland areas in the centre of northern England – some of the highest, wildest and bleakest countryside south of Scotland. Battling against the elements, many walkers find it an endurance test, but not one without rewards. Starting in the Peak District, the trail takes in the South Pennine moors, the best of the Yorkshire Dales (including one of the famous Three Peaks and beautiful Swaledale), the highest pub in England, the stunning High Cup Nick valley, tranquil Teesdale, Hadrian's Wall and the windswept Cheviot Hills. It is, undoubtedly, a classic walk.

In recent years the most notorious stretches of the Pennine Way through moorland bogs have been tamed with lines of rough flagstones. You might not need commando skills to walk it now, but the route still shouldn't be underestimated – swift weather changes can bamboozle even the most experienced walker. You don't get the camaraderie of the Coast to Coast Walk, but you get a real sense of isolation and escape. Whether you choose to do it in one go, or tackle it section by section, the rewards of following the Pennine Way are great, and the walk is now more enjoyable than it's ever been.

HISTORY

The Pennine Way is held in great regard by many British walkers – even those who have never walked it. First proposed by the walkers' campaigner Tom Stephenson in 1935, and inspired by the national trails established in the USA, the idea played a key part in the public-access struggles of the 1930s, which finally led to hikers and ramblers being allowed to cross private land. It was not until 1949, however, that parliament approved the concept and it took until 1965 for the Pennine Way to be officially opened – the first of Britain's LDPs and, later, national trails.

PLANNING

The route is traditionally walked from south to north, with the prevailing winds at your back, but there's nothing stopping you doing it in reverse. It's waymarked with arrows and national-trail acorn symbols, but not uniformly. Some stretches have indicators every few steps, while others will leave you standing bewildered at unclear junctions. You definitely need a map and compass.

You can sprint the route in less than two weeks or stroll it in three; we suggest taking 16 days. The way's official length is 268 miles, which includes various diversions and forays off the route to reach places to stay – reckon on walking at least this distance rather than the 255 miles that's the total of our daily breakdown.

Day	From	To	Miles/km
1	Edale	Crowden	16/26
2	Crowden	Standedge	11/18
3	Standedge	Hebden Bridge	15/24
4	Hebden Bridge	Ponden	11/18
5	Ponden	Malham	22/36
6	Malham	Horton in Ribblesdale	14.5/23.5
7	Horton in Ribblesdale	Hawes	14/22.5
8	Hawes	Tan Hill	16/26
9	Tan Hill	Middleton-in-Teesdale	17/28
10	Middleton-in-Teesdale	Dufton	20/32.5
11	Dufton	Alston	19.5/32
12	Alston	Greenhead	16.5/27
13	Greenhead	Once Brewed	6.5/11
14	Once Brewed	Bellingham	15/24.5
15	Bellingham	Byrness	15/24.5
16	Byrness	Kirk Yetholm	26/42

Alternatives

Mile-eaters could combine Day 2 and 3, or Day 13 and 14. If you want to add in days, options for alternative stops along the way are mentioned in the route description.

If you choose to tackle the route in more manageable chunks, three separate weeks could take you from Edale to Horton in Ribblesdale, then on to Greenhead and finally to Kirk Yetholm. Or you could cover the whole route in a series of day walks following the advice in Kevin Donkin's *Circular Walks along the Pennine Way*.

Maps

Harvey Maps covers the route in three 1:40,000 strip maps: *Pennine Way South* (from Edale to Horton in Ribblesdale), *Pennine Way Central* (Horton in Ribblesdale to Greenhead), and *Pennine Way North* (Greenhead to Kirk Yetholm).

If you want to be fully equipped with OS maps, you will need OS Landranger 1:50,000 maps No 110 *Sheffield & Huddersfield*, 109 *Manchester*, 103 *Blackburn & Burnley*, 98 *Wensleydale & Upper Wharfedale*, 91 *Appleby-in-Westmorland*, 86 *Haltwhistle & Brampton*, 80 *Cheviot Hills & Kielder Water*, 74 *Kelso & Coldstream* and 92 *Barnard Castle & Richmond*.

The OS Explorer 1:25,000 maps are recommended as they show more detail. Listed south to north, these are maps No 1 *The Peak District – Dark Peak Area*, 21 *South Pennines*, 2 *Yorkshire Dales – South & West Areas*, 30 *Yorkshire Dales – Northern & Central Areas*, 31 *North Pennines – Teesdale & Weardale*, 43 *Hadrian's Wall*, 42 *Kielder Water & Forest* and 16 *The Cheviot Hills*.

Books

The official *Pennine Way South* and *Pennine Way North* National Trail Guides by Tony Hopkins combine text with extracts from OS maps, and can almost be used without needing other maps. *Pennine Way* by Martin Collins has smaller-scale OS colour strip maps, route descriptions and cartoons. Other guides include Trailblazer's detailed and practical *Pennine Way* by Ed de la Billière and Keith Carter, and *Pennine Way* by Terry Marsh. For information on the flora and fauna you'll encounter on the walk you'll need *Features of the Pennine Way – Field Guide*, published by the Field Studies Council.

The original version of *The Pennine Way Companion* by Alfred Wainwright dates from 1968. It's wonderfully detailed, fun and part of the Pennine Way tradition, although it's very idiosyncratic (for a start it goes backwards!) and covers a different route from the official one that exists today. The 2004 edition includes updates on the current route.

The Alternative Pennine Way by Denis Brook and Phil Hinchliffe is for those who favour a good meal more than challenging terrain; the authors' 268-mile (431km) route from Ashbourne to Jedburgh passes through several of the places on the official route.

Information Sources

See the walk description for tourist offices on or near the route – all provide information on local accommodation and services in their surrounding area.

For more specific information go to the official trail website at www.nationaltrail .co.uk/PennineWay; from here you can order a series of free leaflets, including the *Pennine Way Accommodation & Public Transport Guide*. The website has up-to-date information on places to stay. Also check the website of the **Pennine Way Association** (www.penninewayassociation.co.uk) for updates on the route and for details of how to get hold of the useful *Pennine Way Accommodation & Camping Guide*.

WARNING

Pennine Way weather conditions can be very changeable and occasionally dangerous. Even in summer, rainfall can be high, and strong winds force temperatures down. Mist is common and signposts irregular, so you must be confident with a map and compass. In the rare event you're blessed with sunny weather, there's very little shade and water is often hard to find on the high ground. You should be well-equipped, carry emergency supplies, be aware of escape routes and check local weather forecasts.

Baggage Services

Brigantes Walking Holidays & Baggage Couriers (☎ 01729-830463; www.brigantesenglishwalks.com) is the only baggage service to cover the entire Pennine Way. **Sherpa Van** (☎ 01748-825561; www.sherpavan.com) operates from Malham northwards.

NEAREST TOWNS
Edale

Surrounded by the majestic Peak District countryside, the tiny cluster of stone houses and the parish church that make up Edale are eye-catching. Tourist information is available at the recently revamped **Moorland Centre** (☎ 01433-670207), 500m north of the train station.

SLEEPING & EATING

Beside the Moorland Centre, **Fieldhead Campsite** (☎ 01433-670386; www.fieldhead-campsite .co.uk; sites for 2 £9) has good facilities.

Cooper's Camp (☎ 01433-670372; sites for 2 £7) is at the far end of the village on a farm. With great views of the hills, it's a little more rustic, but has year-round hot showers.

Two camping barns are **Cotefield Farm Camping Barn** (☎ 0870 870 8808; dm £10) and **Stables Bunkhouse** (☎ 01433-670235; Ollerbrook Farm; dm £8). Both places are less than 1 mile east of the village centre.

Edale YHA Hostel (☎ 01433-670302; edale@yha .org.uk; dm B&B/DB&B £16.50/25; 🖵), in a large, old country house 2 miles east of Edale, is also an activity centre and very popular with youth groups.

Walker-friendly B&Bs include **Mam Tor House** (☎ 01433-670253; www.mamtorhouse.co.uk; s/d with shared bathroom £25/50) and **Stonecroft** (☎ 01433-670262; www.stonecroftguesthouse.co.uk; d £60), which servers an excellent organic breakfast.

In Barber Booth, about 1 mile west of the village, you'll find **Brookfield** (☎ 01433-670227; d with shared bathroom £40).

Sandwiches and full greasy breakfasts are available at **Cooper's Café** (☎ 01433-670401; ☷ breakfast & lunch Wed-Mon), next to the post office, where you can also stock up on food supplies and basic outdoor gear.

There are two pubs. Next to the station is the **Rambler Country House** (☎ 01433-670268; www.theramblerinn.co.uk; s/d £36/72, mains £10; ☷ lunch & dinner), which is also a good place to stay. In the centre of the village, by the official start of the Pennine Way, the **Old Nag's Head** (☎ 01433-670291; self-catering cottage £60, mains £10-15; ☷ lunch & dinner) also has a cottage that sleeps four. Apart from slightly pricey meals, it's a decent enough place for a pint.

GETTING THERE & AWAY

Edale is serviced by **Northern Rail** (www.northern rail.org) on the line between Sheffield (30 minutes) and Manchester (45 minutes, about eight per day Monday to Friday, five at weekends). At weekends and on bank holidays, a bus connects Edale to Castleton (p160; 25 minutes, seven per day).

By road, Edale lies north of the A625 between Sheffield and Chapel-en-le-Frith. Pennine Way walkers can leave their car at the Rambler Country House.

Kirk Yetholm

There's not much to the twee village of Kirk Yetholm, but since 1965 its claim to fame has been secure as the end of the Pennine Way. The official finishing line is held to be the bar of the **Border Hotel** (☎ 01573-420237; www.theborderhotel.com; s/d £45/80, mains £9; ☷ lunch & dinner), on the village green. The current owners continue the tradition of shouting walkers a free half-pint as a celebratory drink and issue certificates to those who have completed the walk in one go. You should also sign the log book, which thankfully was safe when the accommodation part of the hotel suffered a fire in 2006.

Basic hostel accommodation is available at **Kirk Yetholm SYHA** (☎ 01573-229791; www.syha.org.uk; dm £12).

Just down the road from the hostel, **Blunty's Mill** (☎ 01573-420288; ggailrowan@aol.com; s/d with shared bathroom £30/50) offers a couple of spacious, comfortable rooms.

Also very pleasant is **Cross Keys House** (☎ 01573-420727; www.crosskeyshousekirkyetholm.co.uk; s/d/t £35/55/70), on the corner of the green, which also runs a quaint **tearoom** (🕓 1-5pm Wed-Sun).

On the way out the village towards Town Yetholm (where you'll find more accommodation and a small shop – useful if this is your starting rather than finishing point) is **Mill House** (☎ 01573-420604; millhousebb@tiscali.co.uk; s/d from £45/60).

Kelso, 55 minutes away by bus, has a **tourist office** (☎ 0870 608 0404; kelso@scot-borders.co.uk) and all the trappings of a regular town.

GETTING THERE & AWAY

There's a bus between Kirk Yetholm and Kelso (20 minutes, seven daily, three Sunday), where you transfer to another bus to Berwick-upon-Tweed, on the main train line between Edinburgh and London. The last bus from Kirk Yetholm usually leaves around 5.30pm.

You can book a taxi direct to Berwick-upon-Tweed through the Border Hotel (p263) for £27.

THE WALK
Day 1: Edale to Crowden
7–8 hours, 16 miles (26km)
First the bad news: it's a long, tough walk, especially if you get caught by bad weather. The good news is that after a steep ascent, it's mainly across rolling moors and there's a thrilling end to the day, coming down towards Crowden. There's nowhere for lunch so bring supplies.

The official start of the Pennine Way is opposite the Old Nag's Head pub. From here, aim west across fields to **Upper Booth**. Go up the lane to Lee Farm then follow the track to, and steeply up, the impressive stone staircase of **Jacob's Ladder**. You're now on Edale Moor, usually called the Kinder Plateau (from Kinder Scout, the highest part of the moor), and the trail sticks close to the edge. In poor weather, visibility can be minimal and signage is nonexistent, so you'll need a compass and good map.

When the River Kinder is in full flow at **Kinder Downfall**, an impressive waterfall tumbles down. The trail keeps to the plateau edge before dropping then climbing to the cairn and post at **Mill Hill**. Here you turn northeast and strike out over Featherbed Moss – once a horror story through sticky mud, now a doddle along flagstones all the way to the A57 at **Snake Pass**.

Cross the road and continue along the Devil's Dyke and Hern Clough. The trail then wanders across the appropriately named Bleaklow Hill. Keep an eye out for the Pennine Way waymarks here as paths lead in all directions; again a compass could be a life-saver.

Towards the end of the day you leave the plateau, descending steeply through the beautiful, heather-coated Torside Clough to **Torside Reservoir**. Cross the dam to the north shore and walk east on a path that avoids the main road to Crowden.

CROWDEN
There's not much to this hamlet alongside the A628. For camping there's **Crowden Camping & Caravanning Club** (☎ 01457-866057; www.campingandcaravanningclub.co.uk; sites for 2 £11), which has a **shop** (🕓 8.30am-3.30pm), toilets and laundry facilities.

The small and well-run **Crowden YHA Hostel** (☎ 01457-852135; www.yha.org.uk; dm £12) offers dinner to nonresidents.

The closest B&B is the **Old House** (☎ 01457-857527; www.oldhouse.torside.co.uk; s/d £25/50), about 800m west of Crowden along the B6105, on the south side of Rhodeswood Reservoir. Otherwise head into Padfield village, about 4 miles southwest of the Pennine Way, just east of the small town of Hadfield (which fans of the cult UK comedy show *The League of Gentlemen*, will recognise as the fictional Royston Vasey). Here you'll find **White House Farm** (☎ 01457-854695; Main Rd; s/d with shared bathroom £25/40) and the **Peels Arms Hotel** (☎ 01457-852719; 6 Temple St; s/d £25/50), which also serves food and a good range of ales.

The 15th-century **Bull's Head** (☎ 01457-853365; Tintwistle; mains £10; ☾ lunch & dinner) inn is around 3.5 miles west of Crowden along the A628.

Day 2: Crowden to Standedge

5–6 hours, 11 miles (18km)

This is a short and, if the weather is playing ball, very pleasant day over the wild moors squeezed between Manchester and Huddersfield. You'll summit infamous Black Hill, now tamed by flagstone paths, and have time to explore the handsome old mill town of Marsden, which is home to a 19th-century industrial-engineering marvel, the Standedge canal tunnel.

The trail starts by climbing steeply beside Crowden Brook and emerges on the edge of Laddow Rocks, with fine views down the valley. Up on the plateau, flagstones wind across the soggy moors to the broad, peaty summit of Black Hill. For less bleak vistas, continue along the flagstones for excellent prospects north across Dean Clough.

The flagstone path continues across the moors to the A635 at Wessenden Head. The next stretch passes several reservoirs, with a picturesque climb up from Wessenden Reservoir along Blakely Clough and across the northern edge of Black Moss moor, then past the Swellands and Black Moss Reservoirs to reach the A62 at Standedge. At this point you're standing above the **Standedge Tunnel**; head down towards **Marsden** (around 3 miles east of the Way) to inspect it.

STANDEDGE & MARSDEN

Camping and B&B is provided at **Rock Farm** (☎ 01457-870325; rockfarm1@btinternet.com; sites for 2 £10, s/d £25/50), around 400m west of the route; follow the bridleway that heads towards Standedge Foot.

Nearby, past Globe Farm, you'll find **Wellcroft House** (☎ 01457-875017, 0781-687 9244; s/d £25/50), where the friendly owners also provide evening meals (£10).

Less than 800m east of the trail, on the main road, the **Great Western** (☎ 01484-844315; camp sites for 2 £4; ☾ lunch & dinner Tue-Sun) pub allows camping and provides traditional home-cooked meals, including a 'full monty' breakfast for campers from 7am (£6).

A little further east, the **Carriage House** (☎ 01484-844419; ☾ lunch & dinner) is a large pub that has, in the past, provided free camping,

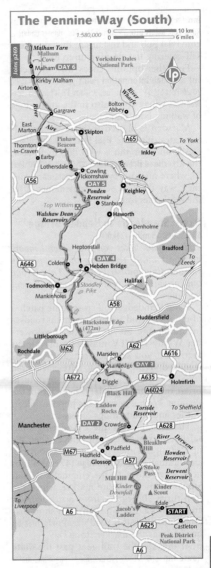

as long as you eat and drink in the pub; this may change, so check first.

Another good local B&B is **New Barn** (☎ 01457-873937, 0797-959 8232; s/d £25/50), less than 1 mile west from the Pennine Way towards Diggle.

Sadly, accommodation is thin on the ground in Marsden. One place is **Tunnel End**

Inn (☎ 01484-844636; www.tunnelendinn.com; Waters Rd; d £60, mains £10; ❤ lunch Thu-Sun, dinner daily), a convivial pub and restaurant that also has a self-catering flat sleeping up to four.

For other options, check with the helpful **Marsden Information Point** (☎ 01484-845595; 20-26 Peel St; ❤ 2-6pm Tue, 9.30am-12.30pm & 1-4pm Wed-Sat), where you'll also find a great range of walking books and maps.

Marsden is blessed with several appealing cafés, plus the **Peel St Chippy** (☎ 01484-844579) and, for those who like their beer, the **Riverhead Brewery Tap** (☎ 01484-841270; Peel St), where micro-brew enthusiasts can work their way through seven ales named after the local reservoirs.

Day 3: Standedge to Hebden Bridge
6–7 hours, 15 miles (24km)
Today's walk takes you over several moors and past many reservoirs that supply the surrounding industrial cities. There's one pub, or you might prefer to be self-sufficient for lunch.

From Standedge you cross some patches of moorland and a couple of main roads – including the A672 – with the towering Windy Hill TV mast as a prominent marker. If you see the orange-and-yellow standard flying above a **refreshments van** (❤ 5.30am-1.30pm Mon-Fri) here, you're in luck; Brian, one of the legendary characters of the Pennine Way, is serving his popular bacon butties and strong mugs of tea.

The trail crosses the thundering M62 safely on its own, elegant bridge. Then it's up Redmires, tamed by flagstones, to rocky and dramatic **Blackstone Edge** (472m). From here, drop down to the enigmatic Aiggin Stone, an ancient route marker, where the trail turns 90 degrees from north to west and follows a 'Roman road' for a short distance (although this road's real origin is as uncertain as the marker stone's).

At the A58 the trail goes past the **White House Inn** (☎ 01706-378456; Blackstone Edge; mains £5-10; ❤ lunch & dinner), a nice pub (dating from 1617) serving good food but without a walkers' bar, so take muddy boots off before entering. Beyond here, the trail turns north past more reservoirs and edges around Coldwell Hill.

At Withins Gate, if you're overnighting at the self-catering **Mankinholes YHA Hostel** (☎ 01706-812340; mankinholes@yha.org.uk; Todmorden;

dm £13), in a converted 17th-century manor house, take the beautifully crafted path known as the Long Drag, a 19th-century famine-relief project. Otherwise, continue on the trail to the prominent **Stoodley Pike monument**, built during the Napoleonic Wars and completed in 1815. Despite its monolithic construction, the monument collapsed in 1854 and again in 1918.

From the monument, the Pennine Way wanders across the high ground then drops down through woods into the narrow and steep-sided Calder Valley, towards the **Rochdale Canal**. The trail crosses the canal and the river to meet the A646. If you're continuing north, go right and then left, up a lane called Underbank Ave. For accommodation options along this route, see the Day 4 description (opposite). Alternatively, follow the canal towpath into Hebden Bridge, about 1.5 miles to your east.

HEBDEN BRIDGE
It's well worth making time to explore the former mill town of **Hebden Bridge** (www.hebden bridge.co.uk), which thrives on its arty, off-centre reputation. It's also a useful entry and exit point to the Pennine Way, being on the Leeds–Manchester train line.

The friendly and helpful **Hebden Bridge Visitor & Canal Centre** (☎ 01422-843831; www.calder dale.gov.uk; Butlers Wharf, New Rd) has a fine stock of maps and leaflets on local walks, including saunters in **Hardcastle Crags**, two unspoiled wooded valleys controlled by the National Trust, 1.5 miles northwest of town; some of the trails here link with the Pennine Way.

Internet access is available at the **library** (☎ 01422-842151). There's a **laundrette** (Bridgegate; ❤ 8am-6pm Wed-Mon) and an outdoor gear shop, **Valet Stores** (19 Crown St).

The pick of the B&Bs is **Mytholm House** (☎ 01422-847493; www.mytholmhouse.co.uk; Mytholm Bank; s with shared bathroom, d with/without bathroom £60/45), a lovely place run by charming hosts.

Also good are **Angeldale** (☎ 01422-847321; www.angeldale.co.uk; Hangingroyd Lane; d £50), in a Victorian mill owner's mansion; and the stylish **Holme House** (☎ 01422-847588; www.holme househebdenbridge.co.uk; New Rd; s/d from £55/70, apt £75), in a Georgian house in the town centre. **Prospect End** (☎ 01422-843586; www.prospectend .co.uk; Savile Rd; s/d £35/50) has long served walkers, but be prepared for the owner's many rules and regulations.

White Lion Hotel (☎ 01422-842197; www.whitelion hotel.net; Bridge Gate; s/d from £46/60, mains £6-11; ☽ lunch & dinner) has rooms both in the 400-year-old coaching inn and in the converted coach house. It's a popular pub and decent restaurant.

Other dining options include the recommended **Crown Fisheries** (☎ 01422-842599; 8 Crown St; mains £5; ☽ lunch & dinner) for takeaways and sit-down fish suppers; the cute **Watergate Tearooms** (9 Bridgegate; ☽ 10.30am-4.30pm); **Nelsons Wine Bar** (☎ 01422-844782; Crown St; mains £6; ☽ breakfast, lunch & dinner Tue-Sun) for inventive vegetarian dishes; the convivial bistro **Mooch** (☎ 01422-846954; 24 Market St; mains £5-8; ☽ lunch & dinner Wed-Mon); and the popular Thai restaurant **Rim Nam** (☎ 01422-846688; Butler's Wharf, New Rd; mains £8; ☽ lunch & dinner Thu-Sun).

Real ale enthusiasts should head to the CAMRA-award-winning pub, the **Fox & Goose** (☎ 01422-842649; Heptonstall Rd).

Day 4: Hebden Bridge to Ponden Reservoir

6 hours, 11 miles (18km)

It's a short walk today, allowing either a lie-in or time to explore Hebden Bridge before setting off. You'll stride across the wild and empty northern moors, setting for both Emily Brontë's Wuthering Heights *and the popular British children's book,* The Railway Children. *Brontë fans can easily divert to Haworth, which can also be accessed by train.*

From Hebden Bridge, return to where the Pennine Way crosses the A646 and go up Underbank Ave, beneath the railway bridge and up a steep switchback to cross a lane east of the village of Blackshaw Head. Near here you'll find **Badgerfields Farm** (☎ 01422-845161; www.badgerfields.com; camp sites for 2 £6; s/d with shared bathroom £35/52), a friendly place where campers can order breakfast (£6).

The trail continues north across the fields to the hamlet of Colden, but you can divert slightly to the west to a cheerful pub, the **New Delight** (☎ 01422-846178; camp sites for 2 £6, mains £5-7; ☽ lunch & dinner), which brews its own beer, serves meals and offers camping with showers. Next door, in a new complex of stone cottages, there's B&B and hostel-style accommodation at **Riverdene House** (☎ 01422-847447; Smithy Lane; dm/s/d £20/35/60).

Closer to Colden, free camping for Pennine Way walkers is offered at **May Farm** (☎ 01422-842897; Edge Lane), where you'll also find an extraordinary shop in a barn selling practically anything you can think of.

Beyond Colden the trail heads northwest across a stretch of moor, until a sharp right (north) turn takes you down past a reservoir channel and steeply down to a stream called Graining Water, then back up the other side and along a road for a short distance. The trail leaves the road and, after about 1 mile, passes between the Walshaw Dean Reservoirs before heading northeast across moors, again by easy paths or flagstone walkways, to the ruins of Top Withins (also called Withens), said to be a possible inspiration for Earnshaw house in Emily Brontë's *Wuthering Heights* – although the claim is tenuous. Regardless, if the weather is fine you can have your lunch on the bench outside and, if not, you can shelter in the grimy outhouse.

The trail continues northeast on a wide track and, about 200m after a farm called Upper Heights (another inspiration?), the Pennine Way turns left (north) heading to Ponden Reservoir.

PONDEN RESERVOIR & HAWORTH

Overlooking Ponden Reservoir, **Ponden House** (☎ 01535-644154; www.pondenhouse.co.uk; camp sites for 2 £10, s with shared bathroom £28, d with/without bathroom £60/50; ☐) is a walker-friendly place, run by nice people who will show you their original artwork by David Hockney.

A short walk east of the route, between Ponden Reservoir and the village of Stanbury, the award-winning **Old Silent Inn** (☎ 01535-647437; www.old-silent-inn.co.uk; d £60, meals £8-12; ☽ lunch & dinner) oozes history, with log fires, low beams, good beer and excellent meals.

Alternatively, head 2.5 miles off the Pennine Way (southeast) to Haworth, home of the Brontës and also a stop on the Keighley & Worth Valley Railway. As a popular tourist centre Haworth has many accommodation options. For more information contact the **tourist office** (☎ 01535-642329; www.haworth-village.org.uk; 2-4 West Lane) and check out www.brontecountry.co.uk.

Day 5: Ponden Reservoir to Malham

9–10 hours, 22 miles (36km)

This is a long, and occasionally challenging, walk across the green and pleasant Yorkshire Dales National Park, heralding a change in scenery and an increase in good lunch and snacking opportunities. Gargrave is an alternative base to Malham, if you want to shorten the walk.

From the western end of the Ponden Reservoir the trail turns north, climbs up past some houses to meet, and briefly follow, a road. It then heads confidently northwest across a wide expanse of moorland, eventually dropping down to a busy main road between the villages of Ickornshaw and Cowling. There are a couple of B&Bs in Cowling, as well as the smart restaurant-bar **Harlequin** (☎ 01535-633277; 139 Keighley Rd; ☺ lunch & dinner Wed-Sun) and the **Cowling Chippy** (☎ 01535-630110; 223 Keighley Rd; ☺ closed Mon).

From Ickornshaw the trail follows a mix of country lanes and field paths for another 2 miles, down into the picturesque village of **Lothersdale**, where the **Hare & Hounds** (☎ 01535-630977; mains £7; ☺ lunch & dinner) serves food. Just along from the pub it's possible to camp at **Lynmouth** (☎ 01535-632744; sites for 2 £10).

From Lothersdale the trail runs across the surprisingly high moors over the hill of Pinhaw Beacon, before dropping across fields. Aim for Brown House Farm and look for the stile on the left just as you approach the farmyard itself. Follow a track for the rest of the way to **Thornton-in-Craven** on the busy A56.

Nearby is the **Earby YHA Hostel** (☎ 01282-842349; earby@yha.org.uk; dm £12). It's self-catering but there's also a nearby pub serving meals (10% discount for those staying at the hostel) and a café in the village serving breakfast.

From Thornton-in-Craven you cross fields again before emerging on the **Leeds & Liverpool Canal** towpath. At **East Marton** an unusual, double-arch bridge crosses the canal. Here you'll find the convivial pub and restaurant **Cross Keys** (☎ 01282-844326; mains £8-10; ☺ lunch & dinner) and, near the canal, the pleasant little café **Abbot's Harbor** (☎ 01282-843207; ☺ lunch Fri-Wed). Next door, in a pretty cottage, is **Sawley House** (☎ 01282-843207; s/d with shared bathroom £30/50).

The trail then leaves the canal and heads through a small wood and fields to Scaleber Hill, and onward to **Gargrave**. This appealing Dales village is well stocked with pubs, antique shops and an ATM at the local Co-op. If you choose to stop here, there's camping at **Eshton Road Caravan Site** (☎ 01756-749229; sites for 2 £8). The **Masons Arms** (☎ 01756-749304;

www.masonsarmsgargrave.com; Marton Rd; s/d £45/65), opposite the church, and the friendly **Old Swan Inn** (☎ 01756-749232; Main St; s/d £35/70) both do B&B and serve standard bar food for £6 to £7.

Don't leave Gargrave without popping into the charming **Dalesman Café** (☎ 01756-749250; Main St; mains £5; ☺ 9am-5pm Tue-Sun), a blast from a sugar-coated past; it also has a Pennine Way signing-in book. For something spicier there's the nearby **Bollywood Cottage** (☎ 01756-749252; Main St; mains £7; ☺ dinner Tue-Sun), while for good old fish and chips there's **Ellisons Fisheries** (☎ 01756-749343; Main St; ☺ lunch Wed-Sat, dinner Wed-Sun).

The route heads north out of Gargrave, crosses the canal again and goes straight on up Mark House Lane before turning off across fields, dropping gently to a bridge over the River Aire. It's a pretty and gentle stroll alongside the river for the next few miles, passing the village of **Airton**. Here, there's the simple **Quaker Hostel** (☎ 01729-830263; dm £8), which is self-catering (and you need your own sleeping bag), or the recommended **Lindon Guest House** (☎ 01729-830418; s/d £35/58). Next door is the **Town End Farm Shop & Tearoom** (☺ 10am-5pm).

Continue through the beautiful valley of Malhamdale, passing the village of Kirkby Malham, where there's the **Victoria Inn** (☎ 01729-830499; s/d £35/50; ☺ lunch & dinner), a friendly little pub with B&B and decent food. Near here you leave the river by Hanlith Hall and Badger House, go up a lane then turn off across fields, heading above the river before dropping down into Malham.

MALHAM

This traditional and very appealing village is a hub of activity, with lots of places to stay and eat. Coming into Malham from the south, you'll pass the excellent **Malham National Park Centre** (☎ 01969-652380; www.yorkshiredales.org.uk); check with the centre about the limited public-transport options to and from the village, including a National Trust bus from Settle that runs on weekends and bank holidays from Easter to October. For more information there's the website www.malhamdale.com. Malham also has a couple of shops selling outdoor gear.

As you enter the village there's camping and B&B at **Miresfield Farm** (☎ 01729-830414; www.miresfield-farm.com; sites for 2 £10, s/d from £30/60).

Leaving the village, there's a well-equipped bunkhouse at **Hill Top Farm** (☎ 01729-830320; Cove Rd; dm £8) and more camping at **Town Head Farm** (☎ 01729-830287; sites for 2 £10).

In the village centre is the top-notch **Malham YHA Hostel** (☎ 01729-830321; www.yha.org.uk; dm £15, d with shared bathroom £32, 3-course dinner £8).

B&B options include the appealing 17th-century country house **Beck Hall** (☎ 01729-830332; www.beckhallmalham.com; s/d from £23/48), just off Cove Rd by the river, which also has a nice tearoom; and **Eastwood House** (☎ 01729-830409; d from £50), back in the centre.

Those with traditional country pub and hotel tastes are well served by the **Buck Inn** (☎ 01729-830317; www.buckinnmalham.co.uk; s/d from £45/65). If you want to keep your boots on, there's also a stone-floored walkers' bar. Moving with the times (Cajun chicken salad on the menu, free internet access in the bar, tasteful décor) is the **Lister Arms Hotel** (☎ 01729-830330; www.listerarms.co.uk; s/d from £50/60; 🖳).

Muddy boots are always welcome at **Old Barn Café** (☎ 01729-830486; snacks £3-5).

Day 6: Malham to Horton in Ribblesdale
7 hours, 14.5 miles (23.5km)

Today's enjoyable walk winds through the heart of the Yorkshire Dales, finishing with Pen-y-ghent, a famous landmark. You pass no cafés or pubs, so bring your lunch.

Leaving Malham the trail climbs steeply up the west side of the curved amphitheatre of cliffs that make up **Malham Cove**, then edges right across the top of the cliffs – a textbook stretch of limestone pavement with wonderful views back down to Malham.

At the east end of the pavement, turn sharp left and head for the natural lake and protected nature reserve of **Malham Tarn**. The trail edges round the east side of the tarn before heading into woods past the field-studies centre **Malham Tarn House** (☎ 01729-830331) then turns north. For 1 mile the trail crosses fields then turns east to cross a road by the prominently signposted Tennant Gill Farm.

Leaving green fields for darker moors, the trail climbs up to **Fountains Fell** (668m) over a series of ridges (each hinting that maybe it's the top) and past a scattering of disused mineshafts to a bleak, stone-walled summit called **In Sleets** – maybe a reference to the weather! As you drop steadily downhill to

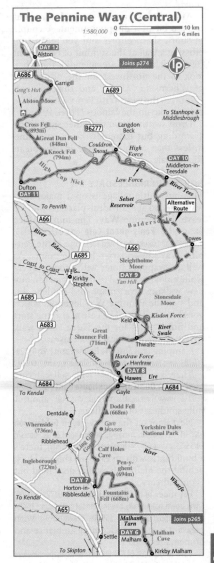

meet a lane called Silverdale Rd, you can look across at the peak you'll shortly have to climb on the other side: the long hump of Pen-y-ghent. The trail almost circles the hill before moving in, marching alongside it for about 1 mile before turning west past Dale Head Farm, then north across to the base of Pen-y-ghent.

After all this foreplay the peak turns out to be a bit of a disappointment. A couple of short, sharp efforts and you're on top, crossing a wall at the summit of **Pen-y-ghent** (694m). The views are splendid, though – look to the northwest for the nearby hill of Whernside (736m), and Ingleborough (723m) to the west. With Pen-y-ghent, these peaks make up the famous 'Three Peaks'.

Drop swiftly down the other side, along a winding but extremely clear path, and in less than an hour you're in Horton in Ribblesdale.

HORTON IN RIBBLESDALE

This busy little village is on a major railway line, so it's an ideal place to join or leave the Pennine Way. The tourist office is in the **Pen-y-ghent Cafe** (☎ 01729-860333; horton@ytbtic.co.uk; ☺ closed Tue), one of the Pennine Way's legendary refuelling points. As well as swapping notes with other walkers while enjoying a meal or drink, you can buy new walking gear, maps and guidebooks, and sign the Pennine Way logbook, which goes back to 1966. The café is also the start and finish point for the Three Peaks walk (p170), a piece of local masochism.

Camping is at **Sutcliffe Holme Farm** (☎ 01729-860281; sites for 2 £10) on the village main street.

There's a bunkhouse with self-catering facilities at **Dub-Cote Bunkhouse Barn** (☎ 01729-860238; www.threepeaksbarn.co.uk; dm £10), about 1 mile southeast of the village.

Next door, at the minty-green **Golden Lion** (☎ 01729-860206; tricia@goldenlionhotel.co.uk; dm/s/d £9/35/55, mains £7; ☺ breakfast, lunch & dinner), there's a bunkhouse with an exposed shower block behind the main pub, which does food but is quite dreary.

Far nicer is the **Crown Hotel** (☎ 01729-860209; www.crown-hotel.co.uk; s with/without bathroom £30/25, d with/without bathroom £59/49, mains £7-9), with pleasant rooms, a welcoming ambiance and homemade food.

The **Knoll** (☎ 01729-860283; www.thepennineway .co.uk/theknoll; s/d with shared bathroom £30/50) is a spotless B&B with charming décor and friendly hosts.

Another option is **Brae Crest** (☎ 01729-860389; s/d with shared bathroom £25/50), in a white-painted semidetached house on the way to the train station.

For self-caterers the **post office shop** has groceries and takeaways.

Day 7: Horton in Ribblesdale to Hawes
6 hours, 14 miles (22.5km)

This is another wonderfully wild Dales day, taking you through country riddled with limestone caves – a mecca for potholers. Once again, there's nowhere to get food, so bring supplies.

The trail departs Horton in Ribblesdale at the north end of the village, and follows a drove road that climbs up onto Birkwith Moor. Three miles north of Horton the trail turns sharply to the west and, shortly afterwards, back north again, passing Old Ing Farm. As it's hidden behind a stone wall you could easily miss the attractive stream tumbling into the mouth of **Calf Holes cave**. Only another 400m along the trail, a short excursion past the barn to the left of the road will bring you to **Browngill Cave**, where the stream emerges. Potholers revel in this watery underground route, but Way walkers may feel wet enough already.

Your next feature is pretty little **Ling Gill Gorge**. You cannot enter this steep-sided valley, but the river bank makes a pleasant picnic spot and there's an interesting old bridge at the head of the gorge. The trail then climbs up to the Roman road route of Cam High Road and starts a lonely trudge northeast, coinciding for a spell with the Dales Way, before turning north to edge around Dodd Fell. At the settlement of **Cam Houses**, down in the valley to the south, the attractive, almost luxurious **Camm Farm** (☎ 07860 648045; www.cammfarm.co.uk; s/d with shared bathroom £45/80) is a possible stop; the rates include evening meal.

The trail follows the northern shoulder of Dodd Fell, and overlooks a wide, deep valley, which is popular with paragliders, before finally dropping down through fields and farms, following Gaudy Lane and a circuitous route through the village of Gayle to reach the town of Hawes.

HAWES

From the Saxon word *haus*, or mountain pass, Hawes is a bustling place. You'll find supermarkets, banks with ATMs, a good outdoor gear shop – **Three Peaks** (☎ 01969-667443; Bridge End) – a laundrette, internet access at the **library** (☎ 01969-667613; per 30 mins £1.25) and scores of B&Bs, cafés and pubs.

The **tourist office** (☎ 01969-667450; www .destinationdales.co.uk) shares the Old Station building with the **Dales Countryside Museum** (adult/child £3/free) – a creatively presented social history of the area. There's also the **Wensleydale Creamery Visitor Centre** (☎ 01969-667664; www.wensleydale.co.uk; admission £2.50), devoted to the production of Wallace and Gromit's favourite powdery-white cheese; you'll also find a café here.

Around 800m east of the town centre, there's camping at **Bainbridge Ings Caravan & Campsite** (☎ 01969-667354; www.bainbridge-ings.co.uk; sites for 2 £7).

Hawes YHA (☎ 0870 770 5854; www.yha.org.uk; Lancaster Tce; dm £14) is a modern, friendly place on the western edge of town.

One of the nicest B&Bs is the comfortable and spacious **Fair View Country Guesthouse** (☎ 01969-667348; www.fairview-hawes.co.uk; Burtersett Rd; s/d £28/59).

Laburnum House (☎ 01969-667717; www.stayat laburnumhouse.co.uk; The Holme; s/d £35/70) combines a quaint tearoom with a B&B.

More upmarket B&Bs are the **Bulls Head Hotel** (☎ 01969-667437; www.bullsheadhotel.co.uk; Market Pl; d from £55) and **Cockett's** (☎ 01969-667312; www.cocketts.co.uk; Main St; d from £59, 2-/3-course meal £15/17; ☺ dinner), in a handsome 17th-century house with delightful rooms decorated in traditional style (two with four-poster beds) and a restaurant.

Several pubs also offer accommodation and food, including the traditional **White Hart** (☎ 01969-667259; www.whitetharthawes.co.uk; Main St; s/d from £28/55, mains £8-10; ☺ lunch & dinner) – try the meat-and-potato pie; and the **Fountain Hotel** (☎ 01969-667206; s/d £30/60; ☺ lunch & dinner), consistently the liveliest hostelry in town.

For more than pub grub try **Herriot's Hotel & Restaurant** (☎ 01969-667536; www.herriotsinhawes .co.uk; Main St; s/d from £45/65, mains £10-15; ☺ dinner Tue & Fri-Sun). There are a couple more accommodation and eating options nearby in Hardraw – see below.

Day 8: Hawes to Tan Hill
7 hours, 16 miles (26km)

Today's route takes you over more lonely high ground, through the quieter northern reaches of the Dales. If you're tired of sandwiches, there are a couple of lunch options.

From Hawes it's only 1 mile to the village of **Hardraw**, home to the atmospheric old pub **Green Dragon Inn** (☎ 01969-667392; www .greendragonhardraw.co.uk; camp sites for 2 £6, s/d £30/60;

mains about £6; ☺ lunch & dinner). You can pay £2 at the pub to see Hardraw Force waterfall – although it's often little more than a trickle. For a total pampering, divert a little way to **Simonstone Hall** (☎ 01969-667255; www.simonstonehall.co.uk; d from £130, mains £10-20; ☺ lunch & dinner), a handsome hotel blessed with wonderful views and a very pleasant bar and restaurant open to nonresidents.

From Hardraw the trail abandons green fields for moorland, often following stone-slabbed paths up to the famous peak and viewpoint of **Great Shunner Fell** (716m). From the summit the trail drops down, through moorland and fields, to the small village of Thwaite, where you can break at the **Kearton Country Hotel** (☎ 01748-886277; www.keartoncountry hotel.co.uk; s/d £40/59, with breakfast £49/78), which has a teashop.

From Thwaite the path climbs high above the **River Swale** with wonderful views across this beautiful section of the upper valley, and then drops to cross the river on a wooden footbridge, briefly coinciding with the Coast to Coast Walk. Grassy river banks overlooking small waterfalls make this an ideal picnic spot. Nearby is the tiny village of **Keld** (p246), which has a couple of camp sites, B&Bs and a teashop. You may need to stop here if today's objective, the Tan Hill Inn, is full.

From Keld, you say farewell to Swaledale as the trail climbs back onto the moor, with a possible short diversion to **Kisdon Force** waterfall. Although the road is never far to the west, the next 4 miles can be a lonely trudge across the moors (take care in mist, there are numerous, unfenced mineshafts nearby) to Tan Hill.

TAN HILL
At 528m (1732ft), the highest pub in England, **Tan Hill Inn** (☎ 01833-628246; www.tanhillinn .com; camping £2, tw/d/t £60/70/80; mains £8; ☺ breakfast, lunch & dinner), is your reward for persevering on today's long walk. As well as offering B&B, and a windswept camp site, the landlord allows walkers to sleep on the sofa in the pub (£10). Any money you save is likely to be spent on the inn's splendid ales and wide choice of food. All this, plus a roaring fire (even in August!), occasional live music and a pet sheep, makes the Tan Hill Inn a unique place to stay, so book ahead as it's the only place up here.

Day 9: Tan Hill to Middleton-in-Teesdale
7 hours, 17 miles (28km)

It's a long walk today, but the good news is that by the time you reach Middleton-in-Teesdale you'll have completed just over half the Pennine Way. This area of the North Pennines is also very beautiful – wild, high fells – and eerie and empty under big skies. If you don't go into Bowes, there are no places to buy lunch, so bring sandwiches.

From lonely Tan Hill the trail slouches across equally lonely Sleightholme Moor for 5 miles. If the weather is dry the walk along the stream can be quite pleasant. In the wet it can be a dishearteningly muddy experience; following the lane and rejoining the trail later may be preferable.

As you leave the moor you have a choice of routes. Going right (northeast) is a slightly longer option into the sleepy village of **Bowes**, where you'll find a ruined castle. The old coaching inn, **Ancient Unicorn** (☎ 01833-628321; www.ancient-unicorn.com; s/d £40/70, mains £6-8; ☺ lunch & dinner) is the only place to stay here unless you have a tent, which you can pitch at **West End Farm** (☎ 01833-628239, 07761-253656; sites for 2 £6) at the west end of the village.

Going left (north) crosses the River Greta on a natural stone slab called **God's Bridge**, before a short detour leads to a tunnel under the busy A66. After 3 miles or so crossing bleak moorland, the two routes converge at **Baldersdale**, a valley full of reservoirs where you can celebrate having reached the half-way point of the Pennine Way. Nearby is **Clove Lodge Cottage** (☎ 01833-650030; www.clove lodge.co.uk; camp sites for 2 £10, s/d with shared bathroom £30/60, 3-course dinner £13), which has washing facilities.

Beyond here the trail climbs up then drops down to more reservoirs, before climbing again and meandering through a maze of fields into Middleton-in-Teesdale.

MIDDLETON-IN-TEESDALE

This handsome little grey-stone town on the banks of the River Tees is well served with shops, ATMs and a **tourist office** (☎ 01833-641001; 10 Market Pl; ☺ 10am-1pm). Internet access is available at the **Teesdale Mercury** (per hr £2).

There's camping at **Dale View Caravan Park** (☎ 01833-640233; sites for 2 £8), passed as the trail comes into town.

In the town centre, B&Bs include **Belvedere Guesthouse** (☎ 01833-640884; www.thecoach house.net; 54 Market Pl; s/d £25/50), an appealing and friendly place with a chandelier above the breakfast table; and pleasant **Brunswick House** (☎ 01833-640393; www.brunswickhouse.net; 56 Market Pl; s/d £35/55, dinner £18).

Also on Market Pl, the **Teesdale Hotel** (☎ 01833-640264; www.teesdalehotel.co.uk; s/d £43/70, mains £10-13; ☺ lunch & dinner) has good accommodation, a smart restaurant and a bar where lunch is available.

Opposite is the **Forresters Hotel & Restaurant** (☎ 01833-640467; www.forrestershotel.co.uk; s/d £35/70, mains £10-13; ☺ lunch & dinner), with contemporary rooms, including DVD players, and a good restaurant.

For freshly baked snacks there's the cosy **Countrystyle Bakery & Tea Shop** (20 Market Pl; ☺ 9am-4.30pm Mon-Sat, 10am-4pm Sun).

Day 10: Middleton-in-Teesdale to Dufton
8 hours, 20 miles (32.5km)

The highlight of today's walk through classic North Pennine landscape is the spectacular High Cup Nick valley. You could grab an early lunch at Langdon Beck, or pack a picnic to enjoy along the way. If you are self-catering, make sure you bring two days of provisions as Dufton no longer has a shop.

For the first 8 miles the trail runs along beautiful Teesdale, following the peaty, amber waters of the River Tees, past **Low Force** waterfall, and then the larger and more impressive **High Force** (entry £1), where a short detour could be made to the old-fashioned **High Force Hotel** (☎ 01833-622222; www.highforce hotel.com; s/d £35/75; mains £6; ☺ lunch & dinner), if an early lunch is needed.

Beyond the waterfalls the trail briefly abandons the Tees to pass close to the village of **Langdon Beck**, where there are a couple of accommodation options. **Langdon Beck YHA** (☎ 01833-622228; langdonbeck@yha.org.uk; dm £12), a model hostel run along environmentally friendly principles, offers organic wines and beers with its meals. Alternatively, there's the friendly **Langdon Beck Hotel** (☎ 01833-622267; www.langdonbeckhotel.com; s with shared bathroom £30, d £60; mains £7; ☺ lunch & dinner).

The trail returns to the north bank of the Tees and follows a beautiful stretch of rocky valley (although the rocky path can be dangerously slippery if wet) to reach **Couldron Snout** waterfall – an impressive sight spoiled only slightly by the large concrete dam upstream. You cross the Tees here and say goodbye to it, aiming southwest (yes, southwest on this northbound path) across wild, empty moors for several miles; the trail is bordered by signs warning of an adjacent army artillery range. For a couple more miles it follows and crosses the sparkling waters of Maize Beck.

There's a breathtaking view a short while later from **High Cup Nick** into a stunning valley cut deep into the high country, with a steep drop shelving down, down, down to a silvery stream in the distance. From here it's just a few more miles downhill (remembering all the time that all this downhill will be paid for tomorrow) into the friendly little village of Dufton.

DUFTON
Entering the village from its southeastern end you'll first pass **Brow Farm** (☎ 017683-52865; www.browfarm.com; camp sites for 2 £6, s/d £28/56), run by a friendly young family.

A little further along is the charmingly old-fashioned **Ghyll View** (☎ 017683-51855; s/d with shared bathroom £23/46).

In the heart of the village is the pleasant **Dufton YHA** (☎ 017683-51236; dufton@yha.org.uk; dm £14, d with shared bathroom £28, dinner £8), which offers meals (all made using local produce and with special diets catered for) to non-guests. Close by, **Hall Croft** (☎ 017683-52902; r.walker@leaseholdpartnership.co.uk; s/d £28/50) is an exceedingly nice B&B offering vegetarian breakfasts and comfortable rooms with video players.

The convivial village pub, the **Stag Inn** (☎ 017683-51608; mains £10; ✆ closed Mon lunch) offers upmarket food and teas during the day.

Day 11: Dufton to Alston
8 hours, 19.5 miles (32km)
You'll need your wits about you for today's route over remote Cross Fell – it's one of the Pennine Way's most serious sections and can be notoriously difficult to navigate if weather conditions are bad, as they frequently are. Make sure you've got a compass and enough rations to survive the day.

The trail climbs out of Dufton, first to **Knock Fell** (794m) and then to **Great Dun Fell** (848m), with its air-traffic-control radar station (including a giant golf ball) visible from far away. Onwards and upwards you go, often along stone-slabbed pathways, to Little Dun Fell and finally **Cross Fell** (893m),

the highest point of the Pennine Way. An 18th-century article commented that Cross Fell was covered in snow for 10 months of the year and cloud for 11. You may think things are much the same now!

A series of tall and wobbly-looking cairns leads across this bleak summit before the trail drops down to the Corpse Rd (this was once a lead-mining area and the bodies of dead miners were carried along the track) and then to **Greg's Hut**, a mountain refuge that will be very welcome in bad weather. From here it's 6 miles across the moors along a rough track, which is easy to follow but uncomfortably covered in awkward, sharp stones.

Reaching the sleepy village of **Garrigill** is a considerable relief; celebrate with a pint at the **George & Dragon** (☎ 01434-381293; ✆ lunch & dinner Wed-Mon). The village's best B&B is **Eastview** (☎ 01434-381561; www.eastview-garrigill .co.uk; s/d with shared bathroom £24/48), a cosy, low-ceilinged cottage with two guest rooms. In the same terrace, **Bridge View** (☎ 01434-382448; www.bridgeview.org.uk; s/d £22/44) has one room for guests and plans to open a tea garden. Across the green there's more accommodation at the **Post Office** (☎ 01434-381257; www.garrigill -guesthouse.co.uk; s/d with shared bathroom £24/48). Next door is the **village store** (✆ closed Tue).

Leaving the village, don't miss **Thortergill** (☎ 01434-381936; www.thortergillforge.co.uk; ✆ 10am-5pm Easter-Oct), which combines a delightful tearoom, a short walk to a picturesque series of waterfalls and the chance to view a working blacksmith's forge.

From Garrigill it's less than 4 miles along a pleasant path beside the River South Tyne to Alston.

ALSTON
With its steep, cobbled main street and sturdy stone buildings, the high-altitude, one-time market town of Alston has often caught the eye of film makers looking for a ready-made set; it was recently used in TV adaptations of *Jane Eyre* and *Oliver Twist*. It's well served with places to stay, a selection of pubs, an outdoor gear shop, banks (with ATMs) and a helpful **tourist office** (☎ 01434-382244; alston.tic@eden.gov.uk; Town Hall, Front St; 💻).

There's camping at **Tyne Willows Caravan Site** (☎ 01434-382515; sites for 2 £8), which has drying facilities.

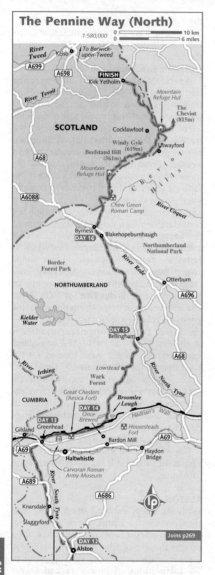

The Pennine Way (North)

1:580,000

Alston YHA Hostel (☎ 0870 770 5668; alston@yha .org.uk; The Firs; dm £13) is a good hostel with meals available.

B&Bs include **Blueberry Teashop & Guesthouse** (☎ 01434-381928; ellisanddoreen@hotmail.com; Market Pl; s/d £29/49, mains £5-7; lunch), and **Highfield** (☎ 01434-382182; Bruntley Meadows; s/d £18/36), just outside the town centre.

The **Cumberland Hotel** (☎ 01434-381875; Townfoot; s/d £33/56, mains £7; lunch & dinner) offers recently renovated rooms, a friendly welcome and decent food.

For a touch more class, head across the road to **Alston House** (☎ 01434-382200; www .alstonhouse.co.uk; Townfoot; s/d £39/79, mains £9-16; lunch & dinner), which has a trendy restaurant and bar serving delicious gastro-pub-style meals.

Down the hill, heading north out of the town, **Lowbyer Manor** (☎ 01434-381230; www .lowbyer.com; Hexham Rd; s/d £33/66) is in a Georgian manor house with period trappings.

The cosy **Angel Inn** (☎ 01434-381363; Front St; s/d £25/40, mains £5-7; lunch & dinner) also offers food and B&B, while further up cobblestoned Front St you'll find the **High Place** (☎ 01434-382300; mains £4; closed Sun) chippy and the **Moody Baker** (☎ 01434-382033; 8am-5pm Mon-Sat), providing tasty baked goods.

Day 12: Alston to Greenhead
7 hours, 16.5 miles (27km)
This is another transition day, mostly along the scenic South Tyne Valley, as you enter Northumberland. Roman remains remind you that Hadrian's Wall is nearby.

From Alston it's a pleasant walk through green farmland, passing the distinct embankments of a **Roman fort**. These are soon followed by reminders of a more recent era as the trail keeps close to an abandoned railway line that once transported lead ore from the area's mines. A number of impressive viaducts remain from this time – shining examples of Victorian engineering.

About 5 miles from Alston you can camp in the village of Slaggyford at **Stonehall Farm** (☎ 01434-381349; sites for 2 £5) or go B&B at **Yew Tree Chapel** (☎ 01434-382525; www.yewtreechapel .co.uk; d £50). A couple of miles further north, in the village of Knarsdale, there's a chance for refreshments at **Kirkstyle Inn** (☎ 01434-381559; lunch & dinner). Here the Pennine Way follows the route of an old Roman road before embarking on a series of field crossings and a brief section of moorland.

Late in the day the walk becomes a bit tedious as it wanders under electricity pylons, over the A69, around a golf course and along an almost imperceptible section of **Hadrian's Wall**, before finally reaching the small settlement of Greenhead (p225). If you're staying at **Holmhead Guesthouse**

(☎ 016977-47402; www.bandbhadrianswall.com; s/d £43/66), don't go into Greenhead; stick to the Pennine Way, over the railway line, past Thirlwall Castle and a river. The trail goes right past the guesthouse.

Day 13: Greenhead to Once Brewed
3 hours, 6.5 miles (11km)
Although today's walk is short it's still quite a work-out, following a roller-coaster route beside Hadrian's Wall. There's plenty to see, including a museum, and several places to buy food, so you won't need to bring along sandwiches. Alternatively, you could sprint this section and the next to get to Bellingham in a day.

For greater detail on the historical background of this section, see p216.

From Greenhead you regain the trail at the ruins of the 14th-century **Thirlwall Castle**, made from recycled blocks from Hadrian's Wall. From here a stiff uphill hike alongside the wall brings you to **Walltown**, where you can grab a snack and nip down the road to visit the **Carvoran Roman Army Museum** (☎ 016977-47485; www.vindolanda.com; adult/child £4/2.50; ⊙ 10am-5pm Mon-Sun mid-Feb–mid-Nov, to 6pm Apr-Sep).

The Pennine Way keeps following the route of Hadrian's Wall, through Walltown Quarry – now a nature reserve – and then along an excellent section of wall, built high on cliffs with great views to the north. Just past **Aesica Fort** (now a farm), a road drops down south; follow it and you'll shortly reach the **Milecastle Inn** (☎ 01434-321372; mains £9; ⊙ lunch & dinner), a cosy pub serving quality homemade food, including some interesting game pies.

Back on the route, well-preserved and impressive stretches of the wall rise and fall over Cawfield Crags and Winshields Crags. Stride along here, centurion-style, until you reach the car park at Steel Rigg. From here a road runs south to reach Once Brewed (p224).

Day 14: Once Brewed to Bellingham
7 hours, 15 miles (24.5km)
There are some more well-preserved and impressive sections of Hadrian's Wall at the beginning of today's route, but you soon leave this behind to wander through Northumberland National Park and the wilds of Wark Forest. In midge season (June to August) this
is where they start to be a nuisance. You'll need to pack your lunch.

From Once Brewed, regain the trail and head east along the wall's ridge-top route. You pass high above Crag Lough – a small lake – and shortly afterwards turn left (north) dropping down from the wall and entering the former land of the barbarians. **Housesteads Fort** (see the boxed text, p225) is less than 1 mile further east, off the route, and warrants a visit.

The trail crosses some marshy country between two larger loughs and enters the southern portion of the giant Wark Forest conifer plantation, before finally emerging to cross farmland, dropping down to Warks Burn and climbing up to Horneystead Farm.

A mile further is **Lowstead**, a fine example of a fortified 16th-century building called a 'bastle-house' and a reminder of that unsettled era when families had to be prepared for outlaw onslaughts. From here the route alternates between path, track and lane, passing the friendly **Shitlington Crag Bunkhouse** (☎ 01434-230330; www.pennineway accommodation.co.uk; camp sites for 2 £5, dm £13), with breakfast (homemade bread and honey) and evening meals available if ordered in advance. From here it's less than 3 miles to Bellingham.

BELLINGHAM
pop 1164
Pronounced 'belling-jum', this thriving little town has a helpful **tourist office** (☎ 01434-220616; Main St) in the same building as the **library** (⊙ 10am-noon Tue, 1.30-7pm Wed, 10am-4pm Fri; 🖳). Also on Main St are a couple of banks, one with an ATM.

Brown Rigg Caravan & Camping Park (☎ 01434-220175; www.northumberlandcaravanparks.com; sites for 2 £10), about 1 mile south of town, on the trail as it runs along the road, is well equipped with showers, a small shop and laundrette.

You can also camp or stay in the bunkhouse at **Demesne Farm** (☎ 01434-220258; www .demesnefarmcampsite.co.uk; sites for 2 £8, bunkhouse £15), in the town centre.

B&Bs include **Crofters End** (☎ 01434-220034; s/d with shared bathroom £22/44), a small place on the trail as you come into town; **Lynn View** (☎ 01434-220344; s/d with shared bathroom £24/44), opposite the tourist office; and the superfriendly **Lyndale Guest House** (☎ 01434-220361;

www.lyndaleguesthouse.co.uk; s/d from £35/60), be-tween Main St and the river. The top place to stay is **Riverdale Hall** (☎ 01434-220254; www .riverdalehallhotel.co.uk; s/d from £65/108; 🔍), which has a good restaurant (two/three courses £18/20), an indoor swimming pool and a gymnasium.

For self-catering there's the fine Village Bakery and a couple of **supermarkets** (🕑 8am-10pm) – stock up as this is the last place for more than basic supplies until the end of the trail.

Fountain Cottage Tea Rooms (☎ 01434-220707; mains £4; 🕑 9.30am-8pm Mon-Sat, to 6pm Sun), next to the tourist office, serves a decent range of light meals and is good value.

Oscar's Café & Bistro (☎ 01434-220288; mains £5-10; 🕑 lunch Mon-Sat, dinner Wed -Sat), just off Main St, allows BYO for its evening meals. The town's premier pub, the **Cheviot Hotel** (☎ 01434-220696; www.thecheviothotel.co.uk; s/d £32/56), also serves food and does B&B.

Day 15: Bellingham to Byrness
6 hours,15 miles (24.5km)

Enjoy this relatively easy walk through the contrasting moorland and forest of the national park before the final day's long slog. Don't forget to stock up on food in Bellingham, and to book ahead for accommodation, as options are very limited in Byrness.

The trail heads east out of Bellingham, crossing a wonderfully lonely sweep of heather moor for about 5 miles before dropping down to the start of a forest plantation. Sheltered by a wall, the trail climbs steeply, and muddily, up the edge of the plantation before levelling out and marching resolutely along, with forest to the left and moor to the right. A succession of marker stones along the fence line bears the letters 'GH': Gabriel Harding was the high sheriff of Northumberland and these reminders of the extent of his lands have stood on this remote moor for nearly 300 years.

The trail dives into the forest and most of the remaining miles are through fir plantations. You leave the trees near the tiny settlement of **Blakehopeburnhaugh** (unsurprisingly, the place with the longest name along the Pennine Way), where you can go through a gate and across the burn to **Border Forest Caravan Park** (☎ 01830-520259; www.border forest.com; sites for 2 £10, s/d £30/48), which offers a couple of comfy, motel-style rooms as well as camping facilities.

From here it's less than 1 mile along the valley to the scattered settlement of Byrness, where the trail crosses a footbridge and brings you to the busy A68 next to a little church.

BYRNESS

The only place to stay other than the Border Forest Caravan Park, the **Byrness** (☎ 01830-520231; thebyrness@jackson6961.fsnet.co.uk; camp sites for 2 £5, s/d £30/50) is something of a life-saver. The dog-loving owners of this B&B are very friendly and can prepare evening meals (£13) and packed lunches (£6), if given advance notice. Campers can also get a hot shower for £2 and order a full breakfast for £6.

Opposite is **Border Park Services** (🕑 café 8am-6pm, shop 8am-7pm), a petrol station that has a café and small shop.

BREAKING THE LAST LEG

The 26-mile haul over the Cheviots from Byrness to Kirk Yetholm is a cruel sting in the tail for Pennine Way walkers, but there are alternatives to doing it in one long slog.

The most convenient halfway stop is **Uswayford Farm** (☎ 01669-650237; nancy@alwinton.net; s/d with shared bathroom £41/72), which is only 1.5 miles southeast from the trail at about the 14-mile mark. The rates include evening meal. Because of its remote location baggage carriers won't pick up from here so, if you are having your bags transported, you'll need to carry an overnight bag with you and have your main bag sent directly to Kirk Yetholm. It's also possible to arrange with B&B owners in Kirk Yetholm to be picked up in **Cocklawfoot**, around 1.5m northwest of the route, and to be run back there the next day to finish off the walk. Both these options involve dropping down off the ridge and climbing back the next day.

If you have camping equipment you can spend the night under canvas, or you could over-night in one of the two mountain refuges along the trail. However, the first refuge (at 9 miles) is probably too early and the second (at 19 miles) is probably too late.

Day 16: Byrness to Kirk Yetholm
10 hours, 26 miles (42km)

The crossing of the Cheviots into Scotland provides a grand finale to the walk. It's also the longest, loneliest stretch on the whole Pennine Way, and can be very hard going, especially if the weather is bad. An early start is essential, as is a packed lunch.

Your blood will be pumping after the steep, 150m ascent out of Byrness. The next few miles are gentle, along the wide ridge overlooking the valley of Cottonshope Burn. After 4 miles you reach the border fence between England and Scotland, which you'll follow for much of the day, staying on the English side.

The trail passes **Chew Green Roman encampment** and the first **mountain refuge hut**, climbing over Beefstand Hill and other moorland bumps, which rejoice in names such as Mozie Law (something to do with controlling the midges?) and Windy Gyle (no comment needed). This latter peak (619m) is topped by Russell's Cairn, a huge pile of stones that was once a Bronze Age burial mound, marking the halfway point on today's walk. About 1 mile further on, a track turns off down to **Uswayford Farm** (see the boxed text, opposite).

After more rising and falling moorland, the trail climbs up to the head of a valley at Cairn Hill, where the border fence and the Pennine Way make a sharp left turn. From this point an official out-and-back diversion off the trail (not an 'option', say the purists) leads to the summit of the **Cheviot** (815m) – a 2.5-mile return trip. It's a straightforward ascent in good weather, but the view is rather dull and nonexistent in mist. ('Stuff it', say tired realists.)

Back at Cairn Hill the trail drops northwest to spectacular Auchope Cairn and then steeply to the second **mountain refuge hut**. (Look back to see the glacial hanging valley at Hen Hole.) From here there's one final slog up the Schil before the trail finally abandons the border fence and crosses decisively into Scotland.

Four miles from the end, there's a choice of routes. One stays low in the valley while the other goes through the hills for the final stretch. You may not want to be bothered with decisions at this stage, but the high route doesn't take much longer. The two routes meet 1 mile from the end to follow a lane into journey's end – Kirk Yetholm (p263), where the route ends at the bar of the Border Hotel.

MORE LONG-DISTANCE WALKS

THE RAVENBER
The Coast to Coast Walk described in this chapter famously takes you across the country, while the venerable Pennine Way leads south to north along the backbone of England. If you want to go coast-to-coast *and* south-to-north, try the 209-mile (336km) challenging route called the Ravenber, taking you from Ravenglass on the Cumbria Coast, through the Lake District, over the North Pennines and Cheviots, along the valley of the River Till to end at historic Berwick-upon-Tweed, on the England–Scotland border. The guidebook you need is *The Ravenber* by Ron Scholes.

NORTH PENNINES
To the north of the Yorkshire Dales and south of Northumberland is an area of hills and mountains called the North Pennines. The landscape is high, wild and impressive, the weather is often severe, the population is thinly dispersed and there are relatively few visitors. It is not a national park but it is an Area of Outstanding Natural Beauty. The tourist board bills it as 'England's Last Wilderness' and cynics say it has probably remained wild precisely because it isn't a national park.

Whatever the arguments, the North Pennines area undeniably has some marvellous walking opportunities. One of the best is Teesdale, the valley of the River Tees, where the Teesdale Way is a 100-mile (161km) route from Dufton, through Middleton-in-Teesdale and Barnard Castle and eastwards to finish at Warrenby on the North Sea coast. The first half of the walk is particularly good and doesn't hit urban developments until it reaches Middlesbrough. Guidebooks include *The Teesdale Way* by Martin Collins and Paddy Dillon.

The other major river valley in the North Pennines is Weardale, also lovely and less frequently visited than Teesdale. Upper Weardale offers more excellent walking, combining river-side paths and wild moorlands with evidence of the area's industrial heritage. Another long route, the 77-mile (124km) Weardale Way, runs along this valley from Killhope to Roper on the North Sea coast. For details see www.weardaleway .com.

YORKSHIRE WOLDS WAY

Billed as 'Yorkshire's best kept secret', the 79-mile (127km) Yorkshire Wolds Way is one of the least trod of Britain's national trails. It starts at Kingston-upon-Hull (always shortened to Hull) on the River Humber and curves north through rolling farmland, quiet villages and deep chalky valleys, to end at Filey Brigg, a peninsula on the east coast south of Scarborough that is also the end of the Cleveland Way (p252).

The Wolds Way is an ideal beginners' walk and is usually possible in five days. It can be done at any time of year, as the landscape is not high or strenuous and the area gets surprisingly little rain, although (as with any part of eastern England) in winter cold winds and snow can blow in from the east. For more details see www

.nationaltrail.co.uk/yorkshirewoldsway, or pick up the National Trails Guide *Yorkshire Wolds Way* by Roger Ratcliffe.

STAFFORDSHIRE WAY

Running for 92 miles (148km) through rural and semirural parts of the county, the Staffordshire Way passes through farmland, the woodlands of Cannock Chase and also skirts the edge of the Peak District National Park. The route starts at Mow Cop (near the town of Congleton) and ends at Kinver Edge (near the town of Stourbridge). A walker from Australia told us: 'We decided on the Staffordshire Way because it was described as 'showing the walker as many aspects of English scenery as possible along its length'. The route also provided easy access to villages and suitable accommodation – namely, old inns. The walk provided us with a truly marvellous experience. There was not one moment that could be described as boring.' For more information on this route, including available leaflets and guidebooks, the Ramblers' website (www.ramblers.org.uk/info/paths/stafford shire.html) is a very good start.

Wales

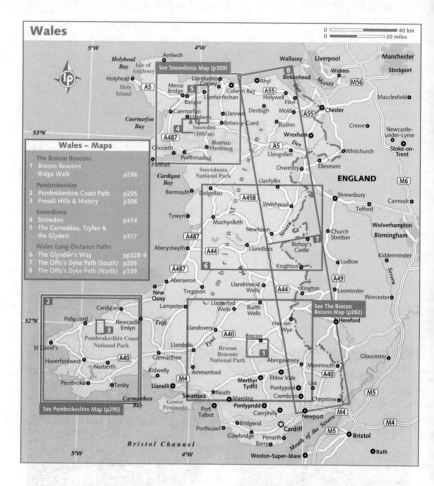

Wales

0 ——— 40 km
0 ——— 20 miles

Wales – Maps

The Brecon Beacons
1 Brecon Beacons Ridge Walk p286

Pembrokeshire
2 Pembrokeshire Coast Path p295
3 Preseli Hills & History p306

Snowdonia
4 Snowdon p314
5 The Carneddau, Tryfan & the Glyders p317

Wales Long-Distance Paths
6 The Glyndwr's Way pp328-9
7 The Offa's Dyke Path (South) p335
8 The Offa's Dyke Path (North) p339

The Brecon Beacons

The Brecon Beacons is one of the largest mountain ranges in Wales, forming a natural border between the wild and rarely visited highlands of the central region and the densely populated southern parts of the country. Although the Beacons cannot compare in dramatic terms with Wales' best-known peaks in Snowdonia, they are the highest mountains in southern Britain, forming a series of gigantic, rolling whalebacks with broad ridges and table-top summits, cut by deep valleys with sides falling so steeply the grass has often given up the ghost to expose large areas of bare rock.

As befitting an area of such dramatic scenery, the mountains and surrounding foothills are contained within the Brecon Beacons National Park (Parc Cenedlaethol Bannau Brycheiniog, in Welsh). Just to keep you on your toes the whole area is also known as Brecknockshire, and if those names weren't enough, there are four separate mountain areas within the national park: in the west is the wild and relatively remote Black Mountain and the lower and less austere hills of Fforest Fawr; to the east are the confusingly named Black Mountains (plural); and in the centre are the Brecon Beacons themselves – the area most favoured by walkers and with the highest summits – giving their title to the whole park.

Within the park you'll find a fantastic choice of day walks. The route we describe is along one of the most frequented sections but it's justifiably popular and provides an excellent introduction to the Beacons' beauty and walking potential. If you're tempted to explore further, we give some ideas for other walks in the area on p287.

HIGHLIGHTS

- Following the airy **ridge path** (p286) between the table-top summits of Pen y Fan and Fan y Big
- Admiring the view of the distant coast in one direction and the faint blue hills of Mid-Wales in the other from the peak of **Corn Du** (p285)
- Sauntering along the sylvan **canal-side path** (p287) into Brecon

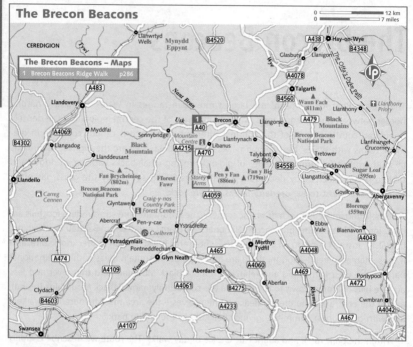

The Brecon Beacons

The Brecon Beacons – Maps
1 Brecon Beacons Ridge Walk p286

INFORMATION
Maps & Books
Most of the Brecon Beacons National Park is covered by Ordnance Survey (OS) Landranger 1:50,000 maps No 160 *Brecon Beacons* and 161 *Abergavenny & The Black Mountains*. For more detail, you will need OS Explorer 1:25,000 maps No 12 *Brecon Beacons – Western Area* (for the Black Mountain, Fforest Fawr and the Brecon Beacons) and 13 *Brecon Beacons – Eastern Area* (for the Black Mountains). Harvey Maps publishes two Superwalker 1:25,000 maps: *Brecon Beacons East* and *Brecon Beacons West*.

Guidebooks covering walking in the area include *Circular Walks in the Brecon Beacons* by local expert Tom Hutton, in the Walks with History series. *Walking in the Brecon Beacons & Black Mountains* by David Hunter suggests 30 routes between 3 miles and 13 miles in length, while *Walk the Brecon Beacons* by Bob Greaves includes a wide range of short and long routes with OS map extracts, colour photos and GPS information.

Guided Walks
The national park runs a very good series of guided walks and other active events during the summer, usually at places that can be reached by the Beacons Bus (opposite). You can get details from tourist offices or at www.breconbeacons.org.

Information Sources
The official national park site is www.breconbeacons.org and there's a lot of good information at www.breconbeaconsparksociety.org.

General tourism websites on the area, covering places to stay and eat, walking options and more, include www.brecon-beacons.net and www.brecon-beacons.com. Outdoor activities sites include www.bootsbikesbunkhouses.co.uk.

The main **National Park Visitor Centre** (Mountain Centre; ☎ 01874-623366; Libanus) is 6 miles south of Brecon. Other tourist offices in (or near) the Brecon Beacons – all with good information on the park – include **Abergavenny** (☎ 01873-857588; www.abergavenny.co.uk), **Brecon** (☎ 01874-622485; brectic@powys.gov.uk), **Crickhowell**

(☎ 01873-812105; cricktic@powys.gov.uk) and **Llan-dovery** (☎ 01550-720693; llandovery.ic@breconbeacons .org). All stock a good range of leaflets, books and maps covering the areas.

There are many YHA hostels in the area – see www.yha.org.uk. Alternatively, www .hostelswales.com lists bunkhouses and backpacker hostels in and around the Bre-con Beacons area, many in excellent walking locations.

GETTING AROUND

The Brecon Beacons area is well served by public transport, and there are two particu-larly useful bus services for walkers. The first is express bus X43, operated by **Sixty Sixty Coaches** (www.sixtysixty.co.uk), running along a dog-leg route through the park between Cardiff and Abergavenny via Merthyr Tyd-fil, Brecon and Crickhowell, with at least five services per day in each direction Mon-day to Saturday, and two services between Merthyr and Brecon on Sunday.

The other very useful service for walkers is the **Beacons Bus** (☎ 01873-853254) network, operating on Sundays and public holidays from late May to early September. Centred on Brecon town, there are interconnecting bus services to/from Hereford (1½ hours), Abergavenny (one hour), Newport (1½ hours), Merthyr Tydfil (45 minutes), Cardiff (1¾ hours) and Swansea (two hours), via all the main villages and attractions within the park, most with at least two services each way per day. You can pick up a timetable at any tourist office. Alternatively go to www .breconbeacons.org and follow the cumber-some links to 'visit the park' then 'Beacons Bus' to find the route map and timetable.

GATEWAYS

The main gateway to the whole Brecon Bea-cons area, and for the route we describe here, is the town of Brecon (p284), eas-ily reached from other parts of Britain by National Express coach, usually via Car-diff or Birmingham, where you may have to change. If you're spending time in the southeast part of the park, Abergavenny makes a good gateway. If you're exploring the west side of the park, gateways include Llandeilo and Llandovery. The Transport chapter (p453) lists public transport inquiry lines that provide details of both national and local bus and train services.

BRECON BEACONS RIDGE WALK

Duration	7½–9½ hours
Distance	14 miles (22.5km)
Difficulty	moderate
Start	Storey Arms
Finish	Brecon (p284)
Transport	bus

Summary A top-class walk, mostly through high, open country with steep ascents, fan-tastic views and a final flat section through peaceful farmland.

The route of the Brecon Beacons Ridge Walk follows, as the name suggests, the most impressive section of the central ridge that runs east–west across the mountain range. This route is popular, and the first few miles can be busy on summer week-ends, but that's simply because it's one of the best days out in the Brecon Beacons.

The route takes in the summit of 886m Pen y Fan (pronounced 'pen-er-van', mean-ing Top Peak), the highest mountain in South Wales, plus three other high sum-mits. On either side of the ridge the ground drops away into vast, bowl-like corries, with U-shaped valleys beyond, all formed by gla-ciers around 10,000 years ago. It's textbook geography and near the start of the walk you may see school groups struggling along the path, pens and soggy notebooks in hand, gamely attempting to take it all in.

In the final few miles you descend from the high mountains and follow the route through tranquil farms and woodland, to finish along the banks of a scenic canal near the meandering River Usk – a striking con-trast to the peaks, ridges, cwms and *bwlchs* (passes) of the high ground.

PLANNING

The walk starts at Storey Arms, a high point on the main road about 9 miles southwest of Brecon town centre. It ends at Brecon. You could do the route in reverse, but this involves a lot more ascent. There are a lot of ups and downs on this route, so with stops you should allow about eight to 10 hours. The route is not waymarked and there are no signposts on the high ground, so you'll need a map and a compass.

You can shorten the route by dropping off the main ridge earlier and aiming north to Brecon, following the old road that leaves the ridge at Bwlch ar y Fan, making the total distance about 10 miles.

On the route itself there's no café or pub for lunch, so take all you need from Brecon town (which has several shops).

When to Walk

You can do this walk at any time of year, although in winter (November to March) you really need to know what you're doing, as snow can block the path and ice can make it treacherous close to the steep cliffs and ridges. Even in other months the rounded nature of the highest part of the Beacons belies their seriousness. It can get wet and cold up here at any time, with winds strong enough to blow you over. Take appropriate clothing, plus a map and compass. You see day trippers with none of these things sauntering merrily along, but you also hear horror stories of people who get lost, sometimes fatally. Don't be one of them.

Maps

The walk route is covered by OS Explorer 1:25,000 map No 12 *Brecon Beacons – Western Area* and Harvey Maps Superwalker 1:25,000 map *Brecon Beacons East.*

WARNING – JAZZ FESTIVAL

Some years ago, a few musicians got together in a pub in Brecon for a bit of jamming. This developed into Brecon Jazz – now one of Europe's leading music festivals, held over three days in early or mid-August and attracting crowds of thousands. If you're into jazz, or just into good times, it's great – but accommodation is almost impossible to find. For more details see www.breconjazz.co.uk.

NEAREST TOWN
Brecon

pop 7901

The old market town of Brecon, on the northern edge of the park, makes a good base for this walk. Its Welsh name is Aberhonddu (pronounced 'aber-hon-thee'), and you'll see this on road signs. As a tourist centre it's busy in the summer, while Friday and Saturday nights are always lively, as pub crowds get reinforced by soldiers from the nearby barracks. As well as the official tourist sites covering the national park (also covering the towns in and around the park) listed on p282, see www.brecon.co.uk. The **tourist office** (☎ 01874-622485; brectic@powys.gov .uk) is in the Old Cattle Market car park.

SLEEPING & EATING

Options include the well-appointed **Brynich Caravan Park** (☎ 01874-623325; www.brynich.co.uk; sites for 2 £14), about 1½ miles east of Brecon; backpackers and walkers with no car pay £5 per person.

Hostel options include **Brecon YHA Hostel** (☎ 0870 770 5718; www.yha.org.uk; dm £14) at Ty'n-y-Caeau (pronounced 'tin-er-kaye') near the village of Groesffordd, 2.5 miles east of Brecon town centre.

There is also **Llwyn y Celyn YHA Hostel** (☎ 0870 770 5936; www.yha.org.uk; dm £14), about 7 miles southwest of Brecon town centre, just off the main road (A470), about 2 miles north of Storey Arms.

There are several independent hostels near Brecon, but all seem to prefer groups, except **Cantref Hostel & Bunkhouse** (☎ 01874-665223; www.cantref.com; dm £12, camp sites per person £3.50), about 2 miles southwest of Brecon, which accepts individual bookings Monday to Thursday. Other facilities include a café, horse-riding, activity centre, 'adventure farm' and Europe's longest sledge run (open all year).

Most B&Bs in Brecon are a few minutes' walk outside the town centre. Along a street called the Watton (the main road towards Abergavenny) are homely **Paris Guest House** (☎ 01874-624205; www.parisguesthouse .co.uk; d from £44); the **Grange** (☎ 01874-624038; www .thegrange-brecon.co.uk; d £40-48), a bright and airy place with good facilities; and the **Borderers** (☎ 01874-623559; www.borderers.com; s/d around £35/50), a former inn with low beams and a cottage-like atmosphere.

On the other side of town, there's more choice along Bridge St, including cheerful and welcoming **Bridge Café B&B** (☎ 01874-622024; www.bridgecafe.co.uk; d £45), which is also a very nice place to eat, with healthy sandwiches and snacks. Nearby is the **Beacons** (☎ 01874-623339; www .beacons.brecon.co.uk; d £42-57), a long-standing and popular guesthouse with a good range of rooms and friendly management.

All of the B&Bs have a range of rooms;

you pay a bit less if you don't mind sharing a bathroom with other guests. Most also have single rooms and family/group rooms available.

Brecon also has several hotels, including the historic **George Hotel** (☎ 01874-623421; www.george-hotel.com; d £65, mains £6-11; ☺ lunch & dinner) in the town centre, with a grand old staircase, comfortable rooms and attached bar and restaurant.

For food, Brecon also has several cafés, teashops and a surprising number of takeaways, including Chinese and Indian – plus, of course, fish and chips. The town centre has a good selection of pubs too, with most doing bar food in the evening, including the **Boar's Head** and the **Bull's Head**.

GETTING THERE & AWAY

Brecon is near the junction of the A470 (the trans-Wales route between Cardiff and Conwy) and the A40 (between Gloucester and West Wales).

It is easily reached from other parts of Britain by National Express coach, usually via Cardiff (1½ hours, daily) or Birmingham (four hours, daily), where you may have to change. If you're coming from the south or east, **Sixty Sixty Coaches** (☎ 01443-692060; www.sixtysixty.co.uk/service.htm) bus X43 runs five times per day through Brecon between Cardiff (1½ hours) and Abergavenny (one hours), via Merthyr Tydfil and Storey Arms.

The nearest train stations are at Abergavenny (via Newport) and Merthyr Tydfil (via Cardiff), both with regular trains to/ from the main line running between London and West Wales. From Abergavenny or Merthyr Tydfil you can get bus X43 (see above).

GETTING TO/FROM THE WALK

The route starts at Storey Arms, about 9 miles south of Brecon town centre on the main road towards Merthyr Tydfil. There was once a pub here, on the highest point of an ancient drove route (later the turnpike road, now the A470) crossing the mountains between South and Mid-Wales. Today the building is an outdoor centre and there's not a beer in sight.

From Brecon, bus X43 runs to Merthyr Tydfil via Storey Arms seven times a day from around 8am Monday to Saturday

(twice on Sunday, from about 1pm, so not much use for walkers on this route). Much handier on Sunday and public holidays are buses on the Beacons Bus network (see p283), running from Brecon to Storey Arms about four times a day from about 10am. Ask the driver to shout when the bus reaches Storey Arms, as it's easy to miss.

To reach Storey Arms by car is easy, and there are car parks nearby. However, if you park here and do the whole route, you have to get back to collect your car afterwards. As buses don't run after late afternoon, you're best bet is to leave your car in Brecon and catch a bus to Storey Arms *before* starting the walk.

If you miss the bus, a taxi from Brecon up to Storey Arms costs roughly £10. There's a taxi rank on the Bulwark (the central square), and drivers are well used to collecting and dropping off walkers.

THE WALK
Storey Arms to Pen y Fan
1½–2 hours, 3 miles (5km)

On the northeast side of very highest point of the main road between Brecon and Merthyr Tydfil, a gate and stile (next to a phone box) leads to a footpath that goes steeply uphill onto the moorland, with a patch of pine plantation on your right (southeast) side. Within a few minutes, you've left the busy traffic behind.

This first section of the route is often busy and the path has been 'pitched' with stones to help prevent erosion; it also makes it very easy to follow as it goes over the first ridge (about 1 mile from the start) and drops down into the valley of Blaen Taf Fawr, crossing the stream and up again to finally reach the ridge crest overlooking the lake of Llyn Cwm Llwch, below the obvious buttress of Corn Du (appropriately meaning 'black horn').

Another path leads down beside the ridge, past **Tommy's Obelisk** (see the boxed text, p286), but our path goes steeply up to the summit of **Corn Du** (873m), the last few steps over blocky rocks. You will have been walking for an hour or so, so maybe it's time for a breather. The summit rewards you with fine views north to Brecon, west over Fforest Fawr and – most spectacularly – east along the ridge, with Pen y Fan and the other table-top summits lined up for inspection. To the south you may catch glimpses of the Severn Estuary, with the coast of England beyond.

From Corn Du, the route is clear – assuming there's no mist! Go down the ridge and steeply up again, with Llyn Cwm Llwch to your left (northwest) and the Blaen Taf Fechan valley to your right (south). A few steep rock steps at the top of the path bring you to the summit of **Pen y Fan** (886m), marked by a large cairn and trig point. Here the views are even better: to the east, beyond Cribyn and Fan y Big, you can see the Black Mountains.

Pen y Fan to Llanfrynach
4–5½ hours, 7 miles (11.5km)
Take care leaving the summit of Pen y Fan, especially in mist. The path does not aim straight for the next summit (Cribyn) but goes south 'off the back' of the table top, with a view south of the Upper Neuadd Reservoir far down in the valley, before it curves round on the ridge crest once again. The Blaen Taf Fechan valley is still to the right (south), but to the left a new valley,

Cwm Sere, opens out, overlooked by steep cliffs on the northeast face of Pen y Fan. About 20 to 30 minutes from Pen y Fan you reach the summit of **Cribyn** (795m).

The path continues south then southeast, dropping over grassy slopes with yet another spectacular corrie (the head of Cwm Cynwyn) to your left. At a low point on the ridge called Bwlch ar y Fan, a track crosses the path. This is actually an old road; it's popular with mountain bikers and in March

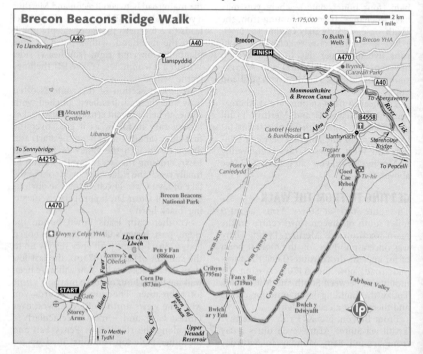

Brecon Beacons Ridge Walk

and September you may also see motorcycles and 4WDs churning it up. Fortunately, for those who come to the countryside for peace and quite it's closed to motor traffic the rest of the year. This track is also an easy-to-follow short cut back to Brecon for walkers – a useful escape route from the high peaks in bad weather.

Assuming the weather is good, our route goes up again; a short, sharp slog up to **Fan y Big** (719m), the final summit and the last chance to take in the wraparound views before descending.

From Fan y Big a broad, grassy ridge leads south, curving east then north round the head of the Cwm Oergwm. The path sometimes gets boggy round the right-angled bend at Bwlch y Ddwyallt, but the going is not too bad.

Several other paths join from the right, coming up from the Talybont Valley. Ignore these and continue northeast down the grassy ridge, with Cwm Oergwm on the left and great views back up the valley to Fan y Big and the other summits dominating the skyline.

About 2 miles from Bwlch y Ddwyallt, the path drops off the ridge, through an area of scattered bushes and small trees. You need to pay close attention to the map as you drop steeply downhill, keeping the tower of Llanfrynach church ahead and to your left as you descend to reach a stile (with a yellow footpath marker) in the corner formed by two fences separating fields from the open hillside. Cross the stile and head north downhill, aiming straight for Llanfrynach church now, through a patch of woodland marked on the map as Coed Cae Rebol.

Footpath markers lead you near to the ruined farm of Tir-hir, then along an old tarred track to meet a lane near Tregaer Farm. Turn right and follow the lane into Llanfrynach village.

This is your first brush with civilisation since leaving Storey Arms, so a pint or a bite in the **White Swan** (☎ 01874-665276; www.the-white-swan.com) in the centre of the village, may be called for – although it's usually closed from 3pm to 6pm. For refreshment of another kind, there's also a water tap in the churchyard wall, opposite the pub. If you want to skip the final part of the walk, bus X43 from Abergavenny comes through

Llanfrynach and on to Brecon every two hours, Monday to Saturday; the last one is at around 6pm.

Llanfrynach to Brecon
2 hours, 4 miles (6.5km)
From Llanfrynach follow the lane out of the village, with the church on your left and the White Swan on your right, to meet a road (marked on the map as the B4558). Turn right and continue for 400m to reach Storehouse Bridge and the **Monmouthshire & Brecon Canal**. Go over the bridge and through the gate onto a towpath, leading northeast before curving round to the northwest towards Brecon.

The towpath is a section of the Taff Trail, a long-distance path from Cardiff to Brecon, so you'll see more walkers and cyclists here. Follow this towpath for about 3 miles – a nice section of flat and easy walking – over an aqueduct and past a lock, into the outskirts of Brecon, to reach the canal basin near the theatre, where both the waterway and this walk terminate.

MORE WALKS

The route we've described here is just the tip of the iceberg (or top of the mountain, as the case may be). There are many more options for walking – as well as other outdoor activities – in the Brecon Beacons National Park.

BLACK MOUNTAINS
The Black Mountains are the easternmost section of Brecon Beacons National Park. You can use Abergavenny as a base but even handier is the pretty little town of Crickhowell, with a good range of B&Bs and hotels. It's on the X43 bus route between Brecon and Abergavenny (see p283) and gives excellent access to the surrounding mountains and valleys. The **tourist office** (☎ 01873-812105; cricktic@powys.gov.uk) stocks books and leaflets covering walks in this area.

The Offa's Dyke Path (p333) runs north along the eastern fringe of the Black Mountains from Pandy to Hay-on-Wye, and this section could be followed as a day walk. The views are spectacular but the route is along a high, grassy ridge that can be very windy. Pandy is on the A465, on the bus route between Abergavenny and Hereford.

If you follow all or part of this route, it's definitely worth dropping down to visit the ruins of Llanthony Priory, where the remaining buildings now house a pub and a delightfully atmospheric hotel.

The highest point in the Black Mountains is Waun Fach (811m). Reaching this on foot is a serious proposition. If you have a car, it's best to drive via Patrishow (an interesting 13th-century church in an idyllic location) to the end of the track in the Mynydd Du Forest. Follow the old railway track up to Grwyne Fawr Reservoir, where a path runs up Waun Fach. Alternatively, the peak can be reached from Llanbedr up to the ridge that runs north via Pen-y-Gadair Fawr. For this route, and others in this area, you need OS map No 13 *Brecon Beacons - Eastern Area* or Harvey's *Brecon Beacons East* map.

FFOREST FAWR & THE BLACK MOUNTAIN

In the western part of the Brecon Beacons National Park, neither Fforest Fawr nor the Black Mountain are visited as often as the main Brecon Beacons range, but they both have great scenery and several good walking opportunities.

To explore Fforest Fawr, the village of Ystradfellte is a good base. Along the rivers and streams to the south there are a number of attractive waterfalls, including Sgwd-yr-eira ('Spout of Snow'). There are other falls at Ponteddfechan and Coelbren; for details on routes, look out for the *Waterfall Walks* leaflet at local tourist offices. The hills of Fforest Fawr can be reached from the main road between Swansea and Brecon (the A4067) via Ponardawe and Ystradgynlais, served by a daily bus in each direction. Jumping-off points include Craig-y-nos Country Park and Dan-yr-Ogof caves, near the village of Gyntawe.

The Black Mountain is the westernmost part of the park. Note the singular, to distinguish this area from the Black Mountains (plural) to the east. The repetition of the name is not surprising, though – when the weather is bad any piece of bare, high ground in the Brecon Beacons deserves to be called 'black'. This western section of the park contains the wildest and least-visited walking country. The area's highest point, Fan Brycheiniog (also known as Camarthen Van; 802m), can be reached from the village of Glyntawe, between Sennybridge and Ystradgynlais, north of the industrial towns of Neath and Swansea. Maps for exploring this area include OS Explorer 1:25,000 map No 12 *Brecon Beacons - Western Area* and Harvey's *Brecon Beacons West*.

THE BEACONS WAY

For a top-class long walk in the Brecon Beacons National Park, you could consider the Beacon Way, a waymarked 100-mile (161km) high-level meander through the best of the area, from Abergavenny on the edge of the Black Mountains in the east to Llangadog on the edge of the Black Mountain in the west. Experienced walkers can do this in a week or eight days. As with all long routes, though, you don't have to do it all. There are some excellent one-day, two-day or three-day sections. For details see *The Beacons Way* by John Sansom or go to www.breconbeaconsparksociety.org and follow the link to the Beacons Way.

A shorter variation is the Black to Black, a 50-mile, five-day route crossing the park from Chapel-y-Ffin, near Crickhowell, to Llanddeusant, near Llandovery, keeping to the high ground and mountain watershed wherever possible.

There's no specific guidebook to this route, so it's ideal if you like to find your own way and have a sense of adventure.

Pembrokeshire

The county of Pembrokeshire sits comfortably in the far southwest corner of Wales, a peninsula jutting out into the waters (and, often, the winds) of the Atlantic. For many visitors, Pembrokeshire's main attraction is its dramatic coastal scenery. Without doubt, this is one of the most beautiful parts of Britain – an array of beaches, cliffs, rock arches, stacks, buttresses, islands, coves and harbours. You have to go to Cornwall to get anything like this, or to northwest Scotland for anything better.

This scenery is contained within Pembrokeshire Coast National Park, as are the offshore islands of Skomer, Skokholm, Grassholm and Ramsey (named by 10th-century Viking invaders). The park also features an impressive array of wildlife, including some of the world's largest populations of sea birds, such as shearwaters and gannets, as well as puffins, kittiwakes, cormorants and gulls, plus rarer choughs and peregrine falcons. Out at sea, seals, porpoises and dolphins are common, and there's even the odd shark. Paradise indeed.

Pembrokeshire's early human inhabitants were Celts, leaving their mark on the landscape in the form of ancient standing stones and burial sites. Even before this time, the menhirs of Stonehenge were quarried here, then transported to their present resting place in southern England.

Inland, and still within the national park, are the little-known Preseli Hills (Mynydd Preseli, in Welsh), the secluded Gwaun Valley (Cwm Gwaun) and the Milford Haven Waterway, one of the world's largest natural harbours, which upstream becomes the tranquil Daugleddau Estuary. These areas have just as much to offer as the more-famous coastline, but they're often overlooked by visitors, so if you're after solitude they could well be the place.

PEMBROKESHIRE

HIGHLIGHTS

- Striding out along the dramatic cliff-top paths round **St David's Head** (p301)
- Sauntering, boots-off, along the beach of **Broad Haven** (p299) at the end of a good day's walking
- Patrolling the ramparts of **Pembroke Castle** (p297)
- Loving the jolly seaside atmosphere of **Tenby** (p293)
- Walking through the mystical landscape of the **Preseli Hills** (p304)

PEMBROKESHIRE

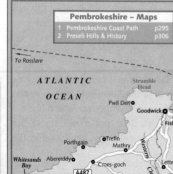

INFORMATION
When to Walk

The area is well known for its relatively mild climate, which means you can walk here year-round, although the coast gets hammered by some spectacular gales, especially in winter.

Maps

For walkers the handiest maps are Ordnance Survey (OS) Explorer 1:25,000 sheet Nos 35 *North Pembrokeshire* and 36 *South Pembrokeshire*.

Information Sources

Pembrokeshire tourist offices are run either by the local tourist board or by the national park authority. Most open daily in summer, with shorter hours and Sunday closing in winter. Tourist offices include **Cardigan** (☎ 01239-613230), **Fishguard** (☎ 01348-873484), **Milford Haven** (☎ 01646-690866), **Newport** (☎ 01239-820912), **Pembroke** (☎ 01646-622388), **Tenby** (☎ 01834-842404) and **St David's** (☎ 01437-720392). The main tourist information website is www.visitpembrokeshire.com.

It's worth noting that the county is often separated by tourist offices into South and North Pembrokeshire (divided by the Milford Haven Waterway), and it's surprisingly hard to get information on the north from a tourist office in the south (and vice versa).

The **national park authority** (www.pembrokeshirecoast.org) publishes a free newspaper called *Coast to Coast*, which is full of information on local events and public transport, plus tide tables and adverts for places to eat, stay or visit; it's available from tourist offices and can be read online at www.visitpembrokeshirecoast.com.

> **MIND THE LINE**
>
> Pembrokeshire's name in Welsh is Sir Benfro. English incomers first arrived in the 11th century (and still pour over the border each summer, usually as holidaymakers). Despite this, the Welsh language is alive and kicking, especially north of an ancient division called the Landsker Line, separating northern Pembrokeshire from the more anglicised south.

GATEWAYS

Pembrokeshire is easy to reach from other parts of South and West Wales, and also very easy to reach from England. The main gateway town is Haverfordwest, in the centre of Pembrokeshire, served by trains (a few per day) and National Express coaches (at least once daily) from London via Bristol, Cardiff, Swansea and Carmathen. There are also coach and train services to/from Birmingham and the Midlands. From Haverfordwest you can reach the other main Pembrokeshire towns of Tenby, Pembroke, Milford Haven and Fishguard by local bus or branch-line train.

PEMBROKESHIRE COAST PATH

Duration	15 days
Distance	186 miles (299km)
Difficulty	moderate–demanding
Start	Amroth
Finish	St Dogmaels
Nearest Towns	Tenby (p293),
	Cardigan (p294)
Transport	bus
Summary	Straddling the line where Wales drops suddenly into the sea, this is one of the most spectacular routes in Britain.

The rugged Pembrokeshire coast is what you would imagine the world would look like if God was a geology teacher. There are knobbly hills of volcanic rock, long, thin harbours formed from glacial melts, and stratified limestone pushed up vertically and then eroded to form natural arches, blowholes and pillars. Stretches of towering red cliff quickly give way to perfect sandy beaches, only to resume around the headland painted black.

The Pembrokeshire Coast Path (PCP) was established in 1970, and takes you from popular holiday spots to long stretches where the only evidence of human existence are the ditches of numerous Celtic forts. In the south, Norman castles dominate many towns and villages, and once held the Celts at bay, creating a frontier that still exists today in the Landsker Line – see the boxed text, left.

The landscape allows for all kinds of outdoor pursuits, whether rock climbing, kayaking, surfing or stretching out on a towel with a trashy novel. Marine life is plentiful, and rare birds make the most of the remote cliffs, with peregrine falcons, red kites, buzzards, choughs, puffins and gannets to be spotted.

It's not all nature and beauty, however. Several military installations require long detours along roads, and two whole days are dominated by the heavy industry of Milford Haven. Still, other manmade structures redeem our impact somewhat – beautiful St David's with its delicate cathedral, haughty Pembroke Castle and the pastel-shaded cottages of Tenby.

PLANNING

We've suggested a south-to-north route on the Pembrokeshire Coast Path, allowing an easy start in highly populated areas to build up to longer, more isolated stretches where you'll need to carry food with you. Some distances look deceptively short, but you must remember the endless steep ascents and descents where the trail crosses harbours and beaches. Referring to a tide table is essential if you what to avoid lengthy delays on a couple of sections.

The weather can be quite changeable, so bring wet-weather gear and something warm, even in the height of summer. During school holidays it pays to book ahead, as B&Bs, hostels and camp sites fill up quickly. Between Whitesands and Fishguard sleeping and eating options are especially limited.

Day	From	To	Miles/km
1	Amroth	Tenby	7/11.5
2	Tenby	Manorbier	8.5/13.5
3	Manorbier	Bosherston	15/24
4	Bosherston	Angle	15/24
5	Angle	Pembroke	13.5/21.5
6	Pembroke	Sandy Haven	16/25.5
7	Sandy Haven	Marloes	14/22.5
8	Marloes	Broad Haven	13/21
9	Broad Haven	Solva	11/17.5
10	Solva	Whitesands	13/21
11	Whitesands	Trefin	12/19.5
12	Trefin	Pwll Deri	10/16
13	Pwll Deri	Fishguard	10/16
14	Fishguard	Newport	12.5/20
15	Newport	St Dogmaels	15.5/25

Alternatives

If you're a strong walker, some days of this itinerary can be combined, particularly Days 1 and 2, or Days 12 and 13.

Using the extensive, cutely named coastal bus services (the Coastal Cruiser, Puffin Shuttle, Poppit Rocket and Celtic Coaster), operating frequently from mid-April to late September (pick up the *Pembrokeshire Coastal Bus Services Timetable* from any tourist office on the route, or online at www .pembrokeshiregreenways.co.uk), it's easy to jump sections or split the walk into manageable chunks. You could, for instance, base yourself in Broad Haven and plan a three-day walk (Herbrandston–Marloes–Broad Haven–Solva), or at St David's for a two-day walk from Solva to Whitesands.

Quite frankly, some segments of the walk are eminently skip-able. On Day 4 we recommend you catch the Coastal Cruiser 2 service from Bosherston to Freshwater West (25 minutes, four daily) to avoid up to 12 miles of dreary road walking. From here continue walking to Angle, where you can pick up the same service to Pembroke (35 minutes, four times daily). The next day, take bus 356 to Milford Haven (45 minutes, hourly Monday to Saturday) and then change to the Puffin Shuttle for Dale (35 minutes, three daily) and resume the itinerary partway through Day 7.

When to Walk

In spring and early summer, wildflowers transform the route with an explosion of colour, and migratory birds are likely to be seen. The height of summer will tend to be drier and more conducive to enjoying the numerous beaches on the route. Other mid- to late-summer advantages include migrating whales, flocks of butterflies and plenty of wild blackberries to snack on – a good payoff for walking in the heat. As you head into autumn, seals come ashore to give birth to their pups. Winter is generally more problematic, as many hostels and camp sites close from October until Easter and buses are less frequent. Needless to say, walking around precipitous cliffs in the wind, rain and chill may not be the most enjoyable (or safe) experience.

Maps & Books

The route is covered by OS Explorer 1:25,000 maps No 35 *North Pembrokeshire* and 36 *South Pembrokeshire*. The official National Trail Guide, *Pembrokeshire Coast Path* by Brian John, includes the coastal section of these same maps, but is cheaper and more manageable – with detailed route descriptions, albeit running north to south. More useful is *The Pembrokeshire Coastal Path* by Dennis Kelsall, which describes the route in the preferred south-to-north direction and includes detailed route descriptions, background information, line maps and an accommodation list. A series of 10 single-sheet *Trail Cards*, available from tourist offices and national park centres, covers the route, with basic maps pointing out sites of interest along the way.

Guided Walks

In May/June national park rangers lead a 14-day walk of the entire path (£180); for details contact ☎ 0845 345 7275.

Information Sources

There are national park centres in St David's, Newport and Tenby (see the route description for details), where you can pick up maps, guidebooks and, most importantly, the annual *Coast to Coast* newspaper (online at www.visitpembrokeshirecoast.com). With a coastal bus timetable and a tide table, it's not just helpful – it's essential. The **national park authority** (www.pembrokeshire coast.org.uk) website is also incredibly useful, with accommodation listings and abundant advice for walkers.

> **WARNING**
>
> The Pembrokeshire Coast Path is safe for sensible adult walkers, but parts of it are certainly not suitable for young children. At the time of writing, no-one has died on the path for 10 years – but fatal accidents have happened in the past. The path is quite narrow and often runs close to the top of sheer cliffs. Take great care, especially when you're tired, visibility is poor, the path is wet or in high wind (when your backpack can turn into a sail).
>
> Don't attempt to swim across river mouths and be aware that some beaches have strong undertows and rips. Particular care should be taken at Whitesands, Newgale, Freshwater West and Marloes Sands when the surf's up. Lifeguards patrol the areas between the flags every day during school holidays. Generally the beaches from Amroth to Tenby, on Day 1, are the safest.
>
> Don't pick up anything shiny in the military firing ranges, and definitely don't attempt to cross these zones when the red flags are flying, even if there's no guard to block your way.
>
> Probably the most dangerous stretches are where the route follows roads with no footpath. A particularly treacherous area is near the grimly named Black Bridge on the way into Milford Haven. Take care also at Wiseman's Bridge and between Little and Broad Havens. For these last two, you're safer crossing on the beach at low tide, but mind that you don't get cut off by the tide. Don't attempt a short-cut along any beach unless you're sure you can make it to the other end. If you get trapped, the best you can hope for is a sodden pack. At worst, you could be in real danger.

NEAREST TOWNS

The route starts at Amroth, near the resort town of Tenby, and ends at St Dogmaels, near the town of Cardigan.

Tenby

pop 4934

Perched on a headland with sandy beaches either side, Tenby is a postcard-maker's dream. Houses are painted from the pastel palette of a classic fishing village, interspersed with the white elegance of Georgian mansions. The main part of town is still constrained by its Norman-built walls, containing a mass of pubs, ice-creameries and gift shops, funnelling holidaymakers through the labyrinthine medieval street scheme. Without the tackiness of the promenade-and-pier English beach towns, in the off season it tastefully returns to being a sleepy fishing village. In the summer months it has a distinct Brits Abroad feel, with packed pubs seemingly all blasting out Status Quo simultaneously.

There's a **national park centre** (☎ 01834-845040; South Pde), a **tourist office** (☎ 01834-842402; unit 2, Upper Park Rd), which can assist you with booking accommodation along the route (for a £2 fee), and the last ATMs and internet café – **No. 25** (☎ 01834-842544; 25 High St; per 20 min £1) – before Pembroke.

It makes sense to arrive the night before starting the walk, leave your bags here and catch the bus to Amroth the following morning.

SLEEPING & EATING

Tenby has dozens of B&Bs and several nearby camp sites. The owners at **Meadow Farm** (☎ 01834-844829; vickyandbobburks@tiscali.co.uk; Northcliffe; sites for 2 £10) have walked the PCP themselves and offer camping right next to the trail, perched on the northern slopes overlooking Tenby.

Deer Park Guest House (☎ 01834-842729; deerpark@hotmail.co.uk; 12 Deer Park; s £18-35, d £36-70) is a pleasant B&B with young owners and a flower-bedecked terrace. More upmarket but just as friendly, **Rebleen Guest House** (☎ 01834-844175; www.rebleen.co.uk; Southcliff St; s £45-65, d £55-75) has some sea views.

It's not the quietest location, but the **Normandie Inn** (☎ 01834-842227; www.normandie-inn.co.uk; Upper Frog St; s/d £45/70) has massive en suite rooms right in the centre of town.

Next to the tourist office there's a **Somerfield** (☎ 01834-843771; Upper Park Rd) supermarket.

Fecci & Sons Ice Cream Parlour (St George's St; cone £1.30) is legendary, and was recently voted third-best in Britain.

For Indian cuisine and spectacular views, visit the **Bay Of Bengal** (☎ 01834-843331; 1 Crackwell St; mains £7-13; ☾ dinner).

If you can justify a splurge so early in the trip, **Plantagenet House** (☎ 01834-842350; Quay Hill, Tudor Sq; mains £15-22; ☾ lunch & dinner) is a gastronome's delight, specialising in fresh local seafood and produce. The house itself, with its massive Flemish chimney, is the oldest in Tenby – possibly from the 10th century.

GETTING THERE & AWAY
Tenby is easily reached by train from Cardiff (2½ hours, seven daily), while National Express runs direct coaches from a number of cities, including London (6¼ hours, three daily) and Manchester (8¼ hours, daily).

Cardigan
pop 4082
While not the most exciting place to celebrate your achievement, Cardigan is an easy walk from the end of the PCP, with a **tourist office** (☎ 01239-613230; Theatr Mwldan, Bath House Rd) and food and accommodation options.

SLEEPING & EATING
Highbury House (☎ 01239-613403; North Rd; s with/without bathroom £27/19, d with/without bathroom £46/37) is not as grand as it sounds, but offers cheap B&B close to the centre of things.

Brynhyfryd Guest House (☎ 01239-612861; Gwbert Rd; s with shared bathroom £21, d £45) is more pleasant, in a quiet side street.

The **Black Lion Hotel** (☎ 01239-612532; www .theblacklioncardigan.com; High St; s/d/tr £40/60/90, mains £7-14; ☺ lunch & dinner) is an atmospheric stone-walled pub with en suite rooms and home-cooked meals.

There's a large **Somerfield** (☎ 01239-615006; Lower Mwlden) supermarket and a great deli, **Ultracomida** (Cardigan Indoor Market, High St; panini £3; ☺ lunch Tue-Sat), which serves fantastic lunches.

Pendre Art (☎ 01239-615151; 35 Pendre; baguettes £3-5; ☺ lunch Mon-Sat) has a café attached, with free wireless internet access and a range of photos and paintings of the Pembrokeshire coast by local artists.

GETTING THERE & AWAY
There are no trains or National Express coaches from Cardigan, so catch a 460 bus to Carmarthen (1¾ hours, nine daily), which has plenty of connections.

GETTING TO/FROM THE WALK
From Tenby catch the 350, 351 or 352 bus from outside the tourist office to Amroth

(40 minutes, seven daily). From St Dogmaels you can walk the 2 miles to Cardigan, wait for local bus 405 (10 minutes, 14 services daily) or ask the pub staff to call you a cab.

THE WALK
Day 1: Amroth to Tenby
3–4 hours, 7 miles (11.5km)
Starting at a wide sandy beach, this short section is the perfect teaser for what's to come, allowing plenty of time for swimming and sightseeing.

A pair of bilingual brass plaques marks the beginning of the trail, near the eastern end of Amroth. Today's destination is clearly in sight, peering out behind rocky little Monkstone, which abuts the point at the south end of the bay. At low tide you can kick off your shoes and follow the shore all the way to Monkstone Point, although the official track takes the road and then follows the cliff tops along what was once a railway track. Just over an hour away, in Saundersfoot, there are places to eat and a **tourist office** (☎ 01834-813672) by the picturesque harbour.

The path continues through a wooded area, taking a short diversion down Monkstone Point before doubling back to come out into the fields near the large **Trevayne Farm Caravan & Camping Park** (☎ 01834-813402; www.camping-pembrokeshire.co.uk; Monkstone; sites for 2 £8). From here there are a few sharp inclines, with ever-nearer views of candy-striped Tenby (p293) along the way.

Day 2: Tenby to Manorbier
3½–4½ hours, 8.5 miles (13.5km)
Another brilliant day with breathtaking cliff-top views. There are a number of steep climbs, but the distance is mercifully short.

Lose the shoes and enjoy the first mile along sandy South Beach. As you near the end you'll be able to see whether the red flag is flying over Giltar Point. Don't get excited and break into *The Internationale* – the revolution hasn't started. It just means the military is using its firing range. Ordinarily the path takes you up around the cliff top, but when the flag is flying you're forced to make a diversion through the nearby village of **Penally**. This isn't all bad, as Penally has a pair of decent pubs and a church containing two Celtic crosses from the 10th and 11th centuries.

PEMBROKESHIRE

You'll eventually rejoin the cliff path to enjoy incredible views over Caldey Island. Head down to caravan-covered Lydstep, about two hours from Tenby, before hooking up the road at the other end of the beach, cutting across the point and regaining the cliffs as the path twists seriously close to sheer drops. Look out for the **Church Doors** limestone formation linking two beaches far below.

Soon you'll pass the futuristic grey-and-yellow **Manorbier YHA Hostel** (☎ 01834-871803; www.yha.org.uk; Skrinkle Haven; dm/d/tr £17/44/61) – a cross between a space station and a motorway diner. It was once part of the military base that still occupies the neighbouring headland, where you're forced to make an-

other detour away from the cliffs, returning high above the extraordinary red-limestone ramparts of Presipe Beach.

It all builds to a spectacular finale, with the path heading alongside a number of sudden, 20m-deep chasms. As you turn the corner and Manorbier comes into view, look out for **King's Quoit**, a Neolithic burial chamber fashioned from massive slabs of rock.

MANORBIER

The beach, 12th-century church and **Manorbier Castle** (☎ 01834-871394; adult/senior/child £4/2.50/1.50; ☼ Mar-Sep) are all worth exploring in this rather spoiled little village.

Friendly **Honeyhill** (☎ 01834-871906; www .bedandbreakfast-directory.co.uk/honeyhillb&b; Warlows

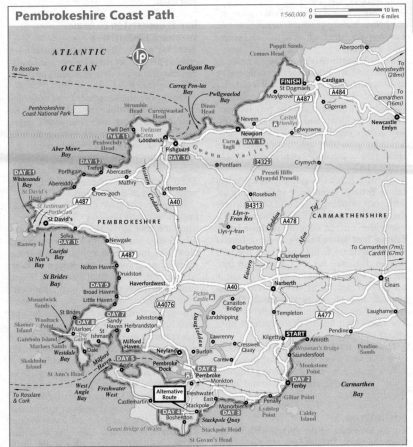

Pembrokeshire Coast Path

Meadow; d £40-50) offers baggage transfers by arrangement (50p per mile).

The **Firs** (☎ 01834-871442; 4 Longfield; s/d £45/65) is nicely renovated and offers a good breakfast selection.

Castlemead Hotel (☎ 01834-871358; www.castle meadhotel.com; s/d £43/86, 2-course meals £15; dinner, closed Dec & Jan) has fantastic views over the church and beach, and an upmarket restaurant.

There are further eating options at the **Chives Tearoom** (☎ 01834-871709; mains £7; lunch) and the **Castle Inn** (☎ 01834-871268; mains £7-14; lunch & dinner), and up the hill you'll find **Manorbier Stores & Post Office** (☎ 01834-871221).

Day 3: Manorbier to Bosherston
5½–7 hours, 15 miles (24km)

A slightly longer day, continually alternating between sheer cliffs and sandy beaches. Lunch options are limited, so consider taking food with you.

From Manorbier it's an easy 3.5 miles to Freshwater East. While not the surfie mecca of its western namesake, it's still a popular holiday destination. After another surging section of cliff you reach the tiny harbour of Stackpole Quay, and then pass two massive arches, one big enough for even large boats to pass through. From Stackpole Head you can proudly peruse your whole walk so far.

About 2 miles further, you reach a bay called Broad Haven (not to be confused with your stopping point on Day 8), where the trail goes inland slightly and crosses a footbridge on the edge of **Stackpole Estate National Trust Nature Reserve**. West of here is another military firing range, and the trail divides. If there's no red flag you can take the path along the coast, past several natural rock arches, to St Govan's Head and visit the tiny 6th-century **St Govan's Chapel**, set into the cliffs. From the chapel you follow a lane 1.5 miles north to reach the little village of Bosherston.

However, if the red flags are flying, you'll have to take a short cut inland through the nature reserve (a very nice route in its own right), over footbridges and round long, thin lily pools to reach Bosherston.

BOSHERSTON
To the southeast of the village, and not far from the track, **Trefalen Farm** (☎ 01646-661643;

trefalen@trefalen.force9.co.uk; sites for 2 £8, s/d with shared bathroom £25/50) welcomes campers and rents rooms. The proprietors have four more rooms at friendly **St Govan's Inn** (☎ 01646-661455; trefalen@trefalen.force9.co.uk; s/d £30/60, mains £4-12; lunch & dinner) in the heart of the village.

Across from the church, **Cornerstones** (☎ 01646-661660; john.jukes@virgin.net; s/d £32/60) is a well-established B&B; the owners will happily suggest other local houses if they have no vacancies themselves.

You can't visit Bosherston without stopping for cream tea at **Ye Olde Worlde Café** (☎ 01646-661216; sandwiches around £2; 9am-6.30pm). It's a local institution, having opened in 1922. It's still run by the original owner's daughter – who's slightly older than the café itself!

Day 4: Bosherston to Angle
5½–7 hours, 15 miles (24km)

There are patches of wonderful coastal scenery, but prepare for some tedious road walking, courtesy of the British Army. For tips to avoid this, see p292.

Quite why the army needs to use some of the most beautiful parts of Britain's coast to test its killing power is anyone's guess. Much of the next stretch is a tank-firing range, meaning that it's permanently off limits to the public. Other parts are open as long as firing isn't actually taking place. There's usually a schedule of the firing times posted in Bosherston.

If you're lucky, you'll be able to head back down to St Govan's Chapel and continue the trail along the coast – a beautiful 3.5-mile stretch with numerous caves, blowholes and natural arches, including the much-photographed **Green Bridge of Wales.** At Stack Rocks you still have to turn inland and begin the 9-mile road walk. With ear-splitting detonations from the range, very little protection from passing vehicles and high hedgerows hiding much of the view, this is not an enjoyable diversion. If you're unlucky and the red flags are flying, you'll have to take the road for an additional 3 miles west from Bosherston. The upside of this is that it saves you a few miles and gives you more incentive to wait for the bus.

You reach the coast again at spectacular Freshwater West, and the trail loops around the Angle Peninsula – another beautiful section with caves, tiny islands and little bays. At popular West Angle Bay you could easily cheat and follow the road 10 minutes to Angle village. Otherwise it's only an hour to Angle Point, where the path curves back into the village.

ANGLE

There's a **village shop** (☎ 01646-641232), a cute wooden-beamed church and a friendly local pub, but no accommodation in the village itself. Despite the 'no riff-raff' sign, the **Hibernia Inn** (☎ 01646-641517; mains £5-14; ✆ lunch & dinner) is very welcoming to scruffy walkers, and serves the usual pub grub.

On the eastern edge of the village, right on the PCP, the **Castle Farm Camping Site** (☎ 01646-641220; sites for 2 £5) offers very basic facilities for campers amongst the ruins.

Near Angle Point, the **Old Point House** (☎ 01646-641205; The Point; s/d £30/60, mains £8-13; ✆ lunch & dinner, closed Tue Nov-Mar) has four rooms available in a 15th-century cottage overlooking the oil refinery. **Hardings Hill House** (☎ 01646-641232; Hardings Hill; s/d with shared bathroom £30/50) has rooms 800m to the south.

Day 5: Angle to Pembroke
5–6 hours, 13.5 miles (21.5km)
Today the scenery turns industrial and there's nowhere to get lunch.

As you enter the Milford Haven estuary, the castles and church steeples that have dominated this landscape since Norman times are now dwarfed by the massive towers and domes of modern oil refineries. When they're not spewing out black smoke there's something almost majestic about the scale of them – although the novelty may wear off after two full days walking in their shadow.

The trail runs around Angle Bay and along the south bank of the estuary, alongside the vast Texaco refinery and past several tanker jetties. Your next highlight is the demolished power station, beyond which tracks, lanes and roads lead through medieval Monkton into Pembroke.

PEMBROKE
pop 7214
Pembroke Castle (☎ 01646-684585; www.pembroke castle.co.uk; adult/concession £3.50/2.50) was the strongest of the chain of keeps used to hold the stroppy Celts at bay. Henry VII, founder of the Tudor dynasty, was born

here in 1457, and the castle remained important until it was sacked and left in ruins by Cromwell's vandals.

Being the largest town since Tenby, there's a **tourist office** (☎ 01646-622388; The Commons Rd), ATMs and plenty of shops. You can check your email or buy licensed Harry Potter wands at **Dragon Alley** (☎ 01646-621456; 63 Main St; per hr £3).

Beech House (☎ 01646-683740; 78 Main St; s/d with shared bathroom £18/35) is a wonderfully kept 15th-century house, blanketed with flowers in season, offering B&B.

While not as classy, friendly **High Noon** (☎ 01646-683736; www.highnoon.co.uk; Lower Lamphey Rd; s/d with shared bathroom £23/49) has comfortable, clean rooms.

Once the townhouse for the Stackpole Estate, 250-year-old **Penfro** (☎ 01646-682753; www.penfro.co.uk; 111 Main St; s £45-70, d £55-80) is a sumptuous option; the grand entry hall has a heritage-listed staircase.

The misnamed **Pembroke Carvery** (☎ 01646-685759; The Commons Rd; mains £6-9; ✆ lunch & dinner) is a Chinese restaurant, right next to the tourist office.

You can't beat the castle views from the waterside deck of **Watermans Arms** (☎ 01646-682718; 2 The Green; mains £7-13; ✆ lunch & dinner), which serves a great beef curry along with local seafood specials.

Day 6: Pembroke to Sandy Haven
6–8 hours, 16 miles (25.5km)
The day starts urban and quickly becomes industrial. Make sure you check your tide timetable before setting out, or you may find yourself with a nasty detour.

The path takes you across the Pembroke River and round the backstreets of Pembroke Dock (a separate town), then over the large Cleddau Bridge, which does at least provide some views. Stay on the road until you cross a second bridge before following the river back down into Neyland. If you're camping, nearby **Shipping Farm** (☎ 01646-600286; Rose Market; sites for 2 £8) comes highly recommended. There's a large new gas terminal and a very dangerous section of pavement-deprived road before you cross the Black Bridge into the grim suburbs of Milford Haven. Beyond the docks there's a final section of grey suburban streets and, just for luck, another bloody gas terminal (Exxon) and – hurrah! – you're back to the national park and the beautiful coast again. From here it's a short hop to Sandy Haven.

The little estuary of Sandy Haven can be crossed (using stepping stones) 2½ hours either side of low tide (a tide table is posted by the slipway on each side). At high tide it's a 4-mile detour via Herbrandston and Rickeston Bridge. At Herbrandston the **Taberna Inn** (☎ 01646-693498; s/d £25/50, mains £10; ☺ lunch & dinner) offers B&B (shared bathrooms) and food in a popular pub.

SANDY HAVEN

Before the crossing, relaxed **Sandy Haven Camping Park** (☎ 01646-695899; www.sandyhavencamping park.co.uk; sites for 2 £9-11) has good facilities.

On the west side of the estuary, close to the trail, **Skerryback Farm** (☎ 01646-636598; www.pfh.co.uk/skerryback; s/d £30/55) offers B&B to weary walkers.

Further towards St Ishmael's, **Bicton Farm** (☎ 01646-636215; jdllewellin@aol.com; s/tw with shared bathroom £20/46, d £50) is another good B&B option.

Day 7: Sandy Haven to Marloes
5–6½ hours, 14 miles (22.5km)
Today takes you back to nature, with more ragged cliffs and deserted beaches, as the industrial plants dissolve into the distance.

From Sandy Haven there's 4 miles of fine, cliff-top walking to the Gann, another inlet that can only be crossed 3½ hours either side of low tide (otherwise it's a 2.5-mile detour via Mullock). The path leads into Dale, where you can grab a sandwich at the **Boathouse** (mains £3-5; ☺ breakfast & lunch), or a more substantial meal at the **Griffin Inn** (☎ 01646-636227; mains £4-12; ☺ lunch & dinner). A 10-minute walk through the village, past Dale castle, to Westdale Bay would save you 2½ hours, but cost you 5 miles of beautiful scenery around St Ann's Head. If you're tempted to linger, **Allenbrook** (☎ 01646-636254; www.allenbrook-dale.co.uk; s/d £35/70) has rooms in a beautiful ivy-covered country house right by the beach.

Two miles after Westdale Bay you'll see the remains of an abandoned **WWII airfield**. Above the impressive sweep of Marloes Sands, the sign to well-positioned **Marloes Sands YHA** (☎ 01646-636667; reservations@yha.org.uk; Runwayskiln; dm/tr £12/36) is three-quarters of the way along the beach.

As with Dale, Marloes village straddles a peninsula. From Marloes Sands head 1.3 miles to the northeast or you can continue on the PCP for a further 4 miles, where the village is less than 1 mile southeast of Musselwick Sands. There are two large camp sites right by the trail towards the bottom of the peninsula. **West Hook Farm** (☎ 01646-636424; sites for 2 £8) isn't far from Martin's Haven, while **East Hook Farm** (sites for 2 £8) is 1 mile further on. Both have similar facilities.

MARLOES
The best organised camp site on the whole route is at **Foxdale Guest House** (☎ 01646-636243; www.foxdaleguesthouse.co.uk; Glebe Lane; sites for 2 £9, s £35, d £56-60). Campers are provided with a bar, café and shop, and there are also rooms available.

Albion House (☎ 01646-636365; s/d £25/50) has basic, comfortable rooms in the heart of the village.

The pumping village pub, **Lobster Pot Inn** (☎ 01646-636233; s/d £25/50, mains £4-8; ☺ breakfast, lunch & dinner), offers rooms as well as standard pub meals.

The **Clock House** (☎ 01646-636527; www.clock housemarloes.co.uk; s £33-38, d £50-60, mains £6; ☺ lunch Tue-Sun, dinner Tue-Sat) is more upmarket and has a great café attached, serving excellent Mediterranean food.

Day 8: Marloes to Broad Haven
4½–6 hours, 13 miles (21km)
Another wonderful stretch along dramatic cliff tops, ending at an impressive beach.

Head back to Marloes Sands where, at the end of the beach, you pass Gateholm Island, a major Iron Age Celtic settlement where the remains of 130 hut circles have been found. You'll pass many such sites today – look out for the earthwork ramparts of promontory forts.

Martin's Haven, at the tip of the peninsula, is the base for **Skomer Island boat trips** (☎ 01646-603123; boat adult/child £8/6, island entry adult/child £6/free) and the office of the Skomer Marine Nature Reserve, with an interesting display on the underwater environment. Set into the wall next to the office is a **Celtic cross** that may date from the 7th century.

Around the headland the cliffs change from red to black, and after an hour you'll reach Musselwick Sands. **St Brides Haven** is a further 2 miles down the track, with the headland dominated by a Victorian faux-castle, once owned by the Barons of Kensington. A reasonably easy 5-mile stretch leads to Little Haven, separated by rocks from Broad Haven. From the path you'll be able to assess the tide and decide whether to follow the busy road or cross via the beach. Little Haven is a pretty village with restaurants and several B&Bs.

BROAD HAVEN

Broad Haven has a surfie vibe, with its wide stretch of sandy beach patrolled by tanned young lifeguards, and a variety of cafés, chippies and surf shops.

The **Broad Haven YHA Hostel** (☎ 01437-781688; www.yha.org.uk; dm/q £17/67; ☾ Apr-Sep) is excellent, with sumptuous sea views from its dining room and deck.

Both **Anchor Guest House** (☎ 01437-781476; www.anchorguesthouse.co.uk; The Seafront; s £25-35, d £50-70) and **Albany Guest House** (☎ 01437-781051; www.albanyguesthouse.co.uk; 27 Millmoor Way; r £54-56) offer rooms close to the beach.

Up the hill between the Havens, **Atlantic View** (☎ 01437-781589; www.atlantic-view.co.uk; Settlands Hill; camp sites for 2 £10, d £64) rewards yet another climb with great views.

The **Sea View Café** (3 Marine Rd; mains £3-6; ☾ breakfast, lunch & dinner) is a cheerful chippie staffed by cool surfie dudes, while **Nautilus** (☎ 01437-781844; Seafront; mains £8-16; ☾ lunch & dinner) is more smart, with a focus on seafood.

Day 9: Broad Haven to Solva
4–5½ hours, 11 miles (17.5km)
Don't be fooled by the distance – today's no easy stroll. There are several steep climbs, but thankfully the scenery remains superb.

Ancient fortifications are even more evident today as you follow the cliffs up from the beach. After an hour you should reach the **Druidstone** (☎ 01437-781221; www.druidstone .co.uk; s £44-48, d £65-143, mains £5-18; ☾ breakfast, lunch & dinner), a rambling old hotel and restaurant at the top of Druidston Haven, offering a range of rooms from basic to downright flash. Just down from the hotel, what looks like a Bronze Age barrow turns out to be an ultramodern home dug into the earth.

A further 30 minutes will bring you to Nolton Haven, a former coal port with a **pub** by the beach. From here the trail gets really steep, sweeping up and down the cliffs towards beautiful Newgale Sands – a

2.5-mile stretch of sand and arguably the best surf beach in Wales. Frustratingly, you can't get down to the beach until you've walked half the distance on the undulating cliff path. **Newgale Camping Site** (☎ 01437-710253; www.newgalecampingsite.co.uk; sites for 2 £10) has well-kept facilities and is perfectly positioned – by the beach and next to the **Duke of Edinburgh** (☎ 01437-720586; mains £4-7; ☾ lunch & dinner) pub.

As you pass over the bridge by the pub, you're crossing the Landsker Line (see the boxed text, p291). From Newgale the trail climbs back onto the cliffs. The 5-mile walk to Solva is along a rugged section with impressive rock formations.

SOLVA

Lower Solva is a touristy little village at the head of a peculiar L-shaped harbour, where the water drains away completely at low tide. Upper Solva is a few minutes further up the trail on the headland.

If you're camping, continue on the PCP a further 45 minutes and turn inland at a wide footpath leading up from a sheltered inlet. **Nine Wells Caravan & Camping Park** (☎ 01437-721809; Llandruidon; sites for 2 £8) has well-kept facilities, next to nine holy wells – popular with sick pilgrims during the Middle Ages.

In Lower Solva, right next to the river, **Gamlyn** (☎ 01437-721542; Y Gribin; s/d £24/55) offers bare-basics B&B. Much nicer is the **Old Printing House** (☎ 01437-721603; 20 Main St; s/d £25/50), with stone walls and hefty beams, which also operates as a tearoom.

Pebble Cottage (☎ 01437-721229; grace-pebble @tiscali.co.uk; 9 Prendergast St; s/d £35/50) is similarly character-filled, while the **Royal George** (☎ 01437-720002; r £60, mains £8-14; ☾ dinner) in Upper Solva is a lively pub with en suite rooms, some with sea views.

The **Harbour Inn** (☎ 01437-720013; 31-33 Main St; mains £7-9; ☾ lunch & dinner) does average pub grub, but it does have an ATM.

Caboose (☎ 01437-720503; 13 Main St; mains £5-7; ☾ lunch) is a bright and cheerful modern café with tables in a garden by the river.

The best restaurant in the area is the **Old Pharmacy** (☎ 01437-720005; 5 Main St; mains £13-36), with an emphasis on fresh seafood and local organic meats.

On your way out of town, you can stock up on supplies at **Solva Minimarket** (☎ 01437-729036; 19 Maes Ewan) in Upper Solva.

Day 10: Solva to Whitesands
5–7 hours, 13 miles (21km)

The spectacular coastline takes a spiritual turn, as you follow in the footsteps of Wales' patron saint.

From Solva, the trail climbs back onto the cliffs and the superb coastal scenery continues. After two hours you'll reach Caerfai Bay, a sheltered sandy beach with two wonderful, walker-friendly camp sites, right on the path. **Caerfai Farm** (☎ 01437-720548; www.caerfai.co.uk; sites for 2 £8) is organic and creates its own electricity from a windmill. Its small shop is your best option for lunch today, unless you decide to detour through St David's. Neighbouring **Caerfai Bay Caravan & Tent Park** (☎ 01437-720274; www.caerfaibay.co.uk; site for 2 £9) has similarly good facilities and sweeping views over St Brides Bay.

Around the next headland is **St Non's Bay**. Named after the mother of St David, this historic pilgrimage site is a supremely peaceful place. If you're cutting to St David's for lunch, it's a 20-minute walk along the marked path through the fields.

Back on the PCP, another half-hour brings you to Porthclais, with a landing stage and some lime kilns. Continuing round the headland there are good views across to **Ramsey Island**. The treacherous rocks close to the island are evocatively known as the Bitches. From the shore you can see and hear the tide rushing through the largest of them, the **Great Bitch**. Another 2 miles of easy walking will bring you to the busy surf beach of Whitesands Bay.

WHITESANDS & ST DAVID'S

There's not a lot at Whitesands, apart from a public toilet, telephone and a seasonal café. If you're lucky enough to find it open,

Whitesands Beach Café & Shop (☎ 01437-720168; packed lunch £3.50; ☺ weekends, daily school holidays & summer) can sort you out for food, caffeine, sun screen or surf gear. The nearby **Whitesands Beach Campsite** (sites for 2 £6) has basic facilities. About 800m uphill is **St David's YHA Hostel** (☎ 01437-720345; stdavids@yha.org.uk; Llaethdy; dm/d £16/40), a converted farmhouse with great views.

The microcity of St David's, 2 miles southeast, has both a **tourist office** (☎ 01437-720392; The Grove) and a **National Trust Shop & Information Centre** (☎ 01437-720385; High St). If you're staying longer, **Thousand Islands Expeditions** (☎ 01437-721721; www.thousandislands.co.uk; Cross Sq) will take you to the Ramsey Island Nature Reserve (adult/child £14/7) or for a three-hour whale- and dolphin-spotting cruise (adult/child £50/25). **TYF Adventure** (☎ 01437-721611; www.tyf.com; 1 High St; half/full day £45/85) seems to stick its oars into just about everything adventure-related – kayaking, surfing, climbing, abseiling and coasteering (everything your mother told you not to do around cliffs).

In St David's, **Y Glennydd** (☎ 01437-720576; www.yglennydd.co.uk; 51 Nun St; s/d £30/55) has a mixture of simple rooms, some with en suites and sea views.

A popular pub serving food, the **Grove Hotel** (☎ 01437-720341; www.thegrovestdavids.co.uk; High St; s £35-55, d £60-90, mains £12-15; ☺ lunch & dinner) inhabits a large Regency house.

Old Cross Hotel (☎ 01437-720387; www.oldcross hotel.co.uk; Cross Sq; s £38-62, d £68-105, mains £7-13; ☺ dinner) offers rooms and food, with friendly staff but a rather ugly restaurant.

Bryn Awel (☎ 01437-720082; www.brynawel-bb.co .uk; 45 High St; r £50) is a laid-back, walker-friendly home, where you can ease those weary legs in en suite bathtubs.

ONCE IN TINY ST DAVID'S CITY

Born in 462 where the ruined chapel stands in St Non's Bay, David was one of a number of missionaries during the pan-Celtic explosion of Christian activity known as The Age of Saints. He founded a monastery in the city that now bears his name and his remains are kept in a casket in the cathedral. It is this fascinating building that makes St David's technically a city – the smallest in Britain. Set in a hollow rather than dominating the skyline, this didn't stop it being sacked three times by Vikings.

The Holy Well at St Non's is said to have sprung up miraculously during the saint's birth. The current Catholic St Non's Chapel takes the form of the original, but was only built in 1934 – using stones sourced from old cottages, which had themselves been built from the ruins of nearby church buildings destroyed during the Reformation.

If you need to stock up on cash or provisions, this is your last opportunity before Fishguard in three days' time. There's a large **CK Supermarket** (☎ 01437-721127; New St) or you could spoil yourself with perishable deli items from **St David's Food & Wine** (☎ 01437-721948; High St).

Coffee is excellent at groovy **Pebbles Yard Espresso Bar** (☎ 01437-720122; Cross Sq; ☾ breakfast & lunch), and you'd be hard-pressed finding a more authentic Welsh country pub than the **Farmers Arms** (☎ 01437-721666; Goat St; mains £7-9; ☾ lunch & dinner).

If you're wanting to treat yourself, **Lawtons at No. 16** (☎ 01437-729220; 16 Nun St; mains £15-32; ☾ dinner, closed Sun Sep-Jun) is the place to do it – with a great wine list and a menu using quality local produce.

Day 11: Whitesands to Trefin
4½–6 hours, 12 miles (19.5km)
Wild St David's Head offers a rugged new landscape at the beginning of a beautiful but taxing walk, with several steep ascents.

From Whitesands the trail quickly takes you to **St David's Head**, an untamed outcrop scattered with boulders, and in summer painted with streaks of yellow and purple flowers. For the next 2 miles the only signs of human habitation are ancient, with the simple **Neolithic burial chamber** on the headland predating the surrounding remnants of Celtic forts. Adding to the primitive feel, herds of horses roam around freely.

After an undulating 3½-hour walk, the beachside settlement of Abereiddy reveals ruins from the industrial age. Another half-hour will bring you to Porthgain, another former quarry town – now a quiet village with a quaint harbour. The **Sloop Inn** (☎ 01348-831449; mains £5-15; ☾ lunch & dinner) provides an all-day bar menu as well as more substantial evening meals, while the **Shed** (☎ 01348-831518; mains £19-23; ☾ lunch & dinner) is an award-winning seafood bistro.

Don't worry too much if the food starts to weigh you down; it's an easy hour from here to Trefin and a well-earned rest.

TREFIN
Blink and you'll miss sleepy little Trefin (pronounced 'Treveen'). **Prendergast Caravan Park** (☎ 01348-831368; www.prendergastcaravanpark .co.uk; sites for 2 £7) is so well sheltered behind its hedges, it's difficult to spot. The facilities are excellent and well maintained, but you'll need to put a coin in the slot to get a hot shower.

Relaxed and friendly **Hampton House** (☎ 01348-837701; viv.kay@virgin.net; 2 Ffordd-y-felin; s/d £25/50) has three simple rooms, including one double with an en suite. **Bryngarw Guest House** (☎ 01348-831221; www.bryngarwguesthouse .co.uk; Abercastle Rd; s/d £40/60) is more established, with some impressive sea views.

The only dinner option is the **Ship Inn** (☎ 01348-831445; mains £7-15; ☾ lunch & dinner), serving typically uninspiring but hearty pub food.

Day 12: Trefin to Pwll Deri
3½–4½ hours, 10 miles (16km)
Today's walk is yet another wonderful experience, with cliffs, rock buttresses, pinnacles, islets, bays and beaches. It's tempered by a distinct paucity of eating and accommodation options.

From Trefin it's an easy 3 miles to Abercastle. Before you reach the small beach, take a short detour over the stiles to **Carreg Sampson** – a 5000-year-old burial chamber with a capstone over 5m long. After another 4 miles you'll reach sandy Aber Mawr beach. One mile to the south, through the woods, **Presell Venture Adventure Lodge** (☎ 01348-837709; www.preseliventure.com; Parcynole Fach; per person £30) is a good sleeping option for groups, but only takes individual walkers on the weekend. Attached to a small outdoor activities centre, you can linger here and indulge in kayaking, coasteering and the like, starting from £39 for a half-day.

The headland of Penbwchdy is the beginning of one of the most impressive stretches of cliff on the whole path. If the weather is good you can see all the way back to St David's Head. If it's windy you may be thankful for the circular dry-stone shepherds' shelter here. Either way, it's a wild 40-minute walk to join the road above the bay of Pwll Deri, where there's another stunning view back along the cliffs.

PWLL DERI
The **Pwll Deri YHA Hostel** (☎ 01348-891385; pwllderi@yha.org.uk; Castell Mawr, Trefasser; dm/tw £15/30) must have one of the finest locations of any hostel in Britain. Apart from the options listed in the route description, there is no other accommodation or food

nearby. If you're a strong walker you could head straight on to Fishguard. Another option would be to catch the Strumble Shuttle to Fishguard (30 minutes, three daily, in winter three weekly) from either Trefasser Cross (1 mile inland) or Strumble Head (3 miles further on the PCP) and then catch it back to pick up the trail the next day.

Day 13: Pwll Deri to Fishguard
3½–4½ hours, 10 miles (16km)

There's excellent cliff scenery and reasonably easy walking on this deserted section, but come prepared or you may be very hungry by the time you reach Goodwick.

From Pwll Deri the trail leads along the cliffs for 3 miles to the impressive promontory of Strumble Head, marked by its famous **lighthouse**. One mile inland you can pitch a tent at **Tresinwen Farm** (☎ 01348-891238; sites for 2 £4). About 3 miles further on you reach Carregwastad Point, where the last invasion of Britain occurred around 200 years ago (see the boxed text, right). Shortly after this, the small wooded valley of Cwm Felin comes as a surprise in this otherwise windswept landscape.

An hour later you round the headland and with a sudden jolt there's Fishguard – the largest town since Milford Haven.

Although close, the villages of Goodwick, Fishguard and Lower Fishguard are quite distinct. Goodwick (Wdig, in Welsh), pronounced 'Goodick', has the train station, the beach and the port for ferries to Ireland.

Glendower Hotel (☎ 01348-872873; glendower hotel@hotmail.com; Goodwick Sq; s/d £39/69) has basic rooms above a popular local pub. A more stylish option is the recently renovated **Hope & Anchor Inn** (☎ 01348-872314; www.hopeand anchorinn.co.uk; Goodwick Sq; d £60-70, mains £10-13; 🕑 lunch & dinner), with an excellent restaurant attached.

The **Rose & Crown** (☎ 01348-874449; Goodwick Sq; mains £5-7; 🕑 lunch & dinner) has a shabby charm, with a chamber-pot collection decorating the lounge bar.

The trail drops down to the port of Goodwick to come out by the ferry quay, then past a roundabout at the bottom of the hill. Nearby, there's a **tourist office** (☎ 01348-872037; The Ocean Lab, The Parrog) with a **cybercafé** (per 30min £2). Along the waterfront there are a series of interesting historical plaques and mosaics illustrating the history of the area.

Alongside the road, Goodwick Moor was the site of the 1078 battle between northern and southern Celtic chieftains (as if they didn't have enough to worry about from the Normans), culminating in a bloody massacre of the southerners. From here the trail climbs steeply up to the cliffs skirting Fishguard. Stay with it until you reach a viewpoint overlooking Lower Fishguard, then go up the street called Penslade, which will bring you out on West St, very near the town centre.

THE FISHGUARD INVASION

While Hastings may get all the press, the last invasion of Britain was actually at Carregwastad Head in 1797. The rag-tag collection of 1400 French mercenaries and bailed convicts, led by an Irish-American named Colonel Tate, had hoped that the British peasants would rise up to join them in revolutionary fervour. Unsurprisingly, their drunken pillaging didn't endear them to the locals, and the French were quickly seen off by volunteer 'yeoman' soldiers, with help from the people of Fishguard, including, most famously, one Jemima Nichols, who single-handedly captured 12 mercenaries armed with nothing more than a pitchfork.

FISHGUARD

Fishguard (Abergwaun, in Welsh) is larger and more interesting than Goodwick, with ATMs, shops and a wider choice of places to stay, eat and drink. The **tourist office** (☎ 01348-873484) is temporarily housed in the library (High St) but due to return to the town hall (Market Sq) in late 2007. There are two stone circles, but before you start preparing to dance skyclad, be aware that they were built in 1936 and 1986 to coincide with the town's hosting of the Eisteddfod.

Hamilton Backpackers Lodge (☎ 01348-874797; www.hamiltonbackpackers.co.uk; 21 Hamilton St; dm/d £14/36) is a cheerful place with good communal areas, including a kitchen.

Avon House (☎ 01348-874476; www.avon-house .co.uk; 76 High St; s £20-33, d £45) offers comfortable, quiet B&B with a mix of rooms with and without en suite.

The walker-friendly **Manor Town House** (☎ 01348-873260; www.manortownhouse.com; Main St;

s £35-40, d £60-75) inhabits a charming two-storey Georgian building with views over the bay. For £5 it will transport your bags anywhere between St David's and Newport. A couple of doors away, in a similar setting, **Basilico** (☎ 01348-871845; 3 Main St; s £45, d £60-70, mains £7-13; ☷ lunch Wed-Fri, dinner Tue-Sun) is predominately a wonderful Italian restaurant, but has a couple of attractive large rooms upstairs.

There's a **Somerfield** (☎ 01348-872566; High St) supermarket, and you won't find it difficult to find a pub – the **Royal Oak Inn** (☎ 01348-872514; Market Sq; mains £7-11; ☷ lunch & dinner) is a must-visit. Loaded with character, the table where the treaty ending the Fishguard Invasion (see the boxed text, opposite) was signed takes pride of place at the back of the dining room.

For a completely different buzz, **barfive** (☎ 01348-875050; 5 Main St; mains £10-14; ☷ lunch & dinner Tue-Sat) is a hip, upmarket bar and restaurant in a cleverly renovated Georgian townhouse. Despite the city-slicker ambience, you might be surprised to know that the owner catches the lobsters and crabs himself.

Lower Fishguard (Cwm, in Welsh) is a sleepy harbour with pretty stone cottages, a pub and not a lot else. It was the location for the 1971 film of Dylan Thomas' *Under Milk Wood*. There are a couple of B&Bs, including quiet **Ael y Bryn** (☎ 01348-874733; aelybrynfishguard@hotmail.co.uk; Glynymel Rd; s £45, d £50-60).

If you continue on the path for a further 2.5 miles there's camping at the **Fishguard Bay Caravan & Camping Park** (☎ 01348-811415; www.fishguardbay.com; Garn Gelli; sites for 2 £10-12), with showers with free hot water, as well as a shop, laundrette and TV lounge.

Day 14: Fishguard to Newport
5–6 hours, 12.5 miles (20km)
There are superb views from the cliffs on this section, but only one lunch option.

Leaving Fishguard, follow the trail round picturesque Lower Fishguard and then out along the cliff tops once again.

About 4 miles on, at the small bay of Pwllgwaelod, **Old Sailors** (☎ 01348-811491; mains £8-12; ☷ lunch & dinner) is a good lunch stop. It's possible to take a short cut to Cwm-yr-Eglwys through the valley that almost divides Dinas Head from the mainland, but

don't be tempted – Dinas Head offers a wonderful walk where you might spot seals and dolphins.

From Cwm-yr-Eglwys it's only 3 miles on to Y Parrog, the old port of Newport, where you'll find the **Morawelon Camping & Caravanning Park** (☎ 01239-820565; carreg@morawelon.fsnet.co.uk; sites for 2 £10), with a café and shop attached. From here, continue to follow the PCP through a small wooded section, turning right at the fingerpost to the YHA and you'll hit the centre of Newport.

NEWPORT
pop 1120
Newport (Trefdraeth, in Welsh) is very Welsh (good luck with the street signs) and a great rest stop. Its modern conveniences (shops, a bank, several bars and excellent restaurants) are matched with a gloomy, ruined Norman castle and a prehistoric burial site, **Careg Coetan**, well signposted from the road just past the Golden Lion. At first glance it looks like the giant capstone is securely supported by the four standing stones. A closer inspection suggests that some druid magic has held if together all these thousands of years, as it's precariously balanced on only two of them.

Trefdraeth YHA Hostel (☎ 01239-820080; reservations@yha.org.uk; Old School Business Centre, Hed Fair Isaf; dm/d/tr £16/35/50) is well set up and central, with a number of bunkrooms of different sizes.

If you're fond of dogs (there's a miniature English bull terrier in residence) and cute 18th-century stone cottages, the **Globe** (☎ 01239-820296; www.theglobepembs.co.uk; Hoel Fair Uchaf; s/d £35/50) has character-filled rooms that share a bathroom.

The **Golden Lion** (☎ 01239-820321; www.goldenlionpembs.co.uk; East St; s £35-40, d £55-60, mains £8-10; ☷ lunch & dinner) is a large, friendly pub with en suite rooms and an overflow cottage across the road with a shared bathroom. Unfortunately, the 2ft-thick walls don't block out the sound of happy punters rolling their way home.

A quieter option is **Cnapan** (☎ 01239-820575; www.cnapan.co.uk; East St; s/d £45/76, 2-course meal £22; ☷ lunch & dinner), which has an upmarket restaurant serving interesting home-cooked meals.

Doctor's Court/Llys Meddyg (☎ 01239-820008; www.doctorscourt.com; East St; s £75, d £90-120; ☐)

PEMBROKESHIRE

IT'S ALL WELSH TO ME

One thing that makes Wales so distinctive is the survival of Welsh as a living language. Welsh, with its long chains of consecutive consonants, is part of the Celtic group of languages, which includes Scots Gaelic, Irish, Manx, Cornish and Breton. The language as it is spoken today, although later influenced by French and English, seems to have been fully developed by the 6th century, making it one of Europe's oldest languages. Despite English colonisation, Welsh is still the first language for many, especially in the north. In 1967 the *Welsh Language Act* ensured that Welsh-speakers could use their own language in court, and in 1994 it became illegal to discriminate against Welsh speakers in employment. Since then Welsh has claimed its rightful place on the airwaves, on street signs and, increasingly, in popular culture.

---

is a great opportunity for a splurge. This Georgian townhouse has handsome rooms with interesting art, walk-in wardrobes and a digital selection of music and movies. If this doesn't tempt you, you can still indulge at the posh restaurant (mains £14 to £19), or have a great relaxed meal in the idyllic Kitchen Garden (mains £8 to £15).

If you prefer feeding yourself, **Bwydydd Cyflawn Trefdraeth** (☎ 01239-820773; East St) has an excellent selection of organic wholefoods. Another relaxed option for lunch or an early dinner is **Café Fleur** (☎ 01239-820131; Hoel-y-farchnad (Market St); mains £5-11; ☼ lunch & dinner).

Day 15: Newport to St Dogmaels
6–8 hours, 15.5 miles (25km)
We've saved the longest, steepest day till last – when those newly formed, rock-like thighs and buns of steel can best handle it. Grab a packed lunch and head for the finish line, enjoying some of the best walking of the whole route.

East of Newport Sands the coast along the first half of this section is wild and un-inhabited, with numerous rock formations and caves. Pwll-y-Wrach, the Witches' Cauldron, is the remains of a collapsed cave. You may see Atlantic grey seals on the rocks nearby. Onwards from Ceibwr Bay is quite tough, but it's a wonderful roller-coaster finale, past sheer cliffs reaching a height of 175m – the highest of the trail.

At Cemaes Head stop and take stock. The end of the trail is nigh but aesthetically this headland is the finish. So, turning your back on the cliffs, follow the lane towards St Dogmaels and Cardigan. The **Poppit Sands YHA Hostel** (☎ 01239-612936; www.yha.org.uk; dm/d £18/40) is 1.5 miles further on, giving you an op-portunity to stop and enjoy the sandy dunes rather than rushing back to normal life.

One mile past the hostel you leave the national park, and a plaque on a wall seems like the end of the trail. Don't celebrate just yet. The actual end is a couple of miles fur-ther on, unmarked, near a carved wooden mermaid as you enter St Dogmaels village. Now you can pop the champagne! There are a couple of pubs nearby to facilitate this, the closest and most upmarket being the **Ferry Inn** (☎ 01239-615172; Poppit Rd; mains £7-21; ☼ lunch & dinner). The friendliest is the **White Hart Inn** (☎ 01239-612099; Finch St; mains £5-12; ☼ lunch & din-ner), if you can bear the walk to the other side of the village, on the way to Cardigan.

PRESELI HILLS & HISTORY

Duration	6–8 hours
Distance	15 miles (24km)
Difficulty	moderate
Start/Finish	Newport (p303)
Transport	bus

Summary A delightful walk through var-ied scenery – farmland, open moorland and wooded valleys – with great views of the coast and a historical flavour.

The Preseli Hills are the highest points in Pembrokeshire, and in the whole of West Wales, but remain relatively little known thanks to the proximity of the much more famous coastline just a few miles away. This means a lack of crowds and the chance to enjoy your walking undisturbed apart from the sound of sheep and birds – and some-times the wind.

The views from the summits are excep-tional, despite their modest altitudes. The bays and beaches of the Pembrokeshire coast can be seen of course, and on a clear day you can see as far as the Gower Peninsula to the southeast and even to the mountains of Snowdonia in the north. In extremely fine conditions you may even see the Wicklow Hills in Ireland.

Nearer at hand, the Preseli Hills area boasts an abundance of monuments from the Iron Age, Bronze Age and Neolithic eras. A glance at a map will show that the landscape is dotted with hut circles, burial chambers, hillforts, old trackways and standing stones. The ancient inhabitants of Britain believed the hills had mystical powers, and the famous menhirs of Stonehenge were carried from here to Salisbury Plain.

The route we describe gives you a taste of this magical, mystical area. From the small coastal town of Newport you cross the moorlands around the peak of Carn Ingli, dip into the tranquil Gwaun Valley, then rise again to wilder moors, before looping back to the start via the woods of Sychbant.

PLANNING
This circuit of the Preseli (sometimes spelled Presely or Preselli) Hills starts and ends at the small town of Newport. Do not confuse this place with the large city of Newport in Gwent, southeast Wales, or any of the several other places in Britain that share the name. The town's Welsh name is Trefdreath (Town on the Beach) and the hills' name in Welsh is Mynydd Preseli.

The route can be walked in either direction, but an ascent of Carn Ingli is best done near the beginning so that you get a preview of the splendours to come. Paths are generally well marked, although indistinct in places and boggy after rain, but this route is not waymarked, so a map is definitely required. There's a reasonable amount of ascent and descent (though nothing very serious), and you should allow about an hour for lunch or looking at ancient monuments – longer if you're a big eater or historian.

Alternative
If you want to trim the distance, from Llanerch you can go straight down the Gwaun Valley to Sychbant, missing out the southern part of the route, making a total of around 8 miles.

When to Walk
You can do this route in any season, but although the hills are not particularly high,

they are exposed. A strong wind (with rain) can blow at any time of year and there's an occasional covering of snow in winter, so take appropriate clothing.

Maps & Books
The OS Landranger 1:50,000 map No 145 *Cardigan/Aberteifi & Mynydd Preseli* fully covers this area. For more detail use the OS Explorer 1:25,000 map No 36 *South Pembrokeshire*.

Guidebooks specifically covering the Preseli Hills include *Walking in the Presely Hills* by Brian John, describing seven circular walks. The same author has also produced *Five Circular Walks around the Upper Gwaun Valley* and *Bluestone Country – The Carningli Walks,* packed full of useful information on history and ecology, as well as route descriptions.

Guided Walks
National park rangers run guided walks in the Preseli Hills. You'll find details at the Newport tourist office, or in the free visitor newspaper *Coast to Coast*. For longer walking trips – guided and self-guided – through the Preselis and other parts of the 'Pembrokeshire Heartlands', see www.greenwaysholidays.com.

Information Sources
Newport's seasonal **tourist office** (☎ 01239-820912; info@newporttic.fsnet.co.uk) can assist with information on the area and accommodation options. If this is closed, contact one of the larger tourist offices listed on p290. See also www.pembrokeshirecoast.org.uk.

GETTING TO/FROM THE WALK
See p291 for details on National Express coaches and trains from outside the region to the gateways of Haverfordwest, Pembroke, Fishguard and Cardigan. There's a daily local bus almost hourly (twice each way on Sunday) between Fishguard (20 minutes) and Cardigan (30 minutes) via Newport.

THE WALK
Newport to Llanerch
2–2½ hours, 3 miles (5km)
From the centre of Newport, take Market St then Church St uphill, past the castle on your right. At a fork in the lane called College Sq, go right, uphill, following narrow

tracks past a couple of farms and houses, up through an area called Carn Cwm to reach a gate leading onto the open hillside of **Carn Llwyd**. Work your way up on grassy paths through the bracken to the summit. It's steep in places, so while you stop to catch your breath, don't forget to look back and admire the view.

From this summit, keep heading south, and still steeply up, to reach the summit of **Carn Ingli**. The name means 'Peak of Angels' and it's certainly a heavenly view. This is also the site of an Iron Age hillfort, fully exploiting the precipitous hillsides as natural defence. It's a scramble over rocks up to the top, so take time here to rest as you admire the 360-degree vista.

From Carn Ingli summit take the path down the southeast side of the hill to reach a lane. Turn right and follow this lane, past the farms of Dolrannog Isaf and Dolrannog Uchaf, where the lane becomes a dirt track, and down through a tranquil stretch of woodland to reach the farm at Llanerch and the lane that runs down the Gwaun Valley.

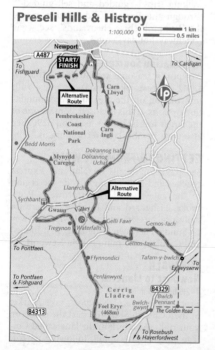

Preseli Hills & Histroy

If you are taking the short cut (see Alternative on p305), turn right (west) along the valley road towards Sychbant.

Llanerch to Sychbant
3–4 hours, 7.5 miles (12km)

If you are going for the southern part of this route, follow the road straight on (southeast) for 200m then, where the lane swings round to the left, you go straight on, over a gate and along a path through some more lovely woodland, alongside pools and waterfalls, uphill to eventually meet a lane at Gelli Fawr.

Turn right and go 300m along this lane, then turn left onto a signposted bridleway. Follow this through the old farm of Gernos-fawr then up through fields to go through the yard of Gernos-fach (still a working farm, so close the gates!). From here a track leads across the moor to Tafarn-y-bwlch.

At Tafarn-y-bwlch you meet the B4329. Turn right and follow it for about 1 mile to Bwlch-gwynt. This road is fairly traffic-free, but if you want to avoid it, a bridleway forks off to the left (south) and meets another bridleway at Bwlch Pennant (*bwlch* is Welsh for 'pass'), where you turn right (west) to reach Bwlch-gwynt. This second bridleway is part of the **Golden Road**, an ancient route across the crest of the Preseli Hills.

From Bwlch-gwynt a permissive path leads up onto the hillside of Cerrig Lladron; the summit itself is called **Foel Eryr** (Hill of the Eagle) and certainly offers bird's-eye views. Then you descend again to meet a bridleway leading over rough moorland, eventually down past the farms of Penlanwynt and Ffynnondici to meet a lane. Cross the lane and go down the drive of a house called Tregynon, where you must follow the markers that take the footpath through the garden. As you cross a stile and enter the woods again, look out for the bumps in the landscape – this is the site of an Iron Age fort.

A narrow path leads down into the densely wooded Gwaun Valley. The boggy valley floor is crossed by a footbridge, and you again meet the lane running down the Gwaun Valley. Turn right (east) along this for about 300m to reach Sychbant, a patch of woodland with some short walking trails, a picnic site and public toilet.

If you need refreshment, you can turn left (west) to reach Pontfaen, 1 mile west of the route, where the **Duffryn Arms** is a single room in the landlady's rather tumbledown house, unchanged for about 50 years. Beer is served in jugs through a hatch, and food is limited to chocolate, crisps and pickled eggs. At one time, many rural pubs were like this, but very few remain in Britain today.

Sychbant to Newport
2–2½ hours, 4.25 miles (7km)
From Sychbant follow the main trail uphill, first on the west side of the stream that runs down the steep little valley of Cwm Bach, then crossing a small bridge to the east side to reach a gate, which you go through to reach open moor. Go right and continue for about 100m, passing a plaque on a tree stump that reads 'Penlan Restoration'. Depending on the age of your map, this area may be shown as a conifer plantation, but when we were researching here in 2006 the trees had all been felled, and some of the walls all but removed too.

The path follows marker posts through the former plantation, leading north towards the top of a hill called Mynydd Caregog, then swings left (west) to meet a lane at a standing stone called **Bedd Morris**. Local myth tells of a highwayman called Morris who was buried here, but it is in fact a Bronze Age marker stone, still used as parish boundary today.

Turn right (northwards) onto the lane. You can follow it all the way to meet the A487 on the western edge of Newport, enjoying the views straight ahead over the coast and out to sea.

Alternatively, about 1 mile from Bedd Morris the lane swings left then does a sharp right at a place called Y Garn. About 100m beyond here, a bridleway crosses the lane. Turn right (east) and follow this for about 800m, past Hill House, traversing the hills above Newport. This eventually meets the top of Mill Lane, which leads straight down into the town centre.

MORE WALKS

THE DAUGLEDDAU ESTUARY
For walkers, the best parts of Pembrokeshire are the coast and the Preseli Hills – both covered in this chapter. But another part of the national park that is often overlooked is the Daugleddau Estuary – a tranquil wetland area where four large rivers meet. So few people come here that it's been dubbed the 'Secret Waterway' by the local tourist organisation. There are several short walking routes, called Secret Waterway Trails, along the eastern side of the river and into the surrounding farmland.

Good points to aim for include the villages of Landshipping and Lawrenny, which can both be reached by public transport from Haverfordwest, Pembroke or Tenby. Also well worth a visit is Carew Castle. There are some historic shipbuilding sites, and several of the villages have pleasant pubs and teashops, which make good lunch stops. The bird-watching is also excellent.

To tie in a lot of these options, you could take the bus between Pembroke and Tenby, get off at Carew, visit the castle, then walk north on one of the Secret Waterway Trails through Cresswell Quay, Lawrenny and Landshipping, to finish at Canaston Bridge, on the bus route between Haverfordwest, Narberth and Tenby. This is over 20 miles (32km), so it would be a long day, but you could always shorten it by getting the bus to/from Lawrenny or Landshipping, or splitting it in two by staying overnight in the area; Lawrenny and Cresswell Quay both have a selection of farmhouse-style B&Bs.

You can get a range of free leaflets covering walking routes, places to stay and things to see, from any tourist office in South Pembrokeshire. Or go to www.greenways holidays.com and follow the 'Pembrokeshire Heartlands' link to 'secret waterways'.

HIDDEN HERITAGE & LANDSKER TRAILS
A series of short and long circular walking routes have been developed to take visitors away from the more popular and crowded areas. Many of these can easily be reached from the Pembrokeshire Coast Path, and make interesting diversions away from the main route. For the short routes, you can pick up leaflets with maps and route descriptions from local tourist offices. For more information on longer routes and organised walking holidays that include accommodation, packed lunches, maps, route guides, baggage transfer and transport to/from train stations, see www .greenwaysholidays.com.

Snowdonia

The high and wild mountain region of North Wales is called Snowdonia, taking its name from Mt Snowdon (1085m), the highest peak in the area. Snowdon is also the highest summit in Wales – and taller than anything in England, too.

The mountains of Snowdonia are the remains of ancient volcanoes, subsequently eroded by ice-age glaciers and leaving us a striking landscape of sharp peaks, jagged ridges and steep cliffs, while beneath the summits are smooth bowl-shaped valleys called cwms. The landscape is more rounded as you go east towards the Carneddau mountains or south towards Cadair Idris, but they still retain a ruggedness that differs from the uplands of England.

This area of mountains and valleys is contained within the extensive Snowdonia National Park. Its name is Parc Cenedlaethol Eryri in Welsh, and Mt Snowdon itself is called Yr Wyddfa. Eryri means 'home of the eagles' or simply 'eyrie' – although these days you're more likely to see falcons and buzzards flying around the mountainsides.

Without doubt, Snowdonia offers some of the best (and most accessible) high-level walking in Britain, so a visit here is highly recommended. If you don't have time to reach Scotland for the really big mountains, then North Wales goes a long way towards supplying the goods.

In this chapter we describe a choice selection of classic mountain day walks. On p320 we outline a few other options, so you can go off and explore more of Snowdonia's treasures on your own.

HIGHLIGHTS

- Making an early start and beating the crowds to the top of **Mt Snowdon** (p311)
- Tramping across the otherworldly landscape of the **Glyders** (p315)
- Throwing caution to the wind, and leaping between the summit stones on **Tryfan** (p317)
- Enjoying fine open walking and spectacular views from the **Carneddau** (p319)
- Completing the **Welsh Three-Thousanders** (p321)

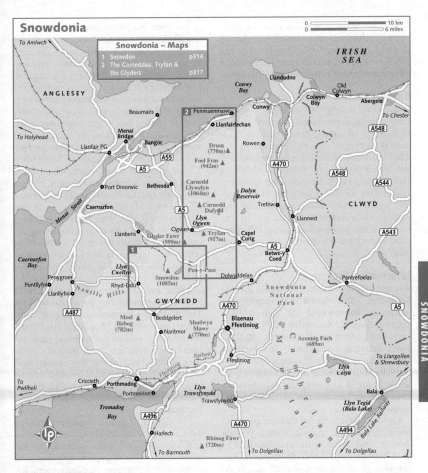

Snowdonia

Snowdonia – Maps	
1 Snowdon	p314
2 The Carneddau, Tryfan & the Glyders	p317

INFORMATION

This chapter covers three different mountain groups in the northern part of Snowdonia – the Snowdon massif, the Glyders, and the Carneddau. Because they're of such high quality, some of these routes are popular and likely to be busy in the high season. But this is a big park – covering an area of over 800 sq miles (around 2000 sq km) – so for less-frequented or remote options, see the More Walks section on p320.

When to Walk

Unless you have the appropriate mountain skills, the high-level routes described in this chapter are not recommended in the winter (between December and March) as they may be partly covered by snow or ice. Even in summer it's important not to underestimate conditions on the summit as they are often very different from those lower down. As in any mountain area, you should check the weather forecast before setting out.

Maps

The Ordnance Survey (OS) Landranger 1:50,000 map No 115 *Snowdon (Yr Wyddfa)* covers the walks described in this chapter, as does OS Explorer 1:25,000 map No 17 *Snowdonia – Snowdon and Conwy Valley*. For wider coverage of the park, you'll need OS Explorer 1:25,000 maps No 18 *Snowdonia – Harlech, Porthmadog & Bala* and 23 *Snowdonia – Cadair Idris & Bala Lake*.

Harvey Maps cover the area in three sheets, each at 1:25,000: *Snowdonia – Snowdon* and *Snowdonia – Glyderau* are required for the routes in this chapter. For further adventures, there's *Snowdonia – Rhinogs*.

Books

Snowdonia is very well covered by guidebooks for walkers. Good starters, with a wide range of routes, are *Snowdonia: Leisure Walks for all Ages* by Terry Marsh and Tom Hutton, and *Snowdonia, Anglesey and the Llyn Peninsula* by Brian Conduit and Neil Coates. For a bit more of a workout, *Hillwalking in Snowdonia* by Steve Ashton covers a wide range of summits and routes, while *Ridges of Snowdonia* by the same author is aimed at hardy hill-types (and includes a few hands-out-of-pockets scrambles).

Information Sources

Tourist offices around Snowdonia include **Beddgelert** (☎ 01766-890615; tic.beddgelert@eryri -npa.gov.uk), **Betws-y-Coed** (☎ 01690-710426; tic .byc@ eryri-npa.gov.uk), **Caernarfon** (☎ 01286-672232; caernarfon.tic@gwynedd.gov.uk), **Llanberis** (☎ 01286-870765; llanberis.tic@gwynedd.gov.uk) and **Porthmadog** (☎ 01766-512981; porthmadog.tic@gwynedd.gov .uk). The tourist office in Llanberis is particularly useful as some staff members are keen local walkers and can advise on routes, maps and so on.

On the internet, official national park and tourism websites include www.eryri-npa .gov.uk and www.visitsnowdonia.info – both have loads of useful information. You can also go to the local council site, www .gwynedd.gov.uk, and click on 'Visiting Snowdonia'. Another good website, covering accommodation, activities and walks, is www.snowdonia-wales.net.

Guided Walks

The Snowdonia National Park rangers organise a series of guided walks throughout the year; you can get details from any local tourist office or the park website. Many of the YHA hostels in the area also offer guided walks and activity courses.

GETTING AROUND

The northern part of Snowdonia described in this chapter is compact and well served by public transport. Handiest for walkers is the **Snowdon Sherpa** (www.visitcaernarfon.com /sherpa/index.html) bus network, with services starting/ending in towns around the edge of the park such as Llandudno, Betws-y-Coed, Porthmadog, Pwllheli, Caernarfon, Llanberis and Bangor, crisscrossing the main Snowdon area via Beddgelert, Capel Curig and Pen-y-Grwyd. You sometimes have to change bus to get where you want, but all-day rover tickets are available. On most routes, buses run every hour or two, typically from about April to September. The network can seem baffling when you're standing at a bus stop in the rain, but get the handy timetable and map from a tourist office and it all falls into place. Note that this service is also used by local people – notably to take children from outlying villages to schools in the main towns, so in school holidays some services are limited; they are also reduced in winter (November to March).

There are also some train services in Snowdonia that are very handy for walkers. The main line between the English Midlands and Holyhead (Anglesey) runs along the northern side of the national park, via Llandudno Junction and Bangor, while branch lines run along the eastern and southern sides of the park through several small towns and villages, including Betws-y-Coed, Blaenau Ffestiniog, Minfford and Porthmadog.

For details of public transport inquiry lines that provide details of both national and local bus and train services, see the boxed text, p456. A good source for local transport information, especially useful for walkers in Snowdonia, is www.countrygoer .org/snowdon.htm.

GATEWAYS

The main gateway towns for northern Snowdonia are Llandudno, Bangor and Caernarfon, from where it's easy to reach the villages and towns near the walking routes we describe. Further south, Porthmadog is another handy gateway, while Betws-y-Coed is a gateway for the northeast area. If you're travelling by coach, all Snowdonia's gateway towns are all easily reached by National Express services from the rest of the country. By train, the mainline stations for northern Snowdonia are Llandudno Junction and Bangor, with regular

SNOWDONIA

MIND YOUR LANGUAGE

Snowdonia is varied not only scenically but socially, too. In the west of this region the people are mainly Welsh-speaking, from farming and slate-mining backgrounds. In the east the communities are closer to the anglicised flatlands of Clwyd, and mainly English-speaking. This contrast has a historical thread, being the remains of frustrated English attempts to occupy Wales in the 13th and 14th centuries, on the heels of the Romans who had similarly failed several centuries earlier.

The survival of the Welsh language is a testament to the Welsh spirit and determination, and when you read, scratched on a rock, 'You English can visit Wales, but please don't come and live here', you'll see that for some the division is alive and kicking. Don't let this put you off, though. The Welsh are known for being friendly and hospitable. Especially if you're not English!

services to/from Crewe in England, where you can connect with trains to the rest of the country. Porthmadog is linked by train to Birmingham via Machynlleth.

A SNOWDON TRAVERSE

Duration	5–7 hours
Distance	7 miles (11.5km)
Difficulty	moderate–demanding
Start	Pen-y-Pass (p312)
Finish	Nantgwynant (p313)
Nearest Towns	Llanberis (p312),
	Nant Peris (p312)
Transport	bus

Summary A high, dramatic, rewarding and relatively straightforward mountain walk on clear paths.

Snowdon is Wales' highest mountain and arguably its most spectacular. Its Welsh name, Yr Wyddfa, means 'burial place' – reputedly of a giant slain by King Arthur. Myths aside, this truly is a place of awe-inspiring beauty, where razor-fine ridges drop in great swooping lines from the summit. Beneath these ridges are cliffs and airy pinnacles, and the steep slopes fall to deep lakes and sheltered cwms.

But Snowdon also has great ugliness. The steam railway chugs noisily from Llanberis all the way to the summit – marked by a grimy station and incongruous (and controversial) café, while on the southern slopes a hydroelectric pipeline cuts an angular scar through the surrounding greenery. It's easy to escape these blemishes though, and we thoroughly recommend a walk on the mountain's ridges and slopes.

The route we describe here is one of many possible traverses of Snowdon, as at least six paths lead up to the summit from the foothills and any two can be joined to cross the mountain, but we think it's one of the best in terms of scenery, variety and access. Once you've had a taste you'll undoubtedly want to try some of the other routes on offer.

PLANNING

The main paths leading up Snowdon are: the Llanberis Path, running roughly parallel to the railway; the Pyg Track and the Miners Track, starting at Pen-y-Pass; the Rhyd-Ddu Path (pronounced 'reed-thee') and Snowdon Ranger Path, on the west side of the mountain; and the Watkin Path to Nantgwynant, south of the summit. The Snowdon Traverse route described here combines the Pyg Track and the Watkin Path, but there are many more possible traverses.

The route we describe is a linear walk and can be done in either direction. We recommend going east to south, as starting from Pen-y-Pass means you're already a good way up the mountain.

In fair conditions, and with an hour for stops, this route will take between six to eight hours in total. If conditions are bad, however, you should allow more time. Just because the paths are good, don't be lured into complacency.

Alternatives

As an alternative to doing the traverse, you can turn this route into a circuit by going up the Pyg Track, and descending the Miners Track back to Pen-y-Pass. For a description of this and other alternatives, see p314.

NEAREST TOWNS

The 'nearest town' to the start of the route is Pen-y-Pass, actually just two buildings (the YHA hostel and a café) about 4 miles southeast of the small village of Nant Peris and about 6 miles southeast of the small town of Llanberis – the main base for walking in the region. The route ends at the tiny settlement of Nantgwynant; there are two sleeping options here, or it's easy to return to Pen-y-Pass or Llanberis by bus.

Pen-y-Pass

At the start of the route, Pen-y-Pass consists of a large car park, a **YHA hostel** (☎ 0870 770 5990; penypass@yha.org.uk; dm £14), and a **café** with some wonderful old photographs of Snowdon on the wall. About 1 mile southeast, towards Capel Curig, the **Pen-y-Gwryd Hotel** (☎ 01286-870211; www.pyg.co.uk; s/d from £28/56; Ⓨ dinner) is steeped in history – it was an old coaching inn – with cosy rooms, creaking stairs and some fine Victorian plumbing. For more history, the ceiling of the wood-panelled climbers' bar is signed by members of the successful 1953 British Everest Expedition.

GETTING THERE & AWAY

Pen-y-Pass is a major hub on the Snowdon Sherpa bus network (see p310) and you can get here from Llanberis on bus S1 (15 minutes, half-hourly), as well as Capel Curig, Caernarfon, Betws-y-Coed, Bethesda (with links to Bangor) and Llandudno.

Pen-y-Pass can be approached from Llanberis on the A4086, or from Capel Curig and Betws-y-Coed on the A5. The car park at Pen-y-Pass costs £4 per day – but often fills in summer, when a 'park and ride' system operates between Nant Peris and Pen-y-Pass. It's also possible to hitch between Llanberis and Pen-y-Pass, as most people in cars are walkers too (but you should always take precautions).

Nant Peris

About 4 miles from Pen-y-Pass, the small village of Nant Peris has **Cae Gwyn Farm** (camp sites for 2 £6), where facilities include basic loos and showers (50p) and…er, that's it. There's no need to book as even in high summer it's never too full – they just open another field. Opposite the camp site, the **Vaynol Arms** has good beer and no-nonsense bar food and is popular with walkers and climbers. Another good camping and bunkhouse option is **Snowdon House** (☎ 01286-870284; sites for 2 £10, dm £10).

Llanberis

This small town is the capital of walking and climbing in North Wales, and an ideal base for any Snowdonia visit. It was once a slate-mining centre (see the boxed text, below) and now thrives on tourism with a high street lined on both sides by a range of hotels, B&Bs, pubs, cafés, food shops, a bank (with ATM) and several outdoor gear shops, plus plenty of visitor attractions. The **tourist office** (☎ 01286-870765; llanberis.tic@gwynedd .gov.uk) is opposite the post office.

SLEEPING & EATING

Budget options include **Llanberis YHA Hostel** (☎ 0870 770 5928; llanberis@yha.org.uk; dm £14) on the edge of town, towards the Snowdon foothills. As well as the usual dorms, it has some en suite double rooms.

MOUNTAIN RESOURCES

While in Llanberis you cannot fail to see the huge (and we mean *really* huge) piles of slate dominating the valley opposite the village – the legacy of a quarrying industry that has existed here for centuries. At one time, Welsh slate was exported around the world, for use mainly on house roofs, but demand dried up in the 1970s and the quarries closed. The railway that once transported slate to the coast now functions as a tourist attraction along the lake.

Today a new industry occupies the old quarry area. A hydroelectric power station has been constructed inside the mountain, with water from the reservoir of Marchlyn, about 600m higher up the mountain, flowing down through underground pipes. Surplus energy is used to pump water from Llyn Peris *up* the underground pipes to Marchlyn, so the water can be reused several times.

Guided tours of the 'Electric Mountain' power station are run daily; details are available from the Llanberis tourist office. If you are unlucky with the weather it's a good alternative to walking on the tops.

The **Heights Hotel** (☎ 01286-871179; www.heights hotel.co.uk; High St; s/d/tr/q £30/45/60/80, mains £7-10) is a long-standing favourite for walkers, climbers, backpackers, local guides and layabouts. The rooms are good value, and there's a bright, noisy bar serving up burgers, pizzas and the like, plus a restaurant. Also available are packed lunches, laundry and drying facilities, pool table and live music some evenings. The flexible and friendly management can advise on outdoor activities and set you up with walking guides or just about anything else required.

For more serene B&B, good walker-friendly places include the well-organised and welcoming **Plas Goch Guesthouse** (☎ 01286-872122; www.plas-coch.co.uk; High St; d from £50), where breakfast includes vegan options, and facilities include wi-fi access and plenty of parking. (The guesthouse website is a mine of local information, too.) Also good is **Dol Peris Hotel** (☎ 01286-870350; High St; s/d from £28/50), with spacious rooms and inspiring views, plus a well-regarded restaurant.

Also popular for food is colourful **Pete's Eats** (☎ 01286-870117; www.petes-eats.co.uk; High St; ☺ breakfast, lunch & dinner; 🖳), a classic café, relaxed, well-organised and frequented for many years by walkers and climbers, where tea comes in pint mugs and you can top up your cholesterol for around £5. There's newspapers, magazines and walking guidebooks to browse through, useful noticeboards, plus showers and accommodation (self-catering apartment, some private rooms and a dorm) upstairs.

A good cheap option is **Seafresh** takeaway and café, serving good fish and chips. Sometimes after a long day on the mountains a big curry is called for: **Balti Raj** (☎ 01286-871983; 32 High St) always does the trick. At the top of the league, **Y Bistro** (☎ 01286-871278; www.ybistro .co.uk; 45 High St; mains £14-17.50; ☺ dinner) fuses fine Welsh ingredients and European cuisine.

GETTING THERE & AWAY
Llanberis is easily reached by local bus from the gateway town of Bangor. Between them, direct bus 85 (45 minutes) and 88 (via Caernarfon, one hour) run at least hourly (every two hours on Sunday).

Nantgwynant
The tiny settlement of Nantgwynant, in the valley of the same name, is at the end of the walk. Places to stay include **Bryn Gwynant YHA Hostel** (☎ 0870 770 5732; www.yha.org.uk; dm £14), a lovely old country house overlooking Llyn Gwynant, with Snowdon as a backdrop. It's about 1 mile northeast of where the Watkin Path meets the main road. Your other option near (in fact, nearer) the end of the Watkin Path is **Bryn Dinas Bunkhouse** (☎ 01766-890234; www.bryndinasbunkhouse.co.uk; dm £10), an excellent bargain option, with beds in heated timber cabins (bring your own sleeping bag) under the trees and a separate self-catering cookhouse.

GETTING THERE & AWAY
Buses S4 and S97 on the Snowdon Sherpa network (see p310) passes through Nantgwynant, from where you can easily return to Pen-y-Pass or Llanberis (although you may need to change at Pen-y-Gwryd).

THE WALK
Pen-y-Pass to Snowdon
3–5 hours, 4.5 miles (7km)
From the car park two paths lead towards the summit of Snowdon. With your back to the café, take the path in the back-right corner. This is the Pyg Track, paved with stone slabs, which leads after about 45 minutes up to a pass called **Bwlch y Moch**. ('Pyg' is sometimes written 'PyG' because it's named after the nearby Pen-y-Gwryd Hotel, although Bwlch-y-Moch means Pass of the Pig – so Pyg is sometimes spelt 'Pig'. Got that?)

At the pass you get your first spectacular view into the great bowl-shaped valley holding Llyn Llydaw and the smaller lake of Glaslyn. From this pass, a path leads steeply up towards the rocky ridge and pinnacles of Crib Goch – this is for very experienced walkers only (those happy using their hands as well as their feet to cross a knife-edge precipice…). Our path goes straight on, crossing through the pass and traversing beneath (south of) the cliffs of Crib Goch, with great views to Llyn Llydaw.

After an hour or so, this path is joined by the Miners Track coming up from the left. You then follow a steep set of switchbacks that lead up to the crest of the ridge, marked by the **Fingerstone** (a rock obelisk).

A few metres beyond the Fingerstone, the railway line comes as a surprise. Try not to be run over by steam trains and follow the path parallel to the railway track for a final 500m of uphill, past the station and café (where you can buy 'Snowdon the Hard Way' T-shirts) and up to the cairn that marks the summit of **Snowdon**. Time to take a breather and admire the 360-degree view from the highest peak in Wales.

Snowdon to Nantgwynant

2–3 hours, 3.5 miles (5.5km)

Although your route lies to the southeast, from the summit of Snowdon it's important to head first southwesterly, down the crest of the ridge from the terrace at the back of the café. After about 150m, by a cairn and standing stone, turn left (east) and zigzag down through steep, broken scree to eventually reach the pass of **Bwlch-y-Saethau** – a popular view point and a possible lunch stop if the summit was too windy or too crowded.

The path is level for a while then reaches a junction. Straight on goes up the ridge path to the west peak of Llewedd (898m). For this walk, however, we go right (south) onto the Watkin Path, which descends steeply and swings southwest into the val-ley of Cwm Llan. From here follow the stream past the old quarry buildings and along the overgrown tramway down into the large valley of Nantgwynant. Below are two lakes, Llyn Gwynant and Llyn Dinas, with much of the surrounding valley covered by thick rhododendron bushes (see the boxed text, opposite). It's easy going downhill now to meet the main road between Beddgelert and Pen-y-Gwryd.

ALTERNATIVE DESCENTS FROM SNOWDON

If you want to return to Pen-y-Pass from Snowdon summit, you can retrace your steps to the Fingerstone and down the steep zigzags to the fork, where the Pyg Track goes east and the Miners Track (which you follow) goes southeast down to the shore of the small lake of Glaslyn then past Llyn Llydaw and along the wide and easy path all the way down to Pen-y-Pass.

If the mist is really bad or you just want to get down from the summit by the easiest route, you can follow the clear path beside the railway tracks all the way to Llanberis. If you're just too tired to walk, you could

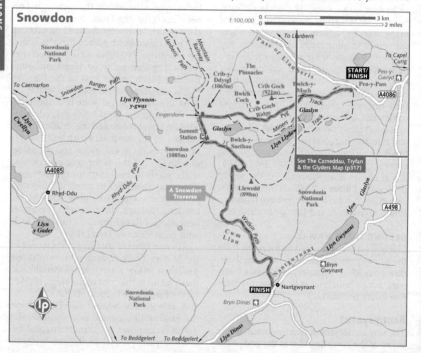

INVASION IN PINK

Walking in Snowdonia in May, you can't fail to notice the profusion of beautiful pink flowers all over the hillsides. You will probably stop to marvel at this amazing floral display, but don't be deceived – these are rhododendrons, the scourge of the hills.

Rhododendrons were introduced to Britain about 200 years ago as an ornamental shrub in the estates of large houses. They thrived in British weather conditions, but it wasn't until the early 20th century, with the break-up of many estates, that they started to spread unchecked. Their environmental impact is devastating, and they now threaten the existence of many indigenous plant and animal species in Snowdonia, and even the very nature of the landscape.

Rhododendron leaves and roots are poisonous, while the dense foliage means that no plants can grow beneath them. This deprives plant-eating animals, birds and insects of a vital food supply, which in turn leads to the decline of carnivorous animals and birds of prey.

So why don't the locals just get rid of them? Not so easy. These plants are almost indestructible. They tolerate all extremes of weather, require minimal daylight for survival, grow back rapidly after cutting and each bush produces several million seeds every year. They are, in short, a conservationist's nightmare. Their single redeeming feature is their spectacular flowers, but if it wasn't for those, they wouldn't have been imported into Britain in the first place.

even hop on the train; one-way standby tickets cost £14 but priority goes to passengers who come up on the train, and it doesn't run when weather conditions are bad. For more details see www.snowdon railway.co.uk.

TRYFAN & THE GLYDERS

Duration	5–7 hours
Distance	5 miles (9.6km)
Difficulty	demanding
Start	Llyn Ogwen
Finish	Ogwen (p316)
Nearest Town	Capel Curig (p316)
Transport	bus

Summary A classic mountain walk through otherworldly scenery; steep ascents and descents, with going a bit rough and slow on the high ground, especially in the wet.

In profile, the peaks of Tryfan appear like a huge dinosaur, with a prickly back curved in a gigantic arc – one of North Wales' most famous sights. The name Tryfan (pronounced 'tre-van') means 'three peaks', with the dramatic rocky summit (915m) flanked by two slightly lower tops.

South of Tryfan are the less obvious mountains of Glyder Fawr and Glyder Fach. Bordered on the north and east by steep cwms and cliffs, they form a broad ridge strewn with shattered stones and contorted boulders, moved by ice to form eerie towers and surreal shapes. This route combines the two Glyder summits with a scramble over Tryfan – a classic Snowdonia outing.

At the foot of Glyder Fawr is the nature reserve of Cwm Idwal. Central to this cwm is the Devil's Kitchen, a dark and austere gorge cutting deeply into the surrounding cliffs. It's a place of Celtic aura and fantasy that befits a landscape steeped in legends of King Arthur. The National Trust protects this delicate and valuable environment. The RAF (Royal Air Force), by contrast, uses the area as a fighter-jet training alley, so on weekdays prepare to be dive-bombed!

PLANNING

The route starts with an ascent of Tryfan, then joins the main Glyder ridge and descends via the Devil's Kitchen. Experienced scramblers will enjoy picking a route up the rocks, but there are easier options, although the range is distinctly rocky and *every* walker needs to use their hands in a few places. For those who are inexperienced or like to keep their hands in their pockets, there's an alternative route on Tryfan that avoids the ridge (and the summit) completely.

We recommend a clockwise circuit, starting with the ascent of Tryfan, because the scrambles are best approached in an uphill direction. The walk measures only 5 miles on the map, but because of the ascents and rough ground, the walking time is longer than you would expect. With stops, about six to eight hours is likely.

When to Walk

The general warning about weather conditions (see p309) applies here, as this whole route is notoriously tricky in bad weather, and not recommended at any time unless you have some skill at using a compass and map.

NEAREST TOWNS

This route starts and ends at Llyn Ogwen, beside the main A5, about halfway between Bethesda and Capel Curig. The 'nearest town' is the tiny settlement of Ogwen, at the western end of the lake of Llyn Ogwen – consisting of a couple of cottages, a car park and some public loos. There are more options 5 miles southeast of Llyn Ogwen, at the scattered village of Capel Curig.

The town of Betws-y-Coed, about 5 miles beyond Capel Curig, has a wider range of places to stay and eat (plus several equipment shops); see www.betws-y-coed.co.uk.

Ogwen

As well as the car park, Ogwen is the site of lovely **Idwal Cottage YHA Hostel** (☎ 0870 770 5874; idwal@yha.org.uk; camp sites for 2 £14, dm £14), in an excellent position and ideally situated for this route. It's self-catering only but there's a good modern kitchen and you can buy food supplies.

Ogwen's only other amenity is a **snack bar** in the car park, also ideally placed – to serve reviving hot food and drinks when you come down off the mountain.

About 2 miles from Ogwen along the A5 towards Capel Curig are two farms offering camping and bunkhouse accommodation: **Gwern Gof Uchaf** (☎ 01690-720294; www.tryfanwales.co.uk; sites for 2 £6, dm £7) is a traditional hill-farm overlooked by Tryfan; the bunkhouse is well maintained, and there's no need to book camping unless you're in a big group – there's always plenty of space. Just 300m further east is **Gwern Gof Isaf** (☎ 01690-720276; www.gwerngofisaf.co.uk; sites for 2 £6, dm £6).

Capel Curig

The village of Capel Curig is spread along the main road (the A5) entering the eastern part of Snowdonia from Betws-y-Coed, just south of its junction with the A4086 (the road towards Llanberis). There are several places to stay and eat; for more details see the village website www.heartofsnowdonia.co.uk.

Walkers and outdoor types are ten-a-penny around here thanks to the presence of **Plas y Brenin National Mountain Centre** (☎ 01690-720214; www.pyb.co.uk; B&B s/d £20/40). This place caters mainly for groups, but spare beds are available to the public (you can book only 48 hours in advance). There's also a good bar serving meals and with free lectures each evening, and you can get a weather forecast here. It's a great place to meet like-minded folks.

Your best budget option is **Capel Curig YHA Hostel** (☎ 0870 770 5746; www.yha.org.uk; dm £16), while walker-friendly B&Bs include **Bron Eryri** (☎ 01690-720240; www.heartofsnowdonia.co.uk/broneryri.htm; d £55) and **Can-yr-Afon** (☎ 01690-720375; www.heartofsnowdonia.co.uk/canafon.htm; d £50).

The **Bryn Tyrch Hotel** (☎ 01690-720223; s/d £40/56) is popular with – you guessed it – walkers and climbers, offering somewhat basic rooms, although the bar (which serves meals) usually has a good atmosphere. Down the road is the smart but friendly **Cobdens Hotel** (☎ 01690-720243; www.cobdens.co.uk; d £70).

In a wholly different league is **St Curig's Church** (☎ 01690-720469; www.stcurigschurch.com; d from £65), now a stunningly imaginative B&B – a conversion that even St Paul would be proud of. Think ultramodern sofas, four-poster beds, hot tubs, chandeliers and stained-glass windows

For food and drinks, Capel Curig has the **Pinnacle Café** (cnr A5 & A4086) – also a well-stocked food store and outdoor equipment shop.

GETTING TO/FROM THE WALK

Llyn Ogwen is on the route of bus S6 on the Snowdon Sherpa network (see p310) between Bethesda (with connections to/from Bangor) and Capel Curig (with connections to/from Betws-y-Coed). There are around five buses per day in each direction. Bethesda to Llyn Ogwen takes 10 minutes; Capel Curig to Llyn Ogwen takes seven minutes.

THE WALK   Map p317
Llyn Ogwen to Tryfan
1½–2 hours, 0.5 miles (800m)

Start from the lay-by on the A5 near the eastern end of Llyn Ogwen, below the North Ridge of Tryfan, where a wall runs down to meet the road. Go through a small gate and follow the wall southwards, uphill, to where it meets a large cliff. This is **Milestone Buttress**, so called (surprise!) because there used to be a milestone on the London-to-Holyhead road here.

It's important to realise that you don't follow the North Ridge from its base, but work your way up to meet the crest about a quarter of the way up the ridge.

From the foot of Milestone Buttress, climb steeply up left (southeast) over loose rocks. A maze of paths weaves through heather and scree. Keep going until you can see down into the valley on the east side of the ridge, then you can turn more to the right (south) and start going up the crest of the ridge proper. (Some old hands say the trick is to look for the building in a small patch of woodland way down in the valley, and line yourself up exactly with the apex of the roof!)

Even when you start climbing properly, keep in mind that this ridge does not have a sharp and well-defined crest, and you should not expect a single easy-to-follow route. In fact, a confusing set of vague paths leads uphill round cliffs, buttresses and boulders. You'll have to use your hands a bit, but if it gets serious you're off the route. (If you don't like using your hands, a precipitous path called Heather Terrace runs along the east side of Tryfan, missing the summit.)

After one to 1½ hours of steady ascent you reach the foot of an imposing rock buttress. Follow the path round its left (east) side to reach a small pass below a fine amphitheatre after another 15 minutes. Descend a little from the pass into the amphitheatre, then go up the first deep and obvious gully (west), under a boulder at the top and back onto the ridge. About 100m further up the ridge is the summit of **Tryfan** (915m), with the standing stones of Adam and Eve marking the spot. Daredevils can leap from one stone to another, to get 'the freedom of Tryfan', but remember that help is a long way away if you break a leg trying. Better to enjoy a rest and the view instead (although one walker we know reported having his lunch disturbed by a rescue helicopter balancing its wheels on the stones – so be prepared).

If you haven't already noticed, the lake of Cwm Bochlwyd, down to the west, looks

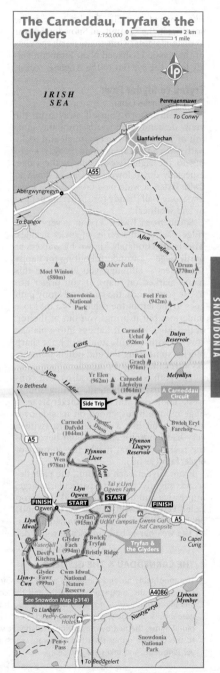

The Carneddau, Tryfan & the Glyders

SNOWDONIA

like a map of Australia. Further away, to the southwest, the summits of Snowdon appear as distant giants, while to the north the view of the classic U-shaped Nant Ffrancon valley leads the eye out to the Anglesey coast.

Tryfan to Glyder Fawr
2–3 hours, 2 miles (3km)

Once you've torn yourself away from the view, descend southwards from the summit of Tryfan. It's a steep, rough and rocky path, with a few cairns along the way, keeping to the right (west) side of the ridge, especially down lower. This leads down to **Bwlch Tryfan**, a wide pass crossed by a large dry-stone wall (handy for sheltering behind in bad weather).

South from Bwlch Tryfan a very steep ridge rises up in a series of rocky needles. This is affectionately known by walkers as **Bristly Ridge** – a wonderful outing for happy scramblers – although you won't see this name marked on maps. If you prefer not to use your hands, the steep and stony path goes to the left of the ridge. It is a bit loose underfoot but it brings you out at the top of the ridge, where it flattens into a plateau covered with a manic jumble of huge sharp blocks, some lying flat and others pointing skywards like jagged pinnacles.

The path is marked by cairns as it continues across this plateau, aiming southwest. Look out for the **Cantilever Stone**, a huge monolith suspended on its side over a drop, a bit like a diving board (with a very bad landing). About 100m beyond is the rock tower that marks the summit of **Glyder Fach** (994m).

From Glyder Fach summit, the path descends slightly, passing a particularly large, impressive and unbelievably spiky outcrop called **Castell-y-Gwynt** (Castle of the Wind) on its left side, and then drops to a pass. (If the weather is bad, an escape route descends from here to Llyn Bochlwyd in Cwm Bochlwyd.)

The main path continues southwest and then west, clearly at first and then over rocks (if there is mist, pay close attention to your navigation), to the summit of **Glyder Fawr** (999m), one of several rock towers standing on the broad summit plateau. Time for a rest and a final look round in this fantastical landscape, before heading towards home.

Glyder Fawr to Ogwen
1½–2 hours, 2.5 miles (4km)

The path leaves the summit of Glyder Fawr heading southwest. Take special care here in bad weather as it's easy to go too far south. The path is marked by a few cairns as it curves and descends over very steep and loose scree, heading generally northwest, down to a flat pass near the small lake of **Llyn-y-Cwn**.

Once again, care is called for to avoid getting lost. Don't go to the lake (unless you want to stop here for a picnic) but aim right (northeast), away from it, to follow a path that takes you to a rocky gap through the cliffs. This path gets steeper, but is paved with rough stone steps. Make sure you find the proper path; any other apparent descent will soon lead you over precipitous cliffs.

As you descend on the path, to your left (north) is the **Devil's Kitchen**, a steep gorge with a waterfall and surrounding cliffs covered with ferns and mosses constantly fed by the mist and dripping water. The mist sometimes looks like smoke from a cooking fire – hence the name.

Beyond the gorge, the path divides, taking you either west or east of the lake of **Llyn Idwal**. There's hardly any difference in distance but the western path is worth taking after heavy rain as there's a deep and

---

THE CARNEDDAU & THE GLYDERS

The mountains around Carnedd Dafydd and Carnedd Llewelyn are known as the Carneddau. *Carnedd* means 'mountain' in Welsh, and the correct plural form is *carneddau*, which means literally 'mountains' – not very helpful if you translate, as there are a great many mountains hereabouts. Strangely, although Carnedd Dafydd and Carnedd Llewelyn are known by the Welsh plural name, the nearby mountains of Glyder Fawr and Glyder Fach are nearly always anglicised to the Glyders, rather than the Glyderau, which is the correct plural form in Welsh. You picks yer language, and takes yer choice.

fast stream on the eastern route. Beyond the lake, an easy paved path takes you down to Idwal Cottage YHA hostel and Ogwen car park, at the west end of Llyn Ogwen, where the snack bar can provide a welcome ice cream or hot coffee – depending on the weather.

A CARNEDDAU CIRCUIT

Duration	4–6 hours
Distance	8 miles (13km)
Difficulty	moderate
Start	Llyn Ogwen (eastern end)
Finish	Nant y Benglog
Nearest Towns	Ogwen (p316),
	Capel Curig (p316)
Transport	bus
Summary A classic route with straightforward walking on mostly good (if faint) paths through a relatively quiet area.	

The group of mountains called the Carneddau (pronounced 'car-neth-aye'), in the northeastern section of the national park, take their name from the two main peaks – Carnedd Dafydd and Carnedd Llewelyn. This area has a more isolated atmosphere than many others in Snowdonia because its mountains are broad and open, although hidden among the grassy slopes are cliffs of a scale more often seen in the Highlands of Scotland. The northern similarities continue further, as in winter the Carneddau attract more snow than other areas, and even in summer the weather can become atrocious on the tops.

PLANNING

The circular route we describe here starts near the eastern end of the lake of Llyn Ogwen, between Bethesda and Capel Curig; it takes in the main summits of the Carneddau and returns to the main road in the valley of Nant y Benglog (universally called the Ogwen Valley), about 1.5 miles east of the start point.

This circular route can be walked in either direction, but clockwise is recommended, as the ascent of Pen yr Ole Wen is better early in the day. On top of the Carneddau you can cover quite a lot of ground fairly quickly. Add at least an extra hour to the walk for lunch and photo stops.

Alternatives

For a longer walk in this area, see the Carneddau Three-Thousanders route description on p320.

GETTING TO/FROM THE WALK

See p316 for details of bus services.

Llyn Ogwen is beside the A5, between Bethesda and Capel Curig. The handiest car parking is at the camp sites of Gwern Gof Uchaf and Gwern Gof Isaf (for details, see p316); parking costs a few pounds for the whole day.

THE WALK   Map p317
Llyn Ogwen to Pen yr Ole Wen
1½–2 hours, 2 miles (3km)

From the eastern end of Llyn Ogwen take the track towards Tal y Llyn Ogwen farm. Just before the farm gate, the path strikes north, uphill, then follows a stream called Afon Lloer, continuing north and uphill. This leads you to a large bowl-shaped valley, Cwm Lloer. Don't go into this valley, but turn left (west) and continue along the ridge that curves round towards the north and leads to the summit of **Pen yr Ole Wen** (978m). This is the first of the Carneddau summits – and the worst of today's ascent over – so time for a breather. There are great views to the south over to the Glyders with Snowdon behind, and northwest to Bangor with the island of Anglesey beyond.

Pen yr Ole Wen to Carnedd Llewelyn
1–2 hours, 3 miles (5km)

From the summit of Pen yr Ole Wen, follow the ridge north, over a bump called Carnedd Fach, then northeast to the summit of **Carnedd Dafydd** (1044m). Once again the views are good; among other summits you can see Carnedd Llewelyn, your next objective, to the northeast.

From this summit it's important not to head straight for Carnedd Llewelyn. First you must head east, along the ridge, with the fittingly titled sheer cliffs of Ysgolion Duon (Black Ladders) dropping down to your left (northwards) at the head of the Afon Llafar valley.

Continue for about 1 mile and then swing northwards, now with a steep drop down to your right (southeast) as well, for a final ascent up to the summit of **Carnedd Llewelyn** (1064m) – the highest in the Carneddau

SNOWDONIA

range. Time for another break, and to marvel at the views. Looking south, the aspect across to Tryfan is now truly magnificent, while in the other direction the other Carneddau summits of Foel Grach, Foel Fras and Drum stretch away to the north. (If you're tempted to follow the broad ridge that links these rounded giants, see Carneddau Three-Thousanders, below.)

SIDE TRIP: YR ELEN
1 hour, 1.5 miles (2.5km)
If you want to bag another Carneddau peak over 3000ft you can take an out-and-back detour to the summit of **Yr Elen** (962m) – very worthwhile if you have the time and the energy. There is a dramatic drop into Cwm Caseg from the summit, so make sure you come back the same way.

Carnedd Llewelyn to Nant y Benglog
1½–2 hours, 3 miles (5km)
From the summit of Carnedd Llewelyn the path leads southeast down a steep, narrow ridge, with some near-sheer drops on either side. This is tricky in mist, so take care.

About 45 minutes from Carnedd Llewelyn you reach the steep-sided pass of **Bwlch Eryl Farchog**. Do not go through the pass, but turn right (south) and follow the steep, zigzagging path that takes you down to the Ffynnon Llugwy reservoir, nestling in the horseshoe of steep mountainsides. Follow the path along its east bank to join the service road, which carries you swiftly down the hill. It's an eyesore but at least you can't lose the way! This brings you down to the A5, where this route ends, opposite the farm and camp site of Gwern Gof Isaf.

If you need to get back to the start, turn right (west) and follow the main road for 1.5 miles to reach the east end of Llyn Ogwen.

MORE WALKS

The routes already described in this chapter are well known and well trodden. But Snowdonia has a lot more to offer, and this section will give you a few ideas for further exploration.

CARNEDDAU THREE-THOUSANDERS
In the Carneddau Circuit section (p319) we described a circular route across three high summits in the Carneddau mountains. Also possible in this area is an excellent linear option taking in seven summits, all in a line and all over the magic 3000ft (914m) contour.

This route starts at Llyn Ogwen and follows the Carneddau Circuit route over the summits of Pen yr Ole Wen (978m), Carnedd Dafydd (1044m) and Carnedd Llewelyn (1064m), and detours out to Yr Elen (962m). The linear route then carries on northwards along the fine broad ridge to Foel Grach (976m), Carnedd Uchaf (926m) and Foel Fras (942m), and eventually to Drum (770m), the final top. From here you descend a broad ridge in a northwesterly direction on a vehicle track to Llanfairfechan. (Alternatively you can head northwest from the pass between Foel Fras and Drum to meet the lane coming up from Abergwyngregyn.)

The route can be walked in either direction, but if you start from Llyn Ogwen you have the advantage of being already at 300m, whereas Llanfairfechan is at sea level. The total distance for this route is 11.5 miles (18km), but the going is fairly good and in fine weather it will take about six to seven hours' walking (seven to eight in total).

A SNOWDONIA COAST TO COAST
If you want a longer walk in Snowdonia, several options exist for crossing the whole area from the north coast to the southwest coast. Perhaps surprisingly, there is no established waymarked multiday route, as in many other national parks. However, the following suggested route crosses some of the finest scenery in the country.

The route is best split into four or five stages, each of a day's duration (although you can just do two or three stages if you want), and it can be walked in either direction. Only the barest directions are given here; the walking is mostly on good paths, but to do this whole route you need to be a fit and experienced walker, confident of your navigation skills in poor weather.

Stage 1
Start at Llanfairfechan on the north coast, going via a small hill called Garreg Fawr to the summit of Drum, from where you cross the Carneddau Three-Thousanders of Foel

THE WELSH THREES

Snowdonia has 14 peaks (some say 15) that rise above the magical 3000ft (914m) contour. A popular challenge for walkers is to get to the top of them all within 24 hours, an outing known as the Welsh Three-Thousanders, or more simply the Welsh Threes. The 'rules' allow the peaks to be bagged in any order, but the nature of the landscape offers two main choices – a north-to-south line or vice versa – starting the clock as you leave the first summit and stopping it on the summit of the last. Assuming a south-to-north line, the route starts with an ascent of Snowdon's three highest summits (as the countdown starts at the *top* of Snowdon, some people use the train to get up here), then descends to Nant Peris. From here the route goes up Elidir Fawr, over Y Garn, and then takes in the Glyders and Tryfan. That's all before you nip across to the Carneddau peaks, which stretch in a line northwards to Llanfairfechan. The whole route can be completed in around 12 hours if you're very fit and don't stop, although a target of 18 hours is more usual (and many people need the full 24 hours). The record for fell runners is under five hours – doesn't it make you sick? For more casual walkers, the 14 peaks (or 15 – Castel y Gwynt is the debatable one) can be split over a few days and enjoyed at leisure. We've even heard about some hardy adventurers doing a variant called the Welsh Freeze – combining a run up some of the mountains with a swim in some of the lakes. Reservoirs are out of bounds, but this is still a challenge best left to super-fit athletes, or the insane.

Fras, Carnedd Uchaf, Foel Grach, Carnedd Llewelyn, Carnedd Dafydd and Pen yr Ole Wen, before descending to Llyn Ogwen.

Stage 2

You have two main choices. The first is a long one: from Llyn Ogwen, follow the route described in the Tryfan & the Glyders walk (p315) to Llyn y Cwn, then continue northwest to Y Garn (947m), then north to Foel Goch (831m). From here the ridge descends to Bwlch y Brecan, from where you can descend to Nant Peris, 3 miles west of Pen-y-Pass.

Your second main choice is much shorter and can be combined with Stage 3. From Llyn Ogwen take the Miners Track (not to be confused with the track of the same name on Snowdon), which leads past Llyn Bochlwyd to Bwlch Tryfan. From here the track continues down to the Pen-y-Gwryd Hotel, from where a short walk along the side of the main road brings you to Pen-y-Pass.

Stage 3

From Pen-y-Pass take the Pyg Track to the summit of Snowdon. From the summit you have more options: you could either descend on the Rhyd-Ddu Path to Rhyd-Ddu or via the Watkin Path into Nantgwynant.

Stage 4

For the final stage you have several options. If you descended yesterday on the Rhyd-Ddu Path, then you could follow the Nantlle Ridge, eventually dropping down to Llanllyfni, near the village of Penygroes, from where you can continue to the coast at Pontllyfni.

If you descended the Watkin Path to Nantgwynant, then for Stage 4 you could go from Beddgelert over the Moel Hebog (782m) and Moel Ddu (552m), eventually to reach the coast at the seaside town of Porthmadog.

A much longer option (requiring two days) leads you south from Nantgwynant via the summits of Moelwyn Mawr (770m) and Moelwyn Bach (711m), or through the valleys between these peaks and Mowl-yr-Hydd, down to the villages of Maentwrog and Trawsfynydd. The final day is through the rough, tough and little visited Rhinogs mountain range. You can proceed either via the summit of Rhinog Fawr (720m) or by skirting the peaks to the west, following tracks and paths that lead eventually down to Barmouth, on the coast of the Irish Sea.

NORTH WALES COAST

If the weather is bad on the high peaks of Snowdonia, there are some great options nearby for coastal walking.

The north and west of the Isle of Anglesey has huge sea cliffs, quaint fishing villages, busy ports and sweeping, sandy beaches. You can choose between short day walks (the area around South Stack, an impressive headland and important nature reserve on the western tip of the island, is a good place to start) and a 120-mile (193km) circuit of the entire island, or something in between. See *Coastal Walks around Anglesey* by Carl Rogers for more ideas.

On the mainland the North Wales Path is a 60-mile (96km) route following the coast from Bangor to Prestatyn (also the end of the Offa's Dyke Path). It is possible to complete the path in four to seven days, or you could explore it in single-day circular outings or linear sections using the frequent buses and trains running along the coast.

This is a popular holiday area, so B&B options are good. The whole route is described in a handy guidebook, *The North Wales Path* by Dave Salter and Dave Worreland.

South of Anglesey, the northwestern extreme of the Welsh mainland is the Lleyn Peninsula. This offers great coastal scenery, particularly between Abersoch and Nefyn, and is quieter than the North Wales Path, although less dramatic than Anglesey. When the weather is bad on the high ground and other parts of the coast, conditions here are often good and it's a great place for a walk.

Wales
Long-Distance Paths

This chapter covers two of the finest long-distance routes in Wales: Glyndŵr's Way and Offa's Dyke Path. They get their own chapter simply because they don't fit neatly into any particular Welsh region, and it's hard to beat either walk for a ground-level lesson in Welsh history and national pride. Both walks trace their roots to the actions of historic figures (Welsh hero Owain Glyndŵr and King Offa of Mercia); both are important illustrations of the extended, often violent tug-of-war between England and Wales; and both wind through wildly varied but consistently gorgeous landscapes.

Horseshoeing out from the Wales–England border, Glyndŵr's Way takes walkers through historically significant sites from Glyndŵr's life amid the beautiful rolling hills, open moors and small farms characteristic of Mid Wales. It's the easier, and the more conventionally pretty, of the two trails. The areas it passes through are pretty far off the tourist circuit, which means walkers could well be the only visitors in most of the towns and villages along the way. A lot of the locals in this largely rural part of Wales will also give you extra credit for arriving on foot.

Offa's Dyke is tougher and more geographically diverse, following King Offa's 8th-century engineering marvel from coast to coast. The trail hops repeatedly back and forth across the border, exhibiting stark differences in the atmosphere of villages just a few miles apart. Covering just about every landscape on offer in this part of the country, it's a rewarding undertaking.

HIGHLIGHTS

- Catching sight of Machynlleth from the ridge above town, then descending via the **Roman Steps** (p330)
- Overlooking Lake Vyrnwy at sunset from the patio outside the **Lake Vyrnwy Hotel** (p332)
- Admiring the 14th-century **Tintern Abbey** (p336)
- Browsing through the bookish town of **Hay-on-Wye** (p337)

THE GLYNDŴR'S WAY

Duration	9 days
Distance	132 miles (212.5km)
Difficulty	moderate
Start	Knighton (p326)
Finish	Welshpool (p326)
Transport	bus, train

Summary This relatively little-used national trail cuts a scenic swath through Mid Wales, meandering across working farmland, gently sloping valleys, thick pine forests and bleak, beautiful moorland.

Very much a well-guarded secret, Glyndŵr's Way opened in 2001 as the newest of three national trails in Wales. It's named after Owain Glyndŵr, the early-15th-century Welsh warrior-statesman who led a fierce but eventually suppressed rebellion against English rule (see the boxed text, opposite). The route passes many sites connected with the rebellion, including the town of Machynlleth where Glyndŵr convened Wales' first parliament. The persistence of a strong Welsh identity, clear at every stop along the trail, is one of the unique pleasures of walking the Glyndŵr's Way.

The area crossed by the trail is sandwiched between Snowdonia to the north and the Brecon Beacons to the south. The landscape is predominantly low moorland and farmland, with lakes, gentle hills and beautiful valleys. A particular highlight is the impressive range of bird life, including buzzards, kingfishers, woodpeckers, red kites, peregrine falcons, flycatchers and wrens.

The Glyndŵr's Way has dual waymarks – the national-trail acorn symbol and a white disc with a red Welsh dragon designed for this route.

NOT THE ONLY LONG WALKS...

If you like to get your teeth into a good long walk, the Glyndŵr's Way and the Offa's Dyke Path are by no means your only options in Wales. Other long routes include the **Pembrokeshire Coast Path** (p291) and a possible traverse of Snowdonia National Park (p320). Some other ideas are given on p341.

PLANNING

Accommodation is scarce along the route, so book ahead. On some of the more remote sections you'll need to pack a lunch and carry enough water for the day.

Because the trail is newer and less frequently used than other national trails, there are points when gaps in the waymarking can baffle even experienced walkers, so it's essential to carry a compass and a good set of maps.

Most people take nine days to complete the walk, and we have divided it accordingly as follows:

Day	From	To	Miles/km
1	Knighton	Felindre	15/24
2	Felindre	Abbeycwmhir	14/22.5
3	Abbeycwmhir	Llanidloes	15.5/25
4	Llanidloes	Dylife	16/25.5
5	Dylife	Machynlleth	14.5/23.5
6	Machynlleth	Llanbrynmair	14/22.5
7	Llanbrynmair	Llanwddyn	17.5/28
8	Llanwddyn	Pontrobert	12/19.5
9	Pontrobert	Welshpool	13.5/21.5

The hilly terrain and difficulty of route-finding, due to a multitude of paths crossing the trail, can make for pretty slow going, so it's wise to allow a little more time than you would for more established trails.

Llanidloes, Machynlleth and Lake Vyrnwy are all worth exploring during rest days, and there's plenty to keep you occupied in Welshpool, so you could conceivably turn this into a leisurely 14-day holiday. If you don't wish to tackle the whole walk, the section from Knighton to Machynlleth has the more spectacular scenery; from Machynlleth you can catch a train to Shrewsbury (via Welshpool).

When to Walk

The walk can be done any time of year, but the lonelier stretches of moorland in particular can be discouraging in cold weather.

Maps & Books

Your best bet is to pick up the *Glyndŵr's Way* official National Trail Guide by David Perrott. Like others in the series, it features extracts from the relevant Ordnance Survey (OS) 1:25,000 Explorer maps for the length of the trail. Be sure your copy includes the

OWAIN GLYNDŴR

Owain Glyndŵr is a Welsh hero but surprisingly little is known about him. Some of the most detailed, but often highly embellished, stories of his life emerge from the writings of the Welsh bards. Glyndŵr was the son of a wealthy landowner, descended from the royal houses of Powys and Gwynedd, and lived in Wales in the second half of the 14th century.

As was common in those times, Glyndŵr became a squire to English nobility, in particular to Henry of Bolingbroke, who later became King Henry IV. Glyndŵr fought for the English army in mainland Europe and Scotland before settling in Mid Wales with his wife and children. Little may have been subsequently heard of Glyndŵr had his neighbour, Reginald de Grey, Lord of Ruthin, not stolen some land from him.

Glyndŵr decided to fight de Grey in court, but most of the English regarded the Welsh as barbarians, and the case was dismissed, reportedly with the words, 'What care we for barefoot Welsh dogs?' At around the same time Henry IV was engaged in a military campaign in Scotland. Glyndŵr refused to take part and was labelled a traitor by the king. He was forced to flee his home for some time, but on 16 September 1400 Glyndŵr met his brothers and a few close associates at Glyndyfrdwy, on the banks of the River Dee. He was proclaimed the Prince of Wales – a deliberate stand against English rule – and so began a long, drawn-out fight for Welsh independence.

Several skirmishes followed, and by the end of 1403 Glyndŵr controlled most of Wales. He called the first Welsh parliament at Machynlleth. But events turned sour when Prince Henry, son of Henry IV and hero of the Battle of Agincourt, appeared. Henry delivered shattering blows to the Welsh army at Grosmont and Usk. The people of South Wales began to renounce the rebellion, and Glyndŵr's position started to look shaky.

Welsh fortunes declined further in 1406. With Prince Henry wreaking havoc in the south, Glyndŵr was forced to retreat to the north. His hopes for a Wales that was free of English oppressors were crushed, and gradually the English regained control. There was no last glorious stand; around 1406 Glyndŵr went into hiding, and the last anyone heard of him was in 1415, according to the Annals of Owain Glyn Dŵr, where the last entry reads, 'Very many said that he died; the seers maintain he did not'.

Theories have Glyndŵr dying anonymously in battle or spending his last years wandering in the mountains, living quietly among friends. The Welsh bards paint a more romantic picture of him sleeping in a hidden cave with his followers, waiting for the right moment to rise again against the English.

loose page of last-minute route alterations; if not, ask for one at a tourist office or download it from www.nationaltrail.co.uk/GlyndwrsWay.

OS Explorer 1:25,000 maps No 201 *Knighton & Presteigne*, 214 *Llanidloes & Newtown/Y Drenewydd*, 215 *Newtown/Y Drenewydd & Machynlleth*, 216 *Welshpool & Montgomery* and 239 *Lake Vyrnwy, Llyn Efyrnwy & Llanfyllin* cover the entire route, except the last 800m as you enter Machynlleth. For this tiny section you'll be able to get by using the Glyndŵr's Way leaflets (see right).

Note that the route indicated for the Glyndŵr's Way on pre-2005 OS maps is the old route, which differs from the current route in many places. The Explorer series published from May 2005 containing 'access to open countryside' information shows the correct route.

Information Sources

Begin your preparations with a visit to the Glyndŵr's Way official website at www.nationaltrail.co.uk/GlyndwrsWay.

See the walk description for tourist offices along the route, all of which can supply you with the *Glyndŵr's Way Accommodation List* plus a series of 16 leaflets called *Glyndŵr's Way*, which describes the route (both are free). Published by the Powys County Council, the leaflets outline the history of the route and surrounding area and contain some wildlife notes.

The **Glyndŵr's Way National Trail officer** (☎ 01597-827562) can answer queries and provide advice and information.

Baggage Services

Llanidloes-based **P&C Taxis** (☎ 01686-412047; www.llanidloes.com/pctaxis) runs a baggage service along the route. Many B&Bs are also happy to transport your bags on to your next stop if you ask when booking accommodation. The fee is usually £15 to £25 per section.

NEAREST TOWNS

Knighton

pop 3043

Knighton, the Glyndŵr's Way's starting point, is an attractive and friendly little market town near the English border. It has some well-preserved Tudor houses and a surplus of excellent pubs, most of which serve good meals. There are also plenty of accommodation options, a supermarket and shops.

Called Tref-y-clawdd in Welsh (meaning 'town on the dyke'), Knighton is also the halfway point of the Offa's Dyke Path, which explains why the **tourist office** (☎ 01547-529424; West St) is in the Offa's Dyke Centre. There's a lot of helpful information here, as well as some interesting displays on local wildlife, geography and the history of both trails.

Other than preparing for your walk, there isn't much to do in Knighton, so if you arrive early enough it's worth considering an immediate start. There's accommodation near the hamlet of Llangunllo (5 miles along the trail), and this makes for a nice late-afternoon walk.

SLEEPING & EATING

Offa's Dyke House (☎ 01547-529816; 4 High St; s/d £30/44), near the clock tower, is the best option for walkers, with spacious, comfortable rooms, friendly and knowledgeable owners and an even-larger-than-average cooked breakfast.

Other options include the basic **Kinsley** (☎ 01547-520753; Station Rd; r from £25), near the train station; the **Fleece House** (☎ 01547-520168; www.fleecehouse.co.uk; Market St; s/d from £35/50), a charming old coaching inn; and the **George & Dragon** (☎ 01547-528532; www.thegeorgeknighton .co.uk; Broad St; s/d £35/55), a dignified pub with cute, rustic rooms in converted stables.

The George & Dragon also serves good pub food (£4 to £10), as does **Nosebag's Brasserie** (Station Rd; lunch £5-7, dinner mains £7-12),

next to the Horse & Jockey pub. The **Horse & Jockey** and the **Red Lion** (☎ 01547-528231; Broad St) are the liveliest pubs after dark.

GETTING THERE & AWAY

The easiest way to get to and from the walk is by train. Knighton is on the **Heart of Wales** (☎ 01597-822053; www.heart-of-wales.co.uk) line between Shrewsbury (one hour) and Swansea (three hours), with four trains a day (one on Sunday). The Knighton Circular bus service runs to Knighton from Newtown (25 minutes, Tuesday and Thursday) and Kington (15 minutes, three per day Monday to Saturday). Knighton is on the A4113 and links with Shrewsbury, Leominster and Hereford by the A49.

Welshpool

pop 5539

Though most people end their walk along Glyndŵr's Way here, making the nickname a little backward, Welshpool is known as the 'Gateway to Wales'. Situated in the Severn Valley, it's separated from England by Long Mountain and the Breidden Hills. Architecturally it's Georgian English but culturally it's Welsh through and through. The **tourist office** (☎ 01938-552043; Church St) has a good supply of books and maps as well as end-of-trail mementos.

SLEEPING & EATING

There's a cluster of places to stay near the attractive St Mary's Church on Salop Rd, of which the pick is the **Westwood Park Hotel** (☎ 01938-553474; r from £25), with its warren of plushly outfitted little rooms above a boisterous pub. If you want a touch more luxury to celebrate the end of your walk, the **Royal Oak** (☎ 01938-552217; www.royaloakhotel.info; s/d £64/94) is right in the centre of town and has just been grandly refurbished.

The Royal Oak offers upscale dining, but there's also an abundance of budget-friendly takeaways in Welshpool. **Andrews Fish Bar** (☎ 01938-552635; 32 High St; mains £2-6; lunch & dinner Mon-Sat) has been named best chip shop in Wales, as the mob of locals crowding its store front confirms.

GETTING THERE & AWAY

Arriva Trains Wales (☎ 08457 484950; www.arriva trainswales.co.uk) Cambrian train line stops at Welshpool on its daily runs between

Shrewsbury (30 minutes) and Aberyst-wyth (1½ hours). **National Express** (☎ 08705 808080; www.nationalexpress.com) coaches run to Welshpool twice daily from London (five hours) via Birmingham and Shrewsbury. Local bus timetables are available in the *Powys Travel Guide*, available from tourist offices, or through **Traveline** (☎ 0870 608 2608; www.traveline-cymru.org.uk). Welshpool is on the A458 to Shrewsbury.

THE WALK
Day 1: Knighton to Felindre
6–7 hours, 15 miles (24km)
Today's combination of bracken-covered moors, rolling hills and quiet farmland is a good sampler for the rest of the walk. Be sure to pack lunch, as the lone pub on the route was closed indefinitely at the time of research.

The Glyndŵr's Way officially begins at the clock tower in the town centre. Walk up the crooked slope of 'narrows' (lined with pretty houses dating from Tudor times), through the back streets of Knighton and on to a track that takes you around the northern side of leafy Garth Hill (346m). Already you'll feel a sense of accomplishment as you've ascended quite rapidly for excellent views over the town.

At Little Cwm-gilla a rough track climbs up to pine-skirted Bailey Hill before descending through a series of hedged fields and another couple of miles of pleasant farmland into the village of Llangunllo.

Apart from a 13th-century church, this tiny hamlet's chief attraction until recently was the Greyhound, a broken-down but friendly little pub – sadly, the Greyhound was closed at the time of research, and its future remained uncertain. Sharing space in Llangunllo with the pub is the village **shop**, which opens at irregular hours. Places to stay in the village include **Craig Fach** (☎ 01547-550605; r from £22).

From Llangunllo, the trail heads north on a road before you venture into farmland again on a path to the left. After crossing a small stream, pass under the railway line and take a path up to Nayadd Fach farm. The track joins a farm road and climbs steadily; behind you are pastoral valley views that will become familiar over the course of the walk but never lose their charm.

For the next few miles, a soft, green track leads you across beautiful heathery moorlands, past Stanky Hill and a few lonely waymarks. As the wide open moors gradually give way to farmland, the path zigzags steeply downhill toward Felindre.

FELINDRE
Book early and plan ahead, as this village is even smaller than Llangunllo. There's a shop with irregular hours, and a friendly pub (no meals). B&B and camping are offered by the comfortable **Trevland** (☎ 01547-510211; sites for 2 £8, s/d £30/55) and the luxurious, faux-rustic **Brandy House** (☎ 01547-510282; www.brandy house.u-net.com; sites for 2 £10, r from £30). The latter has no evening meals, but the owners will drive guests to the excellent **Radnorshire Arms** (☎ 01547-510634, Beguildy; mains from £7) if arranged in advance. If you're in Felindre at lunchtime you'll need to bring food with you.

Day 2: Felindre to Abbeycwmhir
5½–6½ hours, 14 miles (22.5km)
You'll see plenty of sheep on today's relatively easy section of trail, as well as a perfect lunchtime pub stop and a delightful grassy track through high moors and thick forest.

From Felindre the route is well way-marked through gently rising farming country to a short section of road. Where the road turns to the north, you head south

---

THE BEST-LAID PLANS
Little remains of the Cistercian abbey from which the village of Abbeycwmhir takes its name. It was founded in 1143 but never completed, although its plans would have made it one of the largest in Britain, behind York, Durham and Winchester. In 1282 the headless body of Llewelyn the Great was secretly buried here. The abbey continued to support the Welsh princes, so the English Crown cut off funds, but in 1401, after finding most of the monks to be English, Owain Glyndŵr's army destroyed the abbey. The damage was never repaired. The abbey was finally closed in 1536 during Henry VIII's Dissolution of the Monasteries; some of its stones were used to build Dyfaenor, a mansion you'll pass along the trail.

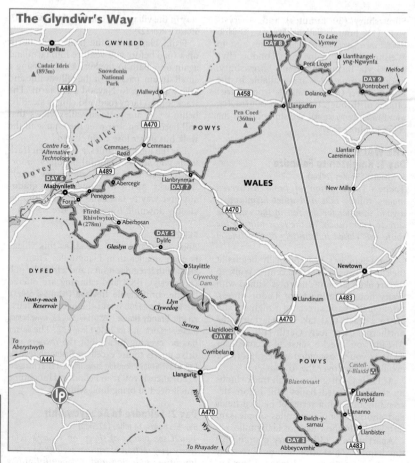

The Glyndŵr's Way

instead, along a byway. The trail takes you steadily uphill, past an old earthwork known as Castell-y-Blaidd (Wolf's Castle), on to a lane and into Llanbadarn Fynydd. Here the **New Inn** (☎ 01597-840378; lanbadarninn@aol .com; r from £20, meals from £5; ☯ breakfast, lunch & dinner) offers comfortable rooms, beautiful outdoor garden seating and hearty meals throughout the day.

From Llanbadarn Fynydd the trail gently climbs to open moor, skirting woods to reach Bwlch Farm. The final stretch of walking to Abbeycwmhir begins with a fine ridge walk rising to a 450m summit, then drops to a clear track through Neuadd Fach wood and down into the valley of Bachell Brook.

ABBEYCWMHIR

Abbeycwmhir is minuscule but has historical significance that belies its size. Cistercians began a huge abbey here in the 12th century, along with a mill; the ruins are visible from the trail (see the boxed text, p327). The lovely little **St Mary's Church** (1870), which may contain stones from the ruined abbey, is worth a look.

There's a shop and a pub, the **Happy Union** (☎ 01597-851203), though it keeps odd hours. (Even if it's closed, be sure to look at the pub sign – note the leek, a symbol of Wales, peeking out of the goat-rider's hat.)

Mill Cottage (☎ 01597-851935; www.abbeycwmhir .co.uk; r from £25), near Mill Bridge (OS reference 059-711), is a homey B&B 800m east of

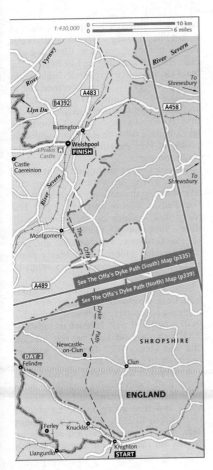

north via the path by the phone box, you cross a rough field and join a road to enter a quiet forest. The landscape opens up and at Blaentrinant, on a clear day, you can see the peak of Cadair Idris (893m) far to the northwest.

Some challenging hills beyond Blaentrinant are rewarded with astonishing views across valleys. The route zigzags wildly, and you have to keep one eye on your map and the other scanning for waymarks. But don't allow this to detract from one of the most glorious stretches of the trail. Eventually you join a quiet road that crosses an arched footbridge into Llanidloes.

LLANIDLOES
pop 2807

This pretty town is best known for its attractive 16th-century **market hall**, a low, half-timbered building on stubby legs in the centre of town. There's also the 14th-century **Church of St Idloes** by the river, with its five magnificent arches brought from Abbeycwmhir in the 1540s. The town itself is set gracefully on the River Severn, and has a **tourist office** (☎ 01686-412605) and all the services a visitor might need.

Llanidloes also has a good range of accommodation and several good pubs; if you have time, it's an ideal spot for a rest day. The pick of the B&Bs is **Dyffryn Glyn Guest House** (☎ 01686-412129; www.dyffrynglyn.co.uk; r from £25), a modernised farmhouse 2 miles out of town with gorgeous views, friendly owners and a head start on the next day's walk. Another good choice is **Lloyds Hotel** (☎ 01686-412284; www.lloydshotel.co.uk; r from £38), on the southeast edge of town, where helpful staff dispense key information about local sights and characters.

Many of Llanidloes' pubs offer meals – try the walker-friendly **Angel** (☎ 01686-412381; High St; mains from £6; ☽ lunch & dinner). On the main street there's a good **takeaway** serving fish and chips, and a **Spar** supermarket open late.

Day 4: Llanidloes to Dylife
6½–7½ hours, 16 miles (25.5km)

After the familiar stiles and fields, today the trail takes you through pine forest, across moorland and alongside a reservoir. Stock up in Llanidloes, as there are no shops until Machynlleth.

the village, with a pretty garden, cosy rooms and evening meals (book in advance).

Day 3: Abbeycwmhir to Llanidloes
6–7 hours, 15.5 miles (25km)

This is a hilly but deeply satisfying day of forests, moorland and grand views. Make sure you carry lunch, as there are no shops on the route.

The walk leaves Abbeycwmhir opposite the Happy Union for a climb along forest roads and farmland. Views grow progressively more spectacular as you ascend. When the forest lane meets a stream, the route climbs the ridge of Upper Esgair Hill. Soon you descend through open moor to the village of Bwlch-y-sarnau. Departing

See The Offa's Dyke Path (South) Map (p335)
See The Offa's Dyke Path (North) Map (p339)

The trail leaves Llanidloes by Long Bridge St, crossing the River Severn to link up with the Severn Way path through an attractive forest. The disused Van Mine, which made Llanidloes' fortune until it closed in 1920, is visible from the trail. Rejoining the main road for 800m, climb steeply and then go left at a cattle grid to pass through Bryntail Farm.

The track descends into the Clywedog Valley, where you can gaze up at the 65m-high **Clywedog Dam** and explore the ruins of the 19th-century **Bryntail lead mine**. Crossing a bridge, a steep climb takes you up the other side of the dam to impressive views of the 6.5-mile-long reservoir Llyn Clywedog, with its 45,000 million litres of captured water.

Follow some steep sections of path along the edge of the lake before passing the Clywedog Yacht Club (with a **café** in summer) and climbing to the extreme edge of the gigantic Hafren Forest pine plantation. A rough track gives way to bleak, open marshland and a picnic site beside the Afon Biga.

From here a forest track re-enters the forest. Amble along a flat and wide track, then back into farmland. Just past Dolydd, another new section of path heads due north; scan the skies here for red kites cruising the air currents. A gradual climb on a grassy trail takes you to the edge of attractive moorland, at which point the trail becomes an ancient Roman road with cart tracks carved into its stone bed. Dylife appears below to the right; leave the trail to descend to the pub for the night.

DYLIFE

This hamlet has just one place to stay – the **Star Inn** (☎ 01650-521345; djlwb@hotmail.com; r from £20, dinner mains from £7), where the lively pub and good food make up for the tired rooms.

Day 5: Dylife to Machynlleth
6–7 hours, 14.5 miles (23.5km)
You'll see some of the finest walking on the route today, as the trail passes through glacial valleys, cool forest and rugged hills to spot hidden mountain lakes and unusual bird life.

Leaving the Star Inn, head back up the hill to rejoin the trail where you left it.

Head west through beautiful, windswept moorland, passing close to a dramatic drop into the rugged Afon Clywedog glacial valley. Descending rapidly to cross the Nant Goch tributary, the trail climbs again through boggy but attractive moorland to the edge of the stunning Glaslyn – a lake and water-bird sanctuary, well worth a detour (it's about a one-hour walk around the lake). Behind the lake is the dark and stoic profile of Foel Fadian (564m), which the trail soon skirts.

You are now at the highest point on the Glyndŵr's Way, with stunning green valleys plunging dramatically to your left and Foel Fadian sloping up to the right. The rocky trail – which can be treacherously slick – drops steeply (330m in just under 1.5 miles) to enter a picturesque and partially wooded valley. The suddenly plush green path passes around 800m south of Aberhosan.

After a demanding climb up Cefn Modfedd, leave the old route, with the new trail swinging expansively southwest, through a short wood and past **Talbontdrain** (☎ 01654-702192; www.talbontdrain.co.uk; r from £25), a beautiful and cheery B&B farmstead with an emphasis on excellent food.

A steep hill leads into a splendid walk above Dyfi Valley, before you climb once more through woodland on Ffridd Rhiwlwyfen and then swing to the far side of Machynlleth to enter town via the '**Roman Steps**,' which may or may not actually be Roman but make for a dramatic approach to the city regardless.

MACHYNLLETH
pop 2147
Machynlleth is ideal for a rest day. A vibrant little town with a rich history, fine architecture and traditional pubs alongside organic restaurants and internet cafés, it's a microcosm of the cultural regeneration being enjoyed by modern Wales. For information on accommodation and attractions in the area, drop into the **tourist office** (☎ 01654-702401; Maengwyn St).

The slate **Owain Glyndŵr Parliament House** (☎ 01654-702827; admission £1; ☿ 11am-3pm Mon-Tue & Thu-Sat, 10am-4pm Wed Easter-Sep), in the main street, postdates Glyndŵr's original venue but probably resembles it closely. Displays explain Glyndŵr's fight for Welsh independence but really the place is rather low key.

Other things to see include the nearby **Centre for Alternative Technology** (☎ 01654-702782; www.cat.org.uk; Pantperthog; adult/child £8/4; ✹ 10am-5.30pm, summer holidays 9.30am-6pm), 1 mile out of town; buses run hourly from the clock tower. The **Museum of Modern Art** (☎ 01654-703355; www.momawales.org.uk; Hoel Penrallt; free admission; ✹ 10am-4pm Mon-Sat) has an interesting collection of work by Welsh artists as well as changing exhibits.

Places to stay include the **White Lion** (☎ 01654-703455; www.whitelionhotel.co.uk; Heol Pentrehedyn; s with/without bathroom/d £38/28, d with/without bathroom £70/50, f £80), with excellent food and a large family room ideal for backpacking groups; and **Maenllwyd Guesthouse** (☎ 01654-702928; maenllwyd@btinternet.com; Newtown Rd; s/d/t £35/55/70). Both are in the centre of town.

For meals there's a large selection of pubs and restaurants, notably the **Quarries** (☎ 01654-702339; Maengwyn St; mains £5), an organic café serving superbly prepared vegetarian meals.

Day 6: Machynlleth to Llanbrynmair
5½–6½ hours, 14 miles (22.5km)
This is a short, easy day with some excellent views over tiny villages and wide valleys. You'll see imposing mountain peaks in the distance and, on a clear day, get a glimpse of the sea.

From Machynlleth, you head down a quiet minor road southeast to Forge, and from there a laneway leads through farmland, back to the main road for 300m and on to Penegoes. Here, a lane juts off from the main road heading due east between hedgerows. Strike up to the left through some fields and then descend steeply through heavy bracken to the small village of Abercegir.

From Abercegir the route once again climbs onto open moorland. Along these hilltops are lovely views of Cadair Idris. Keep a careful eye on your map, compass and waymarks here, as the distinct track up the hill becomes quite vague toward the summit and on the descent to Cemmaes Road.

Among the little cluster of buildings at Cemmaes Road is a **shop**, post office and quiet but adorable **pub** (hours vary, but if you knock on the door and the owner's around, it's open).

After an initial steep climb out of Cemmaes Road, the rest of the 6-mile walk to Llanbrynmair is fairly easy going, across rolling hills and through pleasant, scenic valleys. After climbing to the derelict Rhyd-yr-aderyn farm, the route descends towards Llanbrynmair, before a new section heads northeast up a steepish hill, following the fence-line along a boggy path. A pleasant track takes you 800m through a pine forest. Once out of the forest you reach the brow of a hill with astounding views stretching out before you; descend the hill past a large transmitter tower and along a minor road to Llanbrynmair.

LLANBRYNMAIR
There's not much to Llanbrynmair, except a shop and a great pub, the **Wynnstay Arms** (☎ 01650-521431; A470; r from £25), which serves real ale and good pub meals. Next door is the eccentric and charming **Machinations Museum of Mechanical Magic** (☎ 01650-521635; www.machinations.org.uk; Old Village Hall; adult/child £3/free; ✹ 9.30am-5.30pm), a fascinating collection of mechanised 'automata' that's well worth delaying your walk to see.

Day 7: Llanbrynmair to Llanwddyn
7–8 hours, 17.5 miles (28km)
A long and relatively tough day, this section nevertheless features some spectacular hill-top panoramas – and the well-deserved reward of lovely Lake Vyrnwy at the end.

Leave Llanbrynmair northwards, going under a railway line before heading east through fields. The route soon strikes north again, following a disused vehicle track up a long, steep hill, but the climb is worth it; you can enjoy terrific views of the valley below as you contour for 1 mile or so.

Entering a forest, the trail becomes a broad, open vehicle track – not the most exciting section of scenery, though the flat footing may come as a welcome change – before you cross several fields and meet yet another vehicle track to rejoin the old Glyndŵr's Way near Dolau-ceimion Farm.

You soon climb to the edge of Pen Coed (360m) and cross a particularly lonely stretch of bracken-covered moor. The waymarking has improved here but still keep an eye on your map and compass. After about

1 mile, cross a stream and follow a path to the left that zigzags a little confusingly through a host of farms to take you into Llangadfan. This village has a **shop** at the petrol station, and just up the street, the **Cann Office Hotel** (☎ 01938-820202; s/d/t £26/45/60, sandwiches from £2) is a good place for lunch or an overnight stop.

From here, the walk to Llanwddyn is pretty comfortable. The final 7 miles takes you through the huge plantation of Dyfnant forest, where a well-signposted maze of forestry tracks culminates in one enormous hill before descending rather spectacularly toward Lake Vyrnwy. Watch for pheasants.

LLANWDDYN

Essentially a scattering of houses around **Lake Vyrnwy** and its impressive 33-arched dam, Llanwddyn has an unusual history. In 1881, construction began on a dam and 70-mile-long aqueduct to provide Liverpool with a water supply, but there was a minor obstacle: Llanwddyn. So the builders moved the entire village up the hill. The village's original location is now underwater, and the ruins can be seen when the lake's water levels get low.

There is plenty to do here if you have a spare day, from exploring one of the many nature trails to cycling the 12-mile circuit of the lake. There are also three hides for spotting the many species of local birds (the lake is part of a Royal Society for the Protection of Birds' reserve), plus fishing, sailing and canoeing. There are two small **cafés** (☼ 10am-4pm) with tea and snacks. The helpful **tourist office** (☎ 01691-870346), located inside the craft centre, has information on bicycle hire.

Places to stay in the area include the nice, homey **Gorffwysfa B&B** (☎ 01691-870217; www.vyrnwy-accommodation.co.uk; 4 Glyn Dr; r from £25), run by a lovely couple who will make you want to move in permanently. Nearby, and equally attractive, is the **Oaks** (☎ 01691-870250; mdug99@aol.com; d from £30). There's also the fancy **Lake Vyrnwy Hotel** (☎ 01691-870692; www .lakevyrnwy.com; d from £100, pub mains £7-15), which dominates the hillside and contains the area's only pub and restaurant; the food in the pub is excellent value, and you can dine on the outdoor terrace overlooking the lake.

Day 8: Llanwddyn to Pontrobert

4½–5½ hours, 12 miles (19.5km)

This day marks the end of the harder moorland sections. The trail is quite easy from now on, passing through pretty valleys, pleasant river-side paths and gentle farmland.

The route follows forest tracks and minor roads from Llanwddyn; about 2.5 miles along, look for a waymark post to the right, directing you steeply uphill along a rough green track. Turn left at the top to continue along a forest road. In a short while look for another waymark post to the right, directing you to leave the forest road for an overgrown and rather-hard-to-spot trail. From here it's all ups and downs through fields and woodland toward the village of Pont Llogel, where there's a small post office and shop.

The path follows the River Vyrnwy for 800m before going left again to higher ground. This section meanders through farmland, down a new path towards Dolwar Fach farm (which cuts 1 mile off the old route) and eventually into Dolanog.

The next section is comfortable and attractive, with the route shadowing the Vyrnwy as it undulates through woods before climbing slightly away from the river to follow a lane into Pontrobert.

PONTROBERT

The village of Pontrobert is an attractive place with a terrific pub, the **Royal Oak Inn** (☎ 01938-500243; r from £20, meals from £5), offering B&B and good food. If you're lucky, you may spot kingfishers flashing along the river under the old bridge. If you can't get into the pub, Meifod is only 3 miles or so along the trail.

Day 9: Pontrobert to Welshpool

5½–6½ hours, 13.5 miles (21.5km)

Today is hilly but comfortable, culminating in glorious views over Welshpool as you approach the end of the trail.

Heading east out of Pontrobert, you wander through gentle farmland before crossing the edge of the wooded Gallt yr Ancr (Hill of the Anchorite) and taking a lane into the tidily modern village of Meifod, which has a useful **shop**, plus lovely grounds to relax in at the Church of Saints Dysilio and Mary. The **King's Head** (☎ 01938-500171; s/d £25/50) has B&B and reasonable meals.

POWIS CASTLE

Don't miss visiting **Powis Castle** (☎ 01938-551920; adult/child £10/5; ☼ 1-5pm Thu-Mon Apr, Jun & Sep, 1-4pm Thu-Mon Oct, 1-5pm Tue-Sun Jul & Aug), 1 mile south of Welshpool. Built in the 13th century, it is one of the National Trust's finest properties in Wales, featuring impressive terraced gardens, plus an orangery, aviary and a smattering of niched statues. The castle houses the Clive of India Museum, a collection of artefacts and treasures amassed by the redoubtable Robert Clive during his stint on the subcontinent over 200 years ago. Visit www .nationaltrust.org.uk/wales for garden and restaurant hours.

Leaving Meifod you encounter a steep but pleasant climb through the woods of Broniarth Hill, before looping round Llyn Du (*llyn* means 'lake' in Welsh) and swinging back to the southwest along a minor road. More comfortable farmland walking follows, until you hit the B4392 at Stonehouse Farm. Head south through Figyn Wood and climb uphill to the edge of a golf course for panoramic views and a spectacular feeling of lofty accomplishment. From here, go east through a series of farms to meet the A458, near Welshpool's Raven Sq train station. The main street starts at the nearby roundabout.

A visit to the magnificent **Powis Castle** (see the boxed text, above) will provide a fitting finale to your walk.

THE OFFA'S DYKE PATH

Duration	12 days
Distance	177.5 miles (285km)
Difficulty	demanding
Start	Sedbury Cliffs
Finish	Prestatyn (p335)
Nearest Town	Chepstow (p334)
Transport	bus, train

Summary A popular national trail through varied and historically rich terrain, with a lot of stiles and some testing climbs.

They say good fences make good neighbours, but King Offa may have taken the idea a bit far. The 8th-century Mercian king dreamed up and built Offa's Dyke, Britain's longest archaeological monument, allegedly to keep the unruly Welsh on their side of the border (although many historians say the independent-minded Welsh princes at the time were just fine with King Offa's idea of 'neighbourly'). A grand and ambitious linear earthwork, usually in the form of a bank next to a ditch, the dyke became pivotal in the history of the Marches (the borderlands between Wales and the ancient kingdom of Mercia). Even today, though only 80 miles of the dyke remains, the modern Wales–England border roughly follows the line it defined.

The Offa's Dyke Path National Trail crisscrosses that border around 30 times in its journey from the Severn Estuary in the south through the beautiful Wye Valley and Shropshire Hills to the coast at Prestatyn in North Wales. The trail itself often strays from the dyke, which is overgrown in some places and built over in others. In doing so it covers an astonishing range of scenery and vegetation, including river flat land, hill country, oak forests, heathland and bracken, conifer forest, green fields, high moors and the mountainous terrain of the Clwydian range in the north.

The region's rich and turbulent history is also reflected in the ruined castles and abbeys, the ancient hillforts and remaining sections of Roman road. One of the trail's most exciting features is that you're never really sure what you'll encounter from day to day.

PLANNING

While the Offas' Dyke Path can be walked in either direction, it's best done south to north; the sun and wind will be mostly on your back.

Most people take 12 days to complete the walk, though it's wise to allow at least two rest days, bringing your venture to an even two weeks. The rest days will also allow you to take in some of the notable sights off the trail, particularly Tintern Abbey and Powis Castle.

Offa's Dyke is generally well waymarked by the familiar white acorn indicating a national trail, but many public paths and bridleways crisscross the route, so keep your eyes peeled and carry a good set of maps and a compass.

Day	From	To	Miles/km
1	Sedbury Cliffs	Monmouth	17.5/28
2	Monmouth	Pandy	17/27.5
3	Pandy	Hay-on-Wye	17.5/28
4	Hay-on-Wye	Kington	15/24
5	Kington	Knighton	13.5/21.5
6	Knighton	Brompton Crossroads	15/24
7	Brompton Crossroads	Buttington	12.5/20
8	Buttington	Llanymynech	10.5/17
9	Llanymynech	Chirk Castle	14/22.5
10	Chirk Castle	Llandegla	16/25.5
11	Llandegla	Bodfari	17/27.5
12	Bodfari	Prestatyn	12/19.5

Maps & Books

The best maps are in the OS Explorer 1:25,000 series, conveniently included in the official National Trail Guide *Offa's Dyke Path*. This is also the best guidebook on offer, covering the walk in two books – Sedbury to Knighton and Knighton to Prestatyn – both by Ernie and Kathy Kay and Mark Richards. The books feature straightforward route notes, a taste of the history, colour maps and suggested circular walks off the dyke.

The route is also covered by OS Landranger 1:50,000 maps No 162 *Gloucester & Forest of Dean*, 161 *Abergavenny & The Black Mountains*, 148 *Presteigne & Hay-on-Wye*, 137 *Ludlow & Wenlock Edge*, 126 *Shrewsbury*, 117 *Chester & Wrexham* and 116 *Denbigh & Colwyn Bay*, but the detail is not as helpful.

Also recommended is *Offa's Dyke Path* by Keith Carter, with thorough text and detailed line maps. However, to get a real sense of the trail's rich heritage, you can't go past *Walking Offa's Dyke Path* by David Hunter.

Information Sources

The tourist office at Knighton is appropriately in the **Offa's Dyke Centre** (☎ 01547-528753; www.offasdyke.demon.co.uk; West St), managed by the Offa's Dyke Association (ODA), and it is the best source of information about the route. Here you'll find helpful booklets and pamphlets, including the ODA's indispensable *Offa's Dyke Path – Where to Stay, How to Get There & Other Useful Information*; the handy *Backpackers' & Camping List*; *South to North Route Notes*; and a set of strip maps. Some of these pamphlets are also available at tourist offices along the route.

Also useful are the **Offa's Dyke website** (www.offas-dyke.co.uk) and the official **National Trails website** (www.nationaltrail.co.uk/offasdyke).

Baggage Services

Offa's Dyke Baggage Carriers (☎ 01497-821266; Hay-on-Wye) uses local taxis to collect and transport your luggage along the route. The charge varies depending on the length of the day's walk but you're looking at an average of £15 per person. Many B&Bs provide the same service (termed 'luggage' in the ODA booklet), often at substantially cheaper rates. Inquire about these when booking accommodation.

NEAREST TOWNS
Chepstow
pop 14,195

An industrial town trading in timber, wine and glass, Chepstow originated as a strategic base guarding access into Wales over the River Wye. Though it grew into a prosperous trading port, its importance diminished as river-borne commerce declined. Today, Chepstow is a typical market town, albeit with an unusually pretty river-side setting.

The main attraction is the stout, chunky **Chepstow Castle** (☎ 01291-624065; admission £3.50; ✆ 9.30am-5pm Apr-Oct, to 4pm Nov-Mar), straddling the cliffs of the River Wye. Begun in 1067, the year after the Battle of Hastings, it was the first stone-built castle in Wales. The **tourist office** (☎ 01291-623772) is directly across from the castle but, perplexingly, doesn't always stock important ODA pamphlets, so ensure you have these before you arrive.

SLEEPING & EATING

There is a good range of places to stay in Chepstow. Near the start of the walk there's **Upper Sedbury House** (☎ 01291-627173; Sedbury Lane; r from £23.50), where you can leave your car while you walk. The **Coach & Horses** (☎ 01291-622626; Welsh St; r from £25) has good food all day.

There are plenty of places to eat along High St and Bridge St, including numerous pubs and the more refined **Afon Gwy** (☎ 01291-620158; 28 Bridge St; 2-course meal £14, B&B s/d £40/60; ✆ dinner).

GETTING THERE & AWAY

Chepstow is on the train line between Cardiff (40 minutes) and Gloucester (30 minutes), via Newport, with several trains an hour. **National Express** (☎ 08705 808080; www .nationalexpress.com) long-distance coach 201 passes through Chepstow 11 times a day between Swansea (two to three hours) and Gatwick (four to six hours). There's also a twice-daily route via Chepstow from Cardiff (one to two hours) to London (three to five hours).

By car, Chepstow is reached by leaving the M48 immediately after you've crossed the Severn Bridge coming from England. Ask when you book accommodation about parking your car for the duration of the walk.

Prestatyn

If you weren't high on the triumph of having finished such a long walk, you might notice that Prestatyn, especially in summer, is clogged with tourists and has all the trappings of a typical seaside resort. As it is, though, you'll probably just want to enjoy its exuberance or, at any rate, its vast range of easy-access pubs. The official end of the walk is at the **tourist office** (☎ 01745-889092).

SLEEPING & EATING

There are several B&Bs and camp sites in Prestatyn, including **Roughsedge Guest House** (☎ 01745-887359; roughsedge@ykubler.fsnet.co.uk; 26-28 Marine Rd; r with/without bathroom from £25/23).

Pubs where you can slake your thirst and raise a glass to your success include the **Cross Foxes** (☎ 01745-854984; Pendre Sq, 1 Meliden Rd); the gimmicky **Offa's Tavern** (☎ 01745-886046; 2-10 High St); and, across from the railway station, the impressive 1890s Victoria Hotel. For food, try **Suhail Tandoori** (☎ 01745-856829; 12 Bastion Rd) or any of the ubiquitous fish-and-chip, Chinese or pizza takeaway joints.

GETTING THERE & AWAY

Prestatyn is on the rail line between Chester (30 minutes) and Bangor (45 minutes), with several trains an hour. **National Express** (☎ 08705 808080; www.nationalexpress.com) buses pass through daily on the route from Bangor (1½ hours) to London (via Birmingham), as well as from Pwllheli (3½ hours) to London and Pwllheli to York. Prestatyn is on the A548 between Llandudno and Chester.

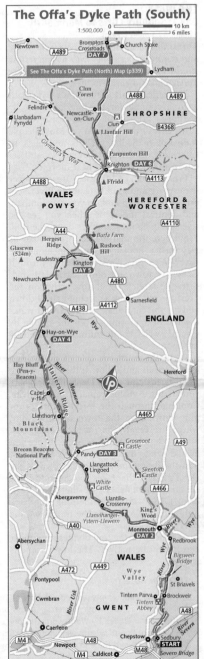

The Offa's Dyke Path (South)

THE WALK
Day 1: Sedbury Cliffs to Monmouth
9 hours, 17.5 miles (28km)

This is one of the longest days on the route and is quite demanding, with several testing climbs, although the sheer beauty of the Wye Valley makes it easier to take.

The official start of the Offa's Dyke Path is by a commemorative marker stone by Sedbury Cliffs, about 1 mile east of Chepstow, across the River Wye. Most people walk out to Sedbury Cliffs and back to Chepstow on the day they arrive, and set out from Chepstow the next morning.

From Sedbury Cliffs there are views over the estuary and mud flats of the River Severn – take a good look so you can compare and contrast the scene when you see the river again about 100 miles down the trail. From here the well-marked trail makes its way past a housing estate and along the River Wye to Chepstow Castle, through Chepstow town. It's not a particularly picturesque stretch so, if you arrive on the previous afternoon, you could stroll down and get this bit done, then start your walking the next morning from the bridge by Chepstow Castle – an infinitely more pleasing spot.

From the northern side of the bridge, join the trail and follow it through several small farms and up to Dennel Hill, where you first see visible remains of the dyke. Continue through the forest before dropping down into the town of Brockweir, where the **Country Inn** (☎ 01291-689548; meals from £4) offers lunch and real ale. Before you head down to Brockweir, there's a path just past the limestone pinnacle, known as the Devil's Pulpit, that takes you down to 14th-century **Tintern Abbey** (see the boxed text, below). You can avoid the long slog back up the hill by following the trail along the river to Brockweir.

At Brockweir the trail divides into upper and lower alternatives. The lower route is an easier and prettier walk along the river but is almost 1 mile longer, while the upper route climbs to follow the line of the dyke through enclosed lanes and minor roads. The routes rejoin at Bigsweir Bridge – if you want to call it a day, there are a few B&B options in St Briavels, 1.5 miles to the east, including a **YHA hostel** (☎ 0870 770 6040; www.yha.org.uk; dm from £18) in an 800-year-old castle.

The trail climbs steeply again to rise and fall through forest and farmland until a descent into Redbrook, where there's a **shop** and several B&Bs. Say goodbye to the dyke now, as you don't see it again until Kington. From Redbrook it's a trudge up another hill and back down to Monmouth.

MONMOUTH

This small, attractive town on the Welsh west bank is at the confluence of the Rivers Wye and Monnow. This strategic position resulted in control of the town changing on a regular basis over the past several hundred years and led the allegiances of war-weary locals to become decidedly local. The town formed its own militia around 1540, a group noted for its propensity to raise arms against both sides whenever caught in the middle of a stoush between powerful neighbours.

Architecturally, Monmouth's main attractions are the beautiful 13th-century stone-gated **bridge** over the River Monnow and the foundations of **Monmouth Castle** – a building that would be far more impressive had generations of local builders not stripped it down for its stone.

The **tourist office** (☎ 01600-713899; Agincourt Sq) is at Shire Hall.

You can camp at **Monnow Bridge Caravan & Camping** (☎ 01600-714004; sites for 2 £8), near the bridge. Most of the 10 or so B&Bs in town charge between £19 and £25; these include the spotless and welcoming **Verdi Bosco** (☎ 01600-714441; Wonastow Rd) and **Burton House**

TINTERN ABBEY

The tall walls and empty, arched windows of **Tintern Abbey** (☎ 01291-689251; ☼ 9.30am-5pm, to 4pm in winter), a 14th-century Cistercian abbey on the banks of the River Wye, have been painted by Turner and lauded by Wordsworth. It's one of the most beautiful ruins in Britain. As a result, the village of Tintern swarms with visitors in summer. The abbey ruins are awe-inspiring, although best visited toward the end of the day after the crowds have dispersed.

(☎ 01600-714958; rogerbanfield@aol.com; St James Sq). For food, try the **Green Dragon** (☎ 01600-712561; St Thomas Sq) for tasty and well-priced meals, or the **Gatehouse** (☎ 01600-713890; Old Monnow Bridge), with a great selection of veggie dishes.

Day 2: Monmouth to Pandy
9 hours, 17 miles (27.5km)
This is another long day but the walking's comfortable, through rolling farmland, though you have to cross a lot of stiles.

Route descriptions are pretty superfluous today as the trail is well waymarked. You go through a seemingly endless succession of farms, with hilly and boggy King's Wood, 1 mile out of Monmouth, the only significant respite from the fields. The day's highlight is undoubtedly the 12th-century Norman stronghold, **White Castle** (£2; ☼ 10am-5pm), about two-thirds of the way along.

You also pass through a few villages that feature lovely old churches, including the isolated but beautiful **Llanvihangel-Ystern-Llewern**, the austere **St Teilo** at Llantilio Crossenny and castle-like **St Cadoc** at Llangattock Lingoed.

Toward the end of the day's walk, a long, flat mountain comes into view – this is Hatterall Ridge, which you'll cross tomorrow.

PANDY
The **Lancaster Arms** (☎ 01873-890699; A465; s/d £26/50) looks after walkers well and serves filling pub food. Nearby, there's also the comfortable **Park Hotel** (☎ 01873-890271; r from £35) and, on the way into Pandy, the pleasant **Llanerch Farm** (☎ 01873-890432; r per person £25). If Hatterall Ridge looks too daunting, Pandy is on the bus route between Abergavenny and Hereford.

Day 3: Pandy to Hay-on-Wye
9½ hours, 17.5 miles (28km)
This is a very long and difficult day through the Black Mountains – among the highest and most exposed sections of the trail. Be prepared for adverse weather, but on a clear day you'll revel in the wildness and the spectacular views.

The trail begins with a long, steady climb to the first summit of the Black Mountains (464m) then continues with an easy, gradual climb to the highest point (703m). The trail alternates between bracken and peat,

and can become very boggy if it's raining. In places the ridge becomes fairly wide and there are a number of confusing paths, so a map and compass are essential. If visibility is poor or the weather atrocious, strongly consider dropping down west into either Llanthony or Capel-y-ffin. You can either spend the night here and hope for better weather tomorrow or follow minor roads and lanes into Hay-on-Wye.

If you opt to stay the night, Llanthony has the small and friendly **Half Moon Hotel** (☎ 01873-890611; s/d £26/47) and Capel-y-ffin has a **YHA hostel** (☎ 01873-890650; capelyffin@yha .org.uk; dm £11).

From Hay Bluff (Pen-y-Beacon), at the northern end of Hatterall Ridge, there are great views to the east, north and west. Have a rest here before you negotiate the steep descent. While Hay might have looked close from the bluff, it's still 4 miles away, mostly downhill through farmland.

HAY-ON-WYE
pop 1400
Take a break from stretching your legs to exercise your intellect at Hay, a pretty little town famous for its wealth of secondhand bookshops. Spend a well-earned rest day here roaming the bookshelves; there are plenty of eating and sleeping options here as well. The **tourist office** (☎ 01497-820144; Oxford Rd) appropriately has a good selection of books.

The welcoming **Clifton House** (☎ 01497-821618; Belmont Rd; d from £55) is ideal for walkers, while the nearby **Rest for the Tired** (☎ 01497-820550; Broad St; s/d £30/50) has nicer rooms in a cute black-and-white house. **Belmont House** (☎ 01497-820718; Belmont St; s/d from £25/40) has cosy rooms, a kitchen and a pretty sunroom in a quiet annexe off the street.

As befits a popular tourist town, most of Hay's many pubs serve good food, and there are plenty of takeaways.

Day 4: Hay-on-Wye to Kington
7½ hours, 15 miles (24km)
This an enjoyable day of contrasts that takes you along the river, through a short stretch of forest and up onto a couple of lovely stretches of moor.

Leaving Hay to the west, cross the River Wye and turn right to follow the trail along its banks for several hundred metres, before crossing several fields up to the A438. After a short walk along this busy road, head up-hill alongside the Bettws Dingle wood – and briefly through its dark and cool heart – to join a minor road and a succession of fields for the next 3 miles into the small village of Newchurch. There's no pub or shop here, but the church offers refreshments to weary ramblers.

Leaving Newchurch, a steep climb takes you up into the undulating moorland of Disgwylfa Hill, where the walking is pleasant and the waymarking clear. Turning left at a clear path, follow the dogleg at Hill House Farm and then negotiate more fields to end up in the village of Gladestry, where there are a couple of B&Bs and the **Royal Oak** pub.

From Gladestry you climb a steep bridleway to the open moors of Hergest Ridge – an enjoyable 3-mile stretch with stunning views that would make your heart race if it wasn't already. The descent starts at a disused racecourse and the trail eventually turns into a minor road to take you into Kington.

KINGTON

Kington gets a bad rap – one local described it as 'looking like it's closed all the time' – but it has the pretty 12th-century St Mary's church, a street or two of attractively rickety black-and-white houses and one exceptional pub.

Accommodation includes the **Royal Oak Inn** (☎ 01544-230081; Church St; s/d £35/55) and, across the road, the **Swan Hotel** (☎ 01544-230510; s/d £40/60). There's also a new **YHA hostel** (☎ 0870 770 6128; www.yha.org.uk; Victoria Rd; dm £14) with enthusiastic, knowledgeable staff and comfy bunks in a former Victorian hospital.

Most of the pubs and inns in Kington serve meals in the £5 to £12 range, with the **Swan** being probably the nicest. There's good Chinese takeaway. Beer geeks should not miss the local treasure that is **Ye Olde Tavern** (Victoria Rd), 10 doors past the hostel, where the house-made ale (try the Early Riser) is worth the 67 miles you've walked to reach it.

Day 5: Kington to Knighton
7–8 hours, 13.5 miles (21.5km)
This stretch is relatively short but very attractive, wandering through rolling hills and featuring some of the best-preserved examples of the dyke along the whole route.

Head north out of town, taking great care crossing the busy A44 before embarking on the first of this day's many ascents. It takes you up through fields to the highest golf course in England (390m). Continuing through fields to Rushock Hill, you rejoin Offa's Dyke itself, which will now be your faithful companion most of the way to Knighton.

The rest of the day takes you up and down a succession of green hills, with impressive views at almost every turn, punctuated by short stretches of pine forest. Highlights of this section include the historic **Burfa Farm**, a restored medieval farmhouse at the base of Burfa hillfort; and the well-preserved section of dyke at Ffridd, which is the last hill before you descend into Knighton (p326).

Day 6: Knighton to Brompton Crossroads
9–10 hours, 15 miles (24km)
This section of trail is so bleak and challenging that satirical poems have been written about it. The relentless pattern is a steep climb, a relatively level section of ridge and then a steep drop, followed immediately by another brutal climb. Get an early start to allow for plenty of rest stops.

Heading north out of Knighton, there's a steep climb to Panpunton Hill, where you rejoin the dyke, which the trail follows almost all day. It's at its most impressive from nearby Llanfair Hill, the dyke's highest point at 429m, with fine views to the ruins of Clun castle.

This section passes 1 mile from the village of Newcastle-on-Clun, where you could split this stage by staying at the **Crown Inn** (☎ 01588-640271; r from £25). Alternatively, about 3.5 miles east of the trail, along the B4368, is the **Clun Mill Youth Hostel** (☎ 01588-640582; dm £12).

Still-more-demanding hills await you between Newcastle and Brompton Crossroads, but the presence of the dyke makes navigation redundant.

BROMPTON CROSSROADS
The hospitable **Drewin Farm** (☎ 01588-620325; r from £22) is right on the path, about 1.5 miles before Brompton Crossroads. A little

further on, the regal **Mellington Hall** (☎ 01588-620456; s/d £50/80) has plush rooms inside a Gothic manor – a real treat, though you might feel self-conscious with mud on your boots.

Day 7: Brompton Crossroads to Buttington
6½–7½ hours, 12.5 miles (20km)

This day is on the short and easy side, with pleasant, flat walking that gradually builds to steep ascents. The path follows the dyke for much of the day.

Leaving the crossroads, the trail follows the dyke straight across the Montgomery plain, passing less than 1 mile from the historic town of **Montgomery**, which is worth a visit if you can spare a couple of hours. After crossing a minor road, you start to steadily rise towards Forden, with today's main obstacle, the Long Mountain, dominating the skyline ahead and to your right.

Following a stretch of road walking, cut through a number of farms before joining a lane, which follows the course of a Roman road. It takes you steeply up and into Green Wood, on the lower slopes of the Long Mountain. From here, zigzag up to the summit, where the trail swings round the edge of Beacon Ring, an Iron Age hillfort.

Keep your eye out for waymarks so that you don't stray on the sharp descent that winds through innumerable fields towards Buttington.

BUTTINGTON
In Buttington itself is the cheery and welcoming **Green Dragon** (☎ 01938-553076; sites for 2 £4), a pub with meals and camp sites. Otherwise, head north to **Mona Broxton's** (☎ 01938-570225; 1 Plas Cefn; r from £17). Less than an hour's walk away, Welshpool (p326) is a much better prospect, with many facilities, including a good range of places to stay and eat.

Day 8: Buttington to Llanymynech
5–6 hours, 10.5 miles (17km)

Today you get a break from your recent exertions with a day of almost completely flat walking. You can make very good time if you stride out, allowing for a visit to Powis Castle if you stayed in Welshpool.

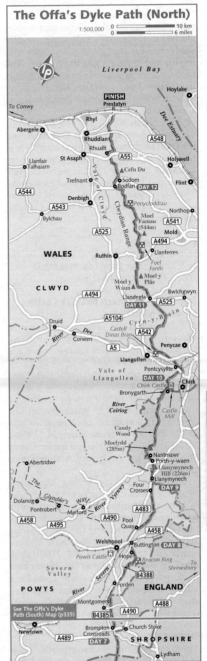

The Offa's Dyke Path (North)

1:500,000

From Buttington the trail joins the serene Shropshire Union Canal and ambles alongside the canal's still waters under shady trees for a couple of miles. After risking life and limb crossing the A483 at Pool Quay, you enter a 4-mile stretch of equally flat farmland that meanders along the River Severn, with the Breidden peaks looming above to the right.

Around lunchtime you reach the Four Crosses, where the **Golden Lion Hotel** and the **Four Crosses Inn** offer refreshment. From here the trail follows the Montgomery Canal all the way to Llanymynech. Just before you hit town, the canal crosses the River Vyrnwy via a stone aqueduct – an arresting sight but only a taste of greater things to come.

LLANYMYNECH

In this small, hospitable town, look for the welcoming **Lion Hotel** (☎ 01691-830234; r from £25), with B&B in oldish rooms.

Day 9: Llanymynech to Chirk Castle
8 hours, 14 miles (22.5km)

In sharp contrast to yesterday's flat terrain, today is a Robin Hood's delight of winding tracks, hills with fine vantage points and dense green forests.

A climb up Llanymynech Hill takes you through a wood, where you will say goodbye to the dyke for a while. Passing through the villages of Porth-y-waen and Nantmawr, you climb once more to take in the fine views from Moelydd (285m), before rejoining the dyke just before Candy Wood. This is a lovely section atop a steep ridge.

Clear waymarking makes the route straightforward over the next several miles of hills and farmland. You eventually drop steadily, and then more steeply, to reach the valley floor, crossing the River Ceiriog and finishing the day at the Castle Mill entrance to **Chirk Castle** (☎ 01691-777701; admission £7; ⌚ noon-5pm Wed-Sun Jul-Oct). If you have made good time, you should consider a visit to the elegant state rooms and manicured gardens of this magnificent 14th-century home.

CHIRK CASTLE

There's camping at Bronygarth, close to Castle Mill, at the friendly **Old School**

(☎ 01691-772546; sites for 2 £6). West, in Llangollen, a popular tourist town and a good place for a rest day, there's a **YHA hostel** (☎ 01978-860330; llangollen@yha.org.uk; Twndwr Hall; dm £12). There are a couple of good places to the north, in Pentre – **Cloud Hill** (☎ 01691-773359; s/d from £20/40) and **Sun Cottage** (☎ 01691-774542; r from £25).

Day 10: Chirk Castle to Llandegla
9 hours, 16 miles (25.5km)

Today offers the most varied scenery of the trail, with added architectural attractions.

From Chirk Castle, take the optional route through the castle's pretty grounds before making your way on minor roads and through fields to the River Dee and the Pontcysyllte aqueduct. Designed and built by engineer Thomas Telford in 1805, the 302m-long arched aqueduct towers 38m over the River Dee and, for those with a head for heights, can be crossed on a narrow walkway.

Next, climb through Trevor Wood and along the Panorama Walk, where a laneway and then a path takes you up the short ascent to the hilltop fort of **Castell Dinas Bran**, which is well worth the 30-minute detour. You end up on a narrow path, traversing a scree slope below Eglwyseg Crags – this is a superb section of walking but it can be slippery in the wet, so be sure to watch your footing.

You next cross a wood, strike across a bracken-covered moor, negotiate a long pine plantation and head into the attractive village of Llandegla.

LLANDEGLA

Llandegla has a good selection of accommodation, including **Hand House** (☎ 01978-790570; s/d £32/54); and **2, The Village** (☎ 01978-790266; camp sites for 2 £6), which has camp sites. The **Willows Restaurant** (☎ 01978-790237; dinner mains £5-£14) offers meals.

Day 11: Llandegla to Bodfari
10 hours, 17 miles (27.5km)

This is one of the longest and most strenuous stages of the walk, with several steep ups and downs offset by the wild beauty of the heather-covered moors along the Clwydian Range.

A few miles of farmland takes you to the base of Moel y Waun, from where you climb steadily to the tumulus at the top of Moel y Plâs, a first taste of today's testing terrain. The well-marked path continues to climb and fall past several more peaks, before a brief respite of more farmland walking. You're going up again soon enough, past the ramparts of **Foel Fenlli** hillfort to the highest point of the Clwydian Range, Moel Famau (544m).

Traverse two more peaks to reach an intensely unfair descent to the valley floor and an equally steep ascent past the apex of conical Moel Arthur, before another drop and climb to **Penycloddiau** hillfort. From here the trail drops around 300m in less than 3 miles to enter the tiny village of Bodfari.

BODFARI
In Bodfari, try **Fron Haul** (☎ 01745-710301; r from £30), which is through the village and up a steep hill – call from the phone box on the A541 for directions.

Day 12: Bodfari to Prestatyn
7 hours, 12 miles (19.5km)
There are several stiff ascents to tackle on this short day, so try to conserve energy in the face of the alluring coastal vistas.

A steep climb out of Bodfari takes you past Sodom village and along one of the many sections of road today up to Cefn Du peak. More road walking, punctuated by short sections through fields, brings you to the busy village of Rhuallt, where the **Smithy Arms** puts on a good lunch.

From Rhuallt, make your way through farmland, along minor roads and over a couple of small peaks to arrive eventually at a hair-raising section of path above a 200m cliff that overlooks Prestatyn. One final descent takes you into Prestatyn. Follow the sedate Bastion Rd down to the sea and the tourist office, which marks the official end of the walk.

MORE LONG-DISTANCE WALKS

As well as the Glyndŵr's Way and the Offa's Dyke Path, there are many other long-distance walking routes in Wales. Some are in the traditionally popular walking areas around Snowdonia and the Wye Valley, while for a true cross-country experience there are routes that cross Wales' entirety. This section outlines some of the best.

THE WYE VALLEY WALK
The River Wye forms part of the border between England and Wales, and the Wye Valley is an Area of Outstanding Natural Beauty (partly traversed by the Offa's Dyke Path). Following the river's entire length is the 136-mile (218km) Wye Valley Walk, starting in Chepstow then running up to Monmouth, through Symonds Yat, which is the most spectacular section of the River Wye, where it flows through a winding, deep-sided valley edged with woodland.

The route then goes past the village of Welsh Bicknor (on the opposite bank to English Bicknor, naturally), and on through Ross-on-Wye and Hereford, before crossing the border back into Wales at Hay-on-Wye, where it follows the upper Wye through the remote mountain country of Mid Wales to the market town of Rhayader.

The walk ends on the slopes of Plynlimon, which is also the source of the River Severn, between the towns of Devil's Bridge and Machynlleth. The walk is described in the *Wye Valley Walk Official Route Guide*.

For more details about the walk see www .wyevalleywalk.org.

THE CAMBRIAN WAY
Long-distance routes that cross Wales include the Cambrian Way, winding between Cardiff and Conwy, traversing just about every bit of high, wild landscape on the way. It is described in *The Cambrian Way* by Tony Drake, the Way's instigator. For experienced walkers this is an excellent trip, although the 274 miles (441km) make it a longer, and much more difficult walk than the Pennine Way.

For more details about the walk see www .cambrianway.org.uk.

SNOWDONIA TO THE GOWER
As well as the Cambrian Way, another trans-Wales route is Snowdonia to the Gower. It's shorter and more direct than the Cambrian Way, although they overlap in the north. Whereas the Cambrian Way goes to/from Cardiff, this route (as its name suggests) ends on the Gower Peninsula, an

Area of Outstanding Natural Beauty further to the west.

Snowdonia to the Gower by John Gillham is an inspirational hardback book with good route descriptions, glossy photos, beautifully drawn aerial views and maps, and fascinating background information. The same author has since produced *A Welsh Coast to Coast Walk: Snowdonia to the Gower*, an ideal guidebook to carry on the route.

Scotland

ANDREW PARKINSON

Scotland

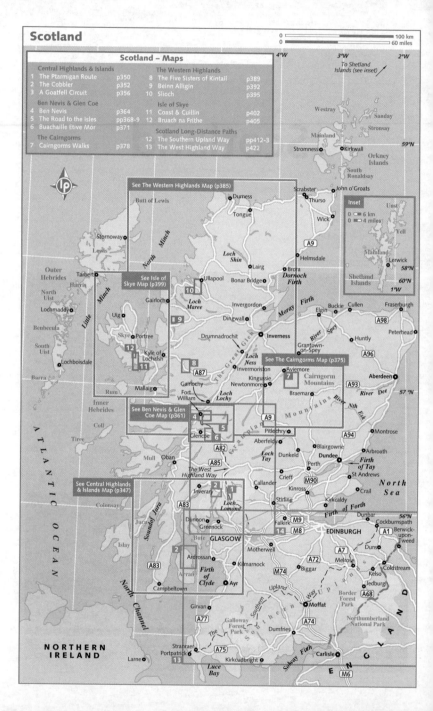

0	100 km
0	60 miles

Scotland – Maps

Central Highlands & Islands
1 The Ptarmigan Route — p350
2 The Cobbler — p352
3 A Goatfell Circuit — p356

Ben Nevis & Glen Coe
4 Ben Nevis — p364
5 The Road to the Isles — pp368-9
6 Buachaille Etive Mòr — p371

The Cairngorms
7 Cairngorms Walks — p378

The Western Highlands
8 The Five Sisters of Kintail — p389
9 Beinn Alligin — p392
10 Slioch — p395

Isle of Skye
11 Coast & Cuillin — p402
12 Bruach na Frìthe — p405

Scotland Long-Distance Paths
12 The Southern Upland Way — pp412-3
13 The West Highland Way — p422

Central Highlands & Islands

Scotland's central Highlands and islands together make a superb area of exceptional natural beauty, brimful of contrasts and rich in alluring challenges. In the far west, floating dramatically in the sheltered waters of the outer Firth of Clyde, the rugged Isle of Arran has something for everyone. There are spectacular, rock-encrusted ridges and peaks, crowned by Goatfell, the island's highest. The peaceful, scenic and very accessible northern coastline offers surprisingly remote, fairly undemanding walking.

Scotland's first national park, Loch Lomond & the Trossachs, embraces a wonderful array of glens, lochs and mountains, extending southwards from the Breadalbane district to the southern end of Loch Lomond, and eastwards from the Arrochar Alps to Loch Earn and Callander. Foremost among the high places are two renowned peaks: Ben Lomond, the southernmost of the country's 284 Munros, affords magnificent views far and wide; while the iconic Cobbler, a fantastical cluster of huge granite tors in the Arrochar Alps, offers a test of nerves and skills almost second to none.

This superb slice of Scotland is compact and easy to reach from Glasgow, Scotland's largest and most vibrant city. There are good public transport services to and around Arran, and to Arrochar. We have divided this chapter into two manageable sections: Loch Lomond & the Trossachs National Park and the Isle of Arran. These are followed by some notes about other walks on Arran and the magnificent wilderness of the remote Isle of Jura on p357.

HIGHLIGHTS

■ Summiting **Ben Lomond** (p349) for an eagle's-eye view of the divide between the Highlands and lowlands

■ Scrambling to the top of the fearsome boulders on the summit of the **Cobbler** (p350)

■ Weaving through jumbled boulders on the ascent of Arran's **Goatfell** (p357)

INFORMATION
Maps & Books
The OS Travel – Road 1:250,000 map No 3 *Southern Scotland* covers the area neatly.

The Southern Highlands by KM Andrew is a rich source of information about geology, geography and routes long and short.

Information Sources
In the main gateways to this region you will find the **Glasgow tourist office** (☎ 0141-204 4400; 11 George Sq) and **Stirling tourist office** (☎ 0870 7200 620; 41 Dumbarton Rd). A useful website for introductory tourist information is www .visitscottishheartlands.com.

GETTING AROUND
Two of the three walks described in this chapter (Goatfell and the Cobbler) can easily be reached by public transport; see the walk descriptions for details. For Ben Lomond, private transport is virtually essential.

GATEWAYS
The main gateway for this area is the city of Glasgow. Scotland's largest city, it's well served by National Express buses and by First ScotRail, GNER and Virgin trains from England and elsewhere in Scotland. From Glasgow, buses and trains link to the Isle of Arran ferry service and to Arrochar for the Cobbler walk. By car, you can bypass the city altogether, while the large, historic town of Stirling makes another handy jumping-off point.

LOCH LOMOND & THE TROSSACHS NATIONAL PARK

Established in 2002, 720-sq-mile (1865-sq-km) Loch Lomond & the Trossachs was Scotland's first national park. It has several fine ranges of mountains, including the Arrochar Alps, the Trossachs and the Breadalbane 'hills', with a total of 21 Munros and 20 Corbetts (see the boxed text, p349). There is also a score of lochs, large and small, woodlands, historic sites, many small towns and villages, major roads and railways, and a fair share of the West Highland Way (p418). Some of these areas were already protected

for their natural values, notably Argyll and Queen Elizabeth Forest Parks, and they are now within the national park.

What benefits can such a large (by local standards) and diverse park bring to residents, the country and visitors? Many people's awareness of the park's superb natural heritage has undoubtedly been strengthened by exhibitions at the visitor centres, publications and activities programs. Perhaps, too, the problems facing park managers in maintaining, let alone improving, access to lochs, glens and mountains have become more obvious. It's probably too soon to pass judgment; perhaps it needs a major threat to an outstanding feature (such as power lines across Ben Lomond) to put it to the test!

Loch Lomond, Britain's largest freshwater loch, straddles the Highland Boundary Fault, the dramatic geological divide between the Highlands and the Lowlands. It's thought that the name Lomond comes from an old Scots word *llumon,* or the Gaelic *laom,* meaning a 'beacon' or 'light'.

PLANNING
When to Walk
The walks in this section are best done between late April and early October, after and before any significant snowfalls.

Maps & Books
Harvey's spiral-bound *Loch Lomond & the Trossachs National Park* atlas has waterproof map pages (at 1:40,000) and lots of background information and contacts.

Loch Lomond, Trossachs, Stirling & Clackmannan by John Brooks covers a wide variety of walks and is recommended.

Guided Walks
Rangers from the **National Trust for Scotland** (☎ 01360-870224) and **Loch Lomond & the Trossachs National Park** (☎ 01389-722100) lead walks in the area, including on Ben Lomond.

Information Sources
The Loch Lomond & the Trossachs National Park's **Gateway Centre** (☎ 0845 345 4978; www.lochlomond-trossachs.org; Balloch) is an excellent first port of call for information about the park, including accommodation; browse the website to get the feel of the place. There is also the more central **Balmaha National Park Centre** (☎ 01389-722100; ✆ Easter-Oct).

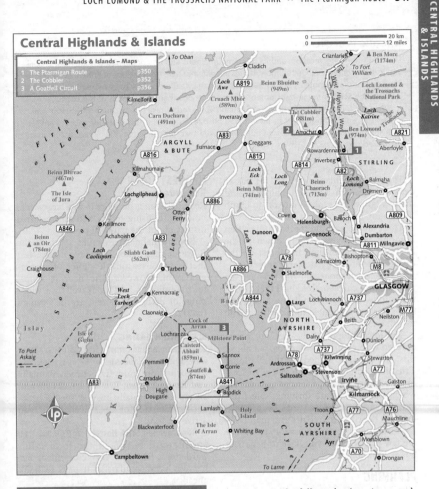

Central Highlands & Islands

Central Highlands & Islands – Maps	
1 The Ptarmigan Route	p350
2 The Cobbler	p352
3 A Goatfell Circuit	p356

THE PTARMIGAN ROUTE

Duration	4½–5 hours
Distance	7 miles (11.5km)
Difficulty	moderate
Start/Finish	Rowardennan (p348)
Transport	ferry

Summary A circuit over one of the most popular mountains in Central Scotland, following clear paths with magnificent views of famous Loch Lomond.

There is no freshwater loch in Scotland larger than Loch Lomond, 22 miles long and up to 4.5 miles wide. Standing guard over the loch is Ben Lomond (974m), the most southerly Munro.

Most people follow the 'tourist route', which starts at the Rowardennan car park, about halfway along the eastern shore of the loch. It's a straightforward ascent on a very well used and maintained path. If the weather is fine, however, we recommend the scenic and slightly less crowded Ptarmigan Route, which is described here. This follows a narrower but still clear path up the western flank of Ben Lomond, directly overlooking the loch. You can then descend via the tourist route, making a satisfying circuit. The Ptarmigan Route involves about 950m ascent. The walking time (around five hours) is the same for the circular walk described and the there-and-back route on the tourist path.

WALKING IN SCOTLAND

Scotland's northerly location, and its more-mountainous and less-populated terrain, have crucial implications for walkers. Quite simply, things are different here from the rest of Britain. Many of the areas you visit are remote by British standards, and the weather is likely to be more severe, making walks in the Scottish mountains potentially more serious than those south of the border.

When planning your walking trip in Scotland you need to take into account the shorter walking season – this is discussed in more detail on p24. Similarly, it is a good idea to be familiar with the Scottish Outdoor Access Code (see boxed text, p351). Rights of way are discussed in the boxed text on p32.

The West Highland Way (p418) passes between the loch and Ben Lomond, and many Way walkers take a day off to climb the mountain.

There are no easy alternative routes; Ben Lomond slopes very steeply down to the loch and tracks through the forest on the eastern side aren't particularly attractive.

On the open moorland you may see the ptarmigan, a chicken-sized bird that blends beautifully with its surroundings; its plumage, speckled-grey in summer, turns white in winter.

The lower slopes of the Ben are partly covered with conifer plantations, but above this, the ground, owned by the National Trust for Scotland (NTS), is open. At least one exclosure – a large fenced area within which native trees are thriving, safe from grazing sheep and deer – has been established. The trust also repairs and maintains the main footpaths in its territory and there are few places where you have to negotiate boggy ground.

PLANNING

Like all Scottish mountains, Ben Lomond can create its own weather, so be prepared for cooler and windier conditions as you ascend.

Maps & Books

Harvey's 1:25,000 map *Glasgow Popular Hills* includes Ben Lomond but isn't much help for identifying surrounding features. For this purpose, either the Ordnance Survey (OS) Landranger 1:50,000 map No 56 *Loch Lomond & Inveraray* or OS Explorer 1:25,000 map No 364 *Loch Lomond North* is preferable.

Loch Lomond, Trossachs, Stirling & Clackmannan by John Brooks covers a wide variety of walks and is recommended.

NEAREST TOWN
Rowardennan

Rowardennan is no more than a large white building, housing toilets and an unstaffed display about the national park.

Beyond Balmaha (6 miles south of the Rowardennan) there are no villages, but there's still a reasonable choice of accommodation. However, the nearest shops, tourist office and ATM, as well as a wider range of B&Bs and hotels, are in Drymen (p421).

SLEEPING & EATING

Cashel Camping and Caravan Site (☎ 01360-870234; www.forestholidays.co.uk; sites for 2 £14) is right on the loch shore, midway between Balmaha and Rowardennan. It has a small café and a shop and is usually busy. A special backpacker rate (£5 for 2) is available if you arrive on foot.

Rowardennan SYHA Hostel (☎ 0870 004 1148; www.syha.org.uk; dm £14), in the former Rowardennan Lodge, is very convenient but it's also very popular, so it pays to book ahead.

Rowardennan Hotel (☎ 01360-870273; www.rowardennanhotel.co.uk; s/d £60/110; ☺ lunch & dinner) does reasonably priced bar meals in the lively Rob Roy bar.

In Balmaha you'll find the **Oak Tree Inn** (☎ 01360-870357; www.oak-tree-inn.co.uk; dm/s/d £25/50/70, mains £7-14), which has comfortable rooms and a four-bed, en suite bunkroom. You can dine in style in the restaurant, or informally in the bar.

GETTING THERE & AWAY

The only public transport to Rowardennan is a small ferry, operated by the Rowardennan Hotel, which plies the loch to and from Inverbeg on the western shore during summer. Take the **Scottish Citylink** (☎ 0870 550

5050) bus service to Inverbeg from Glasgow (one hour, five daily) or Fort William (2¼ hours, five daily), then catch the **passenger ferry** (☎ 01360-870273) to Rowardennan. The ferry departs at 10.30am, 2.30pm and 6pm, and returns at 10am, 2pm and 5.30pm.

By road, from Drymen (20 miles from Glasgow) follow the B837 northwest for 4 miles to Balmaha then continue on the loch-side minor road to Rowardennan.

THE WALK
Rowardennan to Ptarmigan
1½–2 hours, 2.5 miles (4km)

The walk starts and finishes at the large Rowardennan car park, at the end of the road from Balmaha. With your back to the toilet block, walk towards Loch Lomond, where there's a view of the distinctive rounded knob of Ptarmigan, a couple of miles due north. Turn right (north) along the loch-side path, soon passing a granite war-memorial sculpture. The path becomes a gravel road. Soon swing right through a gate in front of the youth hostel, then turn left, following the route of the West Highland Way with the thistle-and-hexagon logo.

Pass Ardess Lodge National Trust for Scotland Ranger Centre and Ben Lomond Cottage on the right, cross a burn and turn right onto a path through the trees. It climbs beside the burn for a short distance

then veers left up the bracken-covered mountainside. As you climb steadily across the slope you're treated to views of the loch and the mountains on its western side and, further on, Ptarmigan summit comes into view. Higher up, above some small cliffs, go through a kissing gate. The path gains more height on an open spur then zigzags steeply up a grassy bluff to the ridge and on to the summit of **Ptarmigan** (731m), near a small lochan. The fine views include virtually the full length of the loch and its cluster of islands, and the Arrochar mountains to the west.

Ptarmigan to Ben Lomond
1 hour, 1 mile (1.5km)

The path leads on along the bumpy ridge, through a chain of grassy, rocky knobs to a narrow gap where stepping stones keep you out of the mud. The final, steep climb begins through the formidable crags, but natural rock steps and the well-maintained path make it quite easy. From a grassy shelf there's one more straightforward, rocky climb to the trig point on the summit of **Ben Lomond** (974m). The all-round view extends from Ben Nevis on the northern horizon, to the Isle of Arran in the southwest, the Firth of Clyde, the Arrochar Alps (notably the awl-like profile of the Cobbler) just across the loch, and the Campsie Fells and Glasgow to the south.

MUNROS & MUNRO BAGGING

In 1891 Sir Hugh Munro, a member of the recently founded Scottish Mountaineering Club (SMC), published a list of more than 500 Scottish summits over 3000ft – the height at which they became 'real' mountains. (The metric equivalent, 914m, somehow loses its mystique in translation.) Sir Hugh differentiated between 283 'mountains in their own right' (those with a significant drop on all sides or with summits well clear of the next peak) and their satellites, now known as 'tops'.

In 1901 Reverend AE Robertson was the first to climb them all, initiating the pastime that has become known as Munro bagging. This has grown to a national passion – there are books, CD-ROMs, charts and maps about Munros. More than 3550 people have completed the full round and the number is growing rapidly. The first person to complete a continuous round was writer Hamish Brown in 1974. Since then at least one continuous round has been completed in winter and the time for the fastest round is lowered regularly. Munro's original list has been revised by the SMC and in late 2006 it totalled 284. List or no list, the great majority of Munros offer outstanding walks with superb views. Of the several websites devoted to the Munros (and other lists) the SMC's is as illuminating as any (www.smc.org.uk).

Once you've bagged the Munros there are other collections of summits to tackle, such as the 219 Corbetts – Scottish mountains over 2500ft (700m) with a drop of at least 500ft (150m) on all sides – and the Donalds, lowland mountains over 2000ft (610m). The extraordinary feat of a complete round of all 728 summits, totalling 351,000m of ascent, was made in 1998.

The Ptarmigan Route

1:95,000

0 — 1 km
0 — 0.5 miles

Ben Lomond to Rowardennan

2 hours, 3.5 miles (5.5km)

The wide path starts to descend immediately, past the spectacular north-facing cliffs on the left. Soon it swings round to the right and makes a series of wide zigzags down the steep slope to the long ridge stretching ahead, which it follows south. Eventually the grade steepens over Srón Aonaich (577m) and the path resumes zigzagging through open moorland. Cross a footbridge and continue into the conifer forest along an open clearing. The path steepens and becomes rockier and more eroded, down through mixed woodland. Eventually it emerges near the Rowardennan car park.

WARNING

The final ascent of the central peak is potentially dangerous, especially when the rock is damp. Take the greatest care if you decide to squeeze through to the narrow ledge and scramble to the top – it's a long way down from the edge of the ledge.

THE COBBLER

Duration	5–5¾ hours
Distance	8 miles (12.8km)
Difficulty	moderate–demanding
Start/Finish	Forestry Commission Cobbler car park
Nearest Town	Arrochar (opposite)
Transport	bus, train

Summary Ascend one of Scotland's most famous and unforgettable peaks; don't forget to pack your head for heights for the final scramble.

Ben Arthur, fondly known as the Cobbler (881m), with its distinctive three-pronged rooster crown, stands majestically apart from its rounded neighbours. While not the highest of the six Arrochar peaks (which include four Munros), the Cobbler is without a doubt the favourite among both walkers and climbers. It dominates the southernmost section of the Arrochar Alps, bounded by Glen Loin, the head of Loch Long and Glen Croe (along the A83) in the south, Loch Lomond in the east and Glen Kinglas in the west. The last Ice Age littered the mountain with moraine and left behind the prominent Narnain Boulders below the Cobbler's peaks.

The popular story of the mountain's name identifies a hunched cobbler (the north and centre peaks) listening to his wife Jean (the south peak). The mountain is inextricably linked to the birth of Scottish rock climbing, especially among young, working-class Glaswegians, and the Cobbler Club, founded in 1866, was Scotland's first climbing group.

The path gains 850m in height and ends with a steep, rocky section from the corrie at the peak's base. Above that is a short, exhilarating scramble. Seen from the corrie, the south peak's steep sides are a popular climber's haunt. The north peak is easily reached along its northern face. The centre peak's final ascent is dramatic and, depending on your experience and the conditions on the day, potentially dangerous. You must squeeze through a body-sized hole (known as the 'needle') in a huge, box-shaped rock to reach the top via a narrow shelf (potentially lethal if damp). People wander about the centre peak, summoning courage or just watching the brave and nerveless (or foolhardy) few 'threading the needle'.

PLANNING
Maps
The OS Landranger 1:50,000 map No 56 *Loch Lomond & Inveraray* covers the area. Better coverage is provided by the Harvey Superwalker 1:25,000 map *Arrochar Alps*.

Information Sources
The **Ardgartan Visitor Centre** (☎ 01301-702432; www.visitscottishheartlands.com; Ardgartan; ✆ Easter-Oct), 2 miles west of the village of Arrochar, is a good source of maps and information about local walks. Staff can also help with accommodation bookings.

NEAREST TOWN
Arrochar
pop 650
A rather scattered village along the shores of Loch Long, Arrochar suffers somewhat from heavy vehicle traffic, but has an unbeatable view across the loch to the Cobbler. There's an ATM in the service station; otherwise the nearest is in Inveraray, 22 miles west.

SLEEPING & EATING
Ardgartan Caravan & Camping Site (☎ 01301-702293; www.forestholidays.co.uk; A83; £15) is 2 miles west of Arrochar, right beside Loch Long.

Inveraray SYHA Hostel (☎ 0870 004 1125; www.syha.org.uk; Dalmally Rd, Inveraray; dm/d £14/28), 22 miles west of Arrochar in a historic town, is the nearest hostel. It has doubles and small dorms.

Ferry Cottage (☎ 01301-702428; www.ferrycottage.com; Ardmay; s/d £35/56, dinner £12), a superbly restored old ferryman's cottage, is 1 mile south of the village. Expect a warm welcome and good home cooking; all rooms have views of Loch Long.

SCOTTISH OUTDOOR ACCESS CODE

Scotland has enjoyed a long tradition of mutual tolerance between landowners and walkers about access to the hills and moors, provided walkers observed what was known as the Country Code, as well as local restrictions during lambing, deer-stalking and grouse-shooting seasons. During the 1990s the number of people going out into the mountains soared, however, and demand for access to lowland walking areas grew.

In 1996 the Access Forum brought together representatives from among land managers, recreation groups and public agencies. It came up with a Concordat on Access, which, essentially, endorsed responsible freedom of access, subject to reasonable constraints for management and conservation. However, it was felt that the agreement merited legal status, and the issue was high on the agenda of the new Scottish Parliament after 1999.

After several years of wide-ranging consultation and, at times, acrimonious debate, the Scottish Parliament passed the pioneering Land Reform (Scotland) Act in 2003 and the following year approved the Scottish Outdoor Access Code. These conferred statutory access rights on many outdoor activities, including walking and wild camping, and on farmers and landowners. These rights don't apply to any kind of motorised activity or to hunting, shooting or fishing.

Access rights can be exercised along paths and tracks and across open ground over most of Scotland, from urban parks and paths to hills and forests, from farmland and field margins to beaches, lochs and rivers. The rights don't apply to buildings or their immediate surroundings, houses or their gardens, or most land in which crops are growing.

When you're in the outdoors the key points are as follows:

■ Take personal responsibility for your own actions and act safely

■ Respect people's privacy and peace of mind

■ Help land managers and others to work safely and effectively

■ Care for your environment and take litter home

■ Keep your dog under proper control

Scottish Natural Heritage administers the Access Code; it has set up a helpful website (www.outdooraccess-scotland.com), which goes into the code in detail; click on the 'Scottish Outdoor Access Code' link. Leaflets outlining the Code are widely available.

Greenbank Licensed Restaurant (☎ 01301-702305; Main St; mains £7-14; ☺ lunch & dinner) is a small, friendly place offering standard fare, including vegetarian dishes and a special Taste of Scotland menu; you certainly won't leave here feeling underfed. It's wise to book a table during the busy season.

The **village shop** (Main St) stocks a reasonable range of supplies. If you have forgotten your map, try the post-office shop.

GETTING THERE & AWAY

Scottish Citylink (☎ 0870 550 5050; www.citylink.co.uk) Glasgow–Campbeltown buses stop at Arrochar (1¼ hours, three daily).

First ScotRail (☎ 0845 755 0033) trains on the West Highland line from Glasgow Queen St to Fort William stop at Arrochar & Tarbet station (1½ hours, three daily), 20 minutes' walk from Arrochar. The overnight sleeper service between London Euston and Fort William also calls here; see p363 for details.

By car from Glasgow, take the M8 towards Loch Lomond and then the highly scenic A82; continue on the A83 to Arrochar from Tarbet.

GETTING TO/FROM THE WALK

The walk starts from a Forestry Commission pay-and-display (£1) car park on the A83 west of Arrochar. It's a good five-minute walk from the western end of the village to the car park, around the head of Loch Long.

THE WALK
Cobbler Car Park to Narnain Boulders

1½–1¾ hours, 2.5 miles (4km)

From the car park, cross the A83 and pass through the timber vehicle barrier signed 'Access to Ben Narnain and Cobbler'. Follow the well-made path as it zigzags uphill to a forestry road. Turn left towards a communications mast then right in front of it. The zigzags continue up through the conifer plantation to a forest track and Allt a' Bhalachain (Buttermilk Burn). A fine vista of the Cobbler's famous three peaks welcomes you to the halfway point of the ascent. Follow the clear path upstream, crossing numerous tributaries, to the distinctive **Narnain Boulders**.

Narnain Boulders to Summit Peaks

1–1¼ hours, 1.5 miles (2.4km)

Over the next few hundred metres the well-made path steers clear of a morass and climbs to the rocky corrie below the three peaks. Scramble up to the saddle between the central and north peaks, marked with a cairn.

For a less arduous, though slightly longer route, follow the path up the glen for another mile to the watershed, where it divides. Take the southern path, climbing steeply up the north ridge on well-built zigzags, to reach the saddle between the central and north peaks.

The central and highest peak lies to the left, while the more easily accessed **north peak**

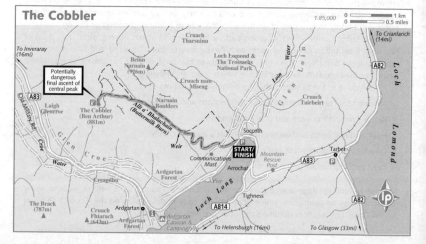

The Cobbler

is to the right. The superlative view takes in Loch Long, Gareloch, the Firth of Clyde, the Isles of Bute and Arran, Ben Lomond and dozens of other peaks to the east.

Summit Peaks to Cobbler Car Park
2½–2¾ hours, 4 miles (6.4km)
Simply retrace your steps back to the car park.

ISLE OF ARRAN

Arran is often called 'Scotland in miniature'; the steep mountains and long, deep glens in the north of the island are reminiscent of the Highlands, while the rolling moorland and the scattered farms of the south resemble parts of the Borders or Dumfries & Galloway. There's even a long, straight valley dividing the north from the south, a minor version of the mainland's Great Glen. Goatfell (874m), the highest peak, overlooks Brodick, the island's capital on the mid-east coast.

The island, in the Firth of Clyde, is only an hour's ferry ride from the mainland and is easily accessible from Glasgow and its hinterland. Consequently, it's very popular with visitors from Easter to October, including many walkers, for whom Goatfell is the main attraction. This section describes a circular route up Goatfell and the More Walks section (p357) outlines an easy-going outing along the scenic north coast and a challenging traverse of the island's northern spine.

PLANNING
Wild camping is not permitted anywhere on Arran without the landowner's permission.

When to Walk/Stalking
Generally walkers are free to roam throughout Arran. However, deer control measures (stalking) are carried out from mid-August to mid-October in the north of the island. Call the **Hillphones** (☎ 01770-302363) service for daily updates on where stalking is to take place and which paths should be used or avoided. Access to NTS properties (Glen Rosa, Goatfell and Brodick Country Park) is unrestricted at all times.

Maps
Arran is covered by two OS maps – Landranger 1:50,000 No 69 *Isle of Arran* and Explorer 1:25,000 No 361 *Isle of Arran*. Harvey's *Arran* map shows the whole island at 1:40,000 and the northern half at 1:25,000. It has lots of practical and background information and is highly recommended.

Books
Alan Forbes' *25 Walks Ayrshire & Arran* includes 10 varied walks on the island. The maps are better than those in Paddy Dillon's *Walking in the Isle of Arran*, which describes 41 day walks. *The Islands* by Nick Williams describes five adventurous Arran outings. *Arran Behind the Scenes* by Gillean Bussell delves into the island's colourful history.

GETTING THERE & AWAY
All public transport timetable details can be obtained from **Traveline** (☎ 0870 608 2608; www .travelinescotland.co.uk).

Stagecoach Western (☎ 01292-613500) bus service X15 links Glasgow to Ardrossan (1¼ hour, twice daily), the ferry terminal on the Ayrshire coast.

A GEOLOGIST'S PARADISE

The Isle of Arran's geology is amazingly varied. Here you'll find all kinds of rock types and evidence of many different geological and landscape-forming processes, which have taken place over countless millennia. In fact, a trip to Arran is virtually compulsory for geology students.

The northern rocky peaks, ridges and deep glens consist of granite, sculpted by glaciers during the last Ice Age. There are several other smaller and more-scattered outcrops of granite in the southern half of the island, including Holy Island, opposite Lamlash. In the north the granite mass is almost totally surrounded by much older schist and slate, and some river sediment. Sedimentary rocks – limestone and sandstone – monopolise the north coast.

To demystify the complexities of Arran's geology, two readable publications are available locally: the first is the *Isle of Arran Trails: Geology* brochure and the second is the more-detailed *Arran & the Clyde Islands: A Landscape Fashioned by Geology*.

First ScotRail (☎ 0845 755 0033; www.firstscotrail .com) operates trains from Glasgow Central to Ardrossan Harbour (55 minutes, four services Monday to Saturday, three Sunday).

Caledonian MacBrayne (☎ 0870 565 0000; www .calmac.co.uk) runs the car ferry between Ardrossan and Brodick (55 minutes, four services Monday to Saturday, three Sunday). It also does a seasonal service between Claonaig (on the Mull of Kintyre, between Lochgilphead and Campbeltown), and Lochranza (30 minutes, at least seven daily March to October).

Ardrossan is about 40 miles southwest of Glasgow via the M8 and A78.

A GOATFELL CIRCUIT

Duration	6–7½ hours
Distance	11.25 miles (18km)
Difficulty	moderate–demanding
Start/Finish	Brodick (opposite)
Transport	bus, ferry

Summary The connoisseur's route to Arran's highest peak, through scenic Glen Rosa and along steep, rock-encrusted ridges to spectacular views from the summit.

There are several routes to the summit of Goatfell. The most popular are from the east – from Brodick, Cladach or Brodick Castle. A quieter and more pleasing approach is from the west, through Glen Rosa to the Saddle and then up the steep, narrow west ridge to North Goatfell and along Stacach Ridge to the summit. The return to Brodick is via the steep, rocky eastern face to moorland and the grounds of Brodick Castle.

The NTS has done a superb job of repairing and building paths and the descent is completely mud-free. There are steep cliffs on both sides of the west ridge and Stacach Ridge, where extra care is needed. It can turn cold, wet and windy very quickly, so make sure you are well prepared, and don't forget a map and compass.

PLANNING

This route can be walked in either direction, but we recommend clockwise as the overall ascent is more gentle, although it still has some steep bits. The summit comes in the latter part of the route. There are signposts where paths leave the road but not on Goatfell itself. The route includes at least 800m of ascent and some minor scrambling.

Alternatives

Of the alternative approaches to Goatfell, Corrie Burn is preferable to Glen Sannox, which is a boggy glen with a hair-raising climb to the Saddle at its head. Corrie is a spread-out village on the east coast, 5.5 miles north of Brodick and well served by local buses. At the southern end of the village, a 'Public Footpath to Goatfell' sign points along a narrow road. After a few hundred metres leave the road at a sharp bend, just before the settlement of High Corrie, and follow a vehicle track then a path up Corrie Burn's glen to a saddle below North Goatfell. It's a steep climb most of the way and the ground can be wet in places.

Guided Walks

The NTS countryside rangers at **Brodick Country Park** (☎ 01770-302462), about 2 miles

---

NATIONAL TRUST FOR SCOTLAND ON ARRAN

The **National Trust for Scotland** (NTS; www.nts.org.uk) has been a big landowner on Arran since 1958, when the Brodick estate was placed in its care after centuries of the Hamilton family's stewardship. Today the 109-sq-mile estate takes in the Goatfell massif, Glen Rosa and its western slopes, and Brodick Castle and its grounds. These last two are the nucleus of **Brodick Country Park** (☼ Apr-Oct), which has a network of waymarked paths, fine formal gardens, a visitor centre, NTS shop, tearoom and, of course, the castle.

Elsewhere, the NTS is encouraging the regeneration of native woodland with exclosures (fenced areas to keep out red deer), where oaks, rowans and other species are making a comeback.

Footpath maintenance and repair is another big commitment, especially around Goatfell, where staff, in cooperation with the Arran Access Trust, wage a constant battle against the elements and the impact of thousands of walkers' feet.

north of Brodick, organise a program of walks (May to October), which range from afternoon wildlife strolls through to low-level forests to days out on Goatfell.

NEAREST TOWN
Brodick
pop 621

Brodick is the ideal walking base in Arran. The mainland ferry docks here and the town is the hub of the island's excellent bus services.

Brodick tourist office (☎ 01770-303774; www .ayrshire-arran.com; The Pier; ☺ daily Easter-Oct, Mon-Sat Oct-Easter) offers an array of leaflets, maps and guidebooks. Staff can help with accommodation reservations. All bus timetables are detailed in the free *Area Transport Guide*. The local weather forecast is displayed daily.

Arran Active (☎ 01770-302416; www.arranactive .co.uk; Cladach Tourist Office; ☺ daily), next to Arran Brewery and opposite the walkers' entrance to Brodick Castle, is the one place where you can purchase the full range of fuel for camping stoves, and much else besides.

SLEEPING & EATING
For accommodation bookings, go to www .ayrshire-arran.com.

Glen Rosa Farm Campsite (☎ 01770-302380; sites for 2 £4), on the Glen Rosa road, is about 2.5 miles northwest of Brodick Pier. It is just a grassy field on the banks of Glen Rosa Burn with a basic toilet block and running water. Check in at the first cottage on the western side of the Glen Rosa road.

Lochranza SYHA Hostel (☎ 0870 004 1140; www .syha.org.uk; Lochranza; dm £14) is the nearest hostel, in a small, peaceful village near the northwestern tip of the island, 14 miles from Brodick. It's not ideal for Goatfell but the island's bus service makes it fairly easy to get around. The nearest shops are in Brodick.

Orwin B&B (☎ 01770-302307; Shore Rd; s/d £25/50) has four comfortable rooms, including a single with lovely views across the golf course. Your hostess is very helpful and obliging.

Hotel Ormidale (☎ 01770-302100; Knowe Rd; mains £8-12; ☺ lunch Sat & Sun, dinner daily) hosts the local Mountain Rescue Team, so the atmosphere is very compatible. The varied menu features local produce, which you can

wash down with draught ales brewed on the island. Save some space for Arran Dark, a wonderfully fruity after-dinner ale.

Oscars of Arran (☎ 01770-302427; Sannox Rd; breakfast £5, mains £6-10; ☺ breakfast, lunch & dinner) sits beside Glen Cloy Burn just off the main road and only about 1 mile northwest of Brodick. It's a small, well-lit place with outside tables, where you can enjoy a range of snacks or more substantial, hunger-satisfying dishes. It also stocks a fair selection of health foods.

For self-catering and picnic lunches, there are two **Co-op** supermarkets on Shore Rd, open daily, but save bread purchases for **Wooleys Bakery** (Shore Rd). The **Arran Brewery** (☎ 01770-302061; www.arranbrewery.com; Cladach; ☺ daily) is very conveniently located beside the Goatfell path. Tours and tastings are available – a good way to finish the walk.

GETTING THERE & AWAY
For Brodick transport details, see p353.

GETTING TO/FROM THE WALK
Stagecoach Western (☎ 01770-302000) bus service No 324 stops at Cladach near the end of the walk (10 minutes, three daily).

THE WALK
Brodick to the Saddle
2½–3 hours, 5.5 miles (9km)

From Brodick, walk generally north beside the main road (A841) for about 1.5 miles (along a path for all but the last 200m) to a major junction. Turn left along the B880 towards Blackwaterfoot. About 100m along this road turn right down a narrow road, the 'Glen Rosa Cart Track'. Follow this to the Glen Rosa Farm Campsite (left), above which the sealed section ends, and continue along a clear vehicle track into **Glen Rosa**. There are superb views of the precipitous peaks on the western side of the glen, culminating in Cir Mhòr (799m) at its head.

The track becomes a path at the crossing of Garbh Allt, the boundary of the NTS property. Aiming unerringly for the Saddle, the low point between Cir Mhór and the massive, rock-encrusted bulk of Goatfell, the path climbs gently, then quite steeply, to the **Saddle**. From here, among the granite boulders, there's a fine view down Glen Sannox to the sea. Cir Mhòr's alarmingly steep crags rise immediately to the left, with the castellated ridge of Caisteal Ab-hail (859m), Arran's second-highest peak, and the notorious cleft of Ceum na Caillich (Witch's Step) to the north. To the right the features of the next stage are clearly visible: bouldery West Ridge, leading steeply up to North Goatfell; and Stacach Ridge, crowned by four small, rocky peaks.

The Saddle to Goatfell

1½–2 hours, 1.25 miles (2km)

From the Saddle, paths lead up the ridge towards North Goatfell. There are some narrow, exposed sections and a few near-vertical 'steps' where you'll need to use your hands. More tricky, though, are the patches of loose granite gravel. After about an hour

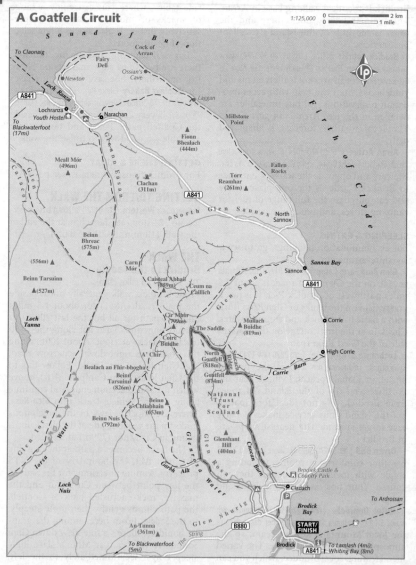

A Goatfell Circuit

1:125,000

the route nears the summit of **North Goatfell** (818m). The final section is a scramble but if this is too intimidating pass below the top, keeping it on your left, and return to the ridge. Turn back to gain the summit of **Goatfell** (874m) from the east.

From North Goatfell you can keep to the crest of the ridge, scrambling over the rocky knobs. Alternatively, drop down to the eastern side of the ridge and follow the less exposed paths below the knobs.

The final section involves hopping over piles of giant boulders to the summit of Goatfell, about 45 minutes from its satellite. The summit is topped by a trig point and a large topographical direction plate, from which you can identify the features in the panoramic view. On a good day, Skiddaw in the Lake District, Ben Lomond and even the coast of Northern Ireland can be seen. The whole of Arran is spread out below, with the conical mass of Holy Island rearing up from the sea in Lamlash Bay.

Goatfell to Brodick
2–2½ hours, 4.5 miles (7km)
From the summit a path winds down the steep eastern face of the peak, then straightens out as the ridge takes shape. At a shallow saddle the path changes direction and leads southeast then south across moorland, down Cnocan Burn glen and into scattered woodland. At a junction in a conifer plantation, continue straight on then turn right at a T-junction. Go down through conifers, cross a sealed road and go on to Cladach and Arran Brewery; the main road is a little further on.

The route into Brodick starts along a footpath on the western side of the main road. Where the path ends, cross the road to a signposted path beside, and then briefly across, Brodick golf course. It leads back to the main road beside Arran Heritage Museum. Follow the roadside path into town.

To reach **Brodick Castle and Country Park** (see the boxed text, p354) turn left 30m after the T-junction in the conifer plantation mentioned above. Follow Cemetery Trail past the eponymous site (the resting place of the 11th and 12th dukes of Hamilton and a wife), over bridges and into the castle grounds. The ranger service office is in the first building on the right. Continue straight on to the NTS shop and tearoom.

MORE WALKS

ISLE OF ARRAN
Cock of Arran
For a change of scene, or if the cloud is too low for a hill walk, the north coast provides fine walking between North Sannox and Lochranza along an almost-level 8-mile (13km) route. There are impressive cliffs, isolated cottages, remains of early coal mining and salt harvesting, and the Cock of Arran itself – a prominent block of sandstone, not named after a rooster but probably from the Lowland Scots word meaning 'cap' or 'headwear'. The views across the Sound of Bute to the mainland, the Isle of Bute and part of the Kintyre peninsula are excellent. There's also a good chance of seeing common seals and a wide variety of birds. The rise and fall of the tide isn't great, so high tide shouldn't complicate things. You will need about four hours, though the boulder-hopping sections and some potentially wet patches could easily increase the time.

The walk starts at a picnic area (with toilets) at the end of a minor road that branches off the A841 about 600m northwest of Sannox. In Lochranza, park by the road at the northwest corner of the Lochranza golf course, or at the end of this road beside Loch Ranza. To return to your car at North Sannox, catch a bus (consult the *Area Transport Guide*, available from the Brodick tourist office, p355) to the North Sannox turn, from where it's about 300m to the picnic area. The walk is described in detail in Lonely Planet's *Walking in Scotland;* carry one of the maps listed on p353.

Glen Rosa to Lochranza
The extremely rugged ridge on the western side of Glen Rosa, and its extension from Cir Mhòr via Caisteal Abhail towards the north coast, offers as fine a ridge walk as you'll find anywhere in Britain. Although it looks impossible from below, there are miraculous ways around those crags and peaks that only experienced rock climbers can traverse. The views all along are tremendous, especially westwards. The 11-mile (18km) walk includes 1360m of climbing, much of which is precipitous and rocky; allow at least seven

hours. The recommended map is Harvey's 1:40,000 *Arran*, which includes coverage of this walk at 1:25,000. Consult Paddy Dillon's *Walking in the Isle of Arran* for more information.

ISLE OF JURA

Jura is a magnificently lonely island, the wildness of its uplands only matched on the Isle of Rum and on Harris in the Western Isles (see p430). Fewer than 200 people now live here, mainly in Craighouse in the southern corner. The rest of the island is uninhabited and unspoiled.

To reach Jura you catch the **Calmac** (☎ 0870 650000; www.calmac.co.uk) ferry from Kennacraig on the Kintyre peninsula to Port Askaig on the Isle of Islay, then the small **Argyll & Bute Council** (☎ 01631-562125) boat to Feolin. From there a local bus regularly goes to Craighouse and north to Inverlussa (twice daily Monday to Saturday).

The OS Landranger 1:50,000 map No 61 *Jura & Colonsay* is the one to have. The SMC's *The Islands of Scotland including Skye* by DJ Fabian, GE Little and DN Williams covers the mountains with a short section on path walks. Much of the island is managed for deer stalking, so the best time for a visit would be from early May to early July. For more information about Jura, visit www.isle-of-islay.com.

The Paps of Jura

A trio of conical peaks – Beinn a' Chaolais (734m), Beinn an Oir (784m) and Beinn Shiantaich (755m) – dominate the island and are visible from afar. A circuit of their summits provides a fairly energetic and outstandingly scenic day; the distance is 11.6 miles (18.5km) with about 1500m of ascent. Allow at least eight hours for the walk – the going is generally rough, the mountains are very steep-sided and paths are generally less well beaten than on mainland mountains.

The West Coast

If you're a coast-walking enthusiast, Jura has enough to justify several return trips. Along the west coast, all 40 miles of it, you'll find raised beaches, caves, rocky headlands and natural arches. To explore the full length would take a couple of weeks of rugged, self-contained walking, as isolated as any in Britain. Feolin makes a convenient starting point; the track to Glenbatrick from the east-coast road (4 miles north of Craighouse) is another possible starting point.

Ben Nevis & Glen Coe

Two of Scotland's most famous place names, especially among walkers – Ben Nevis and Glen Coe – come to life in the southwestern Highlands. Ben Nevis, the highest mountain in Britain, dramatically overlooks the town of Fort William, while magnificent Glen Coe provides an awesome approach to an area graced by some of the most spectacular mountain scenery, and many of the finest walks, in the country.

In this chapter we describe three day walks to illustrate the wide variety of opportunities in the area. The ascent of 'the Ben' follows the main Mountain Track, where you will probably join many other 'pilgrims' and enjoy the camaraderie that soon develops between walkers. You're much less likely to have company along the low-level, historic Road to the Isles, through some of the remotest reaches of the area and following in the footsteps of long-gone cattle drovers. Then there's an exploration of perhaps the most distinctive of the many memorable peaks in Glen Coe, Buachaille Etive Mór, guarding the eastern entrance to the spectacular glen.

The northern half of the West Highland Way linking Glasgow and Fort William, Scotland's most popular long-distance walk, finishes in fine style through the region; you'll find a full description on p418. Fort William is definitely a walker's town and justifiably promotes itself as Scotland's Outdoor Capital. We hope these walks inspire you to linger and explore the area more fully.

HIGHLIGHTS

- Summiting **Ben Nevis** (p360), Britain's highest mountain and, on a good day, being treated to one of the finest views anywhere
- Following the historic **Road to the Isles** (p365) from remote Rannoch Moor to beautiful Steall Meadows and secluded Nevis gorge
- Exploring the lofty ridge and peaks of **Buachaille Etive Mór** (p370), the sentinel guarding the eastern entrance to Glen Coe

INFORMATION
When to Walk
Snow is a factor to be reckoned with to a much greater extent in this area than elsewhere in Scotland. However, by mid- to late May all but the highest reaches of Ben Nevis should be snow-free. At the other end of the season, expect light to moderate snowfalls from late October onwards.

Maps & Books
OS Landranger 1:50,000 map No 41 *Ben Nevis* covers all the walks in this chapter. Details of larger-scale maps are given in the Planning section for each walk.

Walks Fort William by John and Tricia Wombell describes 26 varied walks in the area. *Ben Nevis and Glen Coe* by Chris Townsend also has a good selection of routes. Alternatively, for mountain enthusiasts, there's Nick Williams' Pocket guide *Central Highlands*, which covers the Glen Coe area, among others.

Information Sources
The website www.outdoorcapital.co.uk is a rich source of information about a huge range of outdoor activities, while www.visithighlands.com is the site to visit for accommodation bookings.

GATEWAYS
Fort William (p362) is far and away the largest town in the region. It's well served by daily Scottish Citylink bus services from Glasgow, Edinburgh and Portree on the Isle of Skye, daily First ScotRail trains from Glasgow and the *Caledonian Sleeper* service from London (daily except Saturday).

Glencoe is only other place of any size in the region but it could scarcely be called a transport hub, and isn't on the train line.

BEN NEVIS

Duration	6–8 hours
Distance	9 miles (14.5km)
Difficulty	moderate–demanding
Start/Finish	Ionad Nibheis Visitor Centre
Nearest Towns	Fort William (p362), Glen Nevis (p363)
Transport	bus

Summary A steep, stony path and a long day to the summit of Britain; an immensely rewarding walk with unsurpassed views.

There's something irresistible about climbing a country's highest peak, and hordes of walkers are drawn to Ben Nevis (1344m). The Ben tempts visitors with minimal, if any, walking experience and many discover they have taken on more than they expected. The mountain is a compelling presence above Fort William, often cloud-capped, and displaying a rugged profile from any and every viewpoint. The ascent is bound to be one of the more memorable events in any walker's career, so it's worth allowing a few days during which to stage your climb, to allow for the fickle weather.

Despite, or perhaps because of its dangers, the mountain has a colourful history. During the summers of 1881 and 1882 one Clement Wragge, soon nicknamed 'the inclement rag', made a daily ascent of the Ben to take weather measurements for the Scottish Meteorological Society. In 1883 a weather observatory was built on the summit (it's now a ruin); today's path from Glen Nevis, known as the Mountain Track, follows the pony track constructed at the same time to supply the observers. The observatory closed in 1904 but a small hotel annexe continued in business during

---

BEN NEVIS – AN EXTREME CLIMATE

Not surprisingly, the weather on Britain's highest mountain can be the most extreme in the country. The temperature on the summit is typically 9°C colder than at the foot of the mountain, and this figure doesn't take wind chill into account. An average of 261 gales per year rip across the summit and wind speeds well in excess of 100mph have often been recorded.

Even if skies are clear when you set out, don't be complacent, as the weather can turn arctic all too quickly. The mean annual summit temperature is below 0°C and snow often lies on the mountain until early summer; the summit is only a couple of hundred feet below the level of the permanent snow line. If the views are superb, count yourself lucky – on average the top is cloud-covered six days out of seven.

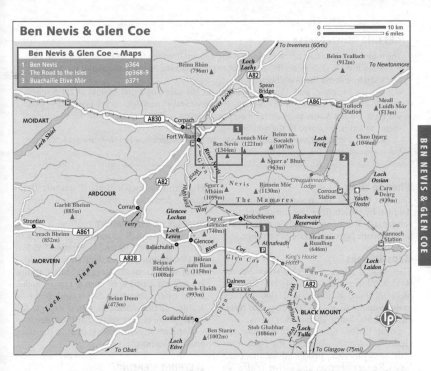

Ben Nevis & Glen Coe

Ben Nevis & Glen Coe – Maps	
1 Ben Nevis	p364
2 The Road to the Isles	pp368-9
3 Buachaille Etive Mòr	p371

BEN NEVIS & GLEN COE

summer until 1918. In 1911 a Model T Ford was 'driven' to the summit as a publicity stunt – a feat that took five days.

A race to the summit was created as a distraction from the daily grind at the observatory. The first timed and recorded ascent was in October 1895: two hours 41 minutes for the return run from Fort William. The race has now become an institution, the **Ben Nevis Race** (www.bennevisrace.co.uk), with up to 500 runners entering the annual 'Ben Race' on the first Saturday of September. In 2006 the records stood at one hour and 25 minutes for men, and 18 minutes longer for women, both set way back in 1984.

PLANNING

No walk up the Ben should be undertaken lightly. You start virtually at sea level and the ascent is continuous, all the way to the top. You should be well prepared with warm, protective clothing and plenty of food and drink. Navigating off the top is notoriously dangerous – sheer gullies cut into the plateau very near to the line of the path. Ensure that you have the bearings

needed to descend from the summit plateau in safety (see the boxed text, p362). Perhaps it is no surprise that among various theories about the meaning of the word 'Nevis', one has it deriving from Gaelic and Irish words meaning 'dread' and 'terrible'.

Alternatives

It may be more convenient to start at the SYHA hostel, about 1 mile further up Glen Nevis; this path meets the Mountain Track above the hostel. Alternatively, if you have your own transport and are coming from Fort William, you can join the path from the car park at the end of the road near Achintee House. The daily weather forecast is posted on a notice board next to a local map. Climb a stile beside a gate; within 100m bear left up the wide path (the Mountain Track).

If you don't want to go all the way to the summit, or if there's snow, ice or cloud high on the mountain, a path from just above Halfway Lochan to the CIC hut affords splendid views of the awesome cliffs of the Ben's northeast face. This option is described in the Alternative Route (p365).

GETTING DOWN SAFELY

The most hazardous part of the Ben walk is the descent from the summit plateau. Particular care is needed if there is snow on the ground or in poor visibility. To reach the top of the Mountain Track safely, use the following bearings:

From the trig point, walk 150m (probably about 200 paces) on a grid bearing of 231 degrees. Then follow a grid bearing of 281 degrees. This should take you safely off the plateau and onto the path. Do not forget to allow for magnetic variation, which is given on the recommended maps, and must be *added* to the grid bearing.

Two useful leaflets, *Ben Nevis Safety Information* and *Navigation on Ben Nevis* are available from the tourist office at the start of the walk.

When to Walk

The best months for an ascent are July and August, by which time the summit plateau is normally free of snow, although it should be safe from June until late September.

Maps & Books

The walk is covered by Ordnance Survey (OS) Explorer 1:25,000 map No 392 *Ben Nevis & Fort William,* and two Harvey maps: Superwalker 1:25,000 map *Ben Nevis* and 1:12,500 Summit map *Ben Nevis.*

Local leaflets covering this route include *Ben Nevis – Walking the Path from June to September,* produced by the Glen Nevis Ranger Service, and *Great Walks No 2,* produced by Fort William & Lochaber Tourism.

Guided Walks

The John Muir Trust organises walks in the area; contact its **Nevis Conservation Officer** (☎ 01397-705049) or the Ionad Nibheis Visitor Centre (opposite) for details.

NEAREST TOWNS
Fort William
pop 9910

Near the head of Loch Linnhe and famously in the shadow of Ben Nevis, Fort William was established as a garrison for the king's troops during the 17th century. These days it promotes itself, with considerable justification, as Scotland's Outdoor Capital, an unrivalled destination for walkers, climbers and outdoor-sports enthusiasts.

INFORMATION

The **tourist office** (☎ 01397-703781; fortwilliam@ visithighlands.com; Cameron Sq, High St; 🖳) stocks maps and books, and can help with accommodation bookings. Pick up a copy of Highland Council's *Public Transport Timetable – Lochaber.*

SUPPLIES & EQUIPMENT

Among the clutch of outdoor gear shops in town, the easiest to find is **Nevisport** (☎ 0845 257 1344; www.nevisport.co.uk; Airds Crossing; 🕓 daily), a short stroll from the train and bus stations. Its **café-bar** (snacks to £6, mains to £13; 🕓 lunch & dinner) offers standard dishes and makes a feature of big steaks; as you'd expect, the atmosphere is very relaxed and congenial.

Morrisons supermarket is next to the train and bus station.

SLEEPING & EATING

The nearest camping ground is in Glen Nevis (opposite).

Although some of the town's streets are wall-to-wall with B&Bs and guesthouses, accommodation can be hard to find during July and August, so it is advisable to book well ahead, especially if you want to stay in a particular hostel or B&B.

Bank Street Lodge (☎ 01397-700070; www.bank streetlodge.co.uk; Bank St; dm/s/d £12/27/46), in a handy central location, has en suite rooms and small dorms, and a kitchen.

Calluna (☎ 01397-700451; www.fortwilliamholiday .co.uk; Heathercroft; r per person £15) is run by a highly experienced mountain guide and his wife. They offer comfortable accommodation in modern, semi-detached, self-contained apartments, available for short stays or week-long bookings.

Lime Tree Studio (☎ 01397-701806; www.limetree fortwilliam.co.uk; Achintore Rd; s/d £40/70) is, refreshingly, more an art gallery with rooms than a conventional B&B; its walls are decorated with the owners' Highland landscapes.

The **Grog & Gruel** (☎ 01397-705078; 66 High St; mains £10-15; 🕓 lunch Mon-Sat, dinner daily) claims to offer the best range of Scottish real ales anywhere. Match one or two of them with a pizza in the Alehouse, or steaks and seafood in the traditional pub-style restaurant.

Crannog Seafood Restaurant (☎ 01397-705589; Town Pier; mains £13-19; ☯ lunch & dinner), with an uninterrupted view over Loch Linnhe, is a great place to go for a celebration seafood feast. The maritime menu includes local mussels and langoustines.

GETTING THERE & AWAY
Fort William is on the A82, 146 miles from Edinburgh, 104 miles from Glasgow and 66 miles from Inverness.

Scottish Citylink (☎ 0870 550 5050; www.citylink.co.uk) buses provide services from Glasgow (three hours, three daily), Edinburgh (four hours, three daily), Inverness (two hours, six services Monday to Saturday, two Sunday) and Portree on the Isle of Skye (three hours, three daily).

First ScotRail (☎ 0845 755 0033; www.firstscotrail.com) operates the *Caledonian Sleeper* service from London Euston to Fort William (13 hours, daily except Saturday) and the service from Glasgow (3¾ hours, three service Monday to Saturday, two Sunday). From Edinburgh, change at Glasgow Queen St.

Glen Nevis
The village of Glen Nevis is really just a collection of amenities 2 miles from Fort William. It can be extremely busy in summer.

INFORMATION
Ionad Nibheis Visitor Centre (☎ 01397-705922; ☯ Easter–mid-Oct) is 1.5 miles up the glen from Fort William. It stocks leaflets with advice

for Ben walkers, maps, books, basic walking equipment, trail snacks and drinks. Displays feature the geology and history of Ben Nevis and the surrounding area. Up-to-date mountain weather forecasts are posted here (and at the SYHA hostel). A voluntary fee is requested for use of the car park.

SLEEPING & EATING
Glen Nevis Caravan & Camping Park (☎ 01397-702191; www.glennevis.co.uk; sites for 2 £10) has an incomparable location and top-class facilities, so is swamped in summer; reservations are recommended.

Glen Nevis SYHA Hostel (☎ 0870 004 1120; www.syha.org.uk; dm £14; ☐) has a few small rooms and several largish dorms, and is ideally located for the Ben.

Achintee Farm (☎ 01397-702240; www.achinteefarm.com; dm/d £11/26, B&B d £30) combines a very comfortable B&B in the old farmhouse, a spacious hostel in which most of the rooms are twins or triples, and **Ben Nevis Inn** (mains £8-14; ☯ lunch & dinner), where you can choose from an extensive menu emphasising local products.

Cafe Beag (☎ 01397-703601; mains £6; ☯ lunch & dinner) offers pretty basic but inexpensive fare, while **Glen Nevis Restaurant & Bar** (☎ 01397-705459; bar mains £9-15, restaurant mains £10-18; ☯ lunch & dinner) does standard bar meals, leavened with daily specials. For something more imaginative, try the restaurant.

GETTING THERE & AWAY
Highland Country Buses (☎ 01463-710555; www.rapsons.com) operates a service between Fort William and Glen Nevis (20 minutes, eight services Monday to Saturday, four Sunday).

LOOKING AFTER THE BEN

The Ben Nevis Estate went on sale in 1999 and the **John Muir Trust** (JMT; www.jmt.org) snapped up the property for around £500,000. The estate extends east into the Grey Corries and west past the upper Glen Nevis gorge. The Trust is a member of the **Nevis Partnership** (www.nevispartnership.co.uk), committed to sustained environmental and visitor management of the Ben Nevis massif and Glen Nevis, in particular through footpath repair projects.

Aware that, in many people's eyes, the Ben's summit had become Britain's highest rubbish tip, the JMT organised several clean-up days, on one of which the remains of a grand piano were unearthed. It turned out that it had once been lugged up there to raise funds for charity. The summit had also become a popular place for leaving mementoes of people who had died on the mountain, a controversial practice, with many walkers and climbers believing that the mountain was being desecrated. In response, the JMT opened a Garden of Remembrance near the tourist office in August 2006, where the memorials placed on the summit were brought together.

GETTING TO/FROM THE WALK

See p363 for details of the Highland Country Buses service through Glen Nevis.

By car, take the A82 east out of Fort William (towards Inverness), going straight on at the roundabout to follow the minor road signed 'Glen Nevis' to Ionad Nibheis Visitor Centre.

To reach Achintee (an alternative starting point), head northeast along the A82, turning off along the road to Claggan Industrial Estate, then follow signs to Achintee, where there's a car park at the end of the road.

THE WALK
Glen Nevis to Halfway Lochan
1½–2 hours, 1.5 miles (2.5km)

From the car park at the Ionad Nibheis Visitor Centre, take the signposted 'Ben Nevis Path' and cross the suspension bridge over the River Nevis. Follow the river bank upstream, then turn left and climb alongside a stone wall to reach the Ben Nevis Path (Mountain Track), where the climb begins in earnest. Gain height steadily on a good path, across the slopes of Meall an t-Suidhe

(Hill of Rest) and past the junction of the steep path up from the SYHA hostel. Continue on over a couple of footbridges; after about 40 minutes the path turns into Red Burn glen. As the gradient eases a little, the path zigzags sharply then levels out as **Halfway Lochan** (its correct name is Lochan Meall an t-Suidhe) comes into view.

This is a good place to take stock. Is the weather still OK? Are you? From here to the top and back takes around three to five hours. If in any doubt, enjoy the view and go back down, or take the alternative route (opposite) to Allt a' Mhuilinn and back.

Halfway Lochan to Ben Nevis
2–3 hours, 3 miles (5km)

Just east of Halfway Lochan the path turns right at a junction (the Alternative Route, described opposite, diverges here) to reach Red Burn Ford. The ruins of Halfway House, used in association with the summit observatory, are nearby. In days gone by walkers were charged one shilling (5p) for walking to the summit, the proceeds being used for path maintenance.

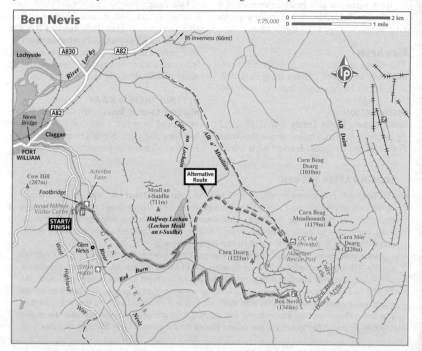

The much rougher path zigzags steeply up across stony slopes. The gradient eases at around 1200m and the path forks beside a large, circular stone shelter. The right-hand path is easier, but either will take you across the plateau to the summit cairn and trig point. Take care on this final section as the last bit of the path goes very close to the edge of the cliffs and gullies on the north face of the mountain. Keep especially well clear of any patches of snow. In poor visibility, don't lose sight of the summit cairn until you're ready to descend.

The summit of **Ben Nevis** isn't perhaps the most scenic of places, with the remains of the substantial walls of the observatory, several cairns and an emergency shelter, as well as the trig point – all set in a boulder-strewn moonscape. However, the views are exceptional, with the islands of Mull, Rum and Skye to the west and a myriad of mountain peaks as far as the eye can see.

Ben Nevis to Glen Nevis
3 hours, 4.5 miles (7km)

To return you must retrace your steps. Remember to watch out for the dangerous summit gullies that cut into the mountain near the path and, in poor visibility, use the bearings listed in the box on p362.

ALTERNATIVE ROUTE: BEN NEVIS LOW-LEVEL WALK
4½–5 hours, 8.5 miles (13.7km)

This route offers a pleasant alternative if you don't want to go all the way to the summit or if there is snow, ice or cloud on the upper part of the mountain. Follow the directions for the main route as far as Halfway Lochan.

From the path junction above Halfway Lochan follow a well-made path that leads north. A short distance along, bear right at a junction (the excellent path to the left goes down to the lochan) to follow a much rougher but clearly defined path north then east, overlooked by the magnificently rugged cliffs of the Ben's northern face. The path leads into the long, deep glen carved by Allt a' Mhuilinn, with the impressive Coire Leis at its head. Continue across the steep, boulder-strewn slope to the stone-built, private **CIC hut**, complete with a small wind generator. It is used by the Lochaber Mountain Rescue Team, one of the busiest in the country. The views into the deep dark gullies and precipitous cliffs below the Ben's summit are truly awesome. Retrace your steps back to Glen Nevis.

THE ROAD TO THE ISLES

Duration	6½ hours
Distance	14.5 miles (23.5km)
Difficulty	moderate
Start	Corrour (p366)
Finish	Glen Nevis upper car park
Nearest Towns	Fort William (p362), Glen Nevis (p363)
Transport	train, bus

Summary A long and remote low-level walk, crossing some rough and wet ground, following a historic route from the wild expanses of Rannoch Moor to spectacular Nevis gorge.

The Road to the Isles means, to most people, the 46-mile route following roads westward from Fort William to the fishing port of Mallaig on the west coast. For walkers it means something just a little more adventurous – the eastern section of this ancient route through the western Highlands, linking central Scotland to the Isle of Skye via Fort William. It was a route much used by cattle drovers (and cattle thieves) heading for the cattle trysts (fairs) at Crieff and Falkirk. Armies, their quarries and refugees have also marched and fled along this route.

An old Scottish song about the Road to the Isles runs: 'By Loch Tummel, and Loch Rannoch and Lochaber I will go'; the walk described here goes through the heart of Lochaber. It starts at Corrour Station (see the boxed text, p366), which, at 408m above sea level, is the highest station on the British rail network. Surrounded by the wilds of Rannoch Moor, it is probably also the most remote, being 11 miles from the nearest public road.

The route follows a right of way all the way to Glen Nevis, past the southern shores of Loch Treig, across wide, grassy, treeless moorland framed by comparatively low peaks. Once you cross the watershed, the scenery becomes much more dramatic, as the lightly wooded glen narrows right down to a mini-Himalayan gorge, the spiky Mamores ridge soars steeply to the south

BEN NEVIS & GLEN COE

and the rugged Grey Corries and mighty Ben Nevis tower above to the north. Simple bothies at Staoineag and Meanach can provide shelter, temporarily or overnight if you bring all the necessary equipment. Both are open and free to walkers year-round.

PLANNING

This route is best done from east to west, to capitalise on Corrour's elevation, and the views are better going this way.

When to Walk/Stalking

This route passes through Corrour and Grey Corries–Mamore Estates, where stalking usually takes place between mid-August and the end of October. Nevertheless, you are free to follow the right of way at any time.

Maps

For detailed coverage of the route consult OS Explorer 1:25,000 maps No 385 *Rannoch Moor & Ben Alder* and 392 *Ben Nevis & Fort William*.

Information Sources

The main tourist office in this area is in Fort William (p362).

NEAREST TOWNS

See Fort William (p362) and Glen Nevis (p363).

Corrour

Corrour begins and ends at the train station, a surprisingly busy place when trains arrive and depart, being popular with walkers, hostellers and train spotters keen to watch a steam train that passes through during summer.

SLEEPING & EATING

As there are only two choices here, it is advisable to book ahead, as you might be unlucky if you turn up unannounced.

Loch Ossian SYHA Hostel (☎ 0870 004 1139; www .syha.org.uk; dm £13) is 1 mile east of Corrour station. As an eco-hostel, it has many environmentally friendly features. Bring your own sleeping bag and supplies.

Corrour Station House B&B & Restaurant (☎ 01397-732236; www.corrour.co.uk; s/d £26/52, breakfast £3, mains £8-15; ☺ breakfast, lunch & dinner) is a friendly, relaxed place offering pleasantly unfussed accommodation and satisfying meals in the former station waiting room. It hopes to open the refurbished bunkhouse in 2007.

GETTING THERE & AWAY

First ScotRail (☎ 0845 755 0033; www.firstscotrail .com) trains from Glasgow (three hours) and Fort William (50 minutes) stop at Corrour. There are three trains Monday to Saturday, and two Sunday. First ScotRail's *Caledonian Sleeper* service from London stops

---

THE WEST HIGHLAND RAILWAY

The West Highland Railway (WHR) runs between Glasgow, Fort William and Mallaig, through some of Scotland's most wild and spectacular mountain scenery, which is also some of Britain's finest walking country. From Arrochar & Tarbet, Crianlarich, Bridge of Orchy, Spean Bridge and Glenfinnan stations you can set off on a seemingly endless range of wonderful mountain walks, direct from the platform. There are several opportunities for circular walks, or you can get off at one station, do a good walk, then catch the train again from another station up or down the line. From Fort William station it's only a few miles' walk to Britain's highest peak, Ben Nevis.

Possibly the most intriguing place to get off the train is at Corrour (above), in the middle of Rannoch Moor. Work on the line began in 1889 and up to 5000 men were employed in its construction, laying foundations of brushwood, ash and earth across miles of bog to support the tracks. It's a tribute to the railway's Victorian engineers that the line is still used. From Corrour there are plenty of peaks to climb and remote glens to explore, including the Road to Isles (p365) walk described here.

Beyond Fort William the magic is undiminished, with the line passing through the rugged country around Glenfinnan and going on to Mallaig, from where it is a short ferry ride to the Isle of Skye.

For a walker this railway is an absolute gift, and for any visitor to Britain a ride on the WHR is a must.

CATTLE DROVING

The Road to the Isles is the most famous of the routes used by drovers on their way from the north of Scotland and the Isle of Skye to the markets in the lowlands. Its destination was Tyndrum, about 10 miles south of Rannoch Moor and a key stop for the cattle droving trade during the 18th and 19th centuries. Herds of small, black Highland cattle and their drovers, who had usually trekked hundreds of difficult miles to this point, sometimes swimming across tidal narrows to reach the mainland (mostly from the Isle of Skye) and then crossing mountain passes and traversing remote glens, moved on from Tyndrum to the trysts (cattle markets) at Crieff or Falkirk, northeast of Glasgow.

Cattle often continued on foot with their new owners across the border into England and the drovers had to start the long journey home. The cattle rustling, thieving and celebrations that accompanied the marches are still commemorated today.

here on request (11½ hours, daily except Saturday). The platform at Corrour is so small that only one door of the train can be opened to let passengers off; the conductor will tell you where best to sit.

GETTING TO/FROM THE WALK

To reach the Glen Nevis upper car park from Fort William, take the A82 east out of Fort William (towards Inverness) and keep going straight at a small roundabout to join a minor road signposted 'Glen Nevis'. Continue up the glen to the large car park at the end of the road.

If you haven't left a car here or haven't arranged to be picked up at the end of the walk, it's a 1.5-mile walk from the car park to the lower falls car park, at the end of the Highland Country Buses' Glen Nevis route (see p363).

THE WALK
Corrour Station to Creaguaineach Lodge

1½ hours, 4 miles (6.5km)

From Corrour Station, on a clear day, you may enjoy a preview of Ben Nevis and its satellites. Cross to the western side of the railway line and follow the track leading northwest, signposted to Fort William (and other destinations). Old railway sleepers help to keep your feet dry across some soft spots and several small burns.

About 20 minutes out, cross a substantial bridge over Allt Lùib Ruairidh and join a wide, firm vehicle track linking Loch Ossian (and the SYHA hostel) and Loch Treig. Soon the track descends steeply to the shores of **Loch Treig**. This is actually an artificial loch, contained by a dam at its northern end. The

level of the original loch was raised as part of the hydroelectric power scheme to supply the aluminium smelter at Fort William. Opened in 1929, the scheme also involved a huge 15-mile-long tunnel through Ben Nevis to the prominent pipes on its western slope carrying water towards the turbines in the power station at the smelter. There are excellent views of the Mamores and shapely Binnein Beag ahead – you'll pass below this peak about three-quarters of the way along this route and it acts as a marker against which you can measure your progress.

The last thing you'd expect to see out here is a house, but **Creaguaineach Lodge**, beside the southwestern corner of the loch, just survived Treig's enlargement. Before you reach the lodge, you need to decide whether to continue along the northern side of Abhainn Rath, following the right of way and the wider path, or to stay on the southern bank, chasing a much narrower and rougher path. The latter route avoids having to ford the stream much further westwards, only a problem if it is in spate.

Creaguaineach Lodge to Meanach Bothy

1½ hours, 3.5 miles (5.5km)

If you choose the northern route, cross the substantial bridge across the burn. The intermittently rocky path wanders along at varying distances from the burn, shaded in places by clumps of beech and birch. About 30 minutes from the lodge, pass **Staoineag Bothy** on the opposite bank, easily reached via a line of stepping stones. The glen here is wide and grassy; within 1 mile it narrows tightly for a short distance and the stream bounces down in a run of cascades. Soon it widens into vast, flat grasslands with

The Road To The Isles

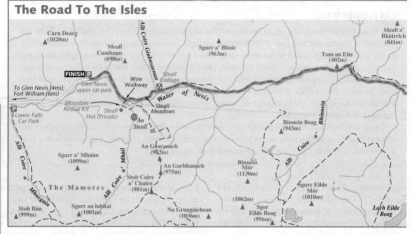

BEN NEVIS & GLEN COE

the peaks standing well back; in places the path is less than obvious but signs of passage aren't difficult to find. **Meanach Bothy** stands all alone in the midst of this; it has two rooms and provides good, weatherproof shelter. Across the river, Lùibeilt is a forlorn, roofless ruin, among a wind-lashed group of trees. A rough, yet driveable, track leads south from Lùibeilt to Kinlochleven, about 7 miles away; an escape route if necessary.

Meanach Bothy to Glen Nevis upper car park

3½ hours, 7 miles (11.5km)

A track leads west from the bothy to the stream, where it's possible to hop across; alternatively, continue upstream on a narrow path until you find a suitable ford. If you do cross here, pick up a rather rough track leading northwest; about 1 mile beyond Lùibeilt the track becomes a path and soon fades. The easiest going is close to the stream. You are now nearing Binnein Beag, which comes into view again on the left. Far ahead is the massive Aonach Beag, with the outer peak of Sgurr a' Bhuic, which you'll soon pass to your right.

Cross Allt Coire a' Bhinnein and head north along the western wide of Allt Coire Rath for a couple of hundred metres to pick up a path leading generally west. It cuts across the slope of **Tom an Eite**, an amorphous lump lying above the narrow watershed between the east-flowing Abhainn Rath and the Water of Nevis. The path, generally easy

to follow, heads downstream in a fairly determined fashion. After 1 mile or so there is, theoretically, a choice between an upper level (and drier) path, and a lower, more clearly defined one, but the parting of the ways is very obscure. Unless there's been a lot of rain recently, the lower path isn't too bad, and you can easily keep your feet dry.

As you leave Binnein Beag behind, many more fine peaks in the Mamores come into sight and there's a dramatic view of Ben Nevis' northeast profile. Eventually you reach the ruins of Steall Cottage and a substantial footbridge over the burn that drains the corrie between Aonach Beag and Ben Nevis. You soon discover the origin of the cottage's name, across on the far side of the Water of Nevis; the beautiful **An Steall** waterfall, a skein of cascades down more than 100m of rock slabs. Steall Hut, also on the other side of the river, is private and reached by a bridge comprising just three wire ropes – try it if you dare, and imagine negotiating it in high winds with a backpack filled for a week's stay! There are usually plenty of people about here, with the falls being a popular destination for a short walk from Glen Nevis.

The path leading out of this sanctuary starts at the base of the cliffs, still on the northern side of the glen. The river takes an abrupt turn to the right and surges down a steep, rocky gorge, the bed of which is filled with massive boulders. A well-constructed path, with a few bouldery sections, clings

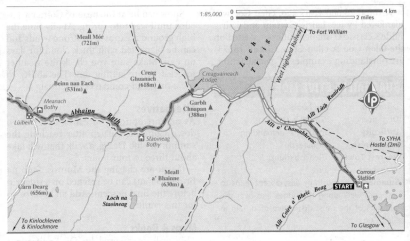

to the steep, wooded slope of the glen. At a sharp turn back to the left there's one last excellent view back up this dramatic gorge to An Steall. The path brings you out at the Glen Nevis upper car park. Unless you have been able to arrange a lift, it is another 1.5 miles down the road to the bus stop at the lower car park.

GLEN COE

Glen Coe is one of the most popular destinations for walkers and climbers in Scotland and one of the most dramatic glens, especially when approached from the east, along the A82. You descend from the vast, open spaces of Rannoch Moor, pass the pyramidal sentinel of Buachaille Etive Mór and drop into the Pass of Glencoe, a notch between Am Bodach (at the eastern end of the awesomely rugged ridge of Aonach Eagach) and Beinn Fhada. Below, the valley floor is pancake flat and no more than 500m wide. To the north, sweeping up from sea level to more than 900m, the ramparts of Aonach Eagach are so steep that you must crane your neck to see the top. To the south the massive buttresses known as the Three Sisters throw shadows across the valley. Partly hidden behind them are the tantalising peaks of Bidean nam Bian and Stob Coire nan Lochan. The view is one of the most arresting in Scotland – and that's just from the car or bus!

The history of Glen Coe has its dark side. It is known as the 'glen of weeping', not because of the rainfall levels (though this is one of the wetter areas of Scotland) but because it was the scene of an infamous massacre of local members of a sept of the MacDonald clan by soldiers led by a Campbell in 1692.

In 1935 Glen Coe became one of the National Trust for Scotland's earliest land acquisitions. Aonach Eagach and Signal Rock were purchased, and two years later the mountains on the south side of the glen were donated to the Trust. The estate now covers approximately 2.1 sq miles. The Trust's mandate is simple: to protect the natural and cultural heritage of the area and to ensure open access for walkers.

ENVIRONMENT

For geologists, too, Glen Coe is an area of great significance. The event that confers such significance occurred towards the end of a period of volcanic activity 60 million years ago. A circular piece of the earth's surface, roughly 6 miles in diameter, fractured and sank into the hot magma below, a phenomenon known as cauldron subsidence. The discovery of the cauldron in Glen Coe marked an important development in geological knowledge. A small quarry near the Clachaig Inn exposes the fault line of the cauldron, which then follows the prominent gully west of Achnambeithach Cottage.

Around 25,000 years ago, Glen Coe was blanketed by ice. Lairig Gartain and Lairig Eilde's classic U-shaped valleys – visited on the Glen Coe & Glen Etive Circuit (p373) are outstanding examples of glacial action.

BUACHAILLE ETIVE MÓR

Duration	5½ hours
Distance	6.5 miles (10.5km)
Difficulty	moderate–demanding
Start/Finish	Altnafeadh
Nearest Town	Glencoe (right)
Transport	bus

Summary A surprisingly easy ascent leads to a superb walk along the ridges and over the summits of the most distinctive mountain in Glen Coe.

Standing sentinel at the head of Glen Coe, Buachaille Etive Mór is one of the most distinctive landmarks in Scotland and the appeal of this mountain for walkers is unmistakable. The initial appearance of the mountain, when viewed from the A82 to the east or from the start of the walk, is one of an impregnable pyramid of buttresses and chasm-like gullies. But looks are often deceiving and a steep, but fairly straightforward, ascent can be made via Coire na Tulaich. The summit, commonly referred to as Buachaille Etive Mór, is actually Stob Dearg (1022m). From this high point, the ridge continues to the west and southwest, connecting another three summits: the sharp cone of Stob na Doire (1011m); Stob Coire Altruim; and the second Munro on the ridge (and the most southerly peak), Stob na Bròige. With deep valleys on either side, the views and feeling of space from the ridge and summits are exceptional.

Once you've gained the ridge from Coire na Tulaich the walking is quite easy, with only a few short ascents required to reach the various summits. The route described here continues along the ridge and across Stob na Doire, then descends into Lairig Gartain via Coire Altruim. Total ascent for the walk is 1080m.

PLANNING

The route is described in a clockwise direction for aesthetic reasons, although it can also be done in the opposite direction.

Snow can lie at the head of Coire na Tulaich until well into spring. At any time the high ground is exposed to strong winds and can be blanketed with thick cloud for days on end. Make sure you check the weather forecast before setting out. The ability to use a map and compass is essential.

Alternatives

As a short option you can simply return down Coire na Tulaich after reaching the summit of Stob Dearg, a walk that will take about three to four hours.

If you are chasing the Munros, Stob na Bròige (956m) can be reached on a side trip before the final descent. Add an hour or so for this jaunt.

Maps & Books

This walk is covered by OS Landranger 1:50,000 map No 41 *Ben Nevis* and the Harvey Superwalker 1:25,000 map *Glen Coe*.

Chris Townsend's *Ben Nevis & Glen Coe* is a reliable guide by one of the most experienced walkers in Scotland.

NEAREST TOWN
Glencoe
pop 360

Glencoe is a picturesque village at the western end of Glen Coe. Fortunately most of it is bypassed by the A82, so it remains fairly quiet, separated from the heaviest traffic.

INFORMATION
The National Trust for Scotland Visitor Centre (☎ 01855-811307; www.glencoe-nts.org.uk; ☼ Mar-Oct), 1 mile east of the village, off the A82, is an award-winning eco-building, and houses displays (£5) about conservation issues and local geology. Videos explore the Glen's natural and cultural history, and a shop stocks a good range of walking guides and maps, including the NTS' own *Glencoe* guide. There is also a **cafeteria** (mains to £3; ☼ 10am-5pm) offering soup and packaged sandwiches. The daily weather forecast is prominently displayed. A diverse program of guided walks and other events is staged from the office; bookings are advisable.

SUPPLIES & EQUIPMENT
Mountain Sports Equipment (A82) stocks outdoor gear and maps. There's a small **Spar** supermarket in the village.

SLEEPING & EATING

Red Squirrel Campsite (☎ 01855-811256; www .redsquirrelcampsite.com; Leacantium Farm; sites for 2 £7), beside the River Coe, offers the rare opportunity to sit around the perfect midge repellent – a campfire.

Glencoe SYHA Hostel (☎ 0870 004 1122; www .syha.org.uk; dm £14; 🖳) is about 1.5 miles east of the village. It is popular, though the largish dorms give it an institutional atmosphere.

Glencoe Hostel & Bunkhouse (☎ 01855-811906; www.glencoehostel.co.uk; camp sites for 2 £10, dm £10; 🖳) is 1¼ miles east of the village. It offers a variety of hostel-style accommodation and has a compact camp site. There's also a small on-site shop.

Clachaig Inn (☎ 01855-811252; www.clachaig.com; s/d £38/84, bar meal mains £9-15) is 2.5 miles east of Glencoe. The inn really comes into its own during the evening, when most outdoor folk in the area congregate in the climbers' bar. The selection of Scottish real ales to wash down the very generous meals is bewilderingly wide and all too tempting; there's the added attraction of regular live music.

The isolated **King's House Hotel** (☎ 01855-851259; www.kingy.com; s/d £35/30, bar meals £7-11), a few miles southeast of Altnafeadh, is the closest shelter and watering place to the walk described here. It is one of Scotland's oldest licensed inns, dating from the 17th century; it was used as a garrison by government troops after the Battle of Culloden in 1746.

GETTING THERE & AWAY

The A82 linking Glasgow and Fort William slices through Glen Coe but bypasses the village.

Scottish Citylink (☎ 0870 550 5050; www.citylink .co.uk) buses between Glasgow (2½ hours, three daily) and Fort William (30 minutes, three daily) stop at the Glencoe crossroads. **Highland Country Buses** (☎ 01463 710555; www .rapsons.com) provides a service between Fort William and Kinlochleven via the Glencoe junction (40 minutes, at least seven Monday to Saturday, three Sunday).

GETTING TO/FROM THE WALK

The walk starts and finishes at the parking area beside the A82 at Altnafeadh.

Scottish Citylink buses (see above) will stop at Altnafeadh if you request this unscheduled stop when you board.

THE WALK
Altnafeadh to Stob Dearg
2 hours, 2 miles (3km)

From the parking area follow a wide 4WD track to a large footbridge. Continue along a good path past Lagangarbh Cottage and gently upwards into Coire na Tulaich. Ignore a path going off to the left (this leads to the many scrambles and rock climbs on the buttresses further east) and follow the path along the right bank of the Allt Coire na Tulaich, which will probably be dry in summer. Higher up, the ground becomes steeper and the stream bed is choked with boulders. The path climbs to the right, onto easier ground, heading for the scree slopes above. Once on the scree, stick to the right, where a well-constructed path leads to the top of some small rock outcrops below the rim of Coire na Tulaich. After that, it is a short scramble to the top and you emerge suddenly on the ridge between Stob Dearg and Stob na Doire (1½ hours from the start).

Turn to the east and climb steadily for 20 minutes over stony, frost-shattered ground to the summit of **Stob Dearg** (1022m). There

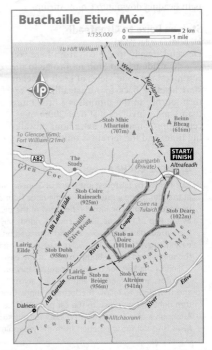

Buachaille Etive Mór

are fine views to the east across vast Rannoch Moor, and to the north and northwest across the shapely summits of the Mamores to the unmistakable, whale-backed profile of Ben Nevis. Closer to home, the eye is drawn to the steep northeast face of Stob na Doire, which is the next mountain on the agenda.

Stob Dearg to Stob na Doire
1 hour, 1.5 miles (2.5km)

Descend back to the top of Coire na Tulaich and head west and then southwest across a lovely, broad ridge with many small lochans filling the depressions between grassy hummocks. Ten or 15 minutes of walking on this ridge should see you at the base of the short, steep haul to Stob na Doire. A well-defined path shows the way to the small summit cairn on **Stob na Doire** (1011m). The vista to the west across Bidean nam Bian now dominates and there are also excellent views south into Glen Etive. To the southwest the Buachaille Etive Mór ridge continues to Stob na Bròige, and immediately below, in a col, you can make out the red erosion scar of a path heading down into Coire Altruim.

Stob na Doire to Altnafeadh
2½ hours, 3 miles (5km)

Descend steeply to the col; from here you can do a side trip to Stob na Bròige to the southwest for good views of Loch Etive, or start heading back to Altnafeadh. The return journey to the summit is a little more than 1 mile, involves just over 200m of ascent (approximately an extra hour of walking time) and the terrain is quite easy.

From the col, the descent into Coire Altruim is steep but quite straightforward, except for a few wet, rocky steps towards the bottom where a little care is needed. Allow an hour to reach the River Coupall, which may be difficult to ford if it is in spate. If so, simply follow the river back to Altnafeadh and cross it on the footbridge used at the start of the walk. If the river is low, cross over and follow the well-defined but boggy path that takes you to the A82, just a few hundred metres west of Altnafeadh (one hour from the col).

MORE WALKS

BEN NEVIS AREA
The Mamores

This shapely mountain range lines the southern side of Glen Nevis and offers Munro baggers a challenging circuit, including the knife-edged Devil's Ridge and magnificent views of mountains both near and distant. Known as the Ring of Steall walk, it starts and finishes at the upper car park in Glen Nevis and takes in Sgurr a' Mhàim, Sgorr an Iubhair, An Garbhanach and An Gearanach.

You will need to allow around eight hours for this moderate–demanding 8.5-mile (13.5km) walk, which involves a total ascent of around 1500m. Consult the OS Explorer 1:25,000 map No 392 *Ben Nevis*. The best of the several guides to the Munros is the Scottish Mountaineering Club's (SMC) *The Munros* by Rab Anderson and Donald Bennet.

GLENCOE LOCHAN

Part-hidden by tall forest just north of Glencoe village (p370), the eponymous Glencoe Lochan sits at the foot of the western end of the ridge bounding the northern side of Glen Coe. On fine days its waters display beautiful reflections of the distinctive profile of Sgorr na Ciche, better known as the Pap of Glencoe. Three colour-coded, waymarked walks around the lochan and through the surrounding forest, owned and managed by the Forestry Commission, make for a pleasantly easy-going afternoon. The walks start at a car park at the end of a rough track, branching from the minor road at the Bridge of Coe at the eastern end of the village.

Follow markers for the blue route steeply up to a lookout for fine views of peaks in western Glen Coe, and in Morvern and Ardgour across Loch Linnhe. Soon, descend steeply to a junction and turn right to follow the lochan's shore. Cross the outlet and a retaining wall to a junction; turn right and go down to the car park. This 1.8-mile (3km) walk should take about 45 minutes. Although a map is scarcely necessary for this stroll, the OS Landranger 1:50,000 map No 41 *Ben Nevis* is useful for orientation from the viewpoint.

The Grey Corries

The Grey Corries lie at the eastern end of the massif crowned by Ben Nevis. A string of graceful, conical summits is linked by a high-level ridge that provides an exceptionally fine walk. The approach is quite long, however, and you will need eight or nine hours for the traverse to Beinn na Socaich, or 10 hours if you go on to Sgurr Chóinnich Beag. Start and finish at Corriechoille, 2.5 miles east along a minor road from Spean Bridge. Unfortunately, public transport (from Fort William) will take you only as far as Spean Bridge. The nearest facilities are here and in Fort William (p362). For the truly heroic, how about the Lochaber Traverse, beginning at Corriechoille and traversing the Grey Corries, Aonach range, Carn Mór Dearg, and finishing with an ascent of Ben Nevis. All in one day of course! Consult OS Explorer 1:25,000 map No 392 *Ben Nevis* and the SMC's *The Munros* by Rab Anderson and Donald Bennet.

GLEN COE
Glen Coe & Glen Etive Circuit

This 10-mile (16km) moderate, low-level walk offers an introduction to the wildness and ruggedness of Glen Coe. Following rough and, in places, wet paths (historic rights of way) that circumnavigate Buachaille Etive Beag, the walk starts on the A82 at Altnafeadh (for access details, see p371), from where it is necessary to follow sections of an old road and the main road verge to the signposted start of the path, 2 miles to the east. The exceptionally scenic route crosses two dramatic passes, Lairig Eilde and Lairig Gartain, and involves 600m of ascent. Consult OS Landranger 1:50,000 map No 41 *Ben Nevis*. The walk is described in *Walks Fort William* by John and Tricia Wombell.

Bidean nam Bian

The ascent of this, the highest mountain in Glen Coe (1150m), is one of the Glen Coe classics. The route squeezes through the steep-sided glens that separate the Three Sisters – the towering buttresses enclosing the southern side of Glen Coe – then climbs onto the main massif and its fine rocky ridges. A 6-mile (9.5km) circuit from near Allt-na-reigh cottage on the A82, involving 1150m ascent, should take six to seven hours. Best done clockwise, the route goes up the tragic Lost Valley (associated with the infamous massacre of Glen Coe), across high ground via Bidean's summit and Stob Coire nan Lochan and down Coire nan Lochan. Carry OS Explorer 1:25,000 map No 384 *Glen Coe* and consult the SMC's *The Munros* by Rab Anderson and Donald Bennet.

The Cairngorms

The Cairngorms are the wildest and most extensive area of uplands in Britain and embrace the largest tracts of land over 600m and up to 1300m high. The climate is the closest in Britain to an arctic regime; consequently the area is of outstanding ecological importance. The greater part of the area is within Cairngorms National Park, the larger of Scotland two national parks, set aside in 2003 (see the boxed text, p376).

The term Cairngorms can refer to the entire area between the River Spey southeast to Braemar on the upper River Dee, but in this chapter the focus is mainly on the vast central Cairn Gorm-Macdui plateau. It's crowned by Ben Macdui (1309m), Britain's second-highest mountain, south of Cairn Gorm (1245m) peak itself. The plateau is separated from neighbouring mountain massifs by the deep gash of the Lairig Ghru in the west and the Lairig an Laoigh in the east, and is pitted with spectacular, cliff-lined corries on its northern and southern faces.

Originally the Cairngorms were called Am Monadh Ruadh, meaning 'red rounded hills' (referring to the large exposures of pinkish-red granite), but the name of the summit most visible from Strathspey was adopted in the 19th century. Oddly, Cairn Gorm means 'blue rocky mountain'.

Don't be put off if you're not keen on venturing into high places. On the northern slopes of the plateau, Rothiemurchus Estate (privately owned by the Grant family, of whisky fame) and Glenmore Forest Park (managed by the Forestry Commission) have many low-level walks, suitable for all and ideal for days when the mountains are cloud-shrouded.

HIGHLIGHTS

- Savouring magnificent views to distant horizons from **Cairn Gorm** (p377), a vast alpine plateau seemingly on top of the world
- Following centuries-old pathways through remote glens to **Lairig Ghru** (p379), the most dramatic mountain pass in Scotland
- Relaxing on the peaceful circuit of secluded **Loch an Eilein** (p382)

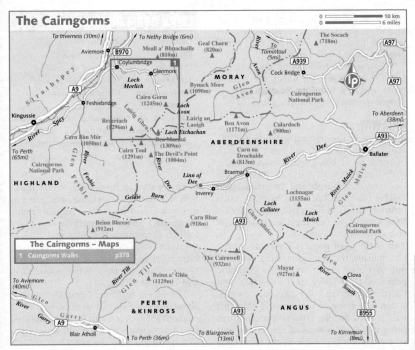

INFORMATION
When to Walk
Since Cairngorm is Scotland's leading ski resort, it's not surprising that snow can lie here (and on the surrounding peaks) until well into May, and can return as early as late October. The season for the Lairig Ghru is slightly longer, but don't forget that hours of daylight are short between mid-October and mid-April.

Maps
Harvey's Superwalker 1:25,000 map *Cairn Gorm* covers both walks very well. The OS Landranger 1:50,000 map No 36 *Grantown & Aviemore* would do as an alternative.

Books
The most comprehensive guidebook is *The Cairngorms* by Adam Watson in the Scottish Mountaineering Club's (SMC) District Guide series. Of the several walking guides covering the area, *Walks Speyside including Glenmore* by Richard Hallewell is very compact and describes 25 varied walks; in similar format, Nick Williams' *The Cairn-*

gorms outlines 40 circular walks, mostly for hardy types. John Brooks' *Cairngorms Walks* has better maps and more generous descriptions. Jim Crumley's *The Heart of the Cairngorms* is a passionate statement of the 'need for wildness' to be recognised in conservation and development proposals.

Information Sources
Cairngorms National Park (www.cairngorms.co.uk) doesn't have a dedicated tourist office; instead local tourist offices carry a selection of park publications. The website is easy to navigate and offers a mountain of information about the park's natural and cultural features, organised Countryside Events, public transport services and publications.

For accommodation bookings, contact the **Aviemore tourist office** (☎ 0845 225 5121; www.visithighlands.com; The Mall; ☉ daily). **Traveline Scotland** (☎ 0870 608 2608; www.traveline-scotland .co.uk) is the most direct source of detailed public transport timetables.

Near the Cairngorm funicular's base station, and close to the Cairngorm car park and bus stop, the **Cairngorms countryside ranger** service (☎ 01497-861703) can give expert advice about walks on the plateau; the weather forecast is posted there daily. It runs a program of guided walks in summer.

Whatever you think about the funicular (see the boxed text on p380), the website of its operator, **CairnGorm Mountain Ltd** (www.cairngormmountain.com), is worth a look.

GATEWAY

Aviemore is the natural gateway for the walks described here, and has a full range of services. It has good transport links, with daily Scottish Citylink buses from Glasgow, Edinburgh and Inverness, and regular First ScotRail trains from the same centres. The GNER service from London King's Cross to Inverness via Edinburgh also stops here.

This is the most popular high walk in the Cairngorms, the highlights being the summit of Cairn Gorm itself, the dramatic peaks of Stob Coire an t-Sneachda and Cairn Lochan, and the awesome corries. It can't be stressed too strongly that this walk is not a doddle. The vast plateau drops precipitously in almost all directions and severe weather is possible at any time; conditions may be fine at Glenmore but up on top it can be completely different. Inexperienced walkers should only tackle this walk in seasoned company. The side trip to Ben Macdui (p379) offers even wider views and a greater sensation of remoteness, out of sight of the northern-slope developments. The path to Ben Macdui diverges from Cairn Lochan southwest across a gap and up to the undulating plateau studded with crowds of cairns. Adding Ben Macdui makes for a full day, but one well within the scope of fit walkers.

WARNING

The Cairngorms is not the place to go for a casual stroll – the plateau is generally above 1000m. The weather is notoriously fickle, with low cloud, mist, strong wind, sleet and snow likely at any time – so always be prepared for the worst. Navigation skills are essential; the paths are well-worn but visibility can quickly deteriorate to zero and finding the way can be decidedly tricky in the absence of prominent landmarks.

CAIRN GORM HIGH CIRCUIT

Duration	4 hours
Distance	7 miles (11.5km)
Difficulty	moderate–demanding
Start/Finish	Cairngorm car park
Nearest Town	Glenmore (opposite)
Transport	bus

Summary An outstanding mountain walk across an exposed plateau with magnificent wide-ranging views and an optional detour to Ben Macdui.

This walk can be done in either direction; it is described clockwise here, going up to Cairn Gorm from the northeast, round the rim of Coire an t-Sneachda, over Cairn Lochan then down the ridge and back to the start. Realistically, the only early escape route on the walk is down Fiacaill a' Choire Chais, the ridge between Coire Cas and Coire an t-Sneachda.

The ascent to Cairn Gorm's summit is about 645m and there's an additional climb of about 155m over Cairn Lochan. The walk isn't a particularly long day, allowing plenty of time for enjoying the views.

NEAREST TOWN
Glenmore

Glenmore (7 miles from Aviemore), beside the Ski Rd up to Cairngorm, is the closest settlement to the start of the walk.

The Forestry Commission's **Glenmore Forest Park Visitor Centre** (☎ 01479-861220) concentrates on the surrounding forest park (within the national park). *Guide to Forest Walks,* available from the centre, includes maps and notes for waymarked walks in the park. There's also a **café** (breakfast £7, lunch £6, dinner £8; ☺ breakfast & lunch daily, dinner Jun-Sep) here.

SLEEPING & EATING

Glenmore Camping & Caravan Site (☎ 01479-861271; sites for 2 £10) is run by the Forestry Commission. Pitches are mostly flat and well grassed; the views are superb.

Cairngorm Lodge SYHA Hostel (☎ 01479-861238; www.syha.org.uk; dm £14; ▣), in a spacious former lodge, has excellent facilities and a great outlook.

Glenmore Lodge (☎ 01479-861256; www.glenmore lodge.org.uk; s/d with shared bathroom £20/40, mains £6-10;

CAIRNGORMS NATIONAL PARK

No one has ever doubted that the Cairngorms is one of Scotland's finest natural assets (which is saying a lot!) but it seemed that this compelling fact was pushed aside in wrangling over the national park boundaries. When it was opened in late 2003 (bizarrely, in a restaurant at the top of the much-opposed funicular), many felt that bureaucrats had won and the Cairngorms had lost, or at least been handed second prize. A sizeable swath of what is generally regarded as Cairngorms country, in the East Perthshire Highlands, had been left out, with the southern boundary generally following that of Highland Council. Nevertheless, the 470-sq-mile park is twice the size of Loch Lomond & the Trossachs; it has four of Britain's five highest peaks, protects 25% of Britain's threatened birds, animals and plants and is home to more than 17,000 people in seven towns.

The park does not, and will not, have a Gateway Centre after the style of Loch Lomond & the Trossachs, nor any dedicated tourist offices. Instead, its many attractive leaflets and brochures are, or should be, available from the several tourist offices within its boundaries, notably **Aviemore** (☎ 0845 225 5121; www.visithighlands.com). Again unlike Loch Lomond & the Trossachs, the Cairngorms National Park Authority does not have the last say in development issues within the park, so it remains to be seen how two of the park's four key aims are juggled: 'To conserve and enhance the natural and cultural heritage of the area' and 'To promote sustainable economic and social development of the area's communities'. It's to be hoped that a coalition of Perthshire movers and shakers, led by a local MP, can win their case when the boundaries are reviewed in 2008. Meantime, the park is still incontestably the finest in Britain, judged by natural values alone.

☺ lunch & dinner), about 1 mile east of Glenmore, houses the National Sports Training Centre. The Lochain Bar has a marvellous view of the Cairngorm plateau and – when you can't see the view – stunning posters of more distant peaks. Accommodation availability depends on courses in progress.

Cas Bar (Cairngorm car park), near the funicular station, is mainly a watering hole, though it does serve snacks and light meals.

Glenmore shop (☎ 01479-861253), next to the camping site, stocks a small range of supplies and liquid fuel and gas; the local forecast is posted outside. There's an adjacent **café** (breakfast £5, lunch mains £5, dinner mains £8; ☺ lunch daily, dinner Jun-Sep).

GETTING THERE & AWAY
Highland Country Buses (☎ 01463-233371; www .rapsons.co.uk) runs a service from Aviemore to Cairngorm via Glenmore (25 minutes, at least 10 daily).

By car, leave the A9 12 miles north of the Kingussie turnoff (or 7 miles south of the Carrbridge turnoff) to reach Aviemore. From here take the B970 to Coylumbridge, then the Ski Rd to Glenmore and Cairngorm car park (at Coire Cas)

GETTING TO/FROM THE WALK
For details of how to reach to the start by bus or car, see above.

THE WALK   Map p378
Cairngorm Car Park to Cairn Gorm
1½ hours, 2 miles (3km)

Start by walking down the road, away from the car park, to a road junction and take the road to the right for about 90m to a stonework drain on the right. A small cairn marks the start of a narrow path on the other side of the ditch, parallel to the road. Follow this old track for about 200m – it becomes wider and clearer up the heather-clad slope. After a while cairns mark the route steadily up, with views unfolding of the corries and spurs of the Cairngorm plateau. The path goes beneath a ski lift and past the top of another, weaving in and out of the picket fences lining the lifts. Having left the heather behind, the path crosses gravelly ground and skirts the Ptarmigan restaurant. Beyond the restaurant a stone-paved path leads steeply up to a boulder field, where cairns and poles clearly mark the route across this minor obstacle course and up to the large summit cairn on **Cairn Gorm** (1245m), with a weather station nearby.

Among the many features in the view are the long, flat plateau of Ben Wyvis (just west of Inverness) to the north; the sprawling bulk of Ben Macdui nearby; beyond it, the sharper profile of Braeriach; and, to the southeast, flat-topped Ben Avon, its summit dotted with granite tors.

Cairn Gorm to Cairn Lochan
1 hour, 2 miles (3km)

Descend sharply west over a jumble of big boulders – initially there's no clear path – towards a wide path on clearer ground below. Then, on a broad saddle, diverge a little to the right to a prominent cairn marking the feature mapped as '1141' at the head of Fiacaill a' Choire Chais (the escape route noted earlier). From the cairn there's a great view of the crags on the eastern side of Cairn Lochan.

Follow the broad path round the rim of cliff-lined Coire an t-Sneachda, its flat floor decorated with swampy lochans (small lakes). A cairned route leads up to **Stob Coire an t-Sneachda** (Peak of the Snowy Corrie;

1176m). Drop down west to a small gap. The path to Ben Macdui (opposite) leads south from here. Otherwise, climb steeply to **Cairn Lochan** (1215m) with its sprawling cairn close to the rim of the plunging cliffs. The beautiful patchwork of broad Strathspey dominates the outlook northwest and west, while Ben Rinnes, a prominent feature along the Speyside Way (p427), stands just to the left of Cairn Gorm's summit.

Cairn Lochan to Cairngorm Car Park
1½ hours, 3 miles (5km)

Continue generally southwest, following a cairned route, then descend the steep, mostly rocky slope to the clearly defined path along the north–south ridge rimming the west-

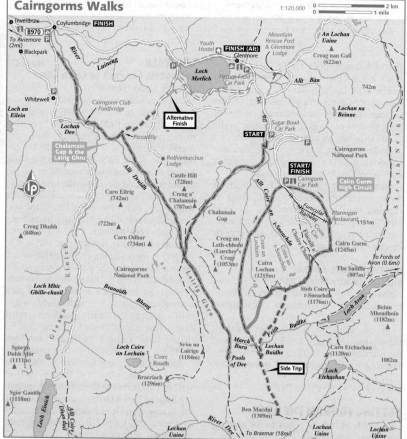

Cairngorms Walks

ern side of Coire an Lochan. The path loses height fairly quickly down the heathery slope as it bends northeast and crosses a small stream. A well-made path takes over – you can be grateful for the huge stepping stones planted across a very boggy stretch. The excellent path leads on, making it much easier to enjoy the superb views of the northern corries, then across Allt Coire an t-Sneachda and on to the Cairngorm car park.

DOTTERELS & DEER

Not only are the Cairngorms outstandingly scenic, they are also exceptionally valuable for wildlife, especially for birds. Golden plovers, ptarmigans and dotterels may be seen on higher ground; siskins, crested tits and redpolls live in more sheltered areas and the pine woodlands on the lowermost slopes. Mountain hares also inhabit the higher ground, red and roe deer are widespread and you may even see reindeer (an introduced species) grazing high up.

SIDE TRIP: BEN MACDUI

2½ hours, 5 miles (8km), 200m ascent

Leaving the gap between Stob Coire an t-Sneachda and Cairn Lochan, follow the clear, narrow path leading south then southwest above the shallow valley of Feith Buidhe and down to a wide saddle cradling Lochan Buidhe. Snow can linger on the north-facing slope, just east of the lochan, into late summer. Beyond Lochan Buidhe you can see the dramatic cliffs of Carn Etchachan, while in the opposite direction, across the depths of the Lairig Ghru, Braeriach's magnificent corries look as if some giant hand has scooped them out of the plateau. Follow a cairned route southeast across boulders then climb the steep slope past a minor peak and on to the summit of **Ben Macdui** (1309m), marked by a lonely survey pillar, near which is a low stone shelter and a direction indicator erected by the Cairngorm Club (Aberdeen) in 1925, identifying the features in the wide view, from Ben Nevis and Creag Meagaidh (west), to Lochnagar (east) and Ben More Assynt (north).

To return to the Cairn Gorm High Circuit route, retrace your steps to the saddle at Lochan Buidhe. From here, keep to the left or westerly path over the broad spur, then

it's down – with an awesome view straight into the Lairig Ghru, overlooked by rugged Lurcher's Crag. Follow this path back to Cairngorm as described in the main route.

CHALAMAIN GAP & THE LAIRIG GHRU

Duration	6 hours
Distance	13 miles (20.8km)
Difficulty	moderate–demanding
Start	Sugar Bowl car park
Finish	Coylumbridge (p380)
Transport	bus

Summary An energetic walk into the finest mountain pass in Britain, following rocky paths and crossing boulder fields, with a choice of return routes.

The Lairig Ghru is generally regarded as the finest mountain pass in Britain and is accessible only to walkers. It was cut by a massive glacier slicing right through the mountain mass, and provides a natural route from Strathspey to Upper Deeside. Lairig Ghru means 'Pass of Druie' – the stream that drains its northern side. It has been used for centuries for trade and cattle droving and is a public right of way. Traditionally, people walked the full distance from Aviemore to Braemar (28 miles) but these days many start from Coylumbridge or Glenmore. At the southern end there's nothing for it but to walk right into Braemar. It's possible to do this in a day, or you could carry a tent, spreading the journey over two days. There is accommodation in and near Braemar.

PLANNING

The walk is a day's outing, through the dramatic Chalamain Gap and up to the top of the Lairig Ghru, then back to Coylumbridge through Rothiemurchus pine woodlands. The best way to do the walk is from Sugar Bowl car park, starting at a point higher than the finish. Crossing Chalamain Gap involves a climb of 240m and it's another 225m up to the top of the Lairig Ghru.

Alternatives

One possible alternative for the return is to walk back to Herons Field car park on the Ski Rd near Glenmore, a distance of 15 miles; the Forestry Commission charges £1 for the use of this car park.

THE CAIRNGORMS

THE CAIRNGORM FUNICULAR

During the 1960s, the northern (and eastern) slopes of the Cairngorms were opened up for downhill skiing with the building of a road from Glenmore into Coire Cas. From there chair lifts ascended via an intermediate station to Ptarmigan, the top station at 1080m. However, the lift was often closed by the strong winds that regularly buffet the plateau.

In 1994 the Cairngorm Chairlift Company proposed a funicular railway similar to those operating in continental European alpine resorts. It would be more reliable and comfortable certainly, and it would, they said, attract up to 100,000 visitors annually, twice then-current numbers. Many jobs would be created and the local economy would thrive.

Walkers, mountaineers and conservation groups protested that the environmental impact of the development would be disastrous in an area of supreme ecological and scenic importance, that it couldn't possibly be economically viable and would probably drive visitors away rather than draw them in. What's more, snowfalls seemed to be on the decline.

Nevertheless, financial backing was secured, Scottish Natural Heritage sanctioned the proposal (subject to mandatory access restrictions to protect adjacent European Union–designated conservation areas) and the Scottish Executive approved the proposal. To minimise the visual impact of the funicular and its support columns, the top 250m of the track to the Ptarmigan Visitor Centre goes through a shallow tunnel, blasted out of the hillside.

The funicular and base station facilities opened in December 2001, and the Ptarmigan Visitor Centre and restaurant the following spring. CairnGorm Mountain Ltd, the operating company, undertook to plough money back into the ski area, including footpath repair and construction.

One very big string was attached to the European funding – the funicular railway must operate as a closed system during summer, to ensure the increased number of visitors doesn't cause severe damage to the fragile mountain environment. This means that between 1 May and 30 November funicular riders are not allowed out onto the mountain, their experience being confined to the displays in the visitor centre and what they can see from the viewing platform and the funicular carriage. Access on foot to the summit is now from the Cairngorm car park in Coire Cas only.

Opponents of the funicular were not amused when the Ptarmigan restaurant was chosen as the site for the official opening of the not-uncontroversial Cairngorms National Park in September 2003, and several who were invited boycotted the ceremony. It remains to be seen whether the summer access restriction withstands commercial pressures as visitor numbers have fallen way short of the optimistic forecasts.

Alternatively, you can reach the Ski Rd near the western end of Loch Morlich via the Rothiemurchus Estate road, although car parking here is less satisfactory. The distance for this version is 12.8 miles. An outline of these alternatives is on opposite.

NEAREST TOWNS
Coylumbridge & Inverdruie

These two places, between Glenmore and Aviemore, are both very small but do have a few facilities.

Rothiemurchus Visitor Centre (☎ 01479-812345; www.rothiemurchus.net; Inverdruie) is run by Rothiemurchus Estate and provides information about the estate, including guided walks led by the estate's own rangers. Under the same roof is the **Farm Shop & Larder**, stocked with seriously tempting Scottish goodies.

Rothiemurchus Camp & Caravan Park (☎ 01479-812800; Coylumbridge; sites for 2 £10) is set in pine woodland beside the Lairig Ghru path.

Junipers B&B (☎ 01479-810405; Inverdruie; s/d £28/50) is welcoming and comfortable.

The **Einich** (☎ 01479-812334; Inverdruie; mains £7-14; ☺ lunch daily, dinner Wed-Sat), next to the visitor centre in an old stone building, is a pleasantly informal restaurant. Local produce is to the fore on the small menu; the soup is second-to-none.

For public transport to Inverdruie and Coylumbridge, see p377.

GETTING TO/FROM THE WALK

The walk starts at the Sugar Bowl car park, on the northeastern side of the Ski Rd, 1.75 miles from Glenmore village. If you're using public transport, the Highland

Country Buses service passes the car park (see p377), although the driver will probably stop below the car park for safety's sake. The same service will stop in Glenmore and Coylumbridge on its way down the mountain.

At the end of the walk, there's a small roadside car park nearby.

THE WALK P378 Map p378
Sugar Bowl Car Park to Allt Druidh
1¾ hours, 3 miles (5km)

From the car park, cross the road and follow the path down to a footbridge across Allt Mór. Climb up to the right, then, on the rim of the bank, veer left along a paved path and continue past a sign warning that you're entering a wild mountainous area, across moorland. The views here are fantastic, taking in the deep corries and sharp spurs of the northern face of the Cairngorm plateau.

The path dips to cross a small stream then climbs to the narrow **Chalamain Gap**. Clamber over the boulders filling its narrow cleft, keeping to the lowest level to avoid the peaty, heathery slopes. It's an eerily quiet place, where rock falls seem to happen frequently. On the far side there are magnificent views across the Lairig Ghru to mighty Braeriach and the cairn-topped Sgòran Dubh Mór beyond. The wide, rocky and occasionally wet path crosses a shallow valley then descends steeply to the Lairig Ghru path beside Allt Druidh.

Allt Druidh to Pools of Dee
1¼ hours, 2 miles (3km)

The path crosses the stream on enormous boulders and climbs the heathery slope, then emerges onto more open ground, but still with the steep slopes towering above, their cliffs scoured by glaciers eons ago. Elongated mounds of moraine, left behind by the retreating glaciers, partly block the valley as you climb towards the pass. The path is marked by occasional cairns; follow these carefully, keeping to the left (east) for the final stretch to the crest. Ahead, the rugged peaks of Cairn Toul and the Devil's Point come into view. Continue for another 500m or so to the **Pools of Dee** – the headwaters of the River Dee – from where you can look far down the southern side of the Lairig Ghru.

Pools of Dee to Piccadilly
2 hours, 5 miles (8km)

Retrace your steps to the point where you joined the Lairig Ghru path and continue downstream from here. The rough path crosses steep, rocky slopes, with Allt Druidh far below in a deep trench cut through the moraine. Continue past a path to the right (to Rothiemurchus Lodge), with fine views of the Monadhliath Mountains on the western side of Strathspey and Meall a' Bhuachaille above Loch Morlich. After just over 1 mile you meet some beautiful Scots pines, the outliers of the Caledonian pine woodland and a precious remnant of the great forests that once covered much of the Highlands. The path junction, known unofficially as Piccadilly, has direction signs to Aviemore (to the left/west) and Loch Morlich (to the right/east).

Piccadilly to Coylumbridge
1 hour, 3 miles (5km)

Follow the track towards Aviemore, beside Allt Druidh, past a stream junction and down to the fine footbridge, built in 1912 by the Cairngorm Club, over Allt na Beinne Moire (mapped as Am Beanaidh). A short distance further on, bear right along a path to Coylumbridge. This leads through dense pines then more-open pine woodland (where the displays of purple heather in August are magnificent), across small burns and through gates. Pass a path to the left (to Gleann Einich) and continue along the broad track, past Rothiemurchus Camp & Caravan Park, to the road at Coylumbridge. There is a small roadside car park to the left.

ALTERNATIVE FINISH: GLENMORE
1¼ hours, 3 miles (5km)

Here we describe two alternative routes to Glenmore, one via Loch Morlich and the other via Herons Field. For both, turn right off the main route at Piccadilly, along the wide path towards Loch Morlich. This leads through pine woodland to a high deer fence, just beyond which you meet the wide gravel road to Rothiemurchus Lodge. Bear left and continue along the gravel road for nearly 1 mile to an unsignposted junction.

To reach the Ski Rd near the western end of Loch Morlich from here, just continue ahead for 300m. There is some roadside car parking here and there's a Forestry Commission car park 200m to the right, where the fee is £1. Glenmore village is 1.25 miles east along the road.

For Herons Field, follow the path from the unsignposted junction to a footbridge across a small burn, then go through a tall gate (where you leave Rothiemurchus Estate and enter Glenmore Forest Park) and left along a wide forest track, skirting the shore of Loch Morlich to the south. Near its eastern end, turn left along a path marked with a red-banded post. Follow the route marked with these posts north and east through cleared land and pines to the Herons Field car park. Sugar Bowl car park, at the start of the walk, is 1.25 miles south along the Ski Rd, while Glenmore is 600m to the east.

MORE WALKS

NORTHERN CAIRNGORMS
Braeriach

Braeriach (1296m), meaning 'Brindled Upland', is Britain's third-highest peak. It's the culmination of a great undulating plateau, with the Lairig Ghru on its precipitous eastern side and its western flank rising steeply from lonely Gleann Einich. For Munro enthusiasts there is also Sgor an Lochain Uaine (1258m) and Cairn Toul (1291m).

The climb starts only after a fairly long walk in from the Whitewell car park. The distance is 18.75 miles (30km) and the ascent 1000m; allow about nine hours. The best map is the Harvey Superwalker 1:25,000 map Cairn Gorm. The SMC's guide The Cairngorms is an invaluable reference.

For a misty overcast day, the walk into Loch Einich and back is well worth doing by itself.

Meall a' Buachaille

This shapely hill (the name means 'Shepherd's Hill') overlooks Glenmore and Loch Morlich and gives superb views of the whole Cairngorm plateau and Braeriach from its summit (810m). A path waymarked with orange-banded posts leads north from behind the Glenmore Forest Park Visitor Centre; the route to the summit is easy to follow. To make a circular walk, continue east to Ryvoan Bothy then follow the vehicle track down past beautiful An Lochan Uaine (Green Lake), back to Glenmore village. Allow three hours for this 6-mile (9.5km) walk, which includes 480m of climbing. It is covered by the Harvey Superwalker 1:25,000 map Cairn Gorm and the OS Landranger 1:50,000 map No 36 Grantown & Aviemore.

Loch Avon

Dramatically beautiful Loch Avon is almost surrounded by cliffs – the precipitous slopes

---

LOCH AN EILEIN

Secluded Loch an Eilein, part hidden in tall forest, sits at the foot of a long ridge northwest of the main Cairngorms massif, within both the Rothiemurchus Estate and Cairngorms National Park. Well-made paths through birch and pine woodland provide an easy 3-mile (5km) circuit of the beautiful loch, which should pleasantly occupy around 1½ hours. To reach the start follow the B970 southwest from Inverdruie (on the Aviemore–Glenmore road) for about 1 mile to the signposted turnoff to Loch an Eilein. The parking area is 1 mile further on; the fee is £2. For more information call at the Rothiemurchus Visitor Centre (p380) in Inverdruie.

By doing the circuit anticlockwise, you can call at the small **tourist office** (☼ Easter-Oct) before you really get going, and learn something of what you'll be seeing during the walk. From the car park, follow a wide path south to the tourist office; the large, partly grassed mound nearby is the remains of a lime kiln. Continue south along the track, close to the shore, and soon the islet that gave the loch its name comes into view, monopolised by the brooding grey ruins of a 14th-century castle. Further on, close to the path on the left, is a memorial to Walter Rice, who drowned while skating here in 1882, reputedly because he misjudged the thickness of the ice. From the end of the track, a path leads on to the left. Beyond the bridged crossing of the stream joining nearby Loch Gahmna to Loch an Eilein, the path leads along the eastern shores, and there are more good views of the castle. At the northern end of the loch, bear left along a shoreline path to the tourist office and turn right to reach the car park.

of the Cairngorm plateau to the north, and Carn Etchachan (1120m) and Beinn Mheadhoin (1182m) to the south. It is the highlight of this long, generally low-level walk round the eastern side of an outlier of the plateau. Parts of the route can be very wet, so keep this walk for a dry spell. The distance is 21 miles (34km), with 470m of ascent; allow around nine hours. Alternatively, take two days, pitching a tent near the tiny Fords of Avon refuge, a windowless stone hut. This would allow time for climbing Bynack More (1090m) and Beinn Mheadhoin nearby. Both the Harvey Superwalker 1:25,000 map *Cairn Gorm* and the OS Landranger 1:50,000 map No 36 *Grantown & Aviemore* cover the walk.

SOUTHERN CAIRNGORMS

Looking south and southeast from the summit of Cairn Gorm, you can see a host of broad-backed hills, many of which are separated by long, deep glens. There's enough high- and low-level walking here to occupy several weeks.

The Lairig Ghru walk (p379) can be extended via Derry Lodge to Braemar on the River Dee. It also links with a right of way southwards through Glen Tilt to the village of Blair Atholl (on the A9 and the railway), and another that you can follow west through Glen Feshie to finish up at Kingussie in Strathspey.

On the eastern side of the Cairn Gorm plateau there's a long-established route, accessible from Glenmore, via the River Nethy and the Fords of Avon through Lairig an Laoigh to Derry Lodge and the Linn of Dee near Braemar. Thus it's possible to circumnavigate the plateau via Lairig Ghru to Derry Lodge and Lairig an Laoigh.

Further east in Deeside, and south of the town of Ballater, are Lochnagar (1155m) and Loch Muick, both deservedly popular walks.

Two Harvey Superwalker 1:25,000 maps cover this area – *Cairn Gorm* and *Lochnagar*. You can also use the OS Landranger 1:50,000 maps No 36 *Grantown & Aviemore*, 43 *Braemar & Blair Atholl* and 44 *Ballater & Glen Clova*. For information visit the **Braemar tourist office** (☎ 01339-741600) and **Ballater tourist office** (☎ 01339-755306).

SPEYSIDE WAY

This long-distance path links Aviemore with Buckie on the north coast and generally follows the course of the River Spey. An outline of this varied route is given p427.

The Western Highlands

The Western Highlands is the earthly equivalent of a walker's heaven. It is a remote and starkly beautiful area, sparsely populated, with beautiful glens and lochs and some of the finest mountains in Britain. In summer the clear air provides rich colours, and (sometimes) great views from the ridges and summits. The sheer number of peaks and their infinite variety attracts walkers from all over the country, year after year. In small and crowded Britain, this is as close as it gets to real wilderness. All this is contained in the area between Glen Moriston and Glen Shiel in the south and Ullapool in the north, and bounded in the east by a line running through Garve.

The wildness integral to this area's charms can make logistics difficult for walkers on a short visit from abroad, especially if you are relying on public transport. If you have the time, the effort will be well rewarded. At any time of year the walking can be difficult, so this is no place to begin learning mountain techniques. But if you are fit, competent, well-equipped and, ideally, have plenty of time, the Western Highlands should be extremely rewarding, even addictive.

The routes we describe in this section are nontechnical (ie no ropes), are easily reached by car or public transport and there is a range of accommodation nearby. They are but a taste of the fine opportunities available, with several other classic walks in each of the Glen Shiel, Torridon and Great Wilderness areas.

THE WESTERN HIGHLANDS

HIGHLIGHTS

- Traversing the **Five Sisters'** (p386) slender, scenic ridge above dramatic Glen Shiel
- Being knocked sideways by the views of Scotland's west coast from atop the **Horns of Alligin** (p392)
- Scaling the heights of **Slioch** (p393), the dramatic peak above Loch Maree, on the threshold of the Great Wilderness

The Western Highlands

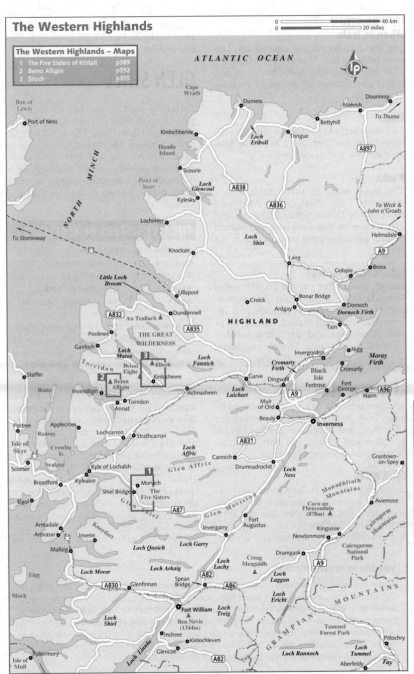

The Western Highlands – Maps	
1	The Five Sisters of Kintail	p389
2	Beinn Alligin	p392
3	Slioch	p395

INFORMATION
When to Walk
The three walks in this chapter are best done between mid-May and early October, after any late-spring snow has gone and before the chances of snowfalls increase dramatically.

Maps
Two maps in the OS Travel – Road 1:250,000 series cover the area: No 2 *Northern Scotland* and No 3 *Western Scotland*.

Books
Two publications by the Scottish Mountaineering Club (SMC), *The Northwest Highlands* by DJ Bennett and T Strang, and *The Munros* by Rab Anderson and Donald Bennet, provide a good introduction to the area.

Information Sources
Gairloch tourist office (☎ 0845 225 5121; gairloch @visitscotland.com) is the main information point for the Western Highlands. It is informative and well staffed, selling maps and guidebooks and providing weather forecasts for the area. The encompassing website for the whole of the Highlands is www.visithighlands.com.

GETTING AROUND
All three areas in this chapter are served by buses from Inverness: Scottish Citylink for Glen Shiel; and Westerbus and Scotbus for Torridon and Slioch. The Fort William–Skye bus also services Glen Shiel.

GATEWAYS
Inverness and Fort William (p362) serve as the main gateways to the area. Both have good daily Scottish Citylink bus and First ScotRail train links to the rest of Scotland, and to London (First ScotRail and GNER).

Inverness is also served by daily flights from Glasgow, Edinburgh, London, Belfast and Dublin.

GLEN SHIEL

Travelling west to the Isle of Skye you pass through what appears to be the impenetrable Glen Shiel. The winding road snakes between steep-sided, rock-encrusted mountains, soaring skywards to the north, and rising almost as steeply and ruggedly to the south. The long spiky ridge to the north of the glen is known as the Five Sisters of Kintail.

THE FIVE SISTERS OF KINTAIL

Duration	6¾–8 hours
Distance	7.5 miles (12km)
Difficulty	demanding
Start	Glen Shiel car park
Finish	Ault a' chruinn (opposite)
Transport	private

Summary One of the finest ridge walks in Scotland – an arduous but immensely scenic walk over rough ground, traversing some narrow ridges along mostly clear, well-used paths.

This chain of elegant, precipitous summits, separated by slits of passes (or bealachs), falls away vertiginously to Glen Shiel on one side and to the more remote and peaceful Gleann Lichd on the other. To the northwest the ridge drops a little less steeply to the shores of beautiful Loch Duich. Three of the sisters are Munros (peaks over 3000ft/914m) – Sgurr Fhuaran (Peak of Springs, 1067m), Sgurr na Càrnach (Rocky Peak, 1002m) and Sgurr na Ciste Duibhe (Peak of the Black Chest, 1027m). The other two, at the north end

---

THE SPANISH CONNECTION
In the long struggle between government and Jacobite forces, which ended at the Battle of Culloden in 1745, a lesser-known battle took place in Glen Shiel. In June 1719 Jacobite troops, including a Spanish regiment, landed at Eilean Donan Castle beside Loch Duich. Government troops came from Inverness and the two sides met about 1 mile west of the starting point for this walk (there is a National Trust for Scotland interpretive sign at the site). The government troops routed the Jacobites and the last to flee were the Spanish, who dashed up the mountainside to the pass now called Bealach nan Spainteach and down into Gleann Lichd.

of the ridge, are Sgurr nan Saighead (Arrows Peak, 929m) and Sgurr na Móraich (Mighty Peak, 876m). And that isn't all: before you even reach the southernmost sister you have to climb over Sgurr nan Spainteach (Peak of the Spaniards, 990m); see the boxed text, opposite, for the history behind this unusual name.

The ridge commands fine views, with the Torridon mountains punctuating the horizon to the northwest, the Isle of Skye spreadeagled across the western skyline and the islands of Canna, Eigg and Rum sailing between the rugged southwestern peaks – and much, much more.

PLANNING

Far and away the best direction for this walk is from southeast to northwest – walking towards the views, starting at a higher point than where you finish, and with a slightly less steep and knee-jarring descent. If you're staying at Morvich or Shiel Bridge, add about 1 mile. The distance isn't unusually long but the ascent of 1530m is nearly 100m more than a romp up Ben Nevis. Keep in mind that even when you've reached the highest point on the walk (Sgurr Fhuaran) the climbing isn't over – there are still two peaks to go.

Alternatives

Once you're on the ridge, escape routes are few. People do go down to Glen Shiel via the spur from Sgurr Fhuaran, but this is seriously steep. Routes to and from Gleann Lichd, on the other side, are feasible and, indeed, have much to recommend them. There is a clear path up to the ridge at Bealach an Làpain from Glenlicht House, and the long ridge thrusting eastwards from Sgurr Fhuaran offers a fairly straightforward climb or descent.

When to Walk

The Five Sisters are very exposed and can be extremely hazardous in poor visibility, strong wind or rain, so it's worth waiting for the right day for this classic ridge walk. This is also important because there's a lot of loose rock along the ridge, especially on the descents into, and climbs out of, bealachs, so considerable care is needed for your own and others' safety. The best times are May and June, and September to early October.

The whole ridge is within the NTS' Kintail Estate, so access is open at all times.

Maps

The Harvey Superwalker 1:25,000 map *Kintail: Glen Shiel* covers the Five Sisters and has some background information and local contacts. The relevant Ordnance Survey (OS) Landranger 1:50,000 map is No 33 *Loch Alsh, Glen Shiel & Loch Hourn*.

Information Sources

At Morvich, about 1.5 miles from the A87, the NTS (☎ 01599-511231; kintail@nts.org.uk) maintains a small, usually unstaffed tourist office featuring the Kintail Estate; the weather forecast is displayed daily. Countryside rangers based here run guided walks during summer.

NEAREST TOWNS
Ault a' chruinn & Shiel Bridge

You can't really call Ault a' chruinn a village – it's more a scattered collection of houses around the junction of the A87 and the minor road to Morvich. Shiel Bridge is a hamlet scattered along the A87, and is a popular refreshment stop on the way to the Isle of Skye.

Morvich Caravan Club Site (☎ 01599-511354; www.caravanclub.co.uk; Inverinate; sites for 2 £19) is about 1 mile north of Ault a' chruinn. Pitches at this secluded, sheltered site are flat and grassy.

Shielbridge Caravan & Camping Site (☎ 01599-511211; Shiel Bridge; sites for 2 £5) is flat and open, with great views of the Five Sisters; facilities are clean and well-maintained.

Kintail Lodge Hotel (☎ 01599-511275; www.kintaillodgehotel.co.uk; dm/s/d £13/50/58; breakfast £10, lunch & dinner mains to £10) offers superior hotel accommodation, the Trekkers' Lodge, with twins and singles, and the Wee Bunk House, offering dorm-style accommodation.

The off-licence **Shielshop** (Shiel Bridge; ◷ daily) has a very good range of supplies and local maps.

Jac-O-Bite Restaurant (☎ 01599-511347; Ault a' chruinn; breakfast £7, lunch mains £4-7, dinner mains £9-20) has a superb outlook. The smallish menu features plenty of local produce and daily specials are offered.

Five Sisters Restaurant (☎ 01599-511221; Shiel Bridge; breakfast £4-7, lunch £4-7) offers standard fare in cheerful surroundings.

GETTING THERE & AWAY

Scottish Citylink (☎ 0870 550 5050; www.citylink
.co.uk) buses stop at Shiel Bridge from Glasgow (4¾ hours, three daily) and the Isle of Skye via Fort William (1½ hours, three daily), as do its buses between Inverness (1½ hours, three daily) and Portree (1½ hours, three daily).

Shiel Bridge is on the A87 trunk road, which branches from the A82 Inverness–Fort William road at Invergarry. From Inverness turn off the A82 at Invermoriston along the A887 to join the A87 near Loch Cluanie.

GETTING TO/FROM THE WALK

The walk starts at a car park beside the A87, 5 miles west of Cluanie Inn. This car park (not signposted at the time of writing) is about 100m west of the one marked on the OS 1:50,000 map. Scottish Citylink buses through Shiel Bridge (see above) stop at Cluanie Inn.

The walk finishes on the minor road to Morvich (which branches from the A87, 1.5 miles from Shiel Bridge) in the hamlet of Ault a' chruinn, beside Loch Duich. The closest parking area is at the nearby Jac-O-Bite restaurant.

THE WALK
Glen Shiel Car Park to Sgurr na Ciste Duibhe

2½–3 hours, 2 miles (3km)

Just uphill from the car park, go through a small gate, immediately right of a burn, and follow a clear path up to a forest track. Just 12m to your right, beside a burn, bear left along a clear path. It follows a generally zigzagging route up beside the burn, through a young conifer plantation, climbing fairly steeply, to a gate in a high fence, leading onto open moorland. Continue on the path, soon bearing left to cross a burn at the foot of a small waterfall. The path leads northwest, up below a crag, zigzags then makes a rising traverse to the remains of an old stone wall. Climb beside or on it for a few minutes then bear left and cross a small stream. From there, in the absence of a clearly defined path, climb the steep, grassy slope to the main ridge, reaching it west of Bealach an Làpain, near Beinn Odhar. Suddenly you're in a different world – surrounded by mountains and deep glens and, for the moment, out of earshot of the traffic on the road below.

Turn west along the ridge crest and follow the well-worn path up to a breezy

---

DEER STALKING

Managing Scotland's wild deer population is an organised and ecologically and economically important business. The 750,000-strong population comprises four species – red, roe, sika and fallow. Red deer are the biggest and most numerous and have the greatest impact on the land. A balance must be maintained between deer numbers and their habitat, so they have enough to eat without wrecking the vegetation.

The **Deer Commission for Scotland** (☎ 01463-725000; www.dcs.gov.uk) has fostered the establishment of deer management groups – voluntary groups of landowners covering areas with distinct herds – in most parts of the country. Regular censuses govern the annual cull, when older and unhealthy animals are shot by experienced professional stalkers using high-velocity rifles. The sport of deer stalking, a good income-earner for estates and local communities, is integrated into the cull.

During the stalking season, mostly between mid-August and mid-October, you can help to minimise disturbance by doing your best to find out where the activity is taking place and by heeding advice on alternative routes. Avoid crossing land where stalking is taking place. Management groups provide detailed on-site information, usually specifying preferred walking routes. This may also be available through the **Hillphones** (www.hillphones.info) service, or perhaps from local tourist offices. The National Trust for Scotland, John Muir Trust, Royal Society for the Protection of Birds, Forestry Commission and Scottish Natural Heritage may conduct stalking on their lands but generally maintain access for walkers throughout the year.

Some estates don't belong to deer management groups and some aren't cooperative. It's worth remembering that access along rights of way is always open, and that shooting doesn't happen on Sunday.

arête and on over the twin bumps of Beinn Odhar. Then comes a shallow dip and a rocky climb to **Sgurr nan Spainteach**. A scramble down the face of a bluff takes you to the amazingly narrow Bealach nan Spainteach. Make your way up through the boulders to the neat summit cairn on **Sgurr na Ciste Duibhe**, the first of the Five Sisters. Here you can look east towards Glen Affric through the gap at the top of Gleann Lichd and, in the opposite direction, contemplate the serrated skyline of the Isle of Skye beyond Loch Duich.

Sgurr na Ciste Duibhe to Sgurr Fhuaran

1½–1¾ hours, 1.5 miles (2.5km)

The ridge changes direction, leading northwest as you continue down to Bealach na Craoibhe (Pass of the Tree), keeping to the highest ground. The line of ascent then turns north to **Sgurr na Càrnach**, the second Sister. From here new features in the panorama include Lochs Affric and Benevean to the east. The first bit of the descent is down a narrow cleft to the left, then it bears right to regain the line of the ridge and go down to Bealach na Càrnach. A steep, rocky, twisting path takes care of the climb to **Sgurr Fhuaran**, the highest point on the ridge and the third Sister. From here the view is just as absorbing as those from her siblings.

Sgurr Fhuaran to Sgurr na Moraich

1¾–2 hours, 2.5 miles (4km)

Leaving the summit cairn, take care to head northwest then north on this awesome and spectacular descent to Bealach Bhuidhe. The path then traverses above the dramatic sheets of cliffs leading up to **Sgurr nan Saighead**, Sister number four. The ridge now changes character with more small, rocky knobs to negotiate on the way down and then up to Beinn Bhuidhe (Yellow Hill). A rough path drops down to a narrow gap, with fine views of Gleann Lichd below. Climb straight up and soon the path follows a more even course among rocky outcrops and, for a pleasant change, across grass and finally up to **Sgurr na Moraich**, Sister number five.

Sgurr na Moraich to Ault a' chruinn

1–1¼ hours, 1.5 miles (2.5km)

Having led northwest from the summit, straight towards the Skye Bridge, the path

The Five Sisters of Kintail

fades. Keep well to the left of the broad spur, generally northwest (or about 300 degrees magnetic), as you descend very steeply over grass and heather, steering away from the small cliffs bristling on the crest of the spur. Keep your eye on the crags on the western side of Allt a' chruinn as a guide to the best route down to a narrow path high above the stream. Follow it down to a stile and continue to a water treatment works. Turn right along a vehicle track, which becomes a sealed road, meeting the Morvich road in Ault a' chruinn, about 200m from its junction with the A87.

TORRIDON

The Torridon mountains dominate a wild area of lochans, moors, deep glens, spectacular corries and rugged peaks.

Within the Torridon group are three major mountains. Liathach (pronounced 'lee-agach' by the locals) is a massive wall of a mountain, festooned with pinnacles and buttresses, crags and boulder fields, its

THE WESTERN HIGHLANDS

main summit being Spidean a' Choire Léith (1055m). To the east is the Beinn Eighe massif (972m), not quite as high as Liathach though its several outliers make it bigger 'on the ground'. Beinn Dearg (914m), a magnificent horseshoe-shaped peak north of Liathach across a wide glen, may be comparatively lowly, but lacks little in the way of ruggedness. And then there's Beinn Alligin, the subject of this section and the ideal introduction to this wonderful area.

The Torridon Estate (2.5 sq miles), purchased by the NTS in 1967, embraces most of these peaks. It adjoins the Beinn Eighe National Nature Reserve, owned and managed by Scottish Natural Heritage (SNH).

BEINN ALLIGIN

Duration	6–8 hours
Distance	6.5 miles (10.5km)
Difficulty	moderate–demanding
Start/Finish	Torridon House Bridge
Nearest Towns	Torridon (above)
Transport	private

Summary An exciting circuit of a horseshoe ridge, crossing two major summits. It involves several steep and exposed sections and some scrambling.

Some Torridon routes are serious undertakings, involving difficult scrambling in very exposed locations, and are beyond the scope of this book. However, Beinn Alligin's summit, Sgurr Mhór (986m) and the peak Tom na Gruagaich (922m) can both be reached without encountering any technical difficulties, although this is still a serious mountain walk and not suitable for the unfit or inexperienced. Sgurr Mhór and Tom na Gruagaich, both Munros, and the spectacular subsidiary peaks, the Horns of Alligin, are linked by a ridge curving round the huge corrie Toll a' Mhadaidh Mor (the Fox Hole). Even more dramatic is the great gash of Eag Dhubh (the Black Cleft) in the back wall of the corrie, running from the summit ridge to the base and appearing to split the mountain in two.

The accepted meaning of Beinn Alligin is 'Mountain of Beauty' or 'Jewelled Mountain'. Either way, it's definitely a gem – a mountain that allows you to get a feel for the high and wild Scottish peaks without having to be a mountaineer or to cover long approach routes. Another plus is that the mountain is owned by the NTS, so access is open at all times.

PLANNING

The recommended direction for this circular walk is anticlockwise, so that you tackle the peaks while you're still fresh. The walk involves around 1300m of ascent.

Even in summer patches of snow lurk in shaded corners, the mist can be thick and the winds strong enough to blow you over if you happen to be caught in a sudden storm. Map-reading and compass skills are essential if the mist comes down, which is always likely. Although there's a well-defined path most of the way, beware of side paths that can lead to dead-end lookouts or potential difficulties.

Maps & Books

The OS Landranger 1:50,000 maps No 19 *Gairloch & Ullapool* and 24 *Raasay & Applecross* overlap on Beinn Alligin. Harvey's Superwalker 1:25,000 map *Torridon* is much more useful.

The SMC's guide *The Munros* by Rab Anderson and Donald Bennet is the most comprehensive guide to this walk (and the others in the Torridon area).

Guided Walks

Countryside rangers lead short walks aimed at introducing the natural and cultural landscape of Torridon between June and August, and high-level guided mountain walks are available by appointment. Contact the NTS Countryside Centre (below) for details.

Information Sources

The **NTS Countryside Centre** (☎ 01445-791221; exhibition £3; ☯ 10am-5pm Easter-Sep) is just off the A896, at the entrance to Torridon village. It stocks maps and a very good range of walking and environment books relating to the local area. Displays feature the scenery and wildlife of the Torridon mountains and Loch Torridon. Mountain weather forecasts are posted beside the entrance daily.

The nearest **tourist office** (☎ 0845 225 5121; gairloch@visitscotland.com; ☯ daily Easter-Sep, Mon-Sat Oct-Apr) is in Gairloch, 31 miles away.

TORRIDONIAN ROCKS

The exposed rocky flanks and summits of many of the peaks in this area display the geological processes that created the region. Ancient Lewisian gneiss, up to 2500 million years old, is the bedrock. In a much-eroded state, it was smothered by desert sands up to 4 miles thick around 800 million years ago when the area was in equatorial regions. The sedimentary material hardened to form a rock so localised it has been named red Torridonian sandstone (though it looks more purple than red). Slioch (p393), with its distinctive double-tiered silhouette, exhibits this rock particularly well, with a broad grey base topped by an 800m-high mound of red sandstone.

Much of this relatively soft sandstone has been eroded, mainly by successive ice ages, wind and rain, which have sculpted wonderful pinnacles and crags on high ridges. The pinnacles on An Teallach (p397) and the Horns of Beinn Alligin are superb examples. These days, the glue-like friction afforded by the fine-grained sandstone makes the area an ideal scramblers' playground.

The third main geological component of the area, Cambrian quartzite, was formed by sediments laid down by tropical seas, which flooded the sandstone some 600 million years ago. At the end of the last Ice Age, this rock was the first to emerge from the ice mantle. It was riven into pinnacles and shattered into scree, notably on Beinn Eighe (p393), which makes it look snow-covered, even in midsummer.

NEAREST TOWN
Torridon

The small village of Torridon, spread out along Loch Torridon's northern shore, at the foot of the towering western reaches of Liathach, is the main settlement in the area. The nearest ATM is in Gairloch, 31 miles away, although the shop may be able to provide a cash-back service for small amounts on UK bank cards.

SLEEPING & EATING

Torridon Campsite (free) is opposite the NTS Countryside Centre. It's basic – just a patch of grass; use the nearby public toilets.

Torridon SYHA Hostel (☎ 0870 004 1154; www .syha.org.uk; dm £13) has mainly smaller-than-average rooms, two lounges with panoramic views and a first-rate drying room.

Ben Damph Inn (☎ 01445-791242; www.bendamph .lochtorridonhotel.com; s/d £50/74, mains £7-12; ⏱ lunch & dinner) occupies a former stable that has been converted to motel-style accommodation, but without the sterile atmosphere that such places can have. The bar, where you can sample some of the 60 malt whiskies on offer, is the centre of evening activity in the area. The only catch is its location, on the south side of the loch, a couple of miles from Torridon village.

Torridon Stores (⏱ Mon-Sat) is small but is well-stocked and carries camping gas, books, maps and a great array of Scottish beers. It's 800m northwest from the junction, along the Inveralligin–Diabaig road.

GETTING THERE & AWAY

Torridon is at the eastern end of Loch Torridon, on the A896 between Lochcarron and Kinlochewe. It is possible to travel by public transport, if you are prepared to fit in with limited connecting services.

First ScotRail (☎ 0845 755 0033; www.firstscotrail .co.uk) operates the service to the nearest train station, Strathcarron, from Inverness (1¾ hours, four services Monday to Saturday, two Sunday) and Kyle of Lochalsh (45 minutes, four services Monday to Saturday, two Sunday).

Donnie Maclennan (☎ 01520-755239) runs a bus service from Strathcarron station to Torridon. He waits for the trains from both Kyle and Inverness that arrive around 12.40pm Monday to Saturday. For the return journey the bus leaves Torridon about 10.30am, arriving at Strathcarron in time for the 12.40pm trains to Kyle and Inverness. The times and services can change, so contact Donnie beforehand.

GETTING TO/FROM THE WALK

The walk starts almost opposite the fairly large car park beside Torridon House Bridge, about 2 miles west of Torridon on the narrow Inveralligin road.

THE WALK
Torridon House Bridge to Sgurr Mhór
3–4 hours, 3.5 miles (5.5km)

From the bridge (which affords a good view of the impressive waterfall and gorge

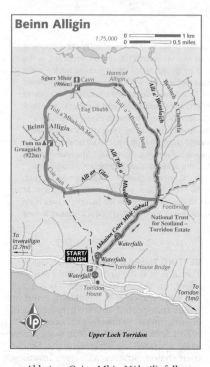

Beinn Alligin

your right (northeast) the view really begins to open out – a beautifully jumbled mosaic of lochans, moors and smaller peaks, with Loch Maree and the coast town of Gairloch beyond. Behind, too, the view keeps on getting better – down the corrie and across Loch Torridon to the mountains around Beinn Damph.

You soon reach **Sgurr Mhór** (986m), and with the extra height the view is almost 360 degrees: range upon range of wonderful peaks spread out in all directions. Most notable to the southwest are the Cuillin peaks on Skye and, to the east, the summits of Beinn Eighe, the quartz scree making them appear eternally snowcapped.

Sgurr Mhór to Torridon House Bridge
3-4 hours, 3 miles (5km)
From the summit, head northwest down a grassy slope, keeping the corrie edge to the left. In poor visibility take particular care on this section as the top of **Eag Dhubh**, the giant gash that dominates the view from below, is hereabouts, just waiting to trap unwary walkers in mist. If, however, the day is clear, the cliffs on either side of the gully frame the view of the glen far below, one of Scottish walking's many classic vistas. *Don't* try to descend this way.

Beyond Eag Dhubh go steeply up again, over large boulders, to reach **Tom na Gruagaich** (922m), about one to 1½ hours from Sgurr Mhór. There's a trig point to lean against as you have a last look at the view before heading down.

The descent is steep but straightforward. Walk south into Coire nan Laogh, between the main western ridge and the ridge extending from Tom na Gruagaich, dropping steeply on an eroded path with several small streams gurgling along beside. The steep walls of the corrie funnel you down to a rocky plateau. Here, if Abhainn Coire Mhic Nòbuil isn't in spate, steer a course slightly south of east to reach Allt a' Bhealaich, just above the footbridge you crossed on the way out. Cross the bridge to reach the path and retrace your steps to the road and car park.

Otherwise, head southeast to avoid crags on the broad ridge and to find a stile for a long deer fence on the eastern fall of the spur. Follow rough paths to the road opposite the car park. The descent from Tom na Gruagaich should take about two hours.

on Abhainn Coire Mhic Nòbuil) follow a path, signposted to Coire Dubh, up through Scots pine woodland and out into moorland. Straight ahead is the blunt western wall of Beinn Dearg. To the right (east) is the western end of Liathach and to the left (west) is Beinn Alligin. About 200m further along, go through a gate in a deer fence. Almost 1km beyond here, the clear path crosses a footbridge and aims roughly north, towards the eastern end of the Alligin horseshoe ridge.

Continue up the crest of the broad and very steep ridge, using your hands for balance while negotiating some rocky steps, and aim for the three **Horns of Alligin**. You reach the base of the first horn about 1½ to two hours from the start. You can scramble over this and the next two rocky peaks, taking care on the steep descent of the first pinnacle. Alternatively, follow the path that skirts the peaks on their southern side.

After the third horn, drop to a small col and then go up again, swinging round to the left (northwest) and keeping the steep drop down into the corrie on your left. To

BEINN EIGHE MOUNTAIN TRAIL

If the clouds are down over the high peaks, or perhaps you have half a day to spare, the Beinn Eighe Mountain Trail provides an excellent introduction to the area. This waymarked route is only 2.5 miles long (though it involves around 550m ascent) and takes in the best low- to mid-level terrain in the Beinn Eighe National Nature Reserve, including beautiful stands of native Scots pine. There is a short, steep section of rocky ground to negotiate to reach the higher section, where the path weaves past secluded lochans and offers a real impression of being in the heart of the mountains. There are also wonderful views of the Beinn Eighe massif and across Loch Maree to Slioch.

The walk starts and finishes at the Glas Leitir parking area beside Loch Maree, a few miles northwest of Kinlochewe (on the main road to Gairloch) and about 18 miles from Torridon. You should allow at least 2½ hours, and take the usual precautions with footwear, waterproofs, food and drink. A booklet produced by Scottish Natural Heritage has a map of the route, and plenty of information about local wildlife and geology. This should be available from the **Beinn Eighe National Nature Reserve Visitor Centre** (☎ 01445-760254; www.nnr-scotland.org.uk; ☯ Easter-Oct), 0.75 miles north of Kinlochewe along the A832. It houses displays about the reserve's habitats and sells maps and natural history guides.

THE GREAT WILDERNESS

The Great Wilderness stretches from Little Loch Broom in the north to Loch Maree in the south, and from the Fannich mountains in the east to the west coast village of Poolewe, an area of about 180 sq miles. For visitors from New World countries in particular, where wilderness areas are on a grand scale, this title may seem presumptuous. But it must be judged by Scottish, indeed British, standards. On these small islands, the fact that it's relatively far from any towns, that there are no roads, only a handful of buildings of any sort, and certainly no pubs or shops within its bounds undoubtedly merits the title.

The landscape is mountainous with many fine, austere peaks. Between the mountains there are lochs of all shapes and sizes, rivers and waterfalls, peat bogs and grassy glens, but very few trees. It may seem strange to see Fisherfield Forest, Letterewe Forest and Dundonnell Forest on the map, but 'forest' here means hunting ground and these names delineate separate estates.

Most of the peaks in the Great Wilderness are rather remote and best climbed in the course of an extended walk of at least two, and preferably three or four, days. Here, however, we describe a day walk to Slioch, on the southwestern threshold of the area, and a superb initiation into its wildness and beauty.

SLIOCH

Duration	7½ hours
Distance	11.8 miles (19km)
Difficulty	moderate–demanding
Start/Finish	Incheril car park
Nearest Town	Kinlochewe (p394)
Transport	bus

Summary A beautiful approach along the wooded shores of Loch Maree leads to a neat mountain horseshoe with excellent views.

The dramatic, double-tiered peak of Slioch (980m) rises majestically from the northwestern shores of Loch Maree. Around 800m of purple-red Torridonian sandstone soars skywards out of a bed of rounded, grey gneiss. When the buttressed flanks of the mountain reflect the evening sunlight, the effect is spellbinding. The mountain is well-named, the most likely meaning being 'spear'.

Unusually among mountain walks in most parts of Scotland, this one starts with a comparatively long walk to the start of the ascent, providing plenty of time to become imbued with the spirit of the place. This is, surely, far preferable to the usual routine of piling out of the car and heading straight up the path to the top. The route to Slioch follows the picturesque Kinlochewe River to Loch Maree, then climbs through wild moorland to the cluster of peaks that make up the Slioch massif. From the summit

---

HEAVY INDUSTRY BESIDE LOCH MAREE

Anything remotely resembling industrial development around Loch Maree would be most unwelcome, of course, but rest assured, it all happened during a brief interlude at least 400 years ago.

On the way to Slioch you cross Abhainn an Fhasaigh; here, between the path and the shore of Loch Maree, largely hidden by thick heather, are the remains of a fairly primitive ironworks (buildings, hearths and furnaces). Using local bog iron ore (which occurs naturally in poorly drained ground), the works probably operated around the end of the 16th century. It is likely that the works helped to encourage entrepreneur George Hay to develop what was probably the first charcoal-fired blast furnace in Scotland, near Letterewe, about 3 miles west of Slioch. Hay shipped iron ore from Fife and felled most of the oak woodlands on the loch shore to produce charcoal. It isn't clear just what he did with the iron produced, but there were ready markets at home and abroad. All activity had ceased by about 1670, leaving the works to crumble almost to nothing, as well as a decimated oak wood and the seemingly incongruous place name 'Furnace' near Letterewe.

---

ridge, views range from the remote heart of the Great Wilderness to the Western Isles. The walk involves a total ascent of 1160m and crosses some rough ground.

PLANNING
When to Walk/Stalking
The route passes through the **Letterewe Estate** (☎ 01445-760311). Contact the estate for advice during its main stalking season, from mid-September to mid-November.

Maps & Books
The OS Landranger 1:50,000 map No 19 *Gairloch & Ullapool* covers this route. Consult the SMC's guide *The Munros* by Rab Anderson and Donald Bennet for background information.

NEAREST TOWN
Kinlochewe
Kinlochewe is a dot on the map in a magnificent location, at the foot of steep, dramatic Glen Docherty and near the head of Loch Maree, with views towards Slioch and the peaks of Beinn Eighe National Nature Reserve. The nearest **tourist office** (☎ 0845 225 5121; gairloch@visitscotland.com; ☉ daily Easter-Sep, Mon-Sat Oct-Easter) is in Gairloch.

SLEEPING & EATING
Beinn Eighe Campsite (☎ 01445-760254; free) is about 1.5 miles north of the village on the eastern side of the A832. Check the distance as there isn't a sign indicating the turn-off. Facilities are minimal but the setting is fantastic.

Hill Haven B&B (☎ 01445-760204; www.kinlochewe .info; s/d £33/56) is a friendly place, renowned for magnificent breakfasts.

Kinlochewe Hotel & Bunkhouse (☎ 01445-760253; www.kinlochewehotel.co.uk; dm/s/d £10/33/70, mains £9-11; ☉ lunch & dinner) offers a warm welcome. The bunkhouse has a kitchen, or you can have all meals in the hotel. In the bar, Isle of Skye beers are on tap, or you can try one of Harviestoun's or Heatherale's brews. The menu changes daily, so everything is freshly prepared; the steak and real ale pie, and the bean stew often appear by popular demand.

The **village shop** (☉ Mon-Sat, Sun 10am-1pm) sells maps, among other things. You can obtain cash from the post office.

There's another tiny shop and the **Tipsy Laird Coffee Shop** (☎ 01445-760227; mains £3-5; ☉ 10am-4pm Wed-Sun) is good for a quick snack; it's next to the petrol station, a little way north along the main road.

GETTING THERE & AWAY
Westerbus (☎ 01445-712255) operates a service between Inverness and Gairloch via Kinlochewe (1½ hours, Tuesday, Thursday and Friday). **Scotbus** (☎ 01463-224410; www .scotbus.co.uk) runs the same route (1½ hours, daily).

GETTING TO/FROM THE WALK
Follow the A832 east from Kinlochewe for about 800m, then turn left along the signposted road to Incheril. Continue for 800m to the large car park at the end of the road.

THE WALK
Incheril Car Park to Abhainn an Fhasaigh
1½ hours, 2.8 miles (4.5km)

From the cairn and plaque (about the Letterewe estate) on the northern side of the car park, go up the steps and through a gate. Turn left, following the sign 'Poolewe by Letterewe'. After a few minutes the track ends; continue along a path and soon go through a gate. The path leads on, past fields and through bracken to another gate, below which is a wide wooden bridge over Allt Chnáimhean.

The well-worn path now climbs slightly, and in less than 10 minutes leads into the first of several lovely woodlands. Soon you're down beside the river, and you catch sight of the mighty ramparts of Slioch for the first time. Just past the end of this woodland is a faint path junction. Bear right and cross grassland, soft in places, or continue straight on, through bracken, for a slightly longer, though generally better, path. The two paths unite a short distance beyond a stony burn. Further on, a short distance beyond another wooded area, you come to another fork. Bear left along a grassy path (a much easier route – the alternative is a nightmare!), generally close to the loch shore. Cross a pebble beach, pass through a silver birch grove and soon you come to the footbridge across thundering **Abhainn an Fhasaigh**.

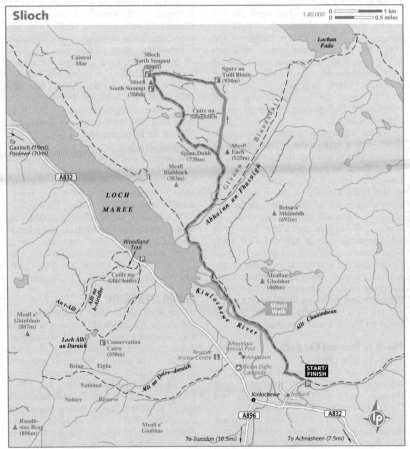

Abhainn an Fhasaigh to Slioch

3 hours, 3.4 miles (5.5km)

Go through a gap in the wire fence on the far side of the bridge and immediately turn right along a path that follows the burn upstream. After 150m the path turns sharply right; this is in fact a fork, which may be marked by a low cairn. Bear left, up across rock slabs and follow the clear path northeast, soon across generally flat ground. About 0.75 miles further on, bear left at a prominent junction, marked by a large cairn. The path leads more or less north, soon near a burn in the shallow depression between Meall Each and Sgurr Dubh.

At the col between these two hills, the main path veers west around the base of Sgurr Dubh directly towards Slioch. Continue north, however, over open ground across Coire na Sleaghaich. Cross the stream that runs down the middle of the corrie and climb the heathery lower slopes of the spur. Veer west to gain easier ground on a rocky shoulder then climb to **Sgurr an Tuill Bhàin** (934m). Enjoy a well-earned rest as you absorb the wonderful view north over Lochan Fada to the remote heart of the Great Wilderness.

Follow the path west from the summit, down onto a narrow ridge. The ridge widens as it climbs towards the northern summit of **Slioch**. In poor visibility stick to the northern edge of the ridge and you will be guided to the top. The northern and southern summits are actually the same height, although the south summit enjoys official status as the higher one. Views from both are stunning, with a panorama of Loch Maree below stretching out to the Atlantic Ocean, and the Western Isles visible on the horizon beyond. From the northern summit make a major change in direction, turning south and swinging slightly east around the top of a steep drop, to reach the trig point on Slioch's southern summit.

Slioch to Incheril Car Park

3 hours, 5.6 miles (9km)

From the summit, descend southeast on a grassy slope. The path twists and turns through rocky ground; cross a rise and then veer further east to drop down the left side of a steep rocky spur and reach the col below, just east of a pair of lochans. The main path heads east into Coire na

Sleaghaich. To complete the full horseshoe, climb the rise to the south of the lochans, veering west slightly to pick up the path that descends to the broad col below Sgurr Dubh. A straightforward climb up the shoulder ahead brings you to the summit of **Sgurr Dubh** (738m). To descend, cross to the northeast side of the summit plateau and go down steeply towards Meall Each. Rejoin the main path at the bottom, turning south and retracing your route back to Loch Maree and the Incheril car park.

MORE WALKS

GLEN AFFRIC

Glen Affric, northeast of Glen Shiel, is considered to be the most beautiful glen in the Highlands with pristine Loch Affric and expanding areas of native pine woodlands.

From the village of Cannich, southwest of Inverness, a road leads to the eastern end of Loch Affric. A public right of way from there traverses the glen to **Glen Affric SYHA hostel** (☎ 0870 155 3255; dm £13; ☒ Apr-Oct). It continues to Morvich on Loch Duich, an inlet from the west coast, via Bealach an Sgáirne or Fionngleann and Gleann Lichd – an outstanding two-day walk. Along the way several fine mountains can occupy a day or three, notably Beinn Fhada (1032m) and Sgurr nan Ceathreamhnan (1151m). Near Morvich there's a good path northwards to the awesome Falls of Glomach.

The Harvey Superwalker 1:25,000 map *Kintail* covers most of this area. The relevant OS Landranger 1:50,000 maps are Nos 25 *Glen Carron & Glen Affric* and 33 *Loch Alsh, Glen Shiel & Loch Hourn*. The SMC guide *The Northwest Highlands* is recommended.

CREAG MEAGAIDH

Rising high above Loch Laggan, between the southern reaches of the Great Glen and Strathspey, is a small cluster of peaks dominated by the magnificent Creag Meagaidh (1130m). The peak is the central feature of Creag Meagaidh National Nature Reserve, owned and managed by SNH. The Creag Meagaidh horseshoe is one of Scotland's classic mountain walks, taking you round the spectacular, cliff-lined Coire Ardair. This 11.8-mile (19km) walk involves 1240m ascent and takes seven to 7½ hours. As well as Craig Meagaidh, the route rewards Munro baggers with Carn Liath (1006m) and Stob Poite Coire Ardair (1053m).

The walk starts at a car park beside the A86, near SNH's Aberarder office, nearly 20 miles from Spean Bridge and 10 miles from Laggan Bridge. The nearest tourist offices for accommodation information are at **Aviemore** (☎ 0845 225 5121; www.visithighlands.com; The Mall) and **Fort William** (☎ 0845 225 5121; www .visithighlands.com; Cameron Sq; 💻).

The best times for the walk are mid-May to mid-June and September; access is generally open at all times but check with **SNH** (☎ 01528-544265) locally about stalking activities.

The OS Landranger 1:50,000 map for the walk is No 34 *Fort Augustus*. The SMC's *The Munros* by Rab Anderson and Donald Bennet, includes this walk, as does Lonely Planet's *Walking in Scotland*.

THE GREAT WILDERNESS
An Teallach

An Teallach (pronounced 'an chelluck') is one of Scotland's finest mountains, standing proudly on the edge of the Great Wilderness and a classic by any standard. Negotiating the trademark pinnacles involves some scrambling along a very exposed ridge; even by following the most cautious alternative paths, it's impossible to avoid crossing steep and exposed ground. For Munro baggers Sgurr Fiona (1060m) and Bidein a' Ghlas Thuill (1062m) can be ticked off here. The walk, best done from south to north, covers 11.5 miles (18.5km) and involves around 1350m of ascent; allow 7½ to 8½ hours.

In bad weather, wet rock and slippery ground make the route distinctly hazardous. Whatever the conditions, it is a serious route and should be tackled only if you have a lot of experience and are adept at scrambling in airy places.

The walk starts at the Corrie Hallie car park, 2 miles southeast of Dundonnell along the A832. Public transport is available to Dundonnell from Inverness with **Westerbus** (☎ 01445-712255) and **Scotbus** (☎ 01463-224410).

Accommodation is centred on the village of Dundonnell, at the east end of Little Loch Broom, about 60 miles west of Inverness on the A832. The nearest information sources are the **Ullapool tourist office** (☎ 0845 225 5121; www.visithighlands.com; 6 Argyle St) and **Gairloch tourist office** (☎ 0845 225 5121; www.visithighlands.com).

For this mountain, a large-scale map is preferable, so consult the OS Explorer 1:25,000 map No 435 *An Teallach & Slioch*, and the SMC's guide *The Munros* by Rab Anderson and Donald Bennet.

KNOYDART

Knoydart is a wild, rugged, virtually road-free area on the west coast, between Loch Nevis to the south and Loch Hourn to the north, and west of Loch Quoich at the head of Glen Garry. It's defined as much by these lochs and its remoteness as it is by the marvellous glens leading into and within its confines, notably Glen Dessary and Glen Barrisdale.

Strictly speaking, it lies outside the area we've delineated as the Western Highlands, but only just. Because it's so special (far more remote than the Great Wilderness with even fewer 'developments') it deserves to be at least mentioned in any survey of walking in Scotland.

The main attractions for walkers are the magnificent Munros, crowned by Ladhar Behinn (1020m). The OS Landranger 1:50,000 map No 33 *Loch Alsh, Glen Shiel & Loch Hourn* covers the area; the SMC's *The Munros* by Rab Anderson and Donald Bennet is your guide.

After long years of mismanagement and conflict, Knoydart is now cared for sympathetically by the **Knoydart Foundation** (www .knoydart-foundation.com) on behalf of the local community, the John Muir Trust and private individuals. The foundation's website will also lead you to the handful of accommodation providers on the peninsula. There's a **ferry** (www.knoydart-ferry.co.uk) from Mallaig to Inverie, Knoydart's only (and tiny) village. Mallaig, in turn, is served by First ScotRail trains and Scottish Citylink buses from Fort William.

THE WESTERN HIGHLANDS

Isle of Skye

The Isle of Skye is blessed with some of the finest scenic splendour and variety in Britain, assets that have attracted writers, artists and travellers to the island for centuries. Since the early 20th century, walkers and climbers have also flocked to Skye to revel in the magnificent hill and coast walking. All manner of visitors also come in search of the island's mystical atmosphere, still little-diminished in many quiet corners, at a safe distance from the seemingly unstoppable growth of tourism and the building of new houses.

The Black Cuillin mountains are all about adrenalin-charged challenge and sublime mountain and sea vistas. Most of these airy peaks are the domain of walkers with experience in scrambling and a head for heights, and are beyond the scope of this book. However, there are a few walks where you can enjoy a close Cuillin encounter without confronting any vertiginous scrambling. In this chapter we describe one of these, a challenging route up Bruach na Frìthe onto the Black Cuillin ridge. To prove that height isn't everything, the Coast & Cuillin walk, into the heart of the Black Cuillin, combines superb coast and mountain scenery.

The name Cuillin (pronounced 'coolin') is derived from the Norse *kjollen,* meaning 'keel-shaped'. The igneous Black Cuillin rocks are mainly gabbro, with sections of smooth basalt on the surface. Glacial action carved out the characteristic bowl-shaped corries and left behind the finely sculpted, jagged ridgeline.

Being rich in iron, the gabbro does strange things to magnetic compasses – a rather important consideration if you're intending to navigate by compass (see the boxed text, p405)!

ISLE OF SKYE

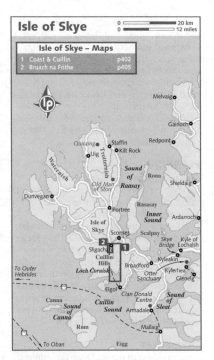

Isle of Skye

Isle of Skye – Maps	
1 Coast & Cuillin	p402
2 Bruach na Frithe	p405

describes 30 walks that range from easy strolls to challenging Cuillin scrambles. *Isle of Skye Including Raasay* by Paul Williams concentrates on walks at the easier end of the spectrum. *Skye 360, Walking the Coastline of Skye* by Andrew Dempster is a personalised account of a month-long journey with just enough detail to follow in his footsteps. *A Long Walk on the Isle of Skye* by David Paterson, in coffee-table format, offers a description of his walk, inspired by his superb photos.

Guided Walks

Highland Council's countryside rangers (☎ 01471-822905; Old Corry Industrial Estate, Broadford) run varied programs of guided walks, with particular emphasis on Skye's natural heritage, from Easter until October. Pick up a brochure at local tourist offices.

Cuillin Guides (☎ 01478-640280; www.cuillin -guides.co.uk; Glenbrittle) has years of solid experience behind it and an unrivalled knowledge of the hills. Its program includes five days of ridge walking and scrambling with a guide-to-client ration of 1:5; the staff are qualified mountain leaders.

Information Sources

VisitScotland's comprehensive www.visit highlands.com website is a good place to start, especially for accommodation bookings. On the island, there are tourist offices in **Portree** (☎ 01478-612137; Bayfield House, Bayfield Rd; ☒ daily Jun-Sep, Mon-Sat Oct-May; ☐) and **Broadford** (☎ 01471-822361; The Car Park; ☒ daily Apr-Oct, Mon-Sat Nov-Mar).

GETTING AROUND

Highland Country Buses operates an island-wide network of services linking Kyleakin (just across the bridge from Kyle of Lochalsh on the mainland), Broadford and Portree, as well as some outlying areas. Some services are very limited or nonexistent on Sundays.

GATEWAY

Broadford is the natural gateway for the walks in this chapter, though the 'capital' of Skye is Portree, further north, with a greater range of accommodation and restaurants. Daily Scottish Citylink bus services from Inverness and Glasgow (via Fort William) pass through Broadford en route to Portree.

INFORMATION

When to Walk

The main walking season on Skye starts around mid-April, perhaps later depending on the depth of snow on the mountains, and generally runs through until mid-October. However, even in midwinter the island can bask in bright (though scarcely warm) sunshine while much of the mainland is being blasted by bitter easterly winds.

Maps

Both the walks described here are covered by Ordnance Survey (OS) Landranger 1:50,000 map No 32 *South Skye & Cuillin Hills*. The OS Explorer 1:25,000 map No 411 *Cuillin Hills* and Harvey's Superwalker 1:25,000 map *Skye: The Cuillin* give greater detail of the Bruach na Frithe walk.

Books

Skye & the North West Highlands by John Brooks and Neil Wilson covers 15 varied walks on Skye. The Ramblers' Association's *Guide to the Isle of Skye* by noted gear expert and wilderness walker Chris Townsend

COAST & CUILLIN

Duration	8 hours
Distance	13.5 miles (21.5km)
Difficulty	moderate
Start	Elgol (opposite)
Finish	Sligachan (opposite)
Transport	bus

Summary A spectacular, low-level route that penetrates into the heart of the Black Cuillin to reach the shores of Loch Coruisk. The route also involves the Bad Step, a short, exposed rock section that some walkers may find problematic.

This low-level route combines coastal paths, mountain views, glen scenery and a short scramble to reach Loch Coruisk in the heart of the Black Cuillin. The section from Elgol to Loch Coruisk is particularly impressive and has justifiably been described as 'possibly the best coastal walk in Britain'.

Loch Coruisk is the jewel in the crown of the Black Cuillin. The jagged ring of peaks that surrounds the loch forms an impressive fortress and a wild setting for its clear blue waters. Boats can be used to access the loch by sea but, without mountaineering skills, there are only three possible routes in to Loch Coruisk on foot. This walk links two of these routes (the other path is more tenuous and leads in from Glenbrittle camp site, to the west).

There is a catch – the route described involves one section of scrambling that may not be to everyone's liking. The Bad Step, about 500m short of Loch Coruisk, is a 6m-long, 60-degree slab with a narrow ledge for the feet and small handholds for support. It is exposed but because it's about 8m above deep water, it's not necessarily dangerous if you can swim well! It should be within the capabilities of most fit walkers, but a cool head is required and heavy packs may also increase the difficulty.

If the idea of the Bad Step is too daunting, there are a couple of options to avoid it – see Alternatives (below) for details.

PLANNING

This walk is best done from south to north for two reasons: transport logistics are easier; and the views in this direction are really stunning.

To really appreciate the magnificent surroundings of the Black Cuillin, it is preferable to split the walk into two days and camp on the shores of Loch Coruisk, completing the walk to Sligachan on the second day. There is also a bothy at Camasunary but tenting at the loch is much more memorable. This is wild terrain and you will need to be entirely self-sufficient.

Alternatives

If the prospect of the Bad Step is completely off-putting, there is another way to reach Loch Coruisk. From Elgol, **Bella Jane Boat Trips** (☎ 0800 731 3089; www.bellajane.co.uk) travel to the landing steps at the loch, a trip of about 45 minutes. From here you can walk the 7.5 miles out to Sligachan, following the walk description from Loch Coruisk to the finish. This option would fit easily into a day and make for a very memorable trip.

SKYE IN TRUST

A good deal of south Skye and the Cuillin mountains is owned and managed by the John Muir Trust (JMT), a conservation organisation that owns and manages several other areas in Scotland. The trust's three separate, but contiguous, estates total around 0.5 sq miles of mountainous and rural Skye. They include several small and active crofting communities, which are directly involved in managing their estates, with a wealth of archaeological sites and plant and animal species.

The first purchase, the Torrin Estate, was made in 1991. Three years later, the much larger and adjoining Strathaird Estate was acquired, ensuring the preservation of land extending into the heart of the Cuillin, including Glen Sligachan, Loch Coruisk and the peaks of Bla Bheinn (an outlier of the Black Cuillin), Marsco and Ruadh Stac in the Red Cuillin. The later addition of the Sconser Estate brought more Red Cuillin summits under the JMT's control.

It could be said that the obvious gap in the JMT's Isle of Skye portfolio is the Black Cuillin mountains themselves. However, their current and future ownership is the subject of a drawn-out and highly controversial debate (see the boxed text, p403).

Alternatively, follow the first part of the route described to Camasunary and then continue straight up Glen Sligachan to Sligachan. A sign on the wall of the house at Camasunary directs you up the glen and the path is generally good. The total distance is 11 miles (17.5km); allow about six hours.

NEAREST TOWNS
Elgol
This tiny village, dependent on fishing and visitors, sits close to the end of the Strathaird peninsula with an incredible view of the Cuillin across Loch Scavaig.

SLEEPING & EATING
Accommodation isn't exactly plentiful, so you'll need to book well ahead to be sure of a roof over your head.

Rose Croft (☎ 01471-866377; www.isleofskye.net /rosecroft; s/d £30/44) is a long-established and friendly B&B with a beautiful garden and lovely views. A light evening meal (£6) is available by arrangement.

Rowan Cottage (☎ 01471-866287; www.rowan cottage-skye.co.uk; 9 Glasnakille by Elgol; s/d £30/60, dinner £20-23) is a traditional cottage with pleasingly furnished rooms a couple of miles along a narrow, winding road east of Elgol.

Coruisk House (☎ 01471-866330; www.seafood -skye.co.uk; s/d £38/76, mains £10-25; ☺ lunch & dinner; 🖳) is a restaurant northeast of the village with rooms in what was originally a thatched cottage to which travellers were first welcomed a century ago. These days, historic photos adorn the walls, the bedrooms are superbly decorated and the restaurant specialises in locally caught fish and seafood, though without neglecting vegetarians.

Cuillin View Gallery & Coffee Shop (snacks to £3; ☺ lunch), above the harbour, is licensed and offers sandwiches and home baking, and the chance to contemplate the work of local artists – and the eponymous view.

The **Post Office Shop** (☺ 9am-5pm Mon-Sat) carries basic supplies and does home baking and hot and cold drinks.

GETTING THERE & AWAY
Highland Country Buses (☎ 01463-710555; www .rapsons.co.uk) operates a bus service from the Broadford post office to the Elgol post office (40 minutes, two services Tuesday and Thursday). This is supplemented by the **Royal Mail Postbus** (☎ 08457 740740; www.postbus .royalmail.com) service (one hour, two services Monday to Friday, one Saturday). The long-distance service covered under Sligachan (below) passes through Broadford.

The A881 to Elgol branches from the A850 Kyleakin–Portree road in the small town of Broadford. There's a car park at the bottom of the first steep descent to the harbour and more parking space opposite the nearby village hall.

Sligachan
Historic Sligachan is just a large hotel, a bunkhouse, camping ground and a bus stop. It has been the gateway to the Cuillin for more than a century and seethes with activity during summer; in fact it's rarely quiet here. Bring all your supplies as you'll search in vain for a shop.

SLEEPING & EATING
Sligachan Campsite (☎ 01478-650204; sites for 2 £8), opposite the hotel at the head of Loch Sligachan, enjoys an outstanding setting.

Sligachan Bunkhouse (☎ 01478-650204; www .sligachan.co.uk; dm £10), on the eastern side of the main road, has that all-important Skye facility – a good drying room.

Sligachan Hotel (☎ 01478-650204; www.sligachan .co.uk; s/d £48/96) is a must, if only for a look at the walls of historic photos of early climbers. The comfortable rooms have either mountain or loch views and you can eat in lively **Seamus' Bar** (breakfast £6-8, mains £6-12; ☺ breakfast, lunch & dinner) or go upmarket at **Cairidh Seafood Restaurant** (mains £12-18; ☺ lunch & dinner).

GETTING THERE & AWAY
Scottish Citylink (☎ 08705 505050; www.citylink .co.uk) bus services from Glasgow, via Fort William to Portree, stop at Sligachan (six hours, three daily), as does the Inverness–Portree service (three hours, three daily).

A highly recommended variation from Inverness is to take the outstandingly scenic **First ScotRail** (☎ 0845 755 0033; www.firstscotrail.com) train trip to Kyle of Lochalsh (2½ hours, four services Monday to Saturday, two Sunday) then connect with the local **Highland Country Buses** (☎ 01463-710555; www.rapsons .co.uk) service to Portree via Sligachan (40 minutes, at least four services Monday to Saturday, two Sunday).

By car, Sligachan is 23 miles from the once-controversial Skye Bridge.

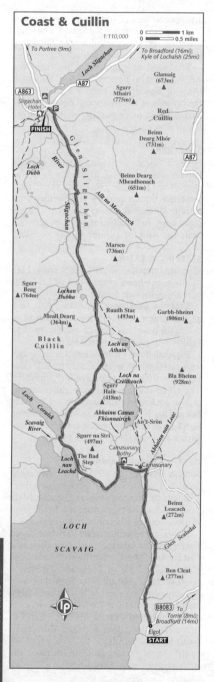

Coast & Cuillin

1:110,000

0 — 1 km
0 — 0.5 miles

To Portree (9mi)
Loch Sligachan
To Broadford (16mi);
Kyle of Lochalsh (25mi)
A863
A87
Sligachan Hotel
P
FINISH
Sgurr Mhairi (775m)
Glamaig (673m)
Red Cuillin
Beinn Dearg Mhór (731m)
A87
Glen Sligachan
River Sligachan
Allt na Measarroch
Beinn Dearg Mheadhonach (651m)
Loch Dubh
Marsco (736m)
Sgurr Beag (764m)
Lochan Dubha
Meall Dearg (364m)
Black Cuillin
Ruadh Stac (493m)
Garbh-bheinn (806m)
Loch an Athain
Bla Bheinn (928m)
Loch na Crèitheach
Sgurr Hain (418m)
Loch Coruisk
Scavaig River
Abhainn Camas Fhionnairigh
An't-Sròn
Abhainn nan Leac
Sgurr na Stri (497m)
Camasunary Bothy
The Bad Step
Loch nan Leachd
Camasunary
Beinn Leacach (272m)
LOCH SCAVAIG
Glen Scaladal
Ben Cleat (277m)
B8083 To Torrin (8mi); Broadford (14mi)
Elgol
START

THE WALK
Elgol to Camasunary
2 hours, 3.5 miles (5.5km)

The walk begins about 300m northeast of Elgol post office, along a lane leading north from the A881, and clearly signposted as a footpath to Camasunary and Sligachan. The road soon disappears, leaving a track that ends at two houses. A footpath (signed to Loch Coruisk) continues directly ahead, between the fences of the two houses, and passes through a gate, leading out onto open hillside. The views are immediately impressive: the Small Isles of Eigg, Rum and Canna lie to the south, while the Black Cuillin ridge dominates the skyline to the northwest.

The well-trodden path contours across grassy, heathery slopes all the way to the beach at Camasunary, with views improving along the way. The drop-off to the west is steep in places as the lower slopes of Ben Cleat and Beinn Leacach are passed, and care is required over these sections. At Glen Scaladal, cross a stile before descending to the pebbly cove, then climb steeply to the broken cliff top from the back of the beach. Duck under the branches of a grove of stunted trees, and follow a track climbing slightly higher up the cliff. Easier ground then leads down to the bridge over the Abhainn nan Leac and a substantial junction of paths, about 3 miles from Elgol.

Of the two buildings at **Camasunary**, the larger house near the bridge is privately owned. The smaller building, 500m further west, is the Mountain Bothies Association (MBA) bothy, which provides free accommodation for walkers and climbers. At the junction of paths, the 4WD track that descends from the shoulder to the east leads to Kirkibost, about 2 miles away. The path that forks right between the bridge and house leads directly up Glen Sligachan to Sligachan, avoiding Loch Coruisk.

Camasunary to Loch Coruisk
2 hours, 2.5 miles (4km)

To continue to Loch Coruisk, take the path that leads west (left at the fork) along the top of the beach and passes in front of the bothy. Ford the Abhainn Camas Fhionnairigh by following its banks upstream for 100m or so and then crossing on stepping stones. The path on the other side climbs slightly to contour round the craggy lower slopes of Sgurr na Stri. The terrain is rougher than previously, and you have to cross several rock steps and angled slabs. As you round the headland another wonderful vista greets the eye; rocky islands nestle at the mouth of the River Scavaig, backed by the looming Cuillin peaks.

The slabs become more numerous as the path veers north and care must be taken not to lose the main route as it splits in various places. Continue towards the white sand and turquoise water of Loch nan Leachd cove. The notorious **Bad Step** is the very last slab that needs to be negotiated before the beach. A cairn marks the stony path that descends to the difficulties. It could be a good idea to undo pack straps, just in case of a slip into the water below. Duck under an overhang and scramble out onto the seaward rock face. Pull yourself up to balance on a ledge that skirts round the slab face, using handholds for support. Shuffle along and at a convergence of fault lines take care to drop diagonally down to the boulders on the beach rather than continuing up the slab.

Cross the boulders to the sand of Loch nan Leachd and follow the path inland across the low saddle at the back of the cove. **Loch Coruisk** is suddenly revealed in all its glory and its banks make a fine rest spot. If you are spending the night here, flat ground for camping can be found just over the stepping stones that cross the River Scavaig.

Loch Coruisk to Sligachan
4 hours, 7.5 miles (12km)
The path from Loch Coruisk to Sligachan leads round the southeastern shore of the loch, and then climbs up the right-hand side of a burn that can be seen tumbling down from a smaller loch above. It is a climb of over 300m to the saddle and the terrain is rocky towards the top. A large cairn marks the saddle and there are fine views west over the serrated north Cuillin ridge. Veer northwest along the ridge to a second cairn 20m away, where a wide, stony path drops down the other side. The path from Camasunary to Sligachan can be seen winding along the valley below. The descent to join it is fairly steep for a section and then evens out, becoming rather wet at the valley floor. Join the main Sligachan path at a large cairn, from where there is a great perspective of Bla Bheinn to the southeast.

From the junction of paths it is about 3.7 miles along the valley to Sligachan. The terrain is largely flat and the going easy, although the Sligachan Hotel soon comes into view and it can seem like a long time before it moves much closer. The final 500m of the route is along a well-made path. Beyond a gate, turn left across the old bridge to arrive at the hotel.

MOUNTAINS FOR SALE?

During the early part of 2000, John MacLeod (chief of the Clan MacLeod) put the Black Cuillin mountains on sale for an asking price of £10 million. Typical of the local reactions reported in the press was the comment of a young lass: 'You cannae sell a mountain'. Environmental and outdoor interest groups were horrified by rumours that wealthy outsiders had expressed interest in purchasing the range. Some feared that the Black Cuillin would be turned into a theme park, or that the long tradition of open access to the mountains would be threatened. The islanders were angered by MacLeod's assumption of title and believed that he should not profit from the sale, and it was unclear whether he actually owned the mountains anyway. MacLeod himself said he needed the money to repair the roof of Dunvegan Castle, one of the island's main tourist drawcards.

The property was later withdrawn, pending an investigation by the Crown Estate Commission (which looks after state-owned land) into the legal title to the mountains. However, it decided not to contest MacLeod's claim and he promptly put the estate back on the market. In July 2001 he offered to give the Cuillin to the nation in exchange for acceptable arrangements to restore his castle. At the time of research, eight organisations were still immersed in an assessment of what needed to be done to the castle; the community at large was to be consulted about looking after the mountains. As one participant observed, 'It is likely to be some time' before the whole thing is sorted out.

BRUACH NA FRÌTHE

Duration	6–7 hours
Distance	8.5 miles (13.5km)
Difficulty	moderate–demanding
Start/Finish	Sligachan (p401)
Transport	bus

Summary A superb, energetic outing with spectacular views of the Black and Red Cuillin, and the chance of some exciting scrambling on the northwest ridge if you are cool-headed and experienced.

Bruach na Frìthe (pronounced 'broo-uch na free-ha') is a turning point on the main Cuillin ridge and provides magnificent views of the range's outstanding rock architecture. At 958m (3142ft) this Munro has been described as the least difficult of the Black Cuillin peaks to climb, being the only one not defended by cliffs. The easiest route is up (and down) Fionn Choire, a steep-sided bowl, following a steep, zigzagging path up through scree and boulder slopes, avoiding all scrambling. The approach is along a right of way from Sligachan to Glenbrittle, over Bealach a' Mhàim (continuing through the pass to Glenbrittle would provide an option in poor weather). The walk involves almost 1000m of ascent.

PLANNING
Alternatives

If you're happy to tackle an easy scramble, which is airy in places, an attractive alternative is to ascend Bruach na Frìthe by the northwest ridge. The impression of exposure is exhilarating. See the Alternative Route on opposite for details.

THE WALK
Sligachan to the Base of Fionn Choire
1½–2 hours, 2.5 miles (4km)

The walk begins about 500m along the A863 Dunvegan road. You can either walk along the road from Sligachan, or use the small car park on the south side of the road, beside the path.

From the car park, follow the track signed 'Footpath to Glenbrittle' that heads towards Alltdearg House. A signed footpath diverts you north of the house, crossing a stretch of boggy ground. The firmest route keeps near to the fence on the left.

You soon pick up a stony path that runs alongside the Allt Dearg Mór, a burn that tumbles down a series of rock ledges. After 2 miles the path begins to level out in Coire na Circe and the going becomes soft underfoot. Continue on, fording a sizable tributary, to reach a large cairn. Here the path for Bruach na Frìthe forks left across

---

IT'S ATTITUDE THAT MATTERS

Standing on the summit of Bruach na Frìthe on a good day, it is difficult to imagine that the Black Cuillin were regarded as unattainable until the early 19th century. Between then and now, when people regularly traverse the entire Cuillin ridge, some even making nonstop traverses of the Greater Cuillin (including Bla Bheinn), lies a fundamental shift in attitude. It wasn't modern climbing gear, boots or clothing that made the difference, but the development of a new approach to the mountains.

In 1835, Reverend Lesingham Smith and local forester Duncan Macintyre visited Loch Coruisk and returned to Sligachan by scrambling across the ramparts of the Druim nam Ramh ridge into Harta Corrie. The following year, James Forbes hired Macintyre as a guide and together they made the first recorded ascent of Sgurr nan Gillean by the now popular (but still tricky) southeast ridge.

With the psychological barrier broken, local men quickly knocked off the other Cuillin peaks, with Sheriff Alexander Nicolson claiming the first ascent of Sgurr Alasdair, the highest summit on Skye (993m). In 1859 a British Admiralty surveyor, Captain Wood, mapped the south Cuillin and identified a pinnacle at 986m as being unclimbable. It only needed that tag to ensure that the first ascent of what is now known as the Inaccessible Pinnacle soon followed. Today it is one of the most popular climbing challenges in the Black Cuillin (partly because it's a Munro), involving one pitch of easy, if airy, rock climbing and a short abseil.

The first traverse of the Black Cuillin ridge fell to Shadbolt and Maclaren in 1911, taking nearly 17 hours. It has since been completed in less than 25% of that time.

boggy ground and crosses another burn (more easily) about 200m after the cairn. Follow the ascending path for about 20 minutes, keeping Allt an Fionn Choire (a burn with small waterfalls pouring from the corrie above) on your left, until you reach a substantial cairn on top of a rock slab. This is a good place for a rest while you decide which route to take to the summit.

Base of Fionn Choire to Bruach na Frìthe

2–2½ hours, 1.5 miles (2.5km)

From the large cairn, stay on the narrow cairned path to the right (west) of the burn. After ascending a short way the path reaches the sill at the corrie's edge. You need to cross the burn to reach a large cairn on the other side; this may be easier above a burn junction. From this cairn there is no discernible path but you can pick out a line of small cairns swinging slightly left across the corrie floor towards some rock slabs in the scree ahead.

After crossing this level stretch a small path ascends to the left of a dry stream bed in a small gorge, where the burn has disappeared below boulders. There are no cairns but an obvious path roughly follows the left-hand side of the burn. Where the ground steepens the route zigzags up the scree and boulders to reach the ridge at **Bealach nan Lice**. Turn right and follow a distinct path around the base of a pinnacle and onto the final rocky ridge leading to the summit of **Bruach na Frìthe** (958m), marked by a distinctive cylindrical trig point. On a clear day the view is one of the best on Skye.

ALTERNATIVE ROUTE: BRUACH NA FRÌTHE VIA THE NORTHWEST RIDGE

2–2½ hours, 2 miles (3km)

From the cairn on top of the rock slab, head up the steep slope of grass, boulders and scree on the right, on a south-to-southwest bearing, with occasional cairns to guide

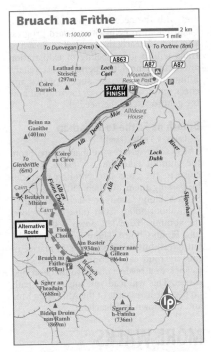

Bruach na Frìthe

you. Climb the steep slope to the left and join a more obvious path (which has come up from Bealach a' Mhàim). This zigzags up steep scree and then grass to a narrowing of the ridge and a short section of easier grade.

Then comes a short, steep ascent to an almost-horizontal narrow section about 150m long. This is a superb situation if you have a head for heights. At the end of this is the main ridge scramble. Difficulties encountered near the ridge crest can be avoided by going to the right, but don't drop too far below the crest or you'll have difficulty climbing back up further on. It's easy enough to pick out the routes that have been taken by those who have gone before,

---

WATCH YOUR COMPASS

The magnetic properties of the Black Cuillin gabbro rock distort compass readings, so this small piece of equipment is virtually useless. Thus you must rely on your map-reading skills, or GPS bearings and/or route-notes interpretation on cloudy days. If you are a bit uncertain in these areas, ensure that the weather is fine and settled for your climb. Even then, extreme caution is necessary as the mountain climate is notoriously changeable.

and with the occasional use of hands for balance and to help with upward progress you should reach the summit of **Bruach na Frìthe** with a great feeling of exhilaration and achievement (or perhaps just relief). Either way, enjoy the superb views and check your compass to see for yourself how the gabbro affects the needle!

Bruach na Frìthe to Sligachan
2½ hours, 4.5 miles (7km)
The descent retraces the main route. From the summit take the east ridge, keeping close to the crest but avoiding obstacles by passing them on their left. Pass below Sgùrr a' Fionn Choire to reach Bealach nan Lice, about 400m from (and 60m below) the summit. Turn left down a stony path into Fionn Choire. There is a burn on the left (west) but this disappears in places. In mist the route can be confusing, but it's best to stick to a reverse of the route described earlier. This will lead you back to the path on the northwest side of the Allt Dearg Mór and then down to Sligachan.

MORE WALKS

TROTTERNISH PENINSULA
The Trotternish Traverse
The Trotternish Peninsula, forming the northern end of Skye, is dominated by a 15-mile-long precipitous escarpment snaking almost its full length. A 14-mile (22.5km), seven-to-eight-hour traverse starts at the Storr Woodlands car park (6.5 miles north of Portree). The route passes the iconic pinnacle of the Old Man of Storr then climbs to the Storr (719m), the peninsula's highest point. It then traverses the sharply undulating ridge to finish at the Quiraing road between Staffin and Uig; by then you'll have coped with 1450m of ascent. The car park on the Quiraing road is about 3 miles northwest of the village of Staffin, where there's a reasonable range of accommodation and a few cafés. OS Explorer 1:25,000 map No 408 *Trotternish & The Storr* covers the area. The walk is described fully in Lonely Planet's *Walking in Scotland*.

The Quiraing
The pinnacles, cliffs and landslides of the Quiraing are a compact and easily explored example of the features that make the Trotternish peninsula so spectacular. A 3.5-mile (5.6km) circuit of around 2¾ hours, following generally good paths, leads past Meall Na Suirmach (543m), down through a pass and past fantastic pinnacles and steep cliffs. It starts and finishes at an informal car park on the Quiraing road, about 3 miles northwest of Staffin. OS Explorer 1:25,000 map No 408 *Trotternish & The Storr* covers the walk, which is described fully in Lonely Planet's *Walking in Scotland*.

Scotland
Long-Distance Paths

What Scotland lacks in its number of long-distance paths (LDPs), it certainly makes up for in their sheer quality and variety. The two paths described in detail in this chapter – the Southern Upland Way and the West Highland Way – are second-to-none for challenging walking, supremely beautiful scenery and fascinating historical associations. Both are well waymarked and signposted, and have an adequate range of accommodation. They follow historic tracks and paths, old railway formations, forest tracks, river-side paths and minor roads.

The Southern Upland Way, threading across the uplands and glens of Dumfries & Galloway and the Borders regions, links Portpatrick on the west coast with Cockburnspath on the eastern shores. It takes you through small villages and towns, across wide-open, rolling moorland, through forests and woodlands and past some beautiful rivers and lochs.

The very popular West Highland Way follows a fairly direct route between Milngavie, on the outskirts of Glasgow, Scotland's largest city, and the town of Fort William, 96 miles to the north. Along the way you travel from the agricultural lowlands of central Scotland into the rugged mountains and deep glens of the Highlands. The Way passes some famous landmarks, including Loch Lomond, wild and lonely Rannoch Moor, Glen Coe and Ben Nevis.

Among other long-distance routes, the Great Glen Way, between Fort William and Inverness, the capital of the Highlands, offers the opportunity to undertake a real Scottish odyssey, continuing on from the West Highland Way. St Cuthbert's Way dangles an even more exciting temptation for long-distance enthusiasts, linking England's mighty Pennine Way and the Southern Upland Way. All you need is time!

HIGHLIGHTS

- Trekking right across the country from the west to the east coast along the challenging **Southern Upland Way** (p408)
- Following in the footsteps of drovers, soldiers and other wayfarers along the magnificently scenic **West Highland Way** (p418)

THE SOUTHERN UPLAND WAY

Duration	9 days
Distance	209.5 miles (338km)
Difficulty	moderate–demanding
Start	Portpatrick (p410)
Finish	Cockburnspath (p410)
Transport	bus, train

Summary An extremely challenging, very long route from one side of the country to the other, through remote country in the west and more settled areas in the east, passing many fascinating historical sites.

The Southern Upland Way (SUW), Britain's first official coast-to-coast LDP, traverses one of the broadest parts of Scotland, through Dumfries & Galloway and the Borders. The route goes across the grain of the countryside, roller-coasting over hills and moorland and through conifer plantations. It also passes through deciduous woodland and agricultural land, mainly on its eastern half.

The going underfoot ranges from sealed roads to muddy forest paths. There are some long stretches (over 2 miles) on sealed (although not busy) road, which some walkers feel should have no place on official routes. There's some comfort in the fact that they do link some very fine paths across the hills and through woodlands.

PLANNING

The majority of people walk from southwest to northeast. It could be said this means the prevailing wind is at your back, but when the Way was originally walked for this book, the persistent north wind was coming either from the side or head-on. There is much to be said, however, for finishing in the east, amid more open, settled countryside, where shorter days are possible, than in the west with some unavoidably big daily distances.

Accommodation is sparse in some areas, so you have to anticipate some long days. Camping or staying in bothies gives more flexibility but all the necessary gear weighs heavily, especially on days of 20 miles or more. These factors, combined with the route's length and remoteness, make it a far more serious proposition than the West Highland Way and most, if not all, national trails in England and Wales. Nevertheless,

the rewards are considerable: a real sense of moving across the country; becoming attuned to gradual changes in the landscape; meeting fellow walkers; and the satisfaction of finally seeing the North Sea on the penultimate day. It's essential to be fit before you start, and preferably to have some long-distance walking experience . It also helps to get into the right mind frame; taking each day as it comes but still keeping the objective firmly fixed – whatever the weather, track condition or distance to be covered.

The route is waymarked with a thistle-hexagon logo and signposts, but you should still carry maps and a compass in case visibility deteriorates on the exposed stretches. Distances between waymarks vary widely, from line-of-sight across moorland to miles apart along minor roads. Sections of the route are changed (often for the better) from time to time, so waymarks should always be trusted over the mapped route.

Many hosts along the Way provide a vehicle back-up service, picking you up from an agreed spot and returning you the next day to continue the walk. Some do this gratis, while others may charge, so check first.

The full walk may take as few as nine or 10 days, or as many as 14 (some people spread the journey over a number of years, doing a bit at a time), depending on your walking speed and number of rest days. The amount of ascent is also a significant factor when planning an itinerary, especially in the central section between Sanquhar and Beattock. Allow some flexibility in your plans, as bad weather, likely at any time, may dictate a change of plans, especially in the more remote and exposed western section.

The following is the nine-day itinerary we suggest:

Day	From	To	Miles/km
1	Portpatrick	New Luce	22.5/36.5
2	New Luce	Bargrennan	17.5/28
3	Bargrennan	St John's Town of Dalry	22/34
4	St John's Town of Dalry	Sanquhar	25/40
5	Sanquhar	Beattock	28/45
6	Beattock	St Mary's Loch	21/34
7	St Mary's Loch	Melrose	30/48.5
8	Melrose	Longformacus	25/40
9	Longformacus	Cockburnspath	18.5/30

Alternatives

The Way crosses some main roads, along which there are bus services, and a railway line with a convenient train station. These enable you to reach the SUW from many major centres and to walk shorter sections of the trail using public transport for access. A brief note on transport connections is included in each day's walk description. Two suggestions for shorter walks are given in the Route Highlight boxed texts on p411 and p415.

When to Walk

You can expect a wide range of weather conditions during a complete crossing. Thick mist and strong winds – and warm sunshine – are likely any time between April and September, the best, if not the only, time for the SUW.

Snowfalls on higher ground are not unknown during winter when short daylight hours make it impossible to complete the day's walk before dark.

Maps & Books

The Southern Upland Way Official Guide by Roger Smith is invaluable, with tons of background information and pointers to the many short walks near the Way. It comes packaged with separate maps extracted from seven Ordnance Survey (OS) Landranger 1:50,000 maps covering the full length of the Way. The cost of the pack is less than half that of buying the maps individually. *Scotland's Coast to Coast Trail – the Southern Upland Way* by Alan Castle also includes full OS maps of the route.

Information Sources

Start planning your trip with the free *Southern Upland Way* brochure (with an annually updated accommodation list). It is available from the **Dumfries & Galloway ranger service** (☎ 01387-260184; Dumfries) and the **Scottish Borders ranger service** (☎ 01835-830281; Jedburgh). They can also provide leaflets on the wildlife, trees and shrubs, geology, history, archaeology and place names of the

---

LAWS & CLEUCHS

As you pore over the maps at home, the names of the hills, rivers and other landscape features of the country you are going to walk through can help give a clearer picture of what it will look like, and can also reveal something of the local history. While Gaelic place names are commonplace in the Highlands and islands to the north, in the Southern Uplands they're largely confined to the southwest, even though Gaelic is now little spoken in these parts. In the Borders, however, the names are mainly from Lallans (Lowland Scots), a distinct language still in use, with origins in the languages of settlers from the east, rather than in the Celtic-Gaelic spoken in the west.

Starting at the beginning of the Way, Portpatrick's origin is obvious, given the Irish connection, although it was originally called Portree, from the Gaelic *port righ*, meaning 'harbour of the king'. The name Killantringan, the location of the fine lighthouse, includes the Anglicised version of the common Gaelic prefix *cill*, meaning 'church' – in this case of St Ringan or Ninian. Balmurrie, the farm near New Luce, has another widespread Gaelic element – *bal*, meaning 'farm' or 'small township', in this case of the Murray family.

Laggangairn, the site of two prehistoric cairns beyond Balmurrie, means 'hollow of the cairns' (*lag* meaning 'hollow'). Further on you climb over Craig Airie Fell – a hybrid of Gaelic and Norse. Craig is derived from *creag*, which is Gaelic for 'cliff' or 'crag'; *àiridh* is Gaelic for 'shieling' (a temporary dwelling); and fell, once a Norse term, is used in a few places to mean 'mountain'. Dalry is from the Gaelic *dail righ*, or 'meadow of the king'. Benbrack, a hill between Dalry and Sanquhar, is the 'speckled *breac* (hill)', while Fingland comes from the Gaelic *fionn gleann*, meaning 'white glen'.

In the east, the Lammermuir Hills feature prominently in the latter stages; the name comes from the Old English for lamb.

Among the most common names for geographical features is *cleuch*, which comes directly from the Lowland Scots for ravine; the similar sounding *heugh* is a cliff. The name *law* pops up all over the Borders and is the equivalent of a Gaelic *beinn* (mountain or hill), often isolated and conical in shape. A *knowe* is also a high sort of place (a small hillock), while a *dod* is a bare, round hill.

Scottish Hill and Mountain Names by Peter Drummond, the Scottish place-names guru, should answer almost any query you can come up with.

area, and booklets describing short circular walks based on the eastern and western sections of the Way. When you've completed the Way, send your details to one of the ranger services to obtain a free completion certificate.

Make sure you check the Way's invaluable official website at www.dumgal.gov .uk/southernuplandway. The commercial site www.southernuplandway.com is helpful for accommodation and other services.

For public transport information contact **Traveline** (☎ 0870 608 2608; www.traveline-scotland .co.uk). Accommodation bookings are most conveniently made through **VisitScotland** (☎ 0845 225 5121; www.visitscotland.com).

For tourist offices along the route, see the walk description.

Baggage Services
Make Tracks (☎ 0131-229 6844; www.maketracks.net; 26 Forbes Rd, Edinburgh) can save you a great deal of hassle by organising almost everything – accommodation, luggage transfer, a pickup and drop-off service, maps and printed notes.

NEAREST TOWNS
Portpatrick
pop 585
The peaceful harbour in Portpatrick village was once the port for ferries from Ireland. These days it looks after anglers, sailors and walkers preparing to set out on the Way. Stranraer, 8 miles northeast of Portpatrick, is a large town with plenty of accommodation. Contact the **tourist office** (☎ 01776-702595; Harbour St; ☉ daily Jun-Aug, Mon-Sat Sep-May) for full details.

SLEEPING & EATING
Galloway Point Holiday Park (☎ 01776-810561; www.gallowaypointholidaypark.co.uk; sites from £10) is less than 1 mile from town.

Carlton Guest House (☎ 01776-810253; 21 South Cres; s/d £30/52), on the seafront, is recommended among the village's several B&Bs.

Harbour House Hotel (☎ 01776-810456; www .harbourhouse.co.uk; 53 Main St; s/d £35/60, bar meals £7-10; ☉ lunch & dinner) offers the opportunity, with luck, to sit outside and enjoy a meal of suitably generous proportions for the miles ahead, washed down with a pint of real ale. The hotel also has several attractive rooms, some with superb harbour views.

There is a small shop, which has a good range of the sorts of things you will need during the first day.

GETTING THERE & AWAY
Stagecoach Western (☎ 01292-613500) operates bus service X77 from Glasgow to Ayr (1¼ hours, half-hourly), connecting with its service to Stranraer (two hours, six services Monday to Saturday). From there, another of the company's routes links Stranraer to Portpatrick (20 minutes, six services Monday to Saturday).

First ScotRail (☎ 0845 755 0033) runs trains from Glasgow to Stranraer (two hours, five trains Monday to Saturday, two Sunday).

By car, from Glasgow follow the M77 and A77 to Stranraer and on to Portpatrick.

Cockburnspath
Cockburnspath is a tiny village just inland from the coast, with minimal facilities for walkers – you have been warned.

SLEEPING & EATING
Chesterfield Caravan & Camping Site (☎ 01386-830459; www.chesterfieldcaravanpark.co.uk; The Neuk; sites for 2 £8) is a very well appointed site a couple of miles from town.

There are a couple of B&Bs on nearby farms: **Mrs Hood** (☎ 01368-830620; The Cornbarn, Cove Farm; d £40), who opens her B&B on weekends only; and **Mrs Russell** (☎ 01369-830465; townhead@ecosse.net; Townhead Farm; d £40).

Unfortunately the nearest pub is at Grantshouse, a few miles south along the A1. At least the small shop in Cockburnspath is licensed.

GETTING THERE & AWAY
Perryman's Buses (☎ 01289-380719) service 253 between Edinburgh (1¼ hours, at least three daily) and Berwick-upon-Tweed (45 minutes, at least three daily), on the main east-coast railway line, stops here.

The village, just off the A1 between Edinburgh and Berwick-upon-Tweed, is 35 miles from Edinburgh and 20 miles from Berwick.

THE WALK
Day 1: Portpatrick to New Luce
8½–9 hours, 22.5 miles (36.5km), 370m ascent
A delightful stretch of about 2 miles along the coast from Portpatrick to Killantringan

lighthouse at Black Head makes a fine start to the Way. The rest of the stage is mainly along minor roads through farmland, with good views.

The Way starts at the foot of a flight of stairs at the northwestern end of the harbour. From here it heads northwest above impressive cliffs (take care, especially in poor visibility) and round scenic coves. The route ahead isn't always obvious but trust the thistle waymarkers to show the way from the shore back up to the cliff top. The lighthouse comes dramatically into view and the SUW joins the minor road leading inland from it.

Minor roads and farm tracks lead to a high point with fine views on a clear day. From here, more minor roads, farm tracks and short, sometimes muddy, paths take you down past the outskirts of Stranraer to **Castle Kennedy**. The village has a small **shop** and the **Plantings Inn** (☎ 01581-400633; camp sites for 2 £5, s/d £35/60, mains to £17) where you can choose a comfortable room or camp in the grounds and eat at the hotel.

From Castle Kennedy a sealed drive takes you through the pleasant, wooded grounds of the ruined castle to a minor road. You soon leave this to follow farm tracks to another minor road, then right round the edge of a cleared conifer plantation. The route descends to a footbridge over a railway line, from where it's down to a suspension bridge over the Water of Luce. New Luce is off the Way, 1 mile north along a nearby road. If you feel like putting a few more miles behind you before stopping at

New Luce, continue across open moorland, past deserted Kilhern and down to a minor road about 1 mile east of New Luce.

NEW LUCE

Here you'll find the fine old **Kenmuir Arms Hotel** (☎ 01581-600218; 31 Main St; s/d £35/56) and its adjacent camping ground (sites for 2 £5, breakfast £5). There's a small shop in the village.

A limited bus service run by **Irvine Coaches** (☎ 01581-300345) links New Luce with Stranraer (30 minutes, one service Tuesday, Wednesday and Friday).

Day 2: New Luce to Bargrennan

6¾–7¼ hours, 17.5 miles (28km), 340m ascent
The Way now starts to feel remote as you traverse almost-empty upland farming country, pine plantations and moorland. It's an easier day than those to come.

Follow very quiet roads to Balmurrie farm, from where the route rises across rough moorland; not far to the east, Artfield Fell has been taken over by a wind farm with around 15 big turbines. The Way then follows a wide, heathery ride (a path specially made for riding on horseback) through a conifer plantation. A short stretch of forest road leads to an open area with a timber, beehive shaped **bothy**, which has only sleeping platforms; there is fresh water nearby. Beside the Way are the 4000-year-old **Laggangairn standing stones**, with information about their history. Beyond a large cairn the Way follows a different route from that on the official map as it climbs over **Craig Airie Fell** (320m) for an excellent 360-degree

---

SOUTHERN UPLAND WAY – ROUTE HIGHLIGHT

In the western half of the SUW the most sustained section of the route across open moorland, with relatively short stretches through pine plantations, is between St John's Town of Dalry (called Dalry) and Beattock, close to Moffat (Days 4 and 5). The Way crosses several relatively high points, including Benbrack (580m), Glengaber Hill (515m) and the highest point on the entire SUW, Lowther Hill (725m). Wanlockhead, an old mining village, has a museum and extensive remains of old lead mines.

On this section of the Way you won't spend too much time walking along sealed roads, with most of the distance along forest and hill tracks. The only drawback is the distance between places to stay. It's 27 miles (43.5km) from Dalry to Sanquhar, although there is Polskeoch Bothy en route. The second section can be split into a short stroll of 8 miles (13km) to Wanlockhead, then a 20-mile (32km) day to Beattock.

Dalry is well served by buses from Ayr and Dumfries, Sanquhar is on the Carlisle–Glasgow railway line and you can reach Edinburgh by bus from Moffat, a short step from Beattock. Accommodation options are covered in the main walk description.

The Southern Upland Way

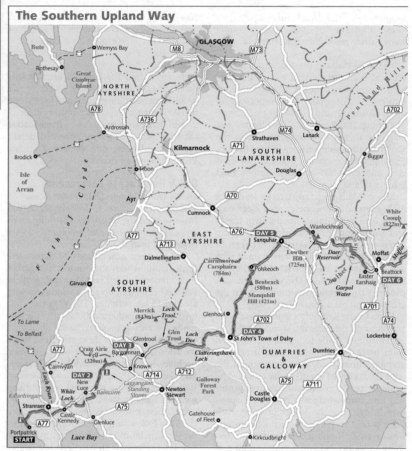

view. The Way then descends past Derry Farm and follows minor roads past Knowe and Glenruther Lodge, over Glenvernoch Fell and down to Bargrennan.

BARGRENNAN & GLENTROOL

Bargrennan and the nearby small village of Glentrool, just west of Loch Trool, offer limited facilities but no shortage of warm hospitality.

Glentrool Holiday Park (☎ 01671-840280; www .glentroolholidaypark.co.uk; Bargrennan; sites for 2 £10), about 800m north along the road, has a small shop.

Historic **House O'Hill Hotel** (☎ 01671-840243; www.houseohill.co.uk; Bargrennan; s/d £35/60, mains to £9; ☑ lunch & dinner) serves hearty bar meals.

Lorien (☎ 01671-840315; moral.lorien61@btinternet .com; 61 Glentrool; s/d £22/44), the only B&B in Glentrool, 1 mile north of the Way, is highly recommended.

King's Buses (☎ 01671-830284) operates route 359 between Bargrennan and Newton Stewart (25 minutes, four services Monday to Saturday) and Girvan (50 minutes, four services Monday to Saturday) on the coast.

Day 3: Bargrennan to St John's Town of Dalry

9–9½ hours, 22 miles (34km), 500m ascent
You now encounter the Galloway Hills, the first significant range of hills along the Way, although the route keeps to lower ground, only reaching an altitude of about 310m.

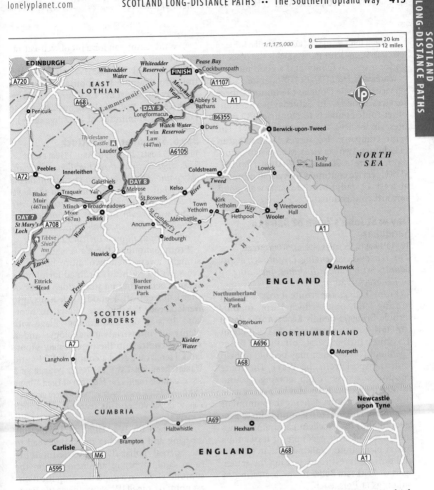

Most of the time you're in Galloway Forest Park; the going underfoot varies widely.

This stage starts along mossy, partly overgrown paths through conifers. After crossing a minor road it passes through pleasant woodland and follows the Water of Trool. It then traverses above Loch Trool, with some good views to Merrick (843m), the highest peak in the Galloway Hills, and drops down to cross Glenhead Burn. Follow the burn briefly then diverge from the mapped route and head southeast to meet a forest road about 1 mile west of Loch Dee. **White Laggan Bothy** is 350m off the route to the south.

Past Loch Dee Angling Club's small hut, the Way crosses the River Dee then traverses a conifer plantation, much of it clear-felled,

and meets the road to Mid Garrary, which you follow west for a short distance.

The Way leaves the road on a good path, heading north through wide clearings between plantations, and then rising across moorland before descending to Clenrie Farm. Further on, well down Garroch Glen, the Way cuts east across Waterside Hill and follows the Water of Ken to a suspension bridge leading to St John's Town of Dalry.

ST JOHN'S TOWN OF DALRY

This large village usually shortens its name to Dalry. There is one small shop.

Mrs Findlay's B&B (☎ 01644-430420; fjames441@aol.com; Main St; s/d £25/50) offers a warm welcome and comfortable bed.

Clachan Inn (☎ 01644-430241; www.theclachaninn
.com; Main St; s/d £30/60, mains to £18) is the place to
go for a spot of luxury and a good meal.

MacEwan's (☎ 01387-256533) operates a bus
service to Castle Douglas (45 minutes, three
services Monday to Saturday), where another route connects to Dumfries (35 minutes, six services Monday to Saturday). The
same company also serves Dalmellington
(1½ hours, two services Monday to Saturday), where a **Stagecoach Western** (☎ 01292-
613500) service continues to Ayr (50 minutes,
at least 12 daily) on the coast, with good
onward connections.

Day 4: St John's Town of Dalry to Sanquhar

10–10¾ hours, 25 miles (40km), 900m ascent
*This is a long, challenging day through empty
country with some stiff climbs, including up
to Benbrack (580m).*

From Dalry, the route crosses rough
grazing land, past Ardoch Farm, to But-
terhole Bridge. Friendly **Kendoon SYHA Hostel**
(☎ 01644-460680; www.syha.org.uk; dm £12) is about
1.5 miles further west, off the SUW, at
Glenhoul (the warden may be able to help
with transport from the Way). The route
continues across rough grazing ground
to Stroanpatrick, then climbs a wide ride
through plantations, skirting the summit of
Manquhill Hill (421m). Continue up to **Benbrack** (580m) for excellent panoramic views
then descend over a couple of lesser tops
into a plantation. Walk past Allan's Cairn
and down a forest road, passing the rather
spartan **Polskeoch Bothy** to the scattering of
buildings at Polskeoch.

About 2 miles along a minor road, the
Way sets off across the ridge to the north
along rough tracks. Sanquhar comes into
view from the top but there's a long descent
into the River Nith valley (Nithsdale) before
you reach the bridge over the river and the
path into Sanquhar (pronounced 'sanker').

SANQUHAR

Castle View Caravan Park (☎ 01659-50291;
ireneriddall@aol.com; Townfoot; sites for 2 £5) is beside
the Way.

Mrs McDowall (☎ 01659-50751; marymcdowell@aol
.com; Town Head; s/d £25/44) offers weary walkers
a warm welcome.

Blackaddie House Hotel (☎ 01659-50270; www
.blackaddiehotel.co.uk; Blackaddie Rd; s/d £40/70, mains to

£20) could tempt you for a bit of well-earned
pampering.

First ScotRail (☎ 0845 755 0033) operates
trains to Glasgow (1¼ hours, six services
Monday to Saturday, two Sunday). **Stagecoach Western** (☎ 01292-613500) bus 246 goes to
Dumfries (50 minutes, at least five daily).

Day 5: Sanquhar to Beattock

10½–11½ hours, 28 miles (45km), 1550m ascent
*This stage includes three highlights: the half-
way point of the Way, the highest point on the
Way – Lowther Hill (725m) – and the highest village in Scotland, Wanlockhead (467m).
Many walkers do manage to complete this
section in a day – probably the hardest day
you'll ever put in on a British LDP.*

From Sanquhar there's a short climb
straight away, then two more bumps to
cross, with Cogshead, a ruined farmhouse,
set between them in a steep-sided valley. A
sharp descent on a good track leads into
Wanlockhead, the highest village in Scotland. It is an old lead-mining village with
plenty of industrial archaeology, and a
striking contrast to the bare, lonely moorland. Here you'll find a couple of B&Bs and
Wanlockhead Inn (☎ 01659-74535; ☯ lunch Sat &
Sun, dinner Wed-Sun). The **Museum of Lead Mining**
(☎ 01659-74387; www.leadminingmuseum.co.uk; admission £6; ☯ Apr-Oct) and its tearoom are worth
a visit.

From here the Way climbs to **Lowther Hill**,
crossing and recrossing the sealed road to
the surreal golf-ball domes (containing
radar equipment) in an enclosure on the
summit. Here, on a good day atop the highest point on the SUW, you can see the Pentland Hills (near Edinburgh) to the north.
The Way continues over the high ground,
steeply up to Cold Moss, then drops down
to the A702 at Overfingland, a large farm
in a wide valley.

Just beyond the A702, in **Watermeetings
Forest**, you reach the halfway point of the
SUW. Cross the wall holding back Daer reservoir (drinking water for Glasgow's southern suburbs) then tackle the long climb over
Sweetshaw Brae, Hods Hill and Beld Knowe
(507m), overlooking the reservoir. This is
inevitably followed by an equally long descent down broad rides through the plantation to Cloffin Burn. **Brattleburn Bothy** is out
of sight, about 400m west of the Way. The
SUW continues generally downhill, still in

THE SOUTHERN UPLAND WAY – ROUTE HIGHLIGHT

The eastern half of the SUW passes through the uplands between Beattock and Melrose, and more settled, agricultural country between there and the coast. The best of the hill country – good views, minimal pine plantations and roads, and plenty of open moorland – is between St Mary's Loch and Melrose. The loch itself, fringed by woodland and overlooked by high hills, is particularly scenic. Between Traquair and Yair, on the River Tweed, the SUW crosses several tops over 500m with fine, wide views.

The walk can be split into two fairly easy days, staying overnight at Traquair or nearby Inner-leithen (12 miles/20km) on one night and then Melrose (18 miles/28km) the next; some details are given in the main walk description.

Moffat, close to Beattock, and Melrose are well served by public transport.

---

dense conifers, across a large clearing and Garpol Water, eventually reaching a minor road at Easter Earshaig. Follow this down to Beattock.

BEATTOCK & MOFFAT

Craigielands Country Park (☎ 01683-300591; www .craigielandsleisure.co.uk; Beattock; sites for 2 £12), about 1 mile south of the Way, has its own restaurant; there's a shop nearby.

Barnhill Springs Country Guest House (☎ 01683-220580; Beattock; s/d £35/60), in a historic building, is right beside the Way.

Moffat, just over 1 mile away, has more accommodation and restaurants but the A701 is very busy, so try for a place that provides vehicle back-up. The **tourist office** (☎ 01683-220620; www.visitmoffat.co.uk; Churchgate; ☉ Mon-Sat Apr-Oct) is near the town entrance from the A74(M).

The **Moffat Camping and Caravanning Club Site** (☎ 01683-220436; www.campingandcaravanning club.co.uk; Hammerland's Farm; sites for 2 £12) has flat, grassy pitches close to the town centre.

Berriedale House B&B (☎ 01683-220427; Beech grove; s/d £25/44), in a large 19th-century villa has huge, comfortable bedrooms in a quiet location.

Bombay Cuisine (☎ 01683-220900; Main St; mains to £11; ☉ lunch & dinner) specialises in unique Laziz Khama cuisine from Samarkand (Uzbekistan), in which each dish has its own sauce. The helpful waiter will explain these absolutely delicious dishes.

The **Co-op supermarket** is next to the well-signposted Moffat Woollen Mill, off the A701, near the tourist office.

MacEwan's (☎ 01387-256533) bus 100 links Edinburgh and Moffat (two hours, three services Monday to Saturday, one Sun). **Stagecoach Western** (☎ 01292-613500) runs a

service between Glasgow and Moffat (1½ hours, three services Monday to Saturday, two Sunday).

Day 6: Beattock to St Mary's Loch

9–9½ hours, 21 miles (33.5km), 1200m ascent

Another tough day, crossing the watershed between streams flowing into the Irish and North Seas at Ettrick Head.

From Beattock go under the A74(M) motorway, across the River Annan, up and over a small hill, then beside Moffat Water. The Way then winds up through a plantation on a forest road and on to a path up a deep valley. This leads to the **gorge** carved by Selcloth Burn; the path traverses this dramatic cleft then climbs to **Ettrick Head** (520m), the boundary between Dumfries & Galloway and the Borders. Beyond here you soon meet a forest road that leads down to **Over Phawhope Bothy** and a minor road beside Ettrick Water. Follow this for 6 miles down the valley, its natural beauty somewhat compromised by blankets of conifers.

Turn off at **Scabcleuch** along a signposted footpath, which climbs up a narrow glen then crosses Pikestone Rig and continues down to **Riskinhope Hope**, a once-solid stone house now a bramble-covered ruin. The route then turns round Earl's Hill and picks up a forest track for the descent to St Mary's Loch.

ST MARY'S LOCH

Historic **Tibbie Shiel's Inn** (☎ 01750-42231; www .tibbieshielsinn.com; s/d £35/60, mains to £10), at the loch, was the scene of the Way's opening in 1984, and offers relatively luxurious accommodation and excellent bar meals. There's also a **camp site** (sites for 2 £6) nearby, run by the inn.

Nearby **Glen Cafe** (☎ 01750-42241; mains to £15; ☺ breakfast & lunch daily, dinner Sat) is also a great place to relax and unwind over a drink.

Houston's Minibuses (☎ 01576-203874) operates a summer-only service between Lockerbie and Selkirk via Moffat (30 minutes, two services Saturday July and August) and St Mary's Loch.

Day 7: St Mary's Loch to Melrose
12–13 hours, 30 miles (48.5km), 1120m ascent
Plenty of variety – lochs, hills and open moorland to Traquair, then forest, heather moor, a relatively suburban interlude around Galashiels and a river-side walk into Melrose. This ultra-long day could be split into two, with an overnight stop at Traquair, 12 miles (20km) from St Mary's Loch. Around 800m of the climbing comes between Traquair and Melrose.

From the inn, pass in front of the Sailing Club building and follow a path then a vehicle track beside the loch; further on, cross Yarrow Water to the A708. The Way crosses the road and returns to open country. Good paths and tracks climb over a spur to Douglas Burn then it's up again, across heathery Blake Muir and down to the hamlet of **Traquair** in the Tweed valley, at the junction of the B709 and B7062.

Accommodation in the village includes **Traquair Mill Bunkhouse** (☎ 01896-830515; dm £13) and the **School House** (☎ 01896-830506; http://old-schoolhouse.ndo.co.uk; s/d £30/56).

There's more accommodation in Innerleithen, about 1 mile north along the B709. **First Edinburgh** (☎ 08708 727271) bus service 62 links Innerleithen with Edinburgh. **Munro's of Jedburgh** (☎ 01835-862253) operates an afternoon-only service between Traquair and Peebles (15 minutes, daily service Monday to Friday), where you can pick up the Edinburgh bus.

Turning your back on Traquair, follow a lane climbing steadily into a plantation. **Minch Moor** (567m) rises on the right and the short detour is well worth the effort for the panoramic view, including the distinctive Eildon Hills near Melrose. The SUW continues along a wide ride through the plantation and rises to **Brown Knowe** (523m), which also provides good views. The next tops are skirted on the right and left. The turn-off to **Broadmeadows SYHA Hostel** (☎ 01750-725506; www.syha.org.uk; dm £13), Scotland's first youth

hostel, is signposted; it is 1 mile or so to the south. If you're considering staying here, note that the nearest shops are in Selkirk, 5 miles away.

The route continues up to a summit distinguished by three massive cairns known as the **Three Brethren**. Then it's down to Yair and a bridge over the River Tweed.

You then climb over a fairly broad ridge and go down across fields, crossing numerous stiles, to woodland on the outskirts of Galashiels. The Way follows a rather devious route through parklands and along suburban streets, skirting Gala Hill. Cross the busy A7 and follow river-side paths and the sealed bed of the old Waverley railway to Melrose.

MELROSE
pop 1656
Attractive Melrose is dominated by a beautiful 12th-century Cistercian abbey. The **tourist office** (☎ 0870 608 0404; www.visitscottish borders.com; Abbey House, Abbey St; ☺ Apr-Oct) is opposite the abbey.

Gibson Park Caravan Club Site (☎ 01896-822969; www.caravanclub.co.uk; High St; sites for 2 £18), close to the town centre, has a few tent sites and excellent facilities.

Melrose SYHA Hostel (☎ 0870 004 1141; www .syha.org.uk; Priorwood; dm £14; 🖳) occupies a fine Georgian mansion overlooking Melrose Abbey.

Braidwood B&B (☎ 01896-822488; www.braid woodmelrose.co.uk; Buccleuch St; s/d £35/56) offers high-standard facilities and a friendly welcome to this 19th-century townhouse.

Marmion's Restaurant (☎ 01896-822245; Buccleuch St; mains to £17; ☺ lunch & dinner Mon-Sat) might seem expensive, but the substantial dishes do represent good value.

There are **Co-op** and **Spar** supermarkets and a few pubs in High St.

First Edinburgh (☎ 08708 727271) runs bus route 62 between Edinburgh and Melrose (2¼ hours, eight services Monday to Saturday, six Sunday).

Day 8: Melrose to Longformacus
9½–10 hours, 25 miles (40km), 900m ascent
The first part of today's walk is through mainly agricultural land, along minor roads and farm tracks, and across fields, which can be very muddy in parts. Essentially the route traverses a long ridge between Allan Water

and Leader Water, tributaries of the River Tweed. From Lauder there's a very different stretch, across extensive grouse moors in the Lammermuir Hills and down to the hamlet of Longformacus.

From Melrose cross the River Tweed, this time by a 19th-century chain suspension bridge for pedestrians and 'light carriages' only. The Way goes back up beside the river then heads north, steadily gaining height. There are fine views on a good day from the highest point around flat-topped **Kedslie Hill**. The route passes through several fields occupied by grazing cows – they're very inquisitive but not aggressive. The steep descent into Lauder skirts the local golf course.

Lauder has three hotels and a couple of nearby B&Bs, of which **Thirlestane Farm** (☎ 01578-722216; s/d £40/60), about 1.5 miles east of the Way beside the A697, is particularly recommended. **Thirlestane Castle Caravan & Camp Site** (☎ 01578-718884; thirlestanepark@btconnect .com; sites for 2 £6) is superbly sited near splendid Thirlestane Castle. In Lauder's main street you'll find an excellent baker, a small supermarket, and the **Flat Cat Coffee Shop**, which is just as well since Lauder is the last place where you can stock up on chocolate and other walking staples before Cockburnspath, at the end of the Way. **Munro's of Jedburgh** (☎ 01835-862253) buses can take you from Lauder to Edinburgh (1¼ hours, 12 services Monday to Saturday, five Sunday).

From Lauder the Way weaves through the grounds of **Thirlestane Castle** (open to visitors). Cross the A697 and follow a lane up through the curiously named Wanton Walls Farm and steeply up to a small plantation. The Way then wanders up and down across open grassland then crosses Blythe Water on a substantial bridge. Continue on to Braidshawrig, part of the Burncastle Estate grouse moor. It's essential to keep to the track (and there's no incentive to stray onto the tussocky moor), especially during the grouse shooting season, which always starts on 12 August. The track climbs across the vast, empty moors, dotted with shooting butts and old tin sheds providing shelter for stock, to the ridge crest. It then turns right to the high point of **Twin Law** (447m), topped with two giant cylindrical cairns, each with a sheltered seat facing southeast. From here the Tweed valley is spread out

before you and the sea is in sight at last. The descent towards Watch Water Reservoir is easy – a good track leads to Scarlaw and a sealed road. If the weather is fine you should find a small **tearoom** (☺ Easter-Sep) here. Continue down to Longformacus (pronounced 'longformaycus').

Whinmore B&B (☎ 01361-890669; junren26@tiscali .co.uk; s/d £35/60, 3-course dinner £15) also offers evening meals.

Day 9: Longformacus to Cockburnspath
7–8 hours, 18.5 miles (30km), 450m ascent
Paths and tracks through farmland and woodland lead to a fine cliff-top walk, but you have to leave the coast to officially finish in the village of Cockburnspath.

After about 1 mile along a minor road east of Longformacus, the Way branches off to climb over moorland, past some small plantations and down to the B6355 road. From here the route follows steep-sided Whiteadder valley through mixed woodland to the hamlet of **Abbey St Bathan**. Cross Whiteadder Water just below where it joins Monynut Water. The Way follows the Whiteadder for a while then turns north; the **Riverside Restaurant** (☎ 01361-840312; ☺ Tue-Sun) is just across the river. Follow paths and lanes, crossing some fields in the process. From a minor road at Blackburn you can catch a last glimpse back to the hills. Then it's down to the busy A1; cross with care. Follow an old road between the A1 and the railway to a pleasant green track into Penmanshiel Wood. It seems cruel at this stage but the route climbs through the wood, fortunately to a very rewarding **view** of the North Sea and the Firth of Forth. A flight of steps takes you down to the A1107, beyond which is Pease Dean Wildlife Reserve, the site of a native woodland regeneration project.

Skirt the serried ranks of vans in Pease Bay Holiday Home Park and walk up the road above the bay. The final cliff-top walk, mirroring the start at Portpatrick, is blessed with impressive coastal scenery, along to colourful Cove Harbour, tucked below. Turn inland, under the A1 and the railway line, to the mercat (market) cross at **Cockburnspath** (pronounced 'coburns-path' or just 'co-path'), the official end of the Way. It takes a while for realisation to sink in that you really have walked from Portpatrick. Congratulations!

THE WEST HIGHLAND WAY

Duration	7 days
Distance	95 miles (153km)
Difficulty	moderate
Start	Milngavie (p420)
Finish	Fort William (p362)
Nearest Town	Glasgow (opposite)
Transport	bus, train

Summary Britain's most popular LDP passes through some of Scotland's finest landscapes, from suburban Glasgow to the foot of Ben Nevis, Britain's highest mountain.

The West Highland Way extends from the outskirts of Scotland's largest city to the base of its highest mountain. The full route is walked by around 15,000 people every year, and many thousands more complete sections of the route; officially, it is the most popular path in Britain.

The walk starts from Milngavie (pronounced 'mullguy'), 7 miles north of Glasgow's city centre, in the lowlands, but the greater part of this walk is among the mountains, lochs and fast-flowing rivers of the Highlands. It runs along the length of Loch Lomond and, in the far north, crosses wild Rannoch Moor and passes through spectacular Glen Nevis to reach Fort William. By the time you finish you will have climbed a total of 3543m (11,624ft), the equivalent of two-and-a-half ascents of Ben Nevis! The route is well signposted and uses a combination of ancient ways, old drove roads (along which cattle were once herded), an old military road (built by troops to help control the Jacobites in the 18th century) and disused railway lines. It's marked with signposts and the thistle-hexagon logo.

PLANNING

The walk is fairly easy going as far as Rowardennan. After that, particularly north of Bridge of Orchy, it's quite strenuous and remote, and the location of accommodation means you will either have some very long days or rather short days. For these reasons, most people start in the south, at Milngavie, and take six or seven days to reach Fort William. You need to be properly equipped with good boots, maps, a compass, food and drink. The weather can turn bad all too quickly, which it's quite likely to do. The

area has a high rainfall, and winds in the narrow mountain glens, and on the more exposed areas, can reach gale force.

Although the route is fully waymarked, you should carry a map and compass and know how to use them.

For a seven-day walk, as described here, the most convenient places to start and end each day are as follows:

Day	From	To	Miles/km
1	Milngavie	Drymen	12/19.5
2	Drymen	Rowardennan	14/22.5
3	Rowardennan	Inverarnan	14/22.5
4	Inverarnan	Tyndrum	13/21
5	Tyndrum	Kings House Hotel	19/30.5
6	Kings House Hotel	Kinlochleven	9/14.5
7	Kinlochleven	Fort William	14/22.5

Alternatives

If your time is limited and you just want to walk a day or two of the West Highland Way, we offer some suggestions for the best day walks along the route in the boxed text on p420.

To do the walk in six days, spend the third night in Crianlarich, the fourth night in Bridge of Orchy and reach Kinlochleven on the fifth night, possibly stopping for lunch at Kings House Hotel.

Many people add a day for an ascent of Ben Nevis (p360), and perhaps another for Ben Lomond (p347).

When to Walk

The Way can be walked at any time of year, although you would need to take account of the short daylight hours, the probability of snow or snowfalls over higher ground, and reduced accommodation during winter. May is the most popular month, before the midges become really active, while September and early October can be particularly beautiful. The Conic Hill section may be closed for lambing during late April and early May, and the section between the Bridge of Orchy and Fort William is often used for the annual Scottish motorcycle trials around the same time. Diversions are set up, but contact the **ranger service** (☎ 01389-722199) for further information. The Way itself is unaffected by deer stalking, but detours from the track should generally be avoided between August and October.

Maps & Books

The Way is covered by OS Landranger 1:50,000 maps No 64 *Glasgow*, 56 *Loch Lomond & Inveraray*, 50 *Glen Orchy & Loch Etive* and 41 *Ben Nevis*, although most people prefer the convenience of a purpose-designed all-in-one route map. The excellent Harvey 1:40,000 Route map *West Highland Way* and the cheap and cheerful Footprint map *West Highland Way* include lots of additional practical information.

The official guide *West Highland Way* by Bob Aitken and Roger Smith comes with the Harvey Route map in a plastic wallet. Also recommended is *West Highland Way* by Charlie Loram, with thorough text and very detailed line maps.

Accommodation

Accommodation should not be too difficult to find, although it's quite limited between Bridge of Orchy and Kinlochleven. During the peak season, from May to August, you must book all accommodation in advance.

There are three SYHA hostels on or near the walk, at Rowardennan, Crianlarich and Glen Nevis, and bunkhouses at Tyndrum, Bridge of Orchy, Kinlochleven and Fort William. Rather more basic are the bothies at Rowchoish and Doune, both on Day 3; they are free and always open.

Camping is permitted on the West Highland Way only in designated areas. There are camping grounds at all but one of the overnight stops (King's House Hotel) in our itinerary and several in between. Some offer wigwams – a halfway house between a tent and a bothy. There are also several free, one-night-only backpacker sites without facilities (no fires allowed).

Most B&Bs provide packed lunches if you ask on arrival. Some B&Bs, particularly those not directly on the route, will send someone to meet you and drive you back next morning for a small charge.

Information Sources

The Official West Highland Way Pocket Companion, a free booklet listing accommodation and facilities along the Way, is available from the **West Highland Way office** (☎ 0845 345 4978; www.west-highland-way.co.uk; Balloch) at the Loch Lomond & the Trossachs National Park headquarters. The website contains all the basic information you should need

to get started, and the *Pocket Companion* should be available as a download.

Baggage Services

Rather than doing all the organising, why not take advantage of the services offered by companies that will arrange all your accommodation and carry your luggage between overnight stops. All you'll have to do is walk! Some outfits go a step further and will provide you with sheafs of information about the Way and the places through which you pass.

Easyways (☎ 01324-714132; www.easyways.com; Haypark Business Centre, Marchmont Ave, Polmont, Falkirk) has years of experience organising accommodation and baggage transfer.

Transcotland (☎ 01887-820848; www.transcotland .com; 5 Dunkeld Rd, Aberfeldy) also has a good track record and will provide detailed directions and plenty of background information.

Sherpa Van (☎ 0871 520 0124; www.sherpavan .com) also offers baggage transfer.

NEAREST TOWNS
Glasgow
pop 629,600

It would be hard to avoid at least passing through Glasgow en route to the start of the Way. The **tourist office** (☎ 0141-204 4400; www.seeglasgow.com; 11 George Sq) is very helpful; it stocks maps, books and *The Official West Highland Way Companion*.

Both **Nevisport** (☎ 0141-332 4814; www.nevisport .com; 261 Sauchiehall St; ☾ daily), in Glasgow's busy, tongue-twisting, shopping street, and **Tiso's** (☎ 0141-248 4877; glasgow@tiso.co.uk; 129 Buchanan St; ☾ daily), in a rather upmarket pedestrianised street, stock the full range of equipment.

SLEEPING & EATING

VisitScotland (☎ 0845 225 5121; www.visitscotland .com) can handle bookings, though all bookings made through it cost an extra £3.

Craigdenmuir Park (☎ 0141-779 4159; www .craigdenmuir.co.uk; Stepps; sites for 2 £12) is the closest camping ground to the city, about 4 miles north; it also has chalets and static caravans.

Glasgow SYHA Hostel (☎ 0870 004 1119; www .syha.org.uk; 8 Park Tce; dm £16) offers quality accommodation in a historic building; all rooms are en suite.

Old School House (☎ 0141-332 7600; oschoolh@ hotmail.com; 194 Renfrew St; s/d £40/60) is a small detached villa, stylishly decorated and excellent value for money.

For self-catering supplies, the **Tesco Metro** (36-38 Argyle St; ✆ daily) is the most centrally located shop.

Bothy (☎ 0141-334 4040; 11 Ruthven Lane; lunch/dinner mains £8/12; ✆ lunch & dinner) is light years removed from any bothy you visited out in the hills. The menu features traditional fare, with a uniquely Scottish flavour.

GETTING THERE & AWAY

National Express (☎ 0870 580 5850; www.national express.com) runs coaches between London Victoria and Glasgow's Buchanan St bus station (8¾ hours, three daily).

Virgin Trains (☎ 08457 222333; www.virgintrains .co.uk) link London Euston and Glasgow Central (5¾ hours, at least 15 daily).

Scottish Citylink (☎ 0870 550 5050; www.citylink .co.uk) bus service 900 links Edinburgh and Glasgow (1½ hours, every 15 minutes).

First ScotRail (☎ 0845 755 0033; www.firstscotrail .co.uk) trains shuttle back and forth between Glasgow Queen St and Edinburgh Waverley (50 minutes, half-hourly).

Milngavie
pop 14,000

Milngavie is a bustling outer suburb of Glasgow, so there's no shortage of shops and restaurants and a fair range of accommodation. The nearest tourist office is in central Glasgow.

The **Iron Chief** (☎ 0141-956 4597; 5 Mugdock Rd), 100m from the start, stocks much of the stuff you might have forgotten.

SLEEPING & EATING

Bankell Farm Camping & Caravan Site (☎ 0141-956 1733; www.bankellfarm.co.uk; Strathblane Rd; sites for 2 £8) is a small, sheltered site 1 mile or so northeast of Milngavie, off the A81. You can leave your car here while you're doing the walk for £2 a day.

Best Foot Forward B&B (☎ 0141-956 3046; BFF Morag@aol.com; 1 Dougalston Gardens South; s/d £35/56) is only a few minutes from the start of the West Highland Way.

Laurel Bank B&B (☎ 0141-584 9400; adam.96@ ntlworld.com; 96 Strathblane Rd; s/d £35/50), in a large Edwardian home, is only five minutes from the train station.

For supplies, there's a **Tesco supermarket** next to the train station.

Toscana Bistro (☎ 0141-956 4020; 44 Station Rd; mains £10-13; ✆ dinner Thu-Sat), a cosy place in the heart of things, offers good value from its extensive Italian menu.

Primo Restaurant (☎ 0141-955 1200; 14 Stewart St; lunch mains £4-7, dinner mains £8-15; ✆ lunch & dinner; 🖳) is all contemporary style and genuine Italian cuisine; start the day with an espresso fix and one of Primo's energy-giving cakes.

GETTING THERE & AWAY

A **Strathclyde Passenger Transport** (SPT; ☎ 0141-332 6811; www.spt.co.uk) suburban train service from Glasgow Central terminates at Milngavie (25 minutes, half-hourly).

Milngavie is 7 miles north of Glasgow. By car, take the M8 and, at exit 17, follow the A82 then the A81. There is a car park close to the train station, off Station Rd.

THE WEST HIGHLAND WAY – ROUTE HIGHLIGHTS

If you want to sample the West Highland Way rather than tackling the full distance, the best stretch (in our opinion) is between Altnafeadh, not far from Kings House Hotel, and Glen Nevis. It is quite possible to complete these two sections in a single day, although the total distance for the day adds up to a fairly lengthy 19 miles (30.5km). Paths are good all the way and you'll only be carrying a day pack. Allow about nine hours for the walk.

Start at the Altnafeadh car park on the A82, 3 miles northwest of Kings House Hotel. **Citylink** (☎ 0870 550 5050) buses from Glasgow and Fort William both pass here and the driver will stop if you ask when you board the bus. At the end of the day you can either stay at Glen Nevis or take advantage of the Highland Country Buses service to Fort William (see p363).

Another highlight of the route is walking along the wooded shores of Loch Lomond, passing several spectacular waterfalls. The section from Inversnaid to Inverarnan covers 7 miles (11km) and can be easily completed as a day walk. A passenger **ferry** (☎ 01877-386223) from Inveruglas, on the western side of the loch, will take you across the water to Inversnaid. Both Inveruglas and Inverarnan are request stops on the Citylink Glasgow–Fort William bus service.

THE WALK
Day 1: Milngavie to Drymen

4½–5½ hours, 12 miles (19.5km)

The first day provides easy walking through rolling countryside and farmland. For about 3 miles the path runs along a disused railway track, which can be muddy if it's wet, then there's a couple of miles along a quiet road. The Beech Tree Inn at Dumgoyne is the only convenient food stop; otherwise you'll need to bring lunch with you.

The official start of the West Highland Way is a granite obelisk beside the bridge over the Allander Water on Douglas St, but for most people the journey begins at Milngavie train station. To reach the obelisk from the station, go through the underpass and up a flight of steps to the pedestrianised centre of Milngavie. Bear left at the exit of the underpass to join Douglas St, passing through a shopping precinct to reach the official starting point.

From the obelisk a small sign on a nearby building indicates a turn upstream; cross Allander Water and follow the stream through the trees to join good paths through **Mugdock Wood**. From the end of the wood, a succession of paths and a track take you past a collection of holiday homes to the B821. Turn left along the road and follow it for about 300m to a stile giving onto a path to the right. As you skirt Dumgoyach Hill look out for Bronze Age standing stones to your right just before the hill. Beyond Dumgoyach Bridge the route joins onto a disused railway track. After about 800m you pass the path to **Glengoyne Distillery** (☼ Apr-Oct); 800m further on you reach the **Beech Tree Inn** at Dumgoyne, a pub that serves food all day. In the village of Killearn, 1.5 miles off the route to the right, there's accommodation, shops and pubs.

Continue along the old railway track to Gartness, from where you follow a road most of the way to the edge of Drymen. One mile beyond Gartness is **Drymen Camping** (☎ 01360-660893; juliamacx@aol.com; Easter Drumquhassle Farm; sites for 2 £10, wigwam for 2 £14, B&B s/d £33/50, dinner £16), where Loch Lomond makes its first appearance.

Pass a quarry and continue along the road; just past a sharp left bend, the Way leaves the road and follows a path to the right. If you're going to Drymen, continue along the road and cross the A811 to enter the village.

DRYMEN
pop 681

The **tourist office** (☎ 0870 720 0611; www.visitscottish heartlands.com; Library, The Green; ☼ May-Sep; 🖳) has a relatively short season; at other times the library staff can help with basic information about accommodation.

It's Great Outdoors (☎ 01360-661148; 1 Stirling Rd; ☼ daily) stocks gas canisters, maps, guides and outdoor gear.

Green Shadows (☎ 01360-660289; greenshadows@ hotmail.com; Buchanan Castle; s/d £28/50) is an outstanding B&B. Well away from the main road, it's beautifully decorated. Breakfast is fantastic, and a pick-up service is also available.

The **Clachan Inn** (☎ 01360-660824; s/d £30/54, mains £8-12; ☼ lunch & dinner) is reputedly Scotland's oldest inn. The mostly standard dishes on the menu are enlivened with spicy sauces, and vegetarians do quite well. The rather small rooms are pleasantly furnished.

For supplies, there's a **Spar** supermarket and the smaller **village shop**.

Day 2: Drymen to Rowardennan

5–6½ hours, 14 miles (22.5km)

Walking on the second day is still easy going, apart from the climb up Conic Hill (358m), and is mostly along undulating paths and the banks of Loch Lomond. The only place for food supplies is Balmaha, around three hours from Drymen.

From where it meets the A811 just outside Drymen, the Way follows the road east for a short distance then veers left to pick up a forest track. It gradually climbs through the dense woods to Garadhban Forest (there is a wild camp site here with no facilities). Near the end of the trees, just over an hour from Drymen, a path to the left leads to the road into Milton of Buchanan, where there are a couple of B&Bs but no shop or pub. This path provides the alternative route when Conic Hill is closed during the lambing season (see When to Walk, p409).

For most of the year the Way continues through the trees, over a stile and onto open moorland. The wide path contours north of the summit of **Conic Hill** (358m), but it's worth the short detour to the top for the wonderful panorama over Loch Lomond. Conic Hill is a boundary point and a landmark for walkers; from here on, you're in the Highlands.

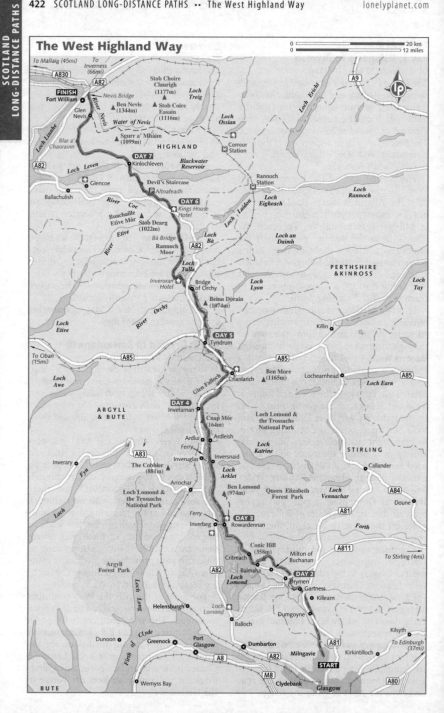

The West Highland Way

0   20 km
0   12 miles

To Mallaig (45mi)
To Inverness (66mi)

A830
A82
A9

Stob Choire
Claurigh
(1177m)
Loch
Treig

FINISH
Fort William
Nevis Bridge
Ben Nevis
(1344m)
Stob Coire
Easain
(1116m)

Glen Nevis
River Nevis
Water of Nevis
Loch
Ossian

Loch Linnhe
Sgurr a' Mhaim
(1099m)
HIGHLAND
Corrour
Station

Blar a'
Chaorainn

A82
DAY 7
Kinlochleven
Blackwater
Reservoir

Loch Leven
Devil's Staircase
Altnafeadh
Rannoch
Station
Loch
Eigheach
Loch
Rannoch

Glencoe
DAY 6
Kings House
Hotel

Ballachulish
River Coe
PERTHSHIRE
& KINROSS

Buachaille
Etive Mór
Stob Dearg
(1022m)
Loch Laidon
Loch
Rannoch

River Etive
Bà Bridge
Loch
Bà
Loch an
Daimh

Rannoch
Moor
Loch
Tulla

Inveroran
Hotel
Bridge
of Orchy
Loch
Lyon
Loch
Tay

Loch
Etive
River Orchy
Beinn Dòrain
(1074m)

Killin

DAY 5
Tyndrum
A85
A85

To Oban
(15mi)
A85
Ben More
(1165m)
Lochearnhead

Loch
Awe
Crianlarich
Loch Earn

Glen Falloch
DAY 4
Inverarnan
ARGYLL
& BUTE
Cnap Mòr
(164m)
Loch Lomond &
the Trossachs
National Park

Ardlui
Ardleish
Ferry
Loch
Katrine
STIRLING

Inverary
Inveruglas
Loch
Arklet
Callander

Loch
Fyne
The Cobbler
(881m)
Inversnaid
Queen Elizabeth
Forest Park
Loch
Vennachar
Doune

Arrochar
Ben Lomond
(974m)
A81
A84

Loch Lomond &
the Trossachs
National Park
Forth
To Stirling (4mi)

Ferry
DAY 3
Rowardennan
A811

Loch
Long
Inverbeg
Conic Hill
(358m)
Milton of
Buchanan

Argyll
Forest Park
Critreach
DAY 2
A82
Balmaha
Loch
Lomond
Drymen
Gartness
Killearn
To Stirling

Helensburgh
Loch
Lomond
Dumgoyne
Kilsyth
To Edinburgh
(37mi)

Balloch
A81
Kirkintilloch

Dunoon
Port
Glasgow
Dumbarton
Milngavie
A80

Greenock
A8
A82
START

Firth of Clyde
M8
Clydebank
A80

BUTE
Wemyss Bay
Glasgow

The path dips through a conifer wood to **Balmaha** and the loch itself, near the **National Park Centre** (☎ 01389-722100; ☿ Easter-Oct). The **Oak Tree Inn** (☎ 01360-870357; www.oak-tree-inn .co.uk; dm/s/d £25/50/70, mains £7-14) offers good hotel rooms and more-simple bunkhouse accommodation; bar meals are available. There's a **shop** in the village.

Continue beside the loch shore, passing a marker commemorating the opening of the West Highland Way in 1980. In less than an hour you reach Milarrochy and **Milarrochy Bay Camping & Caravanning Club Site** (☎ 0870 243 3331; www.campingandcaravanningclub.co.uk; sites for 2 £12), which has a kitchen, drying room and small shop on site. From Critreoch, about 800m further on, the Way dives into a dark forest and emerges to follow the road for about 1 mile. Just after you join the road you'll find the popular **Cashel Caravan & Camping Site** (☎ 01360-870234; www.forestholidays .co.uk; sites for 2 £14). One mile beyond Sallochy House, the Way climbs through **Ross Wood**, its magnificent oaks making it one of Scotland's finest natural woodlands, then returns to the loch side and leads on to Rowardennan (p348). The path to Ben Lomond starts nearby (p347).

Day 3: Rowardennan to Inverarnan
6–7½ hours, 14 miles (22.5km)
Today's walk begins with 4 miles of Forestry Commission track, followed by a 6-mile section down by the loch. The only place for food along the way is the large Inversnaid Hotel, 7 miles beyond Rowardennan.

From Rowardennan follow the unsurfaced road that runs parallel to the loch. Just past Ptarmigan Lodge an alternative path branches left and follows the shoreline, but it's rough and not recommended. The official route provides much easier walking and follows the track higher up the hillside. Ongoing large-scale timber extraction in the area may require path diversions, which will be clearly indicated. The hillsides will be replanted with native broadleaf trees.

From both routes you can reach **Rowchoish Bothy**, a simple stone shelter. About 400m beyond the bothy, the forestry track becomes a path that dives down to the loch for a stretch of difficult walking to Cailness. From here the going improves to Inversnaid, shortly before which the path crosses Snaid Burn, just above the impressive **Inversnaid Falls**. The huge **Inversnaid Hotel** (☎ 01877-386223) could be a good place to stop for refreshments before you tackle the next section, the toughest of all. From March to October the hotel runs a twice-daily ferry service between Inversnaid and Inveruglas, where you could connect with bus services along the A82.

For a couple of miles north from Inversnaid the path twists and turns around large boulders and tree roots, a good test of balance and agility. One mile or so into this, the Way passes close to **Rob Roy's cave**, although there's little to see (see the boxed text, p424). Further on is simple **Doune Bothy** and, almost 1 mile beyond the bothy, at Ardleish, there's a landing stage used by the ferry crossing to **Ardlui Hotel** (☎ 01301-704243; www.ardlui.co.uk; Ardlui; camps sites for 2 £10, s/d £45/60).

From Ardleish you leave the loch and climb to a col on the hill of **Cnap Mór**, where there are good views on a clear day, both north towards the Highlands and south over Loch Lomond. The path descends into Glen Falloch; a footbridge over Ben Glas Burn heralds your arrival at Inverarnan. Just upstream is the spectacular **Beinglas Falls**, a 300m-long cascade that makes a very impressive sight after heavy rain.

INVERARNAN
Beinglas Farm Campsite (☎ 01301-704281; www .beinglascampsite.co.uk; sites for 2 £10, wigwam for 2 £25, B&B d £60, mains £6-10), just north of Ben Glas Burn, is exceptionally well set up, complete with its own bar, restaurant and an off-licence shop selling groceries, drinks and camping supplies.

Across the river, in the village, there's a choice between the **Stagger Inn** and the much older **Drover's Inn**, both doing a good line in traditional Scottish dishes, the latter with the possible added attraction of live music.

Day 4: Inverarnan to Tyndrum
4½–5½ hours, 13 miles (21km)
This day is much easier than yesterday and passes through open country beside a river. Unfortunately, you're also close to the busy road and railway line. Unless you make a detour down to Crianlarich (20 minutes each way), there's nowhere to buy food until Tyndrum.

ROB ROY

Robert Macgregor (1671–1734) was given the nickname Roy as the English version of the Gaelic word *ruadh,* meaning 'red', thanks to his shock of red hair. The Macgregor clan was notorious for violent lawlessness and rebellion so, unsurprisingly, Robert became a cattle trader, making occasional raids to the lowlands to rustle cattle. He owned much of the land around Inversnaid and had effectively become head of the clan soon after he turned 30.

He went bankrupt in 1711 when his head drover absconded with his annual profits, and he was subsequently betrayed and outlawed by the Duke of Montrose, a former ally. When his home was burnt and his family evicted, he took to the hills to begin a campaign of revenge against the duke. Tales of his generosity to the poor and daring escapes from the clutches of the law earned him a reputation as a Scottish Robin Hood. Legends and romantic stories have ensured him a place among the characters of popular Scottish history. The Hollywood film *Rob Roy* (largely shot in Glen Nevis) added a contemporary layer to the legend.

A natural rock cell in a crag about 1.5 miles north of Ptarmigan Lodge, where he is said to have kept kidnap victims, is known as Rob Roy's Prison. The cave where he is supposed to have hidden from the duke's men is north of Inversnaid. Both sites can be visited from the Way but there's nothing much to see, and tales of Rob's use of them can be attributed more to romantic notions than to hard fact.

From Inverarnan the route follows the attractive River Falloch most of the way to Crianlarich. In a short time the valley begins to open out and the river becomes more placid. After about 3.5 miles the path crosses the river and continues along the west bank. About 800m further on it leaves the river and climbs through a small tunnel under the railway line and then crosses under the A82 to join an old military road.

The road climbs out of Glen Falloch towards the trees ahead. At the stile into the forest there's a path leading down to the right towards Crianlarich; this is the approximate halfway point of the West Highland Way.

There's no need to go down to Crianlarich, but the village does have a railway station, a small shop (with an ATM) and accommodation, including **Crianlarich SYHA Hostel** (☎ 0870 155 3255; www.syha.org.uk; dm £16). The **Rod & Reel** pub has a restaurant and is also a great place for a drink.

The Way climbs to the left from the stile, offering good views across to Ben More, then continues through the trees for about 2 miles. Next, it crosses under the railway line and goes over the road. It then crosses the River Fillan via a wooden bridge. Beside the bridge there is a wild camp site (no facilities) on the west bank. Pass the remains of **St Fillan's Priory**, turn left and go on to **Strathfillan Wigwams** (☎ 01838-400251; www

.sac.ac.uk/wigwams; wigwams for 2 £25) at Auchtertyre Farm. The route crosses the A82 once more and, in less than an hour, reaches Tyndrum.

TYNDRUM

This village, originally a lead-mining settlement and now a popular staging point between Glasgow and Fort William, is strung out along the A82.

The **tourist office** (☎ 08707 200626; www.visit scottishheartlands.com; ☼ Easter-Oct) is opposite the Invervey Hotel. **The Green Welly Stop** (☎ 01838-400271; www.thegreenwellystop.co.uk; ☼ daily) includes an outdoor gear shop (that sells maps), an off-licence and the brisk, cafeteria-style **Green Welly Restaurant** (mains to £8), which is liable to be flooded by bus parties. It offers generous servings of standard dishes. The weather forecast is prominently displayed at the store.

By the way (☎ 01838-400333; www.tyndrum bytheway.com; sites for 2 £5, cabins £8-10, dm £15) provides excellent facilities, including a campers' kitchen.

Strathfillan House B&B (☎ 01838-400228; www .tyndrum.com; s/d £24/48) does a special deal for walkers, including pick-up and drop-off.

Invervey Hotel (☎ 01838-400219; www.invervey hotel.co.uk; s/d £28/48, bar meals £6-8) has comfortable rooms and a large bar.

Brodie's (☼ daily) mini-market is an off-licence selling hot takeaway snacks and camping gas.

Day 5: Tyndrum to Kings House Hotel

6½–8 hours, 19 miles (30.5km)

You need to make an early start for this, the longest day of the walk. Mainly on good surfaces, the walk is not difficult but it does cross Rannoch Moor, the wildest section of the West Highland Way. The only places for food are the Bridge of Orchy Hotel and, an hour beyond, the Inveroran Hotel.

From Tyndrum the Way soon rejoins the old military road, affording easy walking with lovely views. Three miles from Tyndrum you cross a burn at the foot of Beinn Dòrain (1074m), the mountain that dominates this section of the path. The path climbs gradually to pass the entrance to Glen Orchy, crossing the railway again en route; here the really mountainous scenery begins.

The settlement of Bridge of Orchy is dominated by the **Bridge of Orchy Hotel** (☎ 01838-400208; www.scottish-selection.co.uk; dm/s/d £15/55/90), where you can live it up in the hotel or stay in the bunkhouse. The latter doesn't have a kitchen, but the bar serves good food. The **West Highland Way Sleeper** (☎ 01838-400548; www.westhighlandwaysleeper.co.uk; dm £15), in the old station building, does have a kitchen, and en suite rooms. There is a free camp site (no facilities) just over the bridge on the right.

Cross the old bridge (built in 1750) and climb through the trees to moorland, from where there are superb views across to Rannoch Moor. The Way follows a good path down to the secluded **Inveroran Hotel** (☎ 01838-400220; www.inveroran.com; s/d £38/70). There's another camp site (no facilities) beside a stone bridge 400m west of the hotel.

The Way follows a road, which soon becomes a track, climbing gently past some plantations and out onto **Rannoch Moor**. There's no shelter for about 7 miles and Bà Bridge, about 3 miles beyond the plantations, is the only real marker point. It can be very wild and windy up here and there's a real sense of isolation. A cairn marks the summit at 445m and from here there's a wonderful view down into Glen Coe.

As the path descends from the moor to join the road again, you can see the chair lift of the Glen Coe Ski Centre to the left. There's a **café** and skiing museum at the base station, about 500m off the Way. Kings House Hotel is just over 1 mile ahead, across the A82.

KINGS HOUSE HOTEL

Dating from the 17th century, the **Kings House Hotel** (☎ 01855-851259; www.kingy.com; s/d £35/60, bar meals £8-12) was used after the Battle of Culloden as a barracks for the troops of George III's troops, hence the name.

The hotel is popular with climbers busy on the peaks in Glen Coe, and if you can't get a bed you could consider taking a bus to Glencoe (p370), 11 miles away. However, during summer any bus could well be full, and you'd be dependent on the first morning bus from Fort William to bring you back.

Day 6: Kings House Hotel to Kinlochleven

3–4 hours, 9 miles (14.5km)

The superb mountain scenery continues. This day is not long, but includes the 330m climb up the Devil's Staircase and a long, knee-cracking descent to Kinlochleven. There's no-where to buy food en route and no shelter.

From Kings House Hotel the route follows the old military road, then goes beside the A82 to a car park at Altnafeadh. This is a wonderful vantage point from which to appreciate the mountainous scenery of Glen Coe. The conical mountain to your left is Buachaille Etive Mór (p370) and the ascent of the peak starts here at Altnafeadh.

From here the Way turns right and leaves the road to begin a steep, zigzagging climb up the **Devil's Staircase**. The cairn at the top is at 548m and marks the highest point of the whole walk. The views are stunning, especially on a clear day, and you should be able to see Ben Nevis to the north.

The path winds gradually down towards Kinlochleven, hidden below in the glen. As you descend you join the Blackwater Reservoir access track and meet the pipes that carry water down to the town's hydroelectric power station. They may not be pretty but they were essential for the now-defunct aluminium smelter, the original reason for the town's existence. Follow the somewhat tortuous route, across the pipes then along minor roads into Kinlochleven.

KINLOCHLEVEN

This town eases you back into 'civilisation' before the sensory onslaught of Fort William. There isn't an ATM but the supermarket can oblige with cash-back on UK bankers' cards. The **Aluminium Story Visitor Centre** (☎ 01855-831663; Linnhe Rd; admission free; ☺ Mon-Fri) is worth a look to make sense of the incongruously massive buildings dominating the village.

Blackwater Hostel & Campsite (☎ 01855-831253; www.blackwaterhostel.co.uk; Lab Rd; sites for 2 £10, dm £12) has well-maintained, pine-panelled dorms with en suite facilities, and grassed tent pitches.

Tailrace Inn (☎ 01855-831777; www.tairaceinn .co.uk; Riverside Rd; s/d £40/70, bar meals £8-14) has tastefully furnished rooms and features live music some evenings.

Macdonald Hotel & Lochside Campsite (☎ 01855-831539; www.macdonaldhotel.co.uk; Fort William Rd; sites for 2 £10, cabin s/d £20/24, B&B s/d £55/80) is at the northern end of the village. The camp site is small and well-grassed; the cabins have four bunk beds. Campers' breakfasts (£4 to £7) are served in the bar.

Ice Factor (☎ 01855-831100; www.ice-factor.co.uk; Leven Rd; mains to £8; ☺ to 6pm, later Tue, Wed & Thu), in part of the former smelter, houses the world's largest indoor ice-climbing wall, plus a normal climbing wall so you can watch people performing amazing vertical feats while you enjoy a big pizza.

Both the **Co-op** supermarket and the **village store** are open daily.

Day 7: Kinlochleven to Fort William
5½–7 hours, 14 miles (22.5km)
The final day is one of the hardest, through varied terrain and with spectacular views that include Ben Nevis. There's little shelter, and nowhere to buy food until Glen Nevis, near the end of the Way.

From Kinlochleven follow the road north out of town and turn off to the right, opposite the school. The path climbs through woodland to the old military road, out in the open; here you can see far up the wide glen ahead. Climb gradually to the highest point (335m), which comes shortly before you reach the ruins of several old farm buildings at **Tigh-na-sleubhaich**. From here the route continues gently downhill and into conifer plantations 2 miles further on. After 1 mile you emerge at Blar a' Chaorainn, which is nothing more than a bench and an information panel.

The Way leads on and up, through more plantations; occasional breaks in the trees reveal fine views of Ben Nevis ahead. After

a few miles, a sign directs you to nearby **Dún Deardail**, an Iron Age fort with walls that have been partly vitrified (turned to glass) by fire.

A little further on, cross a stile and follow the forest track down towards Glen Nevis. Across the valley the huge bulk of Ben Nevis fills your view. A side track leads down to the village of Glen Nevis (p363), which could make a good base for an ascent of 'the Ben' (see p360).

Continue along the path towards Fort William, passing a small graveyard just before you meet the road that runs through Glen Nevis. Turn left here and soon there's a large tourist office (with toilets) on the right. Continue along the roadside down into Fort William (p362). The end of the West Highland Way, like many other British LDPs, is a bit of an anticlimax; just a sign by the busy but rather anonymous road junction on the edge of town, but you can look forward to an end-of-walk celebration in one of the town's several restaurants and bars.

MORE LONG-DISTANCE WALKS

If you are a long-distance enthusiast you may be interested in some of Scotland's other LDPs, especially if the West Highland Way sounds too busy and the Southern Upland Way too long and serious.

THE GREAT GLEN WAY
The Great Glen, the wide, deep trench that almost severs the Highlands from the rest of Scotland, cries out for an LDP. The Great Glen Way (GGW) takes full advantage of this with a magnificently scenic route from Fort William, below Ben Nevis, to Inverness, on the Moray Firth. In between are superb Loch Lochy, Loch Oich, Loch Ness and several fine hills. It follows long stretches of the historic Caledonian Canal's towpath, an old railway formation and quiet roads and tracks.

The GGW is 73 miles (117km) long; spread this over four or five days and you'll have a reasonably comfortable walk. The relatively small amount of climbing involved is mainly at the northeastern end. There is no shortage of accommodation;

the GGW passes through Gairlochy, Laggan, Fort Augustus, Invermoriston and Drumnadrochit. **VisitScotland** (☎ 0845 225 5121; www.visitscotland.com) is the best contact for accommodation bookings.

For up-to-date information about the Way, check the official **Great Glen Way website** (www.greatglenway.com), which includes details of accommodation and services. The Rucksack Readers guide *The Great Glen Way* by Jacquetta Megarry includes background information in a handy format. OS Landranger 1:50,000 maps No 26 *Inverness & Loch Ness*, 34 *Fort Augustus* and 41 *Ben Nevis* cover the route.

Fort William and Inverness are well served by bus and train services from Edinburgh, Glasgow and major English cities, and there are regular bus services through the Great Glen between the two towns.

Fort William is at the northern end of the West Highland Way (p418), so there's the opportunity for a really long walk of 168 miles (270km), linking Glasgow and Inverness.

THE SPEYSIDE WAY

The River Spey is Scotland's second-longest river and one of its most scenic. The Speyside Way has one end at Aviemore, overlooked by the Cairngorms, and the other at Buckie, on the North Sea coast. The Way closely follows the river for many miles and makes use of footpaths, old railway formations, forest roads and quiet rural roads. It passes through Boat of Garten, Nethy Bridge, Grantown-on-Spey, Cromdale, Aberlour, Craigellachie, Fochabers and Spey Bay. A spur route, from Bridge of Avon to Tomintoul (the highest village in the Highlands) provides an attractive walk in its own right. The Way is well signposted and waymarked with thistle-hexagon logos.

The Speyside Way can be followed in either direction, depending on whether you prefer to walk down the river or to travel from the sea to the mountains. The Way is 65 miles (105km) long; the Tomintoul Spur is 14.3 miles (23km) one way. It is possible to do the whole lot in five days, but six or seven allows time for visiting distilleries and the famous Strathspey Steam Railway.

The **Speyside Way Ranger Service** (☎ 01340-881266; www.speysideway.org) publishes a free annual accommodation brochure and a

public transport guide. Harvey's 1:40,000 map *Speyside Way*, the official map of the route, shows facilities and some features of interest. For coverage of the surrounding countryside you'll need OS Landranger 1:50,000 maps No 28 *Elgin & Dufftown* and 36 *Grantown & Aviemore*, which also show the route of the Way.

THE FIFE COASTAL PATH

Although Fife isn't a major walking area, it does have a scenic and varied coastline, much of it accessible via long-established paths. The Fife Coastal Path (FCP) incorporates these paths in a waymarked route linking North Queensferry, on the Firth of Forth in the south, with Tay Bridge, on the Firth of Tay in the north, a distance of 81 miles (135km).

Fife's coastal landscape bears the imprints of its industrial and maritime heritage, and a few less-than-lovely stretches of the FCP are better seen from the window of a bus, train or car. However, the constantly changing vistas across the Firth of Forth and along the subtly indented coast are the highlights of the FCP. The traditional fishing villages of Elie, Pittenweem and Crail are fascinating, bird life is plentiful along the rocky shores, common seals bask on the rocks in several places and the route passes through many fine woodlands.

With the most walker-friendly section in the northeast, North Queensferry is the place to start, saving the best until last; allow at least five days to go the full distance. The FCP's website at www.fifecoastalpath.co.uk has plenty of useful information, detailed maps and contacts for the five tourist offices that can help with accommodation bookings. *Along the Fife Coastal Path* by Hamish Brown, both a local and one of Scotland's best-known walkers, will be an excellent and invaluable companion. OS Landranger 1:50,000 maps No 59 *St Andrews*, 65 *Falkirk & Linlithgow* and 66 *Edinburgh* cover the area concerned. There are good public transport connections to and from the start, finish and intermediate towns.

ST CUTHBERT'S WAY

St Cuthbert's Way links Melrose and Lindisfarne (in Northumberland, England) on a route of great variety and interest, passing through places associated with the life and ministry of the 7th-century Celtic saint. It crosses the Eildon Hills and the Cheviot Hills in Northumberland National Park, follows sections of the beautiful Rivers Tweed and Teviot, and traverses fertile farmland. It follows footpaths, tracks and quiet country roads. At low tide you can cross to Lindisfarne by the causeway or by the Pilgrim's Route across the sands. The route is well waymarked, most prominently with the Way's own Celtic cross logo.

By starting at Melrose you'll follow Cuthbert's lifetime journey and finish with the inspirational experience of crossing the sands to Lindisfarne. The distance of 62.5 miles (101km) includes 1200m of ascent; you will probably need to allow five or six days to fit in with safe crossing times to Lindisfarne. The route links with the Pennine Way (p261) at Kirk Yetholm and the Southern Upland Way at Melrose (p408), thus making possible a grand long-distance walk from Edale in Derbyshire to either Portpatrick or Cockburnspath.

The relevant OS Landranger 1:50,000 maps are No 73 *Peebles, Galashiels & Selkirk*, 74 *Kelso & Coldstream* and 75 *Berwick-upon-Tweed*, while there's also the Harvey 1:40,000 map *St Cuthbert's Way*. The official guide, *St Cuthbert's Way* by Roger Smith and Ron Shaw, comprises a detailed guidebook and the Harvey map.

For accommodation bookings contact **VisitScotland Borders** (☎ 0870 608 0404; www .visitscottishborders.com) and **Berwick-upon-Tweed tourist office** (☎ 01289-330733). Vital information about safe crossing times to Lindisfarne is available from **Wooler tourist office** (☎ 01668-282123) and is displayed there at all times.

More Walks in Scotland

The variety of walking areas in Scotland is immense. The remote island groups of Orkney and Shetland (the Northern Isles) are as far north as you can go in Britain, and offer the finest coast walking anywhere in the country. 'Rocky landscape' takes on a new meaning in the far northwest. Here, vast areas of crags, slabs and cliffs are interspersed with lochs, waterfalls and distinctively shaped peaks. In the long chain of islands to the west you'll find myriad peaks and enough superb coastal walks to fill a lifetime of exploring. The Southwest and Borders is all about big rolling ridges, rounded summits and walks with varied historical themes. A brief outline of the best of these makes up this chapter. For more ideas, chase up Lonely Planet's *Walking in Scotland*.

HIGHLIGHTS

- Saying hello to Orkney's famous sea stack, the **Old Man of Hoy** (p430)
- Walking along the pristine beach at **Sandwood Bay** (p430) en route to the towering cliffs at Cape Wrath
- Revelling in the wild, rugged mountainscapes of Harris from the summit of the Western Isles' highest peak, **Clisham** (p431)
- Imagining yourself following Richard Hannay, hero of *The 39 Steps*, along the **John Buchan Way** (p431)

THE NORTHERN ISLES

Although they're lumped together for convenience, the Northern Isles – the island groups of Orkney and Shetland – are quite distinctive. Orkney, separated from the mainland's north coast by the turbulent waters of the narrow Pentland Firth, is very green, with lush fields cropped by sheep and cattle. Across 60 miles of Atlantic Ocean, Shetland is less fertile and more rugged and remote. The islands do share an attraction for walkers – some of Britain's finest coastal walking. Add a profusion of archaeological sites, countless sea birds and endless hours of summer daylight and you have two inspirational walking destinations.

In **Orkney** the largest island of Hoy is popular for the cliff-top walk to Europe's tallest sea stack, the 137m-high **Old Man of Hoy**. On the rugged west coast of Orkney Mainland, miles of good walking take you past rugged cliffs, deep narrow inlets and rocky islets. The smaller isle of Westray has a waymarked coastal walk, where puffin sightings are almost guaranteed. **VisitOrkney** (☎ 01856-875056; www.visitorkney .com) will get you started with accommodation lists and transport contacts. Ordnance Survey (OS) 1:50,000 Landranger maps No 5 *Orkney – Northern Isles*, 6 *Orkney – Mainland* and 7 *Orkney – Southern Isles* cover the islands. All the walks mentioned are described in full in Lonely Planet's *Walking in Scotland*, while pocket-sized *Walks – Orkney* by Felicity Martin succinctly describes 40 outings, from short strolls to day walks.

The **Shetland** island of Unst is the most northerly part of Britain, and a walk through its **Hermaness National Nature Reserve** is a must, to see the sea birds and Muckle Flugga lighthouse. For the finest coastal walking anywhere, head northwest from the capital, Lerwick, to the **Muckle Roe peninsula**; and to **Eshaness** for spectacularly colourful and rugged coastal scenery and amazingly easy walking. **VisitShetland** (☎ 08701 999440; www.visitshetland.com) is the best contact for planning a visit. The relevant OS 1:50,000 Landranger maps are No 1 *Shetland – Yell, Unst & Fetlar* and 3 *Shetland – Northern Mainland*.

NorthLink Ferries (☎ 0845 600 0449; www.north linkferries.co.uk) operates most of the services to the islands, from Scrabster on the north coast and from Aberdeen.

FAR NORTHWEST

Scotland's most sparsely populated quarter, northwest Sutherland, between Ullapool and the north coast, contains a good share of the wildest and most rugged mountains and glens in the country.

Several peaks offer an immense variety of walks, magnificent views and a keen sense of remoteness. The most northerly Munro, **Ben Hope** (927m), overlooks the north coast between Durness and Tongue. Its neighbour, shapely **Ben Loyal** (764m), graces the view south from the village of Tongue. Mighty **Ben More Assynt** (998m) and its satellite **Conival** (988m) provide a long, exhilarating day in limestone country. The star-shaped **Quinag** (808m), above Loch Assynt, comprises three separate summits. The massive tower **Suilven** (731m) is the icon of the northwest. Also worth mentioning are **Canisp** (847m), **Cul Mor** (849m) and serrated, easily accessible **Stac Pollaidh** (612m).

There are few, if any, finer stretches of coast than that between Oldshoremore and Cape Wrath, including incomparable **Sandwood Bay**. Start from the cape (via ferry and minibus from near Durness) or walk in to the bay from the road at Blairmore, near Kinlochbervie.

Probably the highest waterfall in Britain, **Eas a' Chual Aluinn**, with a drop of 200m to Loch Beag at the head of Loch Glencoul, is the centrepiece of another first-class walk. The usual approach is from the A894 between Skiag Bridge and Kylesku.

The definitive guide to the region is the Scottish Mountaineering Club's (SMC) *The Northwest Highlands* by DJ Bennett and T Strang. The area is covered by OS Landranger 1:50,000 maps No 9 *Cape Wrath*, 10 *Strathnaver*, 15 *Loch Assynt* and 16 *Lairg & Loch Shin*. Contact the **Assynt Visitor Centre** (☎ 01571-844330; www.assynt.co.uk; Lochinver) or the **Durness tourist office** (☎ 01971-511259; www .visithighlands.com) for more information.

THE HEBRIDES

Several of these islands off the west coast provide a wealth of first-class walking, spiced by the experience of being on an island. Here is a selection of what's on offer. For all the walks noted, the best single reference is the SMC's *The Islands of Scotland Including Skye*.

Separated from Morvern in Lochaber by a narrow strait, **Mull** is dominated by Ben More (966m), the only island Munro outside Skye, where magnetic rock plays havoc with compasses. East of Ben More, other groups of hills with long ridge walks worth exploring include those centred around Beinn Talaidh (761m) and Dun da Ghaoithe (766m). The south coast is very fine indeed, especially the cliffs and arches southwest of the village of Carsaig.

The main ferry service goes from Oban to Tobermory, the island's principal town. A small ferry crosses the Sound of Mull between Lochaline and Fishnish. Both are operated by **Caledonian MacBrayne** (CalMac; ☎ 0870 565 0000; www.calmac.co.uk). The **tourist office** (☎ 0870 720 0625; www.visitscottishheartlands .com; Tobermory; ☼ Apr-Oct) is centrally located at the Pier.

These walks are covered by the OS Landranger 1:50,000 maps No 48 *Iona & West Mull* and 49 *Oban & East Mull*.

The **Isle of Rum**, west of the fishing port of Mallaig, is owned by Scottish Natural Heritage (SNH), and its 30-or-so employees are the island's sole inhabitants. The traverse of its Cuillins, less formidable than Skye's mountains of the same name, is an absolutely first-class walk; even the names of the summits are tempting – Hallival (723m), Askival (812m), Trailival (702m) and Ainshval (781m).

The wild and rugged northwest coast is another possibility, and no trip to Rum is complete without an inspection of Kinloch Castle, built by an eccentric former island owner. A CalMac ferry links the island with Mallaig three times weekly. Accommodation is hostel-style in the castle, or in a tent at Kinloch. The Rum midges are ferocious, so a spring visit is recommended.

The OS Landranger 1:50,000 map No 39 *Rum, Eigg, Muck & Canna* and the SMC's *The Islands of Scotland including Skye* are essential. For up-to-date information about accommodation and facilities, contact **SNH** (☎ 01687-462026; www.snh.org.uk).

The **Western Isles**, stretching 130 miles (209km) from the Butt of Lewis in the north to Barra in the south, are a world apart from the rest of Scotland – peaceful, relaxed and a stronghold of Gaelic culture. Of the islands in the group, Harris is the most mountainous, with a cluster of rugged hills topped by Clisham (An Cliseam; 799m). On South Uist there are magnificent Atlantic-coast beaches and the impressive twin peaks of Hecla (606m) and Beinn Mhòr (620m), offering challenges greater than many much higher mainland hills. Tiny Barra has a splendid clutch of hills topping 300m and some fine beaches, one of which is the local airport.

CalMac ferries depart the mainland from Ullapool to Stornoway (Lewis), from Uig on the Isle of Skye to Tarbert (South Harris), and from Oban to Lochboisdale (South Uist) and Castlebay (Barra). The main tourist offices are in **Stornoway** (☎ 01851-703088; info@visitthebrides.com; 26 Cromwell St) and **Tarbert** (☎ 0845 225 5121; www.visitthebrides.com) on Harris. Of six relevant OS Landranger 1:50,000 maps, those most useful are No 14 *Tarbert & Loch Seaforth*, 22 *Benbecula & South Uist* and 31 *Barra & South Uist*.

THE SOUTHWEST & BORDERS

In the far southwest and close to the Southern Upland Way (p408) are the Galloway Hills, of which **Merrick** (843m) is the highest, offering a fine day out and magnificent views. Further east are **Hart Fell** (808m) and **White Coomb** (822m), as well as the beautiful waterfall, **Grey Mare's Tail**.

There's much more to walking in the Borders than tackling mountains, however. The 13.5 mile (22km) **John Buchan Way**, an essentially low-level walk, links Peebles and Broughton. The 65-mile (105km) **Borders Abbeys Way** connects four towns, each with a superb 12th-century abbey. For yet more variety, there's a wonderful 15-mile (24km) **coast path** between St Abb's Head and Berwick-upon-Tweed.

A booklet, *Walking Guide to the Scottish Borders*, outlines the wide range of walks available; two booklets – *Short Walks in the Eastern Section of The Southern Upland Way* and *Southern Upland Way Western Section Short Walks* – describe in some detail short circular walks based on the eastern and western sections of the Southern Upland Way. Several OS Landranger 1:50,000 maps cover the area. The SMC guide *Southern Uplands* by Ken Andrew is a mine of information. For more information contact the **Dumfries tourist office** (☎ 01387-253862; www.visitdumfriesandgalloway.co.uk) and the **Borders Information Service** (☎ 0870 608 0404; www.visitscottishborders.com).

WALKERS DIRECTORY

Walkers Directory

CONTENTS

The information in this chapter is aimed mainly at walkers visiting Britain from overseas (although some of it will also be useful to British walkers). For practical details on specific regions, see the Information Sources sections in the individual chapters. For more general information about the country, you'll need a general guidebook; naturally we recommend Lonely Planet's *Great Britain* guide.

ACCOMMODATION

The accommodation you use while walking in Britain is as varied as the routes you fol-low, and the range of choices (from basic bunkhouses to smart hotels) is all part of the attraction. In all the walk descriptions in this book we list places to stay. The list is not exclusive – they're usually the places we think are the best or most useful for walkers. In many areas you'll find more options. We first give the budget options (up to about £20 per person) then a selection of midrange places (from about £20 to £50 per person). Occasionally we recommend something over £50 because there's not much else in the lower price bands, or simply because we think it's a jolly nice place.

B&Bs & Guesthouses

The B&B ('bed and breakfast') is a great British institution. Basically, you get a room in somebody's house, and at smaller places you'll really feel part of the family. Larger B&Bs may have four or five rooms and more facilities. 'Guesthouse' is sometimes just another name for a B&B, although they can be larger, with higher rates.

B&Bs in country areas often offer a special welcome for walkers. You might stay in a village house, an isolated cottage or a farmhouse surrounded by fields. In towns and cities it's usually a suburban house. Wherever, facilities usually reflect price – for around £20 per person you get a simple bedroom and share the bathroom. For a few pounds more you get extras such as TV or a 'hospitality tray' (kettle, cups, tea, coffee) and a private bathroom down the hall. For around £25 to £30 you get all the above plus an en suite bathroom.

Breakfasts are traditionally enormous – just right to set you up for a day in the hills

---

WALKING CLUBS

There are many walking clubs in Britain, many of them local groups of large national organisations such as the **Youth Hostels Association** (www.yha.org.uk) or the **Ramblers' Association** (www.ramblers.org.uk) – the latter boasts over 500 local groups around the country. Hooking up with a local group is a great way to meet like-minded people. Other national clubs with local groups include the **Long Distance Walkers Association** (www.ldwa.org.uk) for mile-eaters and those who like a challenge, and the **Backpackers' Club** (www.backpackersclub.co.uk) for those who like to walk and camp, and be self-contained in the countryside. For details on individual clubs go to the main website of each organisation and follow the links to (or search for) 'local groups'.

PRACTICALITIES

- Good magazines for walkers include *TGO, Trail* and *Country Walking*, or dip into *Walk*, the magazine of the Ramblers' Association.
- Use electric plugs with three flat pins to connect appliances to the 220V (50Hz AC) power supply.
- Tune into BBC radio for a wide range of content, no adverts and good regular weather forecasts. BBC Radio Scotland carries specific weather forecasts for hill walkers.
- Be ready for a bizarre mix of metric and imperial weights and measures in Britain; for example, petrol is sold by the litre, but road distances are given in miles.

(see the boxed text on below for a rundown on the menu). In country areas, many B&Bs also offer evening meals (from around £10) and packed lunches (from around £3), although these must be ordered at least a day in advance. In these enlightened days, nearly all places will do a vegetarian breakfast, although this may be of the extra-egg-no-bacon type. Some B&Bs only serve breakfast between 8am and 9am, which is annoying if you want to make the most of the day, but places more used to walkers will happily serve breakfast earlier if you ask.

B&B prices are usually quoted per person, based on two people sharing a room (so doubles might be £40 to £60). Solo travellers have to search for single rooms and may pay a premium – around 75% of the double rate. Some B&Bs simply won't take single people (unless you pay the full double-room price), especially in summer.

Here are some more B&B tips:

- Advance reservations are always preferred at B&Bs, and are essential during popular periods. Many require a minimum two-night stay at weekends.
- Rates may rise at busy times (eg August) and differ from those quoted in this book. Conversely, rates may be cheaper in the 'low' (eg winter) season.
- Some B&Bs charge slightly higher rates at weekends.
- If a B&B is full, owners may recommend another place nearby (possibly a private house taking occasional guests, not in tourist listings).
- In cities, some 'B&Bs' are for long-term residents or people on welfare; they don't take passing walkers.
- In country areas, most B&Bs cater for walkers but some don't, so always let owners know if you'll be turning up with dirty boots.
- Some places reduce rates for longer stays (two or three nights) or for groups.
- When booking, check where the B&B is actually located. In country areas, postal addresses include the nearest town, which may be 20 miles away – important if you're walking! – although some B&B owners will pick you up by car for a small charge.

Bunkhouses & Camping Barns

Bunkhouses are simple places to stay, handy for walkers, cyclists or anyone on a budget in the countryside. They usually have a communal sleeping area and bathroom, heating and cooking stoves, but you provide the sleeping bag (and possibly

---

BRITISH BREAKFASTS

If you stay in B&Bs or visit cafés you will encounter a phenomenon called the 'Full English Breakfast' in England, and the 'Full Breakfast' everywhere else. This consists of bacon, sausage, egg, tomatoes, mushrooms, baked beans and fried bread. In B&Bs it's proceeded by cereals, served with tea or coffee and followed by toast and marmalade. In Scotland and northern England (if you're really lucky) you may get black pudding – a mixture of meat and fat and blood.

If you don't feel like eating half a farmyard it's quite OK to ask for just the egg and tomatoes. Some B&Bs offer other alternatives, such as kippers (smoked fish) or a continental breakfast, which completely omits the cooked stuff and may even add something exotic like croissants.

cooking gear). Most charge £7 to £10 per person per night.

Camping barns are even more basic. They are usually converted farm buildings, providing shelter for walkers and visitors to country areas. They have sleeping platforms, a cooking area and basic toilets outside. Take everything you'd need to camp, except the tent. Charges are around £5 per person.

Most bunkhouses and camping barns are privately owned, but the Youth Hostels Association handles information and reservations on their behalf. Other bunkhouses and camping barns are listed in the *Independent Hostel Guide* and website (www .independenthostelguide.co.uk).

MINOR RESERVATIONS

When booking major B&Bs and YHA hostels by phone, you can pay up front by credit card. Smaller B&Bs and independent hostels often accept phone bookings but do not require a deposit. If you book ahead and your plans change, please phone and let your accommodation know. Owners lose money by holding beds for people who never arrive, while turning away others who arrive on spec.

Camping

The opportunities for camping in Britain are numerous – great if you're on a tight budget or simply enjoy fresh air and the great outdoors – although a tent is not essential for any of the walks described in this book.

If you're from overseas, forget the backwoods/bushwalk type of camping of Australasia and North America, where you can pitch a tent anywhere. It just doesn't work like that in Britain, except in very remote areas (and by that we mean more than half a day's walk from an official site or any other form of accommodation) where wild camping *may* be tolerated by landowners.

The usual way of doing things is to camp at a campground (called a camp site in Britain). In rural areas, these range from farmers' fields with a tap and a basic toilet, to smarter affairs with hot showers and many other facilities. For an idea of just how smart some can be, we recommend *Cool Camping: England* by Jonathan Knight, a coffee-table book in the Hip Hotels tradition, listing 40 exceptional camp sites and proving that sleeping under canvas doesn't need to be damp and uncomfortable any more. Volumes covering Wales and Scotland are planned.

Many cities and towns, especially near popular walking areas, have well-appointed camp sites, although these are usually some distance from the centre, which can be awkward if you want to go in for shopping or something to eat.

Rates at camp sites range from around £3 per person at a very basic site, up to around £8 at those with more facilities. Some sites also charge per tent or per car (if that's how you're travelling). To simplify matters, many places charge 'per pitch' – usually the price of a tent and two people. We have quoted 'sites for 2' rates throughout this book, unless the charging structure is different.

If you don't mind carrying a full pack, most national trails and other long-distance paths (LDPs) are fairly well served by camp sites, but you can sometimes find a long section without a camp site. In this case, if you ask nicely, farmers may permit your tent in their field on a one-off basis. Remember that all land is private in Britain, so if you camp without permission you could be moved on rather aggressively. If you can't find anyone to ask, be very discreet. Use your common sense too: don't camp in crop fields, for example, and be meticulous about waste. Leaving a mess spoils things for the next walkers, possibly endangers wildlife and makes landowners less likely to allow camping in the future.

A final note: always carry a stove. Open fires are not normally allowed on official sites or for wild camps. They can be dangerous and quite often there isn't enough wood anyway.

Hostels

There are two types of hostel in Britain: those run by the Youth Hostels Association (YHA) or Scottish Youth Hostels Association (SYHA), and independent hostels. You'll find them in rural areas, towns and cities, and they're aimed at all types of traveller – whether you're a long-distance walker or touring by car – and you don't have to be young or single to use them.

AVOIDING THE BULGE

If you're walking a national trail or other long-distance path (LDP), especially one that's about six or 12 days long, try to avoid starting on a weekend, as that's when most people begin, creating a 'bulge' of demand for accommodation along the route. Several B&Bs on the Coast to Coast Walk, for instance, are often quiet most of the week and then have to turn people away on the busy one or two nights when most walkers come through.

YHA & SYHA HOSTELS

Many years ago, YHA and SYHA hostels had a reputation for austerity, but today they're a great option for budget travellers. Some are purpose-built, but many are in cottages and country houses – even castles – often in wonderful locations. Facilities include showers, drying rooms, lounges and equipped self-catering kitchens. Sleeping is in dormitories, but many hostels also have twin or four-bed family rooms, some with private bathroom.

If you're planning to stay in several YHA or SYHA hostels, you should join the **YHA** (☎ 0870 770 8868; www.yha.org.uk; per year £16, under 26 £10), **SYHA** (☎ 0870 155-3255; www.syha.org.uk, per year £8, under 18 £4) or another Hostelling International (HI) organisation. Accommodation charges vary – small hostels cost around £10 to £13 per person, while larger hostels with more facilities are £10 to £20. SYHA hostels in Edinburgh and Glasgow cost from £18, while London's excellent YHA hostels cost from £25. Students, under-26s and over-60s get discounts. If you're not a YHA/SYHA/HI member (or you're only planning to stay in one or two hostels during your trip and it's not worth joining) you pay around £3 extra per night in England and Wales, and about £1 extra in Scotland.

Most hostels in England and Wales offer meals, and charge about £4 to £5 for breakfasts and packed lunches, and around £6 for good-value three-course dinners. Meals at SYHA hostels are usually not available.

Hostels tend to have complicated opening times and days, especially out of tourist season, so check these before turning up. Small rural hostels may close from 10am to 5pm. Reservations are usually possible – many can be booked through the websites and you can often pay in advance by credit card.

One final warning: the YHA constantly monitors its hostels, and sometimes has to close them down – because they've become too expensive to operate, too old to main-tain, or simply don't get enough guests. All the YHA hostels listed in this book were open at the time of research, but be prepared for some to close down (and some new hostels to open) over the life of this book.

INDEPENDENT HOSTELS

Britain's independent hostels and backpacker hostels offer a great welcome. In rural areas, some are little more than simple bunkhouses (charging around £5), while others are almost up to B&B standard, charging £15 or more.

In cities, backpacker hostels are perfect for young budget travellers. Most are open 24/7, with a lively atmosphere, a good range of rooms (doubles or dorms), bar, café, internet and laundry. Prices are around £15 for a dorm bed, or £20 to £35 for a bed in a private room.

Hotels

A hotel in Britain can be a simple place with a few rooms or a huge country house with fancy facilities, grand staircases, acres of grounds and the requisite row of stag heads on the wall. Charges vary as much as quality and atmosphere, with singles/doubles costing £30/40 to £100/150 or beyond. More money doesn't always mean a better hotel – whatever your budget, some are excellent value while others overcharge.

If all you want is a place to put your head down when travelling between walking areas, and you're unconcerned about style or ambience, chain hotels (often along motorways and busy roads) can offer bargains. For example, **Travelodge** (www.travelodge .co.uk) offers rooms at variable prices based on demand; on a quiet night in November, twin-bed rooms with private bathroom start from £15, while at the height of the tourist season you'll pay up to £45. Other chains include **Hotel Formule 1** (www.hotelfor mule1.com), with rooms from £25.

In London and other cities you can find similar places – motorway-style, in the centre of town – that can be very good value, although often lacking somewhat in soul. These include **Premier Travel Inn** (www.premier travelinn.com) and **easyHotel** (www.easyhotels.com), the latter with no-frills, airline-style rates and rooms.

Pubs & Inns

As well as selling drinks, many pubs and inns offer B&B, particularly in country areas. Staying in a pub can be good fun – you're automatically at the centre of the community – although accommodation varies enormously, from fairly basic rooms with ageing furniture and frayed carpets to stylishly decorated suites with good facilities. Expect to pay around £15 per person at the cheap end, though more usually around £25, and up to around £35 for something better. A major advantage for solo tourists is that pubs are more likely to have single rooms.

If a pub does B&B, it normally also has evening meals, served in the bar or adjoining restaurant. Breakfast may also be served in the bar the next morning – not always enhanced by the smell of stale beer…

Rental Accommodation

If you want to concentrate on walking in one area for a week or two, renting a place can be ideal. You can choose from neat town apartments, quaint old country houses or converted farms (although they're always called 'cottages'), all set up for self-catering.

At busy times (especially July and August) you'll need to book ahead. Cottages for four people cost around £200 to £400 per week. At quieter times, £150 to £200 is more usual, and you may be able to rent for a long weekend.

ACCOMMODATION CONTACTS

The national tourism sites – www.enjoyengland.com, www.visitwales.com and www.visitscotland .com – all have comprehensive accommodation sections. All hotels listed are approved by these tourism boards, but have to pay to be inspected and listed.

For a countrywide view an excellent first stop is **Stilwell's** (www.stilwell.co.uk), a huge user-friendly database for independent tourists, listing holiday rental cottages, B&Bs, hotels, camp sites and hostels. Stillwell's is not an agency – once you've found what you want, you deal with the cottage or B&B owner direct. From the website you can also order a colour holiday-cottage brochure.

Other good agencies for holiday cottage rentals include **Hoseasons Country Cottages** (☎ 01502-502588; www.hoseasons.co.uk), while a good B&B site is **Bed & Breakfast Nationwide** (www.bedand breakfastnationwide.com), both with colour brochures.

Recommended guidebooks include the annually published *Good Hotel Guide* and the *Which? Good Bed & Breakfast Guide*. Both are genuinely independent – hotels have to be good, they can't pay to get in. For walker-friendly accommodation a book called *Walk Britain* is published annually by the Ramblers' Association, and is a very handy planning tool, also listing routes, gear shops, baggage carriers, local guidebooks, maps and more.

For details on hostels, contact the **YHA** (☎ 0870 770 6113, 01629-592708; www.yha.org.uk); the website also has information about bunkhouses, camping barns and YHA camp sites – even places where you can rent a tepee. In Scotland, the equivalent organisation is the **SYHA** (☎ 0870 155 3255; www.syha.org.uk).

The **Independent Hostel Guide** (www.independenthostelguide.co.uk) covers hundreds of non-YHA/ SYHA hostels in Britain and beyond, and is by far the best listing available. It's also available as a handy annually updated book at hostels or direct from the website. North of the border, there's the excellent **Scottish Independent Hostels** (www.hostel-scotland.co.uk).

If you're planning to camp extensively, or combine walking in Britain with touring in a camper-van or motorhome, it's well worth joining the friendly and efficient **Camping & Caravanning Club** (☎ 0845 130 7631; www.campingandcaravanningclub.co.uk; annual membership £30); this organisation owns almost 100 camp sites and lists thousands more in the invaluable *Big Sites Book* (free to members). Membership includes discounted rates on club sites and various other services, including special rates for cars on ferries.

REACH FOR THE STARS

As in most countries, the majority of hotels and B&Bs (and even hostels) in Britain are awarded stars according to their levels of quality and service. Walkers shouldn't worry *too* much about big numbers as many one- and two-star places are small and owner-managed, where guests feel especially welcome. Conversely, some five-star places have loads of facilities but can feel impersonal. In addition, because they have to pay to register with the tourist board before they're awarded any stars at all, many B&Bs don't bother, even though their service is absolutely fine. The moral: if you use official accommodation lists as your only source, you might miss out on a real gem.

Shelters & Bothies

Very simple shelters – often no more than a shed or a long-abandoned shepherd's hut – exist in some remote parts of England and Wales but are most common in Scotland, where they're called bothies. They're not locked or guarded, and those in Scotland are maintained voluntarily by the Mountain Bothies Association (MBA). There's no charge to use a bothy, but you're expected to stay one or two nights only, and groups of more than three are discouraged. There are no facilities and you need your own cooking equipment, sleeping bag and mat. In the last few years some bothies in popular areas have been overused to the point of destruction. Consequently, the MBA prefers the location of others to remain fairly secret. Some walks in this book pass near bothies but, unless essential, they're not listed. Where bothies are already marked on maps they can hardly be considered secret, so are listed. Whatever, if you find a bothy and use it, leave it as you found it (or better).

BAGGAGE SERVICES

Along most of the popular LDPs, commercial companies offer baggage-carrying services, transporting your kit from one B&B or hostel to the next, while you saunter along carrying just the stuff you need for the day. Some outfits cover just one route, and are listed in the relevant chapters. The main players covering several routes include:

Brigantes Walking Holidays & Baggage Couriers
(☎ 01729-830463; www.brigantesenglishwalks.com) Covers most of the popular LDPs in Britain, and is the only firm to cover the entire Pennine Way. Usually requires a minimum of four bags (so if you're solo you pay four times the rate, unless you can hook up with other walkers).

Sherpa Van (☎ 0871 520 0124; www.sherpavan.com) Baggage transfers on a very wide range of walks across the whole of Britain. The website also contains a wealth of information and useful planning tools.

Some baggage services also act as informal buses between destinations – ideal if you twist an ankle and can't walk for a day, or if you just want a rest!. The service is free if your bag is being transferred.

Alternatively, many B&Bs offer baggage transfers (if you're staying with them, of course). You can enquire when booking. In addition, local taxi services in walking areas are quite used to transporting bags rather than people – especially handy if you don't think you'll need this service for the whole route. Local tourist offices and B&Bs can advise on taxi firms offering this service.

Costs for baggage transfer with the commercial companies vary from £5 to £20 per bag per stage, so it's obviously worth shopping around. You may be able to use these services for a couple of stages, while some companies insist you sign up for the whole route. Taxis and B&Bs tend to charge for the journey, rather than the bag – obviously making it cheaper for groups.

BUSINESS HOURS
Banks, Shops & Offices

Monday to Friday, most offices, businesses, shops, banks and post offices operate from 9am to 5pm (possibly 5.30pm or 6pm in cities). On Saturday, shops keep the same hours, while Sunday shopping hours are around 11am to 4pm.

In smaller towns, shops tend to close at weekends and for lunch (normally 1pm to 2pm), and in country areas on Wednesday or Thursday afternoon too. In cities and large towns, there's usually late-night shopping on Thursday – up to about 7pm or 8pm.

London and large cities have 24-hour convenience stores. At the other end of the scale, in the Outer Hebrides some locals adhere strictly to the Scriptures, so on Sunday nearly all shops are shut, most pubs are closed and even the public toilets can be padlocked.

Museums & Sights

When it comes to sightseeing, large museums and major places of interest are usually open every day. Some smaller places will open just five or six days per week, usually including Saturday and Sunday and closing on Monday and/or Tuesday. Much depends on the time of year, too; places of interest will open daily in high season, but may open just at weekends (or keep shorter hours) in quieter periods.

Pubs, Bars & Clubs

Pubs in towns and country areas in England and Wales usually open daily from 11am to 11pm, sometimes to midnight Friday and Saturday. Some may shut from 3pm to 6pm. In Scotland, pubs tend to close later; 1am is normal and 3am is not unusual. Throughout this book, we don't list pub opening and closing times unless they vary significantly from these hours.

In cities, some pubs open until midnight or later, but it's mostly bars and clubs that have taken advantage of new licensing laws in England and Wales ('the provision of late night refreshment', as it's officially called) to stay open to 1am, 2am or later.

Restaurants & Cafés

Restaurants in Britain open either for lunch (about noon to 3pm) *and* dinner (about 6pm to 10pm in smaller towns, up to 11pm or midnight in cities, and often as early as 8pm in country areas), or they might open for lunch *or* dinner only – depending on the location. Restaurants are usually open every day of the week, although some places may close on Sunday evening, or all day Monday.

Café and teashop hours also vary according to location. In towns and cities, cafés may open from 7am, providing breakfast for people on their way to work. Others stay open until 5pm or 6pm. In country areas, cafés and teashops will open in time for lunch, and may stay open until 7pm or later in the summer, catering to tourists leaving stately homes or hikers down from the hill.

In this book, many restaurants and cafés are listed and reviewed, and we indicate if they're open for lunch or dinner or both, but precise opening times and days are given only if they differ markedly from the pattern outlined here.

In winter months in country areas, café and restaurant hours will be cut back, while some places may close completely from October to Easter.

CHILDREN

Many parts of Britain are ideal for walking with children under the age of 10. But many other parts are not – being too high, too steep or requiring too much effort to reach. Several of the routes in this book are suitable for kids aged 11 to 15 – mostly the day walks graded 'easy' – but as much depends on attitude and enthusiasm as on fitness or ability. Long-distance walks are another matter; some young people don't have the stamina for multiday routes, but for those over 16, many of the national trails are feasible, although in some cases the daily distances may need to be trimmed. Lonely Planet's *Travel with Children* contains plenty of useful information. Look out, too, for the excellent *Family Walks* series of guidebooks, published by **Scarthin** (www.scarthinbooks.com).

WHERE THERE'S SMOKE

For years, the regulations concerning smoking in restaurants in Britain have been vague or non-existent. Some places provided no-smoking areas, while others didn't bother – meaning the smokers at the next table wouldn't hesitate to spark up even if you were halfway through your meal. But those days are over: a new Health Act came into force in summer 2007, banning smoking in 'all enclosed public places apart from licensed premises that do not serve or prepare food' throughout England and Wales, replicating similar laws already in force in Scotland. In short, this means all restaurants in Britain will be completely nonsmoking, as will pubs serving food. Pubs that make most of their money from beer, as opposed to food, will probably stop offering dodgy pies and cheese rolls, and allow smoking to continue. Through 2006 a fascinating debate raged: does a packet of peanuts count as 'food'? And what about pickled eggs? By the time you read this book, we'll know.

CLIMATE

In keeping with its geography, the climate of Britain varies widely from place to place. It also varies from day to day, so visitors will soon sympathise with the locals' conversational obsession with the weather.

The winter months (November, December, January and February) are generally least pleasant for walking. It's cold and the days are short, although the hills are less crowded. Snow and ice intermittently cover many highland areas from about December, making walking on hills and mountains potentially dangerous without experience, although nothing can be more exhilarating than a walk in clear sunlight across a snow-covered mountain. Generally, the further east you go the drier it gets and the further north you go the colder it gets (although temperature is also greatly influenced by altitude).

Through the rest of the year (March to October) the weather can be good for walking – it's often dry and cool, and sometimes even warm. In summer, temperatures can become hot and you'll need sunscreen to avoid getting burnt, even if it's windy and overcast.

The following sections provide a bit more detail.

England

Climatologists classify England's climate as 'temperate maritime', for which you can read 'mild and damp'. Light winds that blow off warm seas stop inland winter temperatures falling very far below 0°C and keep summer temperatures from rising much above 30°C. The average high in southern England from June to August is 21°C and the average low is 12°C. It tends to be colder in the north of England, but not as cold as in Scotland. Rainfall is greatest in hilly areas, such as the Lake District and Pennines, but you can expect some cloudy weather and rain anywhere in Britain at any time.

Scotland

'Varied' may be a vague description but it perfectly describes Scotland's climate. One good thing about the weather is that it does change quickly – a rainy day is often followed by a sunny one. In the mountains there are also wide variations over short distances; while one glen broods under cloud, the next may enjoy full sunshine.

Considering the latitude (Edinburgh is as far north as Moscow), you might expect a colder climate, but warm Atlantic winds give the west coast a relatively mild climate, with average summer highs of 19°C. May and June are generally the driest months (as with the rest of Britain, rainfall generally decreases as you go east) and the best time for mountain walking. Note, however, that the Highlands can have extreme weather at any time; in the Cairngorms snow has been recorded in *every* month of the year.

Wales

Temperatures are about on a par with England, but Wales gets a bit more rain. That said, the closeness of the mountains to the coast means you encounter very different climatic conditions within a relatively short distance. In practice this means if it's raining, it will be fine somewhere nearby. It also means you can get sun, then rain, then sun again within a couple of hours.

Weather Information

Walking in Britain is remarkably care-free, but walkers should never underestimate the changeability of the weather, especially in highland or coastal areas, where low cloud, fog, rain and snow can mean trouble for the unprepared. The problem can be minor – you get lost in the mist for a while, or get slightly wet in a rain shower – but things can get much more serious if the fog is thick, or if temperatures drop below freezing.

So before you go walking, always check the weather. General forecasts are available on TV and radio, and it's always worth checking the outlook the day before you walk. In national parks and tourist areas, weather bulletins are posted at tourist offices, hostels, outdoor gear shops and cafés frequented by walkers.

There are also several online and telephone information services. Good places to start, are the **BBC Weather Service** (www.bbc .co.uk/weather) and **Met Office Weather** (www.met office.gov.uk). Both offer next-day and five-day forecasts at a national, regional and local level. The Met Office also has a forecast service especially designed for walkers in the hills at www.metoffice.gov.uk/loutdoor /mountainsafety.

Climate

0   100 km
0   50 miles

Inset 2

SHETLAND ISLANDS

Uist

Lerwick

Foula

60°N

1°W

2°E

58°N

56°N

ELEVATION

1000m (3250ft)
500m (1625ft)
200m (650ft)
100m (325ft)
0m
Below Sea Level

NORTH SEA

LERWICK 82m (269ft)
Temp   Average Max/Min   Rainfall

INVERNESS 9m (30ft)
Temp   Average Max/Min   Rainfall

EDINBURGH 41m (135ft)
Temp   Average Max/Min   Rainfall

NEWCASTLE 81m (266ft)
Temp   Average Max/Min   Rainfall

Westray
Mainland
Hoy

ORKNEY ISLANDS

Cape Wrath

The Minch

Butt of Lewis

Lewis

Little Minch

North Uist

South Uist

St Kilda

OUTER HEBRIDES

Skye

Rum

Coll

Tiree

Mull

Colonsay

Islay

Jura

INNER HEBRIDES

Moray Firth

Inverness

Loch Ness

Spey

Dee

Grampians

Northwest Highlands

Ben Nevis (1344m)

Fort William

Loch Awe

SCOTLAND

GLASGOW

Firth of Clyde

Arran

North Channel

Firth of Forth

EDINBURGH

Lammermuir Hills

Tweed

Cheviot Hills

Pennines

Eden

Southern Uplands

Solway Firth

Nith

Holy Island

NEWCASTLE UPON TYNE

Tyne

ATLANTIC OCEAN

10°W   8°W   6°W   4°W   2°W   0°

FORT WILLIAM 20m (66ft)
Temp   Average Max/Min   Rainfall

GLASGOW 8m (26ft)
Temp   Average Max/Min   Rainfall

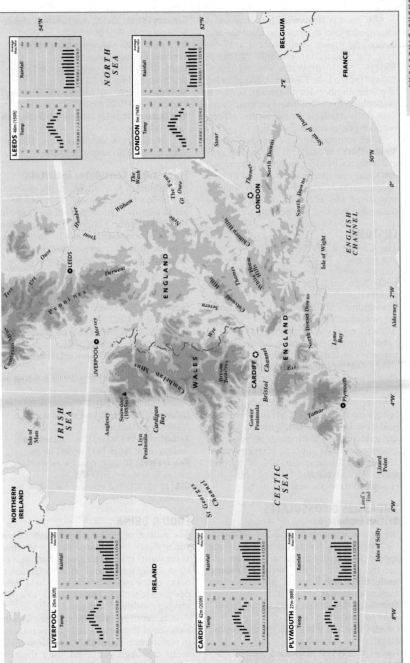

Also good is **WeatherCall** (www.weathercall.co .uk); this site uses information from the Met Office and makes local forecasts available over the phone, for example ☎ 09068-500415 for North Wales and ☎ 09068-500419 for the Lake District. A complete list of phone numbers for all areas in Britain is available on the website, and on small 'business cards' available free at tourist offices, outdoor gear shops and the like.

Other automated phone services include **WeatherCheck** (☎ 0900-133 3111), offering general outlooks; by using the phone keypad you can home into specific areas around Britain. Similar services are advertised in walking magazines and at tourist offices. Calls to these numbers cost 60p per minute.

CUSTOMS

The UK has a two-tier customs system – one for goods bought in from another EU country, where taxes and duties have already been paid; and the other for goods bought duty-free outside the EU. Following is a summary of the rules; for more details see www.hmce.gov.uk or under 'Customs Allowances' at www.visitbritain.com.

For duty-free goods from *outside* the EU, the limits include 200 cigarettes, 2L of still wine plus 1L of spirits or another 2L of wine, 60cc of perfume, and other duty-free goods (including beer) to the value of £145.

There is no limit to the goods you can bring from *within* the EU (if taxes have been paid), but customs officials use the following guidelines to distinguish personal use from commercial imports: 3000 cigarettes, 200 cigars, 10L of spirits, 20L of fortified wine, 90L of wine and 110L of beer – still enough to have one hell of a party.

EMBASSIES & CONSULATES
British Embassies

Below is a selection of Britain's embassies (or consulates and high commissions where appropriate) overseas; for a complete list, see the website of the **Foreign & Commonwealth Office** (www.fco.gov.uk), which also lists foreign embassies in the UK.

Australia (☎ 02-6270 6666; www.britaus.net; Commonwealth Ave, Yarralumla, ACT 2600)
Canada (☎ 613-237 1530; 80 Elgin St, Ottawa, Ontario K1P 5K7)
France (☎ 01 44 51 31 00; www.amb-grandebretagne.fr; 35 rue du Faubourg Saint Honoré, 75383 Paris Cedex 8)

Germany (☎ 030-204 570; www.britischebotschaft.de; Wilhelmstrasse 70, 10117 Berlin)
Ireland (☎ 01-205 3700; www.britishembassy.ie; 29 Merrion Rd, Ballsbridge, Dublin 4)
Japan (☎ 03-5211 1100; www.uknow.or.jp; 1 Ichiban-cho, Chiyoda-ku, Tokyo 102-8381)
Netherlands (☎ 070-427 0427; www.britain.nl; Lange Voorhout 10, 2514 ED The Hague)
New Zealand (☎ 04-924 2888; www.britain.org.nz; 44 Hill St, Wellington)
USA (☎ 202-588 6500; www.britainusa.com; 3100 Massachusetts Ave, NW, Washington, DC 20008)

Embassies & Consulates in Britain

A selection of foreign diplomatic missions in London is given below. This will be of use to tourists from overseas if, for example, you've lost your passport. But remember that these embassies won't be much help if you're in trouble for committing a crime locally; even as a foreigner, you are bound by the laws of Britain.

Australia (☎ 020-7379 4334; www.australia.org.uk; Australia House, Strand, WC2B 4LA)
Canada (☎ 020-7258 6600; www.canada.org.uk; 1 Grosvenor Sq, W1X 0AB)
China (☎ 020-7299 4049; www.chinese-embassy.org.uk); 49–51 Portland Place, London W1B 4JL)
France (☎ 020-7073 1000; www.ambafrance-uk.org; 58 Knightsbridge, SW1 7JT)
Germany (☎ 020-7824 1300; www.german-embassy.org .uk; 23 Belgrave Sq, SW1X 8PX)
Ireland (☎ 020-7235 2171; 17 Grosvenor Pl, SW1X 7HR)
Japan (☎ 020-7465 6500; www.uk.emb-japan.go.jp; 101 Piccadilly, W1J 7JT)
Netherlands (☎ 020-7590 3200; www.netherlands -embassy.org.uk; 38 Hyde Park Gate, SW7 5DP)
New Zealand (☎ 020-7930 8422; www.nzembassy .com/uk; 80 Haymarket, SW1Y 4TQ)
USA (☎ 020-7499 9000; www.usembassy.org.uk; 24 Grosvenor Sq, W1A 1AE)

FOOD & DRINK

The nature of walking in Britain means you're never more than a day's walk (two at the most) from a café, restaurant, pub or shop selling food – and often much closer. Many of the routes in this book have been designed to include a café at lunch, or a pub serving good food at the end of the day.

In larger towns and cities, there's usually a choice of restaurants and takeaways, and in remote areas some B&Bs provide evening meals (although you must order these in advance). Where there's no midway café or pub you'll need to provide your own food, or take advantage of the packed lunches offered by some B&Bs.

If you're camping or self-catering, you can buy supplies as you go. When walking, you're rarely more than a day or two from a village shop selling bread, milk, tinned or dried groceries and fresh fruit and vegetables (although there may be little choice in the last). Shops for resupplying on long walks are listed in the route descriptions.

When it comes to drinking, many walks pass a shop, pub or café, but some don't, so if you're walking for more than a few hours it's worth carrying some water. And if you're going all day without a café stop, then carrying water is definitely recommended – and essential in hot weather.

Where to Eat & Drink

Whether out on the hills or back at base at the end of the day, walkers often have a good choice of places to eat. In rural areas, the British café (often shortened to 'caff') is nothing like its stylish Continental namesake. Most are simple places serving cheap, filling food at reasonable prices (£2 to £4). Around Britain are a number of 'classic cafés' popular with walkers and climbers – and often as famous as the mountain routes nearby. Teashops are slightly more upmarket than cafés, and serve snacks and light meals as well as tea and coffee, usually at slightly higher prices. Note that between about October and March or April, most cafés keep shorter hours, open on weekends only or even shut completely.

The pub (along with the B&B) is a great British institution. One of the great pleasures of walking in Britain is stopping for refreshment at a pub, and a pint or two is always very welcome after a good long walk on the hills. Many walkers plan a route around a midday beer, or go to a certain

---

MINE'S A PINT

Although the Brits are famous for enjoying a 'cuppa' (cup of tea) at any opportunity, among alcoholic drinks Britain is best known for its beer. Typical British beer is technically called 'ale', dark brown to brick red in colour, and generally served at room temperature. It's more commonly called 'bitter' in England and Wales. This is to distinguish it from 'lager' – the drink that most of the rest of the world calls beer – which is generally yellow and served cold. (In Scotland, ales are designated by strength – light, heavy, export, strong – or by a notional 'shilling' scale; so you'd order a 'pint of heavy' or a 'pint of eighty shilling' rather than simply a 'pint of bitter'.)

International lager brands such as Fosters and Budweiser are available in Britain but, as you travel around the country, you should definitely try some traditional beer, also known as 'real ale'. But be ready! If you're used to the 'amber nectar' or 'king of beers', a local British brew may come as a shock. A warm, flat and expensive shock. This is partly to do with Britain's climate, and partly to do with the beer being served by hand pump rather than gas pressure. Most important, though, is the integral flavour: traditional British beer doesn't *need* to be chilled or fizzed to make it palatable. (Drink a cheap lager that's sat in its glass for an hour and you'll see it has very little actual taste.)

And flavour is the key. Once you're used to British beer, you can start experimenting with some of the hundreds of different regional types, all with varying textures, tastes and strengths. The difference between these ales and mass-produced lagers is like the difference between fine wines and industrial plonk, or between gourmet food and a burger. The **Campaign for Real Ale** (www.camra.org.uk) promotes the understanding of traditional British beer – and recommends good pubs that serve it. Look for endorsement stickers on pub windows, or get a copy of the Campaign's very useful and annually updated *Good Beer Guide*. For more depth and flavour, read *The Big Book of Beer* by Adrian Tierney-Jones.

Another key feature of real ales is their 'live' condition, so they only have a shelf life of a few weeks and must be looked after properly (which is why many pubs don't serve real ale). So if you find a pub serving real ale it usually means a willingness on the part of pub landlords to put in extra effort – on food and atmosphere, as well as beer. Beware of places promising real ale where bar staff give the barrels as much care as the condom machine in the toilets. There's nothing worse than a bad pint of real ale.

mountain because the nearby pub is good. There's even a good range of pub-walk guidebooks.

Most pubs – especially those in country areas frequented by tourists – serve snacks or bar meals as well as drinks, and make ideal places to eat at lunchtime or in the evening after your walk. Some cheap pub food doesn't vary much from café fare, but many pubs offer a good, interesting menu and reasonable prices (around £5 to £7). Some pubs are closer to restaurants, with very good food and higher prices (around £10 to £12). Many pubs actually do both, with cheaper food served in the bar, plus a pricier, more formal restaurant.

One final note about pubs: some welcome walkers straight off the path, others are less keen to have mud and other countryside matters deposited on their carpets. Some pubs have a specific bar for walkers with a stone floor and 'Muddy Boots Welcome' signs. Alternatively, where no such sign exists, it is perfectly acceptable to take your boots off and pad around in your socks (look for the other walkers' boots piled up on the porch), although this isn't always advisable if your morning has been a bit sweaty or you've been up to your knees in a peat bog.

FREE BEER?

When walking in the British countryside you'll come across pubs that call themselves a 'Free House'. This, unfortunately, doesn't mean there's no charge for the beer. It means the pub is privately owned, not part of a chain or belonging to a large brewery. These free houses are often worth seeking out as they tend to offer personal management, as well as good beer and food, whereas some chain pubs (like chain hotels) can be a bit impersonal. Pubs owned by (or 'tied' to) small local breweries are often of a similarly high quality.

HERITAGE ORGANISATIONS

For many walkers, highlights of Britain include visiting the numerous castles and other historic sites that pepper the country. If you're going to visit more than a handful of places, membership of Britain's heritage organisations is beneficial: you get free entry to properties, maps, information handbooks and so on.

The main organisations are listed below. You can join at the first site you visit. (If you're from overseas and a member of similar organisations, that membership may get you free or discounted entry at sites in Britain.)

Cadw (☎ 0800 074 3121; www.cadw.wales.gov.uk; annual membership adult £32, 16-20 years £18, child £14, family £37-55) The Welsh historic monuments agency. (The name means 'to keep' or 'to preserve'.) Cadw members are eligible for half-price admission to EH and HS sites.

English Heritage (EH; ☎ 0870 333 1181; www.english -heritage.org.uk; annual membership adult/couple £38/65, seniors £26/42) State-funded organisation responsible for the upkeep of numerous historic sites in England. Some are free to enter, while others cost £1.50 to £6. Alternatively, an Overseas Visitors Pass allows free entry to most EH sites for seven/14 days for £18/22 per person (cheaper rates for couples and families), and half-price entry for HS and Cadw sites.

Historic Scotland (HS; ☎ 0131-668 8600; www.historic -scotland.gov.uk; annual membership adult £36, seniors & students £27, family £68) Manages over 330 historic sites. Membership gives free admission to HS sites and half-price entry to EH and Cadw properties. 'Explorer' passes cost £18 for three days in five, £25 for seven days in 14 and £30 for 10 days in 30. Students and seniors get 25% discount on passes.

National Trust (NT; ☎ 0870 458 4000; www.national trust.org.uk; annual membership adult £40, under 26 years £18, family £55-73) This venerable body protects hundreds of historic buildings (normally around £5 to enter) plus vast tracts of land with scenic importance in England and Wales. Membership fees are reduced by about 25% if you pay by direct debit. Alternatively, a NT touring pass gives free entry to NT and NTS properties for seven or 14 days (£17/22 per person); families and couples get cheaper rates.

National Trust for Scotland (NTS; ☎ 0131-243 9300; www.nts.org.uk; annual membership adult £37, under 25 years £15, senior £27, family £60) The NT's sister organisation north of the border cares for over 100 properties and around 750 sq km of countryside.

HOLIDAYS
Public Holidays

In Britain, most businesses and banks close on public holidays (hence the quaint term 'bank holiday'). In Scotland, bank holidays are just for the banks, and many businesses stay open. Instead, Scottish towns normally have a spring and autumn holiday, but the dates vary from town to town.

Holidays for the whole of Britain (unless specified) are as follows:

New Year's Day 1 January
Good Friday March/April
Easter Monday (except Scotland) March/April
May Day First Monday in May
Spring Bank Holiday Last Monday in May
Summer Bank Holiday (Scotland) First Monday in August
Summer Bank Holiday (England & Wales) Last Monday in August
Christmas Day 25 December
Boxing Day 26 December

In Scotland, 2 January is also a holiday – so everyone can recover from Hogmanay.

Across Britain, if a public holiday falls on a weekend, the nearest Monday is usually taken instead. Some small museums and places of interest close on public holidays, but larger attractions specifically gear up, and this is their busiest time.

Generally speaking, if a place closes on Sunday, it'll probably be shut on bank holidays as well.

Virtually everything – shops, banks, offices, attractions – is closed on Christmas Day, although pubs are open at lunchtime. There's usually no public transport on Christmas Day, and a very restricted service on Boxing Day.

School Holidays

The main school holidays are generally as follows:

Easter Holiday The week before and week after Easter
Summer Holiday Third week of July to first week of September in England and Wales, early July to mid-August in Scotland
Christmas Holiday Mid-December to first week of January

There are three week-long 'half-term' school holidays – usually late February to early March and late May and late October. At school-holiday times, especially in the summer, roads and resorts get busy and prices go up.

INSURANCE

Visitors from overseas should take out a travel insurance policy to cover travel delays, cancellations, theft, loss and medical expenses in case you get ill or injured. Medical expenses are by far the most important component; mountain rescue is free in Britain (see p465 for information about

rescues) but it's imperative that private air ambulances and emergency flights home are covered by your policy. Read the small print too about 'dangerous activities' that are not covered – on some policies this includes walking in the mountains

Buy travel insurance as early as possible to ensure you'll be compensated for any unforseen accidents or delays. If items are lost or stolen get a police report as soon as you can, otherwise your insurer might not pay up.

Although citizens from EU and Commonwealth countries may be eligible for free medical treatment in Britain, this won't include all eventualities, so you still need insurance.

INTERNET ACCESS

Places with internet access are reasonably common in Britain, but you won't find them on every corner. Internet cafés in bigger cities charge around £1 per hour; out in the sticks you can pay up to £5 per hour. Public libraries often have free access, but only for 30-minute slots.

If you're planning to use your laptop to access the internet, your connection cable may not fit in British sockets, although adaptors are easy to buy at electrical stores in airports or city centres. Fortunately, to avoid hassle with wires and sockets, an increasing number of hotels, hostels and coffee shops (even some trains) have wi-fi access, charging anything from nothing to £5 per hour.

MAPS

In theory, Britain has moved to metric weights and measures – although nonmetric (imperial) equivalents are still used in many situations, including mapping. Some maps have a scale of one inch to 1 mile (which is 1:63,360 in case you wondered), while most road atlases are published with scales such as 'one inch to 3 miles' (and don't even quote a ratio figure). Even metric maps with scales of 1:50,000 or 1:25,000 – the most popular for walking – are still called 'one-inch maps' or '2½-inch maps' by die-hard ramblers.

For walkers, there are two main map publishers: **Ordnance Survey** (OS; www.ordnancesurvey.co.uk) and **Harvey Maps** (www.harveymaps.co.uk). OS Landranger maps (at 1:50,000) are ideal for long walks and route planning. OS Explorer

MAPS IN THIS BOOK

The maps in this book are intended to show the general routes of the walks we describe. They are primarily to help locate the route within the surrounding area. They are *not* detailed enough in themselves for route finding or navigation. You will still need a properly surveyed map at an adequate scale – specific maps are recommended in the Planning section for each walk. Most chapters also have a map showing the gateway towns or cities, principal transport routes and other major features. Map symbols are interpreted in the legend on the book's inside front cover.

On the maps in this book, natural features such as river confluences and mountain peaks are in their true position, but sometimes the location of villages and routes is not always so. This may be because a village is spread over a hillside, or the size of the map does not allow for detail of the path's twists and turns. However, by using several basic route-finding techniques, you will have few problems following our descriptions:

▪ Be aware of whether the path should be climbing or descending.

▪ Check the north-point arrow on the map and determine the general direction of the path.

▪ Time your progress over a known distance and calculate the speed at which you travel in the given terrain. From then on, you can determine with reasonable accuracy how far you have travelled.

▪ Watch the path. If there is no path, check your compass bearing.

---

maps (1:25,000) are better for walking in lowland areas, but can sometimes be hard to read in complex mountain landscapes. Harvey Maps produces an excellent range of very clear and accurate maps, mainly covering upland areas and national parks, plus strip maps for routes such as the Pennine Way and Coast to Coast (and many more), especially for ramblers, walkers, mountaineers, and other outdoor types.

If you're new to maps or walking in Britain, or both, a useful book is *Navigation for Walkers* by Julian Tippett – a very accessible guide from a leading expert.

Buying Maps

To buy maps of Britain, large bookshops and outdoor gear shops will usually keep a good stock. Smaller shops and tourist offices will stock maps of the local area.

If you're in London, you can buy in-store or online from **Stanfords** (☎ 020-7836 1321; www.stanfords.co.uk; 12-14 Long Acre, London WC2E 9LP). You can order maps online direct from **OS** (www.ordnancesurvey.co.uk) and **Harvey Maps** (www.harveymaps.co.uk). Other map specialists include **Latitude Maps & Globes** (☎ 01707-663090; www.latitudemapsandglobes.co.uk) and **Maps Worldwide** (☎ 01225-707004; www.mapsworldwide.com); both stock OS and Harvey maps, as well as a good range of walking guidebooks and handbooks.

Large-Scale Maps

The whole of Britain is covered by an excellent series of maps published by OS, once part of the military and now a government agency. Recently published OS 1:25,000 maps have amazingly accurate detail and are ideal for walkers, especially in lowland areas. However, the sheer degree of detail can be confusing in mountain areas and here many walkers prefer 1:50,000 maps instead.

Despite their popularity, OS maps have a number of quirks. One of these is that boundaries (national, county, parliamentary constituency) are marked more clearly than paths – particularly on 1:25,000 maps. In fact, the boundaries *look* like paths, and many inexperienced walkers get lost trying to follow a row of dots on the map that turns out to be a border. OS maps also mark rights of way even when no visible path exists on the ground. Conversely a path may exist that *isn't* shown on the map because it isn't legal. Note also that words that aren't proper nouns have capital initial letters (eg, Ford, Sheepfold, Sinkholes), making it hard to distinguish between features and actual place names. And finally, note that OS uses different symbols on 1:25,000 and 1:50,000 maps (eg footpaths are green dashes on the former and red dashes on the latter). But don't be put off by these gripes. OS maps are still among the best in the world. Once you're used to the idiosyncrasies you'll have no excuse for getting lost.

Harvey maps are becoming increasingly popular with walkers simply because they are specifically designed for them. For example, if a path exists on the ground, it's shown on a Harvey map; if it doesn't exist, it isn't shown. Invisible boundaries are also not shown, so although you may not know when you've passed from Yorkshire to Cumbria, it also means you won't follow the frontier. Another great advantage is that Harvey maps are based on logical walking areas, whereas two OS maps sometimes meet in the middle of a mountain range. Harvey maps are also printed on tough, waterproof paper.

Small-Scale Maps

To get from place to place you'll need a small-scale map of the whole of Britain. Many of the tourist offices listed on p452, and some large tourist offices around Britain, have free introductory maps of the country – and these are enough to give you the basics. If you're combining driving with walking you will need a road atlas showing the smaller roads (as well as the main highways) so you can reach the start of a walking route. The main publishers include OS, Philip's and the Automobile Association (AA), all with atlases at scales of around one inch to 4 miles, most also showing national trails, and costing about £7 to

> ### TRIG POINTS
>
> Trig (short for trigonometric) points are concrete or brick pillars, about 1m tall, used for the making of Ordnance Survey (OS) maps. They're marked on maps, and are a real life-saver if you're walking in the mist and need a bit of navigational confirmation. As the OS does not actually use trig points any more (since most maps are made by aerial surveys), some have been removed. However, in popular walking areas local rambling groups and other interested parties have 'adopted' trig points, promising to keep them in good repair for the benefit of other walkers.

£9. Most road atlases are updated annually, which means old editions are sold off every January – look for bargains at motorway service stations.

In between an atlas of Britain and a very detailed map of a specific walking area, you might also need a regional or area map. OS produce a series of 'Tour' and 'Road' travel maps at various scales; for example, the Lake District, Northumberland and Southwest England.

MONEY

Britain's currency is the pound (£), sometimes called the 'sterling pound', divided into 100 pence (p). Paper money comes in £5, £10, £20 and £50 denominations (and

> ### METRIC MADNESS
>
> Britain is in a state of transition when it comes to weights and measures, as it has been for the last 20 years – and probably will be for 20 more. While most of Europe uses metric measurements based on metres and kilometres, most Brits are happier with imperial units of inches, yards and miles. Most walkers still refer to the height of their favourite mountain in feet (eg 'Ben Nevis is over 4400ft high') although most maps give altitudes in metres only.
>
> For weight, many people use pounds and ounces, even though since January 2000 goods in shops must be measured in kilograms. And nobody knows their weight in pounds (like Americans) or kilograms (like the rest of the world); Brits weigh themselves in stones, an archaic unit of 14 pounds.
>
> When it comes to volume, things are even worse: most liquids are sold in litres, except milk and beer, which often come in pints. Garages sell petrol priced in pence per litre, but measure car performance in miles per gallon. Great, isn't it? And just to make it really interesting, British gallons are not quite the same size as American gallons (and quarts are a different kettle of fish too).
>
> In this book we have reflected this wacky system of mixed measurements. Heights and short distances (800m and less) are given in metres (m), and longer distances in miles, occasionally with kilometre (km) equivalents. For conversion tables, see the inside back cover.

£1 in Scotland), although £50 notes can be difficult to change because fakes circulate. The word 'pence' is rarely used; like its abbreviated written counterpart, it is pronounced 'pee'.

In England and Wales, notes are issued by the Bank of England, and in Scotland, by Clydesdale Bank, Bank of Scotland and Royal Bank of Scotland. All are legal tender on both sides of the border, but if you have any problems, ask a bank to swap them.

A guide to exchange rates is given on the inside back cover, and there are some pointers on costs on p25. Foreign currencies are not accepted if you're buying goods and services, except for a few places in southern England, which take euros.

ATMs

Debit or credit cards are perfect companions – the best invention for walkers and travellers since the backpack. You can use them in most shops, and withdraw cash from ATMs ('cash machines'), which are easy to find in cities and even small towns. But ATMs aren't fail-safe, and it's a major headache if your only card gets swallowed, so take a backup.

Credit & Debit Cards

Visa, MasterCard and Amex cards are widely accepted in Britain, and are good for larger hotels, flights, long-distance travel, car hire etc. Don't rely on these cards totally though, especially when walking in rural areas; many small establishments such as shops, pubs and B&Bs prefer cash (although most B&Bs will accept cheques supported by a bank guarantee card). And as many walking areas are away from towns, you have to plan carefully – and may need to carry enough cash for up to a week.

Since early 2006, nearly all credit and debit cards in Britain use the 'chip & pin' system; instead of signing, you enter a PIN

RIGHTS & ROAMS

The joy, the freedom, the ease of walking in Britain is due in no small part to the right-of-way network – public paths and tracks across private property. Nearly all land in Britain is privately owned, but if there's a right of way you can follow it through fields, woods, even farmhouse yards and country cottage gardens, as long as you keep to the route and do no damage.

The main types of rights of way for walkers are footpaths and bridleways (the latter open to horse riders and mountain bikers too). You'll also see tracks called byways; due to a quirk of history these are open to *all* traffic, so don't be surprised if you have to wade through mud churned up by chunky tyres, or if you're disturbed by the antics of off-road driving fanatics as you're quietly strolling along enjoying the countryside.

Other problems you may encounter is a right of way blocked by a temporary fence, and some farmers have been accused of deliberately putting grumpy-looking bulls in fields crossed by a right of way as a back-door way of keeping walkers off their land. Legally, you're allowed to remove obstacles blocking a right of way (although you have to be careful about damage, so no chain saws allowed and 'removing' two tons of beef might be tricky…), but in reality you're usually better off finding an alternative route and reporting the blocked path to the **Ramblers' Association** (www.ramblers.org.uk).

Generally though, problems like this are rare and you can enjoy walking on thousands of miles of path without the slightest difficulty. It's important to realise though, especially if you're a walker from overseas, that Britain's national trails and other long-distance walks are created by linking together existing rights of way, so many other paths meet and leave the main route at junctions. If specific waymarks (acorn symbols for national trails, for example) exist, make sure you follow them, and don't get distracted by the yellow arrows indicating other paths. (Likewise, the blue arrows indicating bridleways and red arrows indicating byways.)

Thanks to the landmark Countryside Act of 2004, walkers in England and Wales can now move freely *beyond* rights of way in some mountain and moorland areas, though not in enclosed or cultivated fields. This so-called 'right to roam' or 'freedom to roam' legislation opens up thousands of square miles of territory called Access Land previously off limits to walkers, the result of more than 70 years of campaigning by the Ramblers' Association and other groups.

(personal identification number). If you're from overseas, and your card isn't chip-&-pin enabled, you sign in the usual way.

Moneychangers

Finding a place to change your money (cash or travellers cheques) into pounds is never a problem in cities, where banks and bureaus compete for business. Be careful using bureaus, however, as some offer poor rates or levy outrageous commissions. You can also change money at some post offices – very handy in country areas, and rates are usually good.

Taxes & Refunds

In Britain most prices include value-added tax (VAT), which is currently 17.5%. This is levied on virtually all goods except books and food from shops. Restaurants must by law include VAT in their menu prices. Overseas visitors can claim back the VAT on major purchases that are not consumed in Britain, although shops where you buy the goods have to be part of the refund scheme – and not all of them are. Participating shops display a 'Tax-Free Shopping' sign in their window. For more details go to www.visitbritain.com and search on 'VAT Refunds'.

Tipping & Bargaining

In restaurants you're expected to leave around 10% tip, but at smarter restaurants in larger cities waiters can get a bit sniffy if the tip isn't nearer 12% or even 15%. Either way, it's important to remember that you're not obliged to tip if the service or food was unsatisfactory (even if it's been added to your bill as a 'service charge').

At cafés and teashops with table service around 10% is fine. If you're paying with a credit or debit card, and you want to add the tip to the bill, it's worth asking the waiting staff if they'll actually receive it. Some prefer to receive tips in cash.

Just because access is allowed though, it's important to remember that the land is still privately owned. Access Land is occasionally closed, for example if wild birds are nesting or sheep are lambing (from around mid-April to late May), or if the farmer is rounding up stock.

Scotland has a different legal system to England and Wales, with fewer rights of way but a longer tradition of mutual tolerance between landowners and walkers, and relatively free access in mountain and moorland areas. The number of walkers taking to the hills grew massively during the early 1990s, causing landowners and land managers, recreation groups and public agencies to create a Concordat on Access, which essentially endorsed responsible freedom of access, subject to reasonable constraints for management and conservation.

Following on from this, after several years of wide-ranging consultation and (at times, acrimonious) debate, the Scottish Parliament passed the pioneering Land Reform Act in 2003, and the following year approved the Scottish Outdoor Access Code, which conferred statutory access rights on many outdoor activities, including walking and wild camping, and on farmers and landowners. As with the Countryside Act in England and Wales, these rights do not apply to houses, buildings, private gardens or most land where crops are growing. There are also restrictions during the grouse-hunting and deer-stalking seasons. (For information on hunting deer with guns, as opposed to with dogs, in Scotland, and how this impacts walkers, see the boxed text, p388.)

If you're in doubt about whether you can walk in a certain place, Access Land in England and Wales is clearly shown on all new maps, and you can also look out for small discs nailed to gateposts showing the 'open access' symbol (a walker in the hills). Look out too for the 'end of open access area' sign (the same walker and hills crossed through by a diagonal red line) at places when you come down off the high hills into farmland. This means that you have to stick to the rights of way again, but it looks very similar to a 'no walking' sign and many people get confused. It's a shame this landmark legislation wasn't met with clearer thinking on the design front.

For more on walkers' rights and responsibilities, see www.countrysideaccess.gov.uk and www.outdooraccess-scotland.com. See also the boxed texts on p29 and p32.

Taxi drivers also expect tips (about 10%, or rounded up to the nearest pound), especially in London and other big cities. It's less usual to tip minicab drivers.

In pubs, when you order and pay for drinks or food at the bar, tips are not expected. If you order food at the table and your meal is brought to you, then a tip may be appropriate – if the food and service have been good, of course.

Bargaining is rare, although occasionally encountered at markets. It's fine to ask if there are student discounts on items such as books or outdoor equipment.

Travellers Cheques

Travellers cheques (TCs) offer protection from theft, so are safer than wads of cash, but are rarely used in Britain these days, as credit/debit cards and ATMs have become the method of choice for most people. If you do prefer TCs, note that they are rarely accepted for purchases (except at large hotels), so you'll still need to go to a bank or bureau for cash.

PERMITS & FEES

Permits are not required to walk anywhere in Britain, and you don't pay fees to walk in national parks or any other part of the countryside – this ease of access is one of the beauties of walking here. One of the other beauties is the British concept of 'right of way' – see the boxed text, p448.

TELEPHONE

As you walk through Britain, you'll see many iconic red phone boxes on in city streets and in rural areas, although many have been replaced by soulless glass cubicles. Either way, public phones accept coins (minimum charge currently 20p, though this may increase over the life of this book) and usually credit/debit cards, although with the advent of mobile phones (cell phones), many phone booths have been removed and not replaced.

Area codes in Britain do not have a standard format and vary in length, which can be confusing for foreigners (and many Brits). For example: ☎ 020 for London, ☎ 029 for

---

TAKING PHOTOS OUTDOORS *Gareth McCormack*

For walkers, photography can be a vexed issue – all that magnificent scenery but such weight and space restrictions on what photographic equipment you can carry. With a little care and planning it is possible to maximise your chance of taking great photos on the trail.

Light & Filters In fine weather, the best light is early and late in the day. In strong sunlight and in mountain and coastal areas where the light is intense, a polarising filter will improve colour saturation and reduce haze. On overcast days the soft light can be great for shooting wildflowers and running water and an 81A warming filter can be useful. If you use slide film, a graduated filter will help balance unevenly lit landscapes.

Equipment If you need to travel light, carry a zoom in the 28–70mm range, and if your sole purpose is landscapes consider carrying just a single wide-angle lens (24mm). A tripod is essential for really good images and there are some excellent lightweight models available. Otherwise you can improvise with a trekking pole, pack or even a pile of rocks.

Camera Care Keep your gear dry; use zip-lock freezer bags and silica-gel sachets (a drying agent) to suck moisture out of equipment. Sturdy cameras will normally work fine in freezing conditions. Take care when bringing a camera from one temperature extreme to another; if moisture condenses on the camera parts make sure it dries thoroughly before going back into the cold, or mechanisms can freeze up. Standard camera batteries fail very quickly in the cold. Remove them from the camera when it's not in use and keep them under your clothing.

For a thorough grounding on photography on the road, read Lonely Planet's *Travel Photography* by Richard I'Anson, a full-colour guide for happy-snappers and professional photographers alike. Also highly recommended is the outdoor photography classic *Mountain Light* by Galen Rowell.

Cardiff, ☎ 0161 for Manchester, ☎ 01629 for Matlock and ☎ 015394 for Ambleside, followed as usual by the individual number, which can be anything from four to eight digits. For clarity in this book, area codes and individual numbers are separated by a hyphen.

As well as the geographical area codes, other codes include: ☎ 0500 or ☎ 0800 for free calls and ☎ 0845 for calls at local rate, wherever you're dialling from within the UK. Numbers starting with ☎ 087 are charged at national-call rate, while numbers starting with ☎ 089 or ☎ 09 are premium rate, which should be specified by the company using the number (ie in its advertising literature), so you know the cost before you call. These codes and numbers are not separated by hyphen as you always have to dial the whole number.

Note that many numbers starting with ☎ 08 or ☎ 09 do not work if you're calling from outside the UK, or, if they do, you'll be charged for a full international call – and then some.

Codes for mobile phones usually start with ☎ 07 and ringing them is more expensive than calling a land line.

International Calls

To call outside the UK dial ☎ 00, then the country code (☎ 1 for USA, ☎ 61 for Australia etc), the area code (you usually drop the initial zero) and the number.

Direct-dialled calls to most overseas countries can be made from most public telephones, and it's usually cheaper between 8pm and 8am Monday to Friday and at weekends. You can usually save money by buying a phonecard (usually denominated £5, £10 or £20) with a PIN that you use from any phone by dialling an access number (you don't insert it into the machine). There are dozens of cards, usually available from city newsagents – with rates of the various companies often vividly displayed.

To make reverse-charge (collect) calls, dial ☎ 155 for the international operator. It's an expensive option, but what the hell – the other person is paying!

To call Britain from abroad, dial your country's international access code, then ☎ 44 (the UK's country code), then the area code (dropping the first 0) and the phone number.

Most internet cafés have Skype, or some other sort of internet telephony system, so you can make international calls for the price of your time online.

Local & National calls

Local calls (within 35 miles) are cheaper than national calls. All calls are cheaper from 6pm to 8am Monday to Friday and at weekends. From private phones, rates vary between telecom providers. From BT public phones the weekday rate is about 5p per minute; evenings and weekends it's about 1p per minute.

For the operator, call ☎ 100. For directory inquiries, a host of agencies compete for your business and charge from 10p to 40p; numbers include ☎ 118 192, ☎ 118 118, ☎ 118 500 and ☎ 118 811.

Mobile Phones

Around 50 million people in the UK have mobile phones, and thus the ability to tell their loved ones they're on the train. The terse medium of SMS is a national passion, with a billion text messages sent monthly.

Phones in the UK use GSM 900/1800, which is compatible with Europe and Australia but not with North America or Japan (although phones that work globally are increasingly common).

Even if your phone works in the UK, because it's registered overseas a call to someone just up the road will be routed internationally and charged accordingly. An option is to buy a local SIM card (around £10), which includes a UK number, and use that in your own handset (as long as your phone isn't locked by your home network).

A second option is to buy a pay-as-you-go phone (from around £50); to stay in credit, you buy top-up cards at newsagents. A third option is to rent a phone, but if it's for more than a couple of weeks, you're better off buying a cheap phone or SIM card anyway.

TIME

Britain is home to Greenwich Mean Time (GMT), now more commonly called Universal Time Coordinated (UTC). To give you a rough idea, Britain is on the same time (plus or minus one hour) as much of Western Europe, while Eastern Europe is a couple of hours ahead. Sydney is 10 hours ahead of GMT, while San Francisco is eight hours behind and New York five hours behind. Britain uses daylight saving (called 'British Summer Time' or 'BST') so that the whole country is one hour ahead of GMT from late March to late October. Most public transport timetables use the 24-hour clock, but in everyday conversation it is very rarely used; instead people refer to 9am or 9pm etc.

TOURIST INFORMATION

Before leaving home, check the comprehensive and wide-ranging website of **VisitBritain** (www.visitbritain.com), or the more specific sites at www.enjoyengland.com, www.visitscotland.com and www.visitwales.com. Between them, they cover all angles of national tourism, with links to numerous other sites. Details about local and regional websites and tourist organisations are given throughout the regional chapters in this book.

Local Tourist Offices

All British cities, towns and national parks (and some villages) have a tourist office. Most of these are called the Tourist Information Centre (TIC), but you'll also come across Visitor Welcome Centres, Visitor Information Centres or Visitor Information Points; for ease, we've used 'tourist office' throughout this book.

Whatever the name, these places usually have incredibly helpful staff, books and maps for sale, leaflets to give away and loads of advice on things to see or do. They can also assist with booking accommodation (sometimes free, sometimes for a small charge). Most tourist offices keep regular business hours; in quiet areas they close from October to March, while in popular areas they open daily year-round.

Look out too for Tourist Information Points – usually a rack of leaflets about local attractions set up in a post office or shop in a village not big enough to have

its own full-on tourist office. And be aware that some Visitor Information Points are privately owned booking agencies – for local self-catering cottages or similar. You can often pick up leaflets here, but the staff rarely provide additional (or independent) tourism information.

For a list of all official tourist offices around Britain see www.visitmap.info/tic.

Tourist Offices Abroad

VisitBritain's main overseas offices are listed below. Those in other countries are listed on www.visitbritain.com. Offices with a street address can deal with walk-in visitors. For the others it's phone or email only. As well as information, they can help with discount travel cards, often available only if you book before arrival in Britain.

Australia (☎ 02-9021 4400; www.visitbritain.com/au; 15 Blue St, North Sydney, NSW 2060)

Canada (☎ 1 888 847 4885; www.visitbritain.com/ca)

France (☎ 01 58 36 50 50; www.visitbritain.com/fr)

Germany (☎ 01801-46 86 42; www.visitbritain.com/de; Hackescher Markt 1, 10178 Berlin)

Ireland (☎ 01-670 8000; www.visitbritain.com/ie; 22-24 Newmount House, Lower Mount St, Dublin 2)

Japan (☎ 03-5562 2550; www.visitbritain.com/jp; 1F Akasaka Twin Tower, Minato-ku, Tokyo 107-0052)

Netherlands (☎ 020-689 0002; www.visitbritain.com/nl)

New Zealand (☎ 0800 700 741; www.visitbritain.com/nz)

USA (☎ 800 462 2748; www.visitbritain.com/us; 551 Fifth Ave, New York, NY 10176)

VISAS

If you're a European Economic Area (EEA) national, you don't need a visa to visit Britain (you can also work here freely). Citizens of Australia, Canada, New Zealand, South Africa and the USA are given leave to enter Britain at their point of arrival for up to six months, but are prohibited from working.

Visa and entry regulations are always subject to change, so it's vital to check with your local British embassy, high commission or consulate before leaving home. For more information, check www.ukvisas.gov.uk.

Transport

CONTENTS

GETTING THERE & AWAY

London is an international transport hub, so you can easily fly to Britain from almost anywhere in the world. Your other main option for travel between Britain and mainland Europe is ferry, either port-to-port or combined with a long-distance bus trip, although journeys can be long and savings not huge compared to budget airfares. International trains are more comfortable, and the Channel Tunnel allows direct services between Britain, France and Belgium.

ENTERING THE COUNTRY

Entering Britain is straightforward as long as your passport and visa (if required – see opposite) are in order. Immigration officials are firm but fair.

THINGS CHANGE...

The information in this chapter is particularly vulnerable to change. Make sure you understand how a fare (and ticket you may buy) works before parting with your hard-earned cash. You should also be fully aware of visa regulations and the latest security requirements for international travel. Shop carefully. The details given in this chapter are pointers and are no substitute for your own up-to-date research.

Once you're in Britain, travelling between England, Scotland and Wales is effortless. The bus and train systems are fully integrated and in most cases you won't even know you've crossed the border.

Passport

All foreign citizens entering Britain need a passport, valid for at least six months beyond your period of stay. You do not need to show your passport when travelling between England, Scotland and Wales (although since devolution north and west of the border, some Welsh and Scots people may think otherwise...).

AIR

Airports & Airlines

London's Heathrow and Gatwick are the two main airports for international flights. Also near London, Luton and Stansted airports deal largely with charter and budget European flights, while London City Airport specialises in business flights.

Gatwick (code LGW; ☎ 0870-000 2468; www.gatwick airport.com)

Heathrow (code LHR; ☎ 0870-000 0123; www.heathrow airport.com)

London City Airport (code LCY; ☎ 020-7646 0088; www.londoncityairport.com)

Luton (code LTN; ☎ 01582-405100; www.london-luton .co.uk)

Stansted (code STN; ☎ 0870-000 0303; www.stansted airport.com)

Some planes on transatlantic and European routes zip direct to major regional airports such as Birmingham, Edinburgh, Glasgow and Manchester, while smaller regional airports such as Southampton, Aberdeen, Bristol, Cardiff and Newcastle are served by scheduled and charter flights to/from continental Europe and Ireland.

Most major airlines have services to/from Britain, including the following:

Aer Lingus (☎ 0845 084 4444; www.aerlingus.com)

Air Canada (☎ 0871 220 1111; www.aircanada.ca)

Air France (☎ 0845 359 1000; www.airfrance.com)

Air New Zealand (☎ 0800 028 4149; www.airnew zealand.co.nz)

Alitalia (☎ 0870 544 8259; www.alitalia.com)

American Airlines (☎ 08457 789 789; www.american airlines.com)

BMI-British Midland (☎ 0870 607 0555; www.flybmi .com)

British Airways (☎ 0870 850 9850; www.ba.com)

Cathay Pacific (☎ 020-8834 8888; www.cathaypacific .com)

Continental Airlines (☎ 0845 607 6760; www .continental.com)

Delta Air Lines (☎ 0800 414767; www.delta.com)

Emirates (☎ 0870 243 2222; www.emirates.com)

Iberia (☎ 0845 850 9000; www.iberia.com)

KLM-Royal Dutch Airlines (☎ 08705 074 074; www .klm.com)

Lufthansa Airlines (☎ 08708 377 747; www.lufthansa .com)

Qantas Airways (☎ 08457 747 767; www.qantas.com.au)

Scandinavian Airlines (☎ 0870 607 2772; www .scandinavian.net)

Singapore Airlines (☎ 0870 608 8886; www.singapore air.com)

South African Airways (☎ 0870 747 1111; www.flysaa .com)

United Airlines (☎ 08458 444 777; www.united.com)

Virgin Atlantic (☎ 0870 380 2007; www.virgin-atlantic .com)

In recent years, the massive growth of budget ('no-frills') airlines has increased the number of routes – and reduced fares – between Britain and destinations in Ireland or mainland Europe. Fares vary according to demand, and are best bought online. Main players serving British airports include the following:

bmibaby (☎ 0871 224 0224; www.bmibaby.com)

easyJet (☎ 0870 600 0000; www.easyjet.com)

flybe (☎ 0871 522 6100; www.flybe.com)

Jet2 (☎ 0871 226 1 737; www.jet2.com)

Ryanair (☎ 0871 246 0000; www.ryanair.com)

Virgin Express (☎ 0870 730 1134; www.virgin -express.com)

To save trawling several airline sites, services such as www.skyscanner.com and www .lowcostairlines.org have information on many scheduled airlines. For budget airlines try www.whichbudget.com.

Tickets

You can buy your airline ticket from a travel agency (in person, by phone or on the internet), or direct from the airline (the best deals are often available online only). Whichever, it always pays to shop around. Internet travel agencies such as www.travel ocity.com and www.expedia.com (and their country variants, www.travelocity .ca, www.expedia.com.au etc) work well if you're doing a straightforward trip, but for anything slightly complex there's no substitute for a travel agent who knows the system, the options, the special deals and so on.

The best place to start your search for agencies or airlines is the travel section of a weekend newspaper. Another good place is www.lonelyplanet.com/travel_services. Scan the advertisements, check a few websites, phone a few numbers, build up an idea of options, then take it from there. Remember, you usually get what you pay for: cheap flights may leave at unsociable hours or include several stopovers. For quick and comfortable journeys you have to fork out more cash.

Australia & New Zealand

Britain is a very popular destination, with a wide range of fares. From New Zealand some flights go via Australia, but cheaper fares are available via Bangkok or (going the other way) Los Angeles. Round-the-world (RTW) tickets can sometimes work out cheaper than a straightforward return. Online agencies include www.travel.com.au and www .goholidays.co.nz. The major travel agencies, with branches across Australia and/or New Zealand, include the following:

AUSTRALIA
Flight Centre (☎ 133 133; www.flightcentre.com.au)

STA Travel (☎ 1300 733 035; www.statravel.com.au)

NEW ZEALAND
Flight Centre (☎ 0800 243544; www.flightcentre.co.nz)

House of Travel (www.houseoftravel.co.nz)

Canada & the USA

There's a continuous price war on the transcontinental route between Britain and North America, so fares are always keen. Major agencies include the following:

CANADA
Flight Centre (☎ 1888 967 5302; www.flightcentre.ca)

Travel CUTS (☎ 866 246 9762; www.travelcuts.com)

USA
Flight Centre (☎ 1866 967 5351; www.flightcentre.us)

STA Travel (☎ 800 781 4040; www.statravel.com)

LAND
Bus
You can easily get between Britain and numerous cities in Ireland or mainland Europe via long-distance bus. The international bus network **Eurolines** (www.eurolines.com) connects a huge number of destinations; the website has links to bus operators in each country, and gives contact details of local offices. In Britain, you can book Eurolines tickets on the phone, at the website of **National Express** (☎ 08705 808080; www.nationalexpress.com) and at many travel agencies.

Train
The Channel Tunnel makes direct train travel between Britain and continental Europe a fast and enjoyable option. High-speed **Eurostar** (☎ 08705 186 186; www.eurostar.com) passenger services hurtle at least 10 times daily between London and Paris (three hours), and London and Brussels (2½ hours), via Ashford and Calais. A new high-speed rail link on the British side will be completed in 2007, slicing another 30 minutes off the journey.

As well as Eurostar, many 'normal' trains run between Britain and mainland Europe. You buy a direct ticket, but get off the train at the port, walk onto a ferry, then get another train on the other side. Routes include Amsterdam to London (via Hook of Holland and Harwich) and Paris to London (via Calais and Dover).

Travelling between Ireland and Britain, the main train-ferry-train route is Dublin to London, via Dun Laoghaire and Holyhead. From southern Ireland, ferries sail between Rosslare and Fishguard or Pembroke, with train connections on either side.

SEA
Main ferry routes between Britain and the island of Ireland include Holyhead (Wales) to Dun Laoghaire (Republic of Ireland) and Stranraer (Scotland) to Belfast (Northern Ireland). Between Britain and the Continent, ferry routes include Dover to Calais (France), Harwich to Hook of Holland (Netherlands), Hull to Zeebrugge (Belgium) and Rotterdam (Holland), Portsmouth to Santander and Bilbao (Spain), Newcastle to Bergen (Norway) and Gothenberg (Sweden), Rosyth (near Edinburgh) to Zeebrugge, and Lerwick to Bergen. There are many more.

Competition from Eurotunnel and budget airlines has forced ferry operators to offer constant discounted fares, with options varying massively (in budget-airline style), according to demand. Go at a busy time and you pay a lot. Go in the middle of the night outside holiday time and you should get a bargain. Booking early can also help reduce costs. As well as these variants, fares depend on the size of car and the number of passengers. If you're a foot passenger, or cycling, you've got more flexibility.

The best cross-channel deals are return fares – often much cheaper than two singles; sometimes cheaper than *one* single! On longer ferry trips, the fare might include a cabin.

Main ferry operators (and their UK contact details) include the following:
Brittany Ferries (☎ 08703 665 333; www.brittany-ferries.com)
DFDS Seaways (☎ 08702 520 524; www.dfds.co.uk)
Hoverspeed (☎ 0870 240 8070; www.hoverspeed.co.uk)
Irish Ferries (☎ 08705 171717; www.irishferries.com)
P&O Ferries (☎ 08705 202020; www.poferries.com)
SpeedFerries (☎ 0870 220 0570; www.speedferries.com)
Stena Line (☎ 08705 707070; www.stenaline.com)
Transmanche (☎ 0800 917 1201; www.transmanche ferries.com)

Other options are www.ferrybooker.com – an online travel agency covering all sea-ferry routes and train services through the Eurotunnel.

BAGGAGE RESTRICTIONS
Airlines impose very tight restrictions on baggage. No sharp implements of any kind are allowed in carry-on baggage, so pack items such as pocket knives, camping cutlery and first-aid kits into bags that go in the hold. Liquid fuels and gas cartridges for camping stoves are banned from all baggage, and since 2006, most other liquids (including bottled drinks and shower gel) have also been banned, although restrictions may be relaxed in future (ask the airline or agent when buying your flight). Everything you need is available in Britain, so it's easier to buy this kind of stuff when you arrive.

TRANSPORT

GETTING AROUND

For getting around Britain by public transport, your main options are trains and long-distance buses (called 'coach' in Britain). Services between major towns and cities are generally good, although expensive compared to other European countries. Delays are frequent, especially on the rail network, but these tend to afflict commuters rather than visitors: if your train trip from London to Bath runs 30 minutes late, what's the problem? You're on holiday!

AIR

Britain's domestic air companies include British Airways, BMI, bmibaby, easyJet, flybe and Ryanair (see p454). If you're really pushed for time, flights on longer routes across Britain (eg Exeter or Southampton to Newcastle or Edinburgh) are handy, although you miss the glorious scenery in between. On some shorter routes (eg London to Newcastle, or Manchester to Newquay) trains can compare favourably with planes, once airport down-time is factored in. On cost, you might get a bargain air fare, but trains can be cheaper if you buy tickets in advance.

BUS & COACH

If you're on a tight budget, bus is nearly always the cheapest way to get around, although also the slowest – sometimes by a considerable margin.

Local Bus

All cities have good local bus networks year-round, and in rural areas popular with tourists (especially national parks) there are frequent bus services from Easter to September. Elsewhere in the countryside, bus timetables are designed to serve schools and industry, so there can be few midday and weekend services (and they may stop running in school holidays), or buses may link local villages to a market town on only one day each week. It's always worth double checking before you hike to a pretty village on Sunday and then discover that the next bus out is on Thursday.

Long-Distance Coach

In Britain, long-distance express buses are called coaches, and in many towns there are separate bus and coach stations. Make sure you go to the right place!

National Express (☎ 08705 808080; www.nationalexpress.com) is the main operator, with a wide network and frequent services between main centres. Services tie in with those of **Scottish Citylink** (☎ 08705 505050; www.citylink.co.uk), Scotland's leading coach company. If you book online, advance special-offer 'fun fares' can be as low as £1.

Also offering fares from £1 is **Megabus** (www.megabus.com), which operates a budget-airline-style service between about 20 main destinations around the country. Go at a quiet time and book early, and your ticket will be very cheap. Book last-minute, for a busy time and… You get the picture.

PUBLIC TRANSPORT INFORMATION

For any public transport enquiry, **Traveline** (☎ 0870 608 2608; www.traveline.org.uk in England & Wales, www.travelinescotland.com in Scotland) is a very useful portal site covering bus, coach, taxi and train services nationwide (although some areas are better represented than others), with numerous links to help plan your journey. By phone, you get transferred automatically to an advisor in the region you're phoning *from;* to speak to an advisor in the area you want to travel *in* the first advisor will need to transfer you, which can mean twice the wait. To get round this, the website lists keypad short cuts. Other useful contacts include the following:

- **National Cabline** (☎ 0800 123 444) Dial this number from a land-line phone and you'll get put through to the nearest taxi company.
- **National Rail Enquiries** (☎ 08457 48 49 50; www.nationalrail.co.uk) A very good site for help with all train journeys.
- **Train Taxi** (www.traintaxi.co.uk) A list of local taxis serving railway stations.
- **Transport Direct** (www.transportdirect.com) Designed to help with planning door-to-door journeys.

LOCAL TRANSPORT TO/FROM THE WALKS

The start and finish of nearly all the walks in this book can be reached by public transport and full details are given in each route description. In some areas, regular bus and train services mean this is easy, although in other areas the bus services can be patchy, which means you may need to hire a taxi. In countryside areas, local taxi firms are quite used to dropping off or picking up walkers at the end of lonely mountain roads – and split between three or four people the fare isn't much more than the bus anyway. In many cases, local B&B owners (especially those a few miles off national trails and other long routes) provide a drop-off-pick-up service, either free of charge or for a few pounds.

Postbus

A postbus is a van on usual mail service that also carries fare-paying passengers. Postbuses operate in rural areas (and some of the most scenic and remote parts of the country), and so can be useful for walkers – although sometimes the van's schedule doesn't mesh with a long day out in the hills. For information and timetables contact **Royal Mail Postbus** (☎ 08457 740 740; www.royalmail.com/postbus).

Bus Passes & Discounts

National Express offers NX2 discount passes to full-time students and people under 26 years of age. They cost £10, and get you 30% off standard adult fares. Proof and a passport photo are required. People over 60, families and disabled travellers also get discounts.

For touring the country, National Express also offers Brit Xplorer passes, which allow unlimited travel for seven days (£79), 14 days (£139) and 28 days (£219). You don't need to book journeys in advance with this pass; if the coach has a spare seat, you can take it. This deal is only available to non-Brits, though.

Scottish Citylink offer passes if you just want to tour Scotland.

CAR & MOTORCYCLE

Travelling by private car or motorbike you can be independent and flexible, and reach remote walking spots. If you're British, you'll know most of the following information. If you're from overseas, these pointers may be useful.

Driving Licence

If you have an EU licence it's valid in Britain. Other foreign driving licences are valid for up to 12 months.

Fuel & Spares

Petrol and diesel are easy to find, although in remote rural areas it may be 50 miles or more to the next filling station. The cost of fuel rises the further you get from the main centres, and some rural filling stations close on Sundays. Spares and repairs can be located in cities and most towns.

Hire

Compared to many countries (especially the USA), hire rates are expensive in Britain, but they tend to fluctuate with demand. This means you can pay £40 per day for a small car during busy periods, and as little as £3 per day at quiet times. Rates usually include unlimited mileage and full insurance (with perhaps a £50 or £100 excess). Damage to windscreen and tyres usually has to be paid for by the hirer. You normally need to be between 21 and 70 to hire a car. National companies include the following:

1car1 (☎ 0113-387 5866; www.1car1.com)
Avis (☎ 08700 100 287; www.avis.co.uk)
Budget (☎ 08701 565656; www.budget.com)
easyCar (☎ 0906 333 3333; www.easycar.com)
Europcar (☎ 0870 607 5000; www.europcar.co.uk)
Hertz (☎ 0870 844 8844; www.hertz.co.uk)
National (☎ 0870 400 4502; www.nationalcar.com)
Sixt (☎ 08701 567567; www.e-sixt.co.uk)
Thrifty (☎ 01494-751600; www.thrifty.co.uk)

Your other option is to use an internet search engine to find small local car-hire companies who can undercut the big boys. Generally, those in cities are cheaper than in rural areas, and they usually don't have variable rates. Try a rental broker site such as **UK Car Hire** (www.uk-carhire.net).

Another option is to hire a motor home or camper van. It's more expensive than hiring a car but it does help you save on accommodation costs, and gives almost un-limited freedom. Sites worth checking in-clude www.coolcampervans.com, www.wild horizon.co.uk and www.justgo.uk.com.

Motoring Organisations

Large motoring organisations include the **Automobile Association** (AA; ☎ 0800 085 2721; www .theaa.com) and the **Royal Automobile Club** (RAC; ☎ 0800 731 7090; www.rac.co.uk); annual member-ship starts at around £35, including 24-hour roadside breakdown assistance. A greener alternative is the **Environmental Transport Asso-ciation** (ETA; ☎ 0800 212 810; www.eta.co.uk), which provides all the usual services (breakdown assistance, road-side rescue, vehicle inspec-tions etc) but *doesn't* campaign for more roads.

Road Rules

If you're from overseas and plan to bring your own car to Britain, it's illegal to drive without (at least) third-party insurance. Some other important rules:

- Drive on the left.
- Wear fitted seat belts in cars.
- Wear crash helmets on motorcycles.
- Give way to your right at junctions and roundabouts.
- Always use the left-side lane on motor-ways and dual-carriageways, unless over-taking (although so many people ignore this rule you'd think it didn't exist).
- Don't use a mobile phone while driving unless it's fully hands-free (another rule frequently flouted).

Speed limits are 30mph (48km/h) in built-up areas, 60mph (96km/h) on main roads and 70mph (112km/h) on motorways and dual-carriageways. Drinking and driv-ing is taken very seriously; you're allowed a blood-alcohol level of 80mg/100mL (0.08%) and campaigners want it reduced to 50mg/100mL (0.05%).

All drivers should read the *Highway Code*, a handy booklet available from shops and online at www.highwaycode.gov.uk.

HITCHING

Hitching is not as common as it used to be in Britain, maybe because more people have cars and maybe because few drivers give lifts any more. It's perfectly possible, however, if you don't mind long waits, al-though travellers should understand that they're taking a small but potentially seri-ous risk, and we don't recommend it. If you decide to go by thumb, note that it's illegal to hitch on motorways; you must use ap-proach roads or service stations.

However, as is the case with so many other things, it's all different in remote rural areas such as Mid Wales or northwest Scot-land, where hitching is a part of getting around – especially if you're a walker. On some Scottish islands, local drivers may stop and offer a lift without you even asking.

TAXI

There are two main sorts of taxi in Britain: the famous black cabs (some carry adver-tising livery in other colours these days), which have meters and can be hailed in the street; and minicabs that can only be called by phone. In London and other big cities, taxis cost £2 to £3 per mile. In rural areas it's about half this, and for walkers this means when it's Sunday and the next bus is on Thursday, a taxi can keep you moving. If you call **National Cabline** (☎ 0800 123 444) from a land-line phone, the service will pinpoint your location and transfer you to an approved local company.

TRAIN

Long-distance train travel around Britain is generally faster and more comfortable than coach, but can be more expensive, although with discount tickets it's competitive – for a

---

BACK TO THE START

Most of the short (one-day) walks in this book are circular, sharing the start and end point, so you can leave your kit at a camp site or hotel and enjoy the walk unencumbered by a heavy pack. However, most of the long-distance routes go from A to B – where B can sometimes be hundreds of miles from A! If you're on public transport, this is no problem. If you're using a car, B&Bs at the start/end of long-distance routes may offer long-term parking. For a lift back to the start (in addition to public transport) some baggage-carrying services (see p437) also take passengers.

few pounds extra you get more comfort and many railways take you through beautiful countryside.

In the 1990s British rail travel had a bad reputation for delays and cancellations. By 2006 the situation had improved markedly, with around 85% of trains running on (or pretty close to) schedule – and the journeys that are delayed or cancelled mostly impact commuters rather than long-distance leisure travellers.

About 20 different companies operate train services in Britain (for example, First Great Western runs from London to Bath and Bristol; GNER runs London to Leeds and Edinburgh; and Virgin Trains runs a very useful and wide-ranging service all across Britain based from Birmingham, extending to Penzance, Cardiff, Holyhead, Glasgow, Edinburgh, Newcastle, London and Bournemouth), while Network Rail operates track and stations. For passengers this system can be confusing, but information and ticket-buying services are increasingly centralised.

Your first stop should be **National Rail Enquiries** (☎ 08457 48 49 50; www.nationalrail.co.uk), the nationwide timetable and fare-information service. The site also advertises special offers, and has real-time links to station departure boards, so you can see if your train is on time (or not). Once you've found the journey you need, links take you to the relevant train operator or to the centralised ticketing services www.thetrainline.com and www.qjump.co.uk to actually buy the ticket. These websites can be confusing at first (you always have to state an approximate preferred time and day of travel, even if you don't mind *when* you go), but after using them a few times they soon become easy to use, and with a little delving around they can offer some real bargains. For trains in Scotland you can go direct to **First ScotRail** (☎ 0845 755 0033; www.firstscotrail.com).

Classes

There are two classes of rail travel: first and standard. First class costs around 50% more than standard and, except on very crowded trains, is not really worth it. However, on weekends some train operators offer 'upgrades', where for an extra £10 to £15 on top of your standard-class fare you can enjoy more comfort and legroom.

Costs & Reservations

For short journeys (under about 50 miles), it's usually best to buy tickets on the spot at rail stations. You may get a choice of express or stopping service – the latter is obviously slower, but can be cheaper, and may take you through charming countryside or grotty suburbs.

For longer journeys, on-the-spot fares are always available, but tickets are much cheaper if bought in advance. Essentially, the earlier you book the cheaper it gets. Fully discounted tickets for longer trips are usually not available at stations at all and must be bought in advance by phone or online. Advance purchase usually gets you a reserved seat, but do remember that the cheapest fares are nonrefundable, so if you miss your train you'll have to buy a new ticket.

If you have to change trains, or use two or more train operators, you still buy one ticket, valid for the whole of your journey. The main railcards are also accepted by all operators.

If you buy by phone or online, you can have the ticket posted to you (UK addresses only), or collect it at the originating station on the day of travel, either at the ticket desk (get there with time to spare, as queues can be long) or from automatic machines.

For short or long trips, fares are usually cheaper outside 'peak' travel times ('peak' is when everyone else is trying to get to/ from work). It's worth avoiding Fridays and Sundays, as fares are higher on these busy days.

The main fare types are 'open', 'saver' and 'advance', although there are sometimes variations within these main categories (eg, 'super-saver' or 'extra-advance'), and just to keep you on your toes, the different train companies sometimes use different brand names for these products (eg 'sunshine-saver' or 'capital-advance'). The main features of each type are outlined below (with the varying prices of London–York tickets given by way of example).

If you're making a return journey (ie coming back on the same route), open return fares are usually just under double the single fare, while saver returns are often just a few pounds more than saver singles. Advanced return fares are sometimes hard to find, as an increasing number of train operators have followed the lead set by low-cost airlines and offer advance single fares only. This gives you more flexibility and can turn up some amazing bargains, with two advance singles easily undercutting the saver return price.

Advance Available in advance only, up to 6pm the day before travel. Valid only on specified date and time. The earlier you buy, the cheaper the ticket, especially if you travel outside peak times. Nonrefundable. London–York singles £10 to £30.

Saver Available on the spot or in advance. Day of outward travel is fixed, but you can change the time. Changing the day of travel costs £5. Return any day/time. Valid for one month. Some restrictions apply (eg no peak-time travel). London–York single/return £71/72

Open Available on the spot or in advance. Travel any time. Valid for a month. London–York single/return £83/167.

Children under five travel free on trains; those aged between five and 15 pay half-price, except on tickets already heavily discounted. Seniors also get discounts, but again not on already heavily discounted fares.

Train Passes
If you're staying in Britain for a while, discount passes called 'railcards' are available, including the following:

Disabled Person's Railcard

Family Railcard Covers up to four adults and four children travelling together

Network Railcard For train travel in southeastern England

Senior Railcard For anyone over 60

Young Person's Railcard You must be 16 to 25, or a full-time UK student

Passes cost around £15 to £20 (valid for one year, available from major stations) and get you a 33% discount on most train fares. On the Family and Network cards, children get a 60% discount and the fee is easily repaid in a couple of journeys. For full details see www.railcard.co.uk.

BritRail Passes (www.britrail.com) are good value, but they're only for visitors from overseas and are *not available in Britain*. They must be bought in your country of origin from a specialist travel agency. There are many BritRail variants (including 'Flexipass' and 'Consecutive') and versions (eg England only, or the whole of Britain). A BritRail Flexipass offering four days of unlimited travel in Britain within a 60-day period is US$275, eight days in 60 is US$400 and 15 days in 60 is US$600. Children's passes are usually half-price (or free with some adult passes) and seniors get discounts too. For about 30% extra you can upgrade to first class.

For country-wide travel, an All Line Rover (£375/565 for seven/14 days) gives unlimited travel on the national rail network. It can be purchased in Britain, by anyone.

Health & Safety

CONTENTS

Britain is a healthy place to travel. The National Health Service (NHS) provides an excellent service, free at the point of delivery, which is better than most other countries offer. Across the country, hygiene standards are high and there are no unusual diseases to worry about. Having said that, your health while walking and travelling depends on your predeparture preparations, your daily health care and how you handle any medical problem that does develop.

BEFORE YOU GO

Prevention is the key to staying healthy while abroad. A little planning before departure, particularly for pre-existing illnesses, will save trouble later. See your dentist before a long trip, carry a spare pair of contact lenses and glasses, and take your optical prescription with you. Bring medications. If you need a particular medicine, take enough with you in its original, clearly labelled containers. If you can't carry all you need, take part of the packaging showing the generic name, rather than the brand, as this will make getting replacements easier. A signed and dated letter from your physician describing your medical conditions and medications, including generic names, is also a good idea. If carrying syringes or needles, be sure to have a physician's letter documenting their medical necessity.

European Economic Area (EEA) nationals can obtain free emergency treatment on presentation of a European Health Insurance Card (EHIC) – replacing the old E111 form – validated in their home country. Reciprocal arrangements between the UK and some other countries (including Australia) allow free emergency medical treatment at hospitals or general practitioners (GPs) and subsidised dental care. For details, see the **Department of Health** (www.doh.gov.uk) website, following links to 'Policy & Guidance', 'International' and 'Overseas Visitors'.

INSURANCE

If you're coming from overseas for a walking holiday in Britain, travel insurance is highly recommended. EHIC cards cover you for most medical care, but do not cover nonemergencies or emergency repatriation. See p445 for more information.

RECOMMENDED VACCINATIONS

No immunisations are mandatory.

MEDICAL CHECK LIST

This is a list of items to consider including in your medical kit – consult your pharmacist for brands available in your country.

- Acetaminophen (paracetamol) or aspirin
- Adhesive or paper tape
- Antibacterial ointment for cuts and abrasions
- Antidiarrhoeal drugs (eg loperamide)
- Anti-inflammatory drugs (eg ibuprofen)
- Antihistamines (for hay fever and allergic reactions)
- Bandages, gauze swabs, gauze rolls
- Elasticised support bandage
- Iodine tablets or water filter (for water purification)
- Nonadhesive dressings
- Oral rehydration salts
- Paper stitches
- Permethrin-containing insect spray for clothing, tents and bed nets

HEALTH & SAFETY

- Scissors, safety pins, tweezers
- Sterile alcohol wipes
- Steroid cream or cortisone (for allergic rashes)
- Sticking plasters (Band-Aids, blister plasters)
- Sutures
- Thermometer

INTERNET RESOURCES

The **World Health Organization** (WHO; www.who.int/ith) publication *International Travel and Health* is revised annually and is available online. Other useful websites:

www.ageconcern.org.uk Advice on travel for the elderly.

www.fco.gov.uk/travel For Brits going abroad, but also useful for incomers.

www.mariestopes.org.uk Women's health and contraception.

www.mdtravelhealth.com Worldwide recommendations, updated daily.

KNOW BEFORE YOU GO

If you're coming to Britain from overseas, it's a good idea to consult your government's travel-health website before departure:

- **Australia** (www.smartraveller.gov.au)
- **Canada** (www.hc-sc.gc.ca/english/index.html)
- **United States** (www.cdc.gov/travel)

FURTHER READING

Lonely Planet's *Travel with Children* includes advice on travel health for younger children. Other recommended references include *Traveller's Health* by Dr Richard Dawood and *The Traveller's Good Health Guide* by Ted Lankester.

IN BRITAIN

AVAILABILITY & COST OF HEALTH CARE

Good health care is readily available and for minor illnesses pharmacists can give valuable advice and sell over-the-counter medication. They can also advise when more specialised help is required and point you in the right direction. The standard of dental care is usually good, though it is sensible to have a dental check-up before a long trip.

HYGIENE

To reduce the chances of contracting an illness, you should wash your hands frequently, particularly before handling or eating food. Antibacterial soap or hand wipes, available at outdoor gear shops, can be a wise investment.

Take particular care to dispose carefully of all toilet waste when you are on a walk. See the boxed text, p50.

ENVIRONMENTAL HAZARDS
Bites & Stings

There are very few biting and stinging insects to worry about when walking in Britain. Midges (see the boxed text, below) are an annoyance but not a health risk.

Some paths can get overgrown, and if you're from overseas you may not be ready for leafy plants called stinging nettles; they can administer a nasty sting, so you may need to be careful when wearing shorts – especially if you're allergic to this kind of thing.

Hypothermia & Frostbite

If you walk during winter (November to February in England and Wales, October to March in Scotland), especially in the higher mountains, proper preparation will reduce the risk of getting hypothermia. Even on a hot day, the weather in the mountains can change rapidly; carry waterproof garments and warm layers (see p467), and inform others of your route.

Acute hypothermia follows a sudden drop of temperature over a short time. Chronic

---

BEWARE TINY BITES

Between June and August, especially in northern England, and most notoriously in Scotland, millions of tiny biting insects called midges take to the air on cool, windless evenings. They are not a danger, but their bites get very annoying, particularly if you're camping. If you're staying in hostels or B&Bs they're no problem, but the gardens of country pubs can be a bit 'midgey' around sunset. Ways to counter the attack include wearing light-coloured clothing and using midge repellents (available in pharmacies and outdoor gear stores – brands without DDT include Mozi-guard and Swamp Gel). Or going inside.

COMMON AILMENTS

Blisters

To avoid blisters make sure your boots are well worn in before you set out. Your boots should fit comfortably with enough room to move your toes; boots that are too big or too small will cause blisters. Make sure socks fit properly and are specifically made for walkers; even then, make sure there are no seams across the widest part of your foot. Wet and muddy socks can also cause blisters, so even on a day walk, pack a spare pair of socks. Keep your toenails clipped but not too short. If you do feel a blister coming on, treat it promptly. Apply a simple sticking plaster or, preferably, a special blister plaster that acts as a second skin.

Fatigue

More injuries happen towards the end of the day rather than earlier, when you are fresher. Although tiredness can simply be a nuisance on an easy walk, it can be life-threatening on narrow, exposed ridges or in bad weather. You should never set out on a walk that is beyond your capabilities on the day. If you feel below par, have a day off. To reduce the risk, don't push yourself too hard – take a rest every hour or two and take a good-length lunch break. Towards the end of the day, reduce the pace and increase your concentration. You should also eat and drink sensibly throughout the day; nuts, dried fruit and chocolate are all good energy-giving snack foods.

Knee Strain

Many walkers feel the judder on long, steep descents. Although you can't eliminate strain on the knee joints when dropping steeply, you can reduce it by taking shorter steps that leave your legs slightly bent and ensuring that your heel hits the ground before the rest of your foot. Some walkers find that tubular bandages help, while others use high-tech, strap-on supports. Walking poles are very effective in taking some weight off the knees.

HEALTH & SAFETY

hypothermia is caused by a gradual loss of temperature over hours. Hypothermia starts with shivering, loss of judgment and clumsiness. Unless rewarming occurs, the sufferer deteriorates into apathy, confusion and coma. Prevent further heat loss by seeking shelter; hot, sweet drinks; wearing warm, dry clothing; and sharing bodily warmth.

Frostbite is caused by freezing and subsequent damage to bodily extremities. It is dependent on wind chill, temperature and length of exposure. Frostbite starts as frostnip (white, numb areas of skin), from which complete recovery is expected with rewarming. As frostbite develops, the skin blisters and then becomes black. The loss of damaged tissue eventually occurs. Adequate clothing, staying dry, keeping well hydrated and ensuring adequate calorie intake best prevents frostbite. Treatment involves rapid rewarming. Avoid refreezing and rubbing the affected areas.

Sunburn

In summer in Britain, even when there's cloud cover, it's possible to get sunburnt surprisingly quickly – especially if you're on the higher mountains. Use sunscreen, wear a hat and cover up with a shirt.

INJURIES

Sprains

Ankle and knee sprains are common injuries for walkers, particularly in rugged terrain. To help prevent ankle sprains in these circumstances, wear boots with adequate ankle support. If you suffer a serious sprain, immobilise the joint with a firm bandage, and relieve pain and swelling by keeping the joint elevated for 24 hours and, where possible, by using ice or a cold compress. Take simple painkillers to ease the discomfort. If the sprain is mild, you may be able to continue your walk after a couple of days. For more severe sprains, seek medical attention, as you may need an X-ray to rule out the possibility of a broken bone.

Major Accidents

Falling or having something fall on you, resulting in head injuries or fractures (broken bones), is always possible when walking, especially if you are crossing steep slopes or unstable terrain. Following is some basic advice on what to do if a person suffers a major fall:

- Make sure you and other people with you are not in danger.
- Assess the injured person's condition.
- Stabilise any injuries.
- Seek medical attention as soon as possible (see opposite).

If the person is unconscious, immediately check they are breathing – clear their airway if it is blocked. If breathing is absent or abnormal, you should start mouth-to-mouth resuscitation immediately. Move the sufferer as little as possible in case their neck or back is broken, and keep them warm; insulate them from the ground if possible.

Check for wounds and broken bones. Control any bleeding by applying firm pressure to the wound. Bleeding from the nose or ear may indicate a fractured skull. Don't give the person anything by mouth, especially if they are unconscious.

Indications of a fracture are pain, swelling and discolouration, loss of function or deformity of a limb. Don't try to straighten a displaced broken bone. Nondisplaced broken bones can be splinted. Fractures associated with open wounds (compound fractures) require more urgent treatment as there is a risk of infection. Dislocations, where the bone has come out of the joint, are very painful and should be treated as soon as possible.

Broken ribs are painful but usually heal by themselves and do not need splinting. If breathing difficulties occur, or the person coughs up blood, medical attention should be sought urgently, as it may indicate a punctured lung.

Internal injuries are more difficult to detect and, if suspected, medical attention should be sought urgently. Watch for shock, which is a specific medical condition associated with a failure to maintain circulating blood volume. Signs include a rapid pulse and cold, clammy extremities. A person in shock requires urgent medical attention.

Some general points to bear in mind:

- Simple fractures take weeks to heal, so don't need fixing straight away, but should be immobilised to protect from further injury. Compound fractures need much more urgent treatment.
- If you splint a broken bone, check regularly that the splint is not cutting off the circulation to the hand or foot.
- Most cases of brief unconsciousness are not associated with any serious internal injury to the brain but any person who has been knocked unconscious should be watched for deterioration. The sufferer should get a medical check-up within a few days and if there is any sign of deterioration, medical attention should be sought straight away.

TRAVELLING WITH CHILDREN

All travellers with children should know how to treat minor ailments and when to seek medical treatment. Make sure the children are up to date with routine vaccinations, and discuss possible travel vaccines well before departure, as some vaccines are

---

WATER, WATER EVERYWHERE

Wherever you go in Britain, you can usually drink the water that comes out of taps. Where it's not safe to drink (taps in public toilets, at train stations, or in remote rural locations, for example) a sign will usually warn you.

When you're walking in the countryside it's usually not advisable to drink water straight from lakes or lowland rivers. Note also that in some parts of Britain, such as in chalk areas above the spring line, ground water can be hard to find.

In mountain streams, even if there isn't a dead sheep upstream (which there may be), it's still not advisable to drink the water as your insides simply won't be used to it. You should carry all the water you need, or filter or sterilise stream water before drinking.

Having said all that, many hardy walkers do drink water straight from mountain streams – especially in Scotland – with no ill effects. Some say the peaty taste reminds them of a good malt whisky...

WALK SAFETY – BASIC RULES

■ Allow plenty of time to accomplish a walk before dark, particularly when daylight hours are shorter.

■ Don't overestimate your capabilities. If the going gets too tough, give up and head back.

■ Unless you're very experienced, don't walk on your own, especially in remote areas.

■ Leave details of your intended route and return time with someone responsible.

■ Before setting off, make sure you have a relevant map, compass, whistle and spare clothing, and that you know the weather forecast for the area for the next 24 hours.

---

not suitable for children under one year of age. Some advice on walking with children is given on p438.

SAFETY ON THE WALK

By taking a few simple precautions, you'll reduce significantly the odds of getting into trouble while walking in Britain. See the boxed text on above for a list of simple precautions to take. For information on the clothes and equipment you should take when walking, consult the Clothing & Equipment chapter (p467).

DANGERS

When walking through farmland, watch out for temporary electric fences. These are designed to control cattle but they are often placed near (or across) footpaths. They are often no more than a thin strand of wire and can be difficult to see, but they pack a punch, so beware. (It's actually illegal for farmers to put electric fences – or any barrier – across a right of way.)

In farmland, watch out for untethered guard dogs and dangerous bulls, treating both with caution. If confronted, back away slowly and report the situation to police if you consider it dangerous to the point of being unlawful.

Some walks described in this book cross areas of land that are used by the army for training. When manoeuvres may be used, so live ammunition may be used, so walkers are not allowed to enter. Red warning flags are raised around the area at these times. There are usually noticeboards too, listing the days and times when the area is closed to the public. When the red flags are not flying you can cross the land, but you should

still keep to paths and beware of unidentifiable metal objects lying in the grass. If you do find anything suspicious, don't touch it. Make a note of the position and report it to the police after your walk.

CROSSING RIVERS

While walking in mountain areas you may have to ford a river or stream swollen with flood water or snow melt. Trying to cross a fast, deep river is risky and potentially fatal. The first rule is: Don't cross it. Wait for a while to see if the water level recedes, or go upstream to check for a safer crossing place. If this doesn't work, and you really have to get across, here are some tips and methods:

■ Look for the widest part of the river, where the water will flow more slowly.

■ Loosen your backpack straps, so if you slip you can shrug it off and not be pulled under.

■ You're usually more stable if you face upstream and walk across 'crab-wise' (although walking side-on to the direction of flow means your body presents less of an obstacle to the water – basically, ensure you're as stable as possible).

■ Planting your walking poles (or a large stick) upstream gives you greater stability and helps you lean against the current.

■ A river-crossing technique for pairs is for one person to stand behind the other, holding the person in front at the waist as you both walk across crab-wise – it's much harder for the water to knock you all over this way.

RESCUE & EVACUATION

If someone in your group is injured and can't move, leave at least one member of the party with them while at least one other

HEALTH & SAFETY

goes for help. If there are only two in the group, leave the injured person with as much warm clothing, food and water as it's sensible to spare, plus the whistle and torch. Take careful written note of the location (including a map reference) and mark the position with something conspicuous – an orange bivvy bag or perhaps a large stone cross on the ground.

If you need to call for help, use these internationally recognised emergency signals. Give six short signals, using a whistle, a yell or the flash of a light, at 10-second intervals, followed by a minute of rest. Repeat the sequence until you get a response. The response is three signals at 20-second intervals, followed by a minute's pause.

If possible you should get to a telephone. Public phones in country areas are marked on maps, but in real emergency situations the owners of remote farms or houses will let you use theirs. Dial ☎ 999 (the national emergency number) or ☎ 112 (the international distress number) – both are free of charge. When the operator replies and asks 'which service?', ask for mountain rescue. Alternatively, ask for police, explain the situation and the police will coordinate with the mountain-rescue service. Be ready to give information on where an accident occurred (including that all-important map reference), how many people are injured and the injuries sustained. If ringing from a mobile phone, don't forget to leave your own number for further contact.

The mountain-rescue service will include teams and vehicles on the ground, and possibly helicopters. The team members are volunteers, and (unlike in many other countries) mountain rescue is free of charge. These teams are funded by donations from the public. You'll notice collection boxes in pubs and cafés in mountain areas, and even if you've come down safely you may want to make a small donation.

Mobile Phones

In emergency situations, a mobile phone (cell phone) can be useful – but remember they may not get a signal in remote areas, especially if you're in a valley. It's very important to use the mobile for rescue *only* in genuine emergencies. There are too many stories of people calling the mountain rescue team because they got a bit lost or forgot their sandwiches.

A FINAL WORD

Much of the above may sound pretty daunting. That's good. With a bit of luck it will make you respect the mountains and have a safe time while exploring Britain's great outdoors. Most of the advice comes down to common sense, so with some of that and a bit of preparation or training if required, you should be absolutely fine.

HEALTH & SAFETY

Clothing & Equipment

If you're visiting from overseas, you may be coming to Britain to combine walking with 'normal' travel. Most clothing and equipment is suitable for both, but anything you don't have can be bought in markets, shops and outdoor gear stores as you need it.

CLOTHING

A secret of comfortable walking is to wear several layers of light clothing, which you can easily take off or put on as you warm up or cool down. Most walkers use three main layers: a base layer next to the skin; an insulating layer; and an outer, shell layer for protection from wind, rain and snow. The advice here is weighted towards more serious walking on hills or mountains; no special gear is needed for lowland walks in good conditions.

For the upper body, the base layer is typically a shirt of synthetic material such as polypropylene, to wick moisture away from the body and reduce chilling. The insulating layer (eg windproof synthetic fleece or down jacket) traps warm air and retains heat next to your body. The outer shell is a windproof and waterproof jacket.

For the lower body, the layers generally consist of polypropylene underwear ('long-johns') in cold conditions, loose-fitting trousers, and waterproof overtrousers. Of course, when it's hot, shorts are fine. Take the long johns off as well, though.

Outer Shell

The ideal specifications for a jacket are: breathable, waterproof fabric, a hood roomy enough to cover headwear but still allow peripheral vision, a capacious map pocket and a heavy-gauge zip protected by a storm flap. Overtrousers should have slits for access to your trouser pockets and long leg zips so you can pull them on and off over your boots.

Boots & Socks

Training shoes or specifically designed walking shoes are fine for lowland walking in Britain (most of the walks graded 'easy' in this book). For more mountainous routes, across rocks, scree and (the worst) wet grass on a steep slope, boots with ankle support and soles with a good tread are invaluable.

Buy your boots in warm conditions, preferably after a walk in the afternoon, as everyone's feet enlarge slightly during the day. If you buy boots on a cold morning you may find they pinch when you're actually out walking.

Walking socks should be free of ridged seams in the toes and heels.

Gaiters

If you will be walking through snow, scree, deep mud or wet/scratchy vegetation, gaiters protect your legs, keep your socks dry and help keep stones out of your boots. The best are made of strong fabric, with a robust zip protected by a flap, and secure easily around the foot.

EQUIPMENT
Backpack

For day walks your backpack (usually called a rucksack in Britain) can be small – around 20L if it's a warm day and you're not going far, 30L to 40L if you're out all day, going high and the weather may change (which applies to most mountains in Britain). For multiday walks you may need a backpack of 45L to 60L, up to 90L if you're camping.

A good backpack should obviously be strong, with a good, comfortable frame and an adjustable, well-padded harness that evenly distributes weight across your shoulders and hips. Even if the manufacturer claims your pack is waterproof, use heavy-duty liners.

If you're using a baggage-carrying service (see p437), even on long walks you'll need just a small day-pack for lunch, camera, waterproofs etc and the bulk of your stuff can go in a large rucksack or kit-bag.

Sleeping Bag & Mat

For camping in summer lowland conditions, your sleeping bag can be fairly light, but for upland camping in spring or autumn you'll need something rated 'three-season'. Down fillings are warmer than synthetic for the same weight and bulk but, unlike synthetic fillings, do not retain warmth when wet.

An inner sheet helps keep your sleeping bag clean, as well as adding an insulating layer. Silk 'inners' are lightest, but they also come in cotton or polypropylene.

Self-inflating sleeping mats work like a thin air cushion between you and the ground to protect you from any stones under the groundsheet, and (more importantly) to insulate from the cold. Foam mats are a low-cost, but less comfortable, alternative.

Stove

Fuel stoves fall roughly into three categories. Multifuel stoves are small, efficient and ideal for places where a reliable fuel supply is difficult to find. Stoves running on methylated spirits (ethyl alcohol, 'meths') in Britain are often known generically by the name of the most popular brand (Trangia); they are slower and less efficient, but safe,

---

NAVIGATION EQUIPMENT

Maps & Compass

Some paths in Britain are not well signposted, particularly in highland areas, so it's essential that you can read a map and navigate with a compass. As the maps in this book are for guidance only, you should always carry a proper survey map (see p445) and know how to read it.

Before setting off, ensure you understand the contours and map symbols, plus the main ridge and valley/river systems in the area. Also familiarise yourself with the true north–south directions and the general direction you need to be heading. As you go along, confirm your position by identifying major landforms such as mountain peaks or bends in a river and locate them on your map. This will stop you getting lost, and you'll know where you are if the mist comes down.

If you're from overseas and bringing your own compass, you may find it doesn't work properly, as the attraction of magnetic north varies in different parts of the world, so compasses have to be calibrated accordingly. There are five main zones: northern, northern tropical, equatorial, southern tropical and southern. You need the northern type for Britain, and may need to buy it locally. 'Universal' compasses can be used anywhere in the world.

1	Base plate
2	Direction of travel arrow
3	Dash
4	Bezel
5	Meridian lines
6	Needle
7	Red end
8	N (north point)

How to Use a Compass

This is a very basic introduction to using a compass and will only be of assistance if you are proficient in map reading. For simplicity, it doesn't take magnetic variation into account. Before using a compass we recommend you obtain further instruction. For more advice, get a copy of *Navigation for Walkers* by Julian Tippett – a full-colour, illustrated and very user-friendly guide.

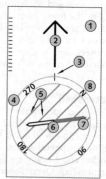

Reading a Compass

Hold the compass flat in the palm of your hand. Rotate the bezel (4) so the red end (7) of the needle (6) points to the N (north point; 8) on the bezel. The bearing is read from the dash (3) under the bezel.

Orienting the Map

To orient the map so that it aligns with the ground, place the compass flat on the map. Rotate the map until the needle is parallel with the map's north/south grid lines and the red end is pointing to north on the map. You can now identify features around you by aligning them with labelled features on the map.

clean, simple to use and fuel is easy to find. Butane gas stoves are clean and reliable, but can be slow. Needless to say, if you use canisters make sure you bring out your empties and dispose of them properly.

Tent

For walking in Britain a tent is not essential, although you may choose to camp for flexibility or economy. A 'three-season' tent will fulfil the requirements of most walkers. The groundsheet and flysheet should have sealed seams and zip flaps. Ideally a two-person tent should weigh less than 3kg. A 2kg tent is even better but costs more. Dome- and tunnel-shaped tents handle windy conditions better than flat-sided tents.

BUYING & HIRING LOCALLY

In popular walking areas, most towns (and even small villages) have outdoor gear shops where you can buy clothing, boots, socks, tents, sleeping bags, maps, guidebooks and anything else you may need for walking. Hiring equipment is much more difficult – very few shops offer this service (none at all in Scotland), and what they do hire may be limited to backpacks and possibly waterproofs (of questionable quality). It is better to have all your own gear.

Taking a Bearing from the Map

Draw a line on the map between your starting point and your intended destination. Place the edge of your compass along this line with the direction of travel arrow (2) pointing towards your destination. Rotate the bezel until the meridian lines (5) are parallel with the north/south grid lines on the map below them, and the N points to north on the map. Read the bearing from the dash.

Following a Bearing

Rotate the bezel on the compass so that the intended bearing is in line with the dash. Place the compass flat in the palm of your hand and rotate the base plate (1) until the red end points to N on the bezel. The direction of travel arrow will now be pointing in the direction that you need to walk.

Determining Your Bearing

Rotate the bezel so the red end points to the N. Place the compass flat in the palm of your hand and rotate the base plate until the direction of travel arrow points in the direction in which you have been walking. Read your bearing from the dash.

GPS

Originally developed by the United States Department of Defense, the Global Positioning System (GPS) is a network of more than 20 earth-orbiting satellites that continually beam encoded signals back to earth.

Small, computer-driven devices (GPS receivers) can decode these signals to give users an extremely accurate reading of their location – to within 30m, anywhere on the planet, at any time of day, in almost any weather. The cheapest hand-held GPS receivers may not have a built-in averaging system that minimises signal errors. Other important factors to consider when buying a GPS receiver are its weight and battery life.

Remember that a GPS receiver is of little use to walkers unless used with an accurate topographical map. The receiver simply gives your position, which you must then locate on the local map. GPS receivers will only work properly in the open. The signals from a crucial satellite may be blocked (or bounce off rock or water) directly below high cliffs, near large bodies of water or in dense tree cover and give inaccurate readings.

GPS receivers are more vulnerable to breakdowns (including dead batteries) than the humble magnetic compass – a low-tech device that has served navigators faithfully for centuries – so don't rely on them entirely.

CLOTHING & EQUIPMENT

EQUIPMENT CHECK LIST

This is a general guide to the things you might take on a walk. Your list will vary depending on the kind of walking you want to do, whether you're camping or staying in hostels or B&Bs, and on the terrain, weather conditions and time of year.

Clothing for the Walk

☐ boots and spare laces

☐ hat (warm) and gloves

☐ overtrousers (waterproof)

☐ shorts and/or trousers

☐ sunhat

☐ T-shirt

☐ gaiters

☐ long-sleeved shirt with collar (if sunny)

☐ rain jacket

☐ socks and underwear (thermal if cold conditions)

☐ sweater or fleece jacket

Clothing for After the Walk

☐ training shoes or sandals

☐ change/s of clothes

Equipment – All Walks

☐ backpack/rucksack with liner (waterproof)

☐ food and snacks (high energy)

☐ map, compass and guidebook

☐ pocket knife

☐ sunscreen and lip balm

☐ toilet paper and trowel

☐ watch

☐ whistle

☐ first-aid kit*

☐ insect repellent

☐ map case or clip-seal plastic bags

☐ sunglasses

☐ survival bag or blanket

☐ torch (flashlight) and spare batteries

☐ water container

Equipment – Multiday Walks

☐ cooking, eating and drinking utensils

☐ matches or lighter

☐ sleeping bag and inner sheet

☐ stove and fuel

☐ toiletries

☐ water purification tablets, iodine or filter

☐ dishwashing items

☐ sewing/repair kit

☐ sleeping mat

☐ tent, pegs, poles and guy ropes

☐ towel

Optional Items

☐ altimeter

☐ binoculars

☐ GPS receiver

☐ notebook and pen

☐ walking poles

☐ backpack cover (waterproof, slip-on)

☐ camera, film or memory card and batteries

☐ mobile phone

☐ swimming gear

* see the Medical Check List (p461)

Major outdoor gear chains include **Blacks** (www.blacks.co.uk), **Cotswold Outdoor** (www.cotswoldoutdoor.com), **Field & Trek** (www.fieldandtrek.com) and **Nevisport** (www.nevisport.co.uk), with stores in the main cities around Britain as well as in small towns and villages near popular walking areas (Llanberis in Snowdonia and Ambleside in the Lake District for example) – plus online mail order. Don't overlook the local, independent shops though – they're often staffed by real outdoor enthusiasts and can offer prices to match the big boys. For a comprehensive list of national and local gear stores see www.ramblers.org.uk/info/equipmentshops.

Glossary

Some English words and phrases commonly used in Britain will be unknown to visitors from abroad, even if they regard English as their first language, so we have translated some of these. We have also focussed on British walking terms, including several Welsh, Scottish and regional English words, mainly to do with landscape, that you are likely to come across during your travels. For those seeking a more in-depth introduction to the English language, pick up Lonely Planet's *British Phrasebook*.

4WD – four-wheel-drive car; all-terrain vehicle

ale – beer, usually brown or red in colour (as opposed to lager, which is usually amber or yellow in colour), often called *bitter*
AA – Automobile Association
aber – river mouth (Wales)
abhainn – river or stream (Scotland)
ABTA – Association of British Travel Agents
afon – river (Wales)
allt – stream (Scotland, Wales)
aonach – ridge
arête – narrow ridge, particularly between glacial valleys
ASL – above sea level
ATM – automatic teller machine; machine for extracting cash from a bank; in Britain usually called a *cashpoint* or cash machine
aye – yes or always (Scotland, northern England)

B&B – bed and breakfast
BABA – book-a-bed-ahead scheme
bach – small (Wales)
bag – reach the top of, as in 'to bag a peak'
bailey – outermost wall of a castle
ban, bhan – white (Scotland)
banger – old, cheap car; sausage (colloquial)
bank holiday – public holiday, ie when the banks are closed
bap – bread roll (northern England)
bastle-house – solidly constructed and well-fortified house (Northumberland)
bealach – pass between hills (Scotland)
beck – stream (northern England)
beinn, ben – mountain (Scotland)
bevvy – any drink (originally northern England; colloquial)
bidean – peak (Scotland)
billion – a million million, not a thousand million

bimble – a short walk or *ramble* (colloquial)
bitter – a type of beer (*ale*)
black pudding – a type of sausage made from meat, fat and dried blood
bloke – man (colloquial)
bothy – hut or mountain shelter (Scotland)
brae – hill or steep slope (Scotland)
bramble – bush with long, thin branches covered in thorns
bridleway – path that can be used by walkers, horse riders and cyclists
broad – lake (East Anglia)
broch – defensive tower (Scotland)
bryn – hill (Wales)
BT – British Telecom
BTA – British Tourist Authority
bun – bread roll, usually sweet
burgh – town (Scotland)
burial mound – ancient burial site characterised by a large circular dome of earth and stone covered by grass; see also *long barrow*
burn – stream (Scotland)
bus – local bus; see also *coach*
butty – sandwich, often filled with something hot, eg bacon or (British speciality) *chips* (colloquial)
bwlch – pass or gap between two hills (Wales)

C2C – Coast to Coast Walk
cadair – chair; stronghold or defended place in the mountains (Wales)
caer – fort (Wales)
cairn – pile of stones to mark path or junction; also (in Scotland) peak
capel – chapel (Wales)
carreg – stone (Wales)
cashpoint – machine for extracting cash from a bank; *ATM*
CCC – Camping & Caravanning Club
chine – valley-like fissure leading to the sea (southern England, especially the Isle of Wight)
chips – hot, deep-fried potato pieces; French fries
clach – stone (Scotland)
cleve – steep-sided valley
clint – the bit of rock sticking up between two *grikes*
clough – small valley
clun – meadow (Wales)
coach – long-distance *bus*
coaching inn – originally an inn along a stage-coach route at which horses were changed
coasteering – working your way round the base of cliffs by scrambling, climbing or swimming
cob – bread roll (northern England)

coch – red (Wales)

coed – forest or wood (Wales)

coire –*corrie* or high mountain valley (Scotland)

col – hill or mountain pass

common – land that may be private but people have traditional rights of access, formerly for grazing animals, more often now for recreation

coombe – valley (southern England)

Corbett – hill or mountain between 2500ft and 2999ft high (Scotland)

corrie – semicircular basin at the head of a steep-sided valley, usually formed by glacial erosion; cirque

crack – good conversation, good times (originally Ireland, also northern England); now also used to mean 'happening', as in 'What's the crack?', ie 'What's going on?' (colloquial)

craig – exposed rock (Scotland)

crannog – artificial island settlement (Scotland)

crisps – salty flakes of fried potato, in a packet (what the rest of the world calls *chips*)

croft – plot of land with adjoining house, worked by the occupiers (Scotland)

cromlech – burial chamber (Wales)

CTC – Cyclists' Touring Club

cut – canal or artificial stretch of water

cwm – *corrie* or valley (Wales)

dale – open valley

DB&B – dinner, bed and breakfast

de – south (Wales)

dead end road   no through road

dear – expensive

dearg – red (Scotland)

din, dinas – fort (Wales)

dinner – usually evening meal, except in some northern regions where it is the noon meal

Donald – lowland hill between 2000ft and 2499ft high (Scotland)

downs – rolling upland, usually grassy, characterised by a lack of trees

drove road – ancient route, once used for bringing cattle and sheep from the farm to the market

drum, druim – ridge (Scotland)

du – black (Wales)

dubh, duibh – dark or black (Scotland)

duvet – thick padded bed cover

duvet jacket – thick padded coat, usually filled with feathers and down, worn by mountaineers or walkers; down jacket

dyke – stone wall or embankment; drainage channel (southern England)

eas – waterfall (Scotland)

East Anglia – eastern England, usually the counties of Norfolk and Suffolk

eilean – island (Scotland)

en suite – a room with an attached private bathroom; also written 'ensuite'

ESA – Environmentally Sensitive Areas

estate – area of landed property, usually large (Scotland)

exclosure – fenced enclosure to protect trees from grazing stock (Scotland)

fag – cigarette

fagged – exhausted (colloquial)

fanny – female genitals (colloquial) – which is why some people giggle when Fan y Big, a mountain in Wales, is pronounced in the English way, rather than in the correct Welsh way as 'van er big'

fawr – big (Wales; colloquial)

fell – large hill or mountain (northern England); hillside or mountain side

fen – drained or marshy low-lying flat land (eastern England)

ffordd – road (Wales)

firth – estuary (Scotland)

fiver – five-pound note (colloquial)

flip-flops – rubber or plastic sandals with one strap over toes (what Australians call 'thongs')

folly – eccentric, decorative (often useless) building

footpath – path through countryside and between houses, not beside a road (that's called a '*pavement*')

force – waterfall (northern England)

fret –worry (colloquial); mist from the sea (Northumberland)

garbh – rough (Scotland)

geal – white (Scotland)

gill, ghyll – small steep-sided valley (northern England)

ginnel – alleyway (mostly northern England)

glan – shore (Wales)

glas – grey, grey-green (Scotland); blue (Wales)

gleann, glen – valley (Scotland)

glyn – valley (Wales)

gorm – blue (Scotland)

GR – grid reference (on maps)

grand – 1000 (colloquial)

grike – narrow fissure, usually in limestone *pavement* areas

gritstone – hard, coarse-grained sandstone containing a heavy proportion of silica

grough – *gully*

gully – small steep-sided valley

gwyn – white (Wales)

gwrydd – green (Wales)

haar – fog off the North Sea (Scotland)

hag – area of peat (northern England & Scotland)

hamlet – small settlement

haus/haws – pass or gap between hills (northern England)

Hogmanay – New Year's Eve (Scotland)

honey pot – crowded place

horseshoe route – curved or circular route, eg up one ridge and down another
hotel – accommodation with food and bar, not always open to passing trade

inch – island (Scotland)
inn – pub, usually with a bar, food and accommodation
inver – river mouth (Scotland)

JMT – John Muir Trust
jumper – sweater

ken – know, as in 'Do you ken what I mean?' (Scotland)
kin – head of a peninsula, lake or sea inlet (Scotland)
kipper – smoked herring (fish)
kirk – church (Scotland)
kissing gate – swinging gate, allowing access to people but not animals or bikes
knoll – small hill
kyle – narrow strait of water (Scotland)

ladder-stile – two small ladders back to back against a wall or fence, to allow people to pass over
laird – estate owner (Scotland)
lairig – pass (Scotland)
lass – young woman (northern England & Scotland)
lay-by – parking space at side of road
LDP – long-distance path
ley – clearing
liath – grey (Scotland)
linn – waterfall (Scotland)
llan – enclosed place or church (Wales)
llyn – lake (Wales)
loch, lochan – lake, small lake or *tarn* (Scotland)
lock – part of a canal or river that can be closed off and the water levels changed to raise or lower boats
long barrow – Neolithic structure, usually covering stone burial chambers
lough – Irish word for lake (Northumberland)
lunch – midday meal

mad – insane (not angry)
Martello tower – small, circular tower used for coastal defence
mawr – big (Wales)
MBA – Mountain Bothies Association
meall – rounded hill (Scotland)
metalled – surfaced (road), usually with tar (bitumen)
mhor, mor – big or great (Scotland)
MoD – Ministry of Defence
moor – high, rolling, open, treeless area
motorway – freeway
motte – mound on which a castle was built
muggy – 'close' or humid weather (colloquial)
mullach – top or summit (Scotland)

Munro – mountain of 3000ft and higher (Scotland)
mynydd – mountain (Wales)

nant – valley or stream (Wales)
navvy – labourer who built canals and railways in the 19th century (abbreviation of 'navigator')
newydd – new (Wales)
NNR – National Nature Reserve
NSA – National Scenic Area
NT – National Trust
NTS – National Trust for Scotland

oast house – building containing a kiln for drying hops
off-license – shop selling alcoholic drinks to take away
ogof – cave (Wales)
OS – Ordnance Survey mapping agency

p – pronounced 'pee', pence (currency)
pasty – hot pastry roll with savoury filling
pavement – sidewalk; any flat area of exposed rock, especially limestone
peat – dark soil, the remains of ancient vegetation, usually wet and glutinous, found in moorland areas
pen – headland or peak (Wales)
pete – fortified houses
PIC – Park Information Centre
Pict – early Celtic inhabitants (from the Latin *pictus*, meaning 'painted', after their painted body decorations)
pike – peak (northern England)
pint – 568mL
pissed – drunk (not angry; slang)
pissed off – annoyed (slang)
pistyll – waterfall (Wales)
pitch – playing field; tent site
pitched – laid with flat stones, eg to improve a path
plas – hall or mansion (Wales)
pont – bridge (Wales)
pop – fizzy drink (northern England, Wales)
porth – bay or harbour
postbus – minibus that follows postal delivery routes and carries passengers
pub – short for public house, a bar, usually with food, sometimes with accommodation
pwll – pool (Wales)

quid – pound (money; colloquial)

RA – Ramblers' Association
ramble – a relatively short or nonstrenuous walk
reiver – notoriously cruel warrior, bandit (northern England & Scotland)
reservoir – artificial lake, usually formed by damming a river
rhiw – slope (Wales)
rhos – moor or marsh (Wales)

ride – path specially made for riding on horseback

round – a natural circuit, mostly along ridges, often in a horseshoe shape

RSPB – Royal Society for the Protection of Birds

ruadh – red (Scotland)

rubber – eraser

rubbish bin – garbage can

RUPP – Road Used as a Public Path

sack – rucksack, pack, backpack

SAE – stamped, addressed envelope

sarnies – sandwiches (colloquial)

Sassenach – an English person or a lowland Scot (Scotland)

scrambling – using hands (as well as feet) to negotiate a steep, rocky section of path

SDW – South Downs Way

sgorr, sgùrr – pointed hill or mountain

shut – partially covered passage

SMC – Scottish Mountaineering Club

sneachd – snow (Scotland)

SNH – Scottish Natural Heritage

spidean – peak (Scotland)

squeeze stile, squeeze gate – narrow gap in wall to let people through, but not animals

sron – nose (Scotland)

SSSI – Site of Special Scientific Interest

stalking – hunting of deer (Scotland)

stile – steps to allow people to pass over a wall or fence

stob – peak (Scotland)

strath – wide valley (Scotland)

stuc – peak or steep rock (Scotland)

subway – underpass for pedestrians

SUW – Southern Upland Way

SWCP – South West Coast Path

sweet – candy

SYHA – Scottish Youth Hostels Association

tarn – small mountain lake (northern England)

tea – British national drink; light meal eaten late in the afternoon; cooked evening meal in those parts of the country where *dinner* is eaten at noon

teashop – smart café, in country areas

thwaite – clearing in a forest

TIC – Tourist Information Centre; tourist office

tom – hill (Scotland)

top – peak over 3000ft (914m), but without a significant drop on all sides

tor – small and pointed hill (England)

torr – small hill (Scotland)

tre – town (Wales)

trig point – pillar, formerly used for the making of Ordnance Survey maps

tube – underground railway

tumulus – ancient burial mound

twee – excessively sentimental, sweet, pretty

twitcher – keen bird-watcher

twitten – passage or small lane

twr – tower (Wales)

ty – house (Wales)

uamh – cave (Scotland)

uig – bay (Scotland)

uisge – water (Scotland)

Unesco – United Nations Educational, Scientific & Cultural Organisation

VAT – value-added tax, levied on most goods and services

verderer – officer upholding law and order in the royal forests

Way – usually a long distance path or trail, eg the Pennine Way

wheal – mine (Cornwall)

WHW – West Highland Way

wold – open, rolling country

WTB – Wales Tourist Board

wynd – lane (Scotland)

YHA – Youth Hostels Association

ynys – island (Wales)

yob – hooligan

ystwyth – winding (Wales)

zawn – very steep-sided *gully* or fissure in a sea cliff (Cornwall)

Behind the Scenes

THIS BOOK

This guidebook was commissioned in Lonely Planet's Melbourne and London offices, and produced by the following:

Commissioning Editor Cliff Wilkinson
Coordinating Editor Andrew Bain
Coordinating Cartographer Andrew Smith
Coordinating Layout Designer Jim Hsu
Senior Editor Helen Christinis
Managing Cartographer Mark Griffiths
Assisting Editors Anne Mulvaney, Nick Tapp, Pete Cruttenden, Pat Kinsella
Assisting Cartographers Ross Butler, Anita Banh, Andy Rojas, Jody Whiteoak
Assisting Layout Designers Tamsin Wilson, Carlos Solarte
Cover Designer Wendy Wright
Project Managers Eoin Dunlevy, Craig Kilburn

Thanks to Sally Darmody, Jennifer Garrett, Trent Paton, Fiona Siseman, Celia Wood, Chris Lee Ack

THANKS
DAVID ELSE

As always, massive appreciation goes to my wife, Corinne, for joining me on the walks and for support when I lock myself away for 12 hours to write the descriptions – and for bringing coffee when it gets nearer 16 hours. Huge thanks also to this book's co-authors, Peter, Simon, Becky, Sandra, Des and Belinda. I'd also like to thank my ever-reliable and usually amiable research assistant Robin Saxby, his partner Sybil Johnson and his daughter Nancy Long, who has long since revised

her opinions about the glamour of travel writing as a career and decided to become a famous actress instead. Out on the track, many people helped me with route-checking, accommodation feedback and historical background: Harry Bitten (Centenary Walk), Etain O'Carroll (Thames Path), Graham Williams (Coast to Coast Walk), Gail Coskrey (Dales Way), Deidre Leonard (Dales Way, Cumbria Way), David McGlade (Hadrian's Wall), John Else (Ridgeway, Kennet & Avon Canal), Jill Leheup (Peak District), Aidan Leheup (Snowdonia), Rachel Hollis (Yorkshire Dales). And finally, thanks to numerous good friends with whom I've enjoyed great days out on the mountains. Without their company, humour, fruit cake and sandwiches I'd never have made it.

SANDRA BARDWELL

Staff at some tourist offices were especially helpful, particularly Robbie at Brodick and Susan at Drumnadrochit. Richard Means (Dumfries & Galloway ranger service) and Mike Baker (Borders ranger service) unstintingly gave advice and up-to-date information, as did Pete Crane (Cairngorms National Park), and Mike McManus (West Highland Way). Jetta also provided invaluable route advice in the central Highlands. Anne unearthed useful archaeological information. David Else's advice and encouragement were also much appreciated. The whole project would have faltered without enthusiastic help from Gavin, Noel and Peter in checking various walks. I may have fallen by the wayside without Hal's companionship, support and help in many ways, including the housework.

THE LONELY PLANET STORY

The story begins with a classic travel adventure: Tony and Maureen Wheeler's 1972 journey across Europe and Asia to Australia. There was no useful information about the overland trail then, so Tony and Maureen published the first Lonely Planet guidebook to meet a growing need.

From a kitchen table, Lonely Planet has grown to become the largest independent travel publisher in the world, with offices in Melbourne (Australia), Oakland (USA) and London (UK). Today Lonely Planet guidebooks cover the globe. There is an ever-growing list of books and information in a variety of media. Some things haven't changed. The main aim is still to make it possible for adventurous travellers to get out there – to explore and better understand the world.

At Lonely Planet we believe travellers can make a positive contribution to the countries they visit – if they respect their host communities and spend their money wisely. Every year 5% of company profit is donated to charities around the world.

BELINDA DIXON

Huge thanks to Cliff, David, Mark and countless others at Lonely Planet for their expertise, guidance and unswerving patience; to Cotswold Way Officer Jo Ronald and the Dartmoor National Park's Michael Nendick for your detailed information; to all the tourist office staff for your universally helpful approach; to every B&B owner, restaurateur and publican who answered strangely detailed questions from an apparently random rambler; to the DNP's Colin Ridgers, whose initial navigational instructions have allowed me to find my way ever since; to Swads for excellent advice on all things bovine, and to J for still making me smile.

PETER DRAGICEVICH

Thanks to all my London friends who helped with encouragement, advice and general friendliness. Special thanks to Tim Benzie for all of the above and a place to crash. Thanks to Ben and Gordon for walking part of the way with me. Extra special thanks to Ben Preston, Adrienne Wong Preston and Jacob Preston for services above and beyond the call of friendship, as ever. Lots of love to my family, especially my father/flatmate Bob Dragicevich.

DES HANNIGAN

Thanks to the many Cornish friends and colleagues who have contributed to my experience and knowledge of the Cornish coast over a lifetime. Special thanks to friends in the National Trust, the Cornwall Wildlife Trust and the Cornwall Archaeological Unit, the real experts, who have tolerated my numerous queries over many years. Thanks above all to family and friends who have explored the truly fabulous Cornish coast with me – by sea, and from level ground through to the vertical.

BECKY OHLSEN

Thanks to Zach Hull and Patrick Leyshock for their exemplary work as bodyguards, punsters and travelling companions; Peter at the Radnorshire Arms in Beguildy for the photograph; Glyndŵr's Way national trail officer Helen Tatchell, as well as everyone at the Offa's Dyke Centre; and David Else for putting this book together and sparking the idea in the first place.

SIMON RICHMOND

Many thanks to the various walkers and locals I met along the two routes who chipped in with their comments and tips. Also thanks to the folks at Sherpa and Brigantes for their logistical assistance; Steve Westwood for updates on the Pennine Way; David Else for dinner and fine CA advice and support; Angie for encouragement; and Tonny as always.

OUR READERS

Many thanks to the travellers who used the last edition and wrote to us with helpful hints, useful advice and interesting anecdotes:

Don Bacon, Vicki Barker, Bob Cromwell, Andrew Forsyth, Antonella Fracasso, Trish Freane, Margaret Gallery, Honey Halpern, R M Heddon, Vance Kerslake, Stephen Land, Edgar Locke, Ed Lucas, Graham Morgan, Thomas Murray, Jean Neil, Rebecca O'Meara, Richard Purver, Anna Ramell, Ted Reader, J Rice, Steve Rudd, Emma Stewardson, Reg Tripp, B Waddington, Richard Wheatley, David Wood

ACKNOWLEDGMENTS

Many thanks to the following for the use of their content:

Globe on back cover ©Mountain High Maps 1993 Digital Wisdom, Inc.

SEND US YOUR FEEDBACK

We love to hear from travellers – your comments keep us on our toes and help make our books better. Our well-travelled team reads every word on what you loved or loathed about this book. Although we cannot reply individually to postal submissions, we always guarantee that your feedback goes straight to the appropriate authors, in time for the next edition. Each person who sends us information is thanked in the next edition – and the most useful submissions are rewarded with a free book.

To send us your updates – and find out about Lonely Planet events, newsletters and travel news – visit our award-winning website: **www.lonelyplanet.com/feedback**.

Note: we may edit, reproduce and incorporate your comments in Lonely Planet products such as guidebooks, websites and digital products, so let us know if you don't want your comments reproduced or your name acknowledged. For a copy of our privacy policy visit www.lonelyplanet.com/privacy.

Index

000 Map pages
000 Photograph pages

INDEX

000 Map pages
000 Photograph pages

INDEX

000 Map pages
000 Photograph pages

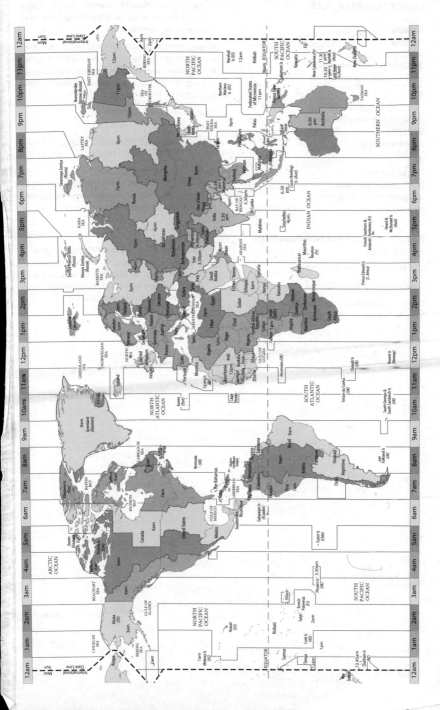

LONELY PLANET OFFICES

Australia
Head Office
Locked Bag 1, Footscray, Victoria 3011
☎ 03 8379 8000, fax 03 8379 8111
talk2us@lonelyplanet.com.au

USA
150 Linden St, Oakland, CA 94607
☎ 510 893 8555, toll free 800 275 8555
fax 510 893 8572
info@lonelyplanet.com

UK
72-82 Rosebery Ave,
Clerkenwell, London EC1R 4RW
☎ 020 7841 9000, fax 020 7841 9001
go@lonelyplanet.co.uk

Published by Lonely Planet Publications Pty Ltd
ABN 36 005 607 983

© Lonely Planet Publications Pty Ltd 2007

© photographers as indicated 2007

Cover photographs: Autumn in the Cheviot Hills – Northumberland, Michael McQueen/Getty Images (front); the Black Cuillin mountains –